JOHN LAURANCE

"You must be content to know the fact is as I have said, and that a great many of the people in those days were not at all what they seemed, nor what they are generally believed to have been."

—*attributed to Supreme Court Chief Justice John Jay by Edward Floyd De Lancey*

Thomas Jones, *History of New York During the Revolutionary War*, edited by Edward Floyd De Lancey (New York: Written between 1783 and 1788, printed for the New York Historical Society, 1879), p. lii.

JOHN LAURANCE

*The Immigrant Founding Father
America Never Knew*

Keith Marshall Jones III

American Philosophical Society
Philadelphia

> Transactions of the
> American Philosophical Society
> Held at Philadelphia
> For Promoting Useful Knowledge
> Volume 108, Part 2

Front cover photo credit:
Oil on canvas (undated), unidentified artist. (Collection of New York Historical Society. Reproduced with permission.)

Copyright © 2019 by the American Philosophical Society for its Transactions series. All rights reserved.

ISBN: 978-1-60618-082-2
US ISSN: 0065-9746

Library of Congress Cataloging-in-Publication Data

Names: Jones, Keith Marshall, author.
Title: John Laurance : the immigrant founding father America never knew / Keith Marshall Jones III.
Description: First edition. | Philadelphia : American Philosophical Society, [2019] | Series: Transactions series, ISSN 0065-9746 ; Volume 108, Part 2 | Includes bibliographical references and index.
Identifiers: LCCN 2019015099 | ISBN 9781606180822 (alk. paper)
Subjects: LCSH: Laurance, John, 1750-1810. New York (N.Y.)
  History 1775-1865 Biography. | Lawyers New York (State)
  New York–Biography. | Legislators New York (State) New York Biography.
  Politicians New York (State)-New York Biography.
Classification: LCC F128.44 .J77 2019 ; DDC 328.73/092 [B]–dc23 LC record available at https://lccn.loc.gov/2019015099

Also available as an ebook (ISBN: 978-1-60618-087-7)

Table of Contents

ACKNOWLEDGMENTS vii
INTRODUCTION: John Who? 1

Part I ... From "Cousin Jack" to Colonel Laurance

ONE: Götterdämerung 13
TWO: Casting Fate to the Wind 17
THREE: Crossing the Bar 29
FOUR: An Officer of the Revolution 41
FIVE: Washington's Courtroom "Von Steuben" 52
SIX: Courtrooms as Battlefields 65

Part II ... The Federal Child of a Thousand Fathers

SEVEN: "Then all the world would be upside down!" 83
EIGHT: New York Lawyer Rising 97
NINE: federalist into Federalist 114
TEN: The Congress of Firsts 136

Part III ... Knight in Washington's "Republican Court"

ELEVEN: Federalist Warhorse 155
TWELVE: Philadelphia Story 173
THIRTEEN: A Farewell to Innocence 185
FOURTEEN: Judicial Safe Harbor 202

Part IV ... The Federalist Hawk Who Fled the Nest

FIFTEEN: The Senator from New York 217
SIXTEEN: Quasi-Warrior in the "Reign of Witches" 230
SEVENTEEN: Slipping the Party Harness 243
EIGHTEEN: The Consolation of Wealth 261

EPILOGUE: Why John Laurance Matters 280
APPENDIX A: General Courts-Martial in George Washington's
             Main Army 1775–1778 284
NOTES..286
BIBLIOGRAPHY...350
INDEX 375

Acknowledgments

I want to thank Kenneth R. Bowling, Adjunct Professor of History emeritus at George Washington University and coeditor of the First Federal Congress Project. The monumental 22-volume *Documentary History of the First Federal Congress of the United States of America* is Ken's life's work, yet he plunged into my raw, unsolicited manuscript for the sheer fun of it! His close and careful reading raised the necessary questions every scholar needs to hear and spooned the editorial cod liver oil every writer—if he knows what's good for him—learns to swallow. Any resistance to Ken's generous advice, along with errors of fact or interpretation, remains my own burden.

JOHN LAURANCE, The Immigrant Founding Father America Never Knew is a New York story whose compass points lay long buried in the bowels of local archival institutions. I am therefore particularly indebted to Tammy Kiter, former Patricia D. Klingenstein Library manuscript reference librarian at New York Historical Society (NYHS), for helping navigate the papers of John Laurance, James Duane, John Jay, Rufus King, Alexander McDougall, and Alexander Hamilton. Thanks also to NYHS Historian Valerie Paley for much-appreciated encouragement at a particularly exasperating time. Thank you, Susan Malsbury, New York Public Library Reference Archivist, for opening up the papers of William Smith Jr. and Robert Troup. Appreciation to Supervising Librarian Christine Bruzzese at the New York City Hall Library Department of Records, Mr. Joseph Patzner at the Chancellor Robert R. Livingston Masonic Library, Mr. Justin White at the Oswego County (NY) Historical Society, and the staff at New York Society Library. Particular thanks goes to Phillip Rodda, research clerk at St. Mylor Parish (Falmouth, England) for traveling on my behalf to the Cornwall Records Office in Truro, England.

I am especially grateful to *Pennsylvania Magazine of History and Biography* Editor Christina LaRocco and her peer readers for elevating my treatment of Laurance's impact on military justice at Valley Forge. Thank you, Carol Herrity at Lehigh Valley (PA) Historical Society in Allentown, for the real scoop on John Laurance's Philadelphia "high society" second wife, Elizabeth Allen. Thank you, Beth Bruno, for the subtle hints only an experienced book editor can dispense. Many thanks to Teresa Exley, who was the production editor. Thanks go to copy editor Janet Krejci, whose invisible hand made my text the best possible version of itself. Thank you, Mary McDonald, Publications Editor at the American Philosophical Society, for gracefully ushering my manuscript into print.

And most of all: *merci*, Judith, for heroically carrying the seven-year spousal deadweight of a preoccupied author.

Posthumous gratitude goes to my forgotten protagonist's grandson George C. McWhorter, whose handwritten 65-page "Biographical Sketches of the Life of John Laurance" illuminated an otherwise blind plunge down the archival rabbit hole. Polished by NYHS President Hamilton Fish in 1869, McWhorter's never-published opus was politely received by the Society over lunch and then diplomatically assigned to the vaults. There it lay until tripped over 143 years later by yours truly.

Introduction

John who? Mention the name John Laurance and all but the most rabid period scholar draws a blank. Understandably so; for we have been educated to comprehend the War for Independence and its Federalist aftermath primarily through the words and deeds of some dozen iconic "Founding Fathers."[1] But the lofty perspectives of Adams, Hamilton, Jefferson, Madison, Washington, and the others conspire with perfect hindsight to render the whole founding experience somehow automatic. Preordained even. Asking, and answering, the question "John who?" invites a scruffier, unscripted, altogether more collaborative perspective of our nation's birth. It is one in which slipping His Majesty's imperial bonds in favor of constitutional government owes to the fortunate confluence of hundreds of unheralded compatriots of resources, talent, and determination consigned to second-tier founding limbo somewhere between shortlist "Fathers" and "We the People."

They called themselves "nationalists" after victory at Yorktown, "pro-government" as the Articles of Confederation proved deficient, and "Federalists" after the Constitutional Convention of 1787. Many were former Continental Army officers and members of the 2,150-strong Washington-inspired Society of the Cincinnati. Most were propertied gentlemen or would-be gentry, if not the "natural aristocracy" that both Adams and Jefferson later idealized.[2] Virtually all had served in colonial or state government; as many as half were lawyers.[3] Their shared commitment to rule of law under strong central government was (as Progressive and Neo-Progressive historians remind us) not without less-than-democratic socio-economic self-interests.[4] As passions enflamed over the character the new nation was to assume, some, like New Yorker Robert R. Livingston and South Carolina's Charles Pinckney, migrated to Madison and Jefferson's Democratic-Republican Party. Most, however, stuck to their pro-administration guns until the pivotal election of 1800 crashed the curtain down on the Federalist era. Soldier, legislator, jurist, and adroit real estate investor, New York lawyer John Laurance (1750–1810) was all of the above.

Sixteen and alone, Laurance in the spring of 1767 clambered off the Falmouth packet in New York harbor with little more than a letter of introduction in his West-Country English waistcoat pocket. Networking his way into the law library of His Majesty's embattled Provincial lieutenant governor Cadwallader Colden, the striving youth five years later hung out his own shingle and—no small feat—passed examination for the American Colonies' most exclusive legal association, the notoriously inbred New York bar. Testimony to his sound character in a rough-and-tumble lower Manhattan salted with chancers, the Fraternal Order of Freemasonry at St. John's Lodge No. 2 welcomed him into their rigorous brotherhood and in 1772—a rare honor for so young a man—selected him Junior Warden.[5]

Even so, the tall, rather thickset young lawyer was not at all what Scottish-born New York Sons of Liberty street leader Alexander McDougall had in mind for his strong-willed 22-year-old only daughter, Elizabeth.[6] Having parlayed the modest fortune amassed as a French and Indian War privateer captain into a prosperous mail-order merchant business, the fiercely Presbyterian Scot above all coveted social respectability from New York's "better sort." Accordingly, "Betsey," as everyone called her, was properly schooled in hope she might attract a moneyed, socially well-placed suitor. Had Laurance hailed from a reputable London family, well, that was one thing, but a Cornwall yeoman's son of middling means was something else altogether. Moreover, he worshipped alongside Crown minions at the Church of England. Yet, the lad's ardent support of the Liberty-Boy cause—and willingness to act on his words—carried the day. Four months before bloody Lexington and Concord, John Laurance and Elizabeth McDougall were man and wife.

It was an opportune marriage that hurled Laurance into Revolution's maw and propelled the erstwhile émigré nobody up the first rungs of the post-war socio-political ladder. No sooner was Independence declared that steamy summer of 1776 than Alexander McDougall was named one of George Washington's generals and his new son-in-law made a personal aide-de-camp. Twenty-two years later, Laurance had eased into high society's most exclusive parlors through his second marriage to Philadelphia's most eligible blue-blood of a certain age, cobbled a significant speculative real estate fortune, and scaled political ranks to become president pro tempore of the United States Senate, two heartbeats from the presidency. Ninety-one men—and one woman—have since the Presidential Succession Act of 1792 stood directly behind the vice president in line of Oval Office succession, but only John Laurance was not native born.[7] Two and a quarter centuries later, his remarkable public service legacy gives lasting lie to the notion that foreign-born citizens lack requisite loyalty or temperament for high national office. What's more, the doughty Cornishman's extraordinary passage from off-the-boat teenage cipher to inner circle of Federalist America's governing elite is a captivating breeches-to-riches story in its own right.

I first chanced across our forgotten protagonist's faint footsteps one blustery autumn afternoon in the College of William & Mary's Earl G. Swem

Library manuscript room. Unexpectedly, he introduced himself from the archives as I burrowed into the wartime military adventures of Supreme Court Chief Justice John Marshall. Imagine my surprise as Marshall's great (times three) grandson to discover that it was John Laurance who launched the redoubtable jurist's life in law. General Washington's order of November 20, 1777, could not have been clearer. "Lieut. John Marshall," declared the headquarters missive, "is by the Judge Advocate General appointed deputy judge advocate in the army of the United States."[8] Judge Laurance, caught short-handed over the Valley Forge winter of privation, had plucked 22-year-old Virginia infantry Lieutenant Marshall from regimental obscurity to help tackle a massive courts-martial backlog.

Laurance's five years in the field as the Continental Army's chief military lawyer and de facto father of today's U.S. Army Judge Advocate Corps is arguably the War of Independence's best kept secret.[9] Eight generations of historians have completely overlooked the officer who embedded the 1776 Congressional Articles of War into America's first professional army; the officer whose Valley Forge military justice set the disciplinary table for "Baron" von Steuben's parade ground drills; and the officer who politely and adeptly prosecuted Major Generals Adam Stephen and Charles Lee out of the army for respective battlefield shortcomings at Germantown and Monmouth.[10] Next came Major General Benedict Arnold's formal reprimand for exceeding his authority in command at Philadelphia. After Arnold turned traitor, it was Judge Laurance as proxy for Washington himself who made the case for dispatching the turncoat's go-between, unfortunate British Major John André, to the gallows for espionage.

Laurance's fingerprints are all over New York City's post-war economic recovery during what nineteenthcentury Massachusetts historian John Fiske deemed the early republic's "critical period."[11] Major General McDougall's ambitious son-in-law wasted little time leveraging wartime prestige into a buzzing law practice convoyed by prodigious community service. Trustee of Columbia University, Trinity Church vestryman, "Worshipful Master" of St. John's Masonic Lodge, city alderman, and founding member of John Jay's Manumission Society, the aspirational Cornishman helped resurrect Manhattan from its ashes. He was elected Westchester County representative to the state general assembly in May 1782 and re-elected the following year by New York County voters. Never defeated for electoral office, Laurance was delegate to the Confederation Congress, a proactive state senate advocate for ratifying the Constitution, and New York City's first United States Congressman.

Representative Laurance turned Federalist warhorse during President Washington's first term, serving on 38 separate House committees and reporting out for six.[12] Acknowledged by House peers for fiscal acuity and maritime law expertise, he spoke for the important appropriations select committees (predecessor of today's powerful Ways and Means Committee) every session of his two-term service. Key voice in the vastly underrated First Federal Congress, the New Yorker linked arms with master parliamentarian James Madison to transform the paper Constitution into machinery of government with an empowered executive branch and robust federal judiciary. When Madison balked at Treasury Secretary Hamilton's sweeping financial agenda, it was Laurance, together with Massachusetts Reps. Theodore Sedgwick and Fisher Ames, who outdueled the formidable Virginian to restructure the national debt, prevent discrimination between original and current note holders, assume state revolutionary war debts at par, and establish a national bank.

In early 1794, President Washington appointed his former judge advocate general to the Federal bench. New York District Judge Laurance soon broke legal ground by refusing to extradite asylum-seeking French naval officer Jean-Baptiste-Henri Barré. Extradition, Laurance determined, was a judicial rather than executive prerogative. Enraged French minister Jean Antoine Fauchet then pressured U.S. Attorney General Edmund Randolph to summon Laurance as *defendant* before the Supreme Court. But to M. Fauchet's dismay, Judge Laurance's precedent-setting lower court decision was swiftly sustained (*The United States v. Lawrence*, 3 U.S. 42, 1795). As relations with France deteriorated into "quasi-war," Laurance resigned the bench to fill fellow Federalist Rufus King's vacated seat as New York's junior U.S. Senator. Staunch supporter of President Adams's defense build-up, he played legislative midwife to America's first real navy. Big frigates *United States*, *Constellation*, and *Constitution* owed their sea legs to Laurance's 1797 senate committee "protections" bill that passed both houses as An Act Providing a Naval Armament.[13]

How, then, to explain the unfathomable absence of any published biography? If not a few pages in the young republic's storybook, why not even a paragraph? Professors Stanley Elkins and Eric McKitrick's masterful Bancroft Prize-winning *The Age of Federalism* (1993) mistakenly identifies Laurance as "a New York merchant."[14] Pulitzer Prize winner Ron Chernow's definitive *Alexander Hamilton* (2004) mentions him in passing as but a "friend," and Gordon Wood's Pulitzer Prize-finalist history of the early Republic, *Empire of Liberty* (2009), soars above Laurance in the trenches. If not for a profile in Volume 14 of George Washington University's important *Documentary History of the First Federal Congress 1789–1791*, Laurance's quarter century of public service would pass virtually unnoticed. How did he become the founding Federalist we never knew?

Lack of a dramatic signature moment is part of the answer; so is a paucity of surviving personal papers and a name that went to ground with his never-married only son. Nor could it help to have been foreign-born during seedtime of the nativist-skewed Great American historical narrative. Laurance was, of course, no alien at all to King George's Provincial authorities when he first scrambled ashore in New York. Rather, he was a bona fide natural-born English subject, as were Virginia-born George Washington, British West Indies-born Alexander Hamilton, and

Scottish-parented Lt. Governor Colden. For King Edward III as early as 1368 had proclaimed that all persons born within the Royal Dominions were "subjects" of the Crown, a status confirmed more than three and a half centuries later by the British Nationality Act of 1730 and its 1740 extension to the American colonies.[15] "Natural born subjects," affirmed eminent jurist Sir William Blackstone two years before Laurance sailed for America, "are such as born within the dominions of the crown of England."[16]

On July 2, 1776, one swoop of a quill pen changed everything. Instantly, Laurance and two-and-a-half million others were transformed from "subjects" into "citizens" when the Second Continental Congress declared the 13 "Free and Independent States" no longer under British rule.[17] But 13 years later, Laurance, Hamilton, and up to 10 percent of white Americans were categorized as something other than native-born citizens. For Article II of the ratified Constitution mandated that no person "except a natural born Citizen" *or* "a Citizen of the United States at the time of the Constitution" was eligible to be president.[18] A subtle distinction certainly, but one—reinforced by the Naturalization Act of 1790— that set Laurance and Hamilton apart from Washington, Jefferson, Adams, and almost everyone else in the governing class.* "He is not a native of the United States," smirked Massachusetts-born John Adams about Hamilton in 1798, "but a foreigner and I believe, has not resided longer, at least not much longer, in North America than [Swiss-born] Albert Gallatin."[19]

Immigration intricacies aside, the most compelling explanation for Laurance's historiographical vanishing act is that he was overshadowed by ideological charisma bomb Alexander Hamilton's soaring intellect, prolific Mozart-like pen, and preternatural genius for turning up at the center of things.[20] Indeed, opposing colossuses Hamilton and Jefferson tower so large over the post-war political landscape that "Great Man" theorists have long relegated like-minded contemporaries to mere follower, sycophant, lieutenant, or protégé. Even President Washington, the premier politician of his generation, is all too often portrayed as little more than an aging, wooden-toothed Hamiltonian tool. Only in recent decades has James Madison truly escaped Jefferson's immense shadow to claim his due as Democratic-Republican Party cofounder, indispensable force helping bring both the Constitution and Bill of Rights into being, and fourth president of the United States.[21]

To be sure, Laurance was no James Madison; but neither was he a mere placeholder in Hamilton's ambitious scheme of capitalist American

---

*The Naturalization Act of March 26, 1790, provided the first rules for granting national citizenship to non-native-born residents. Naturalization was limited to immigrants who were "free white Persons of good character" after two years of residency. Free blacks were not then granted citizenship, although they were permitted to vote in Maryland, Massachusetts, New York, North Carolina, Pennsylvania, and Vermont.

nationalism. However visionary and administratively talented the cerebral treasury secretary may have been, his far-reaching financial wizardry was no more than elegant theory without President Washington at his back and a cadre of strong-willed legislative like-minds to hammer it into law—all-but-forgotten men such as Sedgwick and Ames of Massachusetts, William Smith of South Carolina, transplanted New Yorker Rufus King, New Jersey's Elias Boudinot, and of course Rep. Laurance. For example, the treasury department's vaunted 60-district import-tariff and customs administration owed itself to the Collection Act of July 31, 1789, which primary author Laurance reported out of committee two months before Hamilton took office.[22]

True, John was Alexander's reliable House legislative right arm during Washington's first term, but their long personal and political relationship was far too nuanced for artless puppetry. The two ambitious immigrants first met in mid-1774 as budding revolutionaries in New York Sons of Liberty street-boss Alexander McDougall's campaign to boycott British imports. Hamilton, a King's College student not yet 20, frequented McDougall's library to gather up anti-British pamphlets.[23] Laurance, some five years Hamilton's senior, haunted the reading room for a different reason—McDougall's unmarried daughter Betsey. Although both men served as junior officers under McDougall in the ill-fated 1776 defense of lower New York against William Howe's 30,000 redcoats, it was 50 months together on Washington's headquarters staff that forged an unspoken lifetime bond unique to wartime military comrades.

No sooner had the last British troopship departed New York harbor in November 1783 than Lt. Colonels Laurance and Hamilton spearheaded a covey of young lawyers smelling fortune and reputation to be made litigating property restitution claims in reopened city courts. Within months they collided head-on in a talk-of-the-town court case (*Rutgers v. Waddington*) that addressed judicial review of legislative acts some 25 years before Chief Justice Marshall's monumental *Marbury v. Madison*.[24] Wall Street neighbors, the two rising lawyers hunted grouse together, downed Society of Cincinnati toasts, and partnered in speculative upstate land deals. "I have lately made some cash advances that have run me aground," Alexander confessed (more than once) to his companion, "I will thank you for the loan of a hundred dollars for a few days."[25] It was all part of an intimate 30-year relationship in which Laurance and his mercurial friend usually lived in such proximity there was little need to correspond.[26] Small wonder that John, in the wake of Hamilton's premature death, was named one of three trustees to discharge his cherished country estate, "The Grange."

A large-bodied, dignified man with an Englishman's reserve and a working lawyer's even-tempered pragmatism, John Laurance was no political ideologue. His federalism was simple common sense; what upwardly mobile former Continental officer couldn't see the military, mercantile, and social advantages of a robust central government? Once the Constitution was ratified, though, and a strong, soundly financed federal government put in place, he found himself increasingly put off by personal political agendas, venomous public invective, and rigid "High" Federalist dogma. "I wish you had less Passion and less Party," he lamented in early 1794 to Federalist Senator Rufus King. "They intermix too much in deliberations and measures."[27]

In the spring of 1800, Laurance broke at last with the Federalist Party caucus. The blatantly unconstitutional Senate "Ross" Bill, with its proposed 13-member (Federalist) panel to override the Electoral College, was simply too much to swallow. Matters then came to a head during that year's pivotal presidential election. He rushed from Philadelphia to New York City in an eleventh-hour attempt to help old friend Hamilton turn out the hometown Federalist vote, only to watch well-born second wife Elizabeth Allen die in their Broad Way townhouse the very day polls opened. After Republican Aaron Burr wrested control of New York's 12 electoral votes, the grief-stricken Laurance, his own health failing, rashly resigned his senate seat rather than choose between two friends in Hamilton's divisive behind-the-scenes scheme to dump sitting Federalist President Adams. Whether an act of character, or the lack of it, Laurance had written himself out of the plot as the Jeffersonian Revolution swept the Federalist Party from state and national office to usher in a new chapter in American government. In little more than a decade, he was dead. Left behind were four unmarried daughters from two marriages, rootless only son John McDougall, and a substantial speculative real estate portfolio. And while Alexander Hamilton's public stock has risen and fallen with the ebb and flow of populist capitalism, New York City's first federal congressman awaits his biographical initial public offering.

John Laurance the judge advocate general, lawmaker, jurist, and canny land speculator can be plainly understood, but Laurance the man is more problematic. Indeed, his maddeningly spotty archival record obliges caution. He left no diary or memoir, and apparently destroyed (like Jefferson) his intimate personal correspondence. Bar preparation notes, law practice account books, and courtroom briefs—except for one—are not to be found. Not a letter survives from his two advantageous marriages, so we can only guess the depth of his affection for Betsey McDougall and Elizabeth Allen. All we have of his personal papers fills but a single medium-sized box at the New York Historical Society. They suggest, together with surviving correspondence of Washington, Hamilton, King, and Robert Troup, a conscientious office holder who managed better than most to align personal interests with those of his party and voting constituency. Lacking Hamilton's brilliance, King's diplomatic charm, Troup's garrulous wit, and Livingston/Schuyler/Morris to-the-manor-born resources, Laurance—a skilled orator—compensated with diligence and dedication. About his subordination of self to party, however, Robert Troup, who probably knew him best, observed: "You may be sure he will never forget or forgive."[28]

Yes, the striving Laurance had his flaws: hewing party line in mid-1798, for example, to support the shameful Alien and Sedition Acts during what Jefferson dubbed the "reign of witches" and lacking political stomach for electoral politics after Elizabeth's passing. At the end of the day, however, no better view is to be had of the yeasty rise and fall of America's first political party than from John's front row seat. For New York City, to paraphrase historian Russell Shorto, was an island in the center of the Federalist world.[29] From the initial February 1789 caucus in Edward Bardin's Broad Way tavern nominating Laurance as the city's first federal congressman, to Aaron Burr's devastating electoral triumph of May 2, 1800, Gotham was Federalist ground zero. And all politics aside, John's long relationship with Hamilton reveals a rarely explored side of the "American Bonaparte"—that of loyal and trusted friend.

More important, Laurance reaches across the centuries to remind us that America has always been a nation of immigrants pursuing the main chance. And that Benjamin Franklin was dead wrong to scoff that "Those who come hither are generally of the most ignorant Stupid Sort of their own Nation."[30] Railing against German immigrants, he went on to ask "Why should *Pennsylvania*, founded by the *English*, become a Colony of *Aliens*, who will shortly be so numerous as to Germanize us instead of our Anglifying them?"[31] When Franklin and the others gathered in Philadelphia to craft the Constitution, fear of undue influence by European powers and foreign adventurers was all too real. Future Supreme Court Chief Justice John Jay went so far as to hint by post to Washington "whether it would not be wise and seasonable to provide a strong check to the admission of foreigners into the administration of our national govt."[32]

Jay's apprehensions were soon validated when foreign-born insiders Robert Morris, William Duer, John Nicholson, and Judge James Wilson landed in debtors' prison for speculative real estate excesses.[33] Federalist suspicion was further stoked by the unseemly political meddling of French minister Edmond-Charles Genêt, followed by ambassador Pierre Adet's blatant electioneering against John Adams in the 1796 presidential campaign. Distrust escalated into paranoia with the ugly Alien and Sedition Acts that spawned formal charges against English-born pamphleteer Thomas Cooper, naturalized Irish editor John D. Burk, Scottish-born newspaperman James Callender, and "wild Irishman" editor William Duane for stridently attacking the Federalist administration. That Duane was actually born in New York of Irish heritage made no matter. A bitter xenophobic vein in the body politic was opened that bleeds to this day in the form of "huge" border walls and refugee bans. And although Laurance was not among the "swarthy" Russian, French, and German newcomers that so disturbed the likes of Ben Franklin, the Cornish émigré's rich public service legacy helps to stem the bleeding.

What better time, then, than the current renaissance of all things Hamilton to pry Laurance from his fellow immigrant's autarchic stranglehold on Federalist-era historiography?[34] "Of some of our institutions," wrote respected Stanford history professor John C. Miller, "it may be justly said that they are the lengthened shadow of one man, Alexander Hamilton."[35] For all too long, however, this outsized silhouette has obscured John Laurance's role as a founding father. More than simply an unsung verse of Hamilton's Federalist anthem, Laurance's singular impact on Continental Army military justice, New York's post-war economic resurgence, the First Federal Congress, and the Washington and Adams presidencies merits rightful inclusion in the accepted Federalist-era narrative. Laurance also serves a larger purpose: to remind us that an entire generation of imperfect leaders—not just a worshipful founding handful—fought the War for Independence, kept the United States together under the Articles of Confederation, and established a national government under Constitutional rule of law. It is a civics lesson that citizens of our republic ignore at their peril in an age where democracy itself is under global siege by charismatic "Great Men."

PART I

From "Cousin Jack" to Colonel Laurance

ONE

Götterdämerung

TRINITY EPISCOPAL CHURCH, NEW YORK CITY, JULY 14, 1804. Alexander Hamilton was dead! Thirty-one hours after Vice President Aaron Burr's pistol ball ripped into his abdomen, New York's favorite foreign-born son gently succumbed under the merciful eye of Trinity's Right Reverend Benjamin Moore.[1] Much of America was struck dumb with emotion. "Good God!" exclaimed Philadelphia lawyer Richard Rush, mournful news in hand from Judge Laurance's 29-year-old son, John McDougall. "The gloom in our city," answered Rush, "cannot be less general than in yours."[2] Neither Rush, nor his renowned physician-father Benjamin, nor much of Philadelphia fully embraced Hamilton's capitalistic blueprint for the heavily agricultural new nation, but the visionary New Yorker's role as a founding statesman was indisputable. Energetic promoter of the Constitution, architect of the republic's financial system, and intellectual wellspring of its first political party, the most brilliant — and controversial — public figure of his day was no more.

Aging chests beribboned with bronze eagle pendants dangling from azure silk badges, Judge Laurance and his fellow Cincinnati* stood stone-faced before their departed comrade's open grave near the south wall of Trinity Church burying yard. Behind them milled the muted residue of a funeral procession that had numbered in the thousands. "Not a smile was visible," allowed one newspaperman, "and hardly a whisper was to be heard, but tears were seen rolling down the cheeks of the affected multitude."[3] One of eight pallbearers chosen to shoulder Hamilton's polished mahogany casket, John Laurance at 10 that morning had rendezvoused with eulogist Gouverneur Morris in the Robinson Street visitation parlor of Hamilton's brother-in-law John B. Church. Precisely at noon John assumed his assigned position at the casket's right foot and trudged in silent step behind the Sixth Regiment militia as the funeral cortege made its solemn way to Beekman, Pearl, and Whitehall Streets, then turned up Broad Way.[4] Inching inexorably toward Trinity Church at the head of

---

*Founded June 9, 1783, by General Washington's officers, the Society of the Cincinnati perpetuated the memory of Washington who, like Roman dictator Cincinnatus, resigned public office after military crisis had passed. Lt. Colonels Laurance and Hamilton were both charter members, and Hamilton in 1800 was elected the National Society's second President General. Society badge of membership was the azure-ribbon eagle pendant.

Wall Street, the pallbearers steeled themselves as New York City's foremost citizen grew heavier and heavier. It was all Laurance, aged 54 and diminished by inflammatory rheumatism, could do to bear his share of the weight in the noonday sun.

Episcopal Bishop Moore preceded the corpse, head bowed and shepherding leading lights of the city clergy. Behind the expressionless pallbearers clopped Hamilton's riderless gray horse, dressed in black mourning and led by two white-turbaned black servants. Next came the deceased's family, his four sons grappling heroically with the urge to sob. Further back walked Supreme Court justices, gentlemen of the bar with students of law, the governor, lieutenant governor, mayor, and members of Congress. Silently in their wake trailed civil and military officers of every stripe, foreign dignitaries, and representatives from all segments of society. Observers agreed that no more notable funeral procession had ever graced the streets of New York.[5]

As the muffled thump of military drums slowly beat out the dead march, wartime memories could not help but have flooded into Laurance's balding head. During four spartan years together on General Washington's staff, he had repeatedly summoned Alexander as expert witness to protect His Excellency's back in high-profile courts-martial trials.[6] When Judge Laurance's skillful prosecution chased Major General Charles Lee out of the Army, Hamilton had winked his approval. When John petitioned the Board of War for a full colonel's subsistence pay, Alexander backed up the request with a personal missive to Continental Congress. And when Colonel Hamilton returned victorious that chill October night from his starlight bayonet assault on Yorktown's redcoat redoubt No. 10, John was there to congratulate him.

Accompanied by tolling bells and distant cannon thuds, the melancholy column had continued up Broad Way, passing beneath crowded balconies draped with black crepe and weeping women. When the lead militia platoon reached Trinity Church, Colonel Jacob Morton wheeled his entire regiment by sections to form a lane through which the corpse was borne. On command, muskets were slowly brought to reverse order, the soldiers resting a cheek on the butt in customary martial expression of mourning. Judge Laurance and the other pallbearers gently deposited their burden on a carpeted bier under the lofty portico fronting the church. "Almost every person was in tears," remembered one participant, "even the rabble of boys and negroes who filled the streets seemed to partake of the general grief."[7]

Peg-legged Gouverneur Morris stepped ashen-faced to the dais. Some five years earlier he delivered the New York funeral oration for President Washington and would now render the honors for his friend Alexander. With Hamilton's four wet-eyed sons at his side, Morris spoke in the open air, barely intelligible even to the nearest of the sprawling crowd. While Morris fervently soldiered on, Laurance undoubtedly squinted over a shoulder toward Federal Hall at No. 26 Wall Street. How could he not remember the heady First Federal Congress days of 1790, when packed galleries watched him out-duel formidable James Madison to pass Hamilton's contentious plan for redeeming wartime debt at full face value? Indeed, Federal Hall—New York City's 1789 gift to the new republic—was more John's civic stage than Alexander's. Under its hipped, cupola-crowned roof, Alderman Laurance facilitated the building's lavish refurbishment, Confederation Congress Delegate Laurance jawboned for critical revenue-generating imposts, Congressman Laurance introduced Quaker petitions to abolish the slave trade, and Federal District Judge Laurance pronounced extradition of foreign nationals a judicial rather than an executive prerogative. Further down Wall Street loomed doorway Nos. 13 and 58 where, 20 years before, he and Alexander raised respective families in fashionable townhouses as rising lawyers arguing post-war property cases. Even when President Washington's fledgling Federal government removed to Philadelphia, Rep. Laurance and Treasury Secretary Hamilton resided mere blocks from each other, a short walk from Independence Square.

Eulogy concluded, the graying ranks of New York's Society of Cincinnati directed final burial services; the fallen Hamilton was, after all, their late national president-general. And for the next 30 days, as was Cincinnati custom, a black armband would adorn collective left arms in remembrance of their absent comrade. Slowly the pallbearers hoisted casket to shoulder and moved to the grave. Expressionless soldiers snapped gleaming muskets upright to the command of "present arms." Bishop Moore blessed the corpse, and shovelfuls of gravelly dirt clattered against the lowered coffin. "This Scene," reported Hamilton's grieving *New York Evening Post*, "was enough to melt a monument of marble."[8] Silence . . . then a blue-jacketed platoon executed three crisp volleys. Under lingering plumes of black-powder smoke, the sorrowful crowd melted away. Bells and cannon turned quiet. Trinity churchyard grew empty.

Judge Laurance was no stranger to Trinity. Longtime member of the congregation, he served as post-war vestryman after patriot legislators severed the Church's chartered tie with the King of England. As state senator, he successfully voted to delay state confiscation of Trinity's valuable real estate until a clerk in Hamilton's law office produced a 1705 deed confirming church ownership in perpetuity. Laurance and Hamilton both helped fund the structure's massive 1790 restoration, subscribing for respective pews number 64 and 92.[9] Hamilton, by refusing communion (he relented just before dying), was not formal member of the congregation, but wife Eliza most certainly was.[10] When she and Laurance's second wife Elizabeth imbibed venerable rector Samuel Provoost's Sunday sermons, John and Alexander would have exchanged occasional nodding glances across the serried pews. Although Laurance's exact whereabouts directly after bidding his great friend earthly farewell is lost to history, it would be only natural to have loitered momentarily inside Trinity's welcoming walls to settle his thoughts.

Trinity Church. In the mind's eye, how could he not picture its unmistakable 175-foot wooden steeple tower dominating the skyline as he had sailed into New York harbor some 37 years before? Fresh off the packet ship from England, he had found comfort and continuity in Trinity's familiar Anglican services. Not yet 17, the stocky English lad from Cornwall's rugged southwestern coast could not then possibly have imagined what glorious undertakings lay ahead. Thirty-seven years. How differently might they have unfolded without the outsized figure whose casket he had just borne to ground.

TWO

Casting Fate to the Wind

CORNWALL COUNTY, ENGLAND, FEBRUARY 1, 1751. Some five miles north of Falmouth on England's southwest peninsula, St. Mylor parish church squatted on a sloping ridge overlooking the Fal River estuary known by locals as "Carrick Roads." Said to consecrate the spot where St. Melioris (Melor), son of the Duke of Cornwall, was slain in A.D. 411 for embracing Christianity, the stark, circa 1130 gray Caen-stone structure dated to the reign of Henry I. Inside its dark, arcaded Norman chancel, George Turner, nineteenth Anglican vicar of St. Mylor, stood dutifully at the baptistery.[1] Immersing a babe in the worn twelfth-century baptismal font's granite octagonal bowl, Vicar Turner turned his back to an elaborately carved old Cornish rood screen and intoned the Nicene Creed together with an obligatory cluster of celebrants. And so John Lawrence (his surname was altered in America to Laurance) was welcomed to the family of Christ and the windswept West Country community of St. Mylor Parish.[2]

The infant was likely conceived out of wedlock, for it was less than eight months earlier that "John LAWRENCE of Milor" and "Mary Knuckey of Falmouth" exchanged vows in nearby Redruth Parish another five miles distant along the King's Road from Falmouth.[3] Had the 28-year-old groom descended from Sir John Lawrence (1588–1638), knight, baronet, and wealthy London merchant, his newborn son would likely have never left English soil; but no such fortunate connection is to be found.[4] Plain genealogical truth is that the Lawrence/Lawrance/Laurance surname—first found in Lancashire before the Norman Conquest—had become legion throughout the English shires. And fully one in five Englishmen between 1585 and 1800 answered to the given name of "John."[5] Two John Lawrences of note graced Cornwall in "John of Milor's" day. One was a middling lawyer in the market village of Launceston and the other a captain of militia and proprietor of Trellissick House (presently a National Heritage Trust property). Neither fathered George Washington's future judge advocate general. Instead he would descend from an unremarkable line of yeoman John Lawrences inhabiting St. Mylor Parish as early as 1641.[6] However loving and industrious they may have been, the modest parents of Vicar Turner's baptismal babe exited the church's weathered nave in February 1751 and vanished into genealogical oblivion.

Details of John's youth are equally murky. Parish records show him to have been an only child whose father died in the lad's seventh year.[7] Family tradition boasts of a coveted public school education, superintended most likely by his father's younger brother Richard—a successful Falmouth merchant. Nearest, and by far most academically respected, of Cornwall's public schools was Truro Grammar School, a 42-foot by 28-foot stone classroom in the lee of St. Mary's Church less than 10 miles north of St. Mylor Parish. Anonymously endowed around the year 1549, the venerable Free School with its adjoining library had lately earned a reputation as "the Eton of Cornwall."[8] Headmaster in Lawrence's day was George Conon, an evangelical Anglican churchman known for mercilessly flogging Latin and Greek grammar into his charges. Nonetheless, between 1728 and 1771 Conon's strict classical regimen in the Eton College format attracted gentlemen's sons from throughout the West Country. "The school," boasted one Cornwall historian, "for a long series of years, was of a high character... and saw her scholars both at Oxford and Cambridge."[9]

John Lawrence was not one of them. Fatherless and lacking financial wherewithal for the university, in 1767 he turned "Cousin Jack," as early Cornish émigrés were labeled.[10] What ambitious, educated youth would opt to waste away in semi-feudal St. Mylor Parish? Like most of mid-eighteenth-century western England, the area consisted chiefly of freehold land leased to tenant farmers for life, or a term of years, by lords of the manor as they had done over centuries past.[11] Unless to the manor born, a strapping lad apprenticed himself to agriculture, smuggling, the church, the ocean-trade, went into the tin mines... or left.

No one was better placed to facilitate John's passage to King George's flourishing New York Province than his uncle Richard (1732–1795). A thriving Falmouth factoring agent with important trading contacts from Long Island to South Carolina, Richard was commercially well acquainted with longtime packet agent George Bell and the many packet captains whose fine residences overlooked the harbor from Dunstanville Terrace.[12] Whatever strings Richard Lawrence pulled to secure his nephew's packet berth, John gratefully returned the favor 16 years later by taking his uncle's namesake son into his active New York law practice.[13] And in 1802, well after Richard's death, John slipped 20 gold guineas in a packet courier pouch to aid his late uncle's struggling spinster daughter Mary Ann and her widowed sister Alicia.[14]

Falmouth, a mere 30 miles from Land's End, was Europe's most westerly deep natural harbor. Situated at the mouth of Cornwall County's Fal River and protected by fortified castles, the two-mile-wide estuary served since 1688 as Royal packet station for all mail coming in and out of England. Thirty-seven packet routes connected England with continental Europe, Africa, Asia, and the Americas. The lively Falmouth/New York packet route, commissioned in 1756, transported mail along with Royal dispatches, bullion shipments, and merchant exchange monies. A few cramped cabins five feet wide and perhaps six feet deep were available to paying passengers, but no cargo other than passenger personal baggage was accepted. Passage from Falmouth to New York, at the princely sum of £20 sterling, included meals taken in the officers' dining room.* More affordable to lads of Laurance's moderate station, with the captain's consent, were below-deck bunks in steerage at a going rate of £12.

Monthly passage to New York was a bouncing, plunging adventure under sail into the teeth of prevailing west winds that required between 40 and 100 days at sea. In 1767 four sister ships (*Lord Hyde*, *Harriot*, *Duke of Cumberland*, and *Earl of Halifax*) served the Falmouth/New York route, each completing three round-trips per year.[15] Young Lawrence might have taken any one of the four, but family tradition suggests the most likely was *Earl of Halifax*, departing in early March under Captain John Phillips Boulderson. *Halifax*, launched in 1764 from Collet & Berd's Thames River shipyard, was a three-masted armed schooner built for speed.[16] Eight six-pound cannon ensured that no similar-sized privateer might take her without stiff resistance, but she showed her heels to ponderous 3,000-ton ships of the line with their 800-man crews. Savvy American trans-Atlantic traveler Benjamin Franklin once overheard a packet captain boast his craft notched rates up to 13 knots. "We had on board as a Passenger," chuckled Franklin, "Captain Kennedy of the Navy, who contended that this was impossible, that no Ship ever sailed so fast." Smiling over his eyeglasses, Franklin told of the ensuing wager and how the packet surged forward like a greyhound. "The captain of the Packet (Ludwidge) said he believ'd she then went at the Rate of 13 knots, Kennedy made the Experiment, and own'd his Wager lost."[17]

After precious bags from the London mail coach were duly transferred aboard, Captain Boulderson on March 5, 1767, gave command to haul anchor on the ebb tide. Her canvas filling, *Earl of Halifax* tacked into prevailing westerly breezes and set course for New York. Gliding past the dark guns of St. Mawes fortress to the port side and glowering Pendennis Castle off starboard, the sleek packet worked her way down the Fal estuary and nosed into the fresh wind of open sea. The prominent hilly neck overlooking Falmouth harbor to the northwest was the 3,600-acre St. Mylor Parish, Lawrence's birthplace and boyhood home. He could not know it as he watched Cornwall's soft hills and jagged shoreline cliffs recede in the distance, but John would never see England or his mother again.[18]

Forty-four days later, *Halifax* on April 17 negotiated the curving, treacherous five-mile spit of Sandy Hook, skirted Staten and Governor's

---

*Approximately $2,834 today. A £20 packet fare then represented 4.707 ounces of fine gold according to official London Mint conversion tables. Between 1717 and 1816, the British master of the mint fixed the price for gold at about $20/troy ounce. The Federal Reserve Bank of Minneapolis calculates that in 2018, approximately 30.1 dollars are required to equal the purchasing power of an 1800 dollar. Therefore 4.707 × $20 × 30.1 = $2,833.61.

Islands, and rode the tide into New York harbor. Hard on starboard tack, she would have saluted Fort George with its fluttering Union Jack, coasted along the 600-foot fortified "Battery" wall, and shimmied in to Whitehall Slip (present-day terminal of the Staten Island Ferry) on the very southern tip of Manhattan Island. This Royal dock, restricted since 1730 to vessels conducting the King's business, allied with the like-named street at its head to subtly remind all comers that the long arm of His Majesty's power extended *here* from ministries and departments clustered along London's Whitehall Street. Glancing up at the 10-foot-thick Battery bastion as he stepped ashore, Lawrence made his way up Whitehall Street past newly constructed redcoat military barracks on his left to the triangular "Bowling Green" several hundred feet ahead.[19] Fort George, with its 50 cannon and modest 180-man garrison, did not seem overly intrusive to the clusters of New Yorkers freely strolling the grounds and gardens. In turn, British soldiers and sailors were grudgingly tolerated, if not welcomed, in most city churches, homes, and the many side-street taverns.

Appearances, however, were deceptive. Less than 11 months earlier, those very Fort George guns were trained on the city, whose feisty ranks of mechanics, unemployed seamen, artisans, small shopkeepers, and assorted ne'er-do-wells took to the streets in ongoing anger against Parliament (for its intrusive Quartering Act of 1765), the Provincial General Assembly (for appropriating funds to quarter the King's troops), and the landed gentry (for inviting British regulars to put down recent Hudson River tenant revolts). When provoked, this "lower sort" might at any time erupt into a violent, unreasoning thousand-man armed mob. Talent for provocation was second nature to the bored soldiers and arrogant officers of His Majesty's ill-disciplined Twenty-Eighth Regiment of Foot. Housed in the "upper barracks" near present-day City Hall, the churlish Gloucestershire lads of the Twenty-Eighth Foot had just been marched out of Canada for a history of unnecessary civilian violence. Nor did it help that freshly appointed regimental Lieutenant Colonel Sir John St. Clair viewed the sinecure as a retirement pension, taking up residence in a lordly New Jersey country estate with his young Philadelphia socialite wife. Only six weeks before Lawrence clambered ashore, smirking redcoats had poured from their barracks to trigger street brawls by yet again chopping down the symbolic pole defiantly erected by Sons of Liberty toughs during the Stamp Act imbroglio of 1765.[20] Rift between colonists and Crown minions, John would soon discover, was but an injudicious bayonet thrust from tearing wide open.

Nonetheless, New York with its roughly 20,000 souls was a surprisingly civilized scene to visitors arriving after more than 40 days at sea. "I had no idea of finding a place in America," remarked one dazzled British naval officer, "consisting of near 2,000 houses, elegantly built of brick, raised on an eminence and the streets paved and spacious . . . such is this city that very few in England can rival it in its show."[21] No first-time visitor could miss the mansion at No. 1 Broad Way overlooking Bowling Green and the glacis of Fort George. Built circa 1745 by the father of Ben Franklin's fellow packet traveler, Royal Navy Captain Archibald Kennedy (11th Earl of Cassilis), the spectacular house embodied "the most approved English model" of Georgian elegance with its Palladian central window, columned entry porch, sweeping staircase, and 50-foot-long parlor.[22]

A few doors up Broad Way's west side beckoned proprietor George Burns' City Arms Tavern. Down Great Queen Street to the right, Queen Charlotte smiled from the weathered tavern sign of Samuel "Black Sam" Fraunces' Queen's Head. For news of the day, it was but a short walk down Water Street to the base of Wall Street where Widow Ferrari presided over the two-storied Merchants' Coffee House. There, amid the commotion of backgammon games, animated conversation ranged from exchanging Spanish silver and gold Portuguese "Johannes" for pounds and shillings New York money, to recent whorehouse sackings by "mistreated" redcoat clientele, to stage productions at the newly erected John Street Theatre. The theatre's Chapel Street predecessor, newcomers might be informed with hoary grins, had been pillaged that May by a liberty-shouting mob and carried piecemeal to the common for burning.[23]

What would have captured any visitor's eye was the flock of church spires. Sixteen of them. Anglican, Presbyterian, Moravian, Lutheran, Calvinist, French Huguenot, Old Dutch, New Dutch, and Jewish sects— all but the despised Papists—worshipped their God freely in polyglot New York. Services of an altogether different sort were to be found in dozens of brothels bordering the East River wharves. As early as 1744, an after-dusk stroll on the Battery was "a good way for a stranger to fit himself with a courtesan; for that place was the general rendezvous of the fair sex of that profession after sunset."[24] A quarter-century later, the world's oldest profession had expanded northward to institute a "school of Venus" in the slummy surrounds of King's College, where one visitor optimistically guessed, "above 500 ladies of pleasure keep lodgings."[25] Although much of this brothel district was property of Trinity Anglican Church, winking locals dubbed it "Holy Ground" for more secular reasons.

There is no record of kinsmen meeting John as he disembarked the moored packet, but what youth sails into the great unknown without at very least a distant cousin to contact. Two documents among his personal papers at New York Historical Society connect our "Cousin Jack" to the extensive Lawrence clan populating a section of Queens County, Long Island, then known as Lawrence Point.[26] Located between the East River and the village of Elmhurst in present-day Queens, Lawrence Point was readily accessible from Manhattan by East River ferry to rustic 13-building Brooklands (Brooklyn). From there lay a 10-mile carriage trek northward through the villages of Bedford and Bushwick to present-day Flushing and a dozen Lawrence doorsteps. John's lieutenancy in a Queens County infantry company early in the War for Independence further confirms the local tie, although his exact genealogical relationship with the colonial Lawrences is uncertain.[27]

The Dutch settlement of New Netherland had acquired a sturdy English element—one in every five colonists—well before it surrendered in 1664 to British arms. Earliest on the scene was mercenary military engineer Lion Gardiner (1599–1663), who in 1639 purchased his namesake island from the Montaukett Tribe. In Gardiner's wake came a stream of Puritan refugees, disaffected New Englanders, opportunistic Caribbean traders, and British adventurers. Men with solid Anglo-Saxon names like Doughty, Smith, Fish, Hallett, Moore . . . and Lawrence. Around 1640, Hertfordshire-born brothers John (1618–1699) and William (1623–1680) Lawrence abandoned Puritan Massachusetts's Plymouth Colony for greener pastures in present-day Queens.[28] Twenty-four years later, British colonel Richard Nicolls (assisted by four warships and 300 troops) wrested control of New Netherland's 1,500 souls from the Dutch West Indies Company to advance the finances of James Stuart, Duke of York and brother of King Charles II. Whereupon John Lawrence, who had earlier finagled extensive land patents to present-day Hempstead and Flushing (Vlissigen), endeared himself with the Duke's cronies to become three-time New York mayor, member of the governor's council, and long-serving Supreme Court justice.

Younger brother William was equally accomplished. From his 900-acre Tew's (renamed Lawrence's) Neck residence he became Flushing patent's largest landowner, adding hundreds more acres around Oyster Bay by marrying Smithtown manor grantee Richard Smith's daughter Elizabeth. Early confidant of Dutch governor-general Peter Stuyvesant, William turned adversary when the Long Island towns chafed against New Amsterdam's dominance. With the Union Jack waving over New York, William sensed investment potential in newly created New Jersey Province and purchased substantial acreage from Native Americans around Monmouth Township. One of the most affluent New Yorkers of his day, his estate included plate and personals valued at £4,430 sterling, along with some 10 "Negroes," 32 oxen, 46 cows, 17 horses, and several thousand acres.[29]

In 1665, A third Lawrence brother, Thomas (162?–1703), joined John and William to exploit the Flushing patent. "By purchase from the Dutch settlers," wrote Queens historian James Riker, "he became proprietor of a number of cultivated farms along the East River from Hell-gate Cove to the Bowery Bay."[30] Commissioned a Major of Volunteers by self-appointed Governor Jacob Leisler, Thomas became influential magistrate of the Flushing community when New York Colony in 1683 formalized Queens as one of its 12 original "shires" or counties. Thomas's five sons and three daughters married well and multiplied prodigiously.

All of which brings us to Major Thomas Lawrence's great-grandson, John Jr. One of that day's most eminent New York City merchants, Junior married into perhaps the province's most prominent family, the Livingstons. Of New York's 30 or so great baronial manor grants, three—Rensselaerswyck, Cortlandt, and Livingston—held perpetual seats in the provincial general assembly, invariably filled by the manor lord himself. None was better endowed with "men of rank and ability" than 160,240-acre Livingston Manor, shrewdly ruled by offspring of Robert Livingston the Elder (1654–1728).[31] Linked by blood or marriage to virtually every name in the provincial aristocracy, Livingston hegemony also extended to prosperous lesser families such as the Lawrences. John Jr.'s wife Catherine, for example, was sixth daughter of the Honorable Philip Livingston (1716–1778), merchant, civic leader, and future signer of the Declaration of Independence.

John Jr. and Catherine, alas, could not produce an heir before his passing in 1764 at the age of 43. Accordingly, John Jr.'s last will and testament named four of seven siblings as executors of the estate. And with this document, our Cornwall émigré makes his debut. For not only is the will among Laurance's New York Historical Society papers, but in September 1771, several months before opening his fledgling law practice, the 21-year-old aspiring attorney drew up a property indenture in the collective name of the same four siblings to dispose of "a certain dwelling house and piece of ground lying and being in Montgomery Ward of the City of New York."[32] Because Laurance surely lodged with one or more of the four before hanging out his shingle, their brief acquaintance is worth a moment.

Anne (1731–1798), youngest of the Lawrence siblings, married into one of the bluest of New England blueblood families, the Sacketts of Plymouth Plantation. On Sackett lands near the Queens village of Newtown, she and husband William raised five children. Anne's brother Thomas (1733–1817) was appointed at age 25 to captain of the 18-gun warship *Tartar* during the French and Indian War. Together with wife Elizabeth of the affluent Fish family, Thomas in 1760 settled on a flourishing Flushing Bay farm given to them by her father. As seems to be the case in virtually every Lawrence household, Thomas, too, christened one of his sons "John." Jonathan Lawrence (1737–1812) amassed an early fortune from New York mercantile pursuits and retired aged 34 to the large residence overlooking East River's Hell-Gate* formerly inhabited by his great-grandfather, Major Thomas Lawrence. Jonathan, like brother Thomas, married a Fish girl, Judith, who died unexpectedly in 1767 at the age of 18, to be replaced within a year by Ruth Riker, daughter of

---

*Hell-Gate is a seventeenth-century name for the confluence of the Harlem and East Rivers with Long Island Sound. The narrow passage was treacherous to pass under sail without a strong breeze to offset wicked currents.

a well-to-do Dutch Queens landowner. Brother Daniel Lawrence (1739–1801) wed Miss Eva Van Horn, daughter of esteemed Dutch New York City merchant Abraham Van Horn, and decamped to his fertile Lawrence Point estate to sow, among other crops, the seeds of seven children. (Yes, the firstborn was named "John.") Captain of a troop of horse in the Queens County militia, Daniel would abandon his home when William Howe's British army enveloped Long Island the summer of 1776. And like brother Jonathan, he served the duration of the war as a member of the exiled New York legislature.

Simple fertility mathematics taking its course, Queens County after four generations of descendants was blessed with scores of Lawrence offspring. Cousin Richard served as local militia captain, while cousin Joseph married into the respected family of New York Anglican churchman Benjamin Moore and dispatched a son to Edinburgh to complete his medical education. Captain Samuel Lawrence was among the founders of King's College (later Columbia University), pledging a £200 start-up bond in 1756.[33] County magistrate William Lawrence would in 1776 lead a Newtown militia company in valiant, futile resistance to British General Howe's massive invasion force. Any of these prosperous, well-connected relations would have been more than happy to introduce an educated, promising youth like John Laurance to influential men who could advance his prospects. Indeed, throughout his youth and well into his twenties, John demonstrated remarkable facility for inducing well-placed older men to further his interests. How else could a callow lad from the west country of England have, according to family tradition, "read law" under the sitting lieutenant governor of New York, the Honorable Cadwallader Colden?[34]

Tucked away in the Luce Collection at the Metropolitan Museum's American Wing, Matthew Pratt's 1772 painting reveals the man who received John Laurance. As depicted in figure 1, a prosperous, contented Colden returns our gaze with an intelligent, albeit weary visage. The lieutenant governor, one hand on an unfurled parchment and the other draped over young grandson Warren DeLancey's shoulder, is allegorically posed in the act of transmitting his considerable knowledge to a new generation. Laurance undoubtedly enjoyed similar benevolence because the old man could not help but recall that—more than half a century before—he too had crossed the Atlantic to seek his fortune.

No educated person in New York or London between 1730 and 1776 was unacquainted with the exploits of Cadwallader Colden.[35] He was North America's Ben Franklin before Franklin himself assumed the role. Named first Colonial representative to the powerful Iroquois Confederation, the Irish-born (of Scottish parents) Colden turned historian, publishing *The History of Five Indian Nations*, a 1727 tract read with interest from Bath to Vienna. Colden's Latin taxonomy of upstate New York flora was gratefully included in the acclaimed Swedish botanist Carl Linnaeus's encyclopedia,

FIGURE 1 Cadwallader Colden (1688–1776) and Warren DeLancey (176?–1846). Oil on canvas (ca. 1772) by Matthew Pratt (1734–1805). (Morris K. Jesup Fund, 1969, Metropolitan Museum of New York. Public domain.)

Genera Plantarum (1737). Educated in Edinburgh as a physician, Colden was first to document correlation between filthy living conditions and yellow fever in New York City. And he persuaded the government to do something about it. Later convinced that Isaac Newton erred in matters of physics, Colden authored *An Explication of the First Causes of Action in Matter and of the Cause of Gravitation*, thereby initiating a 20-year correspondence to "correct" the Englishman's mistakes. (Newton prevailed.)

Colden, after only a year as New York Provincial surveyor-general, was in 1721 named by Governor William Burnett to the Governor's Council, where he served for 55 increasingly influential years. And when Lieutenant Governor James DeLancey Sr. was found dead in his library from aggravated asthma in August of 1760, 72-year-old Cadwallader was appointed his successor, a position he would hold the rest of his life.

Over the next 16 years, Colden—dubbed "Silverlocks" for his fine mop of white hair—was King George III's indispensable man on the ground in New York Province. Indeed, he might have been enshrined in American memory had not his loyalty to the Crown been overrun by events. For in Governor Robert Monckton's absence (he never set foot in America from 1763 to 1765), Lt. Governor Colden bore the brunt of protest riots as King George III tightened the screws of empire over his American colonies with a series of ill-conceived measures to pay down £133,000,000 in national debt largely incurred by the Seven Years' War.

Fathoming why a man of Colden's accomplishment would take under his wing a raw aspiring legal apprentice just off the boat requires a closer look at his governing predicament. Two powerful factions had come to dominate New York politics during Cadwallader Colden's day. Led by London-educated James Jr., the DeLancey family along with the Bayards, Jaunceys, and Wattses advanced merchant class interests, while the Livingston/Morris/Smith coalition spoke for large vested landowners. Depending on situational advantage, both factions alternated between supporter and critic of Royal prerogative as they jockeyed for power.

More was at play, however, than simple family rivalry.[36] "Opposite parties," allowed Colden, "have taken their denominations from some Distinguished person or Family," but beneath lay a deeper "fundamental antipathy" rooted in "the different political and religious Principles of the Inhabitants."[37] Livingstons, for example, tended to be Presbyterian, whereas other manor-grant families attended Dutch Reformed Church services. The DeLancey crowd worshipped alongside Colden, together with most of the King's Provincial government, at Trinity Anglican Church. When it came to London politics, Livingston Presbyterians inclined toward the supremacy of Parliament espoused by most liberal Protestant Whigs, while their DeLancey counterparts were staunchly conservative pro-monarch Tories. What with disgruntled tradesmen of all religions and tenant farmer unrest against arbitrary manor-grant landlords, it was all Colden could do during the economically slumping 1760s to maintain a Crown authority eroded by decades of General Assembly assertiveness.

The Livingston faction gained the upper hand in the political fluidity following James DeLancey Sr.'s sudden death in 1760. And a formidable lot they were. Cousins William, Henry, Peter, and Phillip held assembly seats; family patriarch Robert R. Livingston ascended to the Provincial Supreme Court; and Robert Jr. was to emerge as a Manhattan lawyer of consequence. Even acting Provincial Attorney General James Duane was the elder Livingston's ward as well as son-in-law. William Livingston together with like-minded William Smith Jr. (wed to Livingston's cousin) and "bluff, hearty, jovial" John Morin Scott came to dominate the New York bar from the late 1750s through the 1770s. Known as the "Whig triumvirate" for criticism of Royal prerogative in publications such as their weekly *American Whig* and the *Occasional Reverberator*, the Presbyterian trio matriculated from Yale together, clerked at James Alexander and William Smith Sr.'s prestigious law offices, and gathered after hours at the King's Arms "soaking at tavern with a set of noisy fops."[38] A continual pain in Colden's political neck, the threesome strenuously opposed his London-backed initiative to interfere with the Provincial judiciary by imposing tenure "at the Pleasure of the Crown" in place of essentially lifetime terms on good behavior.

Frustrated by rising "Domination of the Lawyers," Colden in 1762 seized upon a civil battery case (*Forsey v. Cunningham*) as a means to restore Crown judicial authority.[39] Under common law, the jury trial judgment against Cunningham was reviewable only by a "writ of error" from the King. Granted appellate authority by Privy Council, Colden directed the Provincial Supreme Court to negate the jury verdict. Robert R. Livingston and his fellow Supreme Court associates refused. For if Colden were accommodated, any jury verdict might then be challenged through "writ of error," enabling the governor and his council to not only re-adjudicate matters but also funnel appeals directly to King George's Board of Trade and Privy Council. It was a travesty of jury trial sanctity that neither the Court, nor then Attorney General John Kempe, nor the plaintiff's savvy co-counsels William Smith Jr. and John Morin Scott would tolerate.

Colden, exasperated by an "incestuous" lawyerly state of political affairs, dashed off a warning to London's Lords of Trade. "Where the Judges and principal Lawyers," he cautioned, "are proprietors of extravagant grants of land, or strongly connected with them in Interest, or family alliances, it is possible that a dangerous combination may subsist between the Bench and Bar."[40] This potent complicity brought Colden to a boil in 1765 when lawyers from both the DeLancey and Livingston factions opposed Lord Grenville's despised Stamp Act. "The lawyers," spat Colden, "influence every branch of our Government. A domination as destructive of Justice as the domination of Priests was of the Gospel; both of them founded on delusion."[41]

Historian, chemist, biologist, and natural philosopher the polymath Colden may have been, but navigating courtroom waters to uphold Crown authority required skilled legal training that he admittedly lacked. "I am no lawyer," the Lt. Governor lamented to the Earl of Halifax after the *Forsey* episode, "and I have not one single person of knowledge of Law to assist me."[42] He could only have been delighted, then, when three years later young John Laurance presented himself, letter of introduction in hand. Not only would Colden gain a malleable apprentice to conduct legal spadework for his Chancery Court rulings, but he could also at last put to use the law volumes in his fine 3,000-book library at Spring Hill, the estate he erected in 1763 some four miles from Lawrence Point.[43] In turn, John would gain privileged insight into the lively Livingston/DeLancey tug-of-war for control of the Provincial legislature as his mentor navigated the two factions to impose the King's Parliamentary will.

Gathering dust in Colden's library stacks were dozens of legal reference books, ordered from London in 1749 for his then so-inclined son John.[44] Among these foundational texts of English jurisprudence were Sir Edward Coke's four-volume *Institutes of the Lawes of England*, Lilly's two-part *Practical Register, Office of Clerk of the Peace*, and Jacob's *Law Dictionary*. No sooner, however, had the books arrived, then poor 21-year-old "Johnny" Colden succumbed in August 1751 to smallpox while superintending family properties in Albany. Some 16 years later, another aspiring law student named John plunged into the little-used volumes. To be sure, the multi-faceted lieutenant governor lacked necessary legal wherewithal to tutor Laurance along the customary clerkship path to the New York bar. Nevertheless, access to Colden's chancery proceedings, provincial archives, and impressive law library provided a crucial first step.

THREE

Crossing the Bar

NEW YORK CITY, AUTUMN OF 1769. Just to the north of Lt. Governor Colden's Fort George administrative chambers, at the corner of Broadway and Exchange Place, stood the fine brick mansion of prim, erudite William Smith Jr., universally regarded as "at the head of his profession of the law." Dubbed the "Weathercock" for his mastery of the political wind-gage, Smith (1728–1793) had lately trimmed activist Whig sails to succeed his father on Governor Sir Henry Moore's royal Provincial Council. Nevertheless, his commitment to professionalize the Provincial legal practice was unwavering. Having twice codified New York laws in collaboration with brother-in-law William Livingston, and in 1757 penned *The History of the Province of New York*, Smith also took particular interest in the proper education of young lawyers.[1] His brief treatise titled "Some Directions Relating to the Law" directed aspiring apprentices to digest no less than 16 necessary English common law publications before even approaching Sir Edward Coke's four-volume landmark tome, *Institutes of the Lawes of England*.[2] Actual mentoring from Smith himself is pure speculation, but John Laurance would have been a freak among his peers not to have perused such Smith requisites as Hale's *History of Commercial Law*, Wood's *Institutes of the Common Law* and *Institutes of the Civil Law*, and Bacon's *Abridgement of the Law*, *Abridgement of Cases in Equity*, and *Chancery Reports and Cases*.

    Young Laurance leavened textbook law with practical precedent by burying his nose in Provincial civil and equity statutes at New York City Hall, the repository of Crown legal records and venue of "Mayor's Court" litigation. After spy-hopping courtroom proceedings, he would have labored mightily as a mere scrivener on mentor Colden's administrative needs, copying and transcribing a mountain of documents. It was all part of understanding firsthand how the Provincial judiciary of specialized courts actually functioned. Each of Great Britain's American colonies had by 1750 evolved its own particular legal system, but none, John soon discovered, more closely resembled the English model than New York with its Courts of Common Pleas and non-juried trio (Chancery, Admiralty, and Prerogative) of King's Courts.[3]

    The bedrock upon which New York's legal code rested was known as the "Duke's Laws." Devised in 1665 by London-trained barrister

Matthias Nichols for the conquering Duke of York, this regulatory code amalgamated fundamentals of English common law with practices of the Massachusetts and New Haven colonies while ensuring that land tenure was only by license from the Duke himself. Although religious freedom was promised to all Christians, the "Duke's Laws" shaped an absolutist state that perpetuated Dutch manor grants and made no provision for local legislative voice. New Yorkers therefore seized the day in 1688 to establish an elective general assembly when the Duke, having ascended to the British throne as King James II, fled to France in face of Parliament's "Glorious Revolution." Three years later, opportunistic colonists instituted a system of courts wholly divorced from both the legislature and the Governor's Council. At its head was the *Supreme Court of Judicature* whose appointed judges exercised the same common law jurisdiction as English courts of the King's Bench. Emboldened by lack of Crown pushback, the General Assembly installed each of the Province's 12 counties with a juried Court of Common Pleas, Court of Sessions (for criminal matters), and popularly elected justices of the peace. New York City's 33-year-old Dutch "Worshipful Court of the Schout, Burgomasters, and Schepens" smoothly transitioned into a court of common pleas that was promptly dubbed the "Mayor's" Court.[4]

Even so, the Province was late to develop a substantial class of competent professional lawyers. Relentless interference with the judiciary by His Majesty's Royal Governors combined with a real aversion to "Boston Principles" (rule of law) among the ruling merchant class to ensure the number of attorneys was unusually small for a colony of New York's wealth and importance. Indeed, no more than 41 lawyers practiced in New York City between 1695 and 1769.[5] Nor was there any coherent sense of professional commonality until 1731, when Governor John Montgomerie, a career soldier turned courtier-bedchamber groom to George II, pocketed a £840 bribe to re-charter the city of New York and grant eight named lawyers exclusive practice before the Mayor's Court.[6] Emergence of a true professional bar, however, was retarded under Montgomerie's successor, the arrogant, grasping Colonel William Cosby. At Cosby's insistence, two of the city's eight chartered lawyers (James Alexander and William Smith Sr.) were arbitrarily disbarred for challenging the legitimacy of Cosby-appointed Supreme Court chief judge James DeLancey during the landmark libel trial of printer Peter Zenger.

Only after Cosby's 1736 death did the reinstated Alexander and Smith settle New York's legal establishment with a colloquial association to supervise education, regulate practice (fix prices), and oversee admission to the Mayor's Court. By 1744 the "Association," as they called themselves, had formalized its stranglehold on membership into colonial America's first professional bar.[7] Consequently, New York, like Massachusetts, eschewed English Inns of Court apprenticeship in favor of "reading law" in the offices of established local lawyers. Of the 115 or so Americans admitted to London Inns between 1760 and 1783, only five were New Yorkers.[8]

Eleven years before Laurance stepped ashore at Whitehall Slip, the decidedly inbred New York Bar Association formally spelled out three qualifications for new clerks: at least two years of college education, a whopping £200 ($22,600 today) down payment, and a binding five-year indenture commitment that was later reduced to three for baccalaureate degree holders.[9] Because there were no Provincial law schools in Laurance's day, sole route to formal license was to clerk for an established lawyer.[10] But John's English public school education was just not commensurate to an Oxford, Cambridge, or King's College baccalaureate. With no clerkship at the London Inns of Court, no father already vested in the bar, and most certainly no £200 in his purse, door to the tightly controlled bar fraternity appeared closed and bolted. Yet, powerful as the bar cabal had become, by 1770 its oligopolistic grip had significantly loosened. Open defiance of admission restrictions in rural districts, legislative enactments to expand the size of the profession, and the arrival of lawyers licensed in other colonies allowed skilled and determined outsider feet in the door.[11]

Exactly how long Laurance read law under Colden is a matter of conjecture. No written record survives to detail his formal clerkship with the lieutenant governor or anyone else. Second-generation Anglo/Irish barrister James Duane may well have played a role in John's training; as acting Provincial attorney general, the former chancery court clerk handled Lieutenant Governor Colden's formal legal matters.[12] Son of an Irish immigrant, Duane (1733–1797) read law under Charter-grandfathered lawyer James Alexander, married a Livingston daughter, was admitted to the New York bar in 1754, and repeatedly turned up in Laurance's later career.

If not James Duane, then another licensed lawyer certainly lent a tutoring hand, for how else, given Colden's lack of formal training in the law, could Laurance have prepared for the bar examination? Even in the best of cases, however, actual tutoring of clerks by their busy masters was problematic. In 1769, for example, a clerk of vaunted William Smith Jr.— Peter Van Schaack by name—declared: "not above one or two attorneys in town do tolerable justice to the obligation to educate their clerks."[13] Whatever the particulars of Laurance's own clerkship, he opened public practice sometime in 1772 and eked out reputation as a sound attorney for rudimentary pleadings in pedestrian debt recovery, admiralty, and property (chancery) matters.[14] But what well-heeled client would hire an unlicensed lawyer to shepherd a case to the Mayor's Court and on to the Provincial Supreme Court?

Unlicensed attorneys such as Laurance were further shackled by the London tradition of smaller professional fees than those due Inns of Court trained "barristers" who hailed from a higher social class. This Old

World practice was first imposed in 1727 when Provincial governor William Burnet's chancery ordinance expressly discriminated in fees between "counsel" and the less prestigious "solicitor."[15] A generation later, ubiquitous William Smith Jr. reiterated the distinction in his 1750 *Scheme for Drawing out Bills of Costs in the Supream Court of New York*.[16] Smith's updated discriminatory fee schedule was later blessed by the City Council, leaving Laurance no choice but seek license before the New York bar if he were to don the more financially rewarding black robe of "counsel." The initial step was to schedule formal examination with at least six established members of the bar, notifying all sitting Supreme Court justices of the dates at least 10 days beforehand. After tacit consent of the justices and written approval from all examiners, the successful candidate applied to the City Recorder for his hard-earned license. Well-born, auspiciously apprenticed clerks might of course be given free pass to the bar without formal examination. Governor Sir Henry Moore, for example, "being well assured of the ability and learning of John Jay, Gentleman," personally authorized him on 1767 to be sworn in as member of the bar.[17]

No such fortunate dispensation devolved on Laurance. Only after posting a "respectable" examination, was Mr. John Laurance, Esq. on January 21, 1775, formally licensed as newest member of the now 62-man New York bar.[18] It was the first recorded instance in which his surname was spelled with a "u" as we now know it. As a freshly minted member of the bar out to ascend His Majesty's colonial social ladder, the tweak was essential to avoid confusion with another John Lawrence already practicing law in the New York area. Also sharing the name was a prominent Westchester County landowner whose 488-acre Tory estate would be forfeited at Revolution's end. Another John Lawrence advertised himself as a city dry goods merchant at No. 182 Queen Street. Two more inhabited Queens County. John B. Lawrence, Esq. was mayor of Burlington, New Jersey, and yet another John Lawrence was Treasurer of Connecticut from 1769 to 1789. In Philadelphia, both the outgoing mayor and a prominent physician answered to the same name.

Barely 24, counselor Laurance might easily have returned to Queens, wed the rosy-cheeked daughter of an affluent Long Island farmer, and settled in to a comfortable ready-made local legal practice. After all, dozens of Queens County Lawrences required wills drawn up, property deeds prepared, debts collected, and estates probated. Instead, the ambitious Cornishman rented quarters around Broad Way and Wall Street in the vicinity of City Hall.[19] Not only were the King's and Mayor's courts a short stroll away, but nearby towered Trinity Anglican Church at the head of Wall Street. Although never flamboyantly missionary, John reserved a special place in his life for Trinity. It was a precious tie to an English childhood and the mother he would never again lay eyes upon. Anglican services of Rector Samuel Provoost (before his 1771 discharge for Whiggish behavior) and Samuel Seabury (staunch Crown loyalist) offered comforting ritual along with opportunity to rub informal shoulders with prominent King's officials such as Colden, Smith, Duane, and Supreme Court Chief Justice Daniel Horsmanden. And there was no better entrée to professional and intellectual society than the elite fellowship of St. John's No. 2 Masonic Lodge, established at Trinity in 1757.[20]

American Freemasonry, starting with the 1730 warrant issued to Daniel Coxe by the Grand Lodge of England, was part and parcel of the transplantation of Anglicized values, culture, and institutions that accompanied rampant commercialization of British colonial seaports from Boston to Savannah. By Revolution's eve, the United Grand Lodges of London had warranted more than 100 American lodges with a 5,000-strong combined membership that included the likes of John Hancock, Ben Franklin, Richard Henry Lee, and George Washington.[21] To suggest that a Washington-centered Masonic clique brought the United States of America into being would severely overstate the case, but there is little doubt that cosmopolitan lodge principles of civility and enlightenment helped shape the values of the founding generation.[22]

Reflecting the character of a London noblemen's club without the nobles, these colonial Lodges offered a genteel commercial and social networking venue to community-conscious merchants, professionals, government officials, and even high-end craftsmen. Requiring faith and moral character—yet throwing up no membership barriers based on politics or religion—the brotherhood, with its rituals, ceremonies, and charitable activities, enabled aspirational young white men of merit such as Laurance to better themselves while enhancing social prospects and honing public speaking skills. Little wonder that John, sometime before today's required age of 21, received the ritualistic Entered Apprentice ceremony of initiation into the Fraternal Order of Freemasonry. It was no token commitment, for the lodge's six-pound initiation fee, eight-shilling Tyler's (door steward) fee, and quarterly five-shilling dues were a serious out-of-pocket expense to any newly licensed young lawyer scratching for business. John evidently thrived among the 70 brethren of St. John's No. 2, because a period Masonic publication lists him as lodge secretary. By 1772, Lodge bylaws show "Worshipful Brother" Laurance had progressed to junior warden.[23]

In addition to boasting five Masonic lodges, New York City in early 1775 brimmed with bright young lawyers with whom to talk shop or blow off steam ... and plenty of taverns in which to do so. Some attorneys, such as Phillip Pell (9,600-acre Pelham Manor) and Robert R. Livingston Jr., descended from elite stock. Others, like home-tutored Richard Varick (clerk-turned-partner of John Morin Scott), came from merchant families or, like Stephen Lush and Jack McDougall, were fathered by flush privateer captains. Most volatile of the lot, with his withered right arm and withering cavalier intellect, was the man who would pen the future written United States Constitution, Gouverneur Morris. A year Laurance's junior, Morris matriculated from King's College at age 16 (1768), clerked for William Smith Jr. while Laurance read under Colden, and quickly gained admittance (1771) to the New York bar. Bred for the law by an aristocratic father, Morris grew up directly across the water from Lawrence Neck at 2,000-acre Morissania Manor.

John Jay, more discrete than the ostentatious Morris, had already developed a reputation as "a man of wit, well-informed, a good Speaker and an elegant writer."[24] Six years older than Laurance, Jay graduated King's College with highest honors (1764) and clerked for noted lawyer Benjamin Kissam before opening his own practice in 1771. Marked early on for distinction, Jay, the youngest member of the New York bar's prestigious "Moot Club," was perhaps the city's busiest lawyer; more than 100 cases were then pending in Supreme Court and another 100 litigations awaited judgment in Westchester County court.[25] Little wonder his 1774 earnings topped £1,000. Jay's marriage that same year to 17-year-old (he was 28) Sarah Livingston, daughter of New Jersey governor William Livingston, was the social event of the season.

Make no mistake. Laurance may have shared a glass or two with the likes of Morris, Jay, and brother-Mason Robert Livingston Jr. at Queen's Head Tavern or the nearby Montayne's, but little more. Although the Queens County Lawrences were prosperous freeholders, they simply did not travel the manor house social circuit. Closer to Laurance's public station was easygoing lawyer Jack McDougall. Graduate of the Presbyterian College of New Jersey (later Princeton), he, like Laurance, was an outsider to the DeLancey and Livingston social networks, for, as might be expected, Jack's uneducated ship's captain-cum-merchant father was far too rough-hewn to crash the gates of "quality" society.

Despite occasional dust-ups between exasperated redcoat sentries and derisive local rowdies, Laurance had disembarked the Falmouth packet in April 1767 into a New York City that was deceptively tranquil. "We have been like the ocean for a long time, tossed with storms and agitated to the bottom," sighed Robert R. Livingston Sr. to the colony's London agent, "and some little time of calm seems necessary."[26] Retraction of the hated Stamp Act momentarily bought time for all factions to regain their breath, no group more so than the Sons of Liberty, a multi-factional collection of mechanics, tradesmen, wharf denizens, small merchants, dissident intellectuals, and generally disenfranchised white males, whose collective need for political voice turned the DeLancey/Livingston rivalry into a three-cornered game.

John had hardly begun reading law when Parliament declared a raft of new tax and regulative measures (Townshend Acts of 1767) to take effect that November. Among them was the New York Restraining Act, a punitive law that specifically forbade the General Assembly from passing any new bills until lawmakers complied with the obnoxious two-year-old Quartering Act to feed and house British troops. Galvanized into action, outraged Sons of Liberty radicals collaborated with both DeLancey merchants and Livingston gentry to boycott all goods British. With an eye to even stronger measures, Liberty Boy secretary John Lamb—an optical instrument-maker turned wine merchant—orchestrated a correspondence network with at least 15 similar-spirited radical groups from New Hampshire to South Carolina. Over the ensuing eight years, the Liberty Boys, despite street-leader factional differences,[27] cajoled, prodded, and shoved New York Province toward independence. Along the way, Laurance progressed from English spectator to Whig sympathizer and ultimately to patriot warrior. And, yes, there was a woman involved. So, to really understand his metamorphosis, we must introduce ourselves to the New York Sons of Liberty and resume acquaintance with gritty street organizer Alexander McDougall.

The slender, fiery son of Scottish milk deliveryman Ranald McDougall, Alexander first went to sea at age 14. Despite a slight stammer, he worked his way from merchant seaman to shipmaster. During the Seven Years' War with France, he commanded the six-gun privateer sloop-of-war *Tyger*, converted the captured *General Barrington* to a 12-gun warship, and marauded the Caribbean under letter of marque to amass a tidy £7,000 fortune in wartime spoils.[28] Barely 28 years old, he then turned mail-order merchant to gain social respectability, acquiring a reputation for somewhat garish dress. Underneath the fancy clothes lay combustible middle-class resentment toward smug, tea-drinking, theatre-going aristocrats who persisted in addressing him as "Captain" rather than the more honorific "Mister."[29] Calvinist Presbyterian to the core, McDougall took his rights as a British subject seriously and seethed with anger at the mere thought of Parliamentary taxation without representation. And like many Scots who had fled heavy-handed English landlords, McDougall bristled at the very sight of wealthy Anglican power brokers with friends in Parliament. Men like James DeLancey Jr.

Junior was a true aristocrat. Namesake firstborn son of former New York lieutenant governor and Supreme Court chief justice James DeLancey (1703–1760), he was educated in England at Eton and then Cambridge. During the Seven Years' War, DeLancey Jr. served with distinction as a King's officer against the French. Upon his father's death, Captain DeLancey resigned His Majesty's commission and relocated to New York to oversee the family's lucrative dry goods business. From his huge inherited Lower Manhattan estate, he indulged the twin passions of hardball politics and thoroughbred horse racing. Member of both the Philadelphia Jockey Club and the Macaroni Club of New York, his stable racked up a long skein of impressive wins from Harlem to Maryland. In perhaps the biggest horse race of all—the election of 1768—the DeLancey conservative faction wrested leadership of the provincial legislature from Livingston opponents by giving lip service to the newly popular Sons of Liberty.

Nudged by the DeLanceys, Provincial lawmakers looked to end the increasingly costly two-year boycott against English goods by conceding to some of London's demands. A window of negotiating opportunity opened in September 1769 with Governor Moore's unexpected death. Whereas Moore enforced Parliamentary policy against printing colonial paper money, acting-Governor Colden was more attuned to local realities. James DeLancey Jr., in return for Colden's green light to issue more fiat money, authorized the Lt. Governor a pay increase and maneuvered the assembly to appropriate £2,000 for supporting the British garrison in New York.[30] As this assembly debate proceeded, the more radical Sons of Liberty tempers boiled. End the boycott? Quarter redcoats in private homes? Had they been duped and sold out by the DeLanceys?

McDougall, having fallen in with the Sons of Liberty during the Stamp Act crisis, determined to take matters into his own hands. The cold night of December 16, 1769, an anonymous figure carrying a large box worked the dark New York streets, pausing from time to time in the shadows.[31] Hidden inside the box was a small boy. As the man stopped to rest, a door at the back of the box opened and the boy quickly pasted a broadside poster to the wall. By dawn, lower Manhattan was plastered with several hundred broadsides titled "To the Betrayed Inhabitants of the City and Colony of New York."[32] Both the DeLancey family and Lt. Governor Colden were accused of subverting the freeholders to secure for themselves "the sovereign lordship of this Colony." To protest the Assembly actions, the unknown author called for a public meeting.

That evening, 1,400 furious New Yorkers gathered on the "Fields" (site of the present-day Town Hall) in response to the broadsheet appeal. Electing John Lamb spokesman, the crowd voted to negate the legislature's grant supporting redcoat troops. Next evening, more than 2,000 citizens materialized in the Fields, followed the subsequent day by an orderly march to the Mayor's office. Soldiers appeared, soon to be surrounded and badly outnumbered. Amid prolonged taunting and jeering, nervous troops fixed bayonets. Blood was drawn, and pockets of fighting continued several hours in what (several months before the "Boston Massacre") became known as "The Battle of Golden Hill." Although several townsfolk were wounded, and five soldiers were disabled, only an elderly sailor was killed and a tavern or two wrecked.[33] Otherwise the storm passed.

Lt. Governor Colden immediately offered a £100 reward for information leading to identification of the mysterious broadsheet author. Soon an apprentice came forward to incriminate his employer, the printer James Parker, who upon securing promise he would not be prosecuted, revealed who had commissioned him to print the poster. "One Alexander McDougall is now in jail," Colden proudly informed London, "He is a person of some fortune, and could easily have found the Bail required of him, but he chooses to go to jail."[34] The canny Scot, as intended all along, became an immediate cause célèbre. Turning his jail cell into a Sons of Liberty publicity office, McDougall filled afternoons with newspaper interviews and supporter appointments. Word spread to Boston, Philadelphia, Williamsburg, and Charleston, inflaming patriots across the American colonies. When witness James Parker unexplainably died (not without suspicion of foul play), the case against McDougall withered. A few weeks later, the Livingston faction posted bail and dispatched formidable John Morin Scott as McDougall's lawyer, whereupon the authorities concluded they had no case and set him free. Though temporarily thrown back in jail by a vindictive general assembly, Alexander McDougall had emerged as acknowledged spokesman for the ascendant Liberty Boys.

Liberty Boy tempers re-inflamed when the Tea Act of 1773 rubbed additional salt in colonial wounds by reasserting yet again Crown right to tax without representation. No sooner had out-of-breath Boston messenger Paul Revere alighted at the door of Merchants' Coffee House with news of the Boston "Tea Party" than the factions of Sears, Lamb, and McDougall consolidated a reinvigorated Sons of Liberty to instigate a more subdued fest of their own. Acting-Governor Colden diplomatically turned his head away, but more powerful heads in London were not amused. Crown retribution for colonial tea dumping was swift and harsh. Parliament closed the Port of Boston to all shipping, suspended the Massachusetts legislature, and passed a series of punishing bills quickly dubbed "The Intolerable Acts."

John Laurance, Esq. by this point had established a fledgling legal practice specializing in admiralty and chancery cases. Though as yet unlicensed before the bar, the Cornish émigré had done well enough to purchase 1,000 acres of land in that part of Albany County that is now Addison County, Vermont.[35] From his Lower Manhattan window he could see and hear street bruisers and redcoat soldiers trade barbs and worse. And by mid-1774 John's spirit, if not his person, was with the Sons of Liberty, for he was courting Alexander McDougall's only daughter, Betsey.

How could an English-born legal protégé of His Majesty's lieutenant governor and member of the Anglican Church fall for the Presbyterian daughter of his former mentor's single most dangerous opponent? When did he evolve into a Colonial Whig, ultimately denounce his King, and become a radical? Never one to advertise deep emotions, Laurance has left us to guess. Certainly, outspoken Queens County kinsman Jonathan Lawrence together with unabashed Whigs John Jay, Robert Livingston Jr., and Jack McDougall influenced his political evolution. Most likely, Laurance's patriotism was less love for his adopted New York and more the cold-blooded self-interest of a striving immigrant with everything to gain by shaking up the established order. Any lingering affinity to King and Parliament stood little chance against passions for Betsey, although perhaps John's west-country rover's blood was simply thicker than Hanoverian water. Whatever the sociopolitical foreplay, by early 1775 Betsey McDougall had become Mrs. John Laurance.[36]

"An agreeable Miss," wrote future President John Adams about Betsey during a five-day late August 1774 New York stopover as he made his way to the First Continental Congress in Philadelphia. Adams thought her stepmother Hannah "a charming woman," taking no apparent note that she was but three years Betsey's senior.[37] Betsey, if her churchgoing garb is any indication, had a mind of her own. Appearing one Sunday in her father's pew, she sported a gaily trimmed bonnet that smacked of "vanity if not frivolity" in the eyes of the Presbyterian minister, the Reverend John Rodgers. Turning to the pew, he is said to have uttered sternly, "Betsey McDougall, I wish you would keep your head quiet; your bonnet disturbs my reflections."[38] It was all part of an independent streak developed after her birth mother Nancy succumbed in 1764 to epidemic fever while McDougall was at sea. Consequently, her youth was spent on Long Island in the care of McDougall's sister Mary, who had wed Scottish sea captain Alexander Stewart. Certainly, Betsey was properly schooled. "You cannot but be very sensible," McDougall directed sister Mary, "of how much importance it is to have a daughter's education properly taken care of and directed."[39] It was an education that the socially aspirational Alexander hoped would attract a "quality" suitor, but, as we earlier learned, future son-in-law John Laurance's keen devotion to the Liberty Boy cause ultimately prevailed.[40]

On July 6, 1774, McDougall chaired a mass meeting in the grassy Fields city common to beat the drum for a renewed boycott on British goods in retaliation for closing the Port of Boston. No doubt the fiery Scot's future son-in-law looked on when a thinly built, fair complexioned, five-foot-seven King's College student is said to have spoken haltingly, then forcefully, as one of many in favor of the proposed boycott. The precocious youth, Alexander Hamilton by name, had recently arrived from under the wing of New Jersey Continental Congress delegate William Livingston. Apparently rolling back his birth date a couple of years, the youth eased admission as a college freshman.[41] No eyewitness account confirms that Hamilton actually addressed the crowd; sole provenance is his son John Church's 1879 *Life of Alexander Hamilton*, published more than a century after the fact. Whether Hamilton spoke in the Fields or not, his extraordinary anti-Tory pamphlets* in response to Loyalist Reverend Seabury's "The Westchester Farmer" led McDougall to befriend the

---

*Hamilton's December 1775 pamphlet, "A Full Vindication of the Measures of the Congress," sharply rebuked Trinity Church Rt. Rev. Samuel Seabury's anti-Continental Congress newspaper invectives under the pseudonym "The Westchester Farmer." Hamilton's second pamphlet, "The Farmer Refuted," was an 80-page tour-de-force that readers found difficult to attribute to so young a man.

collegian in a strong relationship that endured the rest of his years.[42] It was only a matter of time before Laurance, courting Betsey at the time, came to know Hamilton as a frequent visitor to her father's library distributing Sons of Liberty broadsides. The two young striving immigrants, both dependent upon well-placed mentors to advance their careers in the absence of influential fathers, could not help but have recognized themselves in one another.

Although open conflict was expected any day, New Yorkers were nonetheless thrown into a state of alarm when 23-year-old Connecticut express rider Israel Bissell galloped into the city to break the Sunday Sabbath on April 23, 1775 with news of bloodshed at Lexington and Concord. New Yorkers with an educated ear to Massachusetts knew, of course, what thinking men throughout New England knew: a 14,000-strong Bay Colony militia had been training years for that bloody day, and Connecticut, Rhode Island, and New Hampshire would follow their lead. The Boston Tea Party, massive 1774 demonstrations, September's "great powder alarm," the fiery Suffolk Resolves, and the First Continental Congress were but inevitable preliminaries to the shot heard around the world.

Spurred by an outpouring of over 5,000 militant New Yorkers, McDougall and the Sons of Liberty Committee of Observation linked arms with sympathetic Whigs and the Mechanic's Association to form a provisional "War Committee" that gave way to the "Committee of One Hundred" and seized the reins of city government. "The mob," an apprehensive Gouverneur Morris warned fellow gentry about New York's militant commoners, had begun "to think and reason" and "ere noon will bite."[43] And, bite they did. Before Laurance's approving eyes, 110 years of British hegemony unraveled in a matter of weeks. Swarming citizens emptied two supply ships of foodstuffs bound for the King's Boston garrison. Three hundred armed men under Isaac Sears seized the redcoat Customs House arsenal from customs collector Andrew Elliot and promptly shut down all New York harbor shipping. Brawling French and Indian War militia officer Marinus Willet sequestered five carts of "spare" arms from British soldiers retiring to safety aboard 64-gun HMS *Asia* and distributed the weapons to Sons of Liberty roughnecks controlling the streets. Colden, fearing for his life as the redcoat garrison dissipated precipitously from desertion, withdrew from public affairs to his Spring Hill residence.[44] Royal Governor William Tryon, having in late June returned from London, judiciously pulled the remaining—fewer than a hundred—King's troops aboard ships and set up court aboard the *Duke of Gordon* to monitor events from New York Harbor. And James DeLancey Jr., whose practiced political instinct alerted him the game was up, appointed attorneys to dispose of his sprawling Lower East Side estate and hoisted sail for England.

New York's emasculated General Assembly could do no more than watch in horror as a freshly elected Provincial Congress brashly usurped its authority. Headed by Peter Van Brugh Livingston, the new body on

May 25 ordered four infantry regiments raised as New York's contribution to the 20,000-man defense force requested by Continental Congress with General George Washington at its head. And who was chosen to lead the first New York regiment but newly commissioned colonel Alexander McDougall.[45] Washington himself arrived on June 25 by late afternoon boat from New Jersey, providing Laurance an initial look at the man he would serve alongside for more than five years. Larger than life on his prancing charger, the new commander-in-chief's trim blue uniform and fancy-plumed hat exuded confidence. Behind him the immaculate Philadelphia Light Horse reminded striving New Yorkers where the real money lay. There at the head of the welcoming crowd was McDougall, helping an exuberant crowd of soldiers, politicians, and townsfolk escort the tall Virginian to Hull's Tavern, one of the more elegant Sons of Liberty haunts. Next morning, Washington was gone. Leaping into the breach, he headed north to take command at the siege of Boston.

Following news of Lexington and Concord, businessmen of all stripes pulled in their horns. "When I reflect upon the present business of the office," lamented John Jay's clerk Robert Troup, "I am filled with sorrow. Formerly it was extensive and attended with much profit. Now it is confined with very narrow bands, and of course accompanied by little gain."[46] If Jay's business was slow, income for lesser legal lights such as Laurance dried up altogether. Not yet 25 years old and newly married, what was he now to do? John had no military training whatsoever, nor up to this point demonstrated any such disposition. His build, as best can be determined from later portraits, was more round than firm, and his manner more bookish than hawkish. Family papers describe John's personality as "naturally calm, and reflecting his temper, singularly placid."[47] Yet, swept up in "rage militaire" of the day, he determined to draw steel as an officer in the patriot cause.

Laurance might easily have wheedled a commission in his father-in-law's new regiment. But why play third fiddle to brothers-in-law Jack and Ranald Stephen ("Stevey") McDougall, both of whom already sported new lieutenant's uniforms? Instead, the young attorney put his nascent practice on hold, returned Betsey to her father and stepmother Hannah's roof, and hurried to Lawrence Point and a second lieutenant's commission in the Queens County company of a rapidly coalescing Continental Army.

FOUR

An Officer of the Revolution

NEWTOWN, QUEENS COUNTY, NEW YORK, AUGUST 1775. Jaunty beats of the drum had for more than a century summoned Newtown men between 16 and 60 to hoist musket and scramble posthaste for mandatory "training day" on the village common. But this particular late-August assemblage was no drill. Ordered by New York's Second Provincial Congress to "march to Albany with all convenient speed with the men now raised," Captain Nathaniel Woodward's Queens County infantry company readied itself to move out.[1] Second Lieutenant Laurance gathered up soldierly gear, secured his commission of August 3, and reported to Newtown's bustling commons.[2] There, together with 35-year-old First Lieutenant Abraham Riker, he would muster into line the hardscrabble six-month recruits of Captain Woodward's Third Company in Colonel James Holmes's Fourth New York Regiment of the Continental Line.

Forty such infantry companies were being hurriedly raised across 14 New York counties, yet King George's stubbornly neutral shire of Queens could furnish but one. For a decisive majority of Queens County adult men—more than 60% according to a 1775 poll—had refused to identify themselves as either patriot or loyalist.[3] County freemen not only refused to send a delegate to the Continental Congress, but also declined the Provincial Convention and chose not to elect a committee of observation. Newtown was the exception. Patriot island amid a sea of indifference, it was the sole Queens village that voted to attend the 1775 Continental Congress, dispatching Jonathan Lawrence.[4] Three Lawrence men also graced the 17-man Newtown Committee of Correspondence that linked with McDougall's Sons of Liberty, and two, Daniel and William, captained local militia companies. Now their immigrant kinsman, John, was headed into harm's way with the Queens contingent of Westchester County Colonel Holmes's Fourth New York Regiment.

On paper, Woodward, Riker, and Laurance commanded 72 rank and file including three sergeants, a fifer, and two drummers. Hard pressed to enlist two-thirds of that number, Captain Woodward nevertheless in mid-August made ready to march. It was all part of a grand strategy by the Continental Congress to follow up on frontiersman Ethan Allen and Connecticut colonel Benedict Arnold's surprising capture of British forts at Crown Point and Ticonderoga along the Canadian frontier.

Imagining that Canada's French majority would rise up against their British masters, Congress determined to seize thinly garrisoned Montreal and Quebec before reinforcements crossed the Atlantic. New York's four infantry regiments were immediately directed to Albany, swelling Major General Phillip Schuyler and Brigadier General Richard Montgomery's "Northern Army" invasion force to some 2,000 effectives. Without a moment to lose—most patriot enlistments expired at year's end—Schuyler and Montgomery struck out in late August for Canada several weeks before most companies of Colonel Holmes's unequipped regiment made their way up the Hudson to the Albany jumping-off point. If all went well, Quebec would be in American hands before November.

By August 28, five companies of Holmes's Fourth Regiment had reached Albany, but Captain Woodward's company was not one of them.[5] His stubborn Long Island troops were among those mutinously refusing to march from the lower barracks until they received their pay.[6] It was not until mid-September that Woodward's Queens County contingent finally heaved in to Albany, only to learn that "there is no probability of receiving a supply [of arms and clothing] sufficient to answer immediately the demand of the companies of the 3rd and 4th regiments."[7] Bogged down on the west bank of the Hudson some 150 miles from New York, they rummaged for everything from blankets, coats, and tents to cartridge pouches, canteens, haversacks, and muskets and flints, of which there was an alarming absence. As least senior of the four regiments, the Fourth New York was assigned gray, rather than blue, regimentals, making do with an array of gray, brown, and drab coats, all with blue facings.[8] Not until September 25 was Woodward's "grey and blue clad" unit observed boating up Lake George toward Ticonderoga.[9] Though eyewitness accounts leave Lt. Laurance unmentioned over the course of the Canadian expedition, it is inconceivable that Colonel McDougall's son-in-law would, in company of two brothers-in-law, have been a shirker.

Whatever the hue of his own tunic, the Fourth New York's Colonel Holmes could not or would not advance beyond Fort Ticonderoga. (He soon resigned altogether and went over to the British.) Second-in-command Lt. Colonel Phillip Van Cortlandt assumed charge, only to be leveled by fever and removed on extended sick leave. Stepping forward to lead the Fourth New York into Canada was respected French and Indian War veteran Major Barnabas Tuthill of Long Island.[10] Even so, it was not until the last week of October that Schuyler could advise General Washington that "Major Tuthill of Colo: Holmes's, with two hundred & twenty-five" had rendezvoused with the main army.[11] Schuyler, confined to Ticonderoga under illness, then directed 37-year-old Irish-born former King's officer Montgomery to assault the British garrison at Fort Saint-Jean, situated on rugged Isle Richelieu at the extreme northern end of Lake Champlain.

If selected for the attack, Captain Woodward's company would navigate a swampy, timber-covered quagmire, cross a 200- to 300-yard open field completely exposed to cannon and musket fire, scramble over a seven-foot-deep muddy ditch studded with sharpened logs, and scale the splintery points of a 10-foot picket wall to take the fort.[12] Looking around at the Queens County men he had helped train, it was only natural for Lt. Laurance to wonder which ones might perish. Would he be among the dead? And how would his pregnant Betsey handle the news? Then came discouraging word that a strong redcoat relief column had departed Montreal to take General Montgomery in the flank and relieve Fort Saint-Jean. Sounds of gunfire floated in from the north, followed by glorious news that the enemy relief force had been intercepted and turned back by Seth Warner's Green Mountain Boys with a large contingent of New Hampshire militia. British Major Sir Charles Preston, with no hope of reinforcement, dwindling rations, and his own flank uncovered by patriot capture of nearby Fort Chambly, on November 2 surrendered Fort Saint-Jean's 700-man garrison without a final patriot assault. He had held out for 45 days.

Montgomery posted a small contingent under former New York Liberty Boy (now Lt. Colonel) Marinus Willet to secure the captured Fort St. John, and dispatched Captain Jonathan Platt's Fourth Regiment Company back to Ticonderoga to orchestrate army supply logistics for the winter campaign.[13] On November 13, American troops entered the narrow fortified oblong of Montreal without resistance. For British Governor General Carleton understood perfectly that 150 soldiers amid a generally unreliable citizenry could not possibly defend the city, and loaded his small command aboard ship to Quebec. A few days later in the small town of La Prairie on the outskirts of Montreal, Laurance bowed his head in grief as brother-in-law Jack McDougall was laid to final rest in a graystone Catholic church courtyard with full military honors. "Your poor son, Jack, is no more,"[14] wrote Lt. Colonel Rudolphus Ritzema* to Colonel McDougall, who remained in the Provincial Congress at New York City the entire Canadian campaign. "He died this day after a few day's illness of a bilious fever. His corpse attended to the grave by every officer of his own corps and many others."[15] Because young McDougall was Presbyterian, his name was never entered on the local Catholic register.

Familiar with the severity of Canadian winters, General Montgomery halted his invasion campaign behind the walls of Montreal to await spring thaw before assaulting well-defended Quebec. But impetuous, fearless Colonel Benedict Arnold forced matters by leading some

---

*Ritzema (1739–1803) graduated King's College in 1758 and sailed to the Netherlands to study Divinity, followed by a stint in the Prussian army. Member of the "Committee of One Hundred," he gained McDougall's confidence and was made second in command of the First New York Regiment. In November of 1776, he deserted to the British.

800 indefatigable patriots through the backwoods of Maine to emerge on the St. Lawrence at the gates of Quebec. Rather than abandon the heavily outnumbered Arnold to certain defeat, Montgomery secured Montreal with 200 men under Connecticut General David Wooster and embarked the bulk of his New York troops in late November for Quebec aboard a captured prize vessel flotilla. Four days later the New Yorkers climbed ashore to link with Arnold at Pointe aux Trembles and lay siege to redcoat general Guy Carleton's 1,800-strong Quebec garrison.

Unable to breach Quebec City's 30-foot granite block walls with cannon shot from Colonel John Lamb's six-piece battery, and facing expiring enlistments of most New York soldiers the next morning, Montgomery had little choice but to gamble everything on a New Year's Eve surprise assault under cover of darkness.[16] Although the precise size and composition of his attacking detachment remain problematic, Society of Cincinnati records confirm that elements of Major Tuthill's Fourth New York Regiment were present.[17] Queens County historian James Riker (Abraham's brother) places Lt. Riker in Montgomery's bold moonlight sortie, though only family tradition confirms Laurance's participation.[18] With or without Lt. Laurance, Montgomery moved out after midnight. Advancing through swirling snowflakes, the plucky New Yorkers descended from the Plains of Abraham down to Wolf's Cove along the St. Lawrence River and negotiated two slippery miles of icy trail to reach Quebec's Cape Diamond bastion. The silent column then poured into the Lower Town only to be stunned by an unexpected British volley that killed Montgomery and his two chief aides. With their general down, the American attack collapsed and nearly half of Montgomery's command was captured. Colonel Arnold—his simultaneous attack on Quebec's Upper Town having similarly failed—re-grouped American forces and pulled back to the siege line. Although patriot ranks would be later reinforced, the Canadian invasion was for all purposes over.

New York's original four regiments were wrecked beyond repair, none worse than the Fourth New York. Only 1 of its 10 captains volunteered to continue in service, and it was David Palmer, not Nathaniel Woodward. Nor did General Schuyler's February 28 list of serving officers include Lieutenants Riker or Laurance.[19] For the Provincial Congress had determined that remnants of all New York corps in Canada "cannot be usefully formed into one or two regiments."[20] Instead, Provincial lawmakers "superseded their former order to form two battalions out of those troops" and ordered four new Continental regiments to be raised.[21]

Laurance and Riker, their shattered regiment disestablished, had already set out for home with discharged Queens County troops sometime after enlistments expired in the wake of General Montgomery's New Year's Eve debacle. Returning to New York, Laurance discovered that while he had shivered around snowy Canadian campfires, Betsey, on December 15, 1776, had given birth to a healthy baby boy. Together with Colonel McDougall, she had baptized the lad in John's absence on January 17 at First Presbyterian Church.[22] The infant, like his father, and his father's father before him, was named John ... John McDougall Laurance. And while Laurance pondered whether or not to seek a new commission in the reconstituted New York Continental Line, discouraging word came that brother-in-law Stevey McDougall had been captured. Having belatedly arrived at Quebec in the wake of Montgomery's demise, Stevey was taken prisoner when a large reinforcing British fleet overpowered his small retreating schooner, *Mary*, on the St. Lawrence River.[23]

By the spring of 1776, New York City under direction of Major General Charles Lee had become one vast military camp. Trenches, breastworks, barricades, and artillery emplacements were under construction everywhere. On a bluff near Trinity Church, along present-day Rector Street, neighboring General McDougall's residence stood a six-cannon breastwork appropriately christened "McDougall's Battery."[24] From there, as he contemplated his military future, Laurance looked down on Fort George with its two 12-pound guns and four 32 pounders. To the southeast, his vista included the "Grand Battery" whose reinforced walls mounted 22 field pieces, 13 of which were 32 pounders. Nearby Whitehall Battery and Waterbury's Battery served two guns apiece. Swiveling his head toward the Bowery, Laurance could make out the 16-gun heptagonal Bayard Hill Redoubt. In all directions soldiers worked feverishly on dozens more fortifications to house some 121 cannon. Yet, even non-artillerist Laurance readily saw that a single British warship, the 64-gun *Asia* riding at anchor off Governor's Island, equaled half the entire patriot armament.

"What to do with the city," General Lee confided to Washington, "puzzles me ... whoever commands the sea must command the town."[25] Anticipating British General William Howe's massive invasion force, hundreds of New Yorkers drew a similar conclusion and fled. The majority of houses were locked and shuttered. Known Tories were disarmed or escorted out of town. Streets thronged with some 12,000 variously uniformed soldiers drilling, drinking, and whoring away the hours. The surreal presence of Royal Governor William Tryon conducting His Majesty's business aboard *Duchess of Gordon* in New York Harbor only added to the overall state of confusion. Despite open warfare in New England, Tryon, incredible as it may seem, was still maneuvering to engineer a pro-London slate in the defunct General Assembly. Ferried back and forth under flags of truce, New York's leading Crown loyalists solicited Tryon's counsel or negotiated passage to England. Lawyer William Smith Jr., having given up his fine Broad Way residence to General Lee, lobbied to find middle ground that might yet stave off full-scale revolution. Others, like Colonel

McDougall's new second-in-command, Lt. Colonel Herman Zedtwitz,* offered their services to Tryon as British spies.

With His Majesty's courts in disarray, most leading local lawyers opted for a uniform. Gouverneur Morris parlayed family prominence into a lieutenant colonelcy in one of the four reconstituted New York regiments newly raised by Congress. Older brother Lewis was made major general of the Westchester County militia. Robert and Philip Livingston leveraged their powerful name to secure a colonel's rank, 19-year-old cousin Brockholst landed a staff lieutenant colonelcy, and Brigadier General John Morin Scott oversaw all New York County militia. John Jay, although in Philadelphia with the Continental Congress, solicited a vacant militia colonelcy. Decamping Jay's law practice, Laurance's jocular friend Robert Troup (1756–1832) buttoned on a second lieutenant's epaulet in Colonel John Lesher's regiment of New York volunteers.

The affable, thickset Troup was a New Jersey privateer captain's orphaned son who, like Betsey McDougall, was raised by extended family on Long Island. Graduating from King's College a year ahead of Alexander Hamilton, he had lingered an extra six months as the West Indies immigrant's roommate while clerking for patron John Jay. Always one for food and drink, Robert Troup possessed a sense of humor so exuberant that a friend pronounced him "better antidote for the spleen than a ton of drugs."[26] As to his audacious roommate, *Journals of the Provincial Congress* recorded that "Col. McDougall recommended Mr. Alexander Hamilton for Capt. Of Artillery."[27] After satisfactory examination by Captain Stephen Badlam, the enterprising Hamilton was duly appointed captain of the "Provincial Company of Artillery of the Colony." McDougall then forwarded Hamilton £14 to pay his troops, while prodding Jay to furnish uniforms and round up a pair of cannons to actualize the young captain's new command.[28]

Fortunate to survive the Canadian campaign with his health intact, John Laurance possessed neither aptitude nor disposition for raw soldiering. Returning to legal practice, however, was proving impossible; potential clients either fled or squirreled away precious cash. Somehow John would have to put shoulder to the cause in a non-combatant capacity. But what could he do?

The answer came on August 9, 1776: "We the subscribers, Field Officers and Captains in the First Regiment of the New-York troops, in service of the United States of America, do hereby recommend Mr. John Lawrence as a fit person to be appointed as a Paymaster to the said Regiment."[29] Six days later, General Washington confirmed the appointment in his General Orders.[30] As paymaster, John would pass the hours

---

*Zedtwitz, a Prussian who served with the English Light Horse, came to America in 1773 and marched to Canada as a major in the First New York Regiment. Revealed as a spy, he was cashiered from service August 25, 1776.

balancing regimental accounts, maintaining individual pay ledgers for some 340 men, and distributing back pay whenever New York lawmakers raised the money. More important, he was also made personal aide-de-camp to the newly promoted Brigadier General McDougall, at whose table he would make acquaintance with many of the Revolution's leading officers.[31] With one son dead and the other a prisoner of war on parole to Governor Carlton in Quebec, McDougall was not about to risk his only daughter's husband in combat.

Washington, in an ill-conceived attempt to defend both Manhattan and lower Long Island, split his 28,000-man force nearly in half, shuttling troops back and forth as he guessed enemy plans. Consequently, some 11,000 troops found themselves the last week of August trapped on Long Island, outnumbered by more than two to one. British commander William Howe, however, was not about to repeat the carnage of Bunker (Breed's) Hill by marching uphill into heavily fortified patriot guns. In a masterful flanking movement, he instead on the night of August 26 dispatched the flower of his army under Major General Henry Clinton down the undefended Jamaica Pass. Next day, Clinton smashed undetected into the patriot left flank, rolling up the entire American line and killing, wounding, and capturing more than 1,000 men.

Jonathan and Daniel Lawrence saved their own necks by scuttling across Long Island Sound, but brother Richard was not so fortunate. Dragged from his Newtown home, he was thrown in New York's Provost prison where he contracted a fatal illness. Militia captain William Lawrence was also yanked from his Hell-Gate mansion when British Major General Leslie Robertson commandeered the residence and bivouacked his 9,000-troop division on the surrounding grounds. As redcoat troops went door to door cleansing Queens County of rebels, even Crown-loyalist Lawrence brother-in-law William Sackett was hauled in for questioning. "Contriving to make the guard drunk," the story goes, "he slipt away, and was not again called upon."[32]

Paymaster Laurance's First New York Regiment was spared Long Island's bloody carnage. Assigned to protect a battery that Alexander Hamilton's gun company had helped erect on lower Manhattan's Bayard Hill, the First New York's only casualties came a week earlier in the throes of an apocalyptic thunderstorm.[33] "A captain [Abraham Van Wyke] and 2 lieutenants belonging to Genl. McDougall's regiment killed by one thunderbolt," wrote a surviving officer, dumbstruck that "the points of their swords melted off, and the coins melted in their pockets."[34]

Washington, after a council of war at Philip Livingston's fine Brooklyn manor house, directed old sea dog McDougall to evacuate the remnants of the Long Island army across the East River. Under cover of a providential overnight fog of Biblical proportions, the savvy Scot did just that. In a second council in General McDougall's own parlor that aide-de-camp Laurance undoubtedly overheard, Washington then reluctantly determined to abandon New York City altogether.³⁵ Escaping northward just before General Henry Clinton's flanking redcoat division disembarked in his rear at Kip's Bay (a no longer existing inlet at the foot of present-day East 34th to 38th Streets), His Excellency secured a strong defensive position in the Harlem Heights, confiscating as headquarters Mount Morris, the splendid circa 1765 Palladio-inspired Georgian summer home vacated by English Lt. Colonel Roger Morris.

Laurance's accommodations were far less luxurious. Deployed as rear-guard below Harlem Heights, General McDougall and his staff dug in astride the rock-infested Post Road approximately where 135th Street now runs.³⁶ The evening of September 21, John watched the sky turn red over British-occupied New York. A quarter of the city was aflame, torched most likely by departing patriots. Reputedly started in a Whitehall Slip grogshop, the hungry blaze raged northward up Broad Way and Broad Street to City Hall before being contained at the foot of Wall Street. Some 500 buildings were consumed, including Trinity Church. As the flaming 175-foot wooden church steeple crumpled and fell in the distance, John could not help but realize that ties to his English past were irrevocably severed . . . and a once-promising New York legal practice had gone up in smoke.

Seven days later, Laurance's emotional separation from British New York was complete. Unnoticed and of no importance to anyone, 88-year-old Cadwallader Colden died in seclusion at Spring Hill. Having lost Crown confidence five years earlier by permitting the DeLancey General Assembly—in strict violation of Parliamentary decree—to issue additional paper money, Colden was thereafter cold-shouldered by Lord Halifax and the Board of Trade. He had fared no better with his fellow New Yorkers. Near the end, Colden lamented to the Earl of Hillsborough on "having become obnoxious to the People of this Province, and that I am generally disliked."³⁷

Laurance, after the bloody two-hour "hot contest" at Harlem's present-day Morningside Heights, had more than ample time (five weeks before the army moved north) to make his way over to pre-war acquaintance Alexander Hamilton's two-cannon artillery redoubt on the crest of "Breakneck Hill" near present-day 147th Street.³⁸ Over camp coffee they not only had the fate of mutual friend Lt. Troup—one of five officers taken prisoner at Jamaica Pass during the British capture of Long Island—to discuss, but also Hamilton's thrilling news of his personal audience with General Washington himself. His Excellency, after watching the young artillery captain oversee work on a defensive earthwork, "entered into a conversation with him," according to Hamilton's son John Church, then "invited him to his tent," and "received an impression of his military talent."³⁹

It was not until late October that General Howe dispatched a strong flanking force under General Clinton to trap Washington's army on Manhattan Island. Bare hours before Clinton's redcoats closed in his rear, the alert Virginian marched his dwindling command northward across

Kings Bridge and plunged into Westchester County. Like a master of hounds, Howe methodically chased his prey north to the village of White Plains. There, just across the Bronx River, Washington made a stand, rushing General McDougall with some 1,600 Connecticut, Maryland, and New York troops to defend the strategic high ground of Chatterton Hill commanding a plain over which the British would have to advance. Before aide-de-camp Laurance's eyes, a pair of artillery pieces rolled into place, captained by the 21-year-old Hamilton.[40] Peering across the Bronx River, John watched Howe's blue-coated Hessians and scarlet-clad British regulars mass in attack formation. "Its appearance was truly magnificent," gushed one awestruck American officer. "A bright autumnal sun shed its luster on the polished arms; and the rich array of dress and military equipage gave an imposing grandeur to the scene as they advanced in all the pomp and circumstance of war."[41]

Directly in McDougall's center, a strong Hessian battalion under Colonel Carl von Donop fixed bayonets and made ready to cross the Bronx River. Covered by a deafening cannonade that disabled one of Hamilton's two guns, von Donop's growling Hessians began to ascend Chatterton Hill. Howe, sensing victory, wheeled another 10,000 redcoats into place to support the push. McDougall, after an afternoon's bloody work, then directed a disciplined withdrawal that even perpetual critic Major General Lee admitted "lost no credit."[42] Scattered on the Chatterton Hill battlefield in Laurance's first real action under his father-in-law were perhaps 150 to 200 Americans killed and wounded.

Washington, as would become his pattern, refused to further engage his larger, better trained, better equipped, and, yes, better led opponent. Leaving the redcoats in possession of Chatterton Hill, His Excellency fell back to the wild, rugged hills around North Castle, New York. When Howe declined to follow, the Master of Mount Vernon on November 9 crossed the Hudson, veered into northern New Jersey, and pushed south to interpose his rapidly shrinking army between Philadelphia and the Delaware River. Laurance was stationed with General McDougall's brigade in Morristown, New Jersey, some 60 miles behind the main army. Donning his paymaster cap, John in early December galloped back to Peekskill to secure money to pay off the First New York troops at year end. Inside his sleet-spattered greatcoat were three months of pay abstracts and a missive from his father-in-law with instructions to find Colonel Samuel Drake in General Scott's brigade. "He lives about four miles from Peekskill," wrote McDougall. "You should provide yourself with good saddle bags to take care of the money."[43]

Weakened by illness from his Peekskill errand, John made his way back to Morristown only to discover bedridden father-in-law McDougall battling a severe attack of debilitating rheumatism. Laurance's military career, indeed his entire life trajectory, then very nearly became untracked. For McDougall, in a fit of depression, had advised General Washington in mid-December that he was considering resignation. Fortunately, His Excellency would hear none of it, suggesting McDougall instead secure "a little rest."[44]

The 45-year-old Scot was not alone in his despondence. As December of 1776 wound down, Washington's 19,000-man army had shrunk through desertion and militia recalls to a mere 2,400. And many of those might leave when year-end enlistments expired. Others gave serious consideration to William Howe's offer of unconditional pardon for those who laid down arms. Dark moods only worsened with news that Newport, Rhode Island, had surrendered to British arms. "The existing army," remembered Virginia infantry officer (and future Supreme Court chief justice) John Marshall, "except a few regiments affording an effective force of about fifteen hundred men, would dissolve in a few days."[45] It was therefore with profound relief that General McDougall shared with aide-de-camp Laurance His Excellency's startling Trenton victory missive of December 28. "Our men," Washington confided, "surrounded the enemy and obliged 30 officers and 886 privates to lay down their arms without firing a shot. Our loss was only two officers and two or three privates wounded."[46]

FIGURE 2 General Alexander McDougall (1732–1786).

Miniature on ivory by John Ramage (ca. 1784). (Collection of New York Historical Society. Reproduced with permission.)

Five days later, at Assunpink Creek, Washington repulsed three attacks by British reinforcements from New Brunswick under Lord Charles Cornwallis. Overnight the patriot army then silently slipped away, circled behind the sleeping Cornwallis, and pounced on the British garrison at Princeton. Two crack King's regiments were put to rout, suffering more than 400 casualties and prisoners of war. Defeated twice in nine days at a cost of some 1,450 effectives, William Howe ordered General Cornwallis's 7,000-man command back to New Brunswick, thereby abandoning southern New Jersey. Laurance, his father-in-law's rheumatism vanquished by patriot victories at Trenton and Princeton, resumed duties as the aide of the newly promoted major general.

The campaign of 1776 concluded, Paymaster Laurance's First New York was an emaciated skeleton of a regiment reduced by desertion and illness to a handful of men mostly at Fort Ticonderoga awaiting enlistments to expire. Even Captain John Johnson, who had led the small First New York contingent at Trenton and Princeton, confided to General McDougall over a glass of wine that he too was leaving the army. Next spring a new First New York Regiment would bloom as part of the 88-battalion establishment resolved in November 1776 by the Continental Congress. Re-formed and replenished under Colonel Gozen "Goose" Van Schaik, the unit was then detached altogether from General McDougall's brigade to assume garrison duty in the wilds of upstate New York's western frontier. Effective the first of January, regimental paymaster was Abraham Ten Eyck.[47] Laurance, not about to decamp to the rough country of frontier New York, transferred to Colonel Henry B. Livingston's Fourth New York Regiment as paymaster with the rank of captain.[48]

Chafing for a more responsible assignment as February turned to March, John then asked Hamilton to inquire on his behalf about a captain's commission in General Knox's Continental Artillery Corps. Hamilton, just promoted and made aide-de-camp to General Washington, was happy to oblige. "My dear Jack," read the intimate (only his closest acquaintances addressed Laurance by nickname) letter from army headquarters at Morristown. It was from Hamilton, happily informing him that General Knox "was much pleased with the idea, and begged me to urge it upon you."[49] Furthermore, Hamilton added: "As an extra-inducement he desired me to make you a tender of the remains of my old company."[50] Reflecting on the offer, Laurance's eyes surely lingered on his opportunistic comrade's closing words. "If you have not a better prospect," wrote Hamilton, "you will oblige me with a speedy answer, as General Knox will wait until he hears from you, even if he should have an opportunity of filling his vacancies to his satisfaction."[51]

As fortune would have it, John did have a better prospect ... one that would profoundly shape his social and professional future.

FIVE

Washington's Courtroom "von Steuben"

CAMP MORRISTOWN, NEW JERSEY, APRIL 10, 1777. At 11 in the morning, staff majors from the main army's several brigades tramped into the orderly office of Washington's headquarters at Jacob Arnold's Morristown tavern.[1] It was, since the summer of 1775, their daily ritual to collect the commander-in-chief's general orders from his adjutant general and transmit them to regimental adjutants, who in turn passed the directives to first sergeants of the individual companies. Adjutant general this particular April forenoon was grizzled 42-year-old Virginia brigadier George Weedon. After duly communicating the day's password parole ("St. Clair") and countersign ("Muhlenberg"), French and Indian War veteran Weedon briefly paused. "John Laurance Esqr," he resumed, "is appointed Judge Advocate, in the room of William Tudor Esqr. who has resigned."[2] The position came with rank of lieutenant colonel.

Sheer fortune of war had deposited Laurance at Camp Morristown the very day Judge Tudor resigned. Having hand-delivered General McDougall's account of British Lt. Colonel John Bird's destructive March 29 Peekskill raid, Captain Laurance then sought out Paymaster-General William Palfrey to discuss regimental payroll needs when, unexpectedly, His Excellency interceded to arrange 5,000 desperately needed dollars for Colonel Livingston's unpaid Fourth New York troops.[3] Most likely, Washington had already sized up the 27-year-old captain, but if not, William Tudor's empty shoes necessitated a trained lawyer and McDougall's son-in-law, who was a member of the New York bar—and brother Mason*—certainly fit the bill. One thing leading to another, the stoic Virginian eight days later appointed John, with consent of Congress, the Continental Army's ranking lawyer.

---

*Washington, at the age of 20, entered the order of Ancient Free and Accepted Masons (Frederick, Virginia, Lodge #4) in October 1752. Although he periodically attended military Masonic lodge services over the course of the war, and at least 12 of his generals were fellow Masons, there is no evidence that lodge membership influenced Washington's specific command or staff assignments.

And so the new lieutenant colonel made his way to Jacob Arnold's imposing three-story hostelry on the Morristown Green, where Washington had established main army field headquarters. Alexander Hamilton's familiar voice would have welcomed Laurance to His Excellency's military "family," a peripatetic cadre of aides, couriers, and sentries who buzzed about the ground floor parlors. Stepping into the wide center hallway, John faced a broad and winding staircase that led past Washington's rented second-floor chambers up to five third-floor bedrooms shared by headquarters staff, often two to a bed.[4] There he stowed his meager belongings and bounded back downstairs. As newest member of the loosely organized headquarters staff, Lt. Colonel Laurance enjoyed a direct and personal relationship with Washington, because until Valley Forge the General operated without a chief of staff, consulting individually or collectively with up to 20 direct reports as he saw fit.[5] In matters of military justice, he dealt directly with the judge advocate general, particularly when misfortunes of war necessitated general officer prosecutions. Almost a third (9 of 29) of Washington's major generals faced courts-martial between 1776 and 1782. Eight—including father-in-law McDougall—were on Laurance's watch.

"Discipline," the Master of Mount Vernon long believed, "was the soul of an army."[6] Independence, however, was the soul of the untrained New England farmer-patriot multitude awaiting his formal command on July 3, 1775, in the outskirts of Boston. Some 20,000 disordered troops then came and went as they pleased under unprofessional officers, many of their own choosing. Drinking, fighting, unsavory female visitors, and disregard of orders were rampant. Aghast at the pervasive breakdown of military discipline, Washington unilaterally appointed his own judge advocate general. "The necessity was so great," he informed Continental Congress, "that I was obliged to nominate a Mr. Tudor who was recommended to me and now executes the office."[7]

Protégé of feisty John Adams, Boston lawyer William Tudor (1750–1819) tackled head-on the disciplinary challenges of an untrained officer corps and unruly volunteer rank and file. "Almost every day," he lamented to Adams, "a general court martial has sit in one or other Part of the Camp."[8] When experience proved the original 1775 Articles of War naively lenient, Adams, at Washington's desperate urging, championed a more muscular code that Thomas Jefferson helped draft on the heels of the Declaration of Independence over the torrid Philadelphia summer of 1776.[9] The 69 original Articles were expanded to 102, drawing heavily from Great Britain's significantly more severe 1774 Articles of War. In a gesture that would have put a smile on the face of any King's officer, the 39-lash maximum was increased to 100, and the death penalty was expanded to the same wide range of offenses as the British model. Deserters and traitors faced execution, officer or not.

True, Lt. Colonel Tudor was instrumental in securing the revised 1776 Articles of War, but it was Laurance who embedded them into America's first professional army—the three-year men of 1777–1780. Unlike the makeshift patriotic amalgamation of "such negroes, such colonels, such boys, and such great-great-grandfathers," who comprised the 6- and 12-month enlistees of George Washington's early army, the three-year "New Establishment" recruits were mostly able-bodied young men of the "lower sort" for whom soldiering presented their best economic option.[10] Landless, unskilled, transient, and often foreign-born, they were drawn from what historian Charles Neimeyer called the "strolling poor," often serving as paid substitute "scapegoats" to satisfy town recruitment quotas.[11] Most free white private soldiers were of such inferior social status that historian Carolyn Cox thought them likely to have seen themselves as no better than free blacks amidst a rank and file that was almost 10 percent African Americans.[12] Even so, they shared what Cox called "a proper sense of honor" that emanated from sacrifice, service, and a growing sense of martial competence.

Laurance's challenge, therefore, was not simply to weed out criminals and misfits, but to institutionalize ongoing military discipline among evolving professional soldiers who had nothing in common with officers from a different social class. Employing an equable courtroom manner that would make him one of post-war New York's most sought-after lawyers, Judge Advocate General Laurance between April 1777 and June 1782 personally oversaw more than 400 trials while laying the foundation for today's army Judge Advocate General (JAG) Corps. "During the incumbency of Colonel Lawrance," wrote U.S. Army JAG historical officer Colonel William Fratcher, "the legal staff of the army came to include the Judge Advocate General, two judge advocates at headquarters, and one judge advocate for each separate army and territorial department (Northern, Middle, and Southern)."[13]

Preceding the Constitution by 14 years, Continental army courts were the United States' first judicial venue, but, as Laurance quickly learned, Washington's tribunals bore little resemblance to civil courts. Rather, courts-martial were "forums," as one law school dean later observed, "to enforce the Commander-in-Chief's disciplinary policies and inculcate military values."[14] Sentences, in turn, were often public affairs such as running the gauntlet, floggings, or drumming out of the service, all designed to set unmistakable examples and reinforce authority of the army chain of command.[15] While private soldiers suffered gruesome physical punishment, officers (virtually all hailing from the gentleman class) were formally "reprimanded," or in the worst case publicly shamed by being "discharged the service." Between 1775 and 1783, at least 3,315 individual courts-martial were conducted throughout Continental service.[16] Two-thirds of these cases were disposed of in "regimental" (sometimes called "garrison" or "brigade") courts whose five-officer boards adjudicated most private soldier offenses. "General" courts-martial handled the more serious cases. As mandated by Congress, these 13-officer proceedings judged matters involving multiple regiments, senior officers, and all offences requiring the death penalty. Laurance, because of his headquarters' physical proximity as a member of Washington's staff, found his docket almost exclusively scheduled with general courts-martial hearings. Before following the newly minted lieutenant colonel into court, however, a brief overview of official responsibilities is in order.

Judge advocate general was a thankless, behind-the-scenes job. "As to fame," Colonel Tudor bemoaned before resigning the post, "a man might continue Judge Advocate to Eternity without gaining a Particle of it."[17] Judging actual guilt or innocence was the responsibility of a court's presiding officer and his board. So too, sentencing. The judge advocate general's fundamental duty as prescribed by the 1776 Articles of War (after deposing witnesses, swearing-in participants, and soliciting a "guilty" or "not guilty" plea from the accused) was to "prosecute in the name of the United States of America."[18] In the name of fairness, a judge advocate might also advise the defendant who—unheard of today—was denied private counsel to speak in his behalf.[19]

"In every Case where the Evidence is complicated," wrote Judge Laurance's predecessor, "it is expected of me to analyze the Evidence and state Questions which are involved in it."[20] After questions were answered to the court's satisfaction, a vote, beginning with the most junior officer, was taken with verdict and sentence pronounced by the presiding officer. Nearly 8 times out of 10, the verdict was "guilty."[21] No sentence was final until personally approved by Washington, after which it fell to the judge advocate department to work court decisions into His Excellency's daily General Orders and furnish written transcripts to the Congressional War Office, with—if requested—a copy to the accused.[22] Furthermore, Laurance in May 1777 was directed by Board of War Secretary Richard Peters to inform Paymaster General William Palfrey of all appropriate defendant pay stoppages.[23] Little wonder Tudor resigned after "too long Absences from home and bare Livelihood."

Lt. Colonel Laurance had arrived in April 1777 to a Camp Morristown pulsating with armed men. Company after company of raw soldiers, product of the Congress's 88-battalion resolve of September 1776, trickled and then flooded in from all 13 former colonies. Most, at General Washington's insistence, were inoculated for smallpox before leaving home. By July they would number almost 15,000, equipped with thousands of 69-caliber Charleville muskets and clad in blue or brown regimental coats courtesy of the king of France. No sooner had Laurance donned a field officer's twin epaulets than he was inundated by the full disciplinary docket to be expected from such heavy influx of raw recruits. Indeed, second quarter 1777 produced a six-fold caseload increase versus the preceding two quarters (see Appendix A). It was a disciplinary deluge that translated to almost 10 trials per week for Washington's new judge advocate general and his staff.

Outside the courtroom, Martha Washington's welcome presence induced the sweet Morristown springtime countryside to blossom with officers' ladies. Staff dinners at His Excellency's Arnold Tavern headquarters sparkled with female conversation. Joining vivacious Mrs. Theodorick Bland, ebony-haired 22-year-old Catherine "Caty" Greene, and dozens of others, young Betsey Laurance rode into camp "carrying their infant on the pommel of her saddle before her."[24] And soon came welcome news that Washington himself had arranged a prisoner exchange freeing Betsey's brother Stevey McDougall from enemy captivity.

Not until mid-June did the campaign of 1777 really open. Over the next four months, Sir (knighted by King George for his victory at Long Island) William Howe's 27,000-man professional army brushed aside Washington's fledgling light infantry corps at Cooch's Bridge on the Delaware border, manhandled his main army at Brandywine Creek, surprised General Anthony Wayne at Paoli (Pennsylvania) in a midnight bayonet attack that routed an entire division with some 300 casualties, and on September 26 marched uncontested into Philadelphia. Washington, in an audacious dawn assault, subsequently struck Howe's sleeping army at Germantown, only to watch near-victory turn to disaster when late-arriving Continental troops mistakenly fired on one another and advance units ran out of ammunition.

While Washington's army licked battlefield wounds, Judge Laurance engaged in the obligatory face-to-face combat of courts-martial. Most trials were black and white in nature: sleeping on sentry duty (50 lashes), theft (100 lashes), officer cowardice (cashiered from service), or desertion (death). More nuanced questions of senior officer battlefield competence during the Philadelphia campaign schooled Laurance in the gray areas of command responsibility. Irish-born Major General John Sullivan and Brigadier Generals William "Scotch-Willie" Maxwell and Anthony Wayne all faced tough courts-martial questioning for respective shortcomings at Germantown, Brandywine, and Paoli before being acquitted "with honor." Early in November, courtroom gravitas increased another notch when His Excellency tasked Judge Laurance to draw up serious charges against Major General Adam Stephen.

As much as the commander-in-chief valued Generals Wayne and Sullivan, he was wary of Adam Stephen. Second-in-command to Washington in Virginia during the French and Indian Wars, the self-seeking Stephen turned post-war political rival as well as sharp-elbowed competitor in securing prime western Virginia land parcels. Boisterous and a reputed womanizer, the testy Stephen's bouts with alcoholism had entangled him in controversy well before the War for Independence.[25] And recently, he had misrepresented to Washington a brief New Jersey skirmish as a victory when in fact he was put to flight. Character was paramount to the Master of Mount Vernon, and to his mind, Adam Stephen fell short.

If anyone was to blame for turning early October certain victory at Germantown into retreat, it was Stephen. Just when Sir William Howe's reeling troops were about to be cornered in a pincer movement, General Stephen's command had wandered cross-country to collide with another Continental unit and trade volleys. Hearing this musket fire in their rear, the entire American strike force—already low on ammunition—screeched to a halt, withdrew, and then ran. General Stephen, to his credit, exhorted his own scattering ranks to partially reform as a rag-tag rear guard for Washington's retreat, but he was later found slumped against a rail fence in a drunken stupor.

Imbibing alcohol during combat did not per se violate the Articles of War; indeed, Scottish-born New Jersey brigadier William Maxwell was acquitted mere weeks before, despite evidence that he "was disguised with liquor in such a manner to disqualify him in some measure, but not fully, from doing his duty; & that once or twice besides his spirits were a little elevated by spirituous liquor."[26] How, then, was Judge Laurance to proceed? Scanning all 102 Articles of War, he determined to prosecute on the basis of Section XIV, Article 21:

> Whatsoever commissioned officer shall be convicted, before a general court-martial, of behaving in a scandalous, infamous manner, such as is unbecoming the character of an officer and a gentleman, shall be discharged from the service.

It was a benchmark prosecution that articulated "usage and custom of the service" for future military generations regarding behavior unbecoming of an officer and a gentleman, while also establishing prosecutorial precedent in matters of intoxication. Rather than accuse a defendant with drunkenness per se, charge him instead with "behavior unbecoming." Two weeks of frank testimony later, Washington's General Orders broadcast a verdict that may as well have come straight from Laurance's lips. Pronounced guilty of "unofficerlike behavior" in the retreat from Germantown "to the prejudice of good order and military discipline," General Stephen was unceremoniously "dismissed the service."[27]

On December 19, 1777, Judge Laurance moved with Washington's battered but still-potent army west to thickly wooded ground nestled in a cluster of hills enfolding Valley Creek hard on the Schuykill River. Between the creek and Mount Joy lay the 1,008-acre gristmill and refinery forge complex of Isaac Potts, David Potts, and William Dewees, which locals dubbed "Valley Forge." Laurance and the rest of His Excellency's working staff would spend the winter—two or three to a bed—in three upstairs bedrooms of General Washington's rented 22-foot by 27-foot, two-story fieldstone farmhouse (fig. 3) that served as army headquarters.[28]

FIGURE 3 Washington's Headquarters at Valley Forge. Laurance shared one of three upstairs bedrooms with as many as a dozen other headquarters staffers over the winter of 1777/1778. The first-floor parlor to the right of the front entry served as communal workplace and communication center. (Courtesy of the National Park Service. Public domain.)

As early as 1910, the Valley Forge Park Commission thought the site "a sort of myth, and like many traditions of old, a place created of imagination rather than a reality."[29] No image has taken firmer iconic hold on American memory than that of "Baron" von Steuben drilling unshod, disordered, scarecrow soldiers in the bloodied snow. But the Prussian "perfect personification of Mars" did not heave into camp until February 23, 1778, with his two smartly uniformed aides and high-stepping greyhound, *Azor*.[30] Yet another month would pass before first regimental drills began. Until then, Washington employed a pervasive regimen of congressionally sanctioned martial law, backed up by exacting courts-martial justice, to keep 80 regiments from 11 states (South Carolina and Georgia troops were dispatched home) from flying apart during episodes of extreme deprivation.

Judge Advocate General Laurance oversaw a massive three-month courts-martial regimen that supplied necessary disciplinary sinew to hold Washington's ragged, often surly Continentals together until the laughably profane von Steuben's drills took hold.[31] For, as we have learned, the rank and file consisted mainly of spirited young single men who constituted a hasty marriage of hired substitutes, blacks earning freedom through conscripted service, former Hessian prisoners of war, unskilled vagrants, and adventurous farm boys.[32] Yet, an "overweening confidence," as historian Charles Royster put it, in their battlefield competence after the Philadelphia campaign helped most "overcome the strong inducement to desert or mutiny."[33] While General Washington jawboned with the Continental Congress, state governors, and the increasingly meddlesome transitional Board of War to feed, clothe, and pay his desertion-plagued army, Judge Laurance emptied its jails.

"Great numbers of prisoners," wrote former Adjutant-General Weedon (now commanding a Virginia brigade) on December 30, "are now in the provost... Court martials are to be approved tomorrow, and sit every day till all the men that belong to their respective brigades are tried."[34] Brigade courts-martial such as Weedon's did not necessarily require Judge Laurance's personal attention, but he shouldered the full burden of army general courts-martial when well-born Middle Department deputy, Virginia Major John Taylor, opted to winter at Hazelwood, his Caroline County manor. Casting about for a temporary administrative deputy as December had approached, Judge Laurance settled on a young Virginia infantry lieutenant with a reputation for clear thinking. Though but 22 and lacking formal legal training, a first-rate mind lay behind the officer's penetrating dark-eyed gaze. Laurance surely knew the young man's father was an old and trusted Washington friend, but he never could have guessed he had started Lieutenant John Marshall on a path leading to a 34-year tenure as chief justice of the future United States Supreme Court.[35]

Even with Marshall's assistance (he still commanded an infantry company), Laurance staggered under the case backload. "Tho' I have exerted myself to the utmost," he advised Washington on February 5, "I have not been able to complete the business of my department as expeditious as I could have wish'd." Pleading for more resources, he added: "I have made free to mention this matter to Your Excellency as I have understood the Committee of Congress is now here with powers to address any measures they may conceive benefitting the army."[36]

Trials more often than not took place between 8 a.m. and 3 p.m. in the "Bake House," an unrecognizably over-restored building that still stands some 100 yards from Washington's headquarters. Serving as bakery and commissary, the structure also functioned as the venue for junior officer theatrical productions. It was here, in these steamy Bake House confines, that Laurance made his mark on George Washington's main army. In a truly prodigious feat of military justice, the judge advocate general oversaw 179 general courts martial proceedings over the six-month encampment, 139 of which (73.5%) resulted in punishment. (Appendix A explores this regimen in some detail.) In first quarter 1778 alone, Lt. Colonel Laurance prosecuted 51 officers—nearly 1 in 20—as Washington tightened the screws of accountability on an officer corps that had shrunk by 50% to 1,050 men by December's end. Not only did John set the table for von Steuben's drills by ridding the army of 42 of its least competent officers, but he also brought to justice 30 commissary supply-chain cheats and civilians charged with consorting with the enemy.

In late January, an investigatory congressional committee commandeered nearby Moore Hall, the comfortable stone Georgian residence of unrepentant Tory William Moore. Chairman Francis Dana (Massachusetts), along with New York's Gouverneur Morris and three fellow delegates, then settled in to confer with Washington about reorganizing the army and remedying logistical dysfunction that had brought unclothed and starving troops to their knees. Seizing the initiative on issues ranging from supply chain collapse to army reorganization and officer post-war pensions, the General also asked Judge Laurance to recommend alterations that Congress need consider in the 1776 Articles of War.

Top of mind was the army's nagging desertion rate. Between September 27, 1777, and February 28, 1778, at least 871 deserters slipped away to British Philadelphia.[37] Desertion, of course, was a capital offense. But, "Should the greater part of the offenders be punished with death," Laurance cautioned Washington, "the frequency of Examples of that kind might loose that Effect on the Minds of the Soldiers." Even more men might then slip away. "Punishing them with Stripes [lashes]," Laurance continued, "might deter them, . . . but the Number allowed to be inflicted are too few."[38] The solution, to Laurance's mind, was to emulate the British military code granting courts maneuvering room of up to 1,000 lashes per infraction. "I am induced to think," he suggested, "the Honble Congress should repeal that part of the 3rd Article Section 18 of the Articles of War." Rather, he suggested, courts-martial should be "at liberty to sentence offenders to receive as great a number of Lashes, as they conceive an adequate punishment for the crime."[39]

Washington on February 19 laid his judge advocate general's request before Dana and the others, adding for good measure that: "to inflict capital punishment on every deserter" would "incur the imputation of cruelty," while "to give only a hundred lashes to such criminals is a burlesque on their crimes."[40] Reluctant lawmakers, concerned about excessive punishment of free men in a volunteer army, took no action on the increased lash-count suggestion.[41] Instead, Judge Laurance was invited to weigh in on jurisdictional ambiguities involving civilians in the war zone. Directed to bring "records of Congress or laws of this state empowering court methods to try persons other than of the army," John became midwife to the United States' first formal parameters of war zone martial law.[42] Together with Joseph Reed of the Pennsylvania Executive Council, Laurance and the five congressional committeemen (four, including Gouverneur Morris, were lawyers) swiftly resolved that evidence in civilian cases be fully examined before incarceration,[43] and that civilians taken prisoner more than 30 miles from army headquarters must be turned over to civil authority.[44]

Washington's diligent judge advocate general must have made a strong impression on Dana and the others; little more than a month later, Congress resolved to boost his 60-dollar monthly pay to 75 dollars along with forage for two horses.[45] "There is not only an addition to your pay," added Board of War Secretary Timothy Pickering's April 1st confirming missive, "but an adjutant allowed you."[46]

As might be expected of a former regimental paymaster and New York lawyer who knew his way around pre-war admiralty and chancery settlements, Laurance demonstrated an early knack for managing money. Indeed, before joining Washington at Morristown in April, he had squirreled away some $2,000 personal cash with mother-in-law Hannah McDougall "to be delivered to him when called for."[47] It was hardly surprising, then, that his father-in-law's nephew John McDougall in late January solicited John's investment advice. Young McDougall was first lieutenant of the new Philadelphia-built 36-gun frigate *Randolph*. About to ship out again, Lieutenant McDougall named Laurance one of three executors of his will and entrusted his financial nest egg to Laurance's oversight. "I have at present no need for money," McDougall wrote, "and to put it at interest when the currency seems to be growing less valuable every day, I think would be attended with a loss, but think you are the best judge of my situation and business in life at present."[48] With £4,000 of his princely £10,000 prize pot already capitalized in "a good brick house and lot," McDougall asked Laurance to invest the balance. "As I think it probable I shall soon make another addition to my little stock, I would be extremely obliged to you the application of the whole."[49] One can only imagine Laurance's sorrow when word came that the *Randolph* on March 7 had disintegrated off Barbados in one blinding flash, her magazine exploded from a random British cannonball from 64-gun ship of the line HMS *Yarmouth*. Only four of *Randolph*'s 311-man crew survived, and none were officers.

Three days after *Randolph* went down, Laurance prosecuted at an altogether different tragedy. In a general court-martial that would establish army policy for more than two centuries, Third Pennsylvania Lt. Friedrich Enslin was tried for attempted sodomy with private soldier John Monhort. Enslin, after falsely accusing Ensign Anthony Maxwell of slander, was subsequently found guilty of perjury and "dissolute" (homosexual) behavior and "dismissed the service with infamy."[50] At the commander-in-chief's insistence, all the drums and fifes of Valley Forge formed up to literally drum Enslin—his coat turned inside out—from out of the fully assembled army. It would not be until 1993 that harsh military precedent regarding homosexuality would be formally replaced by Defense Department Directive 1304.26, better known as "don't ask, don't tell."

As His Excellency's dependence on Laurance grew, he was periodically pressed into service as aide-de-camp to lend a hand with voluminous headquarters paperwork. For example, he replied on Washington's behalf to British prisoner of war William Nichols's (captain of 16-gun packet HMS *Eagle*) request to be exchanged. Protocol, of course, could never allow His Excellency to respond directly to so junior an enemy. "Sir," Laurance informed the imprisoned captain, "if you are surprised that instead of being indulged with leave to go and negotiate your exchange, you are desired to return to Reading [detention center], it is because your haughty countrymen increase the Horror of War by exercising on their prisoners such cruelties as are reprobated by all civilized nations."[51] Washington himself could not have put it more forcefully.

At day's end, John repaired to the rented stone farmhouse of William Dewees, where Washington's brilliant coterie of young staffers worked and slept. On cold, snowy evenings the general's aides, Lt. Colonels Robert Harrison, Alexander Hamilton, John Laurens, Robert Kidder Meade, and Tench Tilghman, could be found conversing in the front chamber that served as both staff workplace and sitting room. All but Laurance were bachelors, and none were strangers to a glass, or two, of the commander-in-chief's Madeira. Thirty-two-year-old Marylander Robert Harrison was Washington's principal scribe. Known around the army as "Old Secretary," he was the Master of Mount Vernon's pre-war lawyer. At Washington's side since summer of 1775, Harrison enjoyed such editorial trust that he once exclaimed, "I wish to the Lord the General would give me the heads or some idea of what he would have me write."[52]

Whatever Harrison did not pen in Washington's name generally fell to 33-year-old College of Philadelphia graduate Tilghman. Defying his prominent Tory father, Tilghman in July 1775 threw in with the *jeunesse dorée* of Philadelphia's elite, the patriot "Silk Stockings" light infantry unit. He later captained a company in the Continental Army "Flying Camp" and by August 1776 had earned his way into Washington's headquarters family. Of the commander-in-chief's 32 wartime aides, the tall Maryland-born Philadelphian would prove the most loyal, serving until November 1783. "He has a penetrating intellect," observed Laurance's fellow New Yorker James Duane, "that flies like an arrow from a bow."[53]

Hamilton, of course, was just returned from Saratoga, full of juicy tales. Turned out that Horatio Gates's aide-de-camp was none other than Alexander's former college roommate Robert Troup*, who slyly passed word that combative Benedict Arnold—rather than Gates—was true

---

*Troup, following several months aboard a British prisoner "death ship" after his capture in the battle for Long Island, was exchanged in late December 1776. He quickly parlayed a first lieutenancy in Henry Livingston's Fourth New York Regiment into an artillery captain-lieutenancy under General Knox and was later made aide-de-camp to General Horatio Gates with rank of lieutenant colonel.

battlefield victor over British general John Burgoyne. Accompanying Hamilton back from Saratoga was Washington's newly appointed adjutant general, Colonel Alexander Scammell. It was a sort of homecoming for the Massachusetts native who had earned Washington's confidence at Trenton and Princeton before serving with distinction in General Gates's Northern Army. The Harvard-educated ('59) pre-war surveyor-turned-attorney displayed a dry fireside humor that earned him a reputation as master of the "ludicrous anecdote" and second only to Washington himself in commanding the "table after the ladies had left."[54]

Exuberant 20-year-old Marquis de Lafayette and von Steuben's multi-linguistic aide Pierre-Étienne Du Ponceau added a dash of panache along with lively after-dinner conversations *en Français*. Aide-de-camp Richard Kidder Meade, a 31-year-old Virginian who had captained an infantry company since 1775, was a superb horseman trusted by Washington with his most important dispatches. Dashing 23-year-old John Laurens, having graduated from Harrow and barely completed law studies in Geneva before musket balls flew at Concord Bridge, hailed from a prominent South Carolina family (father Henry was then president of Congress) that happily furnished a steady stream of select mealtime provisions. Stirring this sparkling headquarters intellectual punchbowl was His Excellency's congenial wife Martha, who ruled the newly added dining pavilion extending to the rear of the house. Utterly unassuming, full of conversation, and content to give her husband full stage, Martha Washington made headquarters into a real home rather than the gnarly male dormitory it might otherwise have become. "The evening was spent in conversation over a dish of tea or coffee," remembered Du Ponceau. "There were no levees or formal soirees; no dancing, card playing, or amusements of any kind except singing. Every gentleman or lady who could sing was called upon in turn for a song."[55]

By mid-May, Judge Laurance's caseload tapered to but three cases a week as the daily drumbeat of military justice gave way to the stamping feet of von Steuben's close-order drills. And with warmer weather, furloughed veterans drifted back by the hundreds from winter leave. Among them was Abraham Riker, Laurance's fellow Fourth New York lieutenant from the 1775 Canadian campaign. Now 38, with the rank of captain, Riker was back in camp as a company commander in Colonel Philip van Cortlandt's Second New York Regiment. As the days warmed up, however, contagious disease crept into camp like a British light infantry skirmishing line. Encampment huts, despite daily hygienic inspection, housed up to 12 unbathed men who tossed food scraps and trash in dark corners. These dank incubator-like quarters, described by Lafayette as "scarcely gayer than dungeon cells," soon became breeding grounds for influenza, typhus, dysentery, and spotted, yellow, and typhoid fevers. The sick were evacuated from camp to half a dozen hospitals to minimize contagion, and Washington ordered broad-scale smallpox inoculation, but clothing of soldiers who died was often passed on to others. Of the 3,500 men who may have perished at Valley Forge—formal statistics are at best fragmentary—as many as 2,500 to 3,000 succumbed from infectious disease.[56]

"Capt. Riker," Colonel van Cortlandt informed the army, "was taken Sick the 2d of May went out of camp the 3d. Died the 8th and was Buried the 9th."[57] Perhaps three miles from camp in the burying yard of Valley Presbyterian Meeting House, Judge Laurance looked on as his former Canadian campaign comrade was interred with the honors of war. Worrisome questions must have floated through John's mind as the loamy black Pennsylvania dirt was shoveled over Captain Riker's remains. What would become of Riker's wife Margaret and daughter Jane on loyalist-controlled Long Island? Was it only a matter of time before battlefield odds caught up with him too? And what was he doing out here in the middle of a remote country field when he had not seen his wife and son for almost a year?

Within days of Riker's funeral, Laurance inquired to Colonel Timothy Pickering at the Board of War about a vacant secretaryship. "I regret the disappointment," Pickering replied, explaining that the position had been filled. "I forbore response," continued Pickering, "because when I mentioned your desires to my friends there was an objection to your quitting your present office."[58] To the Board of War, if not Washington himself, Judge Laurance after a year on the job had become too valuable to spare.

SIX

Courtrooms as Battlefields

NEW BRUNSWICK, NEW JERSEY, JULY 4, 1778. Judge Laurance gathered his thick frame to full-bodied height in the "large room" of proprietor "Minne" Voorhees's commodious two-story White Hart Tavern and prepared to swear-in the newly formed court. Across the table scowled scarecrow-thin English-born Major General Charles Lee, about to be charged by the judge advocate general on three counts: disobedience of orders, misbehavior before the enemy, and disrespect to the commander-in-chief. It was no secret that Lee, recently exchanged after 16 months in British captivity, believed himself militarily superior to Washington, whom he thought "not fit to command a sergeant's guard."[1] Lee's regard for the rank and file was no better. American soldiers, he had recently warned Congress, would "be laughed at as a bad army by their enemy, and defeated in every encounter which depends on manoeuvres."[2]

Even so, Washington had been honor-bound to offer his senior lieutenant command of a strike force, almost half the army, tasked to engage the rear of Sir Henry Clinton's British column as it made its way to New York from Philadelphia. Rather than attack, however, on ground which neither he nor Washington had reconnoitered, Lee unilaterally withdrew his troops in muddled retreat. Fast on his heels came the flower of Clinton's army in hot pursuit. Fortuitously, Washington arrived that scorching afternoon of June 28 with the fresh divisions of Generals Greene, Stirling, and Lafayette to battle Clinton's redcoats to a bloody draw on the rolling fields below Monmouth Courthouse. "A general rout, dismay, and disgrace," proclaimed an admiring Alexander Hamilton, "would have attended the whole army in any other hands but his."[3] Elated with the army's performance, Washington would likely have excused Lee's retreat, but two insulting letters demanding court-martial to explain his actions induced His Excellency to oblige.

Judge Laurance prosecuted in the name of the United States of America in a 39-day, 26-session marathon as Washington's army marched north through New Brunswick, Morristown, and Paramus, New Jersey, into Peekskill and North Castle, New York.[4] Under Major General William (Lord Stirling) Alexander's presiding eye, the judge advocate general deposed or summoned 5 generals and 20 lesser officers as prosecution witnesses while swearing in 2 generals and 11 junior officers for the defense. Taken together as a whole, eyewitness testimony on both the disobedience and misbehavior charges was divided and inconclusive. Washington's devoted aides Hamilton, Laurens, and Meade, together with Generals Scott and Wayne, remembered Lee's battlefield demeanor as scrambled and his troops disorderly, but several Lee subordinates clearly did not. Laurance's persistent early questioning made abundantly clear that Washington fully expected Lee to engage the enemy; but an equally articulate defendant argued that conditions on the ground precluded any such maneuver. It was not until Laurance addressed the third charge, "disrespect to the Commander-in-Chief," that scales of military justice tipped against the accused. Slowly and deliberately, Judge Laurance hoisted Lee on his own petard by reading into the record word-by-word both of the latter's insulting and disrespectful post-battle letters to Washington.

"The black and white pattern of the proceedings," observed historian Thomas Fleming, "made it clear to the court they were being forced to choose between Washington and Lee."[5] If one believed with Charles Lee that the commander-in-chief was no match for Sir Henry Clinton and that the patriot army could not stand up to Clinton's crack professionals, the decision to withdraw was sound; even worthy of plaudits for turning disaster into a respectable outcome. If, on the other hand, both armies were fairly matched and Washington's intent was to force Clinton's hand so that he might come up with the main army to carry the day, an insubordinate Lee was clearly culpable.

General Alexander's court had little choice but to side with Washington, lest the army become divided and the Glorious Cause itself impaired. Major General Lee on August 12 was pronounced guilty and sentenced "to be suspended from any command in the armies of the Unites States of North American, for the term of twelve months." Washington, without comment, forwarded Judge Laurance's official trial transcript with the court's verdict to Congress to be confirmed or rejected. It was a political hot potato that lawmakers juggled during almost four months of protracted, closed-door discussions before on December 5 confirming Charles Lee "guilty" by a margin of six states to two. Two states were divided and three deferred.[6] Only 23 delegates were in attendance and 7 voted in favor of Lee.

Two-and-a-quarter centuries later, perfect hindsight suggests Major General Lee was likely militarily correct at Monmouth Courthouse. For in 1890, private papers of Sir Henry Clinton surfaced to show he had quickly divined Washington's attack scheme. "Had Washington been blockhead enough to sustain Lee," wrote Clinton, "I should have catched him between two defiles," and his "whole corps would have fallen into the power of the King's army."[7] And perhaps so, unless General Daniel Morgan's detached rifle brigade or Philemon Dickinson's 800-strong, local New Jersey militia belatedly arrived to alter the battlefield equation. But, as Judge Laurance had already learned after 15 months in the field, senior officer courts-martial were as much about politics and the good of the service as about specific case facts. And Like "Old Secretary" Harrison in matters of correspondence, John had acquired a subtle sixth sense for executing His Excellency's unspoken will.

Laurance's insider eye could not help but see that the army had coalesced around their general at Valley Forge, that its officers were bound together by devotion to his person, and that divisive interloper Charles Lee was toxic to the army's performance. How else to explain the judge advocate general's decision *not* to introduce eyewitness testimony from Pennsylvania Major John Clark Jr. . . . testimony that would have justified Lee's retreat. Clark, an officer in whom Washington placed great trust as a spy-master, had been dispatched to General Lee with last minute orders to "proceed with caution and take care the enemy don't draw him into a scrape."[8] Having delivered His Excellency's missive, Clark recalled that Lee then directed him to inform Washington that his regiments were already retiring because they were "thrown into confusion" from "precipitancy by one of his Brigadiers [Charles Scott] and false intelligence."[9] If Clark got it right, General Lee had actually *complied* with Washington's orders by prudently determining not to engage an enemy twice his size with his own troops already in disorder. Laurance, however, was not obligated under the Articles of War to introduce evidence detrimental to his prosecution. Indeed, another 185 years would pass before army prosecutors were mandated to disclose information that might negate defendant guilt or reduce punishment.[10]

Ink on Lee's trial transcript was barely two weeks dry when Judge Laurance was directed to prosecute Continental major general Arthur St. Clair (1737–1818) in a politically charged proceeding that Washington had hoped to avoid. St. Clair, promoted to major general at Washington's urging in wake of victory at Princeton, had in July 1777 conceded Fort Ticonderoga to British general Burgoyne's overwhelmingly superior force without either siege or pitched battle. The American public and Congress were in immediate uproar. Was not the fort with its hundred cannons impregnable? Someone had to be held accountable, and New England firebrands had their sights on both St. Clair and his patrician New York superior, Major General Philip Schuyler. Washington intentionally dragged his feet for more than a year after Congress first demanded St. Clair's prosecution, most likely because he sensed the directive was yet one more piece in the murky scheme of Thomas Mifflin, Joseph Reed, and other members of the so-called "Conway-Cabal" to induce his resignation in favor of Horatio Gates. True, battlefield performance at Monmouth quieted doubts about His Excellency's military ability vis à vis Gates, but an increasingly divisive Congress still wanted greater say in running the army. When a four-person congressional committee—three of whom were suspicious New Englanders—concocted actual charges against St. Clair, Washington had no choice but in late August 1778 to finally schedule the trial.[11]

Section IX of the Articles of War, as every serving officer knew, established courts-martial for the governing of troops by their own senior officers. Nowhere was Congress authorized to usurp the prosecution by drawing up individual charges. What's more, lawmakers patently insulted both Judge Laurance and the commander-in-chief by directing that "two Counsellors learned in the law assist and co-operate with the Judge Advocate in the prosecution."[12] When the attorneys general of Pennsylvania and New Jersey were designated proxy prosecution co-managers, no spectacles were necessary for Laurance to see he was part of a legislative witch hunt with alarming implications for military law.[13] If Congress could arbitrarily prepare courts-martial charges, produce the evidence, and assign special prosecutors, might not they not eventually render verdicts as well?

Washington—no pushover when it came to hardball politics—waited until the eleventh hour before advising congressionally mandated "counsellers" Jonathan Serjeant (Pennsylvania) and Irish-born William Paterson (New Jersey) of trial time and place. When both men demonstrated the good sense not to appear, Judge Laurance wrested control of the proceeding from congressional hands with his opening statement.[14] "It is necessary (previous to my producing the requisite evidence on this trial)," Laurance addressed the court, "that I should inform you of the matters, upon which the charges against Major General St. Clair are founded. They are certain remarks, made by a committee of the Hon. Continental Congress, appointed to examine the evidence collected and state charges."[15] Laurance then proceeded not only to pass over the congressional "evidence," but instead presented a stream of documents and testimonies that, over the next four sessions, *justified* St. Clair's decision to abandon Ticonderoga.

In the end, little remained except for a single accusatory affidavit from civilian commissary Jesse Leavenworth, upon which Congress had relied. Few civilians in such circumstances could withstand detailed cross-examination from senior army officers on matters of military strategy and Jesse was not one of them. A flustered Leavenworth was reduced to amateurish second-guessing when his affidavit was contradicted by a parade of army witnesses as well as his own testimony. As final evidence, Laurance produced a written deposition from Major General Schuyler, confirming that he could not possibly have raised enough troops to relieve Ticonderoga had St. Clair actually hunkered down under siege. Twenty days after trial's onset, the five generals and eight colonels constituting Major General Benjamin Lincoln's court unanimously pronounced St. Clair "NOT GUILTY," acquitting him with "the highest honour." Although Arthur St. Clair would not hold another wartime independent command, the judge advocate general's sympathetic prosecution had not only shielded Washington from legislative vendetta and helped preserve the reputation of a valuable officer, but it also drew a clear line regarding congressional usurpation of individual trial protocol.

Whatever satisfaction John may have savored was short lived. Awaiting him on October 1, some 50 miles north of White Plains near the tiny hamlet of Quaker Hill, was the court-martial of Major General Philip Schuyler. Established in 1731, Quaker Hill was a community of pacifists. The gentle, salubrious surrounds may have provided much-needed peaceful asylum for General Washington and his regiments, but to the Quaker Friends, patriot soldiers were invaders with blood on their hands.[16] Nonetheless, Washington commandeered the Friends Meeting House as a military hospital, and senior officers invited themselves to quarter with the most prosperous burghers. His Excellency established headquarters at John Kane's fine house in nearby Fredericksburg, while Major General Benjamin Lincoln made himself at home in the capacious residence of prosperous farmer Reed Ferris. The latter's large ground floor chamber was rendered into a comfortable courtroom for General Schuyler's trial.

Heir to vast upstate New York manor-grants and linked by marriage to the patroon Van Rensselaer estates, Philip Schuyler's wealth and haughty bearing aroused instant resentment among New England levelers such as Sam Adams and republican Pennsylvanians Thomas Mifflin and Joseph Reed. Unlike the St. Clair case, Schuyler's detractors in Congress had not drawn up specific charges against him nor produced any eyewitness accusations. Indeed, given St. Clair's exoneration, no trial was even necessary. All the same, Schuyler, like Anthony Wayne a year before, demanded an opportunity to clear his name. And so the court—mostly holdovers from the St. Clair trial—was duly called to order. Locking eyes with the man who three years earlier was his commanding general on the march to Canada, Laurance addressed Schuyler with but a single charge: neglect of duty in not being present at Ticonderoga to discharge the functions of his command.[17] The judge advocate did not have any witnesses to call. Three short days later, Schuyler, like St. Clair, was declared "not guilty" and acquitted with "highest Honours." Final word on the matter came from New York legislators who, in a flagrant "favorite son" statement to Schuyler's congressional disparagers, elected him posthaste to the Fourth Continental Congress about to convene in Philadelphia.

Judge Laurance, after 18 grueling months on the courts-martial treadmill, now found himself at tranquil Quaker Hill with time to reflect. At Washington's side from Brandywine to Germantown, Valley Forge, and Monmouth Courthouse, he had overseen hundreds of courts-martials and helped empty the army of unfit officers, all the while teaching the rank and file the consequences of unmilitary behavior. On his watch, the nascent Judge Advocate Corps was firmly implanted as a staff department with deputies George Smith, Henry Purcell, John Taylor, and Henry D. Purcell ensconced, respectively, in New York, South Carolina, Virginia, and Pennsylvania. What more remained to be achieved? Why stay on?

Still licensed before the New York bar, it was back to his home state that John's eyes turned. New York's state legislature conducted its business in Kingston, along the Hudson River only 55 miles northwest of Quaker Hill. Why not resign his commission and join the Kingston establishment in some capacity? Refugee Queens County relatives Jonathan and Daniel Lawrence had served, respectively, as state senator and assemblyman ever since the state's new constitution of 1777 became law. By linking up with them in Kingston, he might then finally share the same roof as wife Betsey, son John (almost three), and infant daughter Mary. General McDougall, as if reading his son-in-law's mind, put in a good word with Governor Clinton for the vacant office of New York City Clerk, a coveted pre-war position that enhanced a young lawyer's future private practice. Hearing of the position, McDougall had praised his son-in-law as an industrious officer who "has preserved his morals in the Army. The gentlemen of the law," he reminded Clinton, "inform me who were present at his examination that he made a respectable one."[18] But it was not to be; the office went to a Livingston devotee. John would remain the army's chief military lawyer for three more years.

"I set out this afternoon for home," Laurance informed Hamilton in late April 1779. "I am obliged to remove my family a considerable distance," he confided, "the delay of which is expensive and inconvenient to them."[19] Before setting off with the commander-in-chief's reluctant permission for the first extended time with his family in two years, John asked a favor of fellow headquarters staffer Hamilton. "Should anything turn up relative to my department of consequence," he asked, "I will thank you to inform me of it by line under cover to General McDougall."[20] John's long-anticipated family idyll lasted little more than two weeks. "As the trial of Genl. Arnold is to come on by the first of June," Washington ordered in mid-May, "you will take care to be at the Headquarters of the army fully in time to make all the necessary arrangements on this occasion."[21] Yet another major general faced court-martial and, as in St. Clair's case, the accusations emanated from civil sources—Pennsylvania's 12-man Supreme Executive Council, which in 1776 replaced the office of Governor.

Philadelphia in the year after British withdrawal was a city on the brink of complete anarchy. Citizens suspected of loyalist collaboration were indiscriminately jailed; state price controls sent tradesmen protesting in the streets over limits on what they could charge; militant gangs accused prosperous merchants of hoarding foodstuffs in favor of hard specie; commissary agents seized provisions that worthless Continental dollars could not buy; supporters of the new state constitution openly quarreled with nationalist factions over what was in best public interest; and marauding bands of disgruntled militia roughed up whomever they pleased. "There are few unhappier cities on the Globe," wrote Connecticut congressional delegate Silas Deane, "than Philadelphia."[22]

Divisiveness only increased when in mid-February 1779 the Supreme Council (some of the very men who earlier questioned Washington's command suitability) publicly accused Philadelphia military commander General Benedict Arnold of gross malfeasance. Although no evidence was given, Arnold was prominently denounced for illegal business transactions, support of a Tory ship owner, and defiance of the independent sovereignty of Pennsylvania. It was an ugly assertion with but one purpose: to remove Arnold from command. Should Washington not comply, the Council threatened to cut off Pennsylvania funds to his army and not call out state militia except in the direst of emergency.

To be sure, His Excellency's choice of Arnold for the Philadelphia command was a glaring mistake. Disturbing signs appeared all too soon, when rumors filtered in that Arnold was too soft on British sympathizers. Some whispered he was using his position for personal financial gain. Whether such hearsay was true or not, it was plain to see that he was living well beyond his means. Where was the money coming from? Tongues wagged even more furiously when General Arnold began courting the much younger Peggy Shippen, a Philadelphia belle who had prominently socialized with British officers. Margaret "Peggy" Shippen was the fourth and youngest daughter of prominent Philadelphia loyalist judge, Edward Shippen IV. After British evacuation, Judge Shippen fled to New Jersey, but he returned after even stricter laws were passed there. Perhaps to insulate her family from patriot retribution, 18-year-old Peggy would become Mrs. Benedict Arnold on April 8, 1779.

By February, however, Pennsylvania's Supreme Executive Council had already seen enough. Eight charges of malfeasance were communicated to the state attorney general, who referred the matter to the Continental Congress. John Jay, then president of Congress, assigned a committee of inquiry. When the Executive Council could produce little evidence to support their charges, the committee relieved Arnold of criminality in six charges, the other two drawing informal rebuke from General Washington. Insulted by the whole affair, General Arnold, on 19 March, resigned his command of the city.[23] But Arnold's mild rebuke and resignation were not sufficient for Joseph Reed and the Supreme Executive Council. To their collective mind, prerogatives of Pennsylvania as an independent government had been trampled during the general's administration of martial law. Bowing to Pennsylvania pressure, Congress reversed itself on the earlier committee report and, fearing a breakdown in state relations might force them to relocate, directed the commander-in-chief to settle matters by court-martial. When Arnold, too, pleaded for prompt military trial to clear his name, Washington on May 16, 1779 summoned Judge Laurance to prepare the case.

Laurance raced back to Camp Middlebrook . . . only to be preempted by battlefield exigencies extending from the New York frontier to the loss of Savannah, Georgia. Not until early December did Washington at last order his judge advocate general to "proceed as soon as possible in the trial of Genl. Arnold."[24] John could not know it, of course, but Arnold five months earlier had begun exploring options with the enemy. Historians for two and a quarter centuries have dissected and debated the turncoat's motivations, more often than not attributing his treason to young Peggy and her expensive upkeep. Arnold, however, may have put it best in a missive to General Washington pleading for early trial:

> Having made every sacrifice of fortune and blood, and become a cripple in the service of my country, I little expected to meet the ungrateful returns I have received from my countrymen, but as Congress has stamped ingratitude as a current coin, I must take it . . . I have nothing left but the little reputation I have gained in the army. Delay in the present case is worse than death.[25]

Yet, delay it had been. For eight months General Arnold and his reputation twisted in the wind of public opinion while Reed's Executive Council sought delays, Congress tip-toed around Council demands, and Philadelphia mobs forced Arnold to arm servants and barricade himself and his pregnant wife inside the Penn mansion.[26] Imagining nowhere else to turn, Arnold (under assumed name) secretly corresponded with British Major John André, offering "his services to the commander in chief of the British forces . . . either by immediately joining the British Army, or by cooperating on some concerted plan with Sir Henry Clinton."[27] By mid-December, Arnold and André had not yet come to financial terms. Apparently, the embittered general was awaiting trial's outcome before selling out.

At 10 a.m. the morning of December 23, Major General Robert Howe gaveled his court to order in militia captain Peter Dickinson's tavern, just northwest of the Morristown green. Administering the mandatory oath of truthfulness to the glowering defendant, Judge Laurance could not help but appreciate the delicacy of his own situation. Benedict Arnold was perhaps the army's most accomplished tactical battlefield commander and a favorite of the commander-in-chief. Every halting step of his crippled right leg reminded the court of his personal sacrifice at Saratoga. The prosecution would have to walk an excruciatingly fine line between achieving military justice and alienating influential Pennsylvania Executive Council leaders whose feathers were already ruffled by Arnold's successful removal of three Pennsylvania officers (Brigadier General Irvine, Colonel Butler, and Lt. Colonel Harmar) as members of Howe's court.

When the trial's fifth session convened the morning of December 29, evidence to date tended on balance to favor General Arnold's acquittal.

Momentum, however, would shift when Judge Laurance addressed the fourth and final charge: "Using public wagons of the State for the transfer of private property." Opening the session with a question reserved for precisely the right moment, he asked Arnold directly if the Captain Moore to whom the wagons were dispatched for loading was the very same Captain Moore who commanded the schooner *Charming Nancy*, a suspected loyalist vessel given special protection by Arnold from Pennsylvania authorities.[28] When Arnold responded in the affirmative, the connection between his private transactions and the protected schooner was laid bare for all to see. With this single devastating question, Judge Laurance had deftly summed up the case against General Arnold: a schooner of questionable loyalty was given protected passage and loaded at public expense with private property possibly purchased improperly under martial law. Following four days of deliberation, the court agreed with the prosecution that Arnold's actions were "imprudent and improper" and ordered his formal reprimand by the commander-in-chief.[29]

The verdict salved Reed and the Pennsylvania Executive Council's aggrieved sense of state sovereignty, thereby relieving considerable tension among military, congressional, and civil authorities. Moreover, Judge Laurance's effective prosecution and respectful demeanor made a strong impression on Council president Joseph Reed. "Acknowledgements for the personal attention shown me," Reed wrote in a post-verdict note to Laurance, "and also for the candid and judicious conduct I have observed on the tryal of Gen. Arnold."[30] The warm and personal message went on to add: "And should you on any occasion visit Phila. I shall be happy in the oppty of making it agreeable to you of rendering you those compliments so justly due."[31]

Winning over Joseph Reed (Princeton '57) was no small feat. A successful London-trained lawyer, the 39-year-old Pennsylvanian had entered Continental service as Washington's initial adjutant general only to walk away after losing confidence in the Virginian's leadership. As head of his state's Supreme Executive Council, Reed was a radical leveler of the first order who enjoyed broad popular backing. Yet, Laurance, in potentially the most politically explosive trial of his judge advocate tenure, managed to satisfy volatile Pennsylvania authorities *and* hold Arnold accountable for his improper behavior *without* costing His Excellency the future services of a valuable fighting general. Much relieved, Washington administered the court-ordered reprimand and welcomed Arnold back to senior command ranks with a "post of honor" in command of the Army's important left wing. Arnold, however, had other plans.

Neither Judge Laurance nor any serving officer could take pleasure in General Arnold's reprimand; virtually all shared the financial duress that drove Washington's "fighting general" to profiteering. Laurance was particularly pinched because civil staff, unlike line officers, received no offsetting compensation for rapidly depreciating wages. Determined to obtain satisfaction or resign his commission, John in mid-October 1779 had set off for Philadelphia to plead his case before Congress. Colonel Hamilton once again unselfishly put himself on the line to advance his good friend's interest. Dashing off an urgent note to New York congressman James Duane, Hamilton reminded the lawmaker of His Excellency's confidence in the judge advocate:

> He will show you a certificate he has lately obtained from the General; though you are I presume, so well acquainted with his character, that no testimonials are requisite to convince you of his merit. From a long and intimate knowledge of him, I esteem him highly as a man of sense and integrity.[32]

Congress evidently agreed, resolving in December that "the subsistence of the judge advocate be the same as the present subsistence of a colonel."[33] The resolution doubled John's daily subsistence allowance, but only on paper. With Continental dollars trading that December at a fortieth of face value, his "raise" was pure illusion, its purchasing value further diluted by British agents circulating millions of counterfeit Continentals, some on the very same paper stock as the originals. Awash in a worthless paper ocean, Congress in November 1779—after printing more than $226 million Continental dollars—shut down presses until a new fiat currency could be established.[34] Lawmakers, just as Benedict Arnold's trial came to a close in early 1780, had no option but to ask the individual states to assume all sums due their native soldiers in Continental service.[35] Nine, including New York, did so, not only adjusting for depreciation but also continuing the payment obligation through 1782.[36] Individual soldier ledger accounts were subsequently kept in hypothetical dollars by army Paymaster-General John Pierce, to be settled at war's end with inflation-adjusted "military" or "depreciation" certificates from the appropriate state treasury. Until then, Laurance somehow continued to survive from his own pocket.

With the staggering dollar on its last legs, financial strains were worsened by the brutal—far more severe than Valley Forge—"hard winter" of 1779–1780. Possibly the iciest month of the eighteenth century, January 1780 blew in "cold enough to cut a man in two," turning sleeping sentries into blocks of ice.[37] Roads were piled with snow 12 feet high and New York harbor froze solid. Shaking collective fists at their own state governments who left them to freeze in the bitterest winter in a century, starving, angry soldiers roasted their shoes for sustenance while officers killed their dogs for food.[38] From this time forward, military operations in the field were supported by impressment of civilian provisions, paid for by as much as $100,000,000 in various state and Continental IOU certificates. Judge Laurance, hearing scuttlebutt that Congress had directed the War Department to set aside some shirts for civil staff, personally asked Board of War Secretary Richard Peters to provide spare clothing for himself and his staff, only to discover the rumor was false. "It would be a precedent for the entire Staff," replied Secretary Peters. "Even if we had the authority it is doubtful we could comply . . . the truth is that we have not nor ever had the least authority to provide for Officers either of the line or Staff."[39]

Courts-martial of restless private soldiers and bored officers went on as usual through the debilitating winter. By the 1st of March 1780, 20 deserters had been sentenced to death by hanging, though Washington in a single theatrical last-minute gallows appearance pardoned seven. Holed up with His Excellency's military family in widow Theodosia Ford's Morristown mansion, Judge Laurance passed the icy days preparing for another high-profile case that promised to make Benedict Arnold's profiteering look like child's play. On March 15, he would prosecute the director general of military hospitals, Dr. William Shippen Jr., for "Malpractice and Misconduct" in a massive medical supply speculation scheme.

Dr. Shippen, like his accusers—Dr. John Morgan and Dr. Benjamin Rush—was a pre-war Philadelphia physician.* The trial itself was final act in a long-festering local drama between Shippen and Morgan that dated back some 18 years to when Morgan reneged on a promise to jointly establish the first medical school in King George's colonies. Shippen evened scores in 1777, convincing Congress to relieve Morgan as director general of military hospitals and install himself as replacement. Two years later, lawmakers reversed themselves and vindicated Morgan of Shippen's accusations, whereupon the enraged Morgan wrote congressional president John Jay, charging his rival with malpractice and declaring himself ready to provide proof.

"He [Shippen] has amassed a princely fortune," Dr. Rush confided to John Adams, "by selling wine and other hospital stores out of the hospital magazines."[40] Another attending physician noted that hospital bedstraw crawled with typhus lice, and that he had known "from four to five patients to die on the same straw before it was changed."[41] Yet another charge claimed Shippen had filed false mortality reports. When Congress directed Washington to conduct a formal inquiry into Dr. Shippen's administration of the army hospitals, His Excellency, in turn, passed the matter to his judge advocate. "I want you immediately to examine the papers," Washington had directed in December 1779, "and to form the charges that he may be arrested."[42]

Judge Laurance, ensconced once again before a roaring fire in Peter Dickinson's cozy Morristown tavern, began the hearing with a lengthy list of accusations from the pen of Dr. Morgan.[43] As heated invectives were hurled back and forth by Morgan, Rush, and Shippen, members

---

*Well-born son of Philadelphia's foremost Colonial physician, William Shippen Jr. was the nephew of Edwin Shippen II, who was the grandfather of Peggy Shippen, Benedict Arnold's young wife.

of the court developed mixed feelings. Was it not Dr. Shippen who conceived of a "flying hospital" that traveled with the army during the dark days of 1776? Was it not Shippen who consolidated the army sick into upper Delaware Valley hospitals and centralized the military hospital system into three military districts, each with a physician-general and surgeon-general? Despite his faults, was not Shippen—unlike Dr. Rush, who resigned the service in 1778—still serving the troops? And how could officers who revered His Excellency forget the peripatetic Rush's two critical (unsigned) public letters castigating Washington during the Gates/Conway episode?

Presiding over the Shippen trial was tall, lean, hawk-faced 36-year-old Brigadier General Edward Hand. Born in Clyduff, Ireland, and holding a medical certificate from Dublin's Trinity College, Hand had served as surgeon's mate in a King's regiment before resigning his commission in 1774 to practice medicine in Lancaster, Pennsylvania. He entered the Continental Army as lieutenanat colonel of a Pennsylvania rifle company, and rushed to Boston shortly after Washington assumed command in July of 1776. A fellow Freemason, Edward Hand earned Washington's battlefield trust at Trenton, commanded the frontier forces at Fort Pitt, and in early 1780 was given charge of the light infantry brigade in Major General Lafayette's division. No other general officer was better suited to probe the medical and battlefield complexities of Dr. Shippen's predicament.

It was not until the last week of June that General Hand's court reached a verdict acquitting Dr. Shippen of all charges by a single vote "without honor." Washington, ever sensitive to state concerns, forwarded the verdict to Congress without comment. Washing their hands of the sordid affair, lawmakers finessed matters in mid-August by neither confirming nor approving the verdict; they simply ordered Shippen "be discharged from arrest."[44] No reputation was enhanced by the Shippen/Morgan affair, but Judge Laurance could at least take some small measure of satisfaction in his even-handed prosecution. The very day presiding officer Hand pronounced his court's verdict, a personal missive from the defendant landed in Laurance's lap. "I can't but express my sentiments," wrote Dr. Shippen, "of your propriety of your impartial conduct on my trial and thank you for your attentive offering to get it finished."[45]

Bitter and humiliated by his recent trial, Benedict Arnold over the summer of 1780 settled on a price for his treason. In return for a general's commission in His Majesty's army, annual pension, and a £6,315 (approximately $834,000 today) lump payment, he promised to deliver into British hands the important military works at West Point.[46] Suddenly informed over breakfast the morning of September 25 that a suspicious "John Anderson" with incriminating papers had been captured near Tarry Town, the turncoat immediately surmised his game was up. "Anderson," as Arnold knew all too well, was the assumed name of his British go-between, adjutant general of the British army, Major John André. With not a moment to lose, Arnold abandoned breakfast and pregnant wife Peggy, dashed to his private Hudson River barge, ordered the oarsmen to row downriver under flag of truce, and escaped to the waiting British warship HMS *Vulture*.

"I am desirous of seeing you without loss of time," Washington hurriedly wrote Judge Laurance, "and request that you will proceed to headquarters, wherever they may be, without delay."[47] In headquarters custody was Major André, captured in civilian clothing. But was he a spy, or, as Alexander Hamilton insisted, a liaison officer from the British command whom Arnold had lured behind American lines? Rather than summarily execute André (as William Howe had done with Nathan Hale in 1776), His Excellency determined to try the prisoner before a Board of General Officers at the Hudson River town of Tappan. As proxy for himself, Washington directed Judge Laurance to "assist in the examination" and present "sundry other papers relative to this matter, which he will lay before the Board."[48]

On September 29, Laurance strode into the cramped parlor of Johannes and Antje DeWint's Dutch Colonial homestead that served as Washington's temporary headquarters at Tappan, New York. Laying his papers on a side table, John recognized the stern faces of 14 general officers about to determine whether Major André lived or died. Major General Nathanael Greene, His Excellency's most trusted lieutenant, would preside. Seated around him were major generals Lord Stirling, St. Clair, Marquis de Lafayette, Robert Howe, Baron von Steuben, and eight brigadiers. Judge Laurance, after André was politely escorted into the room, faced the handsome British officer and read aloud General Washington's personal instructions to the Greene court:

> He came within our lines in the night, on an interview with Major General Arnold, and in an assumed character; and was taken within our lines, in a disguised habit, with a pass under a feigned name, and with the inclosed [sic] papers concealed upon him. After a careful examination, you will be pleased, as speedily as possible to report a precise state of his case, together with your opinion of the light in which he ought to be considered, and the punishment that ought to be inflicted.[49]

Raising his eyes to meet those of André, Judge Laurance asked whether he would either confess or deny the commander-in-chief's accusation. The defendant did neither. Reciting a letter sent to General Washington immediately after capture, André claimed he had departed the *Vulture* in full uniform to meet General Arnold "upon ground not within either army." Thereafter, explained the composed 30-year-old British major, he had against his intention and without his knowledge been conducted behind American lines. It was only when return was made impossible by *Vulture*'s forced move downriver that he donned other clothing to make his way back to New York and was taken at Tarry Town. If indeed such were actually the case, it would be hard to send Sir Henry Clinton's poised and likeable staff officer to the gallows as a spy. But Judge Laurance was not finished. Quietly and deliberately he laid six documents before the board and asked André whether they were found on his person when he was taken. There on the table, for all to see, were ordnance, artillery, manpower, and fortification reports, together with a copy of matters discussed at General Washington's September 6 council of war.

Major André scanned the papers, straightened up, and manfully admitted they had indeed been concealed in his boot. His honor would not permit untruth; nor did his calm demeanor display any sense of guilt. The Board, in an attempt to throw the gallant prisoner a lifeline, then asked whether he had come ashore under a flag of truce. Refusing again to lie—even to save his neck—André replied that "it was impossible for him to suppose he came on shore under that sanction," for if he had, he "certainly might have returned under it."[50]

The examination concluded, André was remanded to custody and escorted from the room. Although never specifically articulated by Judge Laurance, the officers of General Greene's court knew the defendant could be judged nothing but a spy under the common-law principle of *trespass ab inito*, whereby originally lawful entry to premises becomes criminal on subsequent commission of a criminal act.[51] Within hours, General Washington received the written verdict:

> The Board having maturely considered the facts, Do Also Report . . . That Major André, Adjutant General to the British army ought to be considered a Spy from the enemy, and that agreeable to the law and usage of nations, it is their opinion, he ought to suffer death.[52]

When a flurry of letters with Sir Henry Clinton proved futile in exchanging the condemned André for turncoat Arnold, Washington assigned the distasteful task of overseeing the execution to his own adjutant general, Colonel Alexander Scammell. It was an excruciatingly melancholy affair, rendered all the more tragic by the erudite prisoner's graceful bearing and impeccable scarlet-coated full-dress uniform. André, as he was escorted to the gallows, "betrayed no want of fortitude, but retained a complacent smile on his countenance, and politely bowed to several gentlemen whom he knew, which was respectfully returned."[53] Precisely at noon, two days after Washington approved the court's sentence, the prisoner snatched the noose from the blackened-faced hangman, slipped it over his own head, placed the knot behind his right ear, and drew it tightly around his neck.

Judge Laurance was not among the teary-eyed hundreds who lingered nearly half an hour in mournful silence around the Tappan gibbet and its swaying corpse. Not that he lacked the stomach, but rather because he was in court closing the final chapter of the André affair. Within a day of the British major's trial, Laurance had commandeered the Reformed Church of Tappan to prosecute civilian Joshua Hett Smith for alleged complicity in Arnold's treason. Smith, a prominent Duchess County resident who may have been a double—if not triple—agent, had at General Arnold's request provided safe house for André (disguised as "John Anderson") on his stay behind American lines.[54] But which Arnold did Smith obey, the major general in command at West Point or the traitor?

Straightforward and conclusive as was the case against André, evidence against Smith was complex and ambiguous. Mere cooperation was not the same as knowing complicity. Furthermore, Laurance not only had to convince the court of its jurisdiction (versus the State of New York) in such civilian matters, but he also faced a formidable courtroom opponent. For Joshua Hett Smith was both a counselor-at-law and brother to pre-war New York's most respected legal mind, William Smith Jr. "The judge advocate," wrote Smith, "exhibited ten charges against me, so artfully drawn up, that the proof of one would necessarily involve, as by inference, some testimony to support the other."[55] Smith therefore requested that Laurance's multiple charges be consolidated into a single general accusation. When presiding officer Colonel Henry Jackson (Massachusetts) agreed to the defendant's entreaty, Laurance accordingly reduced his case to a solitary charge: "aiding and assisting Benedict Arnold . . . in a combination with the enemy to take, kill, and seize such of the loyal citizens or soldiers of these United States, as were in garrison at West Point."[56]

Over the four-week trial, Washington's judge advocate general wheeled in 14 eyewitnesses, including Major Generals Lafayette and Knox along with the ubiquitous Lt. Colonel Hamilton. It was a testimonial barrage that convinced the court that the accused had indeed facilitated Arnold's secretive rendezvous with British Major André. But simply assisting Arnold did not, to the court's collective mind, constitute treason. Colonel Jackson therefore pronounced the evidence "insufficient" to convict Smith of being privy to Arnold's "criminal, traitorous, and base designs," and set the defendant free.[57]

Smith, like Dr. William Shippen Jr. five months earlier, commended "the candid and impartial manner which the trial was conducted by the judge advocate."[58] Nor did Judge Laurance's fair-minded prosecutorial treatment of John André pass unnoticed. It was generally agreed that Laurance had proceeded with "humanity and civility" in that particularly delicate proceeding.[59] Perhaps because he was born the same year (1750) as the doomed British adjutant general, Laurance was particularly affected by the Englishman's fate. "He seemed most sensitive on the subject," wrote grandson George McWhorter, "and exhibited the greatest reticence, manifesting in a few words indignation at Arnold and sorrows for André."[60] These deep emotions, according to family tradition, were passed on to his children:

> Many years later, after one of his daughters married an English gentleman, she chanced to be with her son in the parlor of Mr. Cox, the London military banker. Transacting some business, Mr. Cox remarked to her that Gen'l Arnold (son of Benedict) was just coming in and asked her to defer her business for a moment. The lady drew herself up, saying: "My father conducted the trial of Major André. Judge Laurance's daughter can never recognize General Arnold." Then, taking the arm of her son, she left the establishment.[61]

PART II

The Federal Child of a Thousand Fathers

SEVEN

"Then all the world would be upside down!"

"If Summer were Spring and the other way 'round
Then all the world would be upside down!"
–Eighteenth-century adaptation of the old English folk tune "Derry Down."

HUDSON HIGHLANDS, NEW YORK, FEBRUARY 1781. Judge Laurance could only watch apprehensively as Main Army ranks withered from expiring Continental enlistments, and state militia units marched home from completed obligations. He knew all too well, having laid before General Greene's board the damning military intelligence secreted in Major André's boots, that 11,400 troops detailed in Washington's private September council had shriveled by January to fewer than 6,000. So did the British high command. Benedict Arnold, less than two weeks after turning traitor, had briefed Crown Secretary of State for North America Lord George Germain on the "Present State of the American rebel army, navy and finances."[1] Washington's "illy clad, badly fed, and worse paid" common soldiers, confided Arnold to Germain, "are exceedingly disgusted with the service."[2]

Washington, aware of rising tension in the ranks, dispersed his regiments over the winter in hope of confusing Sir Henry Clinton as to his true numbers. The New York brigade was dispatched to Albany, the Pennsylvania line to Morristown, and the Jersey line to Pompton. After hutting New England regiments around West Point, the commander-in-chief set up his own winter headquarters in militia colonel Thomas Ellison's modest stone circa 1723 homestead overlooking the Hudson River fortress at New Windsor. Despite wife Martha's incomparable presence, he professed it a "dreary station" with "very confined quarters, little better than those of Valley Forge."[3] Washington's wintry mood only darkened as British strategic focus shifted to the four southern states, sinking war in the north into stalemate. True, January mutiny of the Pennsylvania and New Jersey lines at Morristown and Pompton had been swiftly quashed, but the next courier might well bring word of others. Ill-fitting dentures and nerve-wracking toothaches strained a temper already worn thin dreading the worst from British Brigadier Benedict Arnold's expeditionary force then ravaging Virginia. And suppose the enemy, learning that New

England regiments defending the Hudson Highlands were weakened by discharges, determined to navigate Hudson ice floes and seize West Point.

Judge Laurance's missive of February 20 offered no comfort. "A Cold prevents my waiting Your Excellency in person," he apologized, "I assure Your Excellency that nothing but a peculiarity of situation constrains me to decline, what inclination prompts me to accept."[4] John, in the wake of Alexander Hamilton's abrupt resignation four days earlier, had just turned down General Washington's request to fill his mercurial aide's shoes.

For the best part of four years, Hamilton, Laurance, and fellow headquarters staffers worked, dined, and all too often slept together. Now the talented band was breaking up. First to leave was correspondence secretary James McHenry, who transferred to Lafayette's staff in August of 1780. Two months later, love-struck Richard Kidder Meade returned to Virginia to take a second wife. John Laurens, exchanged from British captivity in November, was now happily bound for France as congressional envoy-extraordinary to the Court of Versailles. Much bothered over his role in the André execution, Adjutant General Alexander Scammell requested line command a few weeks after the hanging. Even long-serving military secretary Robert Harrison hinted he would soon depart to settle family matters in Maryland. And on February 16, senior aide-de-camp Alexander Hamilton rudely hurled his own resignation in Washington's face.

Laurance's ambitious younger friend was at the end of his tether following two and a half years of battlefield inactivity after Monmouth. As the war moved south to Virginia and the Carolinas, Hamilton's opportunity for battlefield glory seemed to be slipping away. His sense of urgency was only heightened by looming responsibilities of recent marriage. By spring of 1779, Alexander knew what he wanted in a wife: "She must be young—handsome . . . sensible, well bred . . . of some good nature . . . as to religion, a moderate stock will satisfy me . . . But as to her fortune, the larger stock of that the better."[5] Who righter to fill the bill than New York Major General Philip Schuyler's lovely second daughter Elizabeth? Smitten with the dark-eyed Eliza on her visit to Camp Morristown in early 1780, Hamilton when winter turned to spring was a "gone man." That December, he and Eliza were married in an intimate family ceremony at General Schuyler's Albany manor house; little more than a month after returning to New Windsor from a pastoral upstate honeymoon, Alexander curtly divorced himself from Washington's staff.

As replacement for Hamilton (or possibly Harrison), Washington naturally turned to Lt. Colonel Laurance, whose calm disposition and dexterity with voluminous paperwork had been displayed for almost four years. That the general thought highly of his loyal judge advocate general is a matter of record. Only three months earlier, he commended Judge Laurance to Congress as an officer of "great uprightness, diligence and ability, by which he has acquired the esteem of the army and merited the consideration of his Country."[6] Still, John was not about to become the commander-in-chief's personal aide. With Main Army headquarters now in the Hudson Highlands, he was finally able to winter with wife Betsey, five-year-old John Jr., and daughter Mary.

Happily, Betsey—after having had a child die in infancy—was in advanced pregnancy with future daughter Ann. General McDougall, to accommodate the growing family, had rented Beverly, the spacious Hudson River farmhouse recently vacated by Peggy Arnold after her husband's treason. McDougall then sped to Philadelphia as New York delegate to Continental Congress, leaving John and Betsey the run of the place, although the children, just inoculated for smallpox, were under house quarantine. Happily, Congress, at Washington's urging, had in November bumped up the judge advocate general's $75 monthly salary appointment to a full colonel's $140/month (including a depreciation rider) and added "a two-horse wagon, complete with forage" for personal baggage.[7] Moreover, the Main Army judge advocate department, bolstered by capable Massachusetts lawyers Thomas Edwards (Harvard '71) and Caleb Strong (Harvard '64), was the strongest it had ever been. With promise of a comfortable Highlands springtime, the last thing John wanted was the demanding dawn-to-dark regimen of His Excellency's aide-de-camp. "I cannot but hope," he wrote in refusing the general's offer, "this incident will not be displeasing."[8]

Whatever disappointment Washington harbored was surely eased six weeks later when Laurance might well have saved His Excellency's toothache-plagued neck. Alarming news had come into John's possession the evening of April 6 from local militia lieutenant Gerard Beekman. Assassination parties from British New York, whispered Beekman, had allegedly been dispatched to murder the commander-in-chief, Governor William Livingston of New Jersey, New York Governor Clinton, and an unidentified fourth patriot leader. Such rumors were not uncommon—British agents sowed previous false alarms—but this one, considering the source, was not to be ignored. The Beekmans, having helped Peter Stuyvesant establish Dutch New Amsterdam, were warp and weft of old New York's social fabric. Like his father before him, Gerard was a prominent pre-war Manhattan merchant whose London commercial contacts ran long and deep. Now removed to their upper manor house near Peekskill, the Beekmans still rubbed social shoulders with Tory neighbors while fending off uninvited redcoat raiding parties. Nonetheless, Gerard's wife Cornelia (Lt. Governor Van Cortlandt's daughter) rejected an approach by local loyalists to "borrow" an American officer's uniform intended for ill-fated British Major John André's return to enemy lines. Little wonder the discreet lieutenant shared his news in confidence with Judge Laurance rather than less tight-lipped militia superiors. To avoid recriminations, Beekman refused to divulge his sources.

Laurance immediately dispatched a courier to Major General William Heath at West Point, who in turn warned the commander-in-chief.[9] A 22-man sergeant's guard hurriedly supplemented Washington's headquarters cordon, while Hudson River vessels, patrols, and sentries hopped to high alert. Whether Laurance's swift action preempted assassination, or the affair was just another deceptive ploy, Washington, Clinton, and Livingston were never attacked. Fully cognizant of what might have been, His Excellency nonetheless confided to General Heath: "I shall be obliged to you to thank Judge Laurance"[10]

Offsetting the bleak Hudson Highlands winter was the glittering promise of French arms, warships, and money to galvanize the campaign of 1781. For the previous July, Jean-Baptiste Donatien de Vimeur, comte de Rochambeau—military war chest bulging with some 250,000 silver French livres—had disembarked 5,740 immaculately uniformed, well-equipped troops at Newport Harbor. Although le Comte placed his expeditionary force at General Washington's disposal, the two men could not agree on how to proceed. His Excellency above all wanted to dislodge Sir Henry Clinton from New York. Rochambeau, on the other hand, declared the fortifications around New York impregnable. And how could Washington ignore the advice of an experienced professional soldier of 40 campaigns and 14 sieges? Le Comte then tried another tack. Learning that his naval counterpart, Admiral François Joseph Paul de Grasse, could be in American waters as early as mid-July 1781, Rochambeau dispatched the swift sailing *Concorde* to strongly hint he sail to the Chesapeake rather than New York. Intentionally kept in the dark by Rochambeau about French naval plans, Washington leapt at de Grasse's August 14 offer to converge at Yorktown and entrap General Charles Cornwallis's 8,000-man army. Hurry he must, for the French fleet could remain no longer than mid-October.

Scrambling the headquarters staff, Washington put his army in motion southward. From Dobbs Ferry on the Hudson, Judge Laurance rode at His Excellency's side to Head of Elk at the northern tip of the Chesapeake Bay and on to Baltimore, Annapolis, and finally Williamsburg, Virginia. Settling into a routine that began as early as 2 a.m. with reveille, John trekked some 430 miles in 44 days before at last pitching his full colonel's 14-foot-long, 8-foot-tall marquee tent about a thousand yards east of Williamsburg's Beaver Creek Dam where the sluggish Warwick River divided French and American infantry encampments.[11]

Riding at anchor in and around the Chesapeake Bay were Admiral de Grasse's 29 powerful ships of the line, reinforced with another nine just arrived from Newport under Admiral Barras. On board, some 24,000 French sailors and 4,500 marines trained more than 2,000 naval guns on Cornwallis's bottled-up garrison. A second French army under Major General Marquis de Saint-Simon (3,300 regulars), plus General George Weedon's Virginia militia (3,100 locals), enabled Washington and Rochambeau in late September to encircle Cornwallis with some 18,100 troops. Against all odds, the trap had snapped close.

No sooner had the Yorktown siege begun, then Judge Laurance's capacious marquee buzzed with courts-martial activity. On the first day of October he pressed charges against Artillery Captain Patrick Duffy for drawing a sword on a fellow captain and snapping an unloaded pistol at another officer. Although Duffy also drunkenly abused a French soldier, his only punishment was to be discharged from the service. Nine other cases followed, including four desertions. As Franco-American relations began to chafe, a New York private was punished for "assisting in robbing a French officer's wagon," and New Jersey Lt. Colonel William De Hart was found guilty of insulting a French soldier and abusing a French sentry on hospital guard duty.[12] Eight more cases were served up on October 12. So it would go until British surrender.

The siege of Yorktown was a formulaic fait accompli conducted according to a script long mastered by English, German, and French generals. For this very purpose, Rochambeau had hauled across the Atlantic a 36-gun siege artillery train and more than 380 artillerists who would now pound Cornwallis's army into submission. But first, Laurance's former headquarters staff-mates Hamilton and Laurens (returned from France) enjoyed a long-awaited taste of martial glory. Fixing bayonets just after sunset the crisp night of October 13, Hamilton dispatched Laurens to the rear of British redoubt no. 10 to corral escapees. Silently, Alexander then led his surging charges across a muddy hundred-yard no-man's-land and over a palisade of sharpened stakes to take the enemy emplacement. Six days later, Cornwallis capitulated.

From atop his horse in Washington's mounted suite, Laurance looked on to a scene of surrender that no soldier of either army would ever forget. British and Hessian regiments marched under cased colors at funerary step, with bayonets fixed, drums beating, and faces lengthening. Humiliated redcoat veterans wept as they marched past flanking columns of allied victors and civilian spectators who stood transfixed in universal silence. Wheeling in ranks of four onto a disarmament field encircled by smug mounted French hussars, His Majesty's troops surrendered 18 regimental standards and sullenly, often violently, grounded their arms.

The "fighting war" was essentially finished, but Judge Laurance's courtroom business most certainly was not. Although terms of disarmament freed as many as 250 loyalists to sail on October 23 for British New York aboard the sloop-of-war *Bonetta,* 24 suspected deserters were not so fortunate. Culled from the ranks of Cornwallis's 7,247 surrendered troops, these two-dozen men faced general courts-martial charges of desertion and bearing arms against the United States. Following Laurance's prosecution, 13 defendants were ordered on November 3 to receive "100 lashes on the bare back" and eight others were to be "hanged by the neck until dead."[13] The remaining three, though pronounced "not guilty" of desertion, were husbanded off to detention camps as prisoners of war.

Having "turned the world upside down," the grand Franco-American alliance dispersed from Yorktown almost as rapidly as it had formed. Major General St. Clair with General Wayne's Pennsylvanians and General Gist's Maryland and Delaware troops were ordered to reinforce Nathaniel

Greene's southern army. The residual Continental regiments marched north to winter camps in New York. On November 4, Washington watched most of Admiral de Grasse's fleet set sail for the West Indies, then headed his own staff west down the Williamsburg Road, bound for Philadelphia. Following a heart-breaking detour to Abingdon Plantation (present-day Dulles International Airport) to bury General Washington's 22-year-old stepson "Jackie" Custis, who had contracted "camp fever" at Yorktown, His Excellency's entourage entered the "City of Brotherly Love." Rhode Island's fully uniformed, almost entirely black infantry regiment—the army's most presentable unit—led the proud column into a Philadelphia set aglow with news hand-carried to Congress by Washington staffer Lt. Col. Tench Tilghmann. It was a lavish welcome complete with tables groaning with food and drink the likes of which the army had never seen, dispensed in obligatory social affairs feted by grateful leading families. Satiated after a few days, Laurance bid Washington temporary farewell and proceeded to the Hudson Highlands for a snug winter with his family of four.

The blustery afternoon of January 7, 1782, found Colonel Laurance and his father-in-law together with several junior officers in General McDougall's parlor conversing around a table amply stocked with spirits. "The glass circulated freely," John recalled, "and the company appeared with unbent minds."[14] As might be expected in such a collegial informal setting, conversation drifted to the many hardships and frustrations of military service. No one was more frustrated than McDougall himself. Although commander of the important West Point fortifications, McDougall reported directly to another major general—"corpulent and bald-headed" William Heath of Massachusetts.[15] To keep both McDougall and Heath in the service, Washington had divided the Hudson Highlands, assigning the latter overall command. Temperamental Alexander McDougall would likely have chafed under anyone except Washington himself, but relations with Heath, a bureaucratic general of modest battlefield ability, had turned particularly prickly.

As the January afternoon progressed into evening and the decanter continued its rounds, General McDougall's face became redder and his words angrier. Surrounded by family and sympathetic officers, the irascible Scot recalled a council of war held in late summer of 1776 at his Nassau Street home just before the Americans evacuated Manhattan. Three officers, "a fool, a knave, and an obstinate honest man," McDougall confided, had then advised General Washington against conceding New York to the enemy.[16] There was little doubt McDougall thought Heath the knave, an eighteenth-century epithet for dishonest scoundrel. Warming to his subject, McDougall elaborated to the rapt audience that Heath admitted "he never thought New York tenable," but "the country in general put so much dependence on it, he thought a retreat would shock them too much at that period."[17] Heath, muttered McDougall with disdain, had espoused the militarily untenable position "merely to gain popularity in the country."

McDougall, looking from Laurance to Captain Ebenezer Sumner, then to Colonel Rufus Putnam, complained that Heath was now deliberately bypassing him and going directly to his West Point subordinates to requisition supplies. "Should this practice prevail," he argued, "it would be in the power of an Arnold to dismantle and fell the garrison at any time."[18]

Several junior officers nodded in agreement. One went so far as to brand General Heath a coward, later urging McDougall to call him out and settle matters by duel.[19] There being few secrets in a garrisoned army, news of such juicy conversation soon reached Heath. Outraged at his junior's insubordination, the portly Massachusetts general drew up seven formal charges, placed McDougall under house arrest, and transferred command of West Point to Brigadier General John Paterson.

Tasked with senior officer court-martial prosecutions, Judge Laurance now faced the disconcerting responsibility of preparing charges against his own father-in-law! This clear conflict of interest was embarrassing enough, but as eyewitness to McDougall's wine-fueled remarks, John would also be summoned to testify against him regarding General Heath's charge of "tending to lessen confidence in the commanding general."[20] Mercifully, General Washington relieved John of the prosecution, but he would still face uncomfortable questioning from his skilled Harvard-educated deputy, future United States senator Caleb Strong. And there is little doubt that Laurance subsequently, as one biographer put it, "touched up" his father-in-law's obstinate defense.[21]

It was not until August 15 that Congress confirmed the verdict acquitting McDougall of all charges but one—denouncing his commanding officer.[22] By then, Judge Laurance's resignation was more than three months old. For on May 17, he had written to the commander-in-chief:

> It is not without much pain, that I induce myself to resign Your Excellency the Commission I hold in the Army; but my circumstances at present render me unable to do it longer, and reduce me to the necessity of now relinquishing a post, which, were they otherwise I should be happy to continue in possession . . . As I am sensible of having received many acts of personal attention and kindness from Your Excellency while in service cannot refrain as I have now left it from serving you, they have made too deep an impression on my mind to be soon Effaced.[23]

Of the half-dozen deputy judge advocates then scattered about Continental service, John promptly recommended as his successor dependable Massachusetts Lieutenant Thomas Edwards. Washington in turn advised Secretary of War Benjamin Lincoln of Laurance's resignation and suggested Edwards as the "only Depy Judge Advocate with the army, of whose capacity to fill the office as a Principal."[24] Congress, on June 8th, accepted Judge Laurance's resignation but ignored Washington's recommendation and instead chose Virginia Lt. Colonel James Innis for the position. Had they heeded Laurance and Washington's original advice, the lawmakers could have spared themselves much time and embarrassment; Innis resigned after only two months, and back-up choice Richard Howell refused the position. It was not until October that Laurance's shoes were filled when New York Delegate James Duane nominated none other than Lt. Edwards. He served until war's end.

Laurance, thanks to his father-in-law's persistent congressional lobbying on behalf of all Continental officers, would not leave the army with empty pockets. Although still unpaid for most of 1777–1780, his 1781 account was duly settled by the State of New York for 12 months of Continental service at $140/month. The lump sum $1,680 payment (netting out $224 previously received from Continental paymaster John Pierce) translated into £582 and 51 pence New York currency.[25] Because New York certificates then commanded no more than 50 percent of face value in hard specie, John apparently pocketed the notes with an opportunistic eye on later exchanging them at full value in post-war real estate ventures.

There was little choice but to resign as judge advocate general when his father-in-law's awkward trial gathered steam, but in truth there was nothing professionally to be gained by remaining in service. The Continental Army after Yorktown had dispersed to half a dozen posts with little more than the usual issues on trial dockets, and paper currency promises were no longer sufficient to feed three young children. Indeed, the most pressing recent case for his department had been the February 28 Philadelphia general court-martial of First Pennsylvania's Colonel Daniel Brodhead for irregularities with public funds at Fort Pitt. It not being worth the judge advocate general's personal participation, Captain "N" White of the Second Canadian Regiment was appointed in his stead to prosecute.[26]

Any New York lawyer could see as the war wound down that the real money beckoned ahead in confiscated property recovery litigation. Hamilton had already scented that very opportunity. Resigning his commission within weeks of Cornwallis's surrender, he removed to the Schuyler mansion in Albany where, in January 1782, he successfully petitioned the New York Supreme Court to grant special waivers from the required three-year internship preceding any bar exam. Only six months' study was necessary for Washington's gifted former aide to pass the New York bar, thanks to having the run of Confederation Congressman James Duane's law library and coaching from pre-war chum Robert Troup, whose own Albany practice was up and running. (The enterprising Troup in early 1780 had resigned as Continental Treasury Board Secretary to read law together with wartime friend Aaron Burr under mild-mannered, but demanding,

New Jersey attorney general William Paterson.) While prepping for the bar exam, the resourceful Hamilton persuaded Robert Morris—Congressional Superintendent of Finance—to appoint him Receiver of Continental Taxes in New York. Then it was on to Philadelphia and a seat in Continental Congress, courtesy of influential father-in-law General Philip Schuyler.

En route to Philadelphia, Hamilton in mid-December dropped in at Laurance's Hudson River residence, only to find him away. "I was . . . sorry, my Dear Friend," read Alexander's note, "that you were absent when I called on your house; I should have been happy to have seen you to converse on many things."[27]

The visit was no mere social nicety. Judge Laurance was now New York Assemblyman Laurance, and Hamilton hoped to pick his brains over state financial plans. John, widely known as the sound patriot who prosecuted both Benedict Arnold and Major André, had, two weeks before tendering his military resignation, been elected one of six Westchester County representatives to the state general assembly.[28] One of only three assemblymen to serve on two standing committees in addition to temporary panels, he quickly established a reputation for diligence. "Laurance," Hamilton advised Superintendent of Finance Morris, "is a man of good sense and good intentions—has just views of public affairs—is active and accurate in business, and . . . is from conviction an advocate for strengthening the Federal government."[29] Morris, on the lookout for like-minded men to institutionalize congressional revenue collection from the Confederated States, then instructed Hamilton to offer Laurance a position as State Revenue Commissioner for either Connecticut or Rhode Island.[30] Assemblyman Laurance, eye on resurrecting his New York City law practice at war's end, politely declined.[31]

John and Alexander were far from alone in their centrist political orientation. Most of General Washington's discharged Continental officers, having fought one Revolution together instead of 13 separately, could not help but favor some form of central government.[32] Judge Laurance's Valley Forge deputy, future Supreme Court Chief Justice Marshall, probably put it best. "I found myself associated," wrote Marshall, "with brave men from different states who were risking life and everything valuable in a common cause . . . I was confirmed in the habit of considering America as my country and congress as my government."[33]

Similar "nationalist"* inclinations had emerged among the propertied class as early as 1780 when the War for Independence reached its nadir,

---

*Longstanding members of Congress with a Continental perspective included John Adams of Massachusetts, New Yorker James Duane, and South Carolinian John Mathews. In 1780, they were augmented by the arrival of James Madison and Joseph Jones of Virginia, Oliver Wolcott of Connecticut, General John Sullivan of New Hampshire, Generals Ezekiel Cornell and James Varnum of Rhode Island, Daniel Carroll and John Hanson of Maryland, and Philip Schuyler and Egbert Benson of New York. See James Ferguson, *Power of the Purse* (Chapel Hill: University of North Carolina Press, 1961), 112–115; and E. Wayne Carp, *To Starve the Army at Pleasure: Continental Army Administration and American Political Culture 1775–1783* (Chapel Hill: University of North Carolina Press, 1984), 200–202.

civilian morale plunged, and complete financial collapse loomed. Guided by the wealthy Liverpool-born Philadelphia merchant Morris, property holders from New England to South Carolina then dispatched "sensible men" to Philadelphia to restore the collective credit and augment congressional powers.[34] Though by no means a true national government by present-day standards, a reenergized Confederation Congress had well before Yorktown embraced Morris's direction.[35] Lawmakers, cushioned by French and Dutch loans, empowered a de facto central bank (Morris's Bank of North America) and applied "correct principles" to economic disarray and inefficient government. In hope of cementing the army to their centralist program, Morris's congressional backers in October 1780 promised half-pay for life to Continental officers who remained in service the duration of the war.

Morris and Washington's centralist vision was shared by New Yorkers Robert Livingston, John Jay, Egbert Benson, Gouverneur Morris, and James Duane, the very men who authored the state's groundbreaking new constitution of 1777 and had pushed the legislature in February 1781 to become the third state to ratify the Articles of Confederation. Dubbed "conservative nationalists" by Bancroft Prize–winning historian Edward Countryman, all (except Benson) had moved on to important Confederation roles after Maryland, as the 13th state to ratify, made the Articles law of the land.[36] Livingston assumed responsibility for the Confederated States' department of foreign affairs while Jay presided over a Confederated Congress in which both Morris and Duane sat as delegates alongside Major General McDougall.

Rep. Laurance's state legislative peers, however, wanted no part of any federal administration with its potential for a standing army and the taxes to pay for it. Led by wartime governor and Continental major general George Clinton, the General Assembly adopted a pronounced New York–first posture accompanied by more than two dozen vindictive measures against Crown loyalists that criminalized their status and taxed their property.[37] No sooner had Laurance taken his Assembly seat than the chamber rammed through the Debt Act of 1782. Better known as the Citation Act, this spiteful measure absolved debtors owing money to people behind British lines from paying any interest on loans after December 1775.[38]

Despite his vengeful July vote, Laurance, because of his English roots, developed an early reputation for even-handed legal treatment of former loyalists. "I am informed Mr. Laurance supports a favorable character," wrote one loyalist refugee to his niece before departing for London, "and bids fair to rise in his profession . . . He will probably be a useful man to you."[39]

John's first Tory law client came knocking that November in the form of Cadwallader Colden's grandson, Gilbert Colden Willet. Five years Laurance's junior, Willet had likely come to know John during his years reading law under the lieutenant governor. Rightly fearing that revenge-minded patriots would confiscate his property when New York City reverted to American hands, Willet made ready to flee. Before doing so, he appointed Laurance—a full year before British troops departed—his "true and lawful attorney to collect all debts and money due as if he were personally present," and to "dispose of the real estate in the United States owned by him and his wife."[40]

Disposing of real estate behind enemy lines was murky business, made even trickier by state legislation designed to punish loyalist landowners. Most severe of New York's anti-Tory measures was "An Act for the Forfeiture and Sales of the Estates of Persons who have adhered to the Enemies of this State."[41] Appropriately dubbed the Confiscation Act of 1779, the punitive measure divided loyalist offenders into two categories. The first consisted of British colonial New York's 59 leading citizens, including the estate of John's deceased pre-war mentor Colden. Pronounced ipso facto guilty in a blatant bill of attainder expressly forbidden 10 years later by the Federal Constitution, the unfortunate 59 were banished from New York under penalty of death. Their personal property was summarily forfeited. All others voluntarily adhering to the Crown were clumped into the Act's second category. Each required individual indictment, but any defendant failing to appear before court was summarily judged guilty and his property seized. Patriot legislators, however, made exception for New Yorkers who had returned to home behind enemy lines without adhering to King George.

Gilbert Colden Willet was no such exception. A New York City merchant who cozily conducted business with both sides, he ultimately donned a British coat as a captain in the Second Battalion of Oliver DeLancey's Brigade. Concluding the game was up after Cornwallis surrendered at Yorktown, Willet determined to liquidate his assets and board ship to England. Had Willett appropriated the property from patriots fleeing William Howe's invading army, no attorney could prevent the rightful owner from reclaiming it. But Gilbert's property was his own, the fruits of a fortunate marriage and successful merchant partnership with widely respected father-in-law Robert Murray. His challenge, now shared by attorney Laurance, was to lawfully dispose of things before indicted in absentia when lower Manhattan returned to patriot control. Quietly and confidentially, Laurance found private buyers before any indictment and forfeiture proceedings could begin.[42]

In a transparent effort to work both sides of the property litigation street, Laurance had a hand in yet another punitive measure concocted by the General Assembly to make life miserable for New York's remaining Tories. This Trespass Act of March 13, 1783 gave patriots carte blanche to sue anyone who occupied, damaged, or destroyed property left behind British lines during the war. The measure not only clearly contravened the established law of nations that spoils of war "belong to the captor as long as he remains in possession of them," but it also went a step further by precluding Tory defendants from appealing decisions of patriot courts.

Assemblyman Laurance, as he voted "aye" on Trespass Act passage, would have been naïve indeed not to anticipate the serious legal battles looming ahead . . . battles that could only enrich lawyers licensed (like himself) before the New York bar.

Fast on the heels of the Trespass Act came another matter affecting Laurance's pocketbook: Continental officer pensions. As the war wound down, Washington's serving officers suspected that a financially strapped Congress would renege on its October 1780 half-pay-for-life commitment. "God grant the union may last," wrote Congressional Delegate Hamilton to Laurance from Philadelphia, "but it is too frail now to be relied upon, and we ought to be prepared for the worst."[43] Fueled by rumors that a preliminary peace agreement had been reached in Paris, collective officer discontent turned to action in mid-March. Angry Continental officers gathered at Camp Newburgh, some 20 miles north of Poughkeepsie along the Hudson, to issue Congress a heated ultimatum. Either lawmakers honor prior pension commitments *before* the army was disbanded *or* officers of the so-called "Newburgh Conspiracy" would march to Philadelphia and take matters into their own hands. They might well have done so, had not General Washington intervened to counsel restraint. Speaking to the assembled officers in what has become known as his fabled "Newburgh Address," the general's apparently off-the-cuff admission that "I have not only grown gray but almost blind in service of my country" stopped disgruntled officers in their tracks.[44]

Shamed from mutiny by His Excellency's words, the Newburgh officers dispatched a compromise to Philadelphia. In lieu of half-pay for life, they would accept a lump sum payment of five years' full salary. Although the proposal, known as "commutation," amounted to $5,000,000 that Congress simply did not have, Washington's urgent plea from Newburgh (along with the officers' unspoken threat not to lay down arms at war's end) prompted the lawmakers on March 22, 1783, to authorize the five years' lump sum commutation while granting enlisted men $80 upon honorable discharge. Within a month, however, Congress diluted the measure. Instead of the five-year lump sum in specie, officers were given six months to collectively approve certificates in that amount bearing 6 percent annual interest.[45] It was, in light of the freshly announced formal cessation of hostilities, the best Washington's long-serving subordinates could expect.

While the army was still encamped at Newburgh, Major Generals Henry Knox and Frederick Steuben determined to bind together lieutenants and generals alike in post-war solidarity by conceiving a hereditary fraternal order, the "Society of the Cincinnati." Within a year, more than 2,150 Continental officers flocked to Society ranks, in no state more so than New York. Headed by Major General McDougall as founding president, the State Chapter ultimately boasted a 475-strong original membership that included Lt. Colonels Laurance, Troup, and Hamilton.[46] Discharged the service in October 1783, more than 200 of these New York officers headed home convinced that some form of strengthened central government was their best hope for collecting promised pensions.[47]

But it was more than that. Soured with bitterness, Connecticut lieutenant colonel Ebenezer Huntington spoke for many officers who resented non-combatants for feathering selfish nests while they had risked health, property, and life itself. "I despise my Countrymen," vented Huntington to his brother. "I wish I could say I was not born in America . . . The insults and neglects which the Army have met with beggars all description."[48] Little wonder Washington's officers subordinated home state devotion in favor of the centralist legitimacy emanating from His Excellency's strong, legislative-sanctioned hand. Every officer knew that during the Valley Forge winter—when Congress dwindled to but 18 members—widespread starvation was avoided when His Excellency took matters into his own hands to seize civilian foodstuffs. Furthermore, it was Washington, not Congress, who dealt directly with state governors in handling state militia, even assuming the role of Continental foreign secretary during the Yorktown campaign to negotiate for troops and ships with Bourbon France. His Excellency, then, was the very model of a modern "Patriot King" to the discharged officers who constituted an advance guard of American federalism.*

More mundane matters were top of mind to Laurance in the waning months of 1783. "I have sent an account for my pay," Laurance advised army Paymaster General Pierce, "from August 1780 to the time I resigned the office of Judge General and an account of the monies I have received in old paper and specie."[49] As to the separate subsistence account, John flung hands in the air, leaving calculations to Pierce: "I have made no charge for my sustenance as I do not know how it stands properly & therefore am willing the matters remaining as it is."[50] Not until July of 1793 did Treasury auditors finally close out his wartime account.[51] Of more pressing concern, however, was the April 1783 pension "commutation" package, because the payment turned out to be less than met the eye. Paymaster General John Pierce had duly issued 6 percent certificates to a list of 2,480 qualified officers, *but there was a huge catch:* the commutation certificates not only lacked a specified payer, they also carried no specific provision for actually paying either interest or principal![52] Immediately the notes plunged to but an eighth of face value in specie. Surviving personal papers offer no details on how Laurance cashed his lieutenant colonel's pension settlement certificate in the amount of $3,600.[53] He was, of course, well aware that New York legislators earlier resolved that Continental pay certificates be accepted at full value toward the purchase of confiscated

---

*English Viscount Bolingbroke's *The Idea of a Patriot King* (1738) described the idealized conduct of a virtuous monarch dedicated to the public good. Written expressly for Prince Frederick of Wales, son of George II, the treatise was well known to John Adams, Thomas Jefferson, and James Madison, if not Washington himself.

loyalist estates and, as we shall see (chapter Eighteen), within months of receiving his commutation certificate, John purchased at least 10 confiscated parcels at public auction.[54]

Confiscated New York City properties were the apple of all eyes on March 24, 1783, when Sir Guy Carleton climbed City Hall steps to read His Majesty's royal proclamation formally suspending hostilities. British and Continental officers set up a joint board of claims to resolve property disputes peacefully, but for thousands of New York loyalists the preferred option was to flee. By the first of July, less than four months after the Trespass Act, as many as 12,000 Crown sympathizers had accepted His Majesty's offer of free passage on departing British ships. Hundreds of others held their breath through November as Carleton and Washington negotiated the logistics of transferring the city to patriot hands. Like a squadron of circling legal vultures, Laurance, Hamilton, and Troup hovered with some dozen other members of the bar at city's edge in wait.[55] "On which event," Hamilton confided to Nathanael Greene, "I shall set down there seriously on the business of making my fortune."[56] And when city courts reopened at last to settle an avalanche of property disputes, a cadre of New York Cincinnati (Burr, Nicholas Fish, Hamilton, Laurance, Morgan Lewis, Brockholst Livingston, Troup, and Richard Varick) would claim a virtual monopoly over the lucrative fee market. For New York legislators had in October 1779 expressly excluded Crown loyalists from the practice of law.[57]

EIGHT

New York Lawyer Rising

NEW YORK CITY, THE BOWERY, NOVEMBER 25, 1783. At the head of Bowery Lane, near present-day Canal Street, stood Richard and Susannah Varian's Bull's Head Tavern. Madame Varian, hostess of the venerable pre-war livestock drover's hangout, had only recently resumed duty while her privateering husband made his way home from British captivity in Halifax. Expectant eyes on the tavern door, a swarm of excited citizens milled about that cold but radiant November forenoon, impatient for General Washington and Governor Clinton to emerge. After seven excruciating years, all hankered for Continental arms to at last reclaim the city. King George's remaining scarlet-clad regiments—less than 2,000 strong—were then pulling out in an orderly, prearranged evacuation.

The Master of Mount Vernon drained his glass of ale shortly after noon, strode from the Bull's Head "straight as a dart and noble as he could be," and mounted his large gray warhorse "Nelson" to join Governor Clinton astride "a splendid bay."[1] Surrounded by a body of Westchester County light horse, Washington and Clinton collected their respective suites and put the train in motion toward an awaiting city. Directly behind, four abreast, followed Lt. Governor van Cortlandt with State Senator McDougall and other members of the "Council for Temporary Government of the Southern District."[2] Colonel Laurance, whose own "Council" membership had terminated in April with his legislative term, may possibly have been alongside his father-in-law but was more likely among the large, animated body of joyful former exiles riding behind tall, lanky state assembly speaker John Hathorn.

Watching Washington expertly guide his mount through the jostling entourage, Laurance could not help but have reflected on his five years alongside the resolute commander-in-chief and the many influential relationships forged in military service. Indeed, sitting Quartermaster General Timothy Pickering was among his first post-war clients.[3] Facing a personal civil lawsuit for congressional nonpayment of certificates issued to confiscate supplies to feed Continental troops, Pickering asked Laurance to prepare his defense. Other serving officers, such as First New York's Major Leonard Bleeker, engaged him to liquidate military pay certificates for cash. "I am conscious these certificates will give you some trouble," confided Bleeker, "however ... they are the only means that will enable me to go on furlough."[4] Dozens of cash-strapped, discharged private soldiers came calling as word of Laurance's services spread to the rank and file. Andrew Rose of the Second New York, for example, and Henry Ennis and Richard Morrison of the First New York appointed John to "solicit and obtain from the state of New York" military land grants promised to discharged veterans.[5] Others, such as Captain of Westchester Light Horse Daniel Delavan turned to Laurance in civil matters.[6] Such was the demand for the legal talents of Washington's former judge advocate that Laurance, six months *before* Evacuation Day, welcomed his English uncle Richard's namesake son fresh off the boat into the promising practice.[7]

A ruined city reeking of filth unveiled itself to Laurance's surveying eye as Washington and Clinton's celebratory procession wound its way past charred timbers, skeletal walls, and collapsed residue of the 1776 and 1778 fires. Neglected gutters ran foul with all forms of garbage and muck. Abandoned lots stank of ordure, droppings, and night stools. At Chatham Square, General Henry Knox and the last soldiers of the Revolution formed from line into column and marched down toward the East River, passing a departing cluster of British troops queuing in the "Fields" where City Hall now stands. "Washington and the rest," remembered militia Captain John van Arsdale, "proceeded on to Wall Street, and up Wall, then the seat of fashionable residences, to Broadway, where both companies again met, and while our troops in line fired a sequential *feu-de-joie*, Washington alighted at the popular tavern . . . kept by John Cape."[8]

Following an emotional, speech-packed reception at Cape's, Governor Clinton hosted a public dinner at Samuel "Black Sam" Fraunces's tavern (whose "Queen's Head" sign was about to come down) at the corner of Great Queen (later renamed Pearl) and Broad Streets. The venerable three-and-a-half-story brick tavern's floorboards groaned that lusty evening as Clinton presided over a jubilant repast for Washington, his few remaining officers, and some three hundred "gentlemen" returned from long exile. Although no guest list survives, a sergeant's guard could not have kept Councilman McDougall and his son-in-law from the joyous occasion. Three days later, on Friday, November 28, former exiles returned the favor with an elegant entertainment at Cape's in honor of the Governor Clinton and his Southern District Council. Amid the hearty toasts and revelry, Laurance, who seven years earlier fled New York an immigrant lawyer of no particular note, could glow in self-absorbed pride at his newfound status. As a state assemblyman who had a hand in the Trespass Act, John, as McDougall's son-in-law and trusted staffer of the commander-in-chief, was among the insiders about to raise the city from its ashes.

Climaxing a euphoric week in the public eye that could only enhance his budding legal practice, it was back to Cape's Tavern on December 2 for a raucous affair compered by Governor Clinton to fete French ambassador Chevalier de la Luzerne, Washington and his officers, plus "upward of 100 gentlemen." Reputedly smashing some 60 wine glasses and 8 cut-glass decanters, revelers consumed "135 bottles of Madeira, 36 bottles of port, 60 bottles of beer, and 30 punchbowls."[9] That evening the entire city turned out for an unequalled display of fireworks orchestrated by New York artillery captain William Price. His program of three stunning aerial sets included Chinese fountains and illuminated stars, moons, and suns, all capped by a grand set-piece finale that dazzled onlookers with some hundred multi-colored rockets. "It far exceeded," wrote Colonel Benjamin Talmadge, "anything I had ever seen in my life."[10]

On December 4, Washington's remaining officers assembled at noon in the Long Room of Fraunces's Tavern to bid His Excellency a final farewell. "Such a scene of sorrow and weeping," wrote Colonel Talmadge, "I had never before witnessed, and fondly hope I will never be called to witness again."[11] A moving scene indeed, but one that, like Valley Forge, has been heavily romanticized, for most names of those tearfully grasping hand with their commander-in-chief have been lost to history. Though perhaps 40 or more officers may have attended, only Generals Knox, McDougall, von Steuben, and James Clinton, along with Colonels Jackson and Talmadge, can be placed in the Long Room with certainty.[12] Nathanael Greene, patriotic legend notwithstanding, was not present.[13] Nor is there evidence Hamilton attended, despite having a few days earlier rented a nearby Wall Street residence.[14] Indeed, most Continental officers, except for those ordered to remain under General Knox, had already returned home with the rank and file.[15] New York City, of course, *was* home to both Laurance and McDougall, so it is highly likely that His Excellency's long-serving judge advocate general was among the Southern District Councilmen whom Washington greeted in the adjacent chamber, if not with his father-in-law and the wet-cheeked Long Room die-hards bidding Washington adieu.

Collecting hat and gloves after little more than an hour, Washington took his leave. Escorted by a sparse body of light infantry, he walked down Pearl Street to Whitehall slip where a barge waited to carry him to Powles Hook on the Jersey shore. From there in company with von Steuben he would sojourn to Annapolis and return his commission to what remained of the Continental Congress. Doffing his hat in silent farewell from the departing barge, the general waved one last adieu to the small cadre of officers among the admiring crowd who had followed. Returning the compliment, the officers dispersed in solemn company as the final curtain fell on the War for Independence.

New York City, its pre-war population reduced by more than half, and perhaps a third of its buildings in ruin, was devastated after seven years of British occupation. Trees, fences, porches, anything that could be burned, had long since been used as firewood. Abandoned military emplacements dead-ended once-open streets. Broken glass, rubble, and filth, together with charred reminders of the 1776 and 1778 fires, were everywhere. Dead animals lay in neglected streets or were dumped in canals. Hogs rooted in the Bowling Green. Although some 29,000 Tories had already departed New York harbor for Nova Scotia, Halifax, Montreal, Quebec, or England itself, gangs of hotheaded patriots agitated for economic revenge against those who remained. Masses of shanties and tents sheltered discharged soldiers whose homes no longer existed or were in uninhabitable disrepair. Hundreds of emaciated, despondent men, recently released from 12 British prison ships anchored off Brooklyn's Wallabout Bay, wandered about or sat dazed on street corners. More than 11,500 former shipmates lay buried in shallow shore-side graves or at the bottom of New York harbor. Skulls in some coastline mud banks lay "as thick as pumpkins in an autumn cornfield."[16]

Of New York's 8,000 or so inhabitants, "the loyalists," remarked one Tory merchant, "are more numerous and much wealthier than the poor despicable Whigs."[17] Although now in firm control, patriot Whigs were not all of like mind. "Ultra-Whigs," wrote Chancellor Robert Livingston, clamored for "expelling all Tories from the State," hoping "to preserve the power in their own hands" and "possess the house of some wretched Tory."[18] Moderate Whigs, eager to preempt thousands of Tory guineas from capital flight, sided with Livingston to "soften the rigor of the laws against the loyalists and not to banish them from . . . social intercourse."[19] Nonetheless, Whigs of all stripes champed at the bit to enforce the punitive Trespass Act and recover patriot property forfeited to Lord Howe's occupying army. To ensure they had their way, state legislators not only forbid former Tories from holding public office, but also in May 1784 deprived most of the right to vote for two years. Little wonder that Whig lawyers captured 8 of 14 aldermen seats together with all nine city seats in the state General Assembly.[20] Among the nine was Lt. Colonel Laurance.

In January 1784, the Southern District Council had no choice but to intercede in affairs at Laurance's Trinity Parish Church. A bitter struggle for parish control erupted when post-war Anglicans put forward assistant Minister Benjamin Moore as new rector, only to be emphatically rejected by irate Episcopalian Whigs led by John Jay and New York mayor James Duane. Presbyterian patriots under Governor Clinton then leaped into the dispute. Had not New York's 1777 Constitution, they asked, formally disestablished the Church of England? Were Trinity's substantial real estate holdings not therefore to be impounded by the state as fortune of war? To settle matters, the General Assembly issued a new Trinity charter and empowered Southern District Councilmen to vest all Church property, real and personal, with a board of nine interim trustees headed by Council president Richard Morris and Mayor Duane.[21]

Trinity's Episcopal Whigs were not about to have Clinton Presbyterians, much less former Crown loyalists, run their devastated church. Gathering in early December at John Simmons's Wall Street tavern, the Whig congregation named Laurance together with Robert Livingston (the Chancellor's namesake son), William Duer, Marinus Willett, and

Robert Troup to a committee bent on ensuring that wartime loyalist Reverend Moore never assumed the pulpit.[22]

Strained negotiations with the interim Trinity vestry in early February produced a pro-Whig majority that directed patriot Rt. Reverend Samuel Provoost (King's College '58) to "take charge of the Episcopal Churches in the City" as Trinity rector.[23] Laurance was promptly appointed to the reconstituted Trinity vestry, where he would serve more than two years.[24] Appalled at the state legislature's attempt to usurp Church real estate holdings, Assemblyman Laurance voted repeatedly over the next year to delay state takeover of the valuable 62-acre Manhattan property known as King's Farm and Garden.[25] Ultimately, Trinity's real estate was spared confiscation when a certain Mr. DeHart in Alexander Hamilton's law office produced its mislaid original chartering deed. Conveyed in 1705 to the vestry by Her Majesty's governor, Lord Viscount Cornbury, the resurrected deed granted undisputed ownership in perpetuity. Property rights assured, Vestrymen Laurance, Duane, and Duer summarily kicked off a fund-raising campaign to consecrate a fully restored Trinity Church edifice by 1790.

Laurance was also instrumental in bringing King's College back from the dead. Its doors closed and shuttered for eight war-torn years, the institution was in early 1784 severed from the Church of England and rechartered as Columbia, "mother of colleges" in a statewide system of higher learning.[26] (Not that there actually was one.) Named to one of the State University Board of Regent seats reserved for residents of New York City, Laurance served for the next 25 years without compensation as a Columbia College trustee.[27] And lest one feel sorry for deposed Trinity Assistant Rector Benjamin Moore, the good reverend was soon appointed professor of rhetoric on the Columbia faculty and 17 years later achieved full redemption as college president, rector of Trinity Church, and ultimately Episcopal bishop of New York.

Thrown together by the politics of Trinity Church, Laurance came to know one of post-war America's most complicated characters, brother Episcopal Whig and immigrant soldier of fortune William Duer. Son of a wealthy West Indies planter, Duer (1743–1799) was born in Devon, some 60 miles east of Laurance's own Falmouth surrounds. The dashing, slender Eton graduate served as Lord Clive's aide-de-camp in India before inheriting his father's Caribbean plantations. Lured to New York by Philip Schuyler as a pre-war trading partner, Duer borrowed £1,400 from his sister to invest in prime upstate timberland, supplying the British navy with masts and spars. In political lockstep with Schuyler, Duer in 1775 became member of the Provincial Congress and two years later earned a seat in New York's General Assembly. As a delegate to the Continental Congress, he later gained Washington's (and likely Laurance's) esteem for helping frustrate the notorious Conway Cabal. From his 1,300-acre Albany estate, Duer prospered during the war by supplying the Continental Army commissary through contracts arranged by Philadelphia financier

Robert Morris; by 1780 he was worth more than £400,000.[28] An inveterate risk-taker with alarmingly few scruples, wheeler-dealer Duer proceeded to fatten his own wartime accounts by coolly arranging to sell flour, cattle—even iron cannon shot—to British quartermasters!

Duer's wealth and charm, together with wife Catherine's hostess skills (she was daughter of the self-styled Lord Stirling, Major General William Alexander), planted him immediately in the first rank of post-war New York society. And Laurance, together with Hamilton and Troup, found their way along with Chancellor Livingston and Mayor Duane to the deep-pocketed Duerses hospitable and richly provisioned table, where "Lady Kitty" lavishly ladled out the portions with two liveried servants at her side.[29]

The spring of 1784, Laurance kicked off his vagabond shoes to establish Betsey and the family at one of the city's more respectable addresses, Wall Street. Time had come to plant family roots after the best part of 6 years as a military nomad and 18 months shuttling between the legislature at Poughkeepsie and father-in-law McDougall's multiple residences. Wall Street, though shabby and neglected from years of hard usage quartering British officers, had fortuitously escaped the fire of 1776 and would soon reclaim a share of its vanished elegance. Assemblyman Laurance's three-story brick residence at No. 13 Wall was rather smallish with its 26 and 1/3-foot street frontage (Samuel Ver Planck's Wall Street mansion boasted 115 feet), but it was splendidly sited—no more than two blocks from City Hall—for John's active post-war law office.[30]

In late February 1784, Laurance set foot in a New York courtroom for the first time in eight years when Mayor James Duane, resplendent in black robe and white jurist's wig, gaveled to order the post-war Mayor's Court opening session. Appointed by Governor Clinton, the burly 51-year-old Duane, son of an Irish Protestant Royal Navy officer from County Galway, was the straw that stirred New York's polyglot drink. Member of the state bar since 1754, the former Provincial Attorney General represented New York for a decade in both the Continental and Confederation Congress. He sat on the committee drafting the state Constitution of 1777, and served in the New York legislature from 1783 to 1790. Ward of Robert Livingston and brother-in-law to Robert Jr., Duane possessed the social clout to get things done. Regarding his political talents, future President John Adams described the mayor as having a "sly, surveying eye . . . very sensible, I think, and very artful."[31]

Duane's hectic opening Mayor's Court session saw 116 writs returned, followed by another 167 at the next seating. Most were Trespass Act suits against former loyalists, several of which involved 34-year-old John Laurance as counsel for the plaintiff. Indeed, a single Laurance client, the Waldron family, entertained 11 separate *capiases* (arrest warrants) dated February 10, 1784, totaling a very respectable £16,430.[32]

Before following John into court, it's worth a moment to briefly revisit New York's post-war legal system. Reassuringly, Article XXXV of the 1777 state Constitution retained the English-based common law that underlay more than 150 years of colonial legislative and judicial action. Chancery Court and Admiralty Court, except for of a clean set of smiling patriot faces, were virtually unaltered from British days. The only striking Constitutional change (other than mandatory retirement at age 60 for the Chancellor, Supreme Court justices, and first judge of county courts) involved appellate review from the State Supreme Court. In place of King George and Privy Council, patriot levelers installed an unwieldy new 31-man tribunal with the equally ungainly name of "Court for the Trial of Impeachments and the Correction of Errors."[33] Even with His Majesty sent packing, every New York County, thanks to Governor Lord Bellemont's ordinance of 1699, still enjoyed a Court of Common Pleas to handle civil common law actions. And just as in pre-war days, the New York City venue was still known as the Mayor's Court. The mayor remained chief magistrate, but he and the city recorder were joined as associate justices by at least four of the seven popularly elected city aldermen.

Counselor Laurance, then, would have noticed only minor differences in court structure, jurisdiction, and procedure from his pre-Revolutionary stint at the New York bar. His practice, however, had changed in two significant ways: the old guard of leading lawyers had moved on, and punitive anti-loyalist legislation created a tide of new business. "After the peace of 1783," wrote future New York Chancellor James Kent (Yale '81), "a few gentlemen of the colonial school resumed their ancient practice; but the Bar was chiefly supplied by a number of ambitious and highly spirited young men, who had returned from the field of arms with honorable distinction."[34] William Smith Jr., finest legal mind of his generation, cast his lot with the British crown and was rewarded with the chief justice-ship of Nova Scotia Province. Most other Loyalist attorneys simply fled. William Livingston, John Morin Scott, and Robert Livingston Jr., the pesky pre-war "Whig Triumvirate," were sitting governor of New Jersey, New York Secretary of State, and Chancellor of all New York Chancery courts, respectively. John Jay, congressional Secretary of Foreign Affairs, was in Europe and Gouverneur Morris represented New York at Congress (and himself with the fair sex). As for Lewis Morris, it was all he could do restoring his huge ruined estate (Morrisania) while serving as state senator and delegate to Congress.

Younger Tory lawyers of promise had fled or, like John Watts and Richard Harrison, become temporarily persona non grata until permitted to practice two years later. The next truly extraordinary New York legal mind to come along, James Kent, had barely opened practice in Poughkeepsie and would not arrive on the lower Manhattan scene until 1793. So, the litigation field pretty much belonged to Laurance, Hamilton, Troup, Aaron Burr, Governor William Livingston's son Brockholst, Morgan Lewis, Egbert Benson, Philip Pell, and the others.

Although Laurance developed an early reputation with paying clients of the loyalist variety, the majority of his early post-war cases were patriots seeking recompense under the Trespass Act.[35] Trespass suits, as John knew so well, were stacked in favor of the plaintiff by statutory provision forbidding as defense "any military Order or Command whatever, of the Enemy." Because the law did not allow removal (appeal) of trial court findings, patriot plaintiffs obtained swift justice without worrisome appeals to the Supreme Court with its stronger procedural safeguards for defendants. Not without good reason, then, did loyalist merchant John Thurman denounce the Trespass measure as mere "food for lawyers."[36]

Unlike Hamilton, whose briefs and notes fill distinguished Columbia University law professor Julius Goebel's five-volume *The Law Practice of Alexander Hamilton*, virtually nothing remains in Laurance's own hand from his professional legal records. The only complete legal brief to survive is a five-page summary of the 1784 Mayor's Court Trespass Act claim by client plaintiffs Elizabeth, Peter, and John Waldron.[37] It reveals an insufferably methodical legal mind wedded to precedent in requesting a £10,000 judgment against deceased loyalist Cornelius Corzine. The Waldrons had fled in the wake of William Howe's 1776 invasion, leaving behind a large Harlem acreage of standing forest, only to discover the land denuded upon returning seven years later. The departed Corzine and very-much-alive partner Cornelis Bogaert had felled some 16,500 trees, including an elegant 500-tree apple orchard, to usurp 3,000 cords of wood and profit from fueling redcoat winter fires.[38] Laurance ultimately prevailed in Mayor's Court but was forced to settle for £6,000 rather than the £10,000 demanded by the Waldrons.

More typical of Laurance's repast at the litigation table was *Helena Brasher et al v. Daniel Ebbets*. Representing the plaintiff, he brought this rather pedestrian Trespass Act case before the Mayor's Court within a month of Chief Justice Duane's courtroom reopening. The Brashers claimed loyalist Daniel Ebbets had damaged a pair of dwelling houses and a starch house, while destroying an outbuilding "and other enormities."[39] The first dwelling house, Laurance argued, was injured by "Carrying away the floor of the cock loft, by taking away and carrying off the staunchions which supported the roof by which means the roof has given way and rotted the beams, by taking up and carrying away the kitchen floor; by pulling off and carrying away the dressers to wit six dressers, by pulling off and carrying away four window frames."[40] On it went for two additional buildings, a starch manufacturing house, and various pieces of equipment, until Judge Duane, as might be expected, ruled for the plaintiff. And lest the defendant avoid payment, who should be New York City High Sheriff responsible for overseeing collection of damages but ex–Liberty Boy street enforcer Marinus Willett.

While vicissitudes of post-war property transfer necessitated litigation, the handover of British New York City's Masonic authority was governed by fraternal courtesy. Departing King's officers and loyalists might have, in a last gesture of British defiance, burned Lodge records and ritualistic paraphernalia before sailing away. Instead, Grand Master William Walters consciously left the Provincial Grand Lodge Organization intact, turning over its London-chartered Grand Warrant to "such brethren as may be appointed to succeed the present Grand Officers."[41] One of the new appointees was Colonel Laurance. Having evidently progressed his Masonic education in one of the 10 of more military lodges during his years on General Washington's headquarters staff, the pre-war St. John's Lodge No. 2 Junior Warden returned not as Junior or even Senior Warden, but as the Lodge "Master." [42]

"The Warrant of St. John's Lodge No. 2," wrote New York Masonic historian Ossian Lang, "was carried away from the city of New York, by a number of the officers and members upon their retirement with the provincial troops in September 1776."[43] Among the absconders was Washington's judge advocate general; but was he the lodge officer who personally harbored the missing St. John's No. 2 Warrant? All we know for certain is that on March 2, 1784, returning patriots surrendered the original St. John's No. 2 Warrant to the New York Grand Lodge. Accepting the document, Grand Lodge brothers "healed" its wayward bearers "as Antients" and installed Laurance as "Master" of St. John's Lodge No. 2.[44] Next day, "Worshipful Brother" Laurance administered Chancellor Robert R. Livingston's ritualistic installation as new Grand Master of the independent Grand Lodge of New York.[45] No sooner had Livingston (pre-war Master of Union Lodge) assumed the trappings of Grand Master than Laurance together with fellow Society of the Cincinnati member James Giles were appointed Joint Secretaries of the Grand Lodge itself.[46]

Although latter-day secret society conspiracy theories have abounded, the brotherhood brooked no such suspicions in Laurance's day. Indeed, Freemasonry spread rapidly in post-Revolutionary New York as patriot and loyalist brethren put aside politics in favor of larger Masonic fraternal principles. By 1825, according to one late-nineteenth-century magazine, some 480 Empire State lodges would house more than 20,000 members.[47]

Laurance, a Freemason well before Lexington and Concord, understood that post-war social and intellectual Masonic fellowship between former enemies was essential to rebuild war-ravaged Lower Manhattan. Administering the brotherhood's local charity was all part of his commitment to community service, for in addition to responsibilities as Trinity Parish vestryman and Columbia trustee, State Assemblyman Laurance was also appointed 1 of 13 commissioners to oversee both the city almshouse and debtor's prison/workhouse (dubbed "Bridewell" after its English predecessor).[48] Neither were mere honorary tasks; almshouse responsibility alone required a thorough on-site visit every Monday afternoon. Few New Yorkers not born a Livingston (or linked to one by marriage like Jay, Duane, Morgan Lewis, and even—indirectly through his wife—William Duer) did more than Washington's former judge advocate general in the year after Evacuation Day to restore New York City to life.

Less than three weeks after British evacuation, Laurance and Wall Street neighbor Hamilton banded with city recorder Richard Varick and attorney Morgan Lewis to solicit from Congress an advance copy of the finalized "Treaty of Paris."[49] The foursome anticipated "great strictness in the Courts of this State," and shrewdly determined that a true copy of the Treaty "under seal of the United States" would help expedite future client judgments. When Laurance actually laid eyes on the ratified document, he, like most of patriot America, surely gasped at Article VI. The Continental Congress of the United States could not have stated its position regarding loyalist property protection any more clearly: "There shall be no future confiscations made, nor any prosecutions commenced against any person or persons ... for or by reason of the part he or they may have taken in the present war."[50]

Fine words, but would the lofty sentiments stand up in court? Every New York lawyer suspected both the Confiscation Act and the Trespass Act violated this act of Congress. And it was common knowledge that the state "Council on Revision" had on January 15 vetoed an "Act declaratory of the alienism of persons therein described" and remanded to the legislature two bills contrary to the treaty with Great Britain. Even so, the Confederation Congress was judicially impotent, a federal constitution lay six years in the future, and the whole idea of judicial review was but academic conjecture. If ever a test case was needed, it was now. The result was *Rutgers v. Waddington*, a landmark collision between the two most prestigious legal teams of New York's pre-Constitutional period.[51] Attorney of record for plaintiff Elizabeth Rutgers was John Laurance.[52] Heading the defense team was Alexander Hamilton.

Hamilton, his ever-aspiring eye on a greater stage, had already championed several high-profile cases publicly addressing congressional legal authority over state legislation.[53] Like Colonel Laurance and most other officers of the Revolution, Alexander learned all too well during the war that self-interested individual states could not and would not function as a national government. Already swirling about his head were themes he, along with James Madison and John Jay, would articulate in favor of centralized government in the *Federalist Papers*. And to Hamilton's mind, fair treatment of ex-Tories and their property under the principle of congressional supremacy went hand in hand with economic prosperity. "Many merchants, of second class, characters of no political consequence," he warned Chancellor Livingston the past August, "each of whom may carry away eight to ten thousand guineas have I am told lately applied for shipping to carry them away. Our state will feel for twenty years at least, the effects of the popular phrenzy."[54] Laurance to a lesser degree shared these higher beliefs, but he was more the pragmatic litigator than legal visionary. Having had a hand in passing the Trespass Act, John saw it as the voice of the people expressed through their elected representatives. If the act was bad law, then the people of New York only need change it. Had not Blackstone himself opined in the first volume of his *Commentaries* that if Parliament erred, "I know of no power that can control it"?[55]

Rutgers v. Waddington (New York Mayor's Court, 1784)

If rising attorney Laurance had expressly set out to mobilize anti-Tory public opinion behind his case, he could not have chosen a more sympathetic client than 75-year-old Elizabeth Rutgers, widow of much beloved pre-war brewery owner Harman Rutgers III. She, like thousands of other New Yorkers, fled William Howe's conquering army the summer of 1776, but her Maiden Lane brewery lay vacant until grabbed up in September 1778 by British merchants Benjamin Waddington and Evelyn Pierrepont. The pair occupied the Rutgers property rent-free until May 1780, when the British commander-in-chief ordered rent paid to a government agent. Waddington and Pierrepont significantly improved the premises, but two days before Elizabeth could reclaim her property on Evacuation Day, a "mysterious" fire turned both the brew house and malt house to ashes. Elizabeth Rutgers's suit, filed in Mayor's Court for £8,000 ($1.06 million today) in back-rent and damages against Joshua Waddington (Benjamin's agent), immediately captured the public fancy. Why, New Yorkers asked, should they honor Article VI of the peace treaty when British troops flagrantly violated Article VII by retaining western frontier forts? Of course, British ministers in turn questioned why they should give up strategic forts at Michilimacinac, Detroit, Oswego, Niagara, Dutchman's Point, and Point-au-Fer along the American-Canadian border when the United States had prevented Crown subjects from recovering debts owed them by American citizens.

Rising to the moment, Laurance and Hamilton both assembled formidable legal teams. John's co-attorney was Egbert Benson, the sitting Attorney General of New York. Nephew to plaintiff Elizabeth Rutgers, the 37-year-old Benson (King's College '65) clerked for the respected John Morin Scott and passed the bar in 1769 to join college classmate John Jay as original members of the bar's exclusive "Moot" Debating Society. An important state legislator and attorney general during the late war, Benson also served a term in Continental Congress. Lead attorney Laurance, as the case's public profile continued to rise, added two additional counsels for the plaintiff: old friend Robert Troup and William Wilcox. Admitted to the bar in 1774, Wilcox (Princeton '69) had come to know Judge Laurance during the war as aide-de-camp to Major General Alexander (Lord Stirling). In turn, Hamilton beefed up his team with defense counsels Morgan Lewis (Princeton '73) and Henry Brockholst

Livingston (Princeton '74). Brockholst, as he preferred to be called, was brother-in-law to Jay, and had served as aide-de-camp to General Schuyler until 1779 when he turned diplomat and accompanied Jay's mission to Spain. Captured at sea by British cruisers on the return trip, Brockholst determined on a law career after being exchanged and was admitted to practice in April 1783. Morgan Lewis (Princeton '73) had clerked for Jay, served chief-of-staff to General Horatio Gates, and in 1779 wed yet another Livingston girl, the sister of Chancellor Robert R. Livingston. Having entered the New York bar in 1782, Lewis would 22 years later become the Empire State's fourth governor.

Laurance and Wilcox opened arguments on June 29 before a court composed of Mayor Duane, Recorder Varick, Aldermen Blagge, Gilbert, Neilsen, Randal, and Ivers. After pronouncing the Trespass Act a remedial statute that clearly applied to both plaintiff and defendant, Laurance and Benson went on to rebut in advance any defense under the law of nations (wartime military possession constitutes de facto ownership) as well as the court's power to construe anything but New York law. Furthermore, they argued that even if the law of nations was integral to English common law, neither was binding on the New York legislature. And while the Articles of Confederation endowed Congress with exclusive treaty-making power, no such power, they asserted, was granted to interfere with the internal laws of the states.

Hamilton's defense team faced a formidable task. To prevail they had to convince the court its role was not to adjudicate state law, but rather interpret it in context of international law and its relationship to the New York state Constitution. Hamilton opened by boldly proclaiming the Trespass Act blatantly against the law of nations, and therefore void. The Waddingtons, he continued, occupied the Rutgers brew house under express authority of the British army during wartime and were therefore protected by universally accepted laws of war. Moreover, argued he and Livingston, such practice *was* embedded in the English common law that New York's Constitution of 1777 had specifically reaffirmed.

Laurance's team leaped to the counter-attack. Supreme law-giving authority in New York State, they argued, was the legislature, accountable only to the people. New York judges, Laurance contended, had no authority to apply law from any other source, be it law of nations or Congress. And so it went, to and fro, as New York's most brilliant lawyers displayed their oratorical wares under the surveying eye of Mayor James Duane.

"Arguments on both sides," Duane later volunteered, "were elaborate, and their authorities numerous."[56] Robert Troup presented his arguments "with simplicity, earnestness, and a winning candor, which commanded invariable attention and respect," while Brockholst Livingston came across as "copious, fluent, abounding in skillful criticism and beautiful reflections."[57] In contrast, Egbert Benson was the very model of an old-school lawyer. "Accustomed to carry his researches back to the recesses and grounds of the law," Benson proceeded, "to rest his opinion and argument on solid elementary principles."[58]

"Laurance," remarked another commentator, "was eminently possessed of what Mr. Hume calls a Delicacy of Taste, an acute Genius connected with a classical Education makes him infinitely my Superior."[59] John's courtroom manner, as we earlier learned from military trials, was methodical, respectful, and restrained. "Colonel Lawrence was graceful, fluent and ingenious," remembered Benson's clerk James Kent, but it was Colonel Hamilton who shone brightest. "By means of his fine melodious voice and dignified deportment," wrote Kent, "his reasoning powers and persuasive address, soared far above all competition. His pre-eminence was at once universally conceded."[60] But had Laurance's deep command of state and common law offset Hamilton's lofty assertion that neither trumped the law of nations?

Arguments concluded, Chief Justice Duane adjourned court within the week. Requesting the briefs from both legal teams, he huddled in deliberation with City Recorder Varick. July passed. Not until August 17 did Duane emerge to announce a split verdict. Ten days later came a written opinion considered "almost studiously ambiguous" by Columbia law professor Goebel, who thought it "a compromise pleasing neither plaintiff or defendant."[61] Duane on the one hand rejected Hamilton's case for voiding the Trespass Act and confirmed Laurance's contention that the Act was a remedial statute that applied to both plaintiff and defendant. Negating the act of a legislature, ruled Duane, would be "to set the judicial above the legislative, which would be subversive to all government."[62] On the other hand, Mayor Duane did just that! Paraphrasing Blackstone's passage authorizing judicial construction of statutes to avoid conflict with common rights, he applied the law of nations to rule that Waddington was *not* liable for the portion of his occupation (1780–1783) that occurred under direct orders from the British military command. Liability, concluded Duane, was limited only to the period (1778–1780) unprotected by the so-called law of nations

As to the Treaty of Paris itself, Duane waffled magnificently, stating that the treaty could not be violated by the state, nor could it provide amnesty for the defendant. Furthermore, the mayor claimed that his court lacked the power to void the Trespass statute because the Articles of the Confederation of the 13 United States did not contain a judicial supremacy clause. And since the legislature did not expressly provide that it intended to violate the treaty, the court, ruled Duane, could not presume that it did. Even so, it was a landmark decision that planted the flag for judicial review of legislative acts a quarter century before John Marshall's transformative Supreme Court decision in *Marbury v. Madison.*

Duane then artfully referred matters to a 12-man jury for determining specific damages. On the second day of September, jurors met at John Simmons's tavern and awarded plaintiff Elizabeth Rutgers less than 10 percent of claimed rent due: a paltry £791, 13 shillings, 4 pence damages plus 6 pence court costs. Duane pounced on the settlement with alacrity, swiftly ordering the sum recorded as judgment of the court. George Washington later weighed in from Mount Vernon, opining to Duane that "reason seems very much in favor of the opinion given by the court, and my judgment yields a hearty assent to it."[63]

Washington may have been pleased, but an outraged patriot New York lambasted Mayor Duane and Recorder Varick for illegally reviewing acts of the legislature. Angry radical Whigs in the state General Assembly went so far as to haul the mayor before the body and move to replace both him and Varick, only to watch the measure go down in defeat 31 to 9.[64] Laurance then produced a "people's writ of error" and

FIGURE 4 James Duane (1733–1797).

Oil on canvas (ca. 1785) by John Trumbull (1756–1843). (New York City Hall Portrait Collection. Public domain.)

forwarded his client's case to New York's Supreme Court. Before any appellate hearing could take place, however, Rutgers and Waddington quietly settled privately for about £800.

John Laurance was on the wrong side of history in *Rutgers v. Waddington* but it did not stop fellow New Yorkers from reelecting him to the Eighth New York State Legislature convening that October.[65] Hamilton's career, on the other hand, was launched spectacularly as newspapers headlined the verdict and introduced his name to future voters from New Hampshire to the Carolinas. To New York loyalists, Duane's compromise opinion was a turning point. Former rank-and-file Tories, convinced they might get a fair shake in court, began filtering back to the city from Canada and other places of refuge. Those not specifically banished by name were restored to full citizenship in 1786 and much of the troublesome Trespass Act was repealed the following April. By 1788 the Citation Act and all other statutes inconsistent with the Treaty of Paris were also repealed. Four years later even Tories expatriated by name were allowed to return. At the polls these grateful former loyalists would not forget that impetus for their restored status came from men becoming known as "Federalists."

Despite sharp confrontation in *Rutgers v. Waddington*, Laurance and Hamilton were never personal adversaries. Within months they represented Dr. John Cochran as co-counsels to petition a water lot grant at Beekman Slip.[66] As both practices flourished, each sought the other's opinion on private cases. And Hamilton, when short of cash, invariably turned to Laurance, confiding on one occasion, "I am just now as poor as Job: & I do not like to go into the bank. If you can accommodate me with 100 Dollars for Ten Days, you will oblidge."[67]

The "bank" was Bank of New York. Although the omnipresent Hamilton is often credited with founding the institution, he was in fact preempted by city merchants. Gathering at Merchants' Coffee House on February 24, leading businessmen approved plans for a "money bank" shortly after learning of Chancellor Livingston's proposed "Letters of Incorporation" to charter a "land-bank" catering to upstate agrarian interests.[68] To be sure, Hamilton had earlier been urged by wealthy London-based brother-in-law John Barker Church to launch a New York bank in which he and business partner Jeremiah Wadsworth would be dominant stockholders. "Unluckily," Hamilton replied to Church in early March, "I entered rather late into the measure; proposals have already been agreed upon."[69] Nonetheless, Hamilton was asked by the coalescing merchants to become one of their proposed bank's 13 founding directors. Laurance could only be amazed that Alexander, in the midst of multiple property litigation cases, then singlehandedly dashed off the bank's intricate 20-article constitution as well as its legislative petition requesting state charter.

There was at the time only one chartered bank (Robert Morris's Philadelphia-based Bank of North America) in the 13 Confederated States. To spare New York City businessmen inconvenient Philadelphia borrowing trips during the city's 1784 "crisis of liquidity," the Albany brokerage firm of Lush and Lansing went so far as to extend downstate lending offers in the *New York Packet*.[70] But only a local institution would do for New York merchants, brokers, and shippers, who desperately needed a bank that catered to their own hard money needs. Chancellor Livingston's real-estate-mortgage-backed "land bank" scheme simply could not provide the liquidity offered by Bank of New York's specie-based capitalization, especially to former loyalists whose purses still clinked with British gold guineas and silver shillings. City businessmen of all stripes wanted a limited-liability institution that could facilitate London trading transactions with hard money, discount Philadelphia bills of exchange, serve as investing platform for purchasing government notes, and was run for the profitability of its subscribers. It mattered little that the spiteful, Clinton-controlled state legislature refused to formally charter the Bank of New York until 1791.

Capitalized at $500,000 (a thousand shares at $500 each), Bank of New York took the form of a limited-liability joint-stock operation accepting payments and receipts only in gold, silver coin, or bank notes.[71] Hamilton, having virtually no funds to invest, acquired but one share, serving primarily as placeholder for deep-pocketed brother-in-law John B. Church and his Connecticut associate Wadsworth.[72] Laurance limited his own founding stake in Bank of New York to three shares ($1,500) because, as we shall learn (chapter Eighteen), his capital was almost entirely invested in land.[73] Nonetheless, he had entrée to the bank's innermost workings because father-in-law McDougall was the institution's first president.

Over the summer of 1784, Laurance and Robert Troup (with Hamilton to a lesser degree) initiated an informal New York real estate investment partnership that would continue until Alexander's death 20 years later.[74] Charter members of the New York Society of Cincinnati, the trio enjoyed theatre, tavern, and courtroom together. Sharing bouncing stagecoaches and smelly boarding rooms, they joined fellow lawyers on the road as court cases carried them into the outlying judicial circuit.[75] And when (at John Jay's instigation) the New York Society for Promoting the Manumission of Slaves formed on February 4, 1785, at the Merchants' Coffee House, who should be among the 32 founding members but Laurance, Hamilton, and Troup.[76] Manumission was no token issue for John; four years later he was elected to the Society's six-member Standing Committee.

The three like-minded lawyers were also Wall Street neighbors. Only a few doors away from John and Betsey at 13 Wall were Alexander and Elizabeth at 58 Wall (later adding 57), and Robert and Jennet Troup at 67 Wall.[77] From courtrooms to financial ventures to quiet parlor dinners, the trio led such intertwined lives that Alan McLane Hamilton listed Laurance and Troup among his famous grandfather's most intimate lifetime friends.[78] Down the street, state legislators conducted business at the Old Royal Exchange, a two-story, cupola-crowned covered marketplace at the foot of Broad Street near the intersection with Water Street. As lower Manhattan merchants and shippers grumbled at Governor George Clinton's restrictive import tariffs and vengeful, Tory-baiting policies, it was only a matter of time until Hamilton and Troup too plunged alongside Laurance into New York's rowdy political waters.

NINE

federalist into Federalist

NEW YORK CITY HALL, APRIL 27, 1785. New York's newest delegate to the Confederation Congress scrambled up the broad front steps of lower Manhattan's "more strong than elegant" three-story brick City Hall and strode purposefully under its grand portico into the large entry chamber. Passing two small apartments reserved for the doorkeeper and city watch, Laurance ascended to the upper floor, entered the buzzing east-wing chamber occupied by Congress, and eased into a morocco leather–trimmed mahogany seat as tall, spare Virginian Richard Henry Lee called the session to order.[1]

John's appointment to the Sixth Confederation Congress was the result of spirited debate in a New York legislature controlled—if not bullied—by brash, iron-willed governor George Clinton.[2] The charismatic Clinton, after seven years of distinctive service as governor, state militia commander-in-chief, and Continental Army general, was popularly embraced as the most powerful man in the Empire State. With taxes running at three cents per pound (£) on improved land, Clinton argued that New York had shouldered a disproportionate share of the war's burden.[3] Therefore, farmers, small business owners, and ex-soldiers alike applauded his "New York first" initiative to reduce local taxes, halt state payments into the Confederation treasury, and slap retaliatory tariffs on British imports. The Confederation Congress, to George Clinton's fiercely anti-federalist followers, was to be tolerated as no more than an administrative appendage of the independent states. When Laurance's predecessors as New York delegate, Walter Livingston, John Jay, and Egbert Benson, proved too federalist, the governor's loyal supporters simply replaced them.

The tide had begun to turn against zealous Tory-baiting when Congress opened its 1785 session, but Clintonian state legislators were not about to let the Confederated body assert itself in matters the governor thought reserved to the states. Two staunch anti-federalists, Melancton Smith and Thomas Haring, were appointed to the upcoming congressional session. Even so, the pro-Congress voice of New York City was not to be ignored. Led by Mayor Duane and State Senator Alexander McDougall, Southern District legislators collaborated with the powerful Livingston faction to name a third delegate who would speak for downstate mercantile and financial interests: John Laurance.[4]

FIGURE 5 George Clinton (1739–1812).
Governor of New York (1777–1795, 1801–1804), and fourth Vice President of the United States (1805–1812). Oil on canvas by Ezra Ames (1768–1836). (Collection of New York Historical Society. Reproduced with permission.)

The Confederation Congress, to the mind of confirmed federalists like delegate Laurance, was defined by impotency. Granted, the body was never intended to supersede state sovereignty, but wartime exigencies in early 1781 had produced a tenuous "nationalist" consensus behind Superintendent of Finance Morris that raised hopes among the army and propertied class for a stronger central government. With independence, however, Morris's influence declined, and his November 1784 departure gave advocates of decentralized government the more subservient body they long wanted.[5] Lacking power to tax or regulate interstate commerce, and completely at the mercy of recalcitrant state legislatures, the Congress of 1785 more nearly resembled receivers of an expiring business

COL. JOHN LAURANCE,
MEMBER OF THE CONTINENTAL CONGRESS

FIGURE 6 Colonel John Laurance.
Lithograph (ca. 1889) by Max Rosenthal (1833–1918). (Courtesy Miriam and Ira D. Wallach Division of Art, Prints and Photographs, New York Public Library.)

than the governing head of an aspiring league of states. Few delegates attended full time; hence, each state maintained a pool of representatives to share the year-round task. Single attendees might help a state constitute quorums, but at least two were required for an individual state's vote to count on any given measure. And both men needed to be of like mind or else an evenly divided state vote would not be tallied. Resolutions only carried when at least seven states produced two or more delegates voting "aye." Nine-state majorities were necessary in matters of defense, foreign treaties, or appropriating monies, but full 13-state unanimity was required to amend the Articles of Confederation.

Delegate Laurance a day after taking his chair was appointed to the important committee overseeing Secretary of Foreign Affairs John Jay.[6] Together with influential fellow committeemen Rufus King (Massachusetts), James Monroe (Virginia), and Charles Pinckney (South Carolina), Laurance would report to the full Congress on matters ranging from establishing consuls in Europe, returning black slaves from

British protection back into hands of owners, ratifying a treaty with Barbary pirates, and reviewing departmental operating expenditures. Other committee assignments ranged from the mundane (arranging a Fourth of July dinner for 50 people), to the practical (defining decimal coinage as official units of United States currency), to the volatile (mediating South Carolina's boundary dispute with Georgia).

By far the most significant pieces of legislation emanating from the Confederation Congress were the land ordinances of 1784, 1785, and 1787 to survey, structure, and administer a "Northwest Territory" from land east of the Mississippi, northwest of the Ohio, and south of the Great Lakes. When Laurance first took his seat, the 1785 ordinance, organizing the 260,000-square-mile territory into 6-square-mile, 36-section townships, had already advanced to its second reading. After his "aye" vote helped ease the measure into law, John later facilitated ratification motions on treaties with the Iroquois Six Nations and other tribes regulating Northwest Territory land use and river navigation rights.[7]

Foreign affairs and Native American treaties aside, the Confederation Congress was more often than not besieged with monotonous individual petitions and memorials requesting compensation due from the late war. Some were rejected outright and others were directed to individual states, while most were relegated to small committees for the thankless task of review and comment. Among eight petitions reported back to the floor in John's hand during 1785 were a $200 gratuity to Christopher Ludwick, former baking department superintendent of the Continental Army,[8] denial of pay and land grants to New York infantry captain James Gilliland,[9] and approval of unremitted back-pay to Boston military hospital ward-master Thomas Walcut.[10] Far juicier in lower Manhattan gossip circles was Laurance's committee investigation of well-heeled fellow Wall Street lawyer Brockholst Livingston's back-pay request for a month of British captivity. For Livingston in April 1782 had been embarrassingly seized at sea en route home after more than two years with brother-in-law John Jay's diplomatic ministry to Spain.[11]

Because the collective states by 1785 had anteed up little more than a quarter of the $8,000,000 originally assessed in 1781, the wolf of insolvency continuously clawed at the congressional door.[12] In mid-July, a grand committee reported that only $708,432 was available to cover estimated annual expenses of $3,708,432 and recommended that states be immediately asked for "cheerful payment" of the difference.[13] Concerned over the government's mounting negative cash flow, Laurance in early August motioned that the Board of Treasury every month lay before Congress an abstract of receipts, expenses, and cash balance from the previous month.[14] It was so moved. Although revenues still fell well short of projected expenses, operating costs could at least be limited to cash in the till—even if it meant trimming necessary governmental operations and further postponing defaulted interest payments on foreign loans.

As Congress slashed away, Laurance voted "aye" on successful motions to replace Court of Appeal judge salaries with a per diem allowance, revert individual wartime reimbursement petitions to the states for payment, and reduce war department staffing. Perhaps most illustrative of lawmaker frugality was the ballyhoo over a $15,000 honorarium to compensate Frederick Steuben (the baron's Americanized name) for wartime services rendered. Although not sharing New England delegate disdain for Steuben as an overrated soldier of fortune, Laurance voted "nay." His vote turned to "aye" at $10,000 but the motion still failed . . . as did a motion for $8,000. Only when tight-fisted lawmakers reduced the sum to $7,000 did Steuben receive his reward.[15]

As 1785 drew to a close and most delegates headed home for the winter, Laurance doggedly soldiered on. The sole New Yorker present on Christmas Eve, he returned to Betsey and the children when only three state delegations materialized. A few days later, his committee of three submitted (in Laurance's hand) a proposed 1786 salary and expense budget for the president of Congress.[16] Yet, another two years would pass before John's all-in recommendation of $12,000 (salary, household rent, wages of private secretary, steward, servants, etc.) was actually settled by the financially hamstrung Confederation lawmakers.

If the Congress of 1785 was school for frustration, the following year's session was a civic embarrassment. The body's newly elected president, John Hancock, failed to materialize the entire term, while proceedings all too often failed to attract the required nine-state quorum. "It is a mere farce to remain here," lamented Massachusetts delegate Rufus King in early 1786. "Three days since last October only have nine states been on the floor."[17] By early February every delegate could see that the United States was unable to repay any principal on French, Spanish, and Dutch loans, much less interest due in excess of $577,000. Worse, the Treasury Board estimated that 1786 operating expenses (including debt interest) of almost $3.8 million would only be offset by some $464,000 in total levies collected from the 13 states over the past 14 months.[18]

Bleeding red ink, the Confederation Congress turned to a special committee of five for answers. Led by Virginia delegate James Monroe, they reported it was "impolitic, if not impossible to borrow more" from abroad.[19] Nor should Congress print more devalued paper bills of credit, "since bearing no interest, they would in effect put the creditors in worse condition then they are in now."[20] Concluding that revenue requisition was the only hope of fiscal relief, Monroe's committee suggested Congress revisit its proposed April 1783 amendment to the Articles of Confederation that empowered the body to levy imposts on imported goods. The original measure, requiring 13-state unanimity, had obtained legislative approval in nine but stalled in Rhode Island, Maryland, Georgia, and New York. When the first three recalcitrant state legislatures responded positively to the urgent new congressional request, all eyes turned to

Laurance's home state as the Confederation government teetered on the brink of insolvency.

Governor Clinton fully understood the economic advantages of New York City's favored location as the Confederation's primary port of entry east of the Delaware River. Into state coffers poured all tariffs imposed on goods entering the port of New York, supplemented by punitive double duties on imports owned in part, or wholly, by British subjects aboard vessels built outside the state. Not only did New York refuse to share the proceeds, but avaricious state legislators also laid tariffs on produce from New Jersey and lumber from Connecticut. When an appalled Confederation Congress in February 1786 demanded New York (and Georgia) surrender delinquent tariff revenues, Laurance voted "aye" on the motion, only to watch anti-Federalist fellow delegate Melancton Smith offset his vote, thus nullifying New York's ballot.[21] Even so, the measure passed. Collecting the money was another matter. With imposts representing between a third and a half of state income, George Clinton and his toll collectors simply would not share their booty.[22]

"Thinking men in New York," wrote Pulitzer Prize–winning historian Allen Nevins, "explicitly recognized the broader implications of the impost question: that it was part of the battle to decide between a strong or a weak federal government."[23] And by voting to transfer state tariff revenue to the Confederation Congress, Laurance laid his cards on the table as a full-blown Federalist. Clintonites to this point had tolerated John's congressional appointment because he had supported the anti-Tory Trespass Act as a Westchester assemblyman and publicly defended the measure against Hamilton in *Rutgers v. Waddington*. Now his true stripes were flashed for all to see, and they were not Clintonian.

Laurance pressed for federal imposts in large part because of his infuriated New York City merchant constituency. Both the Chamber of Commerce and the General Committee of Mechanics had petitioned for uniform continental rates to revive sagging international trade. Local manufacturers had been pushed to the wall by dumping of British goods, shipbuilding had ceased altogether, and financial factors decried a decline of credit. True, the Articles of Confederation reserved matters of trade and commerce to the individual states, but British, French, and Spanish ministers could not be bothered to negotiate with 13 different state legislatures. Manhattan merchants, particularly those who had founded Bank of New York to facilitate hard-specie transactions, were further incensed over Governor Clinton's easy money policy. Derided as "rag money," more than a million dollars in depreciating state bills of credit—designated by Albany as legal currency—diluted their London trade account balances. To the merchant mind, uniform imposts and stiffer hard-specie requirements were two sides of the same coin in squaring their accounts abroad.

As if foreign trade concerns were not enough, Laurance's commercial constituency also harbored a very real fear that neighboring states would combine against them if uniform imposts were not established. And for good reason: toward the end of 1784, state legislators had slapped a 2.5 percent duty on all imported goods and a punitive 5 percent on goods from the British West Indies.[24] "New York [is] like an unchristian Jew," shrieked one Connecticut newspaper, "watching every opportunity to take advantage of their neighbors' necessity."[25] Little wonder New Jersey and Connecticut—over half of whose imports came through the port of New York—threatened to instigate a ruinous trade war that might devastate the local economy.

Laurance's pro-trade voice, however, was negated in Congress by anti-federalists Smith and Haring. Consequently, New York City assemblymen William Duer and Robert Troup, together with a stretcher-borne Senator McDougall,* pressed the state legislature to authorize uniform congressionally collected import levies. Matters came to a head on April 13, when the impost question was finally put to vote. The measure passed 33 to 22 in favor of uniform imposts; but states-rightists under Speaker of the Assembly John Lansing Jr. imposed two intolerable conditions: Albany's complete control of all collections, and payment with state-issued paper money.[26] Declaring New York's conditions unacceptable, the Confederation Congress on July 27 named Laurance the New York member of a select committee chaired by James Monroe to prepare an appropriate response. On August 11, they "earnestly recommended" that Governor Clinton "immediately convene the legislature" to reconsider the impost collection question.[27] Clinton obstinately refused, whereupon Pennsylvania, whose approval of the impost ordinance was conditioned on 13-state unanimity, withdrew its support as well. Thus perished the best hope for the Confederation Congress to avoid looming financial catastrophe.

The plain hard truth was that Governor George Clinton had little use for a soundly financed, independent Confederation Congress. Central government not only would usurp state impost revenues but also would constrain lopsided Native American land-treaty transactions and halt confiscation of loyalist estates, leaving the governor no choice but to saddle farmers and merchants alike with property taxes. New York, to Clinton's mind, could defend its own borders, negotiate necessary treaties with Native American tribes, raise required revenues, issue its own currency, and govern itself. From timber-rich northern forests and fertile Hudson River farmlands to Manhattan's thriving deep-water port, New York State was an empire in the making. As to where the governor perceived himself in the scheme, an elaborate title provides a clue: "His Excellency George Clinton, Esquire, Governor-General and Commander-in-Chief of all the militia, and Admiral of the Navy of the State of New York."

---

*Fifty-three-year-old Alexander McDougall had for the past four years suffered "a complaint of the stone" (inoperable bladder or kidney stones). Following the April vote on "soft" currency, his condition precluded return to the state senate.

Flowery title aside, George Clinton's populist reputation was so strong that artist John Trumbull in 1817 seated him front and center in the background of his famous 12- by 18-foot canvas *Declaration of Independence,* even though Clinton was not present and never signed the 1776 document.[28] Supporters considered him a true man of the people, and with good reason. Many a financially devastated patriot after war's end was helped back on his feet through the governor's political support. And by confiscating loyalist property for public resale and taxing imports, he kept the middling class free of burdensome state taxes. Moreover, a frugal lifestyle endeared him to thousands of small upstate farmers and mechanics who saw him as a bulwark against the powerful manor-house families that had dominated colonial New York. Although rough and uncouth in appearance, and sometimes rash in behavior, the magnetic yeoman governor was a born political operator who skillfully deployed substantial patronage resources and anti-Tory oratory to mobilize America's most effective political machine.

When Laurance cast about for company to share frustration over the obstinate New York governor and an increasingly ineffective Confederation Congress, he needed look no further than charismatic Massachusetts delegate Rufus King, with whom he shared four separate committee assignments. King's father Richard had turned Crown loyalist in 1774 after his home was twice ransacked by leveling mobs for no reason other than his sheer prosperity. However, Rufus and brothers Cyrus and William remained firm patriots. Ambitious and oratorically gifted, the Harvard-educated (first in his class of '77) King was inevitably drawn into "our circle," as Robert Troup later referred to the Wall Street social clique, with Hamilton and Laurance.[29] Then sporting a full head of hair, the handsome, well-formed 31-year-old Massachusetts lawyer sent tongues wagging by pursuing wealthy merchant John Alsop's much sought-after 16-year-old society belle daughter, Mary. Their March 1786 wedding was the toast of New York.

Laurance and King must have instantly warmed to one another. Fellow lawyers, members of the New York Society Library, and former wartime staff officers (King was briefly aide to Continental General John Glover), the Anglophile pair shared an acknowledged expertise in Confederation treasury and financial matters. Both were strongly opposed to slavery; King in 1785 proposed an act of Congress for that very purpose. Avid bird hunters, Laurance and King could not help but discuss replacing the defective Articles of Confederation while bagging grouse together in the fields of rural Long Island. But replace them with what?

On June 10 came news John and Betsey Laurance had dreaded for weeks. General McDougall was no more. Aged 53, the stubborn Scot had died in his Nassau Street home. Mournful New Yorkers of all stripes turned out to honor their fallen Sons of Liberty leader. Amid ringing church bells, uniformed Cincinnati, somber clergy, and grief-stricken family,

FIGURE 7 Rufus King (1755–1827).
Oil on board (1819–1820) by Gilbert Stuart (1755–1828). (National Portrait Gallery, Smithsonian Institution, Washington, DC. Public domain.)

Noah Webster Jr. (founding father of American education) observed: "the Marine Society, members of Congress, foreign ministers and a very numerous and respectable concourse of citizens, in a grand procession escorted the corpse to the Old Presbyterian Churchyard, where minute guns were fired."[30] Little more than three months later, Stevey McDougall followed his father to the grave. Only 34, he never fully recovered from his grueling 1776 stint in British captivity. John and Betsey welcomed friends into their parlor to grieve over the casket, and then led a long train of mourners up Wall Street to deposit Stevey's remains alongside his father in the First Presbyterian burying yard. With her brother's passing, Betsey inherited what survived of General McDougall's much-reduced privateering fortune, "plus a negro man, called Coleraine." And John, as provided by his father-in-law's will, received what remained from the estate of Lt. John McDougall, who in 1778 had perished at sea.[31]

In welcome relief between the two somber McDougall funerals, New York streets came alive on July 4 to celebrate the Declaration of

Independence's glorious 10th anniversary. Cheering crowds packed lower Manhattan for a glimpse of Governor Clinton, Laurance and his fellow congressional delegates, and other state office holders of note as these worthies paraded down Broad Street. By way of Beekman Street, the thirsty dignitaries marched along Broad Way to John Cape's familiar City Tavern. More than one celebratory beverage under their belts, Laurance, Troup, and the New York Society of Cincinnati then dined together in Corre's Tavern at 18 Broad Way just below Little Queen Street.[32] After electing Frederick Steuben to replace McDougall as president, the Society bestowed honorary membership on Robert R. Livingston, James Duane, and William Duer, imbibed an oration by Alexander Hamilton, and downed 13 toasts before breaking up at eight. Those choosing not to cap the festive evening by taking in the grand fireworks display on Governor's Island might have appreciated the irony of a stirring production of "Alexander the Great" at the John Street Theatre.

July 4th celebratory hoopla notwithstanding, the government of the confederated states was technically bankrupt. Already in default on the entirety of loan contracts with the French government, Treasurer Michael Hillegas in late June advised Congress that requisitions from the states for the year would "hardly reach Three hundred thousand Dollars," versus expenses of "at least Three Million and a half Dollars."[33] Not to mention another million and a half dollars in new domestic debt. Rather than abdicate all financial matters back to the states, Laurance and his desperate fellow delegates on July 5 appointed a grand committee of 12 (nearly two out of three dwindling members) to beg state legislatures for "such powers as will render the federal government adequate to the ends for which it was instituted."[34]

Virginia seized the initiative, inviting the states to meet at Annapolis, Maryland, to "remedy defects of the Federal Government." The Virginia legislature, having already retired much of its state war debt, had but minor tweaking in mind, but when only a dozen representatives showed up, the Annapolis delegates audaciously called for a full convention to meet the next May in Philadelphia. Congress concurred, declaring it their "duty to solemnly warn" the several states that "most fatal evils" were about to "flow from a breach of the public faith" if Confederation coffers ran dry.[35] Twelve states, motivated in no small measure by farmer revolts and taxpayer outrage against higher local taxes, responded to the congressional call by dispatching delegates to the Philadelphia convention.[36] Laurance would take no part in the Philadelphia proceedings. Having overplayed his federalist hand on the impost vote, he was not reappointed to the Seventh Confederation Congress when New York's pro-Clinton legislature met on January 26.[37] Indeed, his final days in Congress were in vain, for the moribund body was unable to produce either a president or a quorum from November 11, 1786, until January 17, 1787.[38] Still, John could take heart that the stage, after a decade of disappointment for proponents of central government, was now set for a new constitution that would establish a far more powerful federal entity than anyone then imagined.

Four years after British evacuation, New York had by mid-1787 overcome serious post-war economic depression, aided in no small part by the Clinton-sanctioned emission of "easy" paper money. Plentiful currency—though wreaking havoc with merchant trade balances abroad—not only helped common tradesmen and farmers pay off debts but also facilitated state purchase of interest-paying federal securities to the extent that New York transformed itself into one of the Confederation's wealthiest creditor states. Indeed, the interest on some $2,880,000 in federal securities more than equaled annual requisitions on the state by Congress! Even without uniform tariff rates, total customs receipts (£48,023) increased nearly 50 percent in 1787 over the prior year. In 1788, they would soar another 40 percent to £70,099.[39] That part of lower Manhattan spared from the wartime fires thrived, while the remainder was feverishly recovering from its ruins. Flourishing New York City housed more than 30,600 people in some 3,340 dwellings, supported 330 taverns, and enjoyed the services of 41 lawyers. Thanks to Laurance and his fellow Episcopal vestrymen, Trinity Church reconstruction was well underway.

"The most convenient and agreeable part of the city is Broad Way," bragged Noah Webster Jr., "the street is wide and elevated so as to command a delightful prospect of the town, and the Hudson." Of Laurance's own address, Webster observed: "Wall Street is generally wide and elevated, and the buildings elegant . . . generally built of brick and the roofs tiled."[40] No more than a few blocks from John's fashionable three-story Wall Street residence were the departments of Foreign Affairs (John Jay) and War (Henry Knox), the Board of Treasury (a three-man board with William Duer as Secretary), and Paymaster of the Army (John Pierce). Although still lagging Philadelphia in trade, John Laurance's New York—with the Confederation Congress extending its stay in City Hall—was political ground zero for the 13 United States.

Should John wish to indulge in local politicking, but a brief walk away were eight state senators, nine assemblymen (including newly elected Robert Troup), State Supreme Court Chief Justice Richard Morris, Attorney-General Egbert Benson, and Mayor Duane. Newly married Rufus King increasingly forsook his Massachusetts law practice to remain in town with cultivated young bride Mary, whose wealth, beauty, and gracious manners immediately eased him into fashionable society. Offering more earthy conversation (and a foamy mug or two) was colossally fat Wall Street tavern-keeper John Simmons, who squatted on his wooden doorstep just north of City Hall, offering good-natured salutations to passers-by.[41]

And just a few doors up Wall Street, Colonel Hamilton harbored insider tales from the Schuyler political network. John, in short, was only a conversation away from the pulse of America. But would he cast his own hat back in the ring?

How could freeholders of New York's Southern District the spring of 1787 not have wanted Laurance back in the state legislature? From duty in the General Assembly to community service with Trinity Church, the almshouse, hospital, and Manumission Society, he was regarded as a man of sense, eloquence, and genuine commitment to his adopted city. Professionally, he was, after *Rutgers v. Waddington*, near the head of the legal fraternity. His client portfolio encompassed former loyalists, patriot trespass plaintiffs, and Dutch patroons such as Augustus van Cortlandt and Peter van Zandt. Van Cortlandt alone had just appointed John his attorney for the respectable fee of $500 New York money to collect debts and settle several estates.[42] Little surprise, then, that Laurance on April 26 was elected together with Mayor Duane to represent New York, Queens, Kings, Richmond, Suffolk, and Westchester counties in the Eleventh New York State Senate.

The fundamental task facing state lawmakers when they convened in Albany on the first of January 1788 was whether or not to ratify the new United States Constitution crafted the previous summer in Philadelphia. Hoping to prevent this situation from ever arising, Governor Clinton had in spring of 1787 dispatched two anti-federalist delegates alongside state assemblyman Alexander Hamilton to the Philadelphia Convention. Clinton's plan was for Judge Robert Yates and John Lansing Jr. to override Hamilton and keep New York in the "nay" column, thereby slaying the federal "monster" before it left the womb. Politically astute pro-Constitution Virginian James Madison was not fooled. "Yates and Lansing," he confided to George Washington were "pretty much linked to the antifederal party here, and are likely of course to be a clog on their colleague."[43]

Whether pretending to return home in frustration or genuinely hamstrung, Alexander departed Philadelphia the end of June, only to double back in early August after Lansing and Yates—with no further reason to stay—had vacated the convention. Although his contribution was nominal and his single vote would go uncounted, Hamilton's near-monarchical pro-Federal voice combined with Virginia Plan proponents Madison, William Samuel Johnson of Connecticut, James Wilson of Pennsylvania, and Rufus King to push the convention toward a strong central government.[44] The resulting product's wondrous language is generally credited to the pen of Gouverneur Morris. Presiding over the Philadelphia Convention was 55-year-old George Washington. Although mostly silent, there was little doubt where the Master of Mount Vernon stood in replacing what he earlier dismissed to Virginia delegate Benjamin Harrison as "A half-starved, limping Congress, that appears to be always moving upon crutches, and tottering at every step."[45] Washington could only have been elated on September 27, 1787, to proclaim that a new

United States Constitution had been approved by "unanimous consent of 11 states, and Colonel Hamilton's from New York." Blithely ignoring the 13-state unanimity required by the Articles of Confederation, convention delegates (behind closed doors) unilaterally determined that ratification by two-thirds of the state legislatures would suffice.

Americans were not of one mind about whether the federal Constitution was suitable, or even necessary, for the country. Independence to many—and there *were* many—did not mean replacing one oppressive central government with another. To them, the Articles of Confederation safeguarded hard-won liberty through a defensive union of the states, presided over by a dependent Congress without power of the purse. These adversaries of the proposed Constitution were publicly dubbed "Antifederalists," a label somewhat confusing because it formerly described opponents of the Confederation Congress, many of whom had dismissed the Articles because they were *too weak* and now called themselves "Federalist" in support of the new Constitution.[46] Conversely, many who supported the Confederation Congress as Federalists now found themselves in the Antifederalist camp because they thought the new Constitution too empowering. Whatever their earlier position, the new Antifederalists were bound together by a fervent belief that individual liberties were best secured by state and local governments. Led by Sam Adams and Elbridge Gerry in Massachusetts; Virginians Patrick Henry, Richard Henry Lee, and George Mason; North Carolinians Willie Jones and Timothy Bloodsworth; and New York's powerful George Clinton, all feared a national standing army and thought the proposed Constitution with its strong executive branch smacked of aristocracy if not outright monarchy.[47]

When the new Constitution first appeared in New York's *Daily Advertiser*, Governor Clinton used the barely disguised pen name *Cato* to throw family prestige and the power of 11 years in office against ratification. Joining him was pre-war Sons of Liberty leader John Lamb, whose anti-Constitution "Federal Republican" group pumped out essays and pamphlets while establishing contact with like-minded committees from New Hampshire to South Carolina.[48] State Supreme Court Judge Robert Yates and the plainspoken, dry-humored senator Melancton Smith, along with other now-obscure noms de plume, weighed in to accuse Federalists of attempting an illegal counter-revolutionary coup d'etat. These Antifederalist words rang all too true to upstate farmers and middle-class levelers who mistrusted the blue-blooded John Jay, old-money Chancellor Robert R. Livingston Jr., manor-grant landlord Philip Schuyler, and suspiciously smooth Alexander Hamilton.[49]

Brusque, patrician Philip Schuyler had opposed George Clinton ever since 1777, when as Continental generals the pair contested for governor in New York's first constitutional election. His mother a Van Cortlandt, and wife Catherine a Van Rensselaer, Schuyler reigned as upstate New York's most influential citizen. From his rose-red brick Georgian mansion atop a Hudson River bluff just south of Albany, the tall, sometimes-distant, aristocratic-featured Schuyler directed slaves and tenant farmers working a vast 120,000-acre landholding that would have done any Virginia plantation owner proud. His locally built fleet of Hudson River sloops carried to market the estate's prodigious cargoes of lumber, milled grain, flax, and agricultural products. Although rich in land, Schuyler's livelihood depended on unimpeded access to New York City exporters, neighboring state markets, and the West Indies. And that meant not just eliminating tariff imposts against sister states but also negotiating commercial treaties with foreign powers and funding a navy to protect the coastal trades. Only a muscular central government would do.

If State Senator Schuyler was "boss" of New York's anti-Clinton, pro-government faction, son-in-law Hamilton was its campaign manager and articulate public relations un-hired gun. As New York newspapers came of age, Hamilton countered Clinton with one of America's primal public documents, *The Federalist Papers*. It was an unparalleled publicity coup that gave Federalists the political wind-gage while placing opponents on the defensive. Yoking Jay and Madison (conveniently at hand with the Confederation Congress) to his publicity plow under the collective pen name *Publius*, Hamilton ginned out 85 separate New York newspaper installments between October 1787 and the following August to make the case for ratification. Perhaps even more persuasive was Jay's 19-page April 1788 "Address to the People of New York," asking New Yorkers to unite as a "band of brothers" and at least give the Constitution "fair trial."[50] Assemblyman William Duer, likely at Hamilton's urging, gamely chimed in with four strident, and embarrassingly clumsy, pro-government essays under the pen name of *Philo-Publius*.

John Laurance's early commitment to strong central government was undisputable. Indeed Hamilton, some five years before penning *Federalist Paper No. 1*, lauded State Assemblyman Laurance's "just views" in "strengthening the Federal government."[51] It would be naïve, however, not to surmise Laurance knew full well that ratification of the Constitution could only improve the value of his growing portfolio of speculative land holdings. "Every leading capitalist of the time," observed Progressive historian Charles Beard, "understood the relation of a new constitution to the rise in land values west of the Alleghanies."[52] Moreover, basing the national seat of government in New York would be tonic to John's several investment properties in Manhattan and Westchester County.

Eighteen frustrating months in the Confederation Congress could only have redoubled John's resolve for a powerful federal government, but anonymous pamphlets and factional fireworks were not his style. Rather, he contributed to the ratification process with backroom persuasion, Wall Street jawboning, and state senate speechifying. Again and again, Senators Laurance and Duane argued for their chamber to support the General Assembly's call for a ratifying convention, until on February

3 they prevailed at last by an 11 to 8 margin.[53] Colonel Laurance then championed Duchess County Federalist Benson's proposal that convention delegates be chosen "by all free male citizens of the age of twenty-one years and upwards." Despite Antifederalist opposition and Governor Clinton's coolness, Benson's resolution carried. Every free male citizen 21 years of age was for the first time in New York history, regardless of property requirements, granted right to vote in a statewide election[54]

On the heels of Benson's successful proposition, the freemen of New York duly chose 65 delegates to convene at Poughkeepsie and ratify or reject the new United States Constitution. But Federalist strategy to expand the voting franchise bore disappointing fruit; of the state's 14 counties, only 3 others joined New York City to elect pro-union delegates. Manhattan, anticipating considerable mercantile advantages from the Constitution, dispatched a full slate of nine Federalist delegates to the ratification convention that included Jay, Hamilton, Duane, and Chancellor Livingston. Laurance's absence is at first glance puzzling, given his active pro-government senate stance and recent addition to Governor Clinton's important Commission of Indian Affairs.[55] It was especially mystifying since his name appeared on five separate convention tickets proposed in New York newspapers between March 13 and April 24.[56] Political realities, however, demanded social clout, financial resources, or powerful patronage that the deceased General McDougall's foreign-born son-in-law simply could not bring to bear.

Convention delegates assembled on June 17 in Poughkeepsie's circa 1720 Duchess County Court House. First order of business was of course to elect His Excellency George Clinton as president. And because South Carolina in late May became the eighth state to ratify, Clinton's majority found itself in the unexpected position of deciding the national issue; if New York somehow avoided becoming the ninth and determining vote, the Constitution express just might just be derailed. All such Antifederalist wishful thinking was dashed less than a week into proceedings when Chancellor Livingston suddenly took the floor to announce that New Hampshire had delivered the deciding vote. "The Confederation is dissolved," declared Livingston to his stunned associates. "The question before the committee was now a matter of policy and expediency."[57] Four days later, Virginia also ratified. New York's vote no longer even mattered. And New York City, rather than give up the seat of central government, threatened to join the new Federal union whether Albany did so or not! When Hamilton said as much to the assembled convention, Clinton chided him from the chair for such "highly indiscreet and improper" threats.[58] Still, it was not until July 26 that Jay, Livingston, and Hamilton (conceding to attach a circular letter calling for a second, amending Constitutional convention) finally wore down Antifederalist die-hards by a slender three-vote (30-27) margin.

The City of New York could not be bothered to await a verdict. Three days before Poughkeepsie ratification, Mayor Duane pulled out all stops to mount a grand Federal procession celebrating the new national Constitution. Digging into their collective pockets for more than $8,000—an extraordinary sum for the day—city councilmen and merchants staged an energetic, mile-and-a-half-long parade involving some 5,000 marchers. With Hamilton, Jay, and Livingston still locked in upstate debate, parade place of honor fell to state senator John Laurance and Federalist lieutenants Robert Troup and John Corzine.[59] Bearing oversize copies of the Constitution, the threesome marched at the head of the city's legal community.

The jubilee began in a light drizzle at 8 a.m. when 10 classes of citizens, tradesmen, and artisans were grouped into 10 marching divisions (one for each ratifying state) at present-day City Hall Park, then called the "New Fields." Two hours later, marchers moved out on cue to a 13-gun salute from "Hamilton," a 27-foot model Federal frigate complete with canvas sails. Mounted aboard a huge float drawn by 10 horses and manned by a crew of 30, "Hamilton" would "sail" the entire parade route, cannons belching to the animated throng. In the first division, behind a company of light horse, a squad of trumpeters, an artillery piece, and a man on horseback dressed as Christopher Columbus, marched the uniformed Society of Cincinnati. Then came colorful displays by the coopers, pump-makers, tailors, furriers, hatters, brewers, shipwrights, and all the rest. Like a monstrous serpent, the column wound its way down Broad Way cheered on by thousands lining the streets, through Hanover Square, and north to the city's edge at Grand and Mulberry Streets. Under the guns of Fort George at the base of Broad Way, Laurance watched "Hamilton" joined by another float carrying an 18-foot pilot boat replica filled with New York City dignitaries.

Around noon the procession ended up at the great field of former loyalist John Bayard's large country house, where the entire company decamped for a grand banquet beneath a gigantic dining tent concocted by French-born civil engineer Peter (Americanized from Pierre) L'Enfant, future planner of Washington, DC. "Of the 8000 people who were said to have dined together on the green," marveled one attendee, "there was not a single drunken man or fight to be seen."[60]

No sooner had the Constitution been ratified by 11 states than New York City reveled in anticipation of playing host as first seat of the new Federal government. Beaming with civic pride, New Yorkers licked their collective financial chops over the opportunity to host foreign dignitaries, both houses of Congress, the Supreme Court, and first president of the United States. Mayor Duane, hoping to induce Congress to stay permanently, determined to convert City Hall into Federal Hall, home of the new government. And Laurance, wanting a say in the plan, sought an alderman's seat on the City Common Council. Elected alderman for the East Ward— the city's wealthiest—he joined Duane and City Recorder Varick in choosing architect L'Enfant to renovate and redesign City Hall. John, during his first week on the Council, motioned to withdraw £1,000 from the city account (at Bank of New York, of course) to instigate the transformation.[61]

Authorized by Albany, the Council then assessed city denizens £13,000 in new taxes for the project.[62] Altogether, over £26,000 — more than one-third of the city's annual impost revenues — was lavished on the refurbishment.[63] If Pennsylvanians and Virginians were to banish any hope of returning the seat of government to Philadelphia, nothing could be too good for the New York home of the First Federal Congress.

Replete with an imposing Tuscan-frieze second-floor balcony projecting from beneath a Doric-columned entry portico, the sturdy but unimposing structure was transformed by L'Enfant into America's first example of civic Federal style architecture. Its 40-foot by 30-foot, two-story Senate chamber was a visual tour de force. Advertising New York's burgeoning commercial prosperity, the lavish room boasted tall pilaster-bordered windows curtained in red damask, fireplace mantels of polished variegated American marble, and a two-story arched ceiling adorned with 13 stars surrounding a golden sun. "By far the most extensive and elegant of any building in America," gushed one local newspaper, adding that it was "an edifice that would grace any metropolis in Europe."[64] Even advocates for Philadelphia were impressed. "The building," confessed skeptical Pennsylvania Representative Frederick Muhlenburg, "is really elegant and well-designed — for a trap — but I still hope, no matter how well contrived we shall find Room to get out of it."[65]

While Federal Hall dressed itself for distinguished company and national attention, Alderman Laurance busied himself in Common Council discussions ranging from public water supply to admiralty matters and police oversight. Residents were directed to remove dirt and trash from their street fronts before 10 a.m. or be fined five shillings. Street lamps were relocated from wooden posts to building walls for better light reflection. And as if a full week every three months was not enough as judge of the Mayor's Court of General Sessions, state legislators had in January 1787 granted John and fellow aldermen full Justice of the Peace powers (in company of at least two associates). Other, more curious, duties also devolved on aldermen during days of worship. Sunday in late-eighteenth-century New York was the "Lord's Day," during which traveling, sporting events, tippling, and even commercial merchandising (before 9 a.m.) were forbidden. Should John notice violators en route to Sunday services, he was on the Lord's Day empowered to summarily sentence unfortunate perpetrators on the spot.

There were in 1788 no organized political parties in the new American republic. True, all 13 states produced vocal pro-government factions to ratify the new federal Constitution, but the document itself made no allowance whatsoever for factional parties. It was also true that Governor

George Clinton had skillfully mobilized latent anti-gentry and anti-loyalist sentiments into a powerful New-York-first political organization. Still, neither early Federalists nor Clintonian Antifederalists thought of one another as alternating parties in a two-party system. Rather, each hoped to persuade independent freeholders to share their arguments. If anything, wrote noted political scientist Richard Hofstadter, "political discussion in eighteenth-century England and America was pervaded by a kind of anti-party cant."[66] As far back as the 1640s, Englishmen associated parties with violent differences that spawned religious hostility, threatened liberties, and bordered on treason. From Jonathan Swift to Viscount Bolingbroke to David Hume, English political thinkers pilloried faction and party as canker sores on the body politic. Benjamin Franklin, as late as 1786, warned against "the infinite mutual abuse of parties, tearing to pieces the best of characters."[67] A year later, both Hamilton and Madison disparaged factions in respective *Federalist Papers No. 9* and *No. 10*. "If I could not go to heaven, but with a party," weighed in Thomas Jefferson, "I would not go there at all."[68]

All well and good for coffee house theorizing, but once the Constitution was ratified, thoughtful men had to come to grips with just how much central government was necessary. Although national political parties would not appear until the end of President Washington's first term, pro-government New Yorkers of like mind had begun calling themselves Federalists in the wake of Hamilton, Jay, and Madison's *Federalist Papers*. In February of 1789, America's first political party came into being in a series of nominating meetings at Edward Bardin's Lower Manhattan tavern. The building, formerly Joseph Corre's venerable City Tavern, had just been "fitted up" by new owner Bardin to attract a more upper-class clientele. Boasting cellars stocked with "a variety of the best liquors" and tables "supplied with all the delicacies the markets of this city will afford," Bardin advertised his place "for the reception of the various societies" to meet and partake in formal politics.[69] What better venue for the indefatigable Hamilton to entice local merchant participation as he orchestrated election strategy as chair of New York's 13-man Federalist nominating committee.[70]

Convening in Bardin's comfortable confines, several hundred Federalist stalwarts, including Duer, Troup, Aaron Burr, and deep-pocketed investment banker/merchant William Constable, set out to dethrone Governor Clinton. They went for the jugular from the outset by selecting a former Clinton ally, State Supreme Court Judge Robert Yates, as nominee for governor. Yates was at first glance an odd choice; fervent Antifederalist delegate to the Poughkeepsie Convention, he had publicly opposed ratification under the pseudonyms *Brutus* and *Sydney*. But he unswervingly supported the new Constitution as patriotic duty and his modest means deflected anti-aristocracy criticism from potential rural voters. As Yates's running mate, Hamilton shrewdly proposed Clinton's 78-year-old sitting lieutenant governor, Pierre van Cortlandt, for the same slot on the Federalist ticket. The City Tavern caucus did not produce Federalist choices for the two United States senators despite speculation from some dozen New York and out-of-state newspapers that deadlocked state legislators in Albany had elected State Senator Laurance for one of the positions.[71]

Senatorial rumors notwithstanding, John Laurance Esq. was formally put forward on February 23 by reliable Robert Troup as the Federalist nominee for the combined New York City and Westchester County district in the United States House of Representatives.[72] Three days later, city newspapers carried an open announcement from committee chairman Hamilton inviting freeholders to confirm Laurance's candidacy in a mass meeting at Bardin's Tavern.[73] Hundreds turned up to hear John touted by Hamilton as "a man of integrity, of sense, of information, of early and decided attachment to the Federal Constitution, and of tried firmness of temper."[74] "Mr. Lawrence," Hamilton concluded, "is therefore a very proper person to represent us."[75] Melancton Smith and Marinus Willett spoke against Laurance, and some (preferring a merchant instead of a lawyer) walked out at his nomination; nonetheless both he and Judge Yates were "confirmed by near unanimous vote."[76]

Caucusing at John Lamb's house, Antifederalist Clinton operatives artfully determined to split the heavily pro-government southern New York vote by camouflaging themselves behind moderate Federalist John Broome, "a man of great mercantile knowledge."[77] Broome was an inspired choice. Former colonel in the New York militia and delegate to the state Constitutional Convention of 1777, he was New York City treasurer in 1784, a pioneer merchant in the China trade, and since 1785 the elected head of the Chamber of Commerce. The Broome campaign's cunning eleventh-hour scheme was to divide Laurance's pro-lawyer vote by entering Westchester attorney Phillip Pell as a third candidate. It was a virtuosic ploy, because Pell, like Laurance, was an officer during the late war, as well as Westchester County representative in the state legislature. Broome campaign rhetoric stooped to usurp Laurance's résumé by falsely claiming Pell was a member of General Washington's staff and had served as the final judge advocate.[78]

Laurance backers responded with newspaper and poster advertisements of their own. Distributed mere days before the election under the pen name *ONE and ALL*, the pro-Laurance leaflet bared Broome's secret plot and accused Broome and Pell of a most horrifying subterfuge: plotting to deprive New Yorkers of their fiscal good fortune as temporary seat of Congress:

New York preserved, or the Plot discovered.

Whilst the leaders of the antifederal junto in this city are raising a hue-and-cry against electing a Lawyer, as a Representative for this district, their adherents in Westchester county are supporting with all their zeal, Mr. PELL, another lawyer, and a rank Antifederalist, in opposition to Mr. LAWRENCE. Nor is this all; many of the same party in this city are secretly balloting for Mr. Pell, whilst they are duping Mr. Broome, and those who adhere to him, with professions of support. For shame! Such Federalists as have been deluded with the idea that the present contest was only betwixt a lawyer and a merchant, ought to open their eyes; and those who have not been deluded ought to redouble their exertions to bring out every vote to defeat the artifices of a party whose real object is to destroy the perfect Constitution, and remove the residence of Congress from this city.[79]

New York City was of overwhelmingly Federalist mind when polls opened the first week of March 1789. War veterans welcomed a strong central government as best hope to fund promised pensions. Merchants, ship owners, artisans, and tradesmen alike perceived financial benefits from eliminating commercial tariffs among the states and levying uniform imposts on European imports. Masons, stonecutters, carpenters, and mortar-carriers—variously employed in refurbishing City Hall for the new Congress—anticipated additional Federal building work. Wealthy established gentry families like the Van Cortlandts, Livingstons, and Beekmans relished the order and security of a government controlled by men like themselves rather than unkempt populists. And repatriated loyalists saw stability and safety in a regime resembling the English model. All hoped to share in New York City's substantial economic windfall as the seat of the national government.

Not surprisingly, Federalist candidate Laurance was swept into office with more than 85 percent of the vote. Final returns showed him with 2,418 votes, Broome with 372, and Pell with 33.[80] Clearly the freeholders of New York and Westchester believed John, as an experienced lawyer and cogent orator, was far more likely than any merchant to cajole Congress out of leaving town. The governor's race was a different matter. Of New York State's 340,120 souls, only some 83,700, according to the national census of 1790, were free white males 16 and older.[81] And of these, only unencumbered property-owning (at least £100 value), tax-paying freeholders could vote for governor or state senators. Therefore only 12,353 New Yorkers—a mere 3.6 percent of the state population—visited polling stations the first week of April to elect George Clinton by his narrowest margin since 1777. Judge Yates, despite Hamilton and Schuyler's best efforts, fell 429 votes short of denying the cagey governor a fourth consecutive term. Otherwise, Federalists carried the day. Sweeping Duchess, Columbia, Albany, and Montgomery Counties, all of which had elected Antifederalist candidates the year before, Federalists gained a stunning two-to-one majority in the state assembly while retaining their slim lead in the senate. Of Hamilton and

Schuyler's four candidates for Congress, three (Laurance, Peter Silvester, and Duchess County Federalist kingpin Egbert Benson) prevailed.

Benson, like Laurance and Schuyler, was an important New York nationalist cast by historians as a mere bit-player to Hamilton's larger-than-life leading man. Pre-war Whig and King's College ('65) contemporary of John Jay, he served in the state General Assembly from 1777 to 1781, drafting virtually every significant bill to leave the floor. As a Confederation Congress delegate, he had accompanied Hamilton to the Annapolis Conference. Laurance, of course, came to know Benson intimately both as co-counsel in *Rutgers v. Waddington* and as a pro-ratification ally in the state senate. It was a professional friendship close enough for John to name the longtime bachelor (Benson didn't marry until age 74) co-executor of his increasingly substantial estate.

Philip Schuyler, thanks to the formidable Federalist triumvirate of Jay, Livingston, and his own indefatigable son-in-law, would no longer labor in Governor Clinton's populist political shadow. It was taken for granted that he would inherit one of New York's two federal senate seats. And through Hamilton—Washington's second choice for secretary of the Treasury after Robert Morris declined—Schuyler gained a direct pipeline to the president. The connection was quickly put to use. Party loyalists Richard Harrison and William S. Smith were rewarded with respective posts as Federal Attorney and United States Marshall for the District of New York. Even Robert Troup supped at the federal trough as clerk of the Court of the District of New York.

Chancellor Robert R. Livingston Jr. was aghast. How could the patriarch of a family accustomed to influential say in New York governance for three-quarters of a century now find himself inexplicably sidelined? Slighted to learn the treasury slot he coveted went to Hamilton, Livingston was further insulted to find that Jay—instead of himself—would become first chief justice of the United States Supreme Court. Affront turned to indignation when the gentleman's agreement with Schuyler to fill New York's other senate seat with in-law James Duane was untracked by state legislators in favor of transplanted New Englander Rufus King. Though Duane was soon made federal judge for the District of New York, a spiteful Robert Livingston within the year shepherded virtually his entire clan into George Clinton's welcoming arms.

"The Clintons had *power*," quipped one latter-day biographer, "the Livingstons had *numbers*, and the Schuylers had *Hamilton*."[82] And Hamilton, he might have added, in New York City had Laurance. Nobody had campaigned harder for representative-elect Laurance than Hamilton, but it would be a mistake to attribute John's landslide victory to his good friend's endorsement. As an officer of the Continental Army, prominent lawyer, early defender of loyalist rights, sound businessman, active civic booster, and Alexander McDougall's son-in-law, the English-born Laurance was the complete Federalist, appealing to every key base of his voting constituency. Bankers, gentry, war veterans, repatriated loyalists — and even most merchants — all found something to like. Never, not as state assemblyman, state senator, city alderman, or as a federal congressman, had New York County freeholders failed to embrace his bid for office.

Contemplating his extraordinary run of political upward mobility, the 38-year-old Cornish émigré had good reason to hoist a frothy jar of hard cider. And had uncle Richard kept him abreast of political affairs in his native Cornwall, John would have been a dull man indeed not to down a second jar. For the difference between English and American representative government could not have been starker. His reelected legislative counterpart in the Penryn-Falmouth borough was Sir John St. Aubyn (1758–1839), Fifth Baronet of Clowance, who succeeded to the baronetcy at the age of 14 upon inheriting the family manor near Clowan. Stepping into his father's seat in Parliament from 1780 until 1812, St. Aubyn is remembered primarily for accumulating one of England's best-known fossil collections. (Fittingly, the baronetcy became extinct upon his death.) Of course, challenging Sir John for the Penryn-Falmouth borough in 1780 would have been beyond unthinkable for any son of a mere Cornish yeoman.

TEN

The Congress of Firsts

NEW YORK, FEDERAL HALL, APRIL 30, 1789. Ample-girthed Speaker of the House Frederick Muhlenberg steered Representative Laurance and his freshly elected peers into the gilded second floor senate chamber to fill a phalanx of newly damasked chairs reserved for visiting members of the House. Casting a proud eye over the rich crimson draperies and flanking pilaster columns crowned by fanciful Doric capitals, Laurance must have reveled in the £26,000 City Hall refurbishment he had helped cobble together with local tax hikes, earmarked lottery proceeds, and private donations. Overhead, a gold leaf 13-star-encircled sun graced the room's 20-foot azure-blue arched ceiling.

All heads turned as President-elect Washington entered the room. Dressed in a plain dark-brown American-made suit with white silk stockings, silver shoe buckles, and a formal side sword, the tall Virginian strode to the head of the room, bowing left and right. He was then ceremoniously placed in an elevated, crimson-canopied chair reserved for the president of the Senate, John Adams, who as vice president occupied a chair to his right.[1] At Washington's opposite arm, Speaker Muhlenberg settled into his own officially designated seat.

Informed by Adams that the long-anticipated moment had arrived, Washington rose to his feet and led way to the columned second floor balcony, where that cool, clear afternoon New York Chancellor Robert R. Livingston Jr.—after an embarrassing half-hour's scramble for a Bible at nearby St. John's No. 2 Masonic Lodge—administered the oath of office.[2] Turning to the thousands of upturned faces below, Livingston shouted, "Long live George Washington, President of the United States."[3] A prearranged flag instantly blossomed from atop Federal Hall's third-story cupola, signaling to New York militia captain John Van Dyke the swearing-in had been concluded.[4] On command, 13 cannons crashed in sequence, sending random glass panes of nearby shops into jingling fragments as thousands of onlookers erupted in a flag-waving outburst of spirited huzzas and repeated cries of "God bless our Washington."

Had Laurance peered over Chancellor Livingston's black-robed shoulder, he would have spotted Alexander Hamilton on the opposite side of frenzied Wall Street, looking on from his residential balcony as the new President waved solemnly amid tumultuous cheers.[5] But Washington's most useful wartime aide could do no more than watch him bow again and again to an enraptured throng 10,000 strong that packed the surrounding streets. And though Hamilton had unnecessarily intrigued with seven or eight electors in Washington's landslide victory, he would play no role as America's most significant congressional sessions breathed life into the embryonic Constitution.

Vice President Adams at his side, the president retired to Peter L'Enfant's lavishly redecorated senate chamber and delivered the young republic's first inauguration speech. As Washington self-consciously intoned the humble remarks fellow Virginian James Madison helped prepare, Rep. Laurance could be forgiven for reflecting back to when, a week earlier, Philadelphia's immaculately clad Second Troop of Light Horse had deposited the president-elect's inaugural entourage in Elizabeth Town, New Jersey. There, Laurance, at the behest of Congress, was one of five representatives and four senators to formally receive the president-elect at Boxwood Hall, New Jersey Representative Elias Boudinot's elegant Georgian residence.[6]

Refreshed by a two-hour luncheon catered on Hannah Boudinot's London china and silver, the procession then made its triumphant way to Elizabeth Point, where Laurance boarded one of six dignitary-laden boats that accompanied Washington's magnificent 47-foot barge across the water to New York's Murray Wharf and a giddy city infused with self-importance. As 20 voices in choir from a passing schooner belted out a Washington-worshiping ode to the tune of "God Save the King," a pod of exuberant porpoises burst to the surface just when Spanish royal-packet ship *Galviston* unveiled scores of colorful flags in tribute, her crew at attention in the rigging and battery belching out in salute. "The very water," remembered Boudinot, seemed "to rejoice in bearing the precious burden over its placid bosom."[7] The celebratory entourage stepped ashore at the base of Wall Street, giving way for Governor Clinton and Mayor Duane to cordially embrace Washington amid a cacophony of warship cannonades, artillery volleys, clanging church bells, and huzzaing thousands. Never one to advertise his emotions, Laurance would have been a hard man indeed not to have reflected back 22 Aprils to his own far more plebian entry in this same harbor.

President Washington concluded his soft-spoken inaugural remarks with a flourish of the right hand that "left a rather ungainly impression" to the mind of Pennsylvania Senator William Maclay who thought him "agitated and embarrassed more than ever he was by leveled cannon or pointed Musket."[8] Rising as one with the president, the new government then trooped from Federal Hall into a cheering, militia-lined crowd and made its way down Broad Street to Broad Way's venerable St. Paul's Chapel. There, Laurance, in his own familiar house of worship until Trinity Church was restored, bowed head together with Washington and the others while Episcopal Bishop Samuel Provoost, senate chaplain, sealed the inauguration with prayer.

Now in his prime at the age of 38, Rep. Laurance was a tall, full-bodied man. "He was of commanding stature," recalled grandson George McWhorter, "somewhat portly, very erect in his carriage, according to what the Revolutionaries used to call the Baron Steuben School—and dignified & courteous in his demeanor. He was free from the shyness and stiffness which mark the insular Englishman in the same grade of society."[9] The congressman was also a prodigious reader of broad interests. "His fine library," wrote McWhorter, "was an evidence of his taste and mental inclination; but to know the British drama and classics in those days was deemed indispensible to a gentleman."[10] Frequent borrower from the New York Society Library,* John checked out more than 40 volumes—mostly for indisposed wife Betsey—between July and December 1789, ranging in subject from foreign travel and history to poetry, novels, and drama.[11] The Society Library, conveniently housed on Federal Hall's top floor, was readily accessible to Congress; even President Washington sampled its collection (two volumes remain more than 225 years past due!) during his brief New York residency.

Laurance was one of the most active members of the First Federal Congress, speaking to virtually every key issue in a conclave that more closely resembled a debating society on steroids than a well-oiled legislative machine. Hamilton, no speechifying slouch himself, had urged his friend's election because "our representative should be a man well qualified in oratory to prove that this city is the best station for that honorable body."[12] It was no inflated campaign rhetoric; in the absence of formal party leaders, standing committee chairmen, designated floor whips, or clerical staff of any kind, rhetorical prowess determined a congressman's influence. Laurance's every word—unlike in the closed-door Senate—reached two hanging galleries jammed with curiosity seekers, local newspaper reporters, and his own constituents. Any political faux pas, no matter how slight, provided conversational meat for local dinner tables. It was a voter intimacy that set him apart from 65 House peers who rented, boarded, or commuted to lower Manhattan.[13]

The first United States House of Representatives more often than not operated as a "committee of the whole" to facilitate less formal deliberation without the speaker in the chair. There were no standing committees other than the joint committee of enrolled bills that combined with Senate peers to facilitate inter-chamber communication.[14] Grand Committees, composed of one delegate from each state present, were elected for the most pressing matters. Temporary Committees were pulled together for most everything else. These three- to five-member working groups usually chose their own leaders and disbanded after delivering final reports to the full House. Workloads, as might be expected, were not evenly distributed.

---

*In 1754, William Livingston and other Presbyterian gentry founded New York Society Library as a civic educational alternative to Anglican King's College. It remains open to the public at 53 East 79th Street.

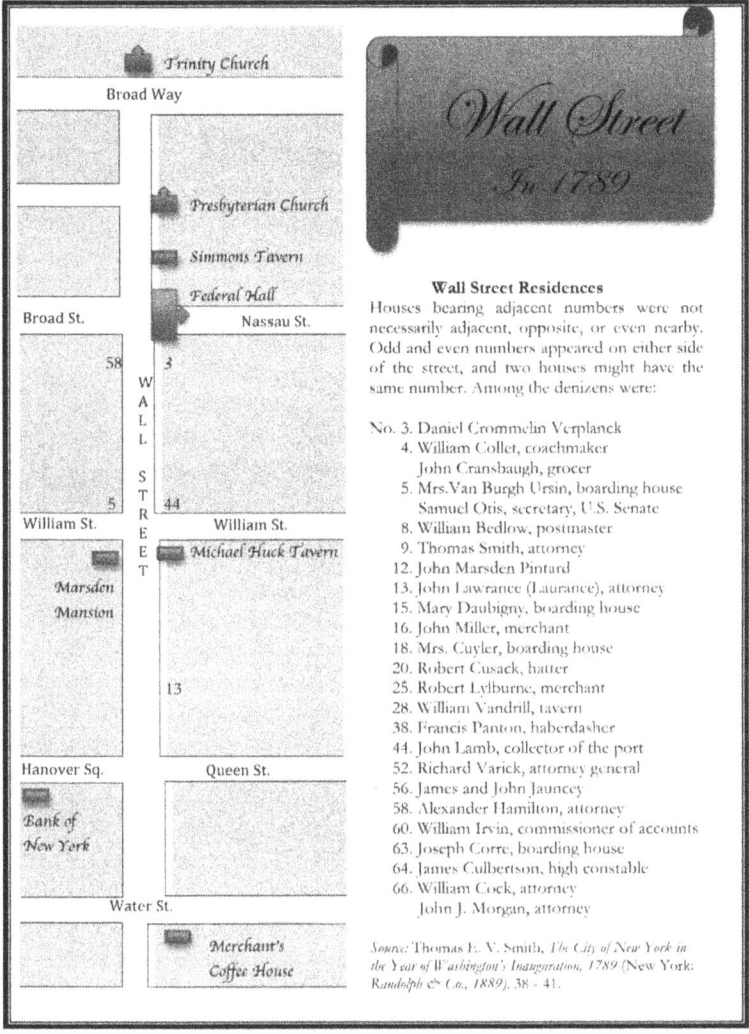

FIGURE 8 Wall Street in 1789.
(Original illustration reproduced with permission of the author.)

Persuasive, hard-working congressmen such as Laurance found themselves in perpetual demand while shirkers barely participated at all.

Speaker of the House Frederick Augustus Conrad Muhlenberg (1750-1801), despite his imperial-sounding name, was a democratic slice of frontier Pennsylvania German country pie. Ordained as a rural Pennsylvania Lutheran minister, he accepted call in 1773 to New York City's German-speaking Swamp Church. Seven years later, he quit the ministry to follow his true vocation as a radical pro-Independence politician. Quickly chosen speaker of the Pennsylvania Assembly, the distinguished-looking, sonorous-voiced former preacher served in the Continental Congress and was named president of the Pennsylvania Convention to ratify the Constitution. Although an early Federalist,

Muhlenberg was a policy moderate who chose not to use his position as a partisan tool.[15] His ready use of the committee of the whole—though promoting overlong debate—was a common touch that earned the confidence of fellow House members. And if congressional legend is to be believed, it was he who suggested the president of the United States should be addressed as "Mr. President" instead of "His High Mightiness" or "His Elected Majesty" as proffered by John Adams and the Senate.

Muhlenberg may have been elected speaker, but prime legislative mover of the First Federal Congress was Virginia Federalist James Madison. At first sight the short, shy, inconspicuous Madison might be taken for a timid black-clad church mouse of a man. Although soft-spoken, his words carried real clout. "The man of soundest judgment in Congress," wrote French minister Louis-Guillaume Otto, "he speaks nearly always with fairness and wins the approval of his colleagues."[16] What's more, the 38-year-old Madison was a legislative workaholic. After setting a near-perfect three-year attendance record in the Confederation Congress, he rarely left his seat except to speak during the sweaty Philadelphia summer of 1787 when the Constitution was hammered out. Possibly because he—like fellow Virginian Thomas Jefferson—fought the war in civilian clothes, Madison's vision of the federal government was rooted in the legislative branch. Nonetheless, he was in 1789 a firm Federalist who thought "excesses" of state legislatures jeopardized "the fundamental principle of republican government" and feared the executive branch was the "weak branch of the Government" in his evolving interpretation of the founding document of which he was a key architect.[17]

Not only did Laurance construe the Constitution more broadly than his influential southern counterpart, he was less concerned with implementing it to check officeholder appetite for power and more interested in employing the "necessary and proper" clause to build a powerful nation.[18] Moreover, John's constituency of northern manufacturers, merchants, repatriated loyalists, and self-interested moneymen gravitated toward London. Madison's electoral base tended to be agrarian, disposed to land banks rather than money banks, pro-slavery, and sympathetic with Revolutionary France. The diminutive Virginian by nature, in stark contrast to Laurance's pragmatic bent, conceived government as a moral force . . . an instrument of virtue that mercantile dependence on England could only taint. Even though both men were suspicious of parochial state government—there were no more than 11 Antifederalists in the first House— Laurance and Madison could not help but increasingly disagree as legislative flesh formed over the constitutional skeleton and debate moved to Treasury Secretary Hamilton's audacious economic agenda.

First priority for the new United States Congress was to stem hemorrhaging finances. While other delegates dawdled for weeks over newspapers and extended breakfasts awaiting a quorum, Madison served notice he intended to be the parliamentary ramrod that got things done.

"The deficiency in our treasury," he announced, "has been too notorious to make it necessary for me to animadvert upon that subject. Let us content ourselves with endeavoring to remedy the evil."[19] Anxious to put the nation's financial house in order, Madison, a week after the House achieved its first quorum, rose from his seat on April 8—three weeks before Washington's inauguration—to introduce a resolution for specific imposts on a broad range of imported goods. It was an ad valorem tax of 5 percent on all imports (exactly as in 1783), to which there was no objection.

On April 24, Madison moved to discriminate between goods landed from domestic and foreign vessels. Yes, American ships must face tonnage duties, he conceded, but at lower rates than foreign bottoms. Furthermore, vessels from countries with commercial treaties with the United States should enjoy favored treatment. Arguing that advantageous duties for American allies would "impress those Powers that have hitherto neglected to treat with us," the cogent Virginian urged his colleagues in effect to discriminate against British goods.[20] Parliament had gone out of its way in its Navigation Act of 1783 to exclude American bottoms from the West Indies trade and impose discriminatory imposts at British ports, so why should vessels flying the Union Jack pay the same tariff as those from France? Madison, piqued that Great Britain enjoyed the lion's share (up to 87 percent) of American trade, was out to break London's virtual monopoly by using duties as an instrument of national policy.[21]

Laurance would have none of it. Because New York merchants depended heavily on the British trade, he stood to challenge Madison's proposal of lower tonnage duties for French shipping than for English. Scanning a packed House gallery, John could not help but know he was playing to a mostly hometown crowd. "I would ask," he countered Madison, "if we have experienced advantages from the powers with which we have treaties, sufficient to entitle them to this preference?"[22] Answering his own question in the negative, John argued that Great Britain's disproportionately large share of America's burgeoning commerce was "not a point for the Government to settle."[23] Rather, he suggested: "The merchants of America are well able to understand and pursue their own interests." And northern merchants knew all too well that tonnage duty discrimination would inevitably lead to ruinous commercial warfare in which—as Laurance realistically pointed out—Great Britain, with only a sixth of her commerce at stake, had far greater capacity to injure America than vice versa.

Madison and Laurance also found themselves at odds over specific article duties. The Virginian's plea to maximize distilled spirit taxes at 15 cents a gallon on moral grounds sent Laurance leaping to his feet. "We are not," John replied, "to reason and determine on this subject as moralists, but as politicians."[24] Because higher taxes meant higher incentive for evasion and smuggling, the representative from New York proposed no more than 12 cents a gallon. Congress, in the end, compromised at 15 cents for rum and 12 on all other distilled spirits. Although differing on proposed molasses tax rates (the House sided with Laurance and Fisher Ames at six cents/gallon), the two emerging adversaries found it in their hearts to agree that imported beer merited an eight-cent duty. Still, the persuasive Madison pretty much had his way with tariffs in the House, including discriminatory rates on British goods. But it was a different matter in the Senate. There, an alarmed mercantile community convinced the body to strike discriminatory foreign duties from the House measure. "The Senate," exulted Massachusetts Rep. Ames, "God bless them, as if designated by Providence to keep rash and frolicsome brats out of the fire."[25] Distrustful of democracies, the 31-year-old Ames (Harvard '74) was an oratorically gifted, flat-out advocate of a strong federal government along the British example. To both his and Laurance's great satisfaction, Madison was unable to reinsert British import discriminations into the Tonnage Act of 1789 that sailed through the House by a 31 to 19 margin.

Rep. Laurance's consistent pro-British stance protecting New York merchants and importers so provoked Senator William Maclay that the prickly Pennsylvanian dubbed him "a mere tool for British Agents & factors."[26] Neither Fleet Street's tool nor Alexander Hamilton's, John instead voiced the interests of his constituency of merchants, shippers, manufacturers, and tradesmen.[27] He walked a fine line, favoring low tax rates on rum, wine, and molasses (imports of New York merchants), while arguing for protectively high import levies on candles and cordage manufactured by the city's artisans. Laurance was of course far from alone in looking out for constituent interests. Representative George Clymer sought protection for Pennsylvania steel and paper, Andrew Moore (Virginia) and Daniel Heister (Pennsylvania) for hemp, Daniel Carroll (Maryland) for glass, Fisher Ames for imported molasses, and Theodorick Bland with Josiah Parker for Virginia coal.[28]

Tonnage and impost matters addressed, House members turned to the administrative challenge that had spelled demise for the Confederated Congress—actually collecting the money. Not only might federal revenues be evaded by well-practiced smugglers working America's thousand-mile Atlantic coastline, but foreign import tariffs still constituted a significant share of state revenues. Laurance, his memory still fresh from New York Governor George Clinton's 1783 impost snub, stepped forward as principal author of the first key revenue collection measure, "House Collection Bill HR-11."[29] Nodding to John's legal experience with Port of New York admiralty and maritime complexities, the chamber followed his lead. After lengthy conversation with the Senate—a delay Senator Maclay guffawed at as mere tactic for New York merchants to pocket duties already added to prices—Laurance reported out the Collection Act of July 31, 1789. It created the young republic's largest civic bureaucracy of its day, establishing 60 federal districts, each with an official port of entry staffed by a naval officer, revenue collector, and surveyor. Ninety-eight secondary ports were designated for delivery only, catering to vessels whose cargo, paperwork, and duties had satisfactorily cleared a primary port of entry. Complete with countersigned permits, multi-copy invoices, official foreign exchange rates, and necessary record logs, the Collection measure could only have been drafted by a New York lawyer! As the Empire State's member of the grand committee for tonnages and imposts, John was also instrumental in producing a fourth revenue-related bill, the Coasting Act of September 1, 1789, as well as the Lighthouses Act of August 7, 1789.

In mid-June, the representatives resolved themselves into a committee of the whole to establish the executive branch. All knew that Article II of the new Constitution, with its economy of words defining executive selection, powers, and duties, was—in an age of kings—a bet-the-republic wager on presidential personal character. It was a bet on George Washington well worth placing, as Laurance knew from wartime experience and the Master of Mount Vernon's 15 years of demonstrated legitimacy and unassailable civic virtue. Even the monarchical fears of firm Antifederalist representatives Aedanus Burke, Elbridge Gerry, Richard Bland Lee, and Thomas Tudor Tucker must have softened somewhat when a humble Washington disclaimed any compensation in his inaugural address, urging Congress only pay for "such actual expenditures as the public good may be thought to require."[30] House Federalists nevertheless resolved to compensate the president whether he wanted it or not. No one desired a stronger federal executive than Rep. Laurance, but he rose to object when his peers proposed to also grant Washington an allowance to pay for house, furniture, carriages, horses, and clerical staff. John thought it an "emolument beyond the compensation contemplated in the Constitution."[31] His concern went much deeper than mere cost shaving; more important was the constitutional issue of presidential economic dependency on legislative whim. If Washington were given an expense account, what would prevent future congressmen from increasing or decreasing it at will to influence presidential decisions? Bowing to Laurance's reservations, lawmakers tactfully avoided the allowance hornet's nest altogether by voting an annual presidential salary ($25,000) sufficiently high to cover his expenses.

There was little debate over presidential appointment powers, for the Constitution expressly granted the office authority to appoint government officials with "advice and consent" of the Senate. But what about removal? "As the constitution has not given the President power of removability," argued wealthy South Carolina plantation owner William (the middle name Loughton was added in 1804) Smith, "it means that he should not have that power."[32] Weighing in to support his southern colleague, Massachusetts's Gerry warned of potential monarchism. "The President," he worried, "would soon swallow up the small security we have in the senate's concurrence in the appointment, and we shall shortly need no other than the authority of the Supreme Executive officer."[33] Gigantic, gruff James Jackson of Georgia went so far as to insist that department heads enjoyed constitutional status.[34]

Laurance and Madison, despite their tonnage duty and impost differences, wanted no part of Jackson's argument. Both supported presidential prerogative to remove incumbent appointees, but for different reasons. Madison, arguably the republic's premier constitutional expert, counseled House colleagues that power to appoint inherently included the power to remove. Laurance's concurring argument was based on practical expediency. Two and a quarter centuries later, his pragmatic words still resonate:

> It appears to me, that the power can be safely lodged here. But it has been said by some gentlemen that if it is lodged here, it will be subject to abuse; that there may be a change of officers, and a complete revolution throughout the whole executive department upon the election of every new President. I admit this may be the case, and contend that it should be the case if the President thinks it necessary. I contend that every President ought to have those men about him in whom he can place the most confidence, provided the Senate approves his choice . . . I see no reason why we should suppose he is more inclined to do harm than good.[35]

Echoing the same theme, Laurance spoke in favor of presidential power to determine administration salaries without senatorial consent under the Foreign Intercourse Act, the president's right to hire and compensate his own secretaries under the Compensation Act, and the president's right to issue writs under the Courts Act. When it came to actually collecting the nation's revenues, John, no doubt remembering doomed Confederation Congress fiscal reliance on state coffers, voted to empower the executive branch with federal collection responsibility.

Laurance and Madison were also simpatico on a potentially highly divisive matter: amending the Constitution to accommodate state concerns over its failure to guarantee basic civil liberties. Indeed, New York, Massachusetts, and Virginia ratifications expressly required such, the latter even mandating a second constitutional convention.[36] On May 6, the New Yorker dutifully presented his own state legislature's mandate for a second convention, although there is no evidence that he cared a whit for one or lifted even token finger to advance it. A second conclave subjecting the entire Constitution to reconsideration would undo the hard-won Philadelphia compromises of 1787. And that was a Pandora's box neither Laurance, nor Madison, nor most of Congress wanted any part of. When the politically astute Virginian on June 8 introduced a nine-amendment draft predecessor to the Bill of Rights, Laurance, rather than revive New York's convention proposal, deftly motioned that the House discuss amendments as a committee of the whole.[37] It was a motion that fellow Federalists Boudinot, Smith, and Delaware's "Jack" Vining refused to support, arguing together with Antifederalist Burke and vehement states-rightist Jackson that more pressing priorities faced the House. But Madison, as historian

Carol Berkin points out, thought the amendments essential to crush lingering Antifederalist opposition to the Constitution, as well as to induce belated ratification by Rhode Island and North Carolina.[38] Refusing to be stifled, the Virginian deftly shunted his nine draft amendments to a grand "Committee of Eleven," which, as committees are wont to do, expanded them into 17 proposed amendments. North Carolina subsequently joined the Union in November, followed by Rhode Island the following spring.

Although Laurance agreed with Madison on amending the Constitution, he differed dramatically on how to go about it. The latter urged amended language be incorporated directly into constitutional text, contending that a separate body of amendments "will create unfavorable comparisons between the two parts of the instrument and embarrass the people."[39] Laurance couldn't disagree more. "If they [amendments] should be engrafted in the body of the Constitution," he argued, "they will make it speak a language different from what it originally did." "Will it not," he asked rhetorically, "be vitiated thereby?"[40] When South Carolina Antifederalist Tucker then attempted to shift debate toward the agenda of five states (including New York) with amendment instructions, Laurance diplomatically set conversation back on track, opining that: "every member on this floor ought to consider himself the representative of the whole Union, not of the particular district which had chosen him."[41] As deliberations continued, John firmly resisted attempts to weave amendments into original constitutional text. Ultimately, with support from Representatives Benson, Boudinot, and Connecticut's Roger Sherman, Laurance's argument for a separate body of amendments prevailed. After a blasé Senate whittled the 17 proposed amendments down to 12, a two-thirds House majority on September 24 dispatched them—today's Bill of Rights—to the president for transmission to the individual states for ratification. The states in their wisdom ratified only 10. (The Eleventh Amendment, delaying laws affecting congressional salary from taking effect until after the next election of representatives, would not be ratified until 1992.)

Rep. Boudinot had on May 19 opened debate on the executive departments by proposing that a Department of Finance be established. Laurance's fellow New Yorker Egbert Benson broadened the discussion to also include Foreign Affairs and War. Little controversy surrounded the ensuing congressional acts establishing the Departments of State and War; but setting up the treasury department invited a warm polemic, for it was no secret that ambitious arch-Federalist Alexander Hamilton was President Washington's choice as treasury head. Could the brilliant West Indies immigrant be trusted to subordinate himself to legislative control? Antifederalist Virginian John Page thought not. Empowering treasury secretaries to "report plans to improve and manage the revenue and support the public credit," warned Page, was "an invitation to monarchy."[42] Having opposed the Constitution altogether, Rep. Tucker vociferously seconded Page. "How," asked Tucker, "can the business originate in this House, if we have it all reported to us by the Minister of finance?"[43] Equally suspicious of executive departmental authority, New Hampshire Rep. Samuel Livermore warned that the power of the purse was "too great, to be entrusted in any hands but those of the representatives of the people, where the Constitution deposited it."[44]

Laurance then demanded the floor to pooh-pooh any fears of congressional loss of control. "I see no danger," Laurance declared, "but a great deal of benefit, arising from the clause." As to the treasury secretary himself, Laurance reminded House colleagues that:

> By making it his duty to study the subject, we may reasonably expect information. Do we give him the power of deciding what shall be law? While we retain this power, he may give us all the information possible, but he can never be said to participate in legislative business; he has no control whatever over this House.[45]

Madison had not yet broken with his *Federalist Papers* coauthor; he was less concerned with Hamilton's appointment than in keeping the office's breadth of authority within constitutional bounds. Still, when the erudite Virginian stood to speak, Laurance must have held his breath ... only to smile when Madison declared to House colleagues: "I am at a loss to see where the danger lies."[46] With Laurance and Madison on the same page, the matter was settled in the House. Vice President Adams—as he had done on the removal issue—then cast the deciding vote in the deadlocked Senate, enabling Washington to sign into being a robust treasury department the second day of September.

Executive departments finally established, Congress turned its collective talent to the judiciary. The fact is that the traditional "capital F" founding figures had little to do with the creation of an empowered federal judicial branch. Indeed, it was Elbridge Gerry, James Wilson, and Gouverneur Morris who had the most to say about judicial prerogative during the Constitutional Convention.[47] And the Constitution itself did no more than mandate a Supreme Court and "such inferior courts as Congress may from time to time ordain." Antifederalists during ratification had regarded the very existence of Article III as a threat to the states. House strict constructionists now balked at the very principle of "inferior courts," claiming that state court jurisdiction would be violated. Madison, who might have been expected to have a hand in any federal courts scheme, was uncharacteristically silent, for he harbored grave concerns over "offensive violations to Southern jurisprudence."[48] Little wonder, then, that House discussion on the federal judiciary was put off until revenue and amendment matters were completed.

No such reservations distracted the overwhelmingly Federalist Senate. Early in April, northern senators seized the initiative to implement Article III in the chamber's very first legislative bill (SR-1). Substantially drafted by Connecticut lawyer Oliver Ellsworth, with contributions from

William Paterson of New Jersey and Caleb Strong of Massachusetts, the bill defined Supreme Court constituency, jurisdiction, and compensation before going on to create inferior federal district and circuit courts. When Ellsworth's 26-section draft reached House desks on July 18, it was not Madison but New Hampshire Rep. Livermore who moved to strike out all language instituting federal district courts. He had stoutly supported ratification as a member of the state constitutional convention but was nonetheless wary of creating "a Government within a Government" by filling "every state in the Union with two kinds of courts for the trial of many cases."[49] Livermore may also have been jealously guarding his own judicial turf, for the Princeton graduate (College of New Jersey '52) had since 1783 served as chief justice of the New Hampshire Superior Court of Judicature.

Laurance, whose wartime experience strongly predisposed him toward federal justice, defended Senate language in the broadest sense. "It is admitted, on all hands," said Laurance, "that necessity requires we should establish superior, and some inferior courts. The only question that then remained was to know how far this extended; it was not, therefore a question on principle, but a question of expediency, and in this view he considered the [Senate] bill to be proper."[50] When Livermore's motion to eliminate district courts was decidedly rejected by a 31 to 11 margin, the tight-fisted New Hampshire representative next contended that proposed $4,500 per annum compensation of the Supreme Court chief justice was too generous, proposing it be slashed to $3,000. Laurance again begged to differ: "To induce gentlemen of the first ability to come forward, and to place them in that situation which shall be above temptation, you cannot give them less a sum." Madison, Sedgwick, and South Carolinian Smith all supported their New York colleague, but only up to $4,000 per annum, a sum the House quickly approved.

Following seven scattered days of debate, the House returned the measure to the Senate with five amendments, but receded four with which the Senate had disagreed before a committee of the whole passed SR-1 without a roll call vote. Signed into law a week later by President Washington, "An Act to Establish the Judicial Courts of the United States" ranked among the First Congress's signal achievements. In a single stroke it created the position of attorney general and established a 6-member Supreme Court, 13 federal district courts, and 6 circuit courts to hear district court appeals, while spelling out precise jurisdictions for each.

When it came to the high-stakes competition for selecting the country's permanent seat of federal government, Rep. Laurance was as parochial as the next man. Because the question might well determine whether America assumed an agrarian or urban character, no subject was more contested. Indeed, almost two-fifths of all roll-call votes in the first two sessions of Congress had to do with the matter.[51] And Laurance as New York City's voice in these informal negotiations missed no opportunity to keep the new government in his own district as long as possible.

Even before Sir Guy Carleton's flotilla set sail for Britain in November 1783, Confederation delegates had jockeyed for position in a self-interested scrum to host the post-war government. Because no single site attracted support from a majority of states, flummoxed lawmakers compromised in October 1783 on rotating between two separate facilities. One near Trenton on the banks of the Delaware appeased northerners, while another near George Town on the Patowmac (as it was then generally spelled) won approval among southerners.[52] Until buildings on both sites were erected, Congress agreed to alternate between Annapolis and Trenton, a range of about 180 miles. In early June 1784, the New Jersey legislature pounced on its best chance to become the peripatetic body's permanent residence. Congress was offered jurisdiction over any district of its choice within the state to the extent of 20 square miles. Trenton sweetened the deal by refurbishing its largest tavern (*The French Arms*) as congressional venue and leasing a fine frame house as official residence for incoming President of Congress, Richard Henry Lee. Delighted at their potential good fortune, the citizens of Trenton proffered "attractive conveniences" including "Good Hay in any quantity," along with "free room and board" to attending delegates.[53] Local physician Dr. David Cowell's last will and testament even bequeathed "one hundred pounds to the United States of America" for erecting public buildings at nearby Lamberton.[54]

Once ensconced in grateful Trenton, the lawmakers resolved—over strong southern resistance—to establish a single federal town and voted to procure suitable buildings in the vicinity for "national purposes" with a sum not to exceed $100,000.[55] Three commissioners were then chosen to "lay out a district of not less than two nor exceeding three miles square on either side of the Delaware."[56] But the simultaneous presence of the New Jersey legislature rendered living quarters too inconvenient. New England delegates grumbled that New York was a more accessible venue, and the southern states, led by Virginia senator William Grayson with George Washington's behind-the-scene support, locked arms to drag out approval of final construction plans for a Trenton-area federal city.[57] Until a Delaware River site was ready for occupancy, delegates decided before adjourning for the Christmas holidays to reconvene in the City of New York on January 11, 1785.[58] Laurance was determined to ensure they never left.

More than simple provincial pride lay behind Laurence's maneuvering. Hosting the seat of government was an unmatched financial boon to his constituency, infusing some £100,000 hard specie per annum into the state.[59] Foreign diplomats and their retinues paid cash money for meals, lodging, and merchant goods, all the while gracing city streets in the latest European fashions. Although the "Buttonwood Agreement" among some two dozen Wall Street brokers to organize securities trading lay three years in the future, capital flowed into Bank of New York as word spread that not only would devalued government securities be refinanced, but state debt would be assumed by the federal government as well. The rising financial tide accompanying the seat of federal government of course lifted all boats, including the well-placed legal practices of Laurance, Troup, and Hamilton.

From House floor maneuvers to backroom wheeling and tavern table jawboning, Laurance labored to keep the seat of government in his own district. Immediately, he disputed the validity of New Jersey congressional elections when the decidedly pro-Philadelphia western New Jersey delegation apparently hijacked the outcome. Not only had polling hours been arbitrarily lengthened in some counties, but Governor William Livingston (who leaned toward Philadelphia in hope of snaring a role for Trenton) also went so far as to declare election winners before pro-New York Essex County votes were even counted. "I think it must result," proclaimed Laurance, "that the election of the present members from New Jersey was not conformable to the law, and therefore not valid."[60] After particularly delicate debate, the specially appointed House committee chose not to intervene, pronouncing—to Laurance's utter dismay—the sitting New Jersey representatives "duly elected and returned."[61] In hope of later derailing momentum for a Potomac location, the New Yorker later motioned (unsuccessfully) to substitute Baltimore as permanent seat of government.[62]

As July turned to August and then to September, a permanent site for the new federal government remained unresolved. "Gentlemen should look," John beseeched his House peers on September 3, "to those parts of the country where was the highest population . . . where was the substantial wealth, the strength of the union, the means by which the United States were to be protected, and the sources from which the government was to draw its principal supports."[63] It was a northern state sales pitch for sure, but delivered so smoothly that the fawning local *Daily Gazette* later pronounced him "so extremely candid and generous" that "it would have been difficult for a spectator . . . to have judged whether he was a representative from the City of New York."[64]

On paper, Laurance's case for keeping New York as temporary seat of government was a strong one. On any given day, a hundred vessels might be glimpsed discharging and loading cargoes along East River wharves. In addition to being on its way to becoming the greatest port in the world (surpassing Philadelphia in tonnage in 1794), New York City possessed the financial capital to ensure a splendid national civic infrastructure. Its population—33,131 in 1790—was arguably largest in the United States.* Its streets were mostly paved and since 1762 had been illuminated with lamps on posts. Boasting a cosmopolitan population, an infatuation with the latest English fashions, 400 taverns, and 7 newspapers, New Yorkers were blessed with a dozen bookstores dotting Franklin

---

*Philadelphia's population was 28,522 without suburbs and 42,444 with them. Only New York, Philadelphia, Boston, Charleston, and Baltimore exceeded 10,000 people in a nation of four million.

Square and Pearl and Water Streets. The John Street Theatre even drew President Washington for its performances. Moreover, Gotham's facility was tangible, as opposed to hypothetical sites touted by the Virginian and Maryland legislatures as well as inhabitant petitioners from along the Delaware, Susquehanna, and Patowmac Rivers.

New York, however, was anathema to Madison, Jefferson, and even Washington's concept of a yeoman republic. Only a Potomac location, argued Madison, would signal to southerners and westerners that northern financial and commercial interests had not usurped the new government. It was a matter of principle in which he simply would not compromise. And southern representatives, their numbers inflated by slaves at three-fifths of a person for districting purposes, had the votes to ensure legislative gridlock on the matter. So despised was Hamilton's home city to Madison and the Virginia delegation that they wanted no part of a late May bargain proposed by New Yorkers conceding the permanent seat of government to the Potomac in return for the temporary residence. Instead, southerners (excepting South Carolina and Georgia) coalesced around Madison to broker an early September backroom deal with Pennsylvania to make Philadelphia the temporary seat of government and fix the permanent site near the Potomac. Learning of the arrangement, New England delegates hurriedly huddled with Rep. Laurance and Senator King to craft a tempting counterproposal, which King and Benjamin Goodhue of Massachusetts laid before the Pennsylvanians.[65] Would Pennsylvania, in return for the permanent seat on the Susquehanna's east bank, insist New York retain temporary seat until the new buildings were completed? Next day, Pennsylvania Senator Robert Morris whispered to King that the Keystone State had agreed to the proposal.

Accordingly, Laurance, Fisher Ames, and George Clymer were appointed by the House to prepare a bill establishing the permanent seat of government on the Susquehanna.[66] Madison, enraged at King and Laurance's complicity, moved at the measure's first reading to strike out New York as temporary residence. When Laurance, then Ames and Smith, rose to squash the motion, the normally reserved Virginian, in a rare moment of public discomposure, vented his frustrations on the outspoken New Yorker. Jaws dropped as the flustered Madison bitterly suggested Virginia would not have ratified the Constitution had it known of such northern tyranny. It was a shocking outburst that Madison later attempted to clarify. "In reply to Mr. Laurance," he wrote, "I was led by his manner and other circumstances of the moment, to declare . . . that if the . . . proceedings on the subject under debate, could have been prophetically brought to that [Virginia] Convention, the State of Virginia might not now be party to the Union."[67] There was just something about the Anglophile, abolitionist New York representative that got under Madison's normally unruffled southern skin.

Madison's reservations notwithstanding, the House on the third week in September voted 31 to 17 to pass HR-25: "An Act to Establish the Seat of Government of the United States." Not only was the Pennsylvania/ New York/Eastern States deal sealed, but the secretary of the treasury was also directed to borrow $100,000 to purchase land and buildings for the permanent site.

Had the Senate approved HR-25 as written, America's 10-square-mile capital district might today grace the Susquehanna rather than the Potomac. But just when the matter appeared settled, Pennsylvania Senator Morris proposed a self-interested amendment that threw the entire arrangement off track. Morris by the fall of 1789 was the most powerful man in the Senate. Fiscal savior of the Confederation Congress as superintendent of finance during the dark days of 1780–1781, he was universally respected for his financial acumen, ability, and public character. Like President Washington, Robert Morris was also of the ethic that blended personal and public values to serve the nation; and like Washington, who harbored similar sentiments for the Potomac, he now thought it not inappropriate for the nation to situate its permanent seat on lands he owned near the falls of the Delaware. In late September, Morris surprised most of the Pennsylvania delegation (and disgusted fellow senator Maclay) by moving to *amend* House Bill HR-25 to include Germantown and parts of Bucks County, some seven miles to the north of Philadelphia.[68] As a construction incentive, he promised $100,000 (more than $3 million today) of his own funds. New York Senators King and Schuyler quickly agreed to support Morris's amendment in return for the promise to block removal from New York for three years. "Indeed," scribbled King, "such a deal passed the Senate!"[69]

Just when southern hopes for a Potomac seat of government appeared dashed, James Madison played a final political card. Knowing that Laurance and his fellow New York delegates would go to any length to keep hope alive for their city as permanent seat, the shrewd Virginian convinced them to support a minor amendment to the bill and return it to the Senate. And there it lay when House Speaker Muhlenberg on September 29 gaveled to a close the remarkable opening session of the First Federal Congress. Not only had Madison successfully played New York against Pennsylvania to keep the Potomac option afloat, but New Yorkers could also take comfort that their own double game postponed indefinitely any removal from Manhattan.

In what had become "a sort of continuing constitutional convention," John Laurance emerged from the First Federal Congress's inaugural session as a forceful, practical voice of nationalistic, commercially ambitious New York City.[70] Before the very eyes of his own constituents, he had ensured that necessary tonnage duties and tariffs did not gut the important London trade. And he helped put real teeth in executive branch departments while endowing broad jurisdiction to the new Federal judiciary. All without Washington, Adams, Jefferson, Jay, or Hamilton in the room. Perhaps most importantly to New Yorkers, he and Senator King had also delayed any decision that might permanently jeopardize the city's lucrative status as political center of the new United States.

With the first session's legislative heavy lifting now behind him, John enjoyed nothing better than hunting grouse in party with friends and political allies. Inquiring of his availability one crisp October day, Vice President Adams was informed by wife Abigail that Laurance, together with Rufus King, Adams's son-in-law Colonel William Stephens Smith, and three others were occupied on Long Island shooting birds.[71] When not in the fields with his friends, John found time for family and church. Restoration of his beloved Trinity was well advanced, but the new structure would not be consecrated until the following spring. In the meantime, Bishop Samuel Provoost's services continued at nearby St. Paul's Chapel, which may as well have been named "Federalist Chapel." John Jay was a warden, Benson, Hamilton, King, and Laurance were regular attendees, and President Washington made it his local house of worship.

Several of the St. Paul's group, in the spirit of the holiday season, gathered for dinner on the 17th of December as guests of President and Mrs. Washington. The president, having not yet moved into the spacious Macomb House on Broad Way whose high-ceilinged public rooms accommodated as many as 27 at table, made do in the fashionable but smaller three-story brick Franklin-Osgood mansion on St. George's Square.[72] Joining Rep. and Mrs. Laurance at the president's table were Bishop Provoost, Supreme Court Chief Justice John Jay with wife Sarah, and Reverend Dr. William Lynn and his lady, together with stout Federalists Egbert Benson and Rufus King.[73] Eccentric Antifederalist Massachusetts Rep. Elbridge Gerry (who had attended the Philadelphia Constitutional Convention but refused to sign the document) rounded out the company for conversational spice.

Conspicuously absent as the president's claret and champagne were drained that festive evening was another St. Paul's churchgoer who had swiftly become the new government's second most powerful man. Alexander Hamilton, appointed secretary of the treasury two weeks before Congress had adjourned, headed the largest civilian department of the new federal structure. Through five principal subordinates, he would direct a treasury staff of more than 30 clerks, a true administrative empire compared to Departments of State (four) and War (three). The long arm of Treasury Secretary Hamilton also extended across a national network comprising hundreds of tax collectors, surveyors, and naval officers who administered customs, revenue, and navigational services. While all of New York savored seasonal holiday joys, the treasury secretary was hard at work. Immediately after taking office he had arranged a $50,000 bridge loan from Bank of New York to cover government operating expenses, and then he had written to Philadelphia's Bank of North America for another $50,000. Late into December, midnight oil burned in the treasury's new office near the Old Exchange at the corner of Broad and Dock Streets as Hamilton crafted an explosive paper that would ignite the First Congress's most acrimonious debate. It was nothing less than a complete retooling of the new republic's financial underpinnings.

PART III

Knight in Washington's "Republican Court"

ELEVEN

Federalist Warhorse

NEW YORK CITY, JANUARY 14, 1790. Five days into the First Federal Congress's second session, Treasury Secretary Hamilton's bombshell *Report Relative to a Provision for the Support of Public Credit* did not so much arrive as to detonate on the House floor. At 165 pages long, the figure-packed 40,000-word tome was a far cry from the informational document congressmen had requested in September. Instead of the expected modest recommendations to pay down the public debt, Hamilton proposed nothing less than sweeping the national financial stables clean. Raising revenue through sales of western land and controversial "whiskey taxes" was only a first step. The centerpiece of the *Report* was a sophisticated menu of borrowing scenarios to refinance the entire national debt as well as assume state obligations. It was a blueprint for funding a strong central government that would pave the way for a capitalist economy in a nation of farmers.

The $77.1 million public debt was a staggering sum, calculated by Harvard Business School Professor Thomas McCraw to have then represented around 31 percent of total United States gross domestic product (GDP).[1] To Secretary Hamilton's mind, this liability consisted of three discomfiting components: 1) foreign debt and accrued interest of about $11.7 million, 2) domestic debt amounting to $40.4 million, and 3) war debts of the states approximating $25 million.[2] First priority was a "sacred obligation" to discharge the foreign debt in full, plus interest. Otherwise the new federal government would be unable to establish credit at a time when ability to borrow was paramount. Next, asserted Hamilton, was the need for government securities (past, present, and future) to trade at full face value, or else the paper would lose liquidity as a circulating hard-specie substitute and thereby erode the value of the fledgling U.S. dollar. A weak dollar, in turn, would undermine the national credit. Secretary Hamilton therefore insisted on paying off the entire $40 million domestic debt at full face value. To do so, he proposed that new federal debt certificates be issued to retire a bewildering array of Continental Loan Office bills of exchange, "Short Bobs" (treasury drafts from the hand of Superintendent of Finance Robert Morris), quartermaster and commissary IOUs, army paymaster-general notes, Confederation Congress warrants, and federal "indents" of interest.

There was more. If backed up by a sinking fund* with publicly scheduled buybacks using surplus post office revenues, Hamilton contended that the new debt certificates could pay lower interest than the retired paper and still hold face value.³ Simply put, much of the accumulated domestic debt bearing 6 percent interest would be refinanced at lower interest rates, while indent certificates on unpaid accrued interest would be slashed to 4 percent (later reduced to 3 percent by the Senate). And with no specific expiration date on the new notes, the government preserved the option of calling them in at a discount if general interest rates fell below 4 percent. With European interest rates hovering at 3–4 percent, Hamilton gambled it was a creditor risk worth taking, particularly since United States government 6 percent notes were then trading at only 70 percent of par value. As to state war debts of $25 million, he offered an eyebrow-raising solution: let the new federal government assume most of them.

House debate over the provocative *Report* began on Monday, February 8. Resolving the chamber into a committee of the whole, Speaker Muhlenberg impartially turned over the chair to Yale-educated 35-year-old former Congregationalist minister Abraham Baldwin of Georgia. Both Muhlenberg and Baldwin saw merit in the treasury secretary's complex proposal, but others feared dire consequences. "It will add strength and power," growled suspicious South Carolina Rep. Burke, "to that faction that brought about the late 2^d revolution [the Constitution], and it will make their princely fortunes."⁴

Paying down the foreign debt was never an issue. Even the staunchly Antifederalist Burke conceded that retiring foreign loans, plus interest, was a matter of national honor. There were, however, in the House of Representatives, two sets of "ready-made enemies" to the treasury secretary's plan of retiring the domestic debt at par.⁵ A frontier faction from Georgia and back-country South Carolina, Pennsylvania, and New Hampshire coalesced around huge, uncouth—yet deceptively articulate—Georgia representative James Jackson. The second faction, led by formidable James Madison, consisted mostly of delegates from the tobacco-growing regions of Maryland, Virginia, and Tidewater North Carolina. Yes, Madison acknowledged Hamilton's need for establishing the public credit, but he was not about to tax southern constituents to support a public debt substantially incurred by the northern states. Jackson's frontier faction opposed paying off the debt at face value for an altogether different reason: it ruined fortune-making schemes to gobble up state-owned western lands using heavily depreciated public securities.

---

*Four years earlier, William Pitt the Younger had employed sinking funds to reduce Great Britain's national debt. First introduced in 1716 by Chancellor of the Exchequer Stanhope and perpetuated by successor Robert Walpole, sinking funds were dedicated pools of money established to repay or purchase outstanding loans and securities. If set up outside of legislative hands (to prevent raiding the fund in crises), sinking funds promoted public confidence, supported securities pricing, and bolstered public credit.

Treasury Secretary Hamilton, for all his genius, never graced the House floor to counter Jackson, Madison, or anyone else's speechifying. Because Article I, Section Seven of the new Constitution mandated that "all bills raising revenue shall originate in the House of Representatives," the primary burden for rendering Hamilton's *Report* into law fell to a now-forgotten cadre of legislative founding Federalists. Over the next three years, Laurance, William Smith of South Carolina, Elias Boudinot of New Jersey, and Massachusetts Reps. Sedgwick and Ames would constitute a pro-administration battering ram that advanced Hamilton's transformative financial agenda and protected his back from vicious political assault.[6] None, however, was personally closer to the treasury secretary than Rep. Laurance, who also brandished presidential trust earned from five years on Washington's wartime staff. Close reading of Gales and Seaton's *History of Debates in Congress* suggests that Laurance, first-session committee leader on both appropriations and revenue matters, was arguably Hamilton's most effective House champion.

True, the treasury secretary's proposed par value refinancing, sinking fund, and use of circulating debt notes as currency were patterned after the English model. But Laurance's whole-hearted backing of Hamilton's *Report* likely owed less to his own English roots or his friend's persuasiveness than to Great Britain's stunning international economic success. By the time Adam Smith published his epic *The Wealth of Nations* (1776), Britain, with its strong central Bank of England, 50 London banks, and 100 country banks had, through fractional-reserve lending, supplanted metallic specie with bank notes for the first time in world monetary history.[7] Every ounce of gold in British vaults multiplied itself several times over through paper notes, drafts, and checks, giving the island nation (backed by its invincible Royal Navy) a significant competitive advantage over Bourbon France, where an ounce of King Louis's gold remained but one ounce. Indeed, since the 1720 collapse of the *Banque Générale*, no French national bank had the power to issue paper money until First Consul Napoleon Bonaparte established the *Banque de France* in 1800. Ever the pragmatist, Laurance advocated the English model because it *worked*, particularly for men of property with capital to invest.

He demanded the floor after a Jackson backcountry follower, Pennsylvania Rep. Thomas Scott, proposed something no British Chancellor of the Exchequer dare suggest: discount the domestic debt. When Scott argued on February 9 that domestic debt was simply too large to retire at face value, Laurance countered sharply. Harking back to congressional promises made to General Washington's army, he reminded lawmakers of their fiduciary duty:

> Shall we go to our officers and soldiers who served during the late war, individually, and say that the balance struck to be due them is an imposition on the public, when the Government itself

has determined that they were entitled to such particular reward? If, at the time those securities were given to them, Government had paid them in money, would any gentleman now contend that their accounts be reliquidated, and every individual called upon to refund a part of what he acquired in conformity to the laws of his country? ... The nature of the case, I conceive is perfectly the same; and we are duty bound to make a full compensation.[8]

As to those who questioned the whole idea of a sinking fund, Laurance again sprang to Hamilton's defense:

My mind, Mr. Chairman, inclines to approve of permanent funds for that purpose; because I believe, more public benefit will result from such a measure than any other; it will destroy that fluctuation which renders a public debt injurious, and will give it that stability necessary to introduce it as a circulating medium, by which numerous advantages will arise to the agricultural, commercial and manufacturing interests.[9]

Laurance could only have been stunned when James Madison rose not to agree but to mount a completely unexpected all-out attack on Hamilton's funding program. Madison at the Philadelphia Convention of 1787 had favored assumption of state debts, all the while opposing discrimination between original and secondary debt holders. How could the Master of Montpelier now stand to argue the very opposite? It was a puzzling reversal that owed in part to a vociferous anti-government earful received from his Virginia constituents between congressional sessions. These strident blasts, together with his earlier unexpected rejection by state legislators for appointment to the U.S. Senate, certainly shaped Madison's new Virginia-first perspective.[10] Political pressures aside, Madison, given his moral probity, was also genuinely bothered that almost three-quarters of domestic debt certificates, having been disposed of at a huge discount, were no longer in the hands of original holders. "There must be, something radically wrong," he lamented to Edmund Pendleton, "in suffering those who rendered a bona fide consideration to lose 7/8 of their dues, and those who have no particular merit towards their country to gain 7 or 8 times as much as they advanced."[11]

Determined to rectify matters (and spare Virginia's public coffers), Madison on February 15 formally motioned to discriminate between original and subsequent holders of domestic debt certificates. Paying off current holders at full face value, he contended, "defrauded" original holders. Why should war veterans, civilian lenders, and those whose property had been confiscated subsidize undeserved windfalls to despised wealthy northern speculators? In Massachusetts, for example, almost 80 percent of all federal securities were no longer with original subscribers.

No sooner had Madison resumed his seat than Laurance requested the floor. Politely acknowledging his Virginia colleague's "talents and knowledge," John reminded House colleagues that public debt certificates were legal contracts.[12] Congress had recognized them as such in its 1783 recommendation to set funds aside to pay interest due. "This recommendation was unequivocal," he continued, "and made no discrimination between the possessor and the original owner."[13] Madison's resolution, John argued, no matter how admirable, "would be a violation of the contract" and there was "no right in the legislature to impair the force of it."[14]

Turning to his peers, Laurance then asked why, if the new government refused to uphold the basic tenets of contracts, would the citizenry and domestic creditors ever want to purchase future issues of federal government debt? Next, he pronounced Madison's policy of discrimination an administrative nightmare in which the logistics of finding original issuers and creditors would prove time consuming and costly, if not impossible. "Part of the army was composed of foreigners," Laurance noted, adding emphatically that "Many had left the country; others were dead."[15] And what, Laurance queried, of the expense to track down original holders of hundreds, if not thousands, of certificates issued by public officers to purchase military supplies in the field? "The scheme of the gentleman from Virginia," he concluded, "would add a considerable sum to the provision proposed by the Secretary and an additional number of officers to carry his plan into execution."[16]

Every man in the chamber knew, of course, that Rep. Laurance's constituency had the most to lose if Madison's discrimination motion carried. New Yorkers held as much as one-sixth of the entire government debt note balance, and New York City was undisputed national center of securities speculation. Influential brokers like Herman LeRoy and William Bayard together with Constable & Co. (whose partners included former congressional financier Robert Morris) established trading prices for the whole country, while a fleet of Manhattan merchants served as clearing house agents for foreign buyers of American notes. From Mayor James Duane to Senators King and Schuyler to William Duer and Gouveneur Morris, most leading New York Federalists had accumulated respectable certificate portfolios. And Laurance himself, though primarily invested in real estate, was a security holder and an "operator in public stocks."[17] Much the same could be said for almost half of his House peers.[18] Even evolving Massachusetts Antifederalist Eldridge Gerry held almost $50,000 in Continental and state securities. Not surprisingly, then, the House on February 22 roundly defeated Madison's discrimination motion 36 to 13.[19] Laurance, Sedgwick, and Ames's collective argument, despite a general suspicion of non-agrarian high finance, carried the issue; sanctity of contracts and preservation of the public credit trumped all.

If domestic debt redemption at par raised the temperature of debate, Hamilton's call for the federal government to assume state war debts was gasoline on the fire. Southern states (excepting South Carolina) had paid down much of their wartime debt and were in no mood to also shoulder a portion of northern state obligations. Assumption, to their anti-administration minds, represented an invasive, unconstitutional consolidation of government that emasculated state autonomy. "Absorption of revenue will certainly follow Assumption of debt," warned agitated Virginia Rep. Richard Bland Lee, "so that our state governments will have little else to do than eat drinke and be merry."[20] Other prominent Virginians were equally vehement. Staunch Antifederalist John Taylor (Laurance's wartime deputy judge advocate) of Caroline County worried the plan would lead to a "court-style English government" that facilitated "accumulation of great wealth in a few hands."[21] On the floor of Virginia's General Assembly, an incensed Patrick Henry and Henry Lee led a formal remonstrance against assumption. And James Madison, having fought Hamilton's financial program at every turn, dug in his feet. What followed was according to Thomas Jefferson "the most bitter and angry contest ever known in Congress before or since the union of the states."[22]

Before the assumption debate could start, Quaker objections to the slave trade unexpectedly burst onto the House floor. If interjecting the slavery issue was not Federalist strategy to drive a wedge between Madison and fellow southerners, it should have been. Madison, although morally opposed to the reprehensible practice, had to tread carefully because of his own constituency's strong pro-slavery bent. During earlier revenue-raising debates, he had floated a $10 per slave tax proposal to "save ourselves from reproaches and our country from the imbecility ever attendant on a country filled with slaves." Economic reality, however, placed the diminutive Virginian at odds with his own words; James Madison owned over a hundred slaves on his 2,650-acre Montpelier estate and, unlike Washington and Jefferson, freed none of them—family lore to the contrary—when he died, not even Paul Jennings, his literate valet of 20 years.[23] Were House Federalists somehow to back Madison on principle into an anti-slavery corner, they just might pocket a bargaining chip to negotiate closure on assumption.

It all began innocently enough on February 11, when Irish-born Pennsylvania Rep. Thomas Fitzsimons—a firm believer in strong federal government and an ardent abolitionist—rose to present a humble address from his Quaker constituents. Wide-eyed delegates then heard the Society of Friends castigate the "national iniquity of trafficking in the persons of fellow men" and demand Congress "to the full extent of your power" endeavor to "produce the abolition of the slave trade."[24] If Laurence didn't orchestrate the slavery brouhaha, he certainly had a hand in things, for no sooner had the Philadelphia Quaker case been made, than he stood to deliver a similar address from the "Quaker Society of Friends in the city of New York."[25] His abolitionist credentials, after all, went back some five years as a founding member of the New York Manumission Society.

No sooner had John resumed his chair then Pennsylvania Federalist Thomas Hartley, as if on cue, motioned "as mark of respect" to refer the addresses to a committee. Virginia Federalist Alexander White quickly seconded. South Carolinian Smith respectfully asked that the matter be tabled altogether, an opinion repeated less delicately by Rep. Jackson of Georgia. Sensing potential explosion of tempers, Mr. Madison reminded his colleagues "not to be alarmed." "They will recollect," he continued, "that the Constitution secures to the individual States the right of admitting, if they think proper, the importation of slaves into their own territory, for eighteen years not yet expired."[26]

Next day, a third anti-slavery petition was read, this one from the Pennsylvania Abolition Society signed by Benjamin Franklin himself. As subsequent discussion heated up, Maryland Rep. Michael Stone warned that if Congress showed serious attention to the Quaker petitions, the price of slave property would decline injuriously to a great number of citizens in the southern states. Laurance responded in words that tell us much about his uniquely pragmatic political character. Although clearly disgusted by the slave trade, he rose to dispute Stone not on moral grounds but on pecuniary ones. "I think the gentleman from Maryland," intoned Laurance, "carries his apprehensions too far, when he fears the negro property will fall in value." Rather, Laurance opined, forces of supply and demand would ensure "the value of a slave would be increased instead of diminished" should Congress "abolish a traffic which is a disgrace to human nature."[27]

Before the debate unleashed by Quaker petitions had run its course, emotions on both sides reached extremes. Slavery, contended Rep. Jackson, was "not only allowed by the Savior but positively commended by the Bible."[28] Laurance interposed to wonder how any Christian could imbibe the Sermon on the Mount and believe it compatible with slavery. Preferring to leave God's will to others, Elbridge Gerry suggested Congress had constitutional right under the commerce clause to use western land sales to purchase and free all slaves in the south. To which South Carolinian Tucker prophetically thundered: "Do these men expect a general emancipation of slaves by law? This would never be submitted to by the Southern States without a civil war."[29] In the end, a House vote of 43 to 14 referred the three Quaker petitions to a select committee that three weeks later filed a sympathetic but toothless report that tabled the controversial matter. The nimble Madison, by voting with the majority while also opining congressional hands were constitutionally tied, had deftly avoided any trap.

On February 23, the House convened as a committee of the whole to address assumption of state debts. "I must own," announced Laurance at the outset, "that I am at present in favor of assuming the State debts; I think I discover great advantages resulting therefrom."[30] After jowly Samuel Livermore proposed the subject was too complex to be addressed so soon, the New Yorker stood to disagree. "The objections made by the gentleman from New Hampshire," John smiled, "may be easily obviated."[31] In the practical voice House peers had come to know, he reminded lawmakers that Treasury Secretary Hamilton clearly ascertained that total claims upon the states did not exceed $25,000,000. And if certain delegates doubted Hamilton's veracity, "Congress may bind them to that amount, that they shall not go further." Dismissing the matter's complexity, Laurance declared:

> I believe it will be much easier, and more productive, for one body to draw forth the resources of the Union, than it will be for many. Supposing the whole [debt] must be satisfied, I am led to conclude it might be done with greater ease, less expense, and more facility if it was all provided for under one general system.[32]

Despite near universal southern opposition to assumption, Laurance found an unlikely ally in prosperous, well-connected South Carolina planter/lawyer William Smith. The sleek, aristocratic-looking Smith, having sat out the War for Independence in London, returned in November 1783 to gain admission to the Charleston bar, marry the second daughter of influential low-country planter Ralph Izard, and fervently support ratification of the proposed Constitution. Although opposing Laurance on the Quaker anti-slavery petitions, he had repeatedly joined him in voting against locating the seat of government on the Potomac. Serving on 33 committees over his four House terms, and reporting out for 13, Smith emerged as Federalist warhorse stable-mate to Laurance, Sedgwick, and Ames.[33] Not surprisingly, federal assumption of South Carolina's massive four-million-dollar war debt was high on his agenda.[34]

Following two nonproductive days of assumption debate by the House sitting as a committee of the whole, Madison shrewdly proposed that each state be required to make a final "settlement" of accounts with the federal government before any assumption plan took place. According to Madison's calculations, Virginia under Hamilton's assumption plan would be responsible for contributing some $5 million to federal coffers in return for only $3 million of assumed debts.[35] "The State which has already paid off what it owed," argued Madison, should not "be burthened to pay the debts of the other states."[36] Laurance politely rejected the Virginian's "settlement" proposal as self-serving: "No State can be a debtor to the United States, because every State has furnished more than she has received from the Union."[37] Still, Madison's amendment eventually passed after long discussion. Final accounting, however, by the Treasury General Board of Accounts later gutted Virginia's settlement claims. Instead of Madison's expected $2,000,000 credit due Virginia, she received but $100,000.[38]

What most peeved Madison and his southern colleagues during the assumption debates was the furious speculation in state government obligations. Every congressman knew that advance word of Hamilton's assumption plan had leaked to Yankee moneymen—not from the scrupulous treasury secretary, but from Assistant Secretary William Duer. Wealthy Philadelphia merchant William Bingham, a close friend of Duer, quickly floated a £60,000 Amsterdam loan for speculative ends.[39] Pocketing an $8,000 bribe, the nefarious Duer directed treasury business to Boston financier Andrew Craigie, who consequently bought up large sums of South Carolina debt from original holders for as little as seven cents on the dollar.[40] Another prominent insider, Connecticut Rep. Jeremiah ("swift vessel") Wadsworth, dispatched two express schooners southward to buy up state certificates for 10 cents on the dollar. And Duer himself, in a conflict of interest as flagrant as it was unprincipled, pooled some $170,000 together with New York financier William Constable into North and South Carolina debt certificates.[41] Such schemes concentrated state debt paper in alarmingly few hands. Fewer than 100 investors, for example, controlled 72 percent of North Carolina's debt.[42] And 78 New Yorkers owned more than 11 percent—some $2,717,754—of all state debt.[43]

Animated congressional debate did not escape President Washington's political antennae. Hoping perhaps to lower political temperatures, the president invited Representatives Madison and Laurance to a social dinner on March 11, along with Speaker of the House Muhlenberg and nine other legislators.[44] Adding color to the evening was artist John Trumbull, premier painter of the War for Independence and brief aide-de-camp to General Washington in 1776. He resigned the army the following year over a dispute regarding the dating of his commission, but in truth, the ascetic Harvard graduate ('73) was not cut out for soldiering.

In 1780, Trumbull traded sword for paintbrush and sailed for Europe to perfect his craft. Returned from London and Paris, the empty-pocketed artist now struggled to make ends meet by catering to a select society portrait clientele. His larger vision was a series of grand canvases commemorating the young republic's most important moments. Having begun the first of these large works (his monumental *Declaration of Independence*) with Jefferson's assistance in Paris, Trumbull next determined to produce a large canvas of New York's presidential inauguration. By filling the background with detailed faces of prominent, recognizable politicians, the penurious artist hoped to fatten future commissions. Apparently for this very purpose, Trumbull in 1792 rendered a flattering nine-inch miniature of a well-fed, pink-cheeked John Laurance (fig. 9) in full powdered wig. The grand inauguration canvas, alas, never came to fruition and Laurance's miniature found its way into family parlors.

On April 12, Hamilton's assumption proposal was put to its first House vote. After sharp exchanges (several members were called to order) fractured the chamber on a North/South fault line foreshadowing disunion, the measure failed to carry. No one rejoiced in the defeat more than fiercely anti-administration Senator William Maclay. Dropping in

FIGURE 9. John Laurance. Oil on canvas (ca. 1792) by John Trumbull (1756–1843). (Collection of the New York Historical Society. Reproduced with permission.)

along with Thomas Jefferson to witness the critical ballot, the gloating Maclay captured Federalist disappointment with indelible color:

> Sedgewick bore the visible marks of weeping... Clymer's ... head neck & Breast consented to Gesticulations resembling those of a Turkey or Goose, nearly strangled in the Act of deglutition ... Benson bungled like a Shoemaker who had lost his End. Ames ... sat torpid, as if his faculties had been benumbed ... happy impudence sat enthroned on Lawrence's brow. He rose in puffing pomp, and moved that the Committee should rise.[45]

The assumption bill fared no better on a second vote. By mid-June of 1790, six months into the congressional session, neither supporters nor opponents of Hamilton's provocative proposal would budge. Enter Thomas Jefferson. Freshly returned from France, the secretary of state was all too aware of dire European consequences if Hamilton's funding plan was not enacted. Some form of compromise was necessary, he confided to fellow Virginian James Monroe, "for the sake of the union, and to save us from the greatest of all calamities, the total extinction of our credit in Europe."[46] To broker a deal, Jefferson invited Hamilton together with Madison to his New York residence at 57 Maiden Lane, a stone's throw from Elizabeth Rutgers's brewery. Hamilton, in return for no serious opposition to assumption, evidently promised to convince northern delegations not to interfere with the Potomac site as the permanent seat of the federal government. Or so the story goes. Whether actually facilitated by Jefferson's dinner bargain or not, Congress on July 16 passed the Residence Act and on August 4, the Funding Act, collectively known in founding father lore as the "Great Compromise of 1790."* Eight days later, a senate resolution thanking New York for its generous hospitality brought the second congressional session to a close.

Laurance, despite Hamilton's personal exhortation, apparently wanted no part of the reputed dinner compromise, for he—indeed all six New York House members—voted against the Residence Act.[47] New Yorkers were outraged. How could the new government abandon Federal Hall after so much treasure had been poured into splendid marble, gold leaf, and damask refurbishment? (Federal Hall reverted to city use until May 14, 1812, when the structure was sold at auction for $425 and the lots on which it stood for $9,500. It was torn down within days.) Convinced that property values would plummet, the *New York Daily Advertiser* charged President Washington with gross ingratitude to the city that had opened its heart (and purse) to him. Not to be outdone, the *New York Morning Post* featured an August 4 cartoon representing the capital being hijacked on the back of Pennsylvania fat-cat Robert Morris. Laurance never forgave the congressional snub of his adopted New York, and voted consistently—as late as 1798 in the Senate—against Peter L'Enfant's city plan for the Potomac site.

The First Federal Congress reconvened that December in Philadelphia, but a devastated Rep. Laurance would make the trip alone. Wife Betsey, following an extended illness, had departed this earth four days after Congress adjourned New York. Only 37 years of age, poor Betsey was laid to rest August 17 alongside her father and brother in the First Presbyterian Church yard following a memorial service at newly restored Trinity Episcopal Church. John and his four shattered children shared the

---

*James Madison, *Papers*, vol. XIII, 295. Jefferson, from a Virginia perspective, got the best of Hamilton in the deal. Not only did Virginia secure the seat of government on its northern flank, but the state also benefited from legislation passed within a month establishing a board to settle accounts with the individual states. "In a pecuniary light," wrote Madison on July 31, 1790, to his father, "the assumption is no longer of much consequence to Virginia."

heartbreaking service from pew no. 64, a special family niche he subscribed less than two months earlier for the respectable sum of £20.[48] Except for his children, John was now completely alone in the world. An only child whose parents were long deceased, he found himself devoid of extended family as well; with Betsey's passing, all of General McDougall's offspring had joined him in eternity.

A gentleman of Laurance's station in late-eighteenth-century America donned black frock mourning coat and black waistcoat for no more than six months. Although society widows of the day were to wear black mourning dress for up to two years and avoid ball-going for one year, active businessmen might resume commercial affairs in a week or two following a wife's funeral. Channeling his sorrow, John flung himself back into a flourishing legal practice until Congress reconvened in December. Business, if his Bank of New York account is any indication, was lucrative, for his surviving June statement reflected a respectable balance of £1,296.[49] Two years in Congress not only justified higher fees, but also added clout and prestige to John's litigation practice. "It will afford my friends at the Bar a great comfort," wrote one Livingston attorney, "if you would favor them with your presence on the opening of court tomorrow. Should you think it proper to give your opinion on the subject," he allowed, "I have no doubt it will give satisfaction to the Bar, the Bench and your sincere friend."[50]

Reputation burnished by selection by Federal Judge Duane as one of only 13 counsel authorized to practice before the District Court and one of six eminent counsel appointed to draw up the Court's procedural protocol, Laurance was named in early 1790 one of the first practicing attorneys admitted to argue before the United States Supreme Court.[51] No doubt for these reasons, he was approached that September by Vice President Adams on a highly personal matter. Was there, Adams inquired, a clerking desk in his law practice for problematic 19-year-old son Charles?[52] The lad's clerkship with Alexander Hamilton had been cut short after three months when the new treasury secretary closed a thriving law practice to assume office, and the vice president wanted his son's nose kept to the grindstone. Young Adams (Harvard '88) on the surface was a bright and affable fellow, but his parents worried about increasing alcohol abuse and a proclivity for "consorting with persons regarded as unsavory." Nor was the vice president thrilled about Charles sharing New York accommodations with Frederick Steuben, whom some historians believe was sexually attracted to men. There was also a dark side to Charles's makeup that ultimately led to depression, alcoholism, financial recklessness, and tragically premature death. Still, Laurance took young Adams into his business for two years, facilitating admittance to the New York bar in 1792.[53]

Facing no organized electoral opposition, Rep. Laurance was re-elected to a second term in April 1790 with a whopping 98.4 percent of the vote over hapless Melancton Smith. Immensely popular with Pearl Street merchants for keeping duties on English goods at parity with those from France, John was equally applauded by Wall Street investors for retiring debt certificate IOUs at full face value. But more was at play than mere personal popularity. The pro-government wave that swept Rep. Laurance back into office was in fact the early flexing muscle of what would become America's first organized political party. New York's 1788 coalition of gentry, merchants, lawyers, speculators, and former Crown loyalists, had spread through Alexander Hamilton's network of treasury agents and like-minded nationalists to the young republic's major cities. "In the process," observed one latter-day political analyst, "what began as a capital faction soon assumed status as a national faction and then, finally, as the new Federalist Party."[54]

Laurance's political world was shifting beneath his feet in December 1790 as the pounding hooves of his carriage team hurried to the relocated United States government in Philadelphia. No longer simply the elected voice of capitalistic New York City, John was now ideologically linked with fellow Federalists from New Hampshire to South Carolina. Indeed, pro-administration members by the end of the First Federal Congress held 39 of 65 House seats and 18 of 26 in the Senate. It would be premature, however, to consider Congressional Federalists of 1790–1791 a national political party. The first "quasi caucus" would not be until the elections of 1796.[55] Nor were Federalist solons mere extensions of Treasury Secretary Hamilton's fertile ideological voice. Senators (who would not be popularly elected until 1913) knew all too well that their six-year appointments owed to respective state legislators, while members of the House ignored at their peril constituent interests. Still, Hamilton's intellectual energy and communicative stamina kept pro-government, pro-bank, and pro-mercantile legislators on the same page. Many of the most influential nationalists—Fisher Ames, William Smith, Jedediah Wadsworth, and Rufus King, for example—were, like Laurance, the treasury secretary's personal friends.[56] And these strong spirits did not require his whispering in their ears to understand that their collective clout was powerful enough to legislate a government of their own design. At last, to paraphrase John Jay's earlier sentiments, those who owned the country would govern it.[57]

Not if James Madison could help it. Earlier in the year, the alarmed Virginian had pulled allies behind closed doors to oppose Hamilton's report on the public credit. Known as the "anti-administration" faction, the group expanded to some 25 mostly southern congressmen that had jelled together over assumption. Jefferson's permanent return from France gave Madison's bloc a strong voice in President Washington's cabinet. In the summer of 1791, Jefferson filled his single departmental patronage job with firebrand New York newspaperman Philip Freneau to launch the anti-administration *National Gazette*. It was the opening gun to what Jefferson campaign manager (and House clerk) John J. Beckley openly called "the struggle between the Treasury Department and the Republican interests."[58]

Ugly political storm clouds gathering in the distance, Rep. Laurance the icy morning of December 6 stepped from Chestnut Street into the 10-foot-wide vestibule of Philadelphia's bustling Congress Hall. Making his way through the large loggia situated beneath a hanging public gallery, John occupied his designated mahogany desk and looked to the dais where dignified Speaker Muhlenberg presided beneath a curtained canopy. The plangent-voiced former minister duly called to order the third and final session of the First Federal Congress, quickly appointing Laurance with two peers to advise President Washington that a quorum had been reached and Congress was ready to do business.[59] Two days later at noon, a black-clad Washington delivered his second annual message to both houses of Congress assembled in the Senate chamber.

It was an address that validated Treasury Secretary Hamilton's financial program and swelled Federalist hearts with self-congratulation. "The abundant fruits of another year," Washington informed the lawmakers, "have blessed our Country with plenty, and with the means of a flourishing commerce."[60] Federal revenues, declared the president, "have been productive beyond the calculations they had been regulated."[61] United States 6 percent notes, which traded at a quarter of par in September of 1789, now commanded full face value. Furthermore, the increased promise of "national respectability and credit" had secured a new three-million-florin loan from Holland. "Further particulars as may be requisite," promised the president, would be forthcoming from the treasury secretary.

Within the week a treasury report indeed arrived, but it had little to do with the Dutch loan. Rather, Secretary Hamilton submitted a breathtaking proposal for imposing additional revenue-raising excise taxes, minting the dollar as national unit of account, and establishing a central banking system anchored by a national bank, the Bank of the United States (BUS). The bank was to be funded by selling $10 million in capital stock to the public, $2 million of which to be purchased by the United States government and the remainder to "any person, copartnership, or body politic."[62] Lending capital was created by requiring $500,000 of the public share be subscribed with hard specie (gold and silver). This hard specie would be leveraged (as practiced for decades by the Bank of England) to provide bank loan amounts several times its number, in this case up to the capitalized limit of $10 million. Hamilton then boldly proposed the United States borrow its $2 million stake from the bank itself![63]

To reassure Congress and the public of the proposed institution's fiduciary independence, the treasury secretary insisted the national bank be a private company chartered for 20 years with 25 rotating directors, only 5 of which were appointed by the federal government. Moreover, the bank was forbidden to buy any government bonds or incur further debt. Its formal role would be as a depository for collected taxes, clearing agent for government payments, facilitator of treasury foreign exchange operations, and potential short-term lending source to cover cash flow gaps. Informally, as Laurance knew from his own Bank of New York experience, the BUS would play a huge role in lubricating the economy. Its bank notes, redeemable in specie, were legal tender that not only expanded the money supply and extended credit to the mercantile community but also enhanced the public credit. And by making government securities redeemable at face value to purchase shares in the new bank, every United States debt instrument was bolstered in value.

All of this smacked of fiscal sorcery to agrarian congressmen deeply suspicious of centralized financial power and the growing strength of the northern merchant faction. Most disquieting of all to southern delegates, the Philadelphia-based national bank promised to become so entwined with the seat of government that permanent relocation to the Potomac might be seriously jeopardized. When the Senate bill authorizing the BUS landed in the House, Rep. Jackson opened debate with an impassioned tirade against any such bank that was "calculated to benefit a small part of the United States, the mercantile interest only." "The Farmers, the yeomanry," he added, "will derive no advantage from it."[64] Nothing, Jackson protested, in the Constitution gave Congress the power to create and charter corporations. Flourishing a bound copy of Hamilton's *Federalist Papers*, the huge Georgian read at length to prove his point.

Instantly, Laurance was on his feet. The power to borrow money was indeed in the Constitution, he lectured, and that power presupposed a right to create capital from which to borrow.[65] Battle over Hamilton's proposed bank was on.

Next afternoon, James Madison with his usual measured eloquence reiterated Jackson's argument. The Constitution, he pointed out in the low, even tone of authority, was intended as a limited document. "Is the power of establishing an incorporated Bank," the Virginian rhetorically asked, "among the powers vested by the Constitution in the Legislature of the United States?"[66] Answering his own question in the negative, Madison argued that all powers not expressly granted in the Constitution were reserved to the states. "The proposed Bank," he continued, "would interfere, so as to indirectly defeat a State Bank at the same place." Therefore, the Senate bill, concluded Madison, "was condemned by the silence of the Constitution" and should "receive its final condemnation by vote of this House." Speaker Muhlenberg accentuated the drama of Rep. Madison's remarks by gaveling the day's session to a close.

Next morning, Massachusetts Federalists Ames and Sedgwick forcefully countered Madison, contending that implied powers of the "necessary and proper" clause of the Constitution clearly justified a national bank. Laurance completed the argument by reminding his colleagues that the Confederation Congress a decade earlier had incorporated Robert Morris's Bank of North America and that surely the present government could not be less powerful than its emasculated predecessor. "The silence of the people on this subject," he added with a flourish, "is strongly presumptive the measure of the bank is not considered by them as unconstitutional."[67] In a subtle jab at southern strict-constructionists,

John concluded with a barb aimed directly at James Madison: "It must be conceded that there is nothing in the Constitution that is expressly against it, and therefore we ought not to deduce a prohibition by construction."[68]

It was—as most delegates had observed by now—Madison's wont to trot out the "un-Constitutional" argument when southern interests were threatened. Fellow Virginia representative Richard Bland Lee was more direct: "He did not wish to sound the alarm, but thought Gentlemen might want to be on their guard" that New York and Philadelphia investors would monopolize bank stock "to the exclusion of holders in the more remote cities and states."[69] Any reference to New York of course guaranteed an immediate reaction from Laurance. "New Yorkers," John opined dismissively, "would receive no particular advantage from the establishment of this bank; they had one of their own."[70] Besides, he reproved Lee, if the BUS charter was reduced from 20 to 10 years, "the Constitutional objections to it might vanish like snow before a warm sun."[71]

Warm debate, though not as impassioned as the assumption discussion, continued in the House until, finally, on Wednesday, February 23, 1791, with steadfast pro-administration Elias Boudinot temporarily in the speaker's chair, the bill to incorporate a bank of the United States was passed by a 39 to 20 margin. When the measure landed on President Washington's desk for signature into law, he balked. What if the bank together with Hamilton's proposed Philadelphia-based national mint proved so convenient that Congress reversed its hard-fought decision to fix the permanent seat of government along his beloved Potomac? Seeking constitutional justification for a bill he was inclined to veto, Washington solicited written opinions from Secretary of War Henry Knox, Attorney General Edmund Randolph, and Secretary of State Jefferson. Knox tersely approved the bill, but both Virginians blasted the measure as unconstitutional.

Tradition has it that Washington inked the bill only after Hamilton's powerful 15,000-word position paper pronounced the national bank constitutional under implied powers of the "necessary and proper" clause. Circumstances, however, suggest that another, less noble, factor was also at play—Washington's economic self-interest. It was no secret that he had ignored both congressional commissioners and legislative-designated parameters in personally choosing the specific capital site on the banks of the Potomac.[72] What's more, the president dispatched a letter to Congress requesting consent to fold in his own hometown of Alexandria (along with some Maryland land south of the Anacostia River).* When Senator Charles Carroll of Maryland formally introduced such a bill, the

---

*As determined personally by the Master of Mount Vernon, the southern-most point of the original District of Columbia was demarcated in Alexandria by a granite boundary stone. One of 36 of the original 40 stones still standing, the Alexandria marker is in Jones Point Park along the seawall just south of the lighthouse. In 1846, Washington's Alexandria portion of the original District was returned to the state of Virginia.

pro-bank Senate forced Washington's hand by postponing Carroll's measure until the final day of the president's bank bill signature window.[73] No national bank, no Alexandria! Washington signed the bank bill into law, and Carroll's measure immediately cleared the Senate to be quickly rubber-stamped in the House.

After spirited debate, House members on January 27 enacted excises (better known as the Whiskey Tax) on both imported and domestic distilled spirits to raise necessary federal revenues to pay bondholder interest on assumed state debts. And it was Laurance, as he had done with the Collection Act 18 months before, who delivered the House select committee's detailed 62-section revenue bill to the chamber floor. Outspoken Rep. Jackson of Georgia rose to protest that a whiskey tax discriminated against southern states lacking orchards and breweries, and Virginia representative Josiah Parker warned the Act "would let loose a swarm of harpies" who would "range through the country, prying into every man's house and affairs."[74] Nonetheless, Laurance steered passage by a 35 to 21 margin.[75]

With President Washington's signature on the Whiskey Act, all that remained undone of the treasury secretary's ambitious financial agenda was his *Report on the Establishment of a Mint*. Until the bank bill was resolved, debate over this Philadelphia facility to coin bi-metallic currency had been put on the back burner. There it would wait, for on March 3 the First Federal Congress adjourned. After three extraordinarily productive sessions, the monumental task of setting up the national government was completed. In spite of growing internal differences, the collaborative Congress of Firsts completely transformed the new republic's financial footing. Not only had some $21,000,000 in state wartime debt been assumed by the federal government, but also a potent treasury department was put in place to pay down foreign debt, roll over domestic debt at lower interest rates, and manage a formal sinking fund to stabilize the market for government securities. Perhaps most encouraging of all, uncollected levies of the Confederation Congress were replaced with a solid federal excise and tariff revenue stream.

If Alexander Hamilton's far-sighted vision for funding the new republic was nothing short of financial revolution, John Laurance was first over the barricades. No member of the First Federal Congress did more to hasten the treasury secretary's proposals into law. Respected for oratorical prowess, financial acumen, and the president's personal regard, John established his bona fides as an influential spokesman in a House whose Federalist majority had lost confidence in James Madison as a pro-administration floor leader. No one was better placed than John to fill the void when the Second Federal Congress convened in late October. Philip Schuyler had said as much when, dumped unexpectedly in favor of Aaron Burr by a Clinton/Livingston state legislative coalition, he exhorted the "illustrious triumvirate" of "King, Benson, and Laurance to carry on the Federalist banner in Congress."[76]

But would the equable Rep. Laurance put himself forward? And if so, would he lead with a distinct voice of his own, or serve as cat's paw for an ascendant administration? Would House colleagues see the John Laurance who ushered Quaker petitions onto the chamber to protest human slavery? The Laurance who delivered the Collection Act of 1789 to administer federal import duties and tariffs? The Laurance who helped facilitate Madison's constitutional amendments? Or would he play the parochial New York lawmaker who executed Hamilton's bidding to pass the West Point Act of July 5, 1790?*

---

*The Act secured 1,795 acres commandeered during the late war from owner Stephen Moore on which the fortifications at West Point were built. Backed by Hamilton and Secretary of War Henry Knox, Moore's 1790 petition was chaperoned by Rep. Laurance to purchase the property for $11,085.

TWELVE
Philadelphia Story

CHRIST CHURCH, PHILADELPHIA, JUNE 30, 1791. A continuous sheet of iron oxide–rich clay underlay the Delaware and Schuylkill River confluence to make William Penn's Philadelphia a red brick city from the outset. Venerable Christ Church was no exception. Founded in 1695 as a parish of the Church of England, it provided Royalist dogmata haven from perceived "wicked and damnable principles and doctrines" of Penn's pacifist Quaker Society of Friends.[1] By 1744, His Majesty's simple house of prayer had been transformed by prosperous Anglican churchgoers into an elegant Georgian cathedral-like monument to colonial craftsmanship, complete with reserved pew for Royal Governors of the colonies. Proud worshippers boasted of the church's silver communion set (presented in 1708 by Queen Anne) and new wine glass–shaped hand-carved pulpit with curving gilded staircase. A massive walnut 600-year-old baptismal font came all the way from All Hallows Church, Barking-by-the-Tower, England. Overhead, an intricate eight-bell chime, cast at London's prestigious Whitechapel Foundry, clanged from beneath Scottish-born master carpenter Robert Smith's somewhat pretentious white octagonal steeple. Few parishioners, of course, would concede the 197-foot-high spire had just been surpassed by New York's resurrected Trinity Church (200 feet) as the country's tallest.

Shorn of Royalist Anglican ties by the sword of Independence, red brick Christ Church and its blue-blood congregation reigned as post-war physical and liturgical epicenter of the Protestant Episcopal Church in the United States. Rector William White (1748–1836) was the nation's pre-eminent churchman. Boasting the country's most impressive ecclesiastical résumé, White was a Pennsylvania College graduate (BA '65, MA '68) and longtime trustee (1774–1836) who, after receiving an honorary Doctorate of Divinity, forged post-war relations with the Anglican Church, and in 1787 was consecrated bishop by the Archbishops of Canterbury and York. As first presiding bishop of America's Protestant Episcopal Church, he was largely responsible for its constitution and canons as well as the *American Book of Common Prayer*. Little wonder White was immediately named cleric to the United States Senate when the federal government unpacked its New York bags. Although his wealthy brother-in-law Robert Morris no longer centered high society, Dr. White—more the practical theologian than inspiring preacher—enjoyed entrée to old Philadelphia's most exclusive parlors. Who better, then, on the final day of June 1791 to bless Colonel Laurance's second marriage?

Laurance had little choice over the previous winter but to leave his son and daughters Mary, Ann, and Elizabeth in New York while attending Congress. Young John Jr. at 14 was well on the way to following his father into the legal profession. Tutored in Greek, Latin, geography, and history by George Wright of the Columbia College Grammar School, he was about to enter the college and had already been made a "freeman" by the New York City Council.[2] The lad was growing up fast, but three girls on the teenage cusp needed a woman's full-time presence. And within 11 months of setting foot in Philadelphia, their father produced one. Befitting the prominent Federalist figure he had become, John married into the crème de la crème of Philadelphia society.[3] Second wife Elizabeth Allen, only child of respected former Pennsylvania Supreme Court Judge John Spratt Lawrence, was among the bluest of Philadelphia's social blood, what with paternal connection to the wealthy Masters family and ties to the Hamiltons, Penns, and Chews.* The ceremony was a private affair so discrete that three months passed before the newlyweds went public. Not until September 30 would President Washington learn from faithful secretary Tobias Lear that "The marriage of Colo. Lawrence and Mrs. Allen is at length avowed by the parties."[4]

Elizabeth was in the spring of 1791 Philadelphia society's most eligible woman of a certain age. Twenty-three years earlier she had married James Allen, son of Pennsylvania Chief Justice William Allen, the founder of Allentown.[5] Reputedly then the richest man in the colony, Judge Allen made a wedding gift of his 3,338-acre Lehigh Valley estate upon which the favored newlyweds in 1770 erected a magnificent stone Georgian summer home christened Trout Hall.[6] (Not to be outdone, Elizabeth's father gave a fine Chestnut Street lot less than two blocks from his own brick three-story townhouse on the northeast corner of Chestnut and Sixth.)[7] James Allen at the outbreak of the Revolution remained tenuously neutral but joined his father and three brothers to seek protection from King George after the Declaration of Independence exposed their vast properties to the leveling mob. Given safe passage by General Washington himself, James ushered pregnant Elizabeth and their three children to safety in British-occupied Philadelphia, only to perish in late 1778 at age 37 from tuberculosis. Elizabeth Allen never remarried. Over the next 13 years, the richly provided-for widow made her Chestnut Street address "one of the

---

*Descended from the Laurenszen's of Amsterdam, Oxford-educated attorney John Spratt Lawrence (1724–1799) fled to England when William Howe vacated Philadelphia. Although sentenced in absentia to death for treason, Lawrence's prestige and integrity earned him pardon upon post-war return to settle on a modest New Jersey farm.

FIGURE 10 Elizabeth Allen Laurance.
Formerly attributed to John Wesley Jarvis, this oil on canvas (ca. 1790) is by an unidentified artist. (Collection of New York Historical Society. Reproduced with permission.)

most popular in the city," while summering at Trout Hall with her three absolutely stunning daughters.[8]

Not yet forty, slender dark-haired Elizabeth and her three graces were much in demand on a select society ball–going circuit energized by descent of the entire federal government.[9] Even the stiff Tuesday afternoon levies that President Washington had begun in New York seemed more elegant in the state dining room of Philadelphia's temporary presidential mansion. Elizabeth knew the opulent rooms well, for her favorite aunt, Mary Lawrence Masters, had raised the splendid High (Market) Street edifice some 20 years earlier. One of America's most imposing residences, the three-and-a-half-story brick Georgian manse served as Sir William Howe's sequestered headquarters during British occupation of Philadelphia. Washington's style of living was just as courtly, and

Martha's fashionable Friday evening receptions lasted up to 10 p.m., later than in New York.

"Crowds of foreigners of the highest rank poured into Philadelphia," sighed Elizabeth's youngest daughter Mary, "and Ministers with their suites from all parts of the world, came to bow to Washington and the Republic."[10] Accompanying the flood of European émigré capital that chased "new world" investment schemes was a wave of refugee aristocrats evading social and political upheaval. These charming, polished men who embellished Washington's "Republican Court" included a fleet of impeccably mannered opportunists such as Franco-Dutch investment agent Theophilus Cazenove, sleek French counter-revolutionary Antoine Omer Talon, and Lafayette's own wartime aide Louis Marie vicomte de Noailles, who Laurance surely remembered from Cornwallis's Yorktown surrender.[11]

"In the numerous assemblies of Philadelphia," the visiting duc la Rochefoucauld-Liancourt would write, "it is impossible to meet with what is called a plain woman."[12] The enraptured Frenchman was of course playing the polite guest; visiting New Yorker Frances Seney was less charitable, remarking to her sister that she had never laid eyes on such a "parcel of ugly women" as at one of Martha Washington's receptions.[13] Even so, Abigail Adams, having gauged London, Paris, and New York's loveliest faces, thought Philadelphia belles quite comely. "How could it be otherwise," she admitted, "when the dazzling Mrs. Bingham and her beautiful sisters were there; the Misses Allen and Misses Chew: in short a constellation of beauties."[14] "As candlelight is a great improver of beauty," she later added with droll Yankee wit, "they appear to great advantage."[15]

"At this time I was not grown up," remembered Mary Allen, "but my Mother and her two elder daughters were equally Belles."[16] Whether by candle or daylight, none sparkled more brightly than incomparable society hostess Mrs. Anne Willing Bingham. One of the most beautiful women of her day, her likeness was purportedly model for Lady Liberty on early United States coins. Wife of nouveau riche merchant prince William Bingham, she entertained in the manner of a French *salonnière* with a seemingly endless series of brilliant balls, sumptuous dinners, and constant receptions at Mansion House, a spectacular 18,000-square-foot stone residence distinguished by America's only freestanding white marble central staircase.

Almost as striking was Mrs. John Jay, who reputedly caused the audience of a French theatre to rise en masse at her entrance, mistaking her for Queen Marie Antoinette. Mrs. Elizabeth (Eliza) Powel, the president's favorite dancing companion, was impossible to overlook. Another star in this favored firmament was Elizabeth Allen's oldest daughter, Ann, who merited at least three portraits by Washington's own limner Gilbert Stuart. "My beautiful sister," remembered Mary Allen, "was a brilliant luminary which seemed to animate everything within its influence."[17] Tradition would have us believe Ann "was one of the most splendid beauties this country ever produced."[18] If so, the peach fell close to the tree, for the raven-haired Elizabeth had not lost her glow. "Mrs. Allen," remarked the not easily impressed Abigail Adams, "is as well bred a woman as I have seen in any country."[19]

Any number of hostesses would have been more than happy to introduce Elizabeth Allen to Colonel Laurance during his lonely 1791 congressional stayover. It might have been at William Bingham's elaborate table, for Laurance had come to know the sociable Philadelphian during his Confederation Congress days if not during the war, when Bingham parlayed business partnership with Thomas Willing and Robert Morris into a fortune supplying the Continental Army. Whatever the venue, Elizabeth displayed poise and social grace that first wife Betsey could never have acquired from her unpolished privateer father. And John, with his commanding stature and Englishman's reserve, must have been equally appealing. "His extensive intercourse with the leading men of the day, his intimate connection with public affairs, his easy ready powers of conversation and amenity of manners rendered him extremely attractive in society."[20] At least that's how George McWhorter remembered the grandfather he never met.

Sorting out the serried ranks of Philadelphia society was no easy task for any newly arrived congressman. Original Quaker aristocrats thought themselves atop a social pyramid whose descending ranks included a second "quality" class of early eighteenth-century Anglican merchant arrivals. Next came distinguished men of the Revolution and well-heeled repatriated Crown loyalists. Further complicating the pecking order was the "court" of President Washington with its legislators, judges, federal administrators, and gaudy flock of foreign diplomats. Alone, Laurance may have floundered, but with Elizabeth on his arm, tricky social waters would be navigated with grace. "With what ease," one knowing socialite observed, "I have seen a Chew, A Penn, an Oswald, an Allen ... entertain a large circle of both sexes, in conversation, without aid of [dance] cards, never flagging nor seeming in the least strained or stupid."[21] Had John intentionally set out to ingratiate himself with Philadelphia society he could not have chosen a better-placed wife.

Philadelphia in those days (fig. 11) was laid out like a chessboard running west, in rectangular fashion, of Delaware River warehouses for some dozen blocks. On every side but the river, adjacent open land was studded with sprawling countryseats of prosperous merchants and gentry. Smack in the middle of town was Statehouse Square, where America's Constitution was hammered out the steamy summer of 1787. Just west of the state house itself (now known as Independence Hall) at Sixth and Chestnut stood Congress Hall, a hurried two-story expansion to the red brick county court house, fitted out as best as possible to resemble New York's more lavish venue. A corresponding brick structure on the court

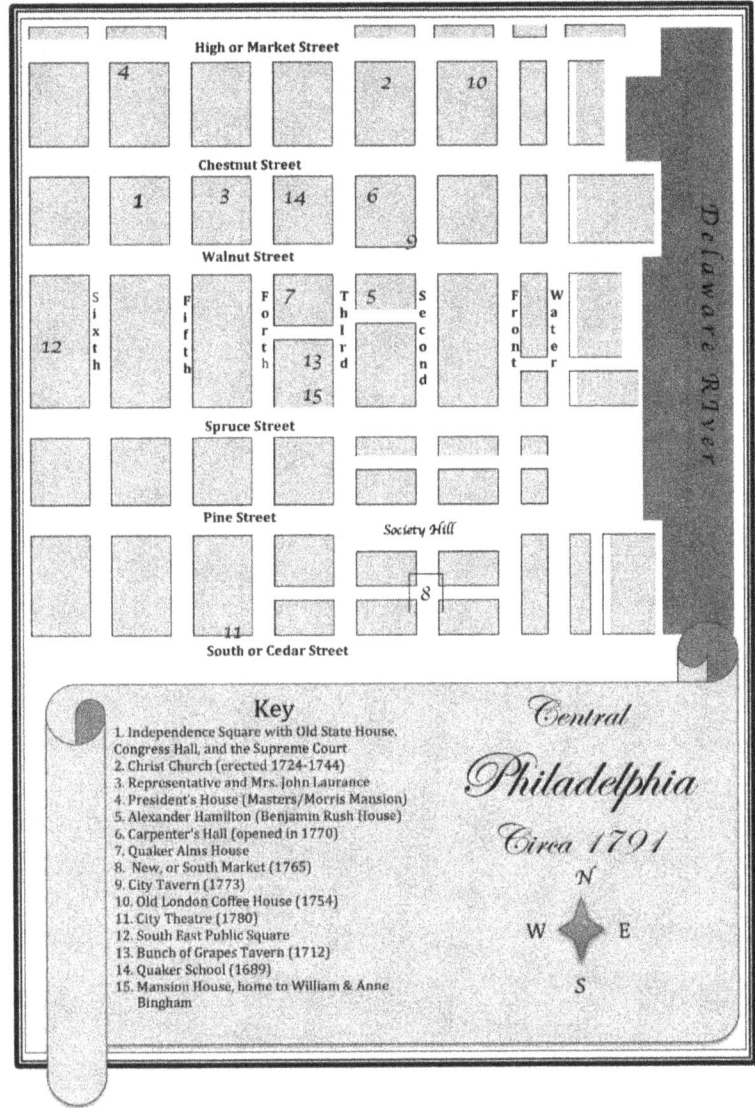

FIGURE 11 Central Philadelphia circa 1791.
(Original illustration by permission of the author.)

house's east side served as venue for the Supreme Court. Although comfortable enough, accommodations for the newly arrived government were noticeably less commodious—and far more republican—than New York's elegant Federal Hall.

Brick-paved, tree-lined Chestnut Street was the center of Philadelphia political, financial, and social life. Stretching westward from the Delaware River, it lay a block south of High Street's buzzing arcaded market stalls. Home to the state house, Congress Hall, Ben Franklin's Library

Company, Bank of North America, and Carpenters' Hall, Chestnut Street was, in short, *the* place to be. Elizabeth Allen's splendid townhouse, situated at Chestnut between Fourth and Fifth Streets, was ideally suited for Rep. Laurance's fall and winter legislative sessions with their accompanying dinners, dances, and levies. Only two blocks from the Laurances, Treasury Secretary Hamilton and his family of five secured Dr. Benjamin Rush's fine house on Walnut and South Third Street. Fellow New Yorker Rufus King left Mary and the family in Manhattan to board at nearby City Tavern, the new Congress's preferred watering hole. Just up the block were President and Mrs. Washington (and their 30-person household) in the "Masters Mansion" at Sixth Street. Lending cosmopolitan panache to the scene, Thomas Jefferson moved into a rented High Street townhouse and proceeded to unload 80 packing cases of imported furniture and paintings from his mission to France. Vice President Adams rented more rustic space at Bush Hill, a huge three-story circa 1740 mansion two miles west of the city. Alarmed to find that they were living beyond their means—four horses were needed for up to three daily trips to city center—Adams later dismissed servants and moved to more modest in-town quarters at Fourth and Arch Streets.

As to the City of Brotherly Love, Abigail Adams was not impressed:

> If New York wanted any revenge for the removal, the citizens might be glutted if they would come here, where every article has risen to almost double its price, and where it is not possible for Congress and their appendages for a long time to be half as well accommodated.[22]

Northerners—none more so than Congressman Laurance—lusted for return of the seat of government to Lower Manhattan, while southerners licked their chops at its promised Potomac sojourn. Philadelphians, on the other hand, were convinced that their city's manifold charms would convince politicians of all stripes to extend its 10-year lease as temporary seat of government. More than a dozen local newspapers ginned out specie exchange rates, commodity prices, and port of entry shipping news to make the city an indispensible nexus of business information. Indeed, Philadelphians were responsible for the first ventures into negotiable ground rents, marine insurance, investment banking, and securities markets. Innovative financiers such as Clement Biddle, Thomas Wharton Jr., Robert Morris, Thomas Willing, and the rising French-born Stephen Girard made Chestnut Street the first "Wall Street."[23] Founded a decade before the Declaration of Independence, the Philadelphia College School of Medicine was second to none. With good reason, civic promoter Benjamin Rush gushed that his city's irresistible cultural, commercial, and social setting would "do more to prolong the residence of a republican Congress among us than ... paving our streets with silver dollars."[24]

The next best thing to actually surfacing Philadelphia thoroughfares with silver coin took place on July 4, 1791. Four days after John and Elizabeth invested in one another at Christ Church, the initial Bank of the United States (BUS) share rights went on sale to the public. These rights, called scrips, were not actual shares but rather a $25 deposit on the full $400 share price. The balance was to be paid in four installments, the last due on July 1, 1793. Within an hour, the entire $8,000,000 of rights open to public subscription was oversubscribed by almost 50 percent.[25] To Jefferson and Madison's disgust, opportunistic New York and Philadelphia insiders scooped up over half the shares, helping themselves to blocks designated for Boston and Baltimore. Among the buyers were no fewer than 30 members of Congress, including the newly married Rep. Laurance.[26]

All too soon, however, the young republic faced its first financial bubble. Only four days after the BUS public offering, the $25/share scrip doubled in value. By August 4 it had tripled. Frenzied speculation soon drove original subscriber rights to $280 in New York and $300 in Boston. It was an unsustainable price that by the end of August tumbled to $150. Concerned that credit was drying up as BUS share-right prices plummeted, Secretary Hamilton moved quickly. With the approval of fellow Sinking Fund Committee members (Adams, Jay, Jefferson, and Attorney General Edmund Randolph), he deployed $350,000 to stabilize BUS scrip share prices with aggressive open market purchases in Philadelphia, and in Manhattan through auspices of the Bank of New York.[27] "You have the blessings of thousands here," a much-relieved Bank of New York cashier William Seton advised Hamilton on September 12. "I feel gratified more than I can ever express, at being the dispenser of your benevolence."[28] Hamilton's swift open market buying strategy had worked. Scrip prices settled and credit lines, for the moment, opened back up.

What Laurance thought of the scrip bubble—or if he even participated—can only be conjectured. Most likely he was a spectator rather than a speculator, for the newlyweds were busy sampling the rustic summer pleasures of Trout Hall. Returning to Philadelphia in September, Laurance livened domestic felicity by installing his own three daughters from New York. Social dynamics, however, of six young women from two marriages under the Chestnut Street roof by month's end proved too complicated. "The Misses Allens," Washington's private secretary Tobias Lear informed him, "have taken up residence with their Grand mother."[29] They never returned full-time to John and Elizabeth's Philadelphia roof. "In the spring," remembered Elizabeth's youngest daughter, Mary, "we went to Fairy Hill, a beautiful spot on the Schuylkill, which belonged to us, and afterwards to Allentown, where we remained till Autumn."[30]

On October 21, John made the short stroll down Chestnut Street to Carpenters' Hall for the first meeting of BUS shareholders. Initial order of shareholder business was to hire Thomas Willing as bank president at an annual salary of $3,000. Having studied law at London's Inner Temple, the well-heeled Willing boasted the nation's most glittering public-finance resume. Willing, former mercantile partner of Robert Morris (1749), was the leading facilitator of the pre-war negotiable ground-rent (liquid IOUs that functioned as mortgages in perpetuity) market, mayor of Philadelphia (1763), Pennsylvania supreme court justice (1767), member of the Continental Congress (1775–1776), and president of the Philadelphia-based Bank of North America (1781–1791). John Kean, former South Carolina delegate to the Confederation Congress, was selected as head cashier to manage day-to-day bank operations. His Charleston roots reassured the bank's southern shareholders, while marriage to a yet another Livingston daughter soothed northern investor concerns.

Laurance and his fellow shareholders elected 25 directors to oversee the bank. Eleven were from Pennsylvania, six from New York, five selected by Hamilton as government placeholders, and three hailed from Massachusetts.[31] Of the 30 members of Congress holding BUS stock, 10, including Reps. Laurance and Bingham along with Senator King, were made bank directors. Only one director—William Smith—hailed from a southern state as northern subscribers scooped up 23,500 of the original 25,000 bank shares. Jeffersonians were not without reason, then, to suspect the bank was destined to become an "engine of state" driven by Hamilton's capitalist allies.

Three days after the BUS shareholder meeting, Laurance was back in his seat at Congress Hall. Just as in the First Federal Congress, he would be an active, prominent member of the Federalist majority (40 of 72 seats) straight from opening day. Assigned with South Carolina Rep. Smith and Virginian Alexander White to commune with the Senate and advise President Washington that Congress was open for business, John then collaborated with Madison and Smith to craft the formal House response to Washington's welcoming address.[32] The New Yorker's rising political stature was further affirmed by important select committee assignments to prepare a bill or bills on the public debt, to reapportion the number of representatives based on recent 1790 census results, and to appropriate necessary funds to support government operations for fiscal 1792. He reported out for the latter two.

Beginning with the short-lived 1789 Committee on Ways and Means, Rep. Laurance had each fall thereafter reported out annual appropriations bills to a House resolved into a committee of the whole.[33] It was by present-day standards a ridiculously simple protocol. Fiscal and calendar accounting year were one and the same, there was no separate capital budget, no individualized executive department accounts, and no hovering flock of outside lobbyists. The House, with no staff of their own, relied entirely upon Treasury Secretary Hamilton to estimate revenues and expenses, to track actual spending versus appropriated funds, and to calculate interest payments on the newly restructured public debt. As might be expected, the inaugural appropriation act in 1789 was a modest document, totaling $639,000 in but four lump-sum ledger accounts: the civil list, necessary Executive Department expenses, discharged wartime treasury warrants, and invalid veteran pensions. Federal revenues were in such surplus that lawmakers appropriated an extra $1,374,656 in August of 1790 to reduce the public debt.[34]

By mid-1791, however, both Madison and Jefferson were troubled by constitutional interpretation so broad as to effectively grant Treasury Secretary Hamilton financial free rein to do virtually whatever he pleased. Indeed, the Taxation Clause—first of the Constitution's enumerated congressional powers—had been controversial ever since ratification. Particularly the phrase in its middle: "to pay the Debts and provide for the common Defense and general Welfare of the United States." To Madison's mind, the Constitution was "a grant of particular powers" to a federal government that was intended to be a government of limited and enumerated power.[35] Therefore he was, from the moment Hamilton's *Report on the Public Credit* landed in the House, at odds with Laurance's interpretation of the "general Welfare" clause, so loose as to give carte blanche to any federal initiative not expressly prohibited by the founding document. It was only natural, then, to suspect the ubiquitous hand of James Madison when Virginia Rep. Josiah Parker rose on Friday, December 2, 1791, to sharply criticize Laurance's proposed appropriation bill for the impending year.

Irascible Josiah Parker (1751–1810), the rare senior Continental Army officer to oppose strong post-war central government, was a bit of a loose cannon. He had distinguished himself as colonel of the Fifth Virginia Regiment at Brandywine, only to later resign his commission in a huff when General Washington refused a furlough request. And he exploded at Governor Jefferson in 1781 when left to his own resources as area militia commander to defend the lower James River from imminent British invasion. One of only four House Antifederalists to gain re-election to the Second Federal Congress, Parker and the others found it impolitic to question the legitimacy of a smoothly operational new constitutional government. Instead, they took cover in strict-constructionism, as political scientist David J. Siemers put it, to "use the Constitution as a refuge from and as a bulwark against activist Federalist policies."[36] Skeptic of Hamiltonian finance Josiah Parker may have been, but he was by no means in James Madison's pocket. True, Parker in May of 1789 had introduced Madison's unsuccessful $10 import tax measure on slaves, but he parted company months later to oppose the whiskey tax. Parker would go on to forcefully declare for an American blue-water navy (spurned by both Madison and Jefferson) and ultimately distance himself altogether from the increasingly anti-administration Madison by gaining reelection in 1797 as a moderate Federalist.

Whether Parker spoke for Madison, or himself, when it came to Laurance's 1792 appropriations proposal, the former objected to "the sum contemplated" for being "nearly double the amount of that granted for a former year."[37] To make his point, Parker had exaggerated (the proposed budget was less than 50 percent more than 1791), but his larger case was that it was the duty of Laurance's committee to "have examined into the expenditure of the former appropriations and called upon them for information" to justify the substantial increase.[38] Was Laurance's committee, Parker intimated aloud, no more than treasury secretary errand boys?

Laurance pushed back forcefully. "It was only the duty of the committee," he reminded Parker, "to examine the estimates contained in the report of the Secretary of the Treasury and report a bill providing for the expenses of the government."[39] The Committee of the Whole, John contended, rather than his Select Committee, would determine which items to fund. "The bill," he added, "had been reported two weeks since" and "Gentlemen knew the subject was before them, and if they had examined into it, their minds would be made up, because there were details on which their opinions could be formed, Relative to the particulars."[40] Leaping to Laurance's defense, South Carolinian William Smith "wished that the Gentleman from Virginia" would have "taken the trouble of examining the accounts from the Treasurer, which have been lying on the table for three weeks."[41] If so, he would have seen enumerated "the increase of our army in consequence of the attacks on our frontiers, the expense incurred in taking the census, and additional claims on Government of the Southwestern Territory."[42]

James Madison demanded the floor. Foreshadowing next year's all-out assault on Secretary Hamilton's reporting veracity and personal integrity, Madison would have no part of simply rubber-stamping the treasury's fiscal 1792 spending estimates. "Representatives," he argued, "were, by the Constitution, made the guardians of the public money . . . they had a right, and it was their duty, to inspect the operations of the Treasury Department."[43] Madison had already begun to distance himself from the Washington administration to lay the strict-constructionist foundation for a legitimate, organized opposition party, but in December of 1791 no House member's words carried more weight.[44] Even pro-administration stalwarts Fitzsimmons and Boudinot rose to support the Virginian's call for additional transparency regarding the proposed 1792 budget. At issue was not distrust of Treasury integrity per se (that would come soon enough), but rather that simple lump-sum expense estimates were no longer sufficient if Congress was to retain power of the purse over a swelling federal government.

Hamilton, with half a dozen assistants at his disposal, responded with alacrity; three days later, House Clerk John Beckley received a detailed account of public money receipts and expenditures for the past fiscal quarter. Reassured from these accounts that the increased civil lists and steepened operating expenses were indeed legitimate, the chamber, Mr. Muhlenberg in the chair, again resolved itself into a committee of the whole. Laurance's committee was remanded to remodel the appropriations bill to "express the several purposes for which the moneys are appropriated, instead of appropriating funds in gross."[45] For the first time in the nascent republic's history, itemized sums would be detailed for each Executive Branch department, backed up by articulated legislative intent.[46] And Laurance, who saw his committee as a conduit for House deliberation of Treasury spending initiatives, readily complied. On December 8, a fully engrossed 1792 appropriations bill in the amount of $1,059,222 — a 43 percent increase over 1791 — was read for the third time and passed.

Since taking office in 1789, John had experienced nothing but success in driving the Hamiltonian agenda. Mr. Madison, despite his parliamentary prowess, had proven no more able to prevent a national bank than to discriminate between original and secondary holders of Continental securities. Yes, he had succeeded in securing a southern location for the nation's permanent seat of government, but when the House adjourned for the Christmas weekend there was every reason to believe that Laurance, together with Sedgwick, Ames, and Smith, would soon wrestle away floor leadership. What sent December parlor conversations humming, however, was neither the reassuring rebound in speculative real estate values since the spring "Panic," nor the coldest winter in a decade, but alarming word that Indian warriors had slaughtered a quarter of America's standing army on the banks of the Wabash River. For on December 9, all of Philadelphia learned that General Arthur St. Clair had been surprised by a confederacy of American Indians under Little Turtle of the Miami and Blue Jacket of the Shawnee. Of the 1,400 engaged officers and soldiers, only 580 had escaped, and but a mere two dozen were completely unblooded.

THIRTEEN

A Farewell to Innocence

PHILADELPHIA, CONGRESS HALL, MARCH 8, 1792. Fierce-eyed Massachusetts Rep. Theodore Sedgwick (1746–1813), perhaps Federalism's bluntest legislative instrument, stood to propose that Treasury Secretary Hamilton recommend the best mode for funding an expanded army to protect the western frontier in wake of General St. Clair's humiliating defeat. No sooner had Rep. Laurance seconded the motion than well-born Virginia Rep. John Page (1743–1808) claimed the floor. Patriarch of Roswell Plantation, the 49-year-old former wartime militia colonel hailed from one of Virginia's First Families and was Jefferson's closest classmate at the College of William & Mary. Page could not get enough of new second wife Mary Lowther's oft-published abstract poetry, but of Alexander Hamilton's assertive treasury department he had had his fill.

"I shall always vote against a motion," barked the balding Virginian, "for applying to the Secretary of the Treasury for information respecting the means of procuring the sums of money necessary for the exigencies of Government."[1] In full Antifederalist throat, he opined that, "The Bills establishing Departments of Government have strong Monarchical features; and have all too often led Congress into the steps of Monarchical Government." Time had come, grumbled Page, for the House to reclaim its constitutional authority and determine for itself "the means of raising the supplies which may be found necessary for the support of the Government."[2] Although he failed by a 31 to 27 margin to prevent Sedgwick's resolution from carrying, it was opening salvo in a Virginia-led campaign to rein in treasury initiative.

Laurance, as Hamilton's House point person on matters financial, could not have thought it mere coincidence when yet another Virginian, husky, pug-faced William B. Giles, stood two weeks later to reject a treasury proposal to expand the $50 million public debt by another $20 million. At issue was the irredeemable portion of the government's original $70 million refinancing of 1790. Hamilton urged that these 3 percent notes with no fixed redemption date should be subscribed to the loan of the United States, lest the nation's credit be impaired. Giles, convinced that "exotic" irredeemable notes had prostrated Great Britain's funding system, motioned to exclude them from the public debt. Laurance was no stranger to argument with Giles; the pair had recently differed on the Post

Office Bill, on bounties on the New England cod fisheries, and on uniform national organization of state militias. Although a pro-administration majority ultimately prevailed on all three measures, the Virginian's assertion that subscribing irredeemable notes to the national loan "would be so fatal to the United States" was more than John could bear. "The credit of the country," Laurance curtly replied, "had been raised from the lowest ebb, and a larger sum of the debt had been paid off than any man in the country had any conception of."[3] Indignant at Giles's slurs against the treasury secretary, John huffed that "such reflections were not merited by an officer who had done so much for his country," and then proceeded to articulate the advantages of irredeemable notes in managing the public debt.[4] The Giles motion was negated 32 to 25.

As if in comic relief, a senate bill for establishment of a United States mint arrived in the House on March 24 with the curious proviso that Washington's face grace the republic's first silver coins. Indeed, some 1,500 prototype copper cent pieces sporting a presidential effigy already jingled in the palms of cabinet officials and members of Congress, courtesy of English die-makers W. and A. Walker in hope of a lucrative contract.[5] Laurance had the good sense to remain silent during a controversial exchange with senate counterparts regarding not only each sitting president's likeness on the coins, but also his name and number of succession. Anti-administration voices (beginning to call themselves "Republicans") combined as one with Virginia's Rep. Page to shout "monarchism" and ship the ill-conceived measure back to its senate authors.[6] Eventually, all factions compromised in favor of beauty, settling on Lady Liberty's bust in Washington's place to pass the Coinage Act of 1792 to establish the United States Mint in Philadelphia. Whether or not Laurance noticed the similarity of Lady Liberty to Mrs. William Bingham's comely profile, he pragmatically endorsed the measure.[7]

Virginia's rising voice in the House of Representatives was rooted in chamber reapportionment debates that began the past October when Speaker John Trumbull gaveled to order the Second Federal Congress. With 1790 census information freshly in hand, the body had formed into a committee of the whole to reapportion its membership according to Article I, Section 2 of the Constitution. The task appeared simple enough: Article I clearly stated that the number of Representatives was "not to exceed one for every thirty Thousand" free persons plus three fifths of the slaves. Virginia, as all could see from census figures, was by far the most populous state, boasting almost 15 percent of the young republic's free white population plus 292,627 slaves (42.1 percent of the national total).[8] Determining just how many additional House seats to assign to James Madison's home state would pit North against South, free states against slave states, and large states against small. On top of which was the controversial matter of how to handle fractional rounding of individual state representation.

Rep. Laurance opened the debate with a straightforward motion that the next House be apportioned consistent with constitutional language calling for one representative for every 30,000 persons.[9] But Sedgwick quickly pointed out that the New Yorker's motion would increase the House from 68 members to an unwieldy 115, or more. Virginia's delegation would then more than double from 10 to 21 because of its huge slave population, an outcome the anti-slavery Sedgwick hoped to forestall. He was "of the opinion that the ratio which would meet the general approbation" was "about one hundred members in the House of Representatives."[10] Amending the law to one representative per 34,000 persons, Sedgwick noted, would produce 100 members, a suggestion seconded by small state Federalist Samuel Livermore of New Hampshire.

Fisher Ames then weighed in to propose the size of the House be determined at a hundred by dividing the ratio of representation into the aggregate national population rather than into the population of respective states.[11] Pro-administration Reps. Barnwell of South Carolina and Clark of New Jersey agreed, arguing that Laurance's proposed ratio would produce too large a House for efficient deliberation. More, of course, lay behind the Federalist hundred-member limit than simple House logistics. It was no secret that more than 35,000 settlers populated Tennessee, double that number had planted foot in Kentucky, and squatters were pouring north of the Ohio River into the Northwest Territories. Because few constituted the educated gentry that Federalists thought best suited to govern the burgeoning new nation, the best way to limit this crude frontier voice was to dilute it with the highest possible per-thousands ratio for House seats.[12]

Countering Sedgwick, Ames, and company, Virginians Giles and White together with Pennsylvania's William Findley contended a larger House better represented the voice of the people. And Hugh Williamson of North Carolina thought the best ratio was one that would leave the fewest fractions. What at first had appeared to be a simple matter soon devolved, as mathematics professor Charles M. Biles succinctly observed, into competing slates of formidable arithmetic, each with its own divisor, fractional rounding formula, and parochial interest.[13]

Laurance now faced a decision: either stick to his literal, nonpartisan reading of the Constitution or join fellow Federalists Sedgwick, Livermore, and Ames to cap the House at a hundred members (and limit Virginia's additional seats) by increasing the representation ratio to 33,000 or 34,000. John's choice tells us much about his ideological independence and personal character. For, rather than taking a Federalist tack, he voted with Madison and the Virginia delegation to ram through his original 1-to-30,000 motion by a 35 to 23 margin.[14] After defeating a late November motion to amend the bill to the ratio of 34,000, Laurance held firm through three readings to pass the House's apportionment bill with an overwhelming 43 to 12 majority.[15]

The Federalist Senate, however, was of different mind. After months of back and forth, Vice President Adams broke a 12 to 12 Senate impasse by altering the House bill to a ratio of 1 to 33,000, an action that slashed Virginia's potential additional seats from 11 to 9. Deadlock between the chambers was then averted in March 1792 by combining Laurance's proposed 30,000 to 1 ratio with a Senate plan that awarded eight additional seats to those states with the largest fractional representative.[16] Perhaps because six of the eight were northern states, President Washington's two cabinet Virginians (Secretary of State Jefferson and Attorney General Edmund Randolph) advised him that fractional rounding was unconstitutional.[17] Washington on April 5 vetoed the bill.

Unable to amass the necessary two-thirds majority to override the president's veto, Speaker Muhlenberg appointed Laurance, Joshua Seney of Maryland, and Jeremiah Smith of New Hampshire a committee to bring in a new bill. Reporting back for the threesome, Laurance read out language that eliminated fractional rounding, but *left the population ratio blank* for the Committee of the Whole to fill in.[18] Next day the House inserted the words "thirty-three" thousand. Whereupon, Laurance, refusing to compromise his original position, voted alongside Madison and the other nine Virginians against the new bill, only to see it pass 34 to 30.[19] Four days later, President Washington signed into law the Apportionment Act of 1792 with a 1 to 33,000 ratio that specified a 105-member House.[20] If the apportionment issue was Laurance's opportunity to establish himself as a moderate Federalist floor leader who could bridge emerging sectional factions, he had failed. Factionalism was on the march, and Theodore Sedgwick and Fisher Ames proved the stronger hands in mobilizing Federalist interests.

What would linger with every congressman well after the session adjourned on May 8 was the harrowing four-month financial rollercoaster ride Treasury Secretary Hamilton had just eased to a halt. It all began the previous December when the Bank of the United States (BUS) first opened its doors for business in Carpenters' Hall. Just as Federalist lawmakers had hoped, merchants, manufacturers, and landowners flocked to the bank with deposits, loan requests, and transfer payments. And just as Hamilton promised, bank notes circulated throughout the states, injecting much-needed paper currency into the commercial economy, facilitating investment in factories, canals, turnpikes, and land companies. The national bank, with deposits approaching $1.3 million and branches slated to open in New York, Boston, Baltimore, and Charleston, instantly became the young country's largest single enterprise.

Republicans' worst fears were soon realized when northern speculators, particularly in Rep. Laurance's constituency, borrowed heavily from the Bank of New York to invest in BUS stock, driving securities prices skyward. The inevitable February price collapse spread like yellow fever to panicky depositors who rushed to withdraw cash from the national bank.

By early March 1792, BUS cash reserves had fallen by some 34 percent, prompting President Willing to call in nearly a quarter of its loans. Similar scenarios played out at the country's four large private banks: Bank of New York, Bank of Massachusetts, Bank of Maryland, and Philadelphia's Bank of North America. By simultaneously curtailing credit, these lenders collectively triggered America's very first large-scale securities crash as speculators scrambled to sell their stocks. The subsequent "Panic of 1792" was a narrowly averted financial meltdown that dramatically altered America's political landscape, so it's worth a moment to understand the event through its largest, most overleveraged speculator: Laurance's fellow West Country English émigré and Trinity Church goer, William Duer.[21]

"Duer could have made a Million," observed New York investment broker William Constable, "if he could Confine himself to any one object— but his Genius will not permit it."[22] Indeed, after being forced to resign as Hamilton's first assistant when reckless speculation in government securities rendered him a political liability, Duer borrowed heavily to support myriad ventures. He rained money into projects ranging from Ohio land schemes to a Boston bridge company, a Pennsylvania canal company, half a dozen bank schemes, and a speculative start-up stake in Hamilton's half-million-dollar 700-acre vision for a "national manufactory" near the Great Falls of New Jersey's Passaic River. With the influential Duer as its founding governor, Hamilton's "Society for Establishing Useful Manufacturers" (SEUM) attracted start-up capital from a "Who's Who" of insider moneymen (William Constable, Andrew Craigie, Nicholas Low, Alexander Macomb, John Pintard, Brockholst, Henry, Phillip Livingston, and more) to swell the original scrip from $19.91 a share toward an eventual high of $50.00.[23] By October of 1791, Duer was also the largest owner of BUS stock, controlling with his close associates 1,200 of the 20,000 shares available to the public.[24]

Determined to capitalize on merger rumors (which he helped spread) between Bank of New York and the national bank, Duer formed a one-year speculative coalition with parvenu Detroit fur trader–cum–New York merchant/shipper Alexander Macomb.* After drawing in Walter Livingston (to the tune of $800,000 of endorsed debt notes) and East India trade merchant John Pintard (up to $1,000,000 of endorsed notes), among others, the partnership set out to drive up BUS share prices.[25] Capitalizing on a seemingly insatiable appetite for public securities, the partners next announced formation of a new "million dollar bank," and hinted of merging the entity with the Bank of New York.[26] Although the new bank

---

*Irish-born Crown loyalist Macomb (1748–1831) pocketed a substantial fortune between 1779 and 1783 billing almost £200,000 in goods to British western garrisons and their Native American allies. In 1785 he acquired 3.6 million upstate New York acres and erected a huge Broadway mansion to shelter his 10 children and 25 servants. The building was so sumptuous that in February 1790, the federal government leased it to serve as Washington's presidential mansion until relocating to Philadelphia.

itself never materialized, more than 20,000 shares—10 times the contemplated evaluation—were subscribed when they went on sale January 16, 1792, sending securities prices soaring across the board. But Duer and Macomb's so-called "million dollar bank" three weeks later turned to mere speculative froth when the General Assembly voted down "An Act to Incorporate a State Bank."[27]

After Bank of New York/BUS merger rumors also proved false, Duer and Macomb—though details are murky—then schemed to acquire a controlling share of Bank of New York stock. Of perhaps 700 available Bank of New York shares, Macomb quickly gobbled up some 400.[28] The idea was to use bank assets to corner the market on 6 percent federal bonds and dole them out at inflated prices to unsuspecting foreign investors and those desperate to pay off required BUS stock purchase installments.[29] Indeed, their scheme just might have worked if securities prices continued to rise; but a rival group of New York speculators spearheaded by Brockholst, Edward, and John R. Livingston wanted security prices to move downward. Opportunity called when Treasury Secretary Hamilton on February 10 urged the Bank of New York to curtail loans because "the superstructure of credit is now too vast for the foundation."[30] Working the ensuing "bear market" with considerable family resources, the Livingston group trapped overextended William Duer in a classic credit squeeze. Together with Boston financier Andrew Craigie and Manhattan merchant/land speculator Theodosius Fowler, Livingston agents sold to Duer the very securities he wanted—but for future delivery—and then maneuvered to cut off Duer's bank credit.[31] On March 9, Duer stopped making payments to his creditors.

As credit defaults began to cascade, banks across the country began calling in loans and anxious depositors withdrew specie, leaving William Duer no choice but to prematurely unwind his long position in government bonds. Double-crossing his partner Macomb, he then began selling 6 percent federal bonds short while the former was still buying long. As security prices tumbled, the vastly overextended Duer scrambled to borrow securities to cover his short sales. Thanks to the Livingstons, however, none were to be had! Desperate for cash, a panicky Duer went so far as to peddle personal IOUs for up to 6 percent interest *per month* to unsophisticated "shopkeepers, widows, orphans, butchers, cartmen, gardeners, market women, & even the Bawd [prostitute] Mrs. Macarty."[32] Wildly exaggerated whispers soon made the rounds that the overreached "King of the Alley" (as Jefferson derisively dubbed Duer) was up to three million dollars in debt.[33] Duer's slippery financial slope only steepened when Secretary Hamilton slapped his former assistant with a federal district court lawsuit for an unsettled $240,000 "discrepancy" still lingering from his earlier stint at the treasury.

Hamilton, recognizing the entire Federalist financial revolution—as well as Bank of New York—was at risk, once again took decisive action.

With the blessing of his Sinking Fund Committee (except Secretary Jefferson), the treasury secretary on March 21 purchased some $243,000 of government 6 percent notes both in open market and by delivering three overnight $50,000 cash transfers for that purpose to Bank of New York cashier Seton.[34]

Having stabilized Federal security prices, Hamilton further bolstered public confidence by announcing that a large loan had just been successfully negotiated from Holland. He then directed Bank of New York head cashier Seton to inject much needed liquidity into the financial marketplace by lending freely when top-quality securities could be had as collateral.[35] Orchestrating similar action in Philadelphia and with Baltimore's Bank of Maryland, Hamilton eased general pandemonium to an end by the first of May. William Duer as much for his physical safety as to prevent flight was ushered into the New Gaol debtors' prison on March 23, followed on April 18 by partner Macomb. Walter Livingston declared bankruptcy and then, boasting to his son-in-law of "hidden assets," sought refuge in the vast upstate family estate.[36] John Pintard, his grandfather's large inheritance devastated, declared New York bankruptcy and escaped to the wilds of New Jersey, only to ultimately end up for a year behind bars in Newark's two-story stone jail.*

On April 11, first-hand reports of the financial carnage reached Laurance in Philadelphia. "Mr. Macomb declared his bankruptcy today at the coffee house," wrote one of John's law clients, while "Mr. Brockholst Livingston declares he is not worth 1000 dollars on earth if his debts are paid." The letter went on to add:

> How many bankruptcies must follow in this City, Philadelphia and & Boston tis improbable to say. The whole fabric of speculation has been so connected that a general failure is supposed to be the inevitable issue amongst the dealers in stocks. Happy are you not to witness the shocking scenes that daily take place here. The depravity of the human mind had been exhibited in its worst stage. The speculators are daily boxing in the streets, cursing and abusing each other like pick pockets and trying every fraud to prey on each others distress ... Our poor friend Duer feels most acutely the general calamity each man lays his misfortunes at his door ... His schemes have been too vast for the resources of this country to support.[37]

---

*John Pintard (1759–1844) never fully recovered his lost wealth but found redemption in three decades of public service. Among other things he became secretary of the New York Chamber of Commerce, founder of the New York Historical Society, cofounder of the American Bible Society, an active Freemason, and founding force behind what became the present-day New York free school system. Pintard also was instrumental in establishing the modern public conception of Santa Claus based upon the Dutch legend of *Sinterklass*, published in 1809 by his friend Washington Irving.

Approached by Duer with a frantic borrowing plea, Laurance according to family tradition consulted John Jay for advice. Jay's icy reply, since lost, was that bailing out Duer was "wrong in principle and prejudicial to the welfare of society."[38] As New York's moneyed society closed ranks to ensure Duer and Macomb received their just deserts, Philadelphia's fiercely Republican *National Gazette* of April 19 trumpeted that rival New York "is in a languishing condition, with vessels laying in wharves without anyone to receive their cargoes—the speculators either in jail, ruminating over bushels of loose paper, locked up in garrets, or fled in to remote and desolate parts of Jersey."[39] Laurance, whose every spare dollar was sunk into upstate New York real estate rather than speculative bonds, watched his property values plummet but emerged otherwise unscathed. Nor was he left holding a piece of the $500,000 capitalization bag along with Robert Troup, Henry Knox, and Philip Livingston when Hamilton's mammoth joint-stock company investment syndicate (Society for Establishing Useful Manufacturers)—its treasury looted by co-investor Duer—collapsed into an accommodation with the state of New Jersey.

Still, Duer's demise must have weighed heavily on Laurance. The two English immigrants had labored together to restore Trinity Parish to life, make the case for congressional imposts to the New York state legislature, and ratify the new federal Constitution. When Duer and "Lady Kitty" removed to their country estate (Raneleigh) below Greenwich Village, Laurance joined Hamilton, Troup, Benson, Jay, and Frederick Steuben as frequent guests over "not less than fifteen sorts of wine at dinner."[40] But even if Laurance had sprung to Duer's financial aid, he could have ameliorated no more than a drop in his friend's vast ocean of debt. In any event, William Duer was financially and emotionally destroyed; three months after his February 1799 release from debtors' prison, the high-living soldier of fortune was dead.

Surrounded by three blossoming daughters from his first marriage, Laurance spent the summer of 1792 at Trout Hall punctuated with visits from wife Elizabeth's trio of Philadelphia belles and the laughing gurgle of their own newly born baby girl, Emily Ann. Still, he would have been blind not to see that societal convulsions from the spring financial panic had heavily poisoned the nation's political atmosphere. "A tendency to ascribe the most extensive evils to Treasury influence," observed Professors Elkins and McKitrick, "and to see in it a steady perversion of public morals, was very widespread."[41] Moralistic newspaper essays denounced the plundering of innocents by New York speculators and called to repeal the BUS charter. Fanning the flame of public suspicion, Madison and Jefferson's newly founded Democratic-Republican Party burst onto the national stage to castigate the entire federal funding system with its program of excise taxes, expanded government payroll, and permanent public debt.

To be clear, Thomas Jefferson cherished the new constitutional government as much as Hamilton and Laurance, but ideological distrust fed deepening personal animosity to convince him by early 1792 that the treasury secretary constituted a mortal threat to the young republic. Where Hamilton saw well-managed long-term public debt as an existential instrument of virtue that increased the money stock, lubricated the national economy, and facilitated national credit, the Master of Monticello saw only transfer of community wealth into the pockets of a corrupt socioeconomic elite who manipulated the debt to pull strings of government for selfish ends. To the agrarian mind, for which everything had its season, there was just something *sinful* about the Funding Act of 1790 — Jefferson's deepest political regret — creating money out of thin air through perpetual federal debt.[42]

Phillip "Poet of the Revolution" Freneau spread the Republican apprehension. Using Jefferson's $250 per year State Department clerkship to launch the privately published *National Gazette*, he had wasted no time creating a platform from which to lambaste the treasury secretary as an incipient monarchist who favored financial speculators, recklessly ran up national debt, and plotted to establish British-style hereditary aristocracy. Enraged by 18 weeks of partisan articles, Hamilton struck back in late July — despite President Washington's plea for restraint — with a newspaper campaign of his own. Of Philadelphia's 12 newspapers, most important was the *Gazette of the United States*, principal recipient of Treasury Department printing contracts. Editor John Fenno, to whom Hamilton occasionally lent money, was delighted to furnish him a podium (under the mask, "An American") to accuse Jefferson point-blank of disloyalty to the president and his administration.

Madison had sounded alarm over the potential perils of perpetual public debt well before Jefferson, but Hamilton's attitude toward his former *Federalist Papers* coauthor was more one of disappointment than personal enmity. "The opinion I once entertained of the candour and fairness of Mr. Madison's character," wrote the treasury secretary in late May to Virginia Federalist Edward Carrington, "has given way to a decided opinion that *it is one of a peculiarly artificial and complicated kind.*"[43] If Laurance harbored similar feelings toward Madison, he kept them to himself. One of the striking characteristics of John's surviving correspondence is the complete absence of personal opinion about his peers, Federalist, Republican, or otherwise. Whether owing to Masonic civility, learned behavior of five years administering military justice, or the essentially collaborative nature of legislative committee work, it was just not his way to judge a man's character or political beliefs in print. Certainly, John, after three years of daily House interaction with Madison, had a clear read on what made the

Master of Montpelier tick. Nobody had clashed more with the diminutive Virginian on the House floor, yet what Hamilton saw as "peculiarly artificial" would have appeared to pragmatic lawmakers the likes of Laurance as obligatory political dexterity essential to bind any representative with his constituency. Besides, he and Madison sometimes—the House apportionment issue and the Coinage Act, for example—found themselves in agreement.

Laurance returned to the City of Brotherly Love in early November for the third and concluding session of the Second Federal Congress, to be immediately charged by Speaker Trumbull as one of three to answer President Washington's State of the Union speech.[44] "There is nothing," the president had urged with an eye to the burgeoning Hamilton/Jefferson animosity, "which can have a more powerful tendency than the careful cultivation of harmony, combined with a due regard to stability, in the public councils."[45] As John helped prepare the obligatory House reply, it was plain to see that the days of harmonious council were nearing the end. For the monumental task of translating the constitutional operating manual into working machinery of a powerful national government was virtually complete. Unfinished business from the historic First Federal Congress had been addressed with last spring's passage of the Postal Service Act making the postmaster-general a permanent cabinet position, the Coinage Act establishing a national mint, and the Militia Acts of 1792 organizing state militias under a uniform federal call-up structure. All that really remained was to create a standing army and effective oceangoing navy; but that would have to wait until 1797 hostilities with Revolutionary France forced the issue.

Looking ahead to the Third Federal Congress about to convene later that March, it was plain to see that advancing the Federalist agenda would meet with stiffer-than-ever Virginia resistance. The Apportionment Act of April 1792 had employed 1790 census data to increase Old Dominion representation from 10 to 19 seats versus New York and Massachusetts's combined gain of six additional seats. The House, based on a new metric of one representative per 33,000 population, would expand to 105 members, enabling southern states (where slaves counted for three-fifths of a person) to combine with the new states of Kentucky and Vermont in the next Congress to give anti-administration voices their first House majority.

The tide of history at his back, James Madison consolidated anti-administration representatives under the emerging Republican umbrella in waning months of the Second Congress to become first true House minority leader. But for all his reservations about slavery's immorality, Madison's economic livelihood depended upon it. Acceding, therefore, to election-year interests of his own constituency, the Virginian in February 1793 flexed real parliamentary muscle to orchestrate "An Act Respecting Fugitives from Justice, and Persons escaping from the service of their Masters." Better known as the Fugitive Slave Act of 1793, the measure guaranteed slaveholders the right to recover their escaped property under a uniform national protocol that assessed anyone who harbored or assisted runaways with a $500 fine and possible imprisonment. Even longtime anti-slavery Federalists Benson, Boudinot, and Sedgwick joined the 48 to 7 House majority rendering the bill into law.[46] To their mind, voluntary cooperation between the states was just not working. The new law, by imposing a magistrate's approval, at least protected free northern blacks from slave-catcher kidnappings.

Laurance, a confirmed abolitionist, could not as matter of principle vote for *any* protocol that returned runaway slaves to a hellish life. Nor, on the other hand, could he bring himself to vote against it; New York—for all its abolitionist talk—was the largest slave state in the north. "Most of the inferior labor of the town is performed by Blacks," observed British traveler William Strickland in 1794 of New York City's 2,500 slaves.[47] Indeed 1,115 of New York's 5,868 white families (19 percent) were slave owners,[48] and not even John Jay's Manumission Society could find the moral wherewithal to exclude slaveholders from its membership.[49] With an eye on his own constituency, Rep. Laurance joined 13 other House members who abstained when the fugitive slave legislation was put to vote. President Washington, whose own 22-year-old slave Ona Judge would flee the Philadelphia presidential mansion in May 1796, and whose Mount Vernon plantation was worked by another 300 slaves, promptly signed the measure into law.[50]

Despite Madison's ascendance as Republican floor general, Laurance in early 1793 did not lack political stature of his own. One of only 25 members of the government to be assigned a code name in confidential communications from Foreign Minister Gouveneur Morris in Paris, John was also the sole New Yorker recommended to President Washington by both War Secretary Knox and Treasury Secretary Hamilton as potential commissioner to negotiate with hostile Northwest Territory Indians.[51] Moreover, confided Vice President Adams to son John Quincy, Laurance was under consideration for the cabinet position of attorney general vacated when Edmund Randolph was made secretary of state in the wake of Jefferson's resignation.[52] John's larger responsibility, however, lay with the select House committee for appropriations from which he reported out a proposed fiscal 1793 operating expenditure of $1,589,044.72—nearly a 50 percent increase versus the previous year.[53] The New Yorker's recommendation was approved without controversy by a lame-duck Federalist majority that for good measure tacked on an amendment authorizing further pay-down of foreign debt at presidential discretion in $50,000 installments.

The overriding business of the third session's final two months was neither appropriations nor revenues, nor even the sordid, drawn-out post-mortem investigation of General St. Clair's bloody defeat at the hands of a Native American coalition in the Ohio Territory. Rather it was a full-scale Republican attack on the character and competence of Alexander Hamilton. Secretary Jefferson, long convinced of Hamilton's corruption, in mid-January 1793 seized on treasury foreign loan reports to conclude that the secretary had without legal authorization diverted into national bank coffers money borrowed in Europe to retire foreign debt, thereby benefitting the private bank at public expense. On January 23, pugnacious William Branch Giles introduced five resolutions demanding exhaustive information on Hamilton's administration of the treasury. After Hamilton complied accordingly, Giles in late February filed nine censure resolutions (likely drawn up by Jefferson) that accused him of maladministration on everything from improperly mixing foreign and domestic debt to sinking fund mismanagement and accounting sleight-of-hand with the national bank.[54] The secretary of state personally climaxed the onslaught by proposing to President Washington an official cabinet inquiry—immediately rebuffed—into Hamilton's department.

Hamilton responded in a tour de force of reportorial stamina, delivering a comprehensive financial overview of his administration in four separate February reports supported by a phalanx of charts and statistics. It was a data trove that Reps. Laurance, Sedgwick, Ames, Boudinot, and Smith—all courtroom-hardened lawyers whom Hamilton counted as personal friends—mined to refute Giles, resolution by resolution. Elias Boudinot's sponsorship of Hamilton stretched all the way back to 1772, when he introduced the immigrant teen to the refined world of books and high culture at Elizabethtown Academy. Behind his ready smile was a grasp of finance that convinced Washington in 1795 to appoint him director of the United States Mint. Sedgwick and Ames, like Laurance, were formidable orators, particularly the 31-year-old Harvard-educated Ames who was regarded as the most eloquent of Federalist voices. But it was William Smith who struck first. By persuading the House to confine itself to the main point—"had the Secretary violated a law"—the astute South Carolinian eliminated Giles's first, second, and ninth resolutions as mere theoretical political abstractions.[55]

Having narrowed the scope of debate, the Federalist quartet then homed in on whether or not Hamilton had breached the law by comingling foreign loans contracted under two separate acts of congress. That Hamilton had comingled the money was beyond dispute; indeed, he had earlier advised the House of such on orders from Washington.[56] Sedgwick and Laurance weighed in, not to dispute these facts but to make the case that mixing of loan funds was not only perfectly legal but also in the national interest by ensuring that government interest payments were met. Furthermore, argued Laurance, the complex transactions had the president's consent. And, "If this mode of paying was within the authority vested in the President," John concluded, "surely the power of drawing [by Treasury as his agent] must have accompanied it."[57] Boudinot and Ames then marshaled treasury data in elaborate detail to prove that neither Hamilton nor the BUS had appropriated a penny of public funds for personal profit. Laurance, shortly before the remaining Giles censure resolutions were rejected by votes ranging from 40–12 to 34–7, rose to pronounce his last say on the matter:

> When the resolutions calling for information from the Treasury Department were first brought forward, the public mind was impressed with an idea that there were monies unaccounted for. This charge is now dropped, and it is honorable to the officer concerned that after much probing, nothing is found to support it.[58]

Fittingly, Laurance's remarks in support of good friend Hamilton were his final words to House colleagues. Next day, Speaker Trumbull adjourned the Second United States Congress, and John would not return. Although Hamilton pleaded that "the next Congress will either anchor the Government in safety or set it afloat," Laurance had the previous October advised him that a third term was out of the question.[59] Two years in Confederated Congress, four years with the federal Congress, and a pair of presidential election campaigns were enough. Never again would he run for elective office.

Why Laurance walked away, aged 42, at the peak of constituency popularity and the threshold of House party leadership has been left for us to guess. Clearly the $6 per diem compensation of a U.S. Representative (he was paid $714 plus travel expenses for 119 days of service in 1792/93) paled against earnings potential of his successful New York legal practice.[60] A trio of coming-of-age daughters from his first marriage, together with socialite second wife Elizabeth and her three graces, not to mention year-old Emily Ann, were certainly *not* low maintenance. Sacrificing income and family was difficult enough when the First Federal Congress buzzed with creative debate, but four years later the daily humdrum of House business droned into dull, increasingly partisan, routine. Fisher Ames may as well have been speaking for Laurance when he lamented: "Congress is not engaged in very interesting work. The first acts were the pillars of the federal edifice. Now we have only to keep the sparks from catching the shavings."[61]

More, however, than simple legislative drudgery wore on Rep. Laurance. Before his eyes the very nature of the chamber had changed from its heady First Federal Congress days, despite almost two-thirds of its members having returned for a second term. Just as Madison had predicted in 1789, a federalist consensus had devolved into "contentions first between federal and antifederal parties and then between Northern and Southern parties."[62] This harsh fact of political life so galled Laurance that in the midst of February's reapportionment debates he stood to reprobate House colleagues for "considering themselves as Representatives merely of particular parts of the Union."[63] To John's mind, the House, as heir to the Confederation Congress, was intended to think and act—as it had generally done in the inaugural federal

Congress—with a national rather than parochial perspective. "The states, as states are represented in the Senate," he argued. "A member of the House from Georgia," John insisted, "is a Representative of the State of New York as much as if he came from the latter state."[64] That he had lobbied to keep the nation's capital in his own district for as long as possible was conveniently disregarded in Laurance's disillusionment with a political agenda that no longer transcended regional and ideological differences.

His decision to forgo a third term also stemmed from increasing disaffection with hardening Federalist Party ideology. More the nationalist than a party ideologue, John had first linked arms with Jay, Schuyler, and Hamilton under the Federalist umbrella to seek public office because he believed American prosperity depended upon a strong, well-financed federal government with an empowered chief executive. To that end, no one had worked more tirelessly in Congress over the past four years. And because his own financial and commercial interests aligned so seamlessly with those of his New York constituency, John's pragmatic legislative style truly advanced Federalist hegemony. Never, however, did his personal political ambition extend beyond the New York state line. As early as the summer of 1791, his increasing estrangement had deeply concerned old friend Robert Troup. "King & I have availed ourselves of every opportunity," Troup confided to Hamilton, "of impressing Laurance with the necessity of his continuing amongst us," but he added, "I fear the impressions we have made are but slight."[65]

With word that Louis XVI in January 1793 had been guillotined and the streets of Paris ran red with blood, Republicans flowered into enthusiastic Francophiles while horrified Federalists solidified pro-British sympathies. As political temperatures rose, Laurance's practical, even-tempered demeanor distanced him from his more ideological associates. "I wish you had less passion and less party," he later confided to Rufus King. "They intermix too much in deliberations and measures."[66] There was just something unbecoming to Laurance about political factions. Indeed, the whole "root idea" in period Anglo-American thought—as far back as early eighteenth-century England—was "that parties are evil."[67] Even President Washington's Farewell Address would warn against "the baneful effects of the Spirit of Party." Although not about to follow Chancellor Robert Livingston and others over to Republican ranks (one set of ideologues was as bad as the other), John was no longer in political lockstep with his Federalist associates. "I think I can see the distance between him and his old friends daily growing wider,"[68] observed Troup.

In truth, Federalist statecraft under Hamilton's architectonic vision *was* becoming more aristocratic, if not the imagined "monarchical plot" Vice President Jefferson had warned President Washington of in mid-1792.[69] The nation's financial capital *was* concentrating in select northern hands, while "high" Federalists Charles Carroll, Richard Goodloe Harper, Oliver Wolcott Jr., and Charles C. Pinckney, together with the so-called

Massachusetts "Essex Junto,"[70] seemed bent on a federal government along the British model that disproportionately favored the wealthy with its powerful military, strong central bank, and a manufacturing-driven political economy. Hamilton professed to be "affectionately attached to republican theory," but he distrusted power in the hands of the arbitrary, impressionable masses; a chariness exacerbated by rowdy pro-Jacobin street demonstrations from newly formed democratic societies. "Hence a disposition on my part," explained the treasury secretary the previous May to Virginia Federalist Edward Carrington, "toward a liberal construction of the powers of the National Government."[71] Although no friend of hereditary distinction, Hamilton spoke for most Federalists by preferring administrative reins of republican government to be firmly in the hands of merit-based members of the educated, propertied sort.

Trouble was, historian Gordon Wood has since observed, "More and more of the Federalist officeholders found that their property, or their proprietary wealth, did not generate enough income for them to ignore or neglect their private affairs."[72] Bankrupt Supreme Court Associate Justice James Wilson fled to North Carolina to avoid debtors' prison, while House Speaker Jonathan Trumbull simply stiffed creditors until departing this earth with an insolvent estate. Faced with the choice between profiteering from office and suffering financial setback, others—like War Secretary Henry Knox, Jeremiah Wadsworth of Connecticut, and eventually Hamilton himself—withdrew from national public service. In March of 1793, so did Rep. Laurance.

Before departing the House chamber for good, John had one last duty to perform. Together with South Carolina Rep. Smith, he was honored to deliver to House Clerk Beckley the Electoral College vote tallied by joint session of Congress to conclude the presidential election of 1792. Laurance then lingered after Speaker Trumbull adjourned final session of the Second Federal Congress to watch Associate Supreme Court Justice William Cushing administer second-term oath of office to President Washington. Clad in black velvet and wearing the same silver side sword as at New York four years before, Washington matter-of-factly delivered the shortest (only 135 words) inaugural address ever given. The exuberance of 1789 was but distant memory.

Six months later, Washington, Vice President Adams, and virtually the entire government fled from a Philadelphia ravaged by the worst epidemic ever to strike an American city. Deadly "yellow jack" virus and the tropical mosquitoes to carry it had swarmed into the Delaware River port with 2,000 French colonial refugees. The malignant fever apparently began on Water Street in the filthy space between Arch and Race Streets near the wharves receiving incoming ships. On August 19, Dr. Benjamin Rush, the most prominent physician of his day, pronounced unfortunate Peter Aston the first yellow fever victim. Unaware that mosquitoes transmitted the fever, Rush and helpless fellow physicians could do little more than rub patients with vinegar, administer calomel purges, and conduct repeated bloodlettings.

Laurance, with no political reason to remain in town, serendipitously relocated his growing family to New York mere days before Mayor Varick quarantined the city of incoming refugees and goods shipped from Philadelphia. By vacating ahead of the epidemic's zenith, John spared Elizabeth the uncomfortable dilemma of choosing whether or not to follow family friend Dr. Rush's "Republican cure" for yellow fever. For, symptomatic of the times, even medical theory had acquired political bias. Republican doctors ascribed the fever to miasmatic local filth and copied the much-esteemed Rush* in bleeding patients with a vigor rivaling Jacobin guillotines. Indeed, Rush's "Republican" treatment with its deaths from harsh purgatives, induced vomiting, and copious bloodlettings was publicly attacked by mudslinging yellow-journalist newspaperman William Cobbett who branded him "a quack" and "a murderer."[73] Ultimately, independent physicians came to less provocative conclusions when the efficacy of Rush's treatments began to wane.

Federalists, on the other hand, blamed yellow jack on the thousands of immigrant Frenchmen fleeing St. Dominique. Instead of bloodletting, Hamilton and his followers adopted the "Caribbean" therapy of exercise, fresh air, restorative fluids, ice-water baths, and mild purging.[74] To those eschewing politics in their cure, respected College of Philadelphia professor of medicine Dr. Adam Kuhn prescribed wine, "The quantity to be determined by the effects it produces." Newspapers trotted out the old medieval medicament to destroy plague by "purifying" the air with charcoal smoke and black-powder musket discharges. Still, the fever spread. By September, Philadelphians were dying at the rate of 20 per day, a toll that in October soared to more than a hundred. By the first hard November frost, almost a tenth of Philadelphia's population (nearly 5,000 people) had perished. It was not until December that Senator King could advise New Yorkers "you need have no apprehensions of the fever, for I really believe the town is free from it."[75]

Nevertheless, John did not return. His distance from fellow Federalists had widened to the point that Robert Troup warned "the force of a feather would almost throw him into the arms of our enemies."[76] Furthermore, Laurance was miffed . . . and for good reason. The nine Philadelphia-based national bank directors, who together with bank president Thomas Willing transacted most of the business, had seized upon

---

*Dr. Rush remained in Philadelphia for the duration of the epidemic, persevering in search of a cure. Victim to the fever himself, Rush demanded his assistants administer the severe bloodletting prescribed to his patients, and he recovered. His heroism during the 1793 epidemic endeared him even to political enemies, but so many fellow members of the University of Pennsylvania College of Physicians opposed his fever theories that Dr. Rush resigned the College on November 5, 1793. During future epidemics, Rush's cure became increasingly discredited.

Laurance's absence to replace him as director with one of their own. Senator King, bowing to Republican pressure for a constitutional amendment to prohibit members of Congress from simultaneously holding BUS office, had already resigned his own directorship so that he might (successfully) oppose the proposed measure without insinuations of self-interest. But Laurance was no longer in Congress. Rather than risk losing him unnecessarily from party ranks, King then threw considerable political weight to reinstate his fellow New Yorker's BUS directorship. "Lawrance is well pleased with his re-appointment," a much-relieved Troup apprised King 10 days later, "and I have informed him of your friendly offices to effect it."[77]

FOURTEEN

Judicial Safe Harbor

NEW YORK CITY, DECEMBER 25, 1793. Laurance, by refusing a third congressional term and quitting Philadelphia to resuscitate his neglected Wall Street law practice, may have bid partisan governmental intrigue adieu, but Alexander Hamilton had not. And so on Christmas Day, John, "confined with a very heavy Cold and Sore throat," hoisted pen to defend the treasury secretary against misconduct accusations leveled by a disgruntled former treasury clerk named Andrew Fraunces.[1]

Fraunces—fired for drunken incompetence the past March—blamed Hamilton personally when treasury officials subsequently refused to redeem questionable Confederation-era warrants for $5,500 hard specie.[2] Hoping to blackmail Hamilton into honoring the disputed warrants, Fraunces (black sheep son of tavern-keeper-turned-presidential-chef "Black Sam" Fraunces) fabricated a threat alluding speculative collusion with jailed, bankrupt speculator William Duer. Bluntly rebuffed by Hamilton as a "despicable calumninator," Fraunces then wrote directly to President Washington.[3] Receiving unsatisfactory reply, he demanded newly selected House Speaker Muhlenberg to investigate the allegedly mismanaged warrants. Hamilton, all too aware that Republican political adversaries were monitoring matters, explained himself to Washington's complete satisfaction, but the House investigatory committee wanted hard proof.

Five exonerating affidavits were in hand as 1793 ticked to a close; only Laurance's sworn testimony was essential to put the affair to rest. Fraunces, it seems, had represented to Washington that "Mr. John Lawrence late in Congress," was offered up by Hamilton to "advance me $2000" on the warrants "until they could be regularly settled at the Treasury."[4] Implication was, of course, that Laurance was in league with Hamilton to secretly arbitrage the dubious warrants. There was no denying that John had in the mid-1780s advanced hard specie to discharged soldiers in return for depreciated pay certificates, and had subsequently speculated on military veteran land-grant certificates; but he was not about to gamble on Fraunces's "iffy" pre-war warrants lacking treasury guarantee. Although John professed a "real aversion" to swearing a written oath "except in court actions," he nevertheless assured Hamilton on Christmas Day that: "I have received your favors and have sent a draft of my answer to your queries to Mr. King to peruse."[5] Laurance's affidavit combined with the others to collapse any specious argument against the treasury secretary.[6] Fraunces's claim was dismissed the following February in its entirety by a predominantly anti-administration House that grudgingly acknowledged Hamilton's honorable handling of matters.

It was only natural, then, for Laurance to suspect the letter of April 30 from United States Attorney General Edmund Randolph somehow involved the coarse Andrew Fraunces. Wariness, upon opening the post gave way to elation. "The President of the U.S.," wrote Randolph, "is desirous of nominating you to the office of district judge of the state of New York. Permit me sir," the attorney general continued, "to request the favor of an answer by the return of the mail whether an appointment to that office would be acceptable to you?"[7]

"You will be pleased to inform him," Laurance immediately responded, "if I am appointed to the Office of Judge of this District I will accept."[8]

Aging incumbent James Duane had for health reasons in mid-March resigned as inaugural United States judge for the District of New York. President Washington, in his 63rd year and visibly declining, quickly offered the vacant federal seat to his former wartime judge advocate general.[9] Senate confirmation came within a week. With its lifetime annual sinecure of $1,500 ($45,150 today) for no more than four short sessions per year, how could Laurance not have reveled in the appointment? He was permanently extricated from the partisan hurly-burly of electoral office while being recognized as at the head of the legal profession in his adopted New York City. And judicial office chambers at Federal Hall were conveniently located—as had become John's public service custom—no more than a few blocks from his new Broadway home.

Yes, Broadway. Upon returning to New York in the fall of 1793, Laurance abjured the former Wall Street residence shared with first wife Betsey and began domestic life anew with Elizabeth Allen in different, more lavish accommodations. "Behold us . . . at 37 Broadway," gushed Elizabeth's delighted daughter, Mary, "living in Splendor and my young heart intoxicated with pleasure."[10] Indeed, their stretch of Broadway was considered the "talk and boast of the city" by aspiring 32-year-old future tycoon John Jacob Astor, who then could only admire its "splendid architecture" from his modest second-floor Water Street workplace.[11]

Broadway was a stage in one's career rather than a mere residence. And Judge Laurance, though not among lower Manhattan's grandee elite, had 26 years after scrambling off the Falmouth packet truly "arrived" in upper-crust New York City. Respected in his profession and wed to the bluest of Philadelphia blood, "Cousin Jack" now resided but two doors from the city's most distinguished address: Alexander Macomb's double-brick, four-story edifice at No. 39 Broadway that had in 1790 briefly served as President Washington's executive mansion. Chancellor Robert Livingston was a long stone's throw away, just off the Bowling Green in William Smith Jr.'s former residence at No. 5 Broadway. Supreme Court Chief

Justice John Jay's old-money manse stood at No. 133, while Rufus and Mary King occupied a newly built townhouse at No. 223. Directly opposite John and Elizabeth's domicile (present-day Broadway and Fulton Street) loomed Trinity Episcopal Parish's elegant Corinthian-columned St. George's Chapel.

Social and architectural centerpiece of tree-lined lower Broadway was the opulent new 137-room City Hotel. Fronting Broadway for 80 feet at No. 115 and extending 120 feet back to Temple Street, the five-story Federal-style structure attracted a select clientele with its concert, dancing, and fine dining venues together with a formidable wine cellar and elegant street-level bar. Little wonder the visiting duc de la Rochefoucauld-Liancourt asserted "There is perhaps in no city of the world a handsomer street than Broadway...The beauty of its proportions render it a choice dwelling place for the richest citizens."[12]

Charming though lower Broadway may have been, New York Harbor was abuzz with unsightly earthwork fortifications as the country girded for potential hostility from abroad. Hardly had Jacobin France declared war against both Great Britain and the Dutch Republic than the British Privy Council on November 6, 1793, issued secret orders for King George's cruisers to capture all ships heading toward or from French colonial ports. By March of 1794, 250 American ships had been impounded as war prizes, their cargoes seized, crews captured, and owners howling for indemnification. Hundreds more ships lay idle, wasting away in West Indies ports. Although dozens of Yankee vessels suffered similar depredation at the hands of French warships, Republicans clamored for action against England. Encouraged by French minister Edmund Charles Genêt, 40 decidedly Francophile "Democratic Societies" then took to streets throughout the county. Had Vice President Adams not cast the defeating Senate vote, Republican legislators would have carried a non-intercourse act against Great Britain.

"The English are absolute madmen," admitted Massachusetts Federalist Ames. "Order in this country is endangered by their hostility no less than by French friendship."[13] Even Laurance, branded a "British tool" five years earlier by Pennsylvania's Senator Maclay, geared for the demise of President Washington's resolute neutrality. "I am really apprehensive," confessed John to Senator King, "the continued injuries we receive from England will oblidge us to take decisive and hazardous measures against her."[14] His premonitions of pending conflict were not misplaced. Lord Dorchester, governor-general of Canada, had in February gathered his Indian allies at Chateau Saint-Louis, a large castle on the cliffs of Quebec's St. Lawrence River, to declare that the Paris Treaty of 1783 had been nullified by American cross-border settlements. As Whitehall hastened powerful ships of the line to North American stations, President Washington requested the states call out militia for potential detention of British commercial vessels, and Congress—bending to the artful James Madison—slapped a 30-day embargo on all ships, foreign and domestic.

Although Washington was empowered to extend the embargo, he was not about to let matters drift into war; Chief Justice Jay was dispatched in mid-April 1794 as minister plenipotentiary to London with instructions to negotiate a politico-commercial treaty. Learning of Jay's appointment and of British Prime Minister William Pitt's newly softened seizure policies, Laurance's own military ardor cooled. "I think from present appearances," he confided to Rufus King, "our condition in relation to a rupture [with Great Britain] is less gloomy than it has been for some time past. We may, with prudence weather the storm." Surveying the burgeoning Governor's Island fortifications from his Broadway window, he also noted with satisfaction that: "our defensive works go on with spirit and make considerable progress."[15]

Determined to steer a neutral course while European powers settled their differences, President Washington the spring of 1794 understood that maritime commerce was the jugular vein of the American economy and that he needed men he could trust on the federal bench at key maritime venues. None more so than New York, where French 32-gun frigate *Embuscade* was refitted the previous summer amid cheering, tricolor-waving crowds after outdueling the British fifth-rate frigate HMS *Boston* off the New Jersey coast. Responding to British captain George Courtenay's challenge. *Embuscade* on July 31, 1793, had bested *Boston*, leaving Courtenay mortally wounded on its battered quarterdeck. The British frigate ultimately escaped to Newfoundland, while French *Capitaine* Bompart returned to New York for refitting. Admiralty cases involving foreign vessels such as *Embuscade* fell under U.S. court jurisdiction. And Washington, as first president, enjoyed a luxury never to be repeated: power to appoint every sitting Supreme Court and district judge according to his own inclinations. Over the course of two terms, he appointed 27 district court judges. All were pro-Constitution, if not outright party Federalists. His 23rd such appointee, John Laurance, was no exception.

The state of New York constituted one of 13 federal judicial districts that Laurance had helped establish with the Judiciary Act of 1789. Known as the "Mother Court" because it was the first federal court in the new republic to hold session, the U.S. District Court of New York was a single-judge venue until 1814, when politics and caseload necessitated division into northern and southern districts. Seated originally at the old "Royal Exchange" building and later removed to Federal Hall, the New York District Court's principal work involved "all civil causes of admiralty and marine jurisdiction, including all seizures under laws of impost and navigation or trade of these United States."[16] Because the Judiciary Act grouped the 13 districts into three appellate circuits—eastern, middle, and southern—Judge Laurance would also sit twice yearly alongside the U.S. Supreme Court Justice(s) assigned to "ride" the Eastern Circuit. Mercifully, a paucity of cases (only 46 between 1789 and 1794), together with frequent inability of Supreme Court justices to attend, ensured the

Circuit Court for the District of New York often adjourned without transacting any business.

John had barely donned his magistrate's robe before dashing to Philadelphia for a joyous fête long anticipated by wife Elizabeth. On the first day of July, her 22-year-old daughter Margaret Elizabeth Allen married rising lawyer William Tilghman in a festive, high-society affair at venerable Christ Church. Son of influential Maryland landowner James Tilghman, young William would go on to become a federal circuit court justice and later serve more than 20 years as chief justice of the Pennsylvania Supreme Court. Amid the ceremonial hoopla, John could not help but reckon the formidable matrimonial math: it was one stepdaughter down, and two more to go. Not to mention three daughters of his own with first wife Betsey and two from his second marriage, for Elizabeth had three months earlier delivered their second child, Frances.

No sooner had the Laurances returned to New York than the Judge faced a high-profile admiralty case bearing significant diplomatic consequences. Not only would the proceeding validate President Washington's confidence in John's Federalist values, but it also landed him as defendant before the U.S. Supreme Court.[17]

The United States v. Lawrence (3 U.S. 42, 1795)

Late in July of 1794 a Pennsylvania warrant crossed Judge Laurance's desk for the arrest of French naval *lieutenant de vaisseaux* Jean-Baptiste-Henri Barré. Captain of the 24-gun corvette *Le Perdrix*, Barré had jumped ship earlier that month after an altercation with his superior, convoy *Capitaine* Mahe of the frigate *La Concorder*. Mahe, his convoy scattered by a more powerful British fleet off the Delaware coast, threatened Barré with the guillotine when he returned to France. Rather than lose his head, Captain Barré used it to slip ashore at Cape Henlopen and take refuge with friends in New York. So far as French authorities were concerned, Barré was a deserter who according to consular convention must be extradited home for punishment. Envoy Plenipotentiary Monsieur Jean Antoine Joseph Fauchet swiftly obtained an arrest warrant from Pennsylvania district judge Richard Peters, only to learn from Judge Laurance that it was invalid in New York State. The French vice-consul in New York then respectfully approached him to resolve matters with a new warrant.

Extraditing 26-year-old *Lieutenant de vaisseaux* Barré was, as Laurance well knew, a death sentence. More than 17,000 people had vanished in a sea of blood during the French reign of terror, including several who served in America during the late war. The head of Admiral comte d'Estaing had already rolled. And was not General Rochambeau awaiting disposition behind bars while Lafayette himself bided time in an Austrian prison? To avoid similar fates, many noblemen, like Louis Le Bégue Du Portail — General Washington's wartime chief engineer — disappeared into hiding in the American backcountry. Even French minister Genêt refused to return home when recalled, opting instead for quiet upstate New York retirement as husband to Governor George Clinton's daughter Cornelia.

Judge Laurance's jurisdiction in the Barré matter was indisputable. Shortly before he assumed the bench, exclusive right of U.S. courts over admiralty cases had been established by Supreme Court Chief Justice Jay (*Glass v. Sloop Betsey*, 3 U.S. 6, 1794), thereby denying the French consul from conducting any such proceedings on American soil. As Laurance fingered the invalid Pennsylvania arrest warrant, he knew whatever actions he took would establish precedent, for it was the young republic's first significant extradition case under the five-year-old Constitution.[18] He therefore determined to adhere strictly to express language of his country's 1788 consular treaty with France. "Before a warrant could issue," Laurance informed French vice-consul Louis Arcambal, "the applicant should prove by the register of the ship (*role d'equipage*) that Captain Barré was in fact one of the crew of *Le Perdrix*."[19]

Arcambal replied that the ship's register was not in his possession and protested that he should be able to submit collateral proof without being obliged to produce the actual register itself. Judge Laurance disagreed, countering: "The mode of proof mentioned in the 9th article of the Convention was the only legitimate one, and that he could not dispense with it."[20] The vice-consul next transmitted a certified copy of the ship register under consular seal to Judge Laurance. Contending this formal copy was sufficient under Article 5 of the Consular Convention, Monsieur Arcambal demanded his warrant. Judge Laurance refused to budge. Declaring that he did not consider the copy of the register to be the proof designated by the ninth article, Laurance ruled: "that till the proof specified by the express words of the article was exhibited, he could not deem himself authorized to issue a warrant."[21]

The original role d'equipage, it seems, was nowhere to be found. Legal options exhausted, French Envoy Plenipotentiary Fauchet then presented his case to President Washington's new secretary of state, former Attorney General Randolph. Anxious to keep the matter from escalating into diplomatic debacle, Randolph offered Laurance a convenient way out of the delicate affair. "So solicitous is the President," wrote Randolph, "that our treaty, which he has uniformly respected, should be interpreted in a manner, strictly right: that, if you think proper, the Attorney for the district of New York shall be instructed to take the most effectual and expeditious measure, which the law allows."[22]

All Judge Laurance had to do was let the New York district attorney handle matters and, *voilà,* he was off the hook. Doing so would, however, establish precedent for extradition as an executive prerogative rather than a judicial one. And this, he would not concede. Refusing Randolph's proposal, he reiterated that there would be no extradition without the original ship register. An indignant Monsieur Fauchet then persuaded

Secretary Randolph to direct U.S. Attorney General William Bradford Jr. to take matters "expeditiously" to a higher court.[23] Accordingly, Bradford on January 31, 1795, advised Judge Laurance of his intent to move directly to the Supreme Court with a *writ of mandamus* (an order from a court of superior jurisdiction commanding an inferior tribunal to act) against *him*.[24]

Laurance could not have known it at the time, but Secretary of State Randolph's Republican sympathy with Revolutionary France had recently gotten the best of him. Randolph's duplicity, however, would not come to light until July 1795 when British minister George Hammond presented President Washington with captured French papers implicating that Randolph had divulged state secrets. There was also evidence that Randolph had colluded with Envoy Fauchet to bribe Pennsylvania officials during the recently suppressed "Whiskey Rebellion."[25] Confronted by Washington before the full cabinet, Randolph in August resigned as secretary of state. By then, however, ink on the Supreme Court decision regarding Judge Laurance was six months' dry.

As target of the attorney general's mandamus, Judge Laurance might have chosen to postpone or obstruct; instead he agreed to shortcut procedures so the controversy might be settled in the upcoming February 1795 Supreme Court term. "I had no desire to retard a Decision," he advised Bradford. "If the Letters and Answers, which passed on the subject were laid before the Court, I should be content; as the Principle I had contended for, in the Interpretation of the Article would be discovered."[26] Had John chosen delay over expediency, the matter would not have been adjudicated until the following August session. With Randolph's complicity then exposed, American relations with France might have turned truly ugly.

On February 7, 1795, this inaugural extradition case under the Constitution was formally docketed as "United States v. John Lawrence, Judge of the district of New=York." Argument 11 days later commenced before acting Chief Justice John Rutledge and five associates. And who should be Judge Laurance's lead defense attorney, but his new stepson-in-law, William Tilghman. As his stepfather-in-law looked on from the defendant's box, Tilghman and firm Federalist co-attorney Jared Ingersoll argued that Congress had endowed district judges with the authority to enforce the consular convention, and that Judge Laurance—according to his interpretation of treaty language—had properly exercised that authority. Neither Congress nor the consular treaty, contended Tilghman, constrained any federal judge from construing treaty language strictly as it was written. In which case, he concluded, the Supreme Court had no reason to interfere.

Before Tilghman could even finish his summation, the justices rendered their decision in a brief *per curiam* (unanimous) opinion. Attorney General Bradford's petition for writ of mandamus was denied. There would be no judgment against Laurance, because issuing an arrest warrant for extradition was no mere *ministerial* duty, in which a judge enjoyed no discretion, but rather a *judicial* one. "It is evident," declared Associate

Justice Ellsworth for the Court, "that the District Judge was acting in a judicial capacity . . . and (whatever might be the difference of sentiment entertained by this Court) we have no power to compel a judge to decide according to the dictates of any judgment but his own."[27]

Judge Laurance had prevailed. Precedent was established. A foreign power could not mandate extradition of one of its citizens on U.S. soil. For generations to come, the Supreme Court had established that the right to *habeas corpus* (personal liberty) of all persons—even French sailors—was for the judiciary, not the executive branch, to decide. Moreover, French authorities would have to tread lightly in recovering future mutineers. Of such consequence was the matter to Fauchet that he requested authorization from Paris to negotiate a new treaty regarding mutineers from French warships.[28] The request was denied.

Still, one wonders. Did Laurance insist on the original ship roster listing Barré as captain because he suspected any copy might be forged? Or, did he simply take advantage of a technicality to both save Barré's neck and shield the U.S. government from the ignominy of supporting French terror? Judge Laurance, after returning to New York, may well have shared his private motivations over dinner with Supreme Court Associate Justice James Iredell.* Then in Manhattan to "ride" circuit on the constitutionally mandated Eastern State Federal Court of Appeals, the English-born Iredell dined the evening of April 8 at John and Elizabeth's Broadway table. Conversation surely drifted to Iredell's fellow Supreme Court justice James Wilson, who at the age of 51 had recently proposed to 19-year-old Hannah Gray, an "amiable young lady of Boston" only two days after first making her acquaintance.[29] Over a shared glass or two of Port, Laurance and Iredell had good reason to joke over Miss Gray's immediate acceptance, before moving to the more serious matter of extraditing foreign citizens such as Captain Barré. But all Iredell had to tell his own wife Hannah of his repast with the Laurance's was that "His wife [Elizabeth Allen] is really a very agreeable woman."[30]

Laurance could only have been delighted that Hamilton, after resigning from Washington's cabinet in late January 1795, opted to dally a few weeks in New York City en route to a long-anticipated Albany respite. There was much to catch up on as the two friends sat down the last day of February with 200 local merchants and bankers to an enormous

---

* Born in the Sussex country town of Lewes, James Iredell (1751–1799) sailed to America in 1768 to be King George's comptroller of customs in Edenton, North Carolina. An outspoken proponent of American independence and strong proponent of the Constitution, Federalist lawyer Iredell was appointed by President Washington to the Supreme Court in February 1790.

dinner fêted in Alexander's honor by the Chamber of Commerce at the Tontine Coffee House.[31] Almost two years had transpired since Laurance departed Philadelphia, and several shared upstate real estate ventures (chapter Eighteen) were in play. Indeed, Hamilton little more than a month earlier deposited $1,500 with Laurance apparently for that very purpose.[32] And with George Clinton's announcement that, after 18 years as governor, he would not run for reelection, rumors flew that Hamilton might seek the vacant chair. In such a case, New York's Federalist apparatus would shift into full gear and John, never defeated at city ballot boxes, would be drawn into his friend's campaign.

Hamilton was not about to run for governor, or any other office for that matter. Having sunk deeply in personal debt while he squared away the republic's finances, the former treasury secretary determined to "take a little care of my own, which need my care not a little."[33] He was as good as his word. Indeed, Hamilton never returned to government service; in 1798, he refused appointment to the Senate rather than "sacrifice the interest of my family to public call."[34] Establishing temporary quarters at No. 56 Pine Street, Alexander set about filling personal coffers with a blue-ribbon clientele as New York's most sought-after lawyer. Clinton kept his word as well, turning over the governor's chair to John Jay, who was elected in absentia while still in London as President Washington's treaty emissary to the Court of St. James.

Out of public office Hamilton may have been, but out of the public eye he could never be. At noon on July 18, 1795, an agitated crowd surged outside Laurance's Federal Hall chambers, summoned by Edward, Philip, and Brockholst Livingston to debate the Jay Treaty in the intersection where six years earlier Washington had taken the oath of president. Across the street, Hamilton, though no longer part of Washington's cabinet, ascended a venerable Dutch building's stoop to defend the newly signed treaty with England.

So lopsided in favor of Anglophile interests was the Jay Treaty that the president cloaked it in impenetrable secrecy for months. And for good reason; the treaty granted British imports most-favored-nation status with no reciprocal concession for American imports. Although Britain allowed for arbitration by American merchants whose cargo had been impounded, illegal impressment of American sailors by Royal Navy cruisers was never remedied, nor was reparation for slaves carried off at the close of the Revolution. On the first day of July, Republican Senator Stevens T. Mason of Virginia leaked the full treaty text to the Philadelphia newspaper *Aurora*, whereupon Jay and his treaty were trashed in a public uproar the likes of which American politics had never seen. From Charleston to Boston, angry mobs burned Jay effigies, hurled stones at government buildings, and stomped on the Union Jack. The controversial treaty not only ended House Speaker Frederick Muhlenberg's political career, it almost cost him his life; in retribution for casting the tie-breaking House vote in favor of the treaty, Muhlenberg was violently stabbed by his mentally unstable brother-in-law Bernard Schaeffer.[35]

Near Judge Laurance's chambers the July 18 crowd, augmented by seamen from French ships in New York Harbor, grew restive as Peter R. Livingston began to speak against the Jay Treaty. That American economic life, particularly marine commerce, would flourish as never before in the wake of the treaty was of little matter to those whose sense of national self-esteem was slighted by yet another blunt reminder that Britannia ruled the waves.[36] When Hamilton spoke up in the treaty's defense, loud murmurs turned to heckling and then to flinging stones. Reportedly grazed in the forehead, Hamilton withdrew. Pamphleteering and protests continued for weeks, during which time a United States marshal seized the French armed schooner *La Vengeance* in New York Harbor.

United States v. La Vengeance (3 U.S. 297, 1796)

La Vengeance, returning from a voyage to Port-de-Paix, St. Domingo, had captured a Spanish prize, *La Princessa de Asturias,* and carried her into New York Harbor. Demanding restitution, prize owner Don Diego Pintardo filed a *libel* (written declaration) in Judge Laurance's District Court claiming that *La Vengeance* had illegally fitted out in New York for privateering—a flagrant violation of the 1794 Neutrality Act. United States District Attorney Josiah Hoffman then doubled down with the same allegation, adding *ex-officio* (by right of office) that U.S. Marshall Aquila Giles had already seized *La Vengeance*. Further complicating matters for Laurance, a third libel was filed by District Attorney Hoffman alleging *La Vengeance* had carried cannons, muskets, and gunpowder from the port of New York to a foreign country. If true, Hoffman's allegation constituted a direct violation of the May 1793 Congressional Act prohibiting arms and ammunition export from American shores to foreign nations.

La Vengeance's owner, French citizen Jacques Rouge, immediately filed a denial claim. Monsieur Rouge did not deny his vessel had transported muskets and gunpowder to the French West Indies colony of St. Domingo. Rather, he contended with straight face, the muskets were simply private property and not for resale. As to the gunpowder, Monsieur Rouge asserted it was French government property that he had legally transferred to a proper office of the republic at Port-de-Paix.

Because all three libel claims were *in rem* (not touching the offender's person), Judge Laurance determined the case was civil rather than criminal in nature and therefore did not require a jury. After arguments, he dismissed Pintardo's claim—and by association the district attorney's—that *La Vengeance* had fitted out in New York. There simply was no convincing evidence to that effect. And since Spain was then at war with Revolutionary France, the *La Princessa de Asturias* according to the "law of nations" was a perfectly legal prize. Whatever satisfied smile crossed *La Vengeance* owner Jacques Rouge's face was short-lived after Laurance addressed the third libel claim. It was, after all, common knowledge that the French Republic used Port-de-Paix as a St. Domingo base for predatory naval activity. Therefore, Judge Laurance ruled in favor of the United States on the illegal arms transport charge and ordered *La Vengeance* forfeited.[37]

La Vengeance's owner appealed the ruling to the Federal Circuit Court where Judge Samuel Chase confirmed Judge Laurance's two dismissals, but overturned his decision on the illegal arms transport libel. Whereas Laurance had strictly applied the express letter of the law, Chase went a step further in its interpretation, certifying his reversal on an interesting technicality. It seems the offending 40 boxes of gunpowder had never touched shore in New York when downloaded from French frigate *Semillante* as government property bound to the French base at St. Domingo. Therefore, the Congressional Act of May 1793 had not been violated. From this judgment, U.S. Attorney General Charles Lee (no relation to the disgraced Revolutionary War general) then sought and received a writ of error to bring the matter before the Supreme Court. On August 11, Chief Justice Oliver Ellsworth affirmed Judge Chase's circuit court decision and overruled Laurance on the matter of illegal arms transport.

La Vengeance's 40 controversial kegs of gunpowder and Captain Barré's earlier high-profile acquittal were but temporary high drama. For the most part, Laurance's district court tenure consisted of petty smuggling cases interspersed with the occasional civil lawsuit. Every week, diligent federal customs agents dutifully produced a stream of impounded rum, gin, brandy, porter, coffee, fine fabrics, and gunpowder confiscated from offending sloops, schooners, sailboats, brigs, brigantines, and ships.[38] And each and every seizure required some sort of district court adjudication.

The monotonous procession of customs proceedings was interspersed with an important new administrative task that Judge Laurance must have relished: formally approving new citizenship applications. Although county courts served as a venue for most of the early republic's naturalization ceremonies, the federal district court proved more convenient for many lower Manhattan immigrants. Having had a hand in the Naturalization Act of March 26, 1790, former Congressman Laurance knew all too well that naturalization was restricted to "free white persons" of "good character" with established residence of at least two years. Still, as a naturalized immigrant himself, John must have taken a certain pride in swearing in more than 50 new United States citizens during his two-and-a-half-year district court tenure.[39] And knowing Laurance, he surely imagined each and every new American a potential purchaser for some of the thousands of upstate farm lot acres he (chapter Eighteen), Robert Troup, and Hamilton had acquired for speculative resale.

As 1795 wound down, Judge Laurance lost his national bank directorship in Philadelphia for good. It was really only a matter of time because the original bank charter prohibited more than three-fourths of prior-year directors from returning in each annual election. Nonetheless, Alexander Hamilton once again extended helping hand to advance his comrade's career. During the late war, he had not only arranged an artillery captaincy under General Knox (that John refused) but also covered for him during family-related absences and lobbied Congress in support of Judge Advocate Laurance's subsistence pay hike. After proposing Laurance as congressional candidate on the 1789 Federalist ticket, Alexander had tirelessly campaigned for his friend's election. And now he maneuvered to help John save face over the lost bank directorship.

"Lawrance is hurt," confided Hamilton to Rufus King in Philadelphia, "and as far as I see not without some reason given the particular circumstances at being left out of the Direction of the Bank."[40] Concerned for his friend, Hamilton urged Senator King to work the Federalist old-boy network* to orchestrate Laurance's appointment as director of the national bank's New York branch. "It will be balm to his feelings," wrote Hamilton, "& I believe it will be an improvement of the Direction to do it. Speak to Bayard of our City and Wharton in Philadelphia. This is a suggestion of my own, for Lawrance rides a rather high horse upon the occasion."[41] And that is how Judge Laurance in early 1796 served simultaneously as director of the Bank of the United States in his own federal judicial district—a blatant conflict of interest unthinkable today.

---

*Behind the Federalist public faces of Hamilton, King, Laurance, Sedgwick, et al., lay a cadre of wealthy capitalists. Men like George Cabot, Stephen Higginson, and John Lowell of Boston; William Bingham, George Clymer, Robert Wharton, and Thomas Willing in Philadelphia; James and William Bayard, William Constable, Royal Flint, and Herman LeRoy in New York, along with scores of forgotten merchants, brokers, and shippers who stocked the New York, Philadelphia, Baltimore, and Boston Chambers of Commerce.

PART IV

The Federalist Hawk Who Fled the Nest

FIFTEEN

The Senator from New York

NEW YORK CITY, MAY 23, 1796. On this day, against both Alexander Hamilton and John Jay's urging, Rufus King resigned as New York's senior senator to accept President Washington's appointment as the United States minister plenipotentiary to Great Britain.[1] "You must know," King had confided to Hamilton a week before Congress adjourned, "that I am not a little tired with this separation from my family and drudgery in the senate."[2] Moreover, the senator was thoroughly worn out after nearly two years of partisan agitation over the Jay Treaty. What better sabbatical than a few years on the glittering social circuit enfolding diplomatic service to the Court of St. James? Boarding the American ship *James*, King, on a cloudy 20th of June, sailed for England accompanied by strikingly attractive 27-year-old wife Mary and four handsome sons.

New York legislators were in no hurry to replace him. The Senate would not reconvene for another six months and George Clinton no longer filled the governor's chair. So why rush? With fresh majorities in both legislative houses, Empire State Federalists could afford to leisurely mull their options for King's vacant seat. The party cupboard of proven New York heavyweights, however, was startlingly bare. Jay's term as governor had two more years to run and Egbert Benson, the most obvious choice, was happily seated on the state Supreme Court alongside 19-year bench veteran John Sloss Hobart. The Livingston and Van Cortlandt families had decamped for greener political pastures in the Republican fold, Gouverneur Morris was in Paris as minister plenipotentiary to France, and gout-ridden 63-year-old General Philip Schuyler struggled to attend the state senate. Venerable James Duane was near death's door, Richard Varick was reappointed New York City's mayor, affable Robert Troup had his eye on Laurance's district judgeship, and Hamilton was not about to return his growing family to the brink of financial insolvency attending public office. By early October, King's senate seat was still unfilled.

"Hamilton, Henderson,* and myself made an excursion to Long Island for 5 days," wrote Laurance in mid-October. "We got a few grouse.

---

*Dr. Thomas Henderson (1743–1824) was then a Federalist congressman from New Jersey. It was he who in 1778 as brigade-major informed General Washington of Charles Lee's infamous retreat at Monmouth Court House. Laurance would have come to know Henderson at Lee's subsequent court-martial, if not before.

And the ride restored Hamilton's digestion."[3] Hamilton (newly settled down the street at No. 26 Broadway) may have bagged more than grouse, for Judge Laurance little more than a month later resigned his judgeship in order to keep Rufus King's vacated position a Federalist fiefdom.[4] "Our good friend," Troup happily informed King in mid-November, "has been appointed to take your seat in the senate. There was but one dissenting voice in both branches of our legislature."[5] And who should be confirmed to fill John's shoes as federal New York district judge, but reliable party soldier Robert Troup.

Laurance no doubt thought long and hard before giving up a lifetime judicial sinecure in favor of Philadelphia's rough-and-tumble legislative politics. Forty-six-year-old Elizabeth was certainly a consideration. Having delivered their second daughter (Frances Caroline) 10 months before, nothing could please her more than Chestnut Street's familiar social milieu. Easing the decision, John was apparently promised a future seat in the state judiciary in return for sacrificing his district judgeship.[6]

New York's newest senator in mid-November packed his finest clothes into an awaiting carriage and hurried to Philadelphia. Not to attend Congress, but for the November 27 wedding of Mary Masters Allen, youngest daughter from wife Elizabeth's first marriage. And what a wedding it was. Groom Henry Walter Livingston, son of Walter Livingston and Cornelia Schuyler, embodied two of New York's most prominent bloodlines. What with the Livingstons, Schuylers, Penns, and all their connections, the guest list was, according to one Livingston biographer, "probably the most brilliant that could be assembled," with President Washington perhaps gracing the exclusive affair.[7] Stepfather to the 20-year-old bride, Laurance surely beamed with satisfaction as he watched the favored couple pledge their troth before Reverend Bishop White's historic Christ Church altar. The senator himself may even have introduced the handsome pair on one of Mary's many New York stayovers, for Livingston, recently returned from a two-year Paris stint as private secretary to Minister Gouverneur Morris, was atop everyone's parlor invitation list. Well launched in a promising New York law practice, young Walter (Yale '86) was not only a rare family Federalist but also a living conduit to every immigrant's aspirational dream: blood ties with New York's most influential clan.

Two of three stepdaughters now splendidly wedded, Senator Laurance on December 8 strode two blocks from Elizabeth's Chestnut Street townhouse to the familiar red brick confines of boxy Congress Hall at the corner of Sixth Street. Making his way to the intimate second floor Senate chamber, John duly presented credentials to secretary Samuel Allyn Otis (former speaker of the Massachusetts legislature) and settled into one of the room's 32 individual mahogany secretary desks.

"The senate chamber," remarked a visiting Englishman in 1795, "is furnished and fitted up in a much superior style to that of the lower house."[8] From heavy red window drapes to local rug-maker William Sprague's deep blue carpet adorned with shields of the 13 original states, the Senate exuded a gravitas unmatched by the simple downstairs House chamber, where 105 representatives shoe-horned themselves into three semicircular rows of shared table-desks. Although never formally designated an "upper" chamber by the Constitutional Convention, the Senate's older minimum age (30 versus 25), more lengthy citizenship requirement (nine versus seven years), and indirect election by state legislatures (versus popular vote) were all designed to produce a wiser body that might check House impetuosity. It was only human nature, then, given the constitutional power of "advice and consent" and the informal practice of "senatorial courtesy" (presidential consultation with affected senators *before* making state-level appointments) that six-year Senate appointees perceived themselves senior statesmen to the transitory two-year denizens a floor below.

Familiar figures from Laurance's House days extended welcoming hands well before Vice President Adams gaveled to order the second session of the Fourth United States Senate. There was hawk-nosed, fierce-eyed Massachusetts High Federalist Theodore Sedgwick with whom John had defended Hamilton from accusations of treasury malfeasance three years before. And how could he not remember high-minded, long-jawed Benjamin Goodhue (Massachusetts), intensely Antifederalist Timothy Bloodsworth (North Carolina), common-sensed Delaware lawyer "Jack" Vining, and tight-fisted, sharp-witted Samuel Livermore (New Hampshire), who was distinguished by "force of his talents" rather than any "mildness of his temper, or the amenity of his manners."[9] From the Second Federal Congress stepped forward fervently anti-slavery arch-Federalist James Hillhouse (Connecticut), not to mention London-educated South Carolina lawyer Jacob Read with whom John had shared Confederation Congress frustrations way back in '85. Fellow New York senator Aaron Burr was of course no stranger, but no friend either; five years as a chamber Clintonian marked him as sharp-elbowed political adversary.

The fiftyish Senator Laurance who looks directly into our eyes from figure Eleven is a far cry from the bewigged, boyish striver of John Trumbull's earlier portrait. An unidentified artist, possibly young John Wesley Jarvis, presents the former federal judge as a serious statesman, comfortable enough in his own skin to comb sparse ringlets of thinning hair forward over a balding pate. No longer Washington's military lawyer, Alexander McDougall's son-in-law, or Hamilton's legislative champion, the sitter was, perhaps for the first time, captain of his own political destiny. It couldn't hurt that former House adversary James Madison had at long last announced his hiatus from national office to tend his neglected Orange County estate.

Respected member of a lopsided two-to-one Federalist senate majority, Laurance, together with colleagues Goodhue and Livermore, was

FIGURE 12 John Laurance.

Oil on canvas (undated), unidentified artist. (Collection of New York Historical Society. Reproduced with permission.)

immediately charged to review compensation of both legislators and government officers "with a view of making a more just and liberal provision for them."[10] (A proposed 25 percent increase for both houses of Congress met with warm approval.) Over the next 10 weeks, John displayed the same high work ethic that characterized his House terms, serving on eight additional committees dealing with state boundary disputes, postal roads expansion, the military establishment, settlement of state credits with the national treasury, and individual property reimbursement memorials. It was the kind of relatively nonpartisan, pragmatic lawmaking he truly seemed to relish.

Legislation ground to a standstill in early 1797 as all eyes turned to the electoral vote determining President Washington's successor. The election campaign of 1796 was mercifully short, lasting but two months due to the late timing of Washington's farewell address. Neither Adams nor Republican opponent Jefferson left home. The latter abdicated electioneering to James Madison and campaign manager John Beckley while the former declared himself "a silent spectator of the silly and wicked game."[11] Perhaps the most active campaigner of all was Pierre Adet, French minister to the United States, who openly lobbied Republican congressmen and warned of potential war if Jefferson was not elected, going so far as to sponsor newspaper broadsides lambasting Vice President Adams. Even so, Jefferson let it be known that if the election ended in a tie, he would defer to Adams to forestall acrimonious transition of government. And one thing upon which both could agree was a mutual antipathy toward Alexander Hamilton.

Members of the Electoral College were chosen by all 16 states between November 4 and December 7, 1796, but ballots, according to law, would not be opened before the second Wednesday in February. To formalize ballot counting procedures, Laurance and fellow Federalists Sedgwick and Read were appointed, not without Republican suspicion, to a temporary Senate select committee instructed to liaise with House counterparts.[12] Senator Laurance then witnessed one of the strangest spectacles in American history: Vice President Adams as president of the Senate stood before a joint session of Congress to announce *himself* Washington's successor by a mere three-vote margin. Even more bizarre, Thomas Jefferson—rather than Federalist Charles C. Pinckney—came in second, exposing a constitutional quirk that had never happened before, or ever again: vice president and president were of opposing political parties!

"It appearing to me proper that the Senate of the United States should be convened on Saturday the fourth day of March instant," Washington dryly advised Laurance of the Adams inauguration, "you are desired to attend."[13] Shortly after 10 o'clock that March morning, Laurance, who had lost out to William Bingham to become Senate president pro tempore, watched Bingham administer the vice presidential oath of office to Thomas Jefferson.[14] Rising as one, the senators then trooped downstairs to the House chamber where, just before noon, Chief Justice Oliver Ellsworth swore in Adams—humbly attired in a suit of gray broadcloth intentionally devoid of ornamentation—as second president of the United States. One unassuming attendee, clad in an outfit of simple black velvet, caught Senator Sedgwick's discerning eye:

> The company was numerous, respectable, and behaved with that decent gravity which the solemn occasion demanded; but the circumstance the most interesting was the presence of the late President. He came unattended and on foot, with the modest appearance of a private citizen. No sooner was his person seen, than a burst of applause such as I had never before known.[15]

It was a moment for the ages ... a tableau that Laurance (who attended both Washington inaugurations) and his fellow lawmakers could never forget. For in a day of hereditary monarchs, the reins of power peacefully changed hands between two publicly elected heads of state. Together one last time on the same stage stood the three patriots who, more than any others, embodied the Revolution: short, pudgy, Massachusetts plow horse John Adams and the two tall Virginia thoroughbreds, Washington and Jefferson.

As applause for the former president subsided, thinking men could not help but reflect that the person of Washington—though officially nonpartisan—was the unspoken face, body, and soul of American Federalism ... and that no ideology, however brilliantly articulated, could take his place. Indeed, Washington's 132 electoral votes of 1792 had shockingly shriveled almost by half in John Adams's near-run 71 to 68 win. Weakening Federalist grasp on voters was ominously clear; six of the eight states choosing presidential electors by popular vote had moved into the Republican fold.[16] Even the former bastion of South Carolina, despite William Smith and Thomas Pinckney's best efforts, bestowed all eight of its electoral votes to Jefferson. With the political elephant of a generation departing the room, would his followers evolve into what historian Manning Dauer labeled "Adams Federalists"?[17] Or would they instead heed Alexander Hamilton's "High" Federalist siren call to even more powerful central government?

Hoping to bully the United States into repudiating the contentious Jay Treaty, Revolutionary France's five-member Directory in November 1796 rudely refused new American minister Charles Cotesworth Pinckney and—violating international law as well as the 1778 Treaty of Amity—belligerently ordered Gallic cruisers against the American merchant marine.[18] By the following April, more than a hundred American vessels had been seized and their cargoes confiscated. Any American found aboard a British vessel, public or private, was (in blatant Jay Treaty retaliation) declared a pirate to be hung upon capture. Amid soaring insurance rates for American shipping, the Directory heaped on further insult by demanding all American ships carry the rôle d'équipage, a document required of no other maritime nation.[19] National self-respect demanded something be done, leaving newly elected President Adams no choice but to summon the republic's first special session of Congress.

Senator Laurance listened hard the morning of May 16, 1797, to the president's maiden speech. It was a sweeping call to enlarge the militia, commission privateers, strengthen seacoast fortifications, build warships for protecting the merchant fleet, and levy direct taxes to pay for it all. Legislative initiative for this military escalation, as John well understood, would fall to the Federalist Senate because a powerful Francophile Republican minority in the House promised to water down or delay necessary taxes to finance the ambitious program.

No doubt owing to his hawkish Anglophile inclination and amicable 20-year relationship with Adams, Laurance was immediately named one of three to respond to the president's policy address. A week later John was elected to the five-man committee tasked to deal with Adams's message regarding security and protection of American commerce. Consisting of Federalists Laurance, Bingham, Goodhue, Uriah Tracy (Connecticut), and unpredictable James Gunn (Georgia), the panel would, according to Senate historian Roy Swanstrom, "attain repute as the most productive Senate committee of the entire Federalist period."[20] Laurance next joined Livermore and Read on the important select committee charged to bring in bills "building and equipping cruisers" and "fitting out privateers."[21] Nodding to John's hand in the Militia Acts of 1792, Senate colleagues also included him among the five tasked to organize, arm, and discipline the several state militias.[22]

Putting a finger on Laurance's individual sway—for that matter any senator's—in the Fifth United States Senate is particularly difficult; not only do the *Annals of Congress*, *Journal of the United States Senate*, and the *Journal of the Executive Proceedings of the Senate of the United State*s exclude details of chamber debate, but much of Federalist strategy was plotted at closeted conferences where no records were kept. Senatorial correspondence, except for Theodore Sedgwick's cross-Atlantic exchanges with Rufus King and ongoing dialog with Hamilton, rarely disclosed the inner springs of party stratagem. True, the Philadelphia-based *Gazette of the United States*, *National Gazette*, and the *General Advertiser* (better known as the *Aurora*) covered Senate sessions, but all, as historian Jeffrey L. Pasley has observed about the period press, were shaded by epithet-laden partisan political predisposition.[23]

What is certain about the Fifth United States Senate is that chamber leaders under the Washington administration, exhausted from two grueling years of defending the Jay Treaty, had moved on. Oliver Ellsworth, equivalent of the latter-day Senate majority leader, resigned his seat to replace Jay as Supreme Court chief justice; Robert Morris had all he could do to balance massive real estate overspeculation with pending debtors' prison; Caleb Strong and George Cabot returned to private interests, and Rufus King was, of course, in London. "There is no danger of an anti-Federal Senate," admitted one Federalist congressman, "but the loss of tried characters is a misfortune . . . There is now left only a bare majority of good men in the Senate."[24] Stepping up to assume leadership of the two-to-one Federalist majority were two firm Hamilton allies, fiery Uriah Tracy of Connecticut and Theodore Sedgwick, both fresh from three years of battling Republicans in the House.[25] In matters of national security, Laurance would play a particularly influential role, for he was the only senator named to all three committees charged to turn the president's maiden defense speech into action.

Laurance, together with Senators Bingham, Goodhue, Hillhouse, Livermore, Sedgwick, Stockton, Read, Ross, and Tracy, constituted an aggressive Federalist bloc that responded wholeheartedly to the president's call to arms. On June 7 they anchored an 18 to 8 majority to authorize an additional corps of artillery and regiment of engineers.[26] Two days later, Laurance facilitated a 15 to 13 vote recommitting back to the House Senator Read's proposed "Act prohibiting, for a limited time, the exportation of arms and ammunition."[27] On the 14th, John voted to raise an additional corps of light dragoons, only to watch the measure be defeated when Hillhouse and Ross sided with chamber Republicans.[28] And Senator Laurance on the 21st reported out his own committee's unamended approval of the House bill to beef-up harbor defenses.[29]

Birthing a navy was the most essential task on the new president's defense agenda, and the Federalist Senate served as the nascent fleet's legislative nursery. Senators Laurance and Goodhue's "protections" bill was critical first step. Delivered out of their committee in mid-June for third and final reading, "An Act providing for the protections of the trade of the United States" provided powerful escort frigates to protect three quarters of a million tons of combined domestic and foreign shipping subject to French harassment. Despite stiff Republican opposition, and economic reservations by inland-state members of Laurance's own party, the measure carried by a 16 to 13 margin.[30] Immediately dispatched to the House, it constituted the young republic's most serious attempt yet to fund a standing United States navy.

Stark reality was that in May of 1797, except for a few patrol boats and a dispatch cutter, there was no United States navy. Only the warships *Deane*, *General Washington*, and *Alliance* survived the War for Independence, all three of which Laurance had witnessed a funds-starved Confederation Congress dispose of by December 1785. True, the new Constitution had authorized Congress "to provide and maintain a navy," but all that emerged was a 1790 Senate report suggesting one be cobbled together "as soon as the state of our finances permit." States concerned with western development or southern agriculture cared not a whit for a handful of seamen in North African prisons, and even less about Boston and New York ship owner losses. It was not until January 1794 that outrageous pillaging of American vessels by Tunisian and Algerian pirates off the Barbary Coast forced Congress to act. Even then, House Federalists met with acrimonious debate, prevailing by a mere two votes over Rep. Madison's opposition to provide a six-frigate naval force.

Construction of the half-dozen proposed frigates was for the sake of political expediency spread among six separate Atlantic coast shipyards running from Portsmouth, New Hampshire, to Norfolk, Virginia. Work, however, was halted in September 1795 on all but three of the vessels in wake of a humiliating million-dollar treaty concession to the Dey of Algiers that mollified the Barbary piracy threat. By the time Laurance assumed Senator King's vacated seat in November of 1796, the three partially completed frigates still rested on Boston, Philadelphia, and Baltimore shipyard blocks.

Fully aware that potential war with France would be fought primarily if not exclusively at sea, House appropriations committee leader William Smith warmly embraced Laurance and Goodhue's June 1797 senate "protections" bill calling for an American navy. But it was not until Secretary of State Timothy Pickering reported that 316 American ships had fallen prey to French cruisers that House Republicans reluctantly agreed to fit out the three uncompleted frigates for action. On July 1, An Act Providing a Naval Armament authorized the president to launch 44-gun frigates *United States* and *Constitution* and the 36-gun *Constellation*.[31] Readying the big frigates for sea, Secretary of War James McHenry requested $200,000 (he received $172,000) along with another $100,000 to man and supply them. A jubilant John Adams then sped to seafaring Massachusetts for the inaugural September 20 launch of *Constitution* from Edmund Hartt's Boston shipyard.

Adams's motivation for naval respectability stretched all the way back to 1785, when as minister to the Court of St. James he was politely received . . . then pointedly ignored. "They really do not think us much consequence," he lamented to cousin Samuel Adams, "We have no Navy; and we are Aukward in Uniting in anything."[32] Unaware that Hamilton had effectively ghostwritten (through pliable Secretary of War McHenry) major tenets of his May 16 congressional address, Adams in the summer of 1797 steamed full speed ahead to restore the U.S. Navy to respectability while tolerating his party's increasing demand for a standing "provisional" army.[33]

Republican newspapers responded hostilely to the Federalist defense build-up. Castigated for "gasconading like a bully, swaggering the hero, and armed cap-a-pie, throwing the gauntlet to the most powerful nation on earth," the president was smeared as "vile leader of a British faction" who was the "representative of George the Third."[34] Benjamin Bache's Philadelphia *Aurora* repeatedly branded the "Three-Vote President" a mere tool of Hamilton and High Federalist war hawks. Sabre rattling notwithstanding, Adams had no intent of plunging into a suicidal war. More military joke than a threat, the young American republic fielded a standing army of only 3,500 troops (France had more than a quarter-million under arms) and a three-frigate navy (French frigates and ships-of-the-line numbered almost 200). Little wonder the prickly Adams determined to balance defense initiatives with diplomacy by dispatching a trio of envoys to Paris in hope of producing an equitable settlement. No such presidential emissaries could, of course, be appointed without advice and consent of the Senate. Nonetheless, Adams, having presided over that august body for eight years as Washington's vice president, knew that nominating power had become squarely lodged in the Executive Office. "But," he bemoaned, "I soon found that if I had not the previous consent of the heads of departments [his Cabinet], and the approbation of Mr. Hamilton, I run the utmost risk of a dead negative in the Senate."[35]

"Take my ideas and weigh them," Hamilton in March 1797 had advised Secretary of War McHenry, who, unlike Secretary of State Pickering and Treasury Secretary Oliver Wolcott Jr., initially favored the president's three-man delegation to France. "A special extraordinary mission," Hamilton counseled, "is at least necessary to know what measure of redress will satisfy, if any is due."[36] And if France rebuffed Adams's negotiators, "the great advantage," continued Hamilton, "results in showing in the most glaring light to our people of her unreasonableness" while simultaneously "disarming [Republicans] of the plea that all has not been done that might have been done."[37] Urging McHenry to form a provisional 25,000-man army, Hamilton closed his missive by warning that "no mortal" must "know its contents."[38]

Alexander Hamilton, more than two years departed from the government, hovered like a High Federalist Banquo's ghost over the new administration. No sooner had Adams assumed office than Hamilton dispatched the new president an unsolicited "long, elaborate letter" with "a whole system of instruction for the conduct of the President, the Senate, and the House of Representatives."[39] Adams detested the letter as much as he despised its author, but Washington cabinet holdovers McHenry, Pickering, and Wolcott continued to correspond with their former colleague on important matters. Hamilton's detractors may have overstated his influence over the threesome, for Wolcott and Pickering were sometimes profoundly at odds with him; still, all three—particularly McHenry—consulted incessantly with the former treasury secretary on confidential policy issues, apprising him of the government's every move and valuing his judgment above that of an increasingly isolated Adams.[40] "I was as President a cipher," Adams complained 25 years later, "the government was in the hands of an oligarchy consisting of a triumvirate who governed every one of my five ministers."[41] If so, Adams had no one to blame but himself. Not only did he not replace the three holdovers with his own ministers after assuming the presidency, but he also virtually abdicated the office for months at a time on sabbatical to his Quincy farm.

Propensity for self-pity notwithstanding, Adams pretty much had his way on the diplomatic mission to France. And so Laurance in early June voted with a bipartisan Senate majority to appoint two southern Federalists, Charles Cotesworth Pinckney and Virginian John Marshall, together with Massachusetts jurist Francis Dana (replaced by Congressman Elbridge Gerry) as "Envoys Extraordinary and Ministers Plenipotentiary to the French Republic."[42] Tasked by Adams to preserve the peace and halt confiscation of American vessels, Pinckney, Marshall, and

Gerry were further directed to gain compensation for recent seizures and produce a commercial treaty along the lines of Jay's British agreement. It was a daunting presidential gambit that would produce unexpected consequences.

No correspondence exists to link Senator Laurance with Hamiltonian cabinet intrigue during the Paris envoy appointments or any other such shadow-presidency schemes during the Adams administration. Laurance, by renouncing his House seat and serving two years on the Federal bench, had served notice that his days as the former treasury secretary's legislative champion were over. Indeed, surviving period posts between the two New Yorkers have only to do with their multiple joint real estate interests.[43] Mostly it was a matter of accommodating Hamilton's cash flow exigencies, for the senator was now financially as well as politically his own man. Still, it's inconceivable—given their long and close relationship—that Hamilton's detailed eight-point defense plan for war against France could have escaped Laurance's eyes. Especially since the military blueprint was in the hands of mutual friend Rep. Smith (who steered House appropriations) more than a month before President Adams convened that May's special congressional session.[44] Nor could Laurance possibly have been blind to his old friend's ambition for a standing army with himself at the head. It was plain to see that Hamilton, from the creation of General Anthony Wayne's Legion in early 1792 to the Whiskey Rebellion militia call-up of 1794, had progressed through ever-larger military budgets toward institutionalizing a permanent army.[45] Western Pennsylvania Scots-Irish Republican Rep. William Findley may have overstated the case when he accused Hamilton of deliberately provoking the Whiskey Rebellion to create an excuse for taking the field to repress it, but wild horses could not have kept Alexander from assuming charge (together with Governor Henry Lee of Virginia) of 13,000 troops Washington assembled in October 1794 to quash insurgent western Pennsylvania whiskey producers.[46]

Laurance to a large extent shared Hamilton's national security vision for additional federal boots on the ground.[47] Indeed, most Federalists believed that military power was interdependent with fiscal power, commercial power, and the ability to enforce treaties.[48] He also understood that Great Britain was fulcrum of the balance of international power, and that too muscular a navy, as relations worsened with Revolutionary France, might threaten Federalist hopes for a closer British–American union that depended on unchallenged Royal Navy supremacy. Nevertheless, John demonstrated an unwavering commitment for a strong American navy. It was a personal conviction spurred no doubt by New York and Philadelphia mercantile interests clamoring to protect the multinational carrying trade. And with good reason: American foreign trade tonnage had exploded from 124,000 gross tons in 1789 to almost 500,000 tons nine years later.[49] European powers plundering one another's merchant fleets ensured that a barrel of flour fetching eight dollars in New York might garner 18 in Amsterdam, but profits were decimated by insurance rates that had skyrocketed from 6 percent of cargo value to 30 percent.[50] With Navy cruisers to sweep the coastline of French privateers, insurance costs could only go down while the odds of cargo reaching Amsterdam soared. Why depend upon the Royal Navy to protect American interests in the Caribbean when Yankee seamanship was up to the task?

Maritime economics aside, Laurance had another—more personal—interest in seeing *United States*, *Constitution*, and *Constellation* out to sea with their combined 124 guns. Alexander McDougall in February of 1781 had been selected by the Confederation Congress to become the first and only United States secretary of the Marine.[51] Although McDougall only served for six months, he spoke for a potent navy, and Laurance, by ushering one into being, could only enhance his deceased father-in-law's legacy.

On July 10, an exhausted, tetchy Congress adjourned for the summer. By month's end, yellow fever again raged in sweltering Philadelphia. More were aware early of their danger than in 1793 but were no more knowledgeable of its mosquito-borne cause, and two-thirds of the population again fled the city. President Adams relegated the government to his mostly holdover cabinet and decamped on a four-month retreat to Quincy. Senator Laurance removed with Elizabeth (then about to deliver daughter Margaret) and the family to the familiar pleasures of Trout Hall in present-day Allentown. As he made September rounds of his upstate New York investment properties, John could only have been stunned by newspaper reports of a sensational scandal involving Hamilton. Known as the "Reynolds Affair," it was a web of adultery, blackmail, and alleged Treasury Department corruption dating back to 1791 that linked Hamilton to a swindler's wife named Maria Reynolds. Jefferson, Madison, and James Monroe had long agreed, as gentlemen, to keep silent on the matter, but a muckraking writer for the Philadelphia *Aurora*, James T. Callender, had no such scruples. Bent on stamping Hamilton a corrupt debaucher, Callender broke the unsavory story in a damning series of pamphlets innocently titled "The History of the United States for the Year 1796."

Hamilton manfully owned up to the adulterous escapade with Maria—hush money and all—in a late-August 95-page rejoinder that vehemently denied any governmental financial improprieties.[52] Admirable as the candid apology may have been,* the former treasury secretary's career in high public office was seemingly finished. Even steadfast Robert

---

*Not all historians accept Hamilton's account at face value. Distinguished Princeton University Professor Julian Parks Boyd in 1963 expressed his concerns in a 62-page appendix to the 18th volume of his Jefferson series. Boyd argues that Hamilton misled the three congressmen investigating James Reynold's statements and that he fabricated 20 forged letters attributed to Maria Reynolds in his August 25, 1797, pamphlet. See also Robert C. Alberts, "The Notorious Affair of Mrs. Reynolds," *American Heritage* vol. 24, no. 2 (1973).

Troup conceded that the "ill-judged pamphlet has done him inconceivable injury."[53] Whatever the uncertainties of Hamilton's political future as 1798 dawned, keeping financial accounts square with Laurance was not one of them. For on December 29, the former treasury secretary dispersed $1,500 to Laurance to satisfy their joint $6,000 speculative debt obligation to mutual friend Robert Lenox, a fellow director of the New York branch of the Bank of the United States.[54] And, perhaps for the first time, it was Laurance, rather than Hamilton, whose star was on the rise.

SIXTEEN

Quasi-Warrior in the "Reign of Witches"

PHILADELPHIA, NOVEMBER 22, 1797. As presidential envoys Pinckney, Marshall, and Gerry labored gamely in Paris to present credentials to a disinterested, newly reconstituted Jacobin French Directory, South Carolina Federalist Jacob Read dutifully convened the second session of the Fifth United States Senate. Vice President Jefferson, as was becoming habit, found himself detained at Monticello.[1] No sooner had a newly appointed Tennessee senator by the name of Andrew Jackson been duly read in than President Pro Tempore Read named Senator Laurance one of three to respond to President Adams's perfunctory welcoming address. By early December, the New Yorker also sat on committees tackling Tennessee boundary issues and North Carolina harbor matters, and (nodding to his experience on the federal bench) legislating necessary amendments to the 1789 Judiciary Act.

On December 27, Laurance's health completely gave way. "He was flat on his back with the return of his old enemy, the inflammatory rheumatism," observed Robert Troup. "In size He is reduced at least 30 percent . . . and he expresses to me much regret for having gone [back] into public life."[2] The senator did not return to Congress Hall until March 5, 1798, an absence of 67 days. Unrecognizably gaunt, Laurance was uncharacteristically subdued until the 19th when he rose to introduce an addition to the 1789 "Act establishing the Judicial Courts of the United States."[3]

Laurance's Courts Bill (granting the Supreme Court authority to review civil suits filed in circuit court against federal revenue collectors) had barely completed its second reading on April 3 when news from abroad rendered Congress thunderstruck. So disturbing were fresh dispatches from envoys Marshall and Pinckney that a visibly agitated President Adams asked that galleries be cleared in both chambers before the contents were read aloud. Marshall's shocking narratives revealed the American diplomatic mission had encountered nothing but corruption and humiliation as guileful French Foreign Minister Talleyrand orchestrated a gauntlet of bribery shakedowns and loan requests to line his own pockets through unofficial channels. After more than six months of rebuffing Talleyrand's outstretched palm, the three American envoys had yet to even present their formal credentials. When made public, this national insult burst into a political conflagration instantly dubbed the "XYZ Affair" and escalated strained French relations into "Quasi-War."*

"Since the publication of the five dispatches, from our Ministers at Paris," wrote Laurance to Ambassador King, "public opinion has undergone a material change, in our country. We have hitherto," he continued, "acted on the defensive except on our coast; how soon we must act otherwise, cannot be long in doubt."[4] As public support hardened behind President Adams, congressional Federalists beat the drum for additional military readiness to the tune of an incremental two million dollars in new taxes. On April 27, Adams was green-lighted to build 12 new vessels of up to 22 guns apiece.[5] A week later came an $80,000 authorization for up to 10 small armed vessels.[6] Nearly a million dollars was then voted to actualize Senator Laurance's committee proposal for additional harbor fortifications and cannon foundries.[7] By mid-July, 20 separate defense measures had made their way to the president's desk.

Payoff on the naval investment was immediate: Captain Stephen Decatur's 20-gun sloop-of-war *Delaware*—on her maiden voyage—the first week of July captured French 12-gun privateer schooner *La Croyable* off the Jersey coast. Congress, emboldened by the heavily armed wooden walls of King George's powerful Royal Navy standing between French bluster and American shores, suspended trade with France and its dependencies and rubber-stamped Adams's initiative reviving commerce with St. Dominique (modern Haiti), whose slave revolt had thrown off French rule. The president then slapped the final stamp on the undeclared Quasi-War by unilaterally revoking the authority of French consuls in the United States.

Secretary of War McHenry was simply not up to the task of administering the full plate of defense measures. Indeed, President Washington had only offered him the position in early 1796 after three others refused. Hamilton, who even then thought the man "wholly insufficient for his place," two years later considered him "loaded beyond his strength."[8] Nowhere were McHenry's management shortcomings more glaring than in naval matters, where waste and delay led Virginian Josiah Parker's House committee on naval affairs in early 1798 to investigate substandard bookkeeping practices and possible fraud. "The purchase, building & providing of the ships falls on me," complained a frustrated Treasury Secretary Wolcott about McHenry's deficiencies, "and you know that my

---

*Three of Talleyrand's minions, code-named X, Y, and Z, served as medium for the French foreign minister's bribe solicitations and loan demands as preconditions to presenting diplomatic credentials to the governing Directory. To open the door for negotiations, they demanded a 1.2 million-livre *douceur* (bribe), a $12,000,000 loan, and President Adams's apology for indelicate comments. Rather than pay a penny, Marshall and fellow delegate Charles Pinckney aborted the diplomatic mission and returned home as heroes. Gerry stayed on another four months, ultimately facilitating fruitful resumption of negotiations.

other duties are enough. Mr. Lawrence & Mr. Bingham," he added, "have frequently created much embarrassment" over the matter.[9]

Senator Laurance had genuine cause for concern. Ten months had passed since his select committee authorized completion of frigates *Constellation*, *Constitution*, and *United States*; yet by April 1798 none of the vessels had been completely fitted out. A contractor supplying *Constitution* with "wet provisions" (salted beef or pork) warned the casks might go rancid after languishing four months in a storehouse awaiting proper paperwork.[10] Moreover, necessary live oak procurement was behind schedule, 24-pound naval guns were in short supply, and construction logistics of six separate shipyards had combined with yellow fever, fires, and bad weather to raise serious questions about the secretary of war's very competence. McHenry, to his credit, asked in early March that Congress augment the war department with a "commissioner of the Marine," but Senators Laurance and Bingham had seen enough. When Bingham on the second day of April motioned to establish a separate executive department of the navy, Laurance helped facilitate chamber passage by a 19 to 6 margin. Sailing through the House, the bill signed into law a navy department consisting of Secretary Benjamin Stoddert, six clerks, and a messenger at an annual cost of $9,152.[11]

Confident that naval mismanagement had been addressed, Laurance and his fellow committeemen in mid-June authorized the president to procure via private subscription up to a dozen additional warships on credit. One, thanks to John's fine legislative hand, was to be christened *New York*.[12] No sooner were the purchase details finalized than Laurance's proud constituents, unconstrained by government specifications or oversight, took up public subscription to lay keel of the Samuel Humphries–designed frigate *New York* in Peck and Carpenter's lower Manhattan shipyard. Last frigate to be launched and commissioned during the Quasi-War, the 144-foot *New York* carried 35 long guns along with a standard complement of 305 officers and crew.

Like Department of War Secretary McHenry, self-righteous, fiercely Anglophile holdover Secretary of State Timothy Pickering was not President Washington's first choice for the job. In the wake of Edmund Randolph's embarrassing 1795 resignation, six previous candidates (including Rufus King) turned Washington down. As June passed into July with no hope of negotiations with France, overwrought Secretary of State Pickering decided to take matters into his own hands. "The Rubicon is passed," he confided to his son in Lisbon, "War is inevitable."[13] Against Hamilton's express counsel, Pickering then mobilized a "war faction" in Adams's cabinet to precipitate formal hostilities against Revolutionary France whether the president agreed or not.

Artfully playing to Pickering's resolve, British minister Robert Liston—who thought him "one of the most violent anti-Gallicans I have met"—proposed (unsuccessfully) through diplomatic channels a startling naval alliance. In return for access to United States seamen to man Royal Navy ships, Liston confided that he was authorized to dedicate a full British squadron to defend American shores.[14] Sea lanes protected by His Majesty's warships, an American "provisional army" could then intercede in the rumored conspiracy of French and Spanish operatives with western separatists in Tennessee and Kentucky. Or perhaps even snatch Florida from Spanish hands and proceed unimpeded into colonial South America. And to Timothy Pickering's mind, only Alexander Hamilton possessed the administrative and leadership wherewithal to command the provisional force.[15] Thrice (according to Hamilton's grandson) the secretary of state insisted President Adams put Hamilton in charge rather than summon George Washington from retirement.[16]

Determined to put his plans into action, on the evening of July 1 Pickering summoned McHenry, Wolcott, Sedgwick, and dependable party members from both houses of Congress to gather at Senator William Bingham's opulent mansion on the corner of Spruce and Third Streets.[17] "The Subject," proclaimed that day's stridently Republican Philadelphia *Aurora*, was "A Declaration of War against France." Only Congress, of course, was constitutionally empowered to declare war—presidential war-making would have to wait until James Polk's 1846 Mexican land grab—so Pickering scrambled to mobilize full Federalist Party backing at Bingham's conveniently situated mini-Versailles. No attendee list survives, but the senator from New York would have been impossible to exclude. Laurance, it may be remembered, had come to know Bingham socially in the intoxicating days of Washington's early republican court. Not only was wife Elizabeth a socialite blueblood intimate of hostess extraordinaire Mrs. Bingham, but both men were directors of the Bank of the United States, and though Bingham operated on a hugely larger scale, the two senators shared a common speculative interest in upstate New York real estate. Committed to establishing an oceangoing navy to be reckoned with, the pair had voted in hawkish lockstep on Adams's initiatives throughout the Fifth United States Senate. Would they now sanction outright war with France behind the president's back?

Exactly what transpired at the Bingham conclave is a shadowy, well-kept Federalist secret. Apparently, newly elected Senate President Pro Tempore Sedgwick—rather than Secretary Pickering—formally motioned for a show of hands in favor of declaring war. Sedgwick, who had earlier boasted that every Federalist senator except Bingham favored immediate declaration of war, found himself misinformed.[18] Moderate "Adams Federalists" such as Joshua Coit of Connecticut and Samuel Sewall of Massachusetts, convinced that the House would reject any such measure, reportedly mustered a majority of five votes to quash what one historian pronounced "the most serious attempt in American history to declare war without a recommendation by the President."[19] A defense hawk

Senator Laurance may have been, but he likely sided with the moderates, for he was too much the pragmatist to unnecessarily risk fledgling America's delicate neutrality during France and England's superpower clash. Nor could he have forgiven Pickering for supporting the tawdry 1778 cabal to undercut General Washington, and for continuing to attribute victory to brilliance of the general's aides rather than the Master of Mount Vernon's leadership.[20]

Still, John was not averse to a firm diplomatic shot across the Jacobin Directory's bow; little more than two weeks earlier he and Bingham had reported to the Senate floor a bill "declaring void the treaties between the United States and the French Republic." Five days after the Bingham conference, the measure cruised through the Federalist House by a 47 to 37 margin to formally pronounce all "treaties heretofore concluded with France, no longer obligatory on the United States."[21] Nonetheless, first-term Connecticut Rep. John Allen pressed for a House resolution to consider declaration of war against France. And just as Adams moderates had foreseen, the question was "negatived without a division [roll call]."[22]

Within a week, President Adams signed the Treaty Act into law and, without consulting Congress or his cabinet, pushed the Quasi-War to its very nondeclared limit. "You are hereby authorized, instructed, and directed," Adams ordered commanders of all 21 deployed United States gunships, "to subdue, seize, and take any armed French vessel, or vessels, sailing under any authority or pretense of authority from the French Republic which shall be found within the jurisdictional limits of the United States or elsewhere on the high seas."[23] Next day, an Act for Establishing and Organizing a Marine Corps created the United States Marine Corps with a seagoing battalion of 500 privates led by a full complement of officers and noncommissioned officers. Laurance's Senate select committee then led the way for congressional authorization of three additional big frigates, *Congress*, *Chesapeake*, and *President*.[24]

Military bit in their teeth, Federalist legislators finally steamrolled into being the provisional army that Antifederalist and Republican counterparts had successfully opposed since adopting the Constitution. There is no evidence that Senator Laurance went so far as to join Ambassador King in embracing Hamilton's alleged scheme to wrest Florida territory from Spanish King Charles IV, but the *Annals of Congress* show him among the Federalist majority voting to raise an "Additional" 10,000-man standing army and authorize a 50,000-strong provisional army, supplemented with 30,000 stands of arms for the state militias.[25] As might be expected, Laurance was also among the senators whose unanimous "advice and consent" spurred President Adams on July 3 to summon George Washington from retirement.

"In a moment like the present," Washington responded, "when everything we hold dear and sacred is so seriously threatened, I have finally determined to accept the commission of Commander-in-Chief of the

Armies of the United States."[26] After assuming the specially created rank of lieutenant general, the 66-year-old president-emeritus made his service contingent upon offering Alexander Hamilton the major-generalship he craved as the army's second-in-command inspector-general. With this stipulation, Washington, who had raised Hamilton from anonymous artillery captain to wartime headquarters prominence, made him the nation's first treasury secretary, and backstopped his audacious financial agenda, now transcended lingering Reynolds-scandal stigma to restore his talented protégé to the national stage. "You crammed Hamilton down my throat," an infuriated Adams later snapped to Massachusetts High Federalist Senator Goodhue after reluctantly signing the ubiquitous New Yorker's commission on the same day—to save face—as those of fellow major generals Henry Knox and Charles Pinckney.[27]

Hamilton sprang to the task. It was a long-cherished chance to establish a true military academy and build a national officer corps in the mold of the great European powers. With hundreds of officer slots to fill by patronage, he solicited names from staunch Federalists across the states. Senator Laurance replied by recommending "sprightly young Alexander Macomb Jr." and two others.[28] Although likely doing the young man's financially broken father a Federalist courtesy, John displayed a genuine eye for talent; Macomb Jr. would rise to rank of major general and ultimately command the entire United States Army!

Major General Hamilton, in yet one more favor to good friend Laurance, scribbled the name of the senator's son John McDougall high (no. 6) among the 150 junior officers from New York that he proposed to Secretary of War McHenry. "A clever young man," Hamilton noted, who—though completely without experience—would make a "good Lt."[29] Generous gesture it may have been, but the senator wanted no part of any military adventure for his 22-year-old namesake son. "Mr. Laurance," Hamilton later sheepishly confessed to McHenry, "somewhat abruptly, regrets that I promoted his son's nomination . . . as it was his desire that he should continue to pursue his [legal] profession."[30] John McDougall may not have seen eye to eye with his father on the matter; New York records show him six years later as a "Captain in the 3rd Regiment of Militia in the City and County of New York."[31]

There was a second front in the undeclared war with France, an internal front of divisiveness and distrust. By early summer of 1798, John Adams's presidency had deteriorated into increasingly bitter political animosity between the "War Party" (Federalists) and the "French Party" (Republicans). "The legislature is much divided," complained exasperated Pennsylvania senator James Ross, "and the parties in it as much embittered against each other as it is possible to conceive."[32] Indeed, bitterness had earlier erupted into violence on the House floor when Irish-born Republican Matthew Lyon of Vermont spat in the face of Connecticut Federalist Roger Griswold for sarcastically referring to the former's (unjust) cashiering for cowardice during the Revolution. When Griswold later retaliated by savagely striking Lyon with a stout hickory cane, the Vermonter then grabbed a pair of fire tongs to send the pair grappling like common street thugs. Scuffling continued at intervals throughout the day until the House adjourned on Massachusetts Rep. Harrison Otis's merciful motion.

Party lines only tightened when tall, bony-figured Federalist Speaker of the House Jonathan Dayton (New Jersey)—alarmed at Napoleon Bonaparte's armies sweeping across Italy and Austria—went so far as to proclaim (without foundation) that France was also massing troops at its western ports to invade America.[33] Replicating Dayton's paranoia, the *Gazette of the United States* (9 June) and *Federal Gazette* (7 and 20 July) trumpeted that Philadelphia was to be burned by a "French Party" out to deliver the country into Gallic hands. To High Federalists such as freshman Senator James Lloyd of Maryland—who demanded (unsuccessfully) the death penalty in sedition cases—formal hostilities represented an opportunity to once and for all crush Jeffersonian Francophiles. "Declaration of war," wrote Lloyd to General Washington, was "necessary to enable us to lay our hands on traitors."[34] If the Master of Mount Vernon objected, his reply is yet to be found.

The ensuing Federalist witch hunt against Senator Lloyd's perceived "traitors" and the accompanying all-out assault on the Republican press are better understood by revisiting a party caucus held earlier that year at Senator Bingham's mansion. Not to be confused with Secretary Pickering's later assemblage under the same roof, the spring caucus was conceived to forge a solid senate Federalist voting bloc during the upcoming legislative session. Exactly how many of the 29 Federalist senators were in the room is unclear, but, "It was proposed and agreed to," reported the fiercely anti-Federalist Philadelphia *Aurora*, "that all members present should solemnly pledge themselves to act firmly on all measures agreed upon by the majority of those present at the caucus."[35] By a purported vote of nine to eight, in what John Adams would later dub one of those "nocturnal caucuses at the pompous Mansion House,"[36] High Federalists were reported by the *Aurora* to have prevailed over moderates to commit attendees to lockstep party discipline across the full spectrum of legislative issues.[37] Veracity of *Aurora* reporting is difficult to prove, but close reading of the *Senate Journal* over the subsequent session reveals a remarkable Federalist unanimity. "There is," concluded Professor John F. Hoadley's statistical analysis of Fifth United States Senate voting patterns, "no evidence of any substantial division within the Federalist bloc."[38]

Bingham dissented in his own parlor vote, but no record survives to tell us whether or not Laurance was among the other seven dissidents.

In any event, the senator from New York was subsequently honor-bound to abide by the majority decision. This pledged commitment to party voting solidarity was put to test over the summer of 1798 when Federalists, concerned that an influx of French refugees and surfeit of Irish immigrants invited a breeding ground for foreign agents, set out to curtail immigrant naturalization and criminalize political opposition to the administration. The result was a shameful series of punitive laws that President Adams, who since assuming the presidency had dealt with the Senate at arm's length, never requested: the reprehensible Alien and Sedition Acts.[39]

Today, this barefaced mockery of First Amendment rights to free speech appears without justification. But in 1798, with the nation at undeclared war with France, Federalist fears of Gallic subterfuge—if not outright invasion—were far from ungrounded. Hadn't French minister Pierre Adet in 1795 procured a copy of the still-secret Jay Treaty for unauthorized publication in Bache's pro-Republican Philadelphia *Aurora*? Didn't Adet plot to use United States soil as the staging area for General Victor Collet's invading military coup in Spanish Louisiana, and didn't he later openly campaign against the Adams presidency? Suspicion of French deceit extended well beyond minister Adet. Hadn't botanist Andre Michaux fomented frontier rebellion in league with former French minister "Citizen" Genêt? And what of the French privateer that in February refit in Charleston before flagrantly seizing the English merchant ship *Phoebe Ann* at the harbor's mouth? Were there not 25,000 or more French émigrés in America whose French newspapers, booksellers, boarding houses, schools, and restaurants were scattered about the states? What about scores of sympathetic tricolor-cockade-wearing "democratic society" parades? Not to mention a vast body of blacks in the south that French agents, à la alliance with Toussaint L'Ouverture against the British in St. Dominique, might inspire into armed insurrection. Obsession with a perceived Jacobin conspiracy loomed so large that the president of Yale University, Timothy Dwight, went so far as to orate in the flowery manner of his day: "Shall our sons become the disciples of Voltaire, and the dragoons of Marat; or our daughters the concubines of the Illuminati?"[40]

First of the Alien and Sedition laws was the Naturalization Act of June 18, 1798, lengthening from 5 to 14 years the waiting period for immigrants to become fully naturalized citizens. It was a ploy pure and simple to deprive the Republican party of foreign-born voters. Next came the Alien Act, granting President Adams power to deport without cause any foreigner deemed dangerous to the peace. On June 25, Vice President Jefferson, who branded the whole affair a "reign of witches," walked away from his role as Senate chair when a Federalist majority (including Senator Laurance) voted 14 to 5 to render "null and void" all treaties and alliances with the French Republic.[41] The Alien Enemies Act of July 6 empowered the president to declare as enemy any American residents who were citizens of countries at war with the United States. Eight days later, the Sedition Act made it a crime to speak or publish anything of "a false, scandalous, and malicious" nature against the government or Congress.

Individual responsibility for the Alien and Sedition Acts is difficult to assign, but Senator Laurance to his lasting shame voted lockstep with the Federalist majority on all four vindictive measures.[42] As early as April 26, he was named along with High Federalists Sedgwick, Read, Livermore, and Hillhouse to a select Senate committee tasked to consider Hillhouse's motion "respecting such aliens resident in the United States, as may be dangerous to its peace and safety."[43] A former immigrant himself, John's heart surely was not in the matter; Sedgwick said as much two weeks earlier, describing him as only "so-so" in a letter to Rufus King recounting ideological intensity of individual Party legislators.[44]

Laurance took no leadership role in drafting the four repugnant laws and did not speak on the floor in their favor. Although pro-British on mercantile matters and a pronounced defense hawk, he had for the best part of his Senate term been a pragmatic moderate on domestic issues. Whether deciding state boundary disputes, amending the Judiciary Act, or balancing state credits with the federal treasury, Senator Laurance was respected for his measured practicality. How, then, to explain his hewing ideological party line with the Alien and Sedition Acts? Hamilton was certainly not a factor; his biographers agree on an early ambivalence, if not outright concern that the Sedition Act "more than anything else may engender civil war."[45] Nor has Laurance left anything in his own hand to clarify just what he was thinking. Gallic distrust may well have simply gotten the better of him, but more likely he played good party soldier, adhering all too well to consensus pledged under Bingham's luxurious roof. A man's personal honor was only as good as his word, and honorable eighteenth-century men did not publicly go back on their word. Still, the Bingham caucus must have festered on Laurance's conscience, undoubtedly contributing to his eventual decision to walk away from party politics altogether.

Character flaw it may have been, but John's silence regarding the regrettable Alien and Sedition measures was not because he had turned Senate slacker; on less ideological matters of national importance he assumed the lead. Senator Laurance reported out and pressed for closure on bills to revise the Federal Judiciary Act, punish frauds against the national bank (Bank of the United States), provide relief for persons in debtors' prison, support orphans and wives of deceased war veterans, and settle state financial accounts with the federal government. Stubbornly clinging to lost parochial hope of returning the government to New York, he voted yet again in vain against appropriations to complete architect Peter L'Enfant's new capitol in Washington, DC.

Unexpectedly, on September 9, 1798, 26-year-old stepdaughter Margaret Elizabeth Tilghman tragically died in childbed at Trout Hall while bearing a baby daughter. The senator rushed to Allentown to join wife Elizabeth for the burial. There he would remain until first freeze of winter, for in late summer the dreaded yellow fever virus again returned to Philadelphia. And this time there was no escape to New York. "Yellow Fever in NY avg. 45 a day," warned Robert Troup, going on to observe, "1400 dead to the first of October ... 2/3 of people left for the country ... Phila worse at 70 a day."[46]

"Laurance is now at Albany," Troup continued, "attending the commission appointed to try and settle claims to military lands ... he says he is tired of wandering with his family and he has thoughts of buying a farm and settling down ... most probably near Mrs. Laurance's daughter Mrs. Livingston in the upper Manor."[47] Troup, as usual, had a reliable finger on his friend's pulse, for John had lived a truly peripatetic existence in the wake of the government's removal to Philadelphia eight years before. Repeated shuttling between Elizabeth's Chestnut Street residence, Allentown's Trout Hall, upstate New York real estate holdings, and his own lower Manhattan townhouse had acquainted him all too well with the back seat of over-the-road carriages. Sporadic bouts of inflammatory rheumatism were now an unpleasant fact of life. With three daughters under the age of seven, it truly was time to slow down. Especially since wife Elizabeth's health after bearing daughter Margaret was beginning to fail.

Yet, on December 5, there he was in Philadelphia's Congress Hall when the Senate re-convened. Finding no quorum, John and four other punctual senators returned home. Next day the first order of business was—in Vice President Jefferson's continuing absence—to elect a president pro tempore to administer the chamber. John Laurance that morning received the highest honor his peers could bestow. Selected president pro tempore of the Senate (the fourth of six who would preside in lieu of the disgusted Jefferson), he served as such the next 20 days.[48] The apogee of John's public career, the moment was unique in American history. To this day, he is the only non-natural-born citizen to stand behind the vice president in succession to the presidency.

John's first act as Senate head was to lead his colleagues downstairs to the House floor, where President Adams's forcefully written pro-defense speech was read aloud to both chambers of Congress. Backing Adams to the hilt, President Pro Tempore Laurance on December 11 personally delivered the Senate's written reply:

> We are of opinion with you, sir, that there has nothing yet been discovered in the conduct of France which can justify a relaxation of the means of defense adopted during the last session of Congress, the happy result of which is so strongly and generally marked. If the force by sea and land which the existing laws authorize should be judged inadequate to the public defense, we will perform the indispensable duty of bringing forward such other acts as will effectually call forth the resources and force of our country.[49]

Continued defense buildup assured, Laurance next presented Treasury Secretary Oliver Wolcott's report on the sinking fund. Happily, Wolcott advised that no new purchases of United States debt had been made since December of 1797, and that more than $1.1 million of the debt had since been retired by sinking fund payments (just as Hamilton had promised). It then fell to Laurance to preside over the very first impeachment proceeding in United States history when the chamber on December 17 resolved itself into a court of impeachment for the trial of expelled Tennessee Republican senator William Blount.[50] The Blount affair* began back in July of 1797 when the House of Representatives, acting on information provided by President Adams, voted to authorize senate impeachment of Blount for allegedly conspiring to allow Great Britain control of Louisiana in return for free access by American merchants to New Orleans and the Mississippi River. Blount, on the brink of bankruptcy, stood to profit by inflating the value of some quarter million acres of speculative western land affected by Mississippi River commerce. The Senate immediately sequestered Blount's seat, whereupon the unseated senator vanished into the western backcountry. Nearly a year and a half went by as Republican legislators searched for collusion between the Adams administration and Great Britain, while Federalists hoped to find a French connection. With no evidence of either, the formal Senate trial itself proved anticlimactic: Blount by narrow vote was found to be "unimpeachable."

Laurance's brief chamber presidency terminated in mid-trial when Vice President Jefferson on December 27 descended the steps of his Francis Hotel quarters, trod three blocks down Market Street to Congress Hall at State House Square, and reclaimed the Senate chair. No sooner had John relinquished the gavel than he was again stricken with rheumatism. Bedridden all of January, he returned on February 16 to help pass a bill giving the president authority to call up state militia to suppress insurrection and repel invasion.[51] During this latest bout of inflammatory arthritis, family tradition offers a rare glimpse of the respect he engendered from senate opponents:

> The physician desired that he should be put in a hot bath. But it was a difficult matter to lift so tall and heavy a man—one too in great pain. There chanced to be in the legislature at that session a Republican member of great size and personal strength. He was decidedly hostile to Laurance both as a Federalist and

---

*After the House on July 7, 1797, voted to impeach Blount, the Senate next day voted 25 to 1 to "sequester" Blount's seat. Blount, after posting bail, fled to Tennessee, never to return. The Senate on February 5, 1798, issued an arrest order and dispatched its sergeant-at-arms to Tennessee, but he returned empty-handed. On January 11, 1799, Vice President Jefferson presided over a 14 to 11 vote that concluded the Senate lacked impeachment trial jurisdiction because the absent Blount no longer held office. Seven of 18 Federalists joined seven Republicans in the majority. Senator Laurance, bedridden with rheumatism, was absent.

as a large landholder. Hearing however of the position in which his enemy was placed, he went immediately and took him up in his arms and carried him to the bath and put him carefully in the tub.[52]

Despite his painful disability, Laurance was not about to miss the opportunity to strengthen his cherished new United States Navy. With word of the frigate *Constellation*'s impressive pummeling of French 50-gun *L'Insurgent*, he conveyed himself to Congress on February 19 to help vote one million dollars to construct six 74-gun ships of the line and six small sloops.[53] Another $200,000 was allocated for timber, and $135,000 set aside to purchase land for six new navy yards.[54] Before Laurance and his fellow congressional sea hawks were satisfied, the Navy would boast of 54 ships, 750 officers, and 5,000 sailors, together with 1,085 officers and men of the newly formed Marine Corps.[55] Building, arming, and maintaining this nautical force cost taxpayers some $2.5 million between 1794 and 1798, but long-serving Navy chief clerk Charles Goldsborough estimated insurance savings by American ship-owners in 1798 alone amounted to $8,655,566.[56] A handsome return on investment indeed, on top of which came a fat diplomatic dividend. American envoys, thanks to the unmistakable West Indies presence of three big Yankee frigates, had negotiated with Britain "not as petitioners but as participants, pursuing a course of common interest" against French machinations in Haiti.[57] If President Adams was, as most historians agree, "Father of the American Navy,"[58] the Federalist Senate was its legislative nursery and Laurance and Bingham its collaborative midwives.

Leveled yet again by nagging rheumatism, John returned to New York in late spring 1799 after senate adjournment. "Laurance is here in a crisis," Troup informed Rufus King in early May, "and is indisposed with the remnants of a pretty severe attack during the last winter of inflammatory rheumatism. Mrs. Laurance is also in bad health," he continued. "After next winter Laurance will give up the senate and remove with her family to this city."[59]

The gossipy Troup made it his business throughout King's six-and-a-half-year London residency to pass along news of Laurance and Hamilton in his weekly correspondence. As the year wore on, however, the letters acquired a darker tone. "I believe both Mr. & Mrs Laurance," he confided on June 5, "are much impaired in health, and that they must be careful if they mean to continue somewhat longer with us. I do not know when I have ever seen a man more altered in size than Laurance is."[60] By early November John's crisis appeared to have passed, but Elizabeth's travails only worsened. "Laurance," Troup confessed, "has returned to Philadelphia with his family. He and Mrs. Laurance have been on a visit to the springs above Albany during the summer, where Mrs. Laurance found herself much recruited, but since her return to Pennsylvania she has relapsed. I fear that she is also in decline." Troup worriedly added that "Laurance will quit public life in the spring, and I can not conjecture who will replace him."[61]

Black crepe armband on his left arm, Senator Laurance the melancholy morning of December 26, 1799, left Elizabeth to her Chestnut Street convalescence and made his way to a Congress Hall hung with black curtains. "Before my eyes and in front of the Speaker's chair," wrote one congressman, "lies a coffin covered with a black pall, bearing a military hat and sword."[62] George Washington, first placeholder in the nation's heart, was dead. Twelve days earlier the former president had calmly died in his bed as he had lived—with masterly self-control. As New York's senior senator, John was immediately named one of seven to collaborate with the House in expressing their collective grief to Martha Washington and a mournful nation. Now the former president's symbolic coffin reposed in state at Congress Hall in order for the government to pay its last respects. Sharply at noon, a mounted trumpeter led two black-scarfed marines bearing the empty casket into the street, trailed by a symbolic riderless horse. Laurance and his congressional colleagues together with senior military officers filed in funeral procession from Sixth and Chestnut Streets to Philadelphia's capacious German Lutheran Church, the only facility large enough to accommodate some 4,000 mourners. There, Episcopal Bishop William White led a memorial service attended by President Adams and virtually the whole government. A somber Alexander Hamilton hurried down from New York; but Vice President Jefferson, in transit to Philadelphia from his Virginia home, avoided calling attention to himself by avoiding the doleful affair.

Laurance could not help but be affected by his wartime leader's passing. The trust earned as General Washington's judge advocate general proved the steppingstone to his successful post-war law practice and had opened the door to political office. It was a confidence reaffirmed in 1794 when President Washington appointed him federal district judge. From Revolutionary courtrooms to Philadelphia ballrooms, the Master of Mount Vernon had been a 20-year steadying presence. Like the older brother John never had, George Washington was always . . . well, always *there*. Indeed, the era of firsts so fluently characterized by historians Elkins and McKitrick as the "Age of Federalism" might as well have been named the "Age of Washington." Now, the indispensable man was gone.

SEVENTEEN

Slipping the Party Harness

PHILADELPHIA, MARCH 1800. "Poor Mrs Laurance is on her deathbed," confided Robert Troup glumly to Rufus King across the Atlantic. "In a letter Laurance wrote the day before yesterday, he relinquishes all hope for her recovery."[1] Before the senator's disheartened eyes, Elizabeth wasted away to the ravages of consumption, an inflammatory lung disease known today as pulmonary tuberculosis. Product of infectious aerobic bacteria whose assault sporadically waxed and waned as it wore down the immune system, consumption showed little or no symptoms in its early stages. Once embedded in hospitable lung tissue, it became a slow, relentless killer. Crisp mountain air and healing effervescent mineral waters of Ballston Spa (three miles south of Saratoga Springs, New York) had furnished Elizabeth some relief over the past year, but only temporarily.

Perhaps as distraction from the inevitable, John immersed himself in Senate business, sitting on 12 committees between January and May of 1800.[2] None proved more controversial than the five-member panel appointed to consider a startling motion from western Pennsylvania Federalist James Ross. On January 23, the fiercely anti-populist Ross—who reputedly "saw no good in any kind of election"—had motioned to establish a "Grand Committee of Thirteen" to function as a kind of super Electoral College for resolving potential individual state elector voting disputes.[3] No votes promised to be more disputed than in Ross's home state, where John Adams four years earlier received but 1 of 15 electoral votes. In December, Pennsylvania's Federalist state senate, hoping to gain an elector or two in the upcoming national election, had rejected a lower chamber bill for choosing presidential electors on a statewide basis; rather, state senators proposed to alter procedure to vote by district. When the legislature adjourned with the matter unresolved, Federalist-turned-Republican governor Thomas McKean refused to call a special session to break the deadlock, hinting that he would call on the people to choose electors. And waiting until the new legislature met—as Senator Ross well knew—meant leaving the choice of presidential electors dangling in uncertainty. Thomas Jefferson immediately grasped the implications for the upcoming presidential election of 1800. "If Pennsylvania votes," he confessed to Madison, "then either Jersey or New York giving a Republican vote, decides the election."[4]

To Ross's mind, Governor McKean's refusal to call state legislators into a special session violated Article II of the Constitution, which indisputably entrusted state legislators, rather than the people, with picking electors. Therefore, Ross—still smarting from McKean's trouncing him in the nasty 1799 gubernatorial race—rose from his seat on January 23 to propose that six members each from the Federalist-dominated Senate and House confer in secret with the chief justice (also Federalist) to decide the legality of future elector votes. Next day, Federalists Ross, Laurance, Livermore, and Dexter of Massachusetts were named along with South Carolina Republican Charles ("Blackguard Charley") Pinckney* to a select committee charged to "report out a bill or otherwise." Whether or not a secret Federalist caucus—as the *Aurora* trumpeted—had in fact strategized the matter behind closed doors before Ross first spoke, Laurance could not have failed to understand the larger implications: disqualify enough of Pennsylvania's Republican electors, hold on to New York, and the presidency would remain in Federalist hands.[5]

Laurance soon found himself in the center of a political firestorm. Sparks flew when fellow committeeman Pinckney pronounced the Ross measure blatantly unconstitutional, but Philadelphia combusted into political flame when three alarmed Republican senators went public on the matter. The trio, suspecting Federalist subterfuge to swing the presidential election in favor of incumbent Adams, anonymously leaked proposed "Ross Bill" contents to hard-hitting Philadelphia anti-administration newspaperman William Duane.

The 40-year-old Duane (no relation to James Duane) was a New York-born refugee Irish firebrand journalist whose Calcutta start-up newspaper, *The World*, criticized East India Company policies so fiercely that British authorities in 1794 forcibly shipped him back to England. Two years later he was welcomed aboard the single-sheet triweekly Philadelphia *Aurora* by censorious 29-year-old owner/editor Benjamin Franklin Bache—Franklin's grandson—to become a thorn in Federalist flanks. When Bache succumbed to yellow fever mere days before his trial on trumped-up charges of libel and sedition, Duane not only forcefully defended his former employer as martyr to a free press, but also turned up editorial heat against the Adams administration. "If the Aurora is not blown up," one Federalist senator is said to have muttered, "Jefferson will be elected in defiance of everything."[6]

Dark-haired, roguishly handsome William Duane wasted no time sensationalizing his juicy leaked Senate tidbit, but he mistakenly printed that the Ross Bill had actually cleared the chamber. Indignant Federalist

---

*A moniker devised by Federalists to distinguish the "father" of South Carolina Republicans from Federalist kinsmen Thomas and Charles Cotesworth Pinckney. Delegate to the Continental Congress, the Congress of the Confederation, and the Constitutional Convention, Senator Charles Pinckney (1757–1824) was appointed minister to Spain (1801–1805) by President Jefferson and elected governor of South Carolina upon his return.

senators pounced upon the error to form a five-man "Committee on Privileges" to determine whether Duane's disclosure breached the sanctity of chamber confidentiality. To no one's surprise, the Committee decreed that *Aurora*'s "false, defamatory, and malicious" reporting had violated the Sedition Act, a verdict promptly adopted on March 20 by the full Senate. Before sentencing the newspaperman outright, Privileges Committee chairman Jonathan Dayton summoned him to explain his actions. Duane duly complied, but discovering the proceeding was more trial than a hearing, asked for a lawyer. Allowed a two-day continuance by Vice President Jefferson to confer with counsel, the wily newspaperman presciently surmised that his lawyers would be muzzled by Senate "privileges" and disappeared into safe hiding. Senator Laurance then dutifully voted with a party-line majority to arrest the fleeing Duane, and Jefferson as Senate president reluctantly signed the warrant.[7]

Next morning, Laurance set aside the Ross/Duane affair to bring closure on a legislative task he had begun more than a decade earlier: passage of an "Act to establish a uniform system of bankruptcy throughout the United States."[8] Independence had not only left unaltered the varied individual state practices defining debtor and creditor relationships, but also the harsh English common law tradition of debtors' prison as final resort for insolvency. Although it is not exactly clear what delegates at the Constitutional Convention had in mind, article I, section 8, clause 4 of the document authorized Congress to enact uniform bankruptcy legislation. Accordingly, Laurance, barely two months into the First Federal Congress, was appointed with Reps. Smith and Ames to draft the new republic's first bankruptcy bill. All went for naught, however, when unfinished House business was forced to begin anew on the government's removal to Philadelphia.

In November 1791 and yet again following the "Panic of 1792," the New Yorker was named to committees charged to report out bills establishing a uniform system on bankruptcies.[9] And though such bills surfaced in one form or other in virtually every subsequent session, it was not until December of 1798, after debtors were jailed by the hundreds in wake of the burst 1796 land speculation bubble, that the House finally produced a draft bill.[10] The 49-section measure squeaked past fierce anti-Federalist opposition thanks to Speaker Theodore Sedgwick's tie-breaking vote, and landed in February 1800 on the senate docket. Given Laurance's earlier spadework, it was only fitting that he shepherded the belated bill through three chamber readings to report out on March 28 his committee's unamended endorsement for a final floor vote.[11] Approved by a 16 to 12 margin, it was signed into law as the Bankruptcy Act of 1800 within a week.*

---

*Republicans repealed the Bankruptcy Act of 1800 three years later, claiming it was designed to free former senator Robert Morris from jail and that implementation was both arbitrary and discriminatory. More than a few suspected that Senator Laurance supported the Bankruptcy Act because of empathy for Morris and pending bankruptcy proceedings against stepson-in-law William Greenleaf, but John's early commitment to bankruptcy relief long predated their jail stints.

Knowing Laurance, any personal elation over passage owed less to humanitarian concern and more to facilitating a national credit system that fueled speculative investment in canals, turnpikes, factories, banks, and land companies. For the new law, largely based on the British 1732 bankruptcy statute of George II, was designed to protect creditors, not debtors.[12] Only at banker, merchant, or broker creditor request were federal district judges empowered to appoint nonjudicial commissioners to oversee and help administer bankruptcy proceedings. Agrarians and southerners cried foul at a law that offered little relief to farmers and the small creditor, while federalizing what to their mind might be accomplished more speedily and less expensively in state courts. And to a skeptical general public, the new bankruptcy law invited another round of chicanery by manipulative big city moneymen. Still, by tempering the cruel English common law practice of debtors' prison as consequence for insolvency, Senator Laurance helped pioneer the first—albeit flawed—step in a debt relief process that culminated in the "Chandler Act of 1938," giving all debtors voluntary access to a uniform bankruptcy system.[13]

Bankruptcy measure settled, senators resumed consideration of the controversial Ross Bill. The Pennsylvanian's original motion to establish a "grand" (overwhelmingly Federalist) committee to discard "disputed" electoral votes was provocative enough, but the reported-out measure went even further. Not only would the proposed grand committee meet behind closed doors, but there would also be no record of their deliberations and no appeal of their verdict. Senator Pinckney, lone Republican on the select committee reporting out the measure, took the floor to passionately condemn it as a legislative machination that perverted the Constitution. Congress's only constitutionally specified duty, insisted Pinckney, was to count state electoral votes in a convention of both houses. Undeterred, a 16 to 12 Federalist majority approved the Ross Bill as an "Act prescribing the mode of deciding disputed elections of President and Vice President of the United States."[14] Laurance, who sat with Pinckney on the Ross panel, might have been expected to champion its passage; instead, he stunned Federalist colleagues by abstaining! It was the first time he broke party ranks on a constitutional matter since assuming Rufus King's seat almost four years earlier.

The senator from New York was not alone in his growing estrangement from Federalist ideologues; it was plain to see that public zeal for the administration was withering. Agrarian America wanted no part of Major General Hamilton's inchoate "provisional" army with its adventurous Louisiana scheme and the taxes to pay for it. Distrust of a standing army was compounded by widespread disgust at a flat-out partisan assault on the Republican press and the odious Senate-sponsored Sedition Act. Popular petitions against the repressive measure rolled into the House, with 18,000 names received from Pennsylvania alone.[15] And though Federalists still enjoyed a clear majority in both houses of Congress, they had not lately—other than the Bankruptcy Act squeaker—carried an important measure in the House, where both middle state and southern members of the party had become increasingly moderate. Despite his disaffections, Laurance was not about to defect to the Republican camp along with the Livingstons, Burr, Pennsylvania governor McKean, Senator Pinckney, and enigmatic former South Carolina congressman Pierce Butler. Nor would he temporarily cross the aisle as Kentucky Federalist colleague Humphrey Marshall had done on both the Duane arrest warrant and Ross Bill votes. It was also not his way to publicly reject party dogma as Virginia Federalist John Marshall had brazenly done during the Alien and Sedition debates. So, when a measure such as the Ross Bill was a bridge too far, Laurance withheld his vote . . . just as in 1793 with the Fugitive Slave measure.

Six days later, Laurance abstained again! At issue this time was Senator Pinckney's proposed constitutional amendment to preclude sitting federal judges from accepting any other federal or state positions. Pinckney, like most Republicans, was justifiably concerned that diplomatic service on behalf of the president, such as Chief Justice Ellsworth's current mission to Paris, violated constitutional separation of powers. After the South Carolinian contended that judges vacating their posts unfairly increased the caseload burden on their peers, Laurance was named to a Senate committee of five to formally report out Pinckney's measure. Following debate, Laurance withheld his vote when a motion to authorize a third reading was negated 14 votes to 12.[16]

Savoring Laurance's moral dilemma to the fullest, a secretly sequestered William Duane opined in the *Aurora* of April 7 that the New Yorker's abstention was no act of principle at all, but rather "cowardly submission to party pressure."[17] If John dreaded similar press second-guessing when the contentious Ross Bill was returned from the House, he need not have worried; the measure, as Jefferson smugly observed, "underwent a revolution in the House of Representatives."[18] Not only did Federalist John Marshall (who chaired the select committee to which the bill was referred) forcefully oppose the proposed Senate-centric procedures for secretly vetting electors, but a raft of House amendments so completely eviscerated the bill that it collapsed under its own unconstitutional weight when both chambers of Congress refused in early May to recede from irreconcilable positions.

Three weeks before the Senate adjourned for the summer, Laurance on Friday, April 25, excused himself to devote full attention to Elizabeth and the poignant Saturday marriage of stepdaughter Ann (Nancy) Penn Allen in an intimate ceremony administered by assistant rector Dr. Robert Blackwell at venerable Christ Church.[19] Thirty-one, and one of the beauties of her day, Nancy Allen (fig. 12) had dallied the past five years with a gentleman of prominent Boston parentage but a complicated past—land speculator James Greenleaf. With her mother at death's door, Nancy could put off marriage no longer.

Fine-looking in a delicate, aristocratic way, the smartly dressed Greenleaf arrived in Philadelphia in late 1793 after an embarrassingly brief stint as consul at the United States embassy in Amsterdam. His "rascality" rivaled that of the jailed William Duer. Rumored to have wed Baroness Antonia Scholten van Aschat to gain access to Dutch banking circles, Greenleaf lined up his financing, amassed a million-dollar fortune arbitraging American bonds to unsuspecting European investors,

FIGURE 13 Ann Penn Allen (1769–1851).

Oil on canvas (ca. 1795) by Gilbert Stuart (1765–1828) (Courtesy of the Pennsylvania Academy of Fine Arts, Philadelphia. Bequest of Mrs. Mary W F Howe in memory of her father J Gillingham Fell Reproduced with permission.)

fathered two children with the baroness, and then fled Amsterdam for a long-distance New York divorce.[20] Thrown out of brother-in-law Noah Webster's lower Manhattan townhouse after hosting a raucous party, the slick Bostonian partnered with financiers Robert Morris and John Nicholson to control nearly half the federal government's salable land in the development of Washington, DC, only to default.[21] Greenleaf then doubled down on an already precarious indebtedness by borrowing some $37,000 to acquire Landsdowne, the magnificent Philadelphia mansion formerly owned by Nancy's grandfather John Penn. Next, he shelled out $28,000 for General Dickinson's splendid Chestnut Street residence a few doors from the Allen sisters. When he and Nancy Allen sat in late 1795 for individual Gilbert Stuart portraits, they had become more than friends.

Two years later, James Greenleaf's lavish Philadelphia idyll crashed to earth. Massively overreached in land speculation, he lost everything. Lansdowne was seized for sheriff's auction and General Dickenson—citing delinquent mortgage payments—foreclosed on his former Chestnut Street property. Following a year in Philadelphia's Prune Street debtors' prison, Greenleaf in February 1799 found himself again in bankruptcy court, this time in a Maryland case that would be discharged three years later under protection of Senator Laurance's Bankruptcy Act of 1800. Nancy may have been smitten with the roguish Greenleaf, but she was nobody's fool. The auburn-haired beauty shrewdly sheltered her substantial inheritance from her new husband's weaker instincts by placing everything in trust under twin executorships of Senator Laurance and her trusted brother-in-law, attorney William Tilghman.[22] It was a bittersweet April 26 wedding indeed.

In November 1800, 138 electors from all 16 states would choose the young republic's third president. Because each state scheduled its own balloting date between April and October, the election of 1800 was national in name only. Five states selected presidential electors by popular vote instead of legislative appointment, but New York was not one of them. It was therefore imperative that Alexander Hamilton, when Empire State polls opened between April 29 and May 1, keep Federalist bottoms in all 13 New York City seats of the state general assembly. Otherwise, New York's 12 electoral votes would end up in Republican hands. And without New York, Federalist chances for retaining the presidency were dim.

Former senator Aaron Burr, Hamilton's politically savvy 44-year-old New York Republican counterpart, was a formidable, street-smart opponent. In a shrewd, altogether deceptive ploy, state assemblyman Burr in February 1799 conned Federalist New York legislators, Governor Jay,

Mayor Varick, and Hamilton himself into chartering the start-up Manhattan Company as a water utility to help spare the city from future yellow fever epidemics. Buried in the fine print, however, was permission for Manhattan Company to deploy "surplus capital" as if it were a bank. Raising two million dollars in share capitalization, the mundane water utility then transformed itself into a Wall Street lending institution, offering credit to Republican merchants and tradesmen.[23] Six months before Election Day, Burr's Manhattan Company bank opened its discount window to a New York weary of restrictive Federalist lending policies by Hamilton's Bank of New York and Laurance's local national bank (Bank of the United States) branch.

Burr melded upstate Clinton agrarians and Livingston patricians together with New York City artisans, craftsmen, and mechanics into a powerful Republican voting bloc that was publicly endorsed by Chancellor Livingston himself. Naming Brockholst Livingston campaign co-manager, the shrewd Burr waited until Hamilton showed his hand with a mediocre slate, then unveiled a stellar Republican ticket headed by former Governor Clinton that included Revolutionary "Hero of Saratoga" Horatio Gates, Colonel Henry Rutgers (namesake donor of the University), and former Postmaster General Samuel Osgood. Joining them was Laurance's congressional opponent of 1789, John Broome, now president of the New York Life Insurance Company.

Stellar as was his ticket, Burr's edge lay in Manhattan's immigrant-laden outer wards, where tradesmen were wooed with a promise to alter voting laws that disenfranchised three-fourths of city mechanics by limiting alderman elections to property-holders. Additional Republican strength came from the city's Democratic Society, one of hundreds of such self-created groups that sprang up across the country in the mid-1790s in sympathy with Revolutionary France and antipathy to the Alien and Sedition Acts. Between 100 and 200 strong, the New York Democratic Society boasted both Edward and Brockholst Livingston as past presidents, along with the Scot Donald Fraser who headed the local Caledonian Society, and many "heroes and the sons of those heroes" who helped gain independence.[24] It was a vocal, demonstrative group that, together with the Tammany Society, Mechanics' Association, Humane Society, Friendly Sons of Saint Patrick, and half a dozen other organizations, drew immigrant Scottish, French, German, and Irish voters toward the Republican camp. With "one in seven or eight New Yorkers probably at least nominally Catholic,"[25] Republican block wardens homed in on the heavily immigrant Fifth, Sixth, and Seventh Wards, denouncing Federalists as an anti-immigrant, anti-Catholic "British junto" controlled by former loyalists and Anglophiles antagonistic to independence for Ireland. Indeed, Irish tempers were stoked by the very mention of Federalist Rufus King's name, for as minister to England he had persuaded London not to permit captured revolutionaries from the United Irish uprising of 1798 to seek exile in the United States.[26]

As April wore on, Burr and Hamilton with their respective ward captains worked the streets with extraordinary stamina and professional courtesy, addressing street corner crowds and buttonholing friends in search of votes. But there was a marked difference in style; the outspoken Hamilton said what he believed, while shrewd Aaron Burr used the lively new Republican newspaper, the *American Citizen*, to tell voters what they wanted to hear. What's more, the Republican ground game was by far superior. Turning his home into round-the-clock campaign headquarters, Burr canvassed every ward, raised money from supporters, collected information on thousands of possible voters, and dispatched party workers to cajole and persuade. Campaign aides Theodorus Bailey, Matthew Davis, John Swartout, and others individually targeted nearly two-thirds of eligible voters, including free blacks. To the heavily German Seventh Ward, Burr assigned fluent German speakers. When a potential voter fell short of the minimum property requirement, Burrites are said to have bundled him with as many as 20 others in a practice known as "faggoting" on joint-tenancy deeds just large enough to meet franchise qualifications.[27]

Undermanned Federalists countered the best they could. "I have not eaten dinner for three days," lamented an exhausted Robert Troup, "and have been constantly upon my legs from 7 in the morning til 7 in the afternoon."[28] No amount of legwork, however, could compensate for a weak Federalist ticket of political mediocrities. "It is next to impossible," Troup lamented to Rufus King, "to get men of weight and influence to serve."[29] Indeed, all but two of New York City's 13 Federalist incumbents had opted not to run for general assembly reelection, and their replacement slate was dismissed by Abigail Adams as "men of no note, men wholly unfit for the purpose."[30] Hamilton's misfortunes only worsened when a British warship on election eve heaved into New York harbor with seized American merchantmen in tow to remind voters one last time of Federalist ties with Great Britain.

Senator Laurance well understood that his own political future was on the line along with New York's 12 electoral votes when city polls opened the end of April. And how could he not support old friends Hamilton and Troup's desperate eleventh-hour attempt to solicit votes from property-owning freemen as they scurried to city polling stations? True, the cobbled-together Federalist slate of "two grocers, a ship chandler, a baker, a potter, a bookseller, a mason, and a shoemaker," was ordinary at best, but the senator could still twist a few arms on familiar streets of his local neighborhood ward.[31] Directly after Nancy's April 26 wedding, he gathered deathly frail Elizabeth to his side and sped by coach to New York.[32]

"There are at present four stages that ply between this city and New York," announced J. Hardie's *Philadelphia Directory & Register*, "two of which set off at three o'clock in the morning and arrive at New York that evening."[33] The Laurances might have taken either, but given the awkward departure hour more likely opted for Swift Sure Stage Line's 8 a.m. coach departing the Bunch of Grapes Tavern some three blocks from Elizabeth's Chestnut Street residence. Inaugurated in 1799, the Swift Sure Line shaved time off the rigorous journey by taking the Old York Road to Coryell's Ferry 15 miles above Trenton and crossing the Delaware into New Jersey en route to Newark and on to the Paulus Hook ferry to lower Manhattan. Fare, including baggage, was four dollars a person.

As it turned out, Laurance played no role whatsoever in the New York election. For on April 29, very morning polls opened, and three days after daughter Nancy's wedding, Elizabeth passed away in the senator's Broadway townhouse.[34] She was not yet 49. That Elizabeth died in New York City is beyond dispute, but exactly why she braved an arduous coach ride to accompany her husband from Philadelphia remains a mystery. Family tradition has it that before leaving Philadelphia she was reassured by her doctor to be on the road to recovery.[35] Insisting the (unnamed) physician put his hand on her Bible, so the story goes, she asked him to swear before God that it was so. Although the good man complied, it was not to be. "Died Mrs Elizabeth Allen," read Benjamin Rush's belated journal entry for 29 April, "one of the belles of Philadelphia."[36] Laurance, along with responsibility for grieving daughters Emily (age seven), Frances (five), and Margaret (almost three), was left with the unconscionably macabre thought that—although her days were numbered—he had accelerated his wife's death in a hurried journey of political expediency.

While the senator mournfully orchestrated necessary logistical and social arrangements for Elizabeth's Philadelphia burial, the election campaign shifted into yet higher gear. A determined Hamilton speechified at each polling location, reputedly riding from poll to poll on a white horse amid cheers in some wards and catcalls in others. Burr assigned guards of his own to keep an eye on federal army officers posted at several polling spots to oversee ballot tabulations. "All manner of carriages, chairs and wagons," reported the *New York Gazette*, were made available by Burr operatives for elderly Republicans lacking transportation to their polling station. On the final day, indefatigable Aaron Burr stationed himself for 10 straight hours in the all-important Seventh Ward to influence every last voter. The morning of May 2 it was all over. Stunning the young nation, Burr's Republican slate carried New York City's 13 seats with a cumulative majority of some 500 votes.[37] And to Federalist horror, George Clinton was reelected governor in a Republican sweep of both houses of the state legislature. Alexander Hamilton's Federalist home turf was no more.

Nevertheless, the election outcome was a very near thing. "It is perfectly truthful," observed Edward Channing's 1926 Pulitzer Prize winning *History of the United States*, "to say that a change of less than two-hundred fifty votes in the city of New York in the May election of 1800 would have given New York's vote to Adams and made him President."[38] Echoing Channing's words, distinguished twenty-first-century historian David

McCulloch reminds us that with this 250-vote swing "Adams would have prevailed with an electoral count of 71 to 61."[39] It would be tempting, then, to lay partial blame for the Federalist demise of 1800 at Senator Laurance's tragically absent feet. After all, John had *never* been personally defeated at the polls by New York City voters. Not as ward alderman, state legislator, or U.S. congressman. Might his presence, then, at Hamilton and Troup's Tontine Coffee House Party caucus of April 15 have helped produce a stronger Federalist ticket? Would weeks of hard personal campaigning in his adopted home town have slowed the Burr steamroller and sent a Federalist slate to Albany?

Closer examination of the city voting results suggests otherwise. Laurance indeed retained clout in the "bluestocking" Second and Third Wards where Federalist victory was assured, but Republican triumph was the product of lopsided wins in the impoverished Sixth and Seventh outer wards where rent-collecting English-born landlord John Laurance—he owned at least four properties in the heavily German Seventh Ward— lacked influence or allure.[40] Indeed, Republicans captured almost two-thirds of Seventh Ward votes despite the fact that 65 percent of ward households were propertyless.[41] Whatever street appeal Laurance earlier earned, as an immigrant lawyer, gritty Alexander McDougall's son-in-law, and patriot soldier, had long since dissipated. By 1800 John was the very picture of a Broadway socialite who frequented exclusive upstate spas and commuted by carriage from an elegant townhouse to the branch Bank of the United States, only to slam lending windows shut for ordinary merchants. No, Hamilton's absent friend could not have tipped the balance in the downscale outer wards. Last word is best left to Aaron Burr. When asked by an opponent how he managed to pry New York from Federalist hands, Burr replied: "We have beat you by superior Management."[42]

Nineteen days after the New York polls closed, Senator Laurance on an unseasonably warm 20th of May conveyed Elizabeth's mortal remains to earth at Philadelphia's venerable Christ Church burying yard.[43] Had his grieving eyes searched out nearby markers, they would have landed on final resting places of her mother Elizabeth (Francis) Lawrence, paternal grandfather Thomas Lawrence, first husband James Allen, and her only son, James Jr., who had perished in August 1788 at the age of 10. As John bid his wife a final farewell, the Philadelphia chapter of his own life was nearing closure. Not just because the Republican sweep of New York left him a political lame duck out of water when his term expired next March, but without Elizabeth there was really no further reason to remain in town. Although membership in the prestigious Philadelphia bar dated all the way back to 1780, his ticket to local inner society was no longer punched without Elizabeth on his arm.[44] And, as if to bring down the final curtain on the city's glittering decade as seat of the "Republican Court," irreplaceable hostess extraordinaire Anne Bingham would in a matter of months set sail with her family for Lisbon, never to return.*

After George Washington passed, only a shared distrust of France and Jefferson's "French Party" kept the Hamilton and Adams wings of the fracturing Federalist Party from flying apart. All hope for party unity had been dashed by President Adams's bold—characteristically unilateral— November 1799 decision to dispatch Chief Justice Oliver Ellsworth and two fellow envoys on another treaty-seeking mission to Paris. Utterly opposed to the mission, High Federalists and pro-Britain "Essex junto" extremists agitated to replace Adams. A derisive Fisher Ames scoffed to Pickering that moderates who supported President Adams were no better than "Jacobins and the half-federalists."[45] Gouverneur Morris, "considering Mr. Adams unfit for the office he now holds," went so far as to beg George Washington to consider a third term; but the man of the ages was dead before the letter arrived.[46] Little wonder Secretary of War McHenry saw "rocks and quicksands on all sides, and the administration in the attitude of a sinking ship."[47]

It was a floundering vessel that McHenry, Pickering, and Wolcott in the early months of 1800 had determined to abandon. Strategizing with Hamilton, the cabinet trio in March conspired with recently named Speaker of the House Sedgwick, outspoken South Carolina Rep. Robert Goodloe Harper, and Senators Carroll, Dayton, and Hillhouse to supplant Adams as party presidential nominee in the upcoming national election.[48] In his place they favored two-time senator and sitting Chief Justice Ellsworth, then still in Paris as one of Adams's envoys. On or about the third of May, the first full-fledged party presidential caucus in our nation's history is said by the gossipy *Aurora* to have taken place when Federalist legislators gathered at Senator Jacob Read's residence (more likely they met in the Senate chamber) to propose Charles Cotesworth Pinckney and Pickering as the Federalist ticket.[49] But word of Hamilton's crushing New York Federalist defeat, together with Ellsworth's complete disinterest and honorable silence from Pinckney, forced an expedient conciliatory consensus: pressure would be placed on party electors to instead cast their two votes equally for Adams and High Federalist Pinckney. Common understanding was that the latter would become vice president.

Learning of the party caucuses, Adams at long last understood that McHenry and Pickering's primary loyalty lay with Hamilton and not himself. Two days later he demanded and shortly received McHenry's resignation.

---

*Diagnosed by her physician with consumption, Anne Willing Bingham departed with her husband for Lisbon in the hope that warm climate might arrest her decline. She died May 11, 1801, on the island of Bermuda. Distraught William Bingham removed three months later to England, where he died in the spa city of Bath on February 7, 1804.

When the obstinate Pickering refused to step down, he was cashiered. The president, advised by his envoys that Napoleonic France truly wanted peace, then lost no time dismantling the republic's "provisional" army. After slashing the ranks on May 20 by 12 regiments, he rid himself of Major General Hamilton in June by scuttling the army altogether.[50] Hamilton, never consulted on the Paris mission and irked at not being promoted into Washington's empty shoes as military commander-in-chief, was furious. Dreams of military glory ruined and plans for a select national officer corps gutted, his smoldering resentment combusted into personal vendetta when derogatorily branded in private by Adams as a "British lackey" and "Creole bastard."[51]

Hamilton's behind-the-scenes manipulations to supplant Adams with Pinckney (or even Jefferson!) placed Senator Laurance in an untenable spot. The president was more than just a political bedfellow; though a frustratingly irascible bundle of peptic insecurities, he was still a friend.[52] Their relationship traced all the way back to the summer of 1774, when Adams, on his way to the Continental Congress in Philadelphia, stopped for a week in New York City hosted by Sons of Liberty leader Alexander McDougall.[53] Laurance, then an aspiring pro-Sons attorney courting McDougall's daughter Betsey, could not help but have supped and conversed with the noted Boston lawyer. It was, of course, Adams, who had as virtual one-man head of the Congressional Board of War and Ordinance swiftly blessed Laurance's April 1777 appointment to judge advocate general. After the war, Laurance not only took Adams's son Charles into his Manhattan practice to read law, but he and Elizabeth also became close to the president's daughter Abigail ("Nabby") and her perpetually financially dissipated husband William S. Smith. The two men during federalism's halcyon days of the early 1790s took pleasure bird hunting on Colonel Smith's Long Island farm and dabbled on more than one occasion together in upstate land speculation. As one of but three senators to support the president's nomination of Smith for a provisional army generalship, it subsequently fell to Laurance (together with William Bingham) to personally inform Adams that it was not to be.[54] As consolation, the senator from New York within six months helped ease through Congress Smith's Quasi-War commission as lieutenant colonel of the Twelfth Regiment of Infantry.[55]

By mid-summer of 1800, Senator Laurance found himself with one foot awkwardly on either side of the widening Adams/Hamilton schism. Never one for backroom political intrigue, John, rather than choose camps, turned his back on the national election and walked away altogether from the Federalist Party he had helped bring into being. Indeed, after Elizabeth's death, he refused to play fundraiser, speechmaker, or even backroom arm-twister for Hamilton, Adams, Pinckney, or anybody else. It was a decision facilitated by blunt reality that Philadelphia's decade as the seat of national government had come to an end. With removal of Congress to the distant, mosquito-infested District of Columbia, how could he possibly juggle six daughters from two marriages and a dwindling legal practice with periodic bouts of rheumatism, much less manage Albany land investments from another 140 miles to the south?

As wagons clattered toward the Potomac with all vestiges of the federal government, John turned his eye to New York City, first and true home in America. "Laurance has put his children at school," Troup in late June informed King, and "is about renting his house in Philadelphia, and means to come and settle here. He has," added Troup, "not yet resigned his seat in the senate. He is said he will not do it until the French Treaty be decided on."[56]

After Republicans wrested New York from Hamilton's supporters, the national election turned truly ugly. Federalists spared no poison depicting Jefferson as a demonstrable coward who avoided military service, reneged on his debts, schemed to unleash southern slaves, and panted like a godless Jacobin to usher in a reign of mob terror. More virulent critics hissed of a lascivious "Congo-harem" and "dusky Sally Hemmings" at Monticello.[57] Ridiculed as "His Rotundity," Adams in turn was accused of plotting his daughter's marriage with a son of King George III in a dynastic ploy to establish a monarchical American royal bloodline. Some called him insane. Other partisan flights of fancy accused chubby 64-year-old Adams of smuggling a bordello of prostitutes into the presidential mansion. Even deceased President Washington, earlier abused as "vain and inept with monarchical tendencies," was now called "traitor, a robber, and a perjurer."[58] It was a nasty torrent of abusive mudslinging that continued until the electors met in their individual states on the first Wednesday of December to each cast two votes for president.

Laurance meanwhile bided his time visiting upstate properties to collect rents and recuperate his health at Albany area spas. "His intent," wrote Troup in early August, "is to quit public life until his lands put him out of debt, and do a little less traveling."[59] Formal accord with Napoleonic France would hopefully be reached before Congress resumed session in mid-November, for Senator Laurance was not about to occupy spartan rental quarters along the Potomac, only to pass indeterminate days under the roof of amateur architect William Thornton's unfinished new Capitol building until the treaty was consummated. Negotiations, however, had foundered when Napoleon in early May dashed from Paris to lead his army across the Saint-Bernard Pass and drive Austrian armies from Italy in the decisive Marengo campaign. As August drew to a close, Laurance's patience wore thin. One month before Joseph Bonaparte inked the *Convention of Môrtefontaine* to formally end the "Quasi-War," John, on August 20, 1800, resigned his Senate seat and abandoned elective politics for good. How apt then, that his very last public act affirmed the abolitionist cause he so long supported. For the congressional record shows that Laurance, six days before burying his wife, had on the adjourning day of the first session of the Sixth United States Senate voted with a 14 to

5 majority to negate "An act to permit, in certain cases, the bringing of slaves into the Mississippi Territory."[60]

Resigning his seat into Republican hands, at a time when every Federalist vote was crucial to implement the party's judiciary-packing exit strategy, was a shortsighted, self-interested decision that cost John's reputation dearly. But he had wearied of the increasing political toxicity that accompanied elective office. Three-term Federalist Massachusetts congressman Samuel Lyman may as well have been speaking for Laurance in his own decision not to seek another term. "There is a division," Lyman lamented about party factionalism to his constituents, "as to the degree of hatred and animosity necessary to be used in order to destroy all opposition to the government."[61]

Hamilton—as if his and Laurance's stars were somehow catastrophically aligned—in late October forked written manure down his own political well. Although strongly cautioned otherwise by influential George Cabot, Fisher Ames, and Treasury Secretary Wolcott, Hamilton recklessly distributed a belligerent circular letter scathingly critical of President Adams. Inevitably the 54-page vilification, "Concerning the Public Conduct and Character of John Adams," fell into the hands of the opposition press. Philadelphia's *Aurora* gleefully proclaimed it "the most gross and libelous charges against Mr. Adams that have ever yet to be published or heard of."[62] A euphoric James Madison could hardly contain himself. "I rejoice with you," he wrote to Jefferson, "that Republicanism is likely to be so <u>completely</u> triumphant."[63] No one was more damaged by the sulfurous letter than Hamilton himself, for there is no evidence that any specific elector withheld his vote for Adams because of it. New England High Federalist pastor/geographer Jedediah Morse spoke for many when he confided to Wolcott that Hamilton's divisive anti-Adams tirade "will administer <u>oil</u> rather than <u>water</u> to the fire."[64]

On February 11, 1801, John Laurance, for the first time in the history of the republic, was not on hand when elector votes were formally tallied in Congress. If present, he would have wagged his head in amazement after Vice President Jefferson read aloud all but South Carolina's ballots. Astonishingly, John Adams—despite Hamilton's best efforts—clung to a three-way tie with both Jefferson and Burr at 65 electoral votes apiece. South Carolina then rendered Adams a single-term president by giving all eight ballots to Republicans Thomas Jefferson and Aaron Burr. To avoid Republican deadlock, one anonymous South Carolina elector was supposedly to have omitted Burr's name from his ballot, but for whatever reason neglected to do so. "It is very well ascertained," Laurance observed matter-of-factly from his Broadway armchair, "that Mr. Jefferson and Mr. Burr have an equal number of votes, and both a majority; but it is yet uncertain who will be elected by the House of Representatives voting by States."[65]

Constitutionally mandated procedure threw the decision into the outgoing Federalist-controlled House of Representatives, where each state possessed one vote. Thirty-five agonizing ballots, however, failed over six frustrating February days to produce the required nine-state majority to elect either Jefferson or Burr. The Federalist House caucus had on January 5 decided for Burr, but Hamilton in one final desperate assertion of his waning influence dashed off letters urging they choose Jefferson over the "selfish . . . profligate . . . unprincipled" Burr, whom he branded a "complete *Cataline*."[66] Whether influenced by Hamilton or not, Federalist James Bayard* (sole representative of Delaware) broke with the party caucus on the 36th ballot and together with like minds in Maryland and Vermont left his ballot blank. Consequently, Maryland and Vermont went to Jefferson. And with Delaware's vote negated, the Master of Monticello emerged with a 10-state majority.

Much has been written to explain the demise of Federalism in wake of the election of 1800, but former Massachusetts High Federalist Senator George Cabot (1752–1823) probably hit the nail squarest on its sociopolitical head. "The spirit of our country," reflected Cabot after election dust had settled, "is doubtless more democratic than the form of our government."[67] For as Cabot well knew, the Constitution's framers, ambivalent about a fickle populace, vested power of setting voting requirements with the states, who in turn limited the franchise to property-owning or tax-paying free white adult males—about 6 percent of the population.[68] Trouble was, for the likes of George Cabot, a tide of Republican-inclined immigrants had expanded the country's white adult male population by more than 35 percent since 1790, while voting suffrage simultaneously widened from perhaps 60 percent of adult white male freeholders in the early 1780s to 80 percent by 1800.[69] The "Monarchical Republic," as John Adams approvingly dubbed it upon returning in 1789 from the Court of St. James, had in little more than a decade evolved right under Federalist noses into a Democratic Republic.[70]

"American democrats," observed historian Seth Cotlar, "began to interpret their new nation's emerging forms of land speculation and finance capitalism as updated versions of old aristocratic privilege."[71] The result was a populist tide against Federalist elitism that Laurance experienced firsthand in April when immigrant-laden outer wards threw New York City into the Republican fold. True, only New York, New Jersey, Pennsylvania, and North Carolina explicitly enfranchised free black males on the same terms as their white counterparts, but the trend toward universal (male) suffrage was unmistakable. North Carolina, New Hampshire, and Pennsylvania replaced freeholder property qualifications with a light poll tax, while Kentucky and Delaware eliminated such qualifications

---

*Bayard later allowed that he left his ballot blank because Jefferson had privately agreed (through friends John Nicholas of Virginia and Samuel Smith of Maryland) to Bayard's demands he honor the public credit, maintain the navy, and not remove those holding government office . . . a conversation Jefferson vehemently denied.

altogether. Propertied women were allowed to vote in New Jersey until state legislators reversed themselves in 1807. Popular election of the governor in nine states further jolted higher voter turnout than four years before. This grassroots surge carried four (Kentucky, Maryland, North Carolina, and Virginia) of the five states selecting electors by popular vote, giving Republicans a huge House majority and first-ever control of the Senate. Even the Federalist stronghold of Massachusetts found itself with half its 14 House seats in Republican hands. A confident Thomas Jefferson put the nation's secular democratic evolution into words when he bluntly promised that, "I shall sink federalism into an abyss from which there shall be no resurrection for it."[72]

"The Federalists," lamented Fisher Ames, perhaps their most articulate voice, "hardly deserve the name of a party. Their association is a loose one, formed by accident, and shaken by every prospect of labor or hazard"; particularly in the crop-growing areas of Pennsylvania, western South Carolina, and Maryland, where dissatisfaction with the Jay Treaty and the Sedition Act, distrust of northern banking interests, and a residual antipathy to Hamilton's whiskey tax spurred departure from Federalist ranks. Baltimore County, for example, which in 1796 chose the Adams elector by more than two to one over his Jeffersonian counterpart, turned overwhelmingly Republican four years later, giving the Jefferson elector a 1,497 to 438 vote victory.[73] With the Constitution universally embraced, federal government firmly installed, national finances secure, and George Washington no longer figurehead, the Federalist Party lacked clear public raison d'être to a populace in which 9 of 10 men were farmers.[74]

Tired as Federalist ideology had become, all too many party leaders were equally exhausted by a decade of defending "their" constitutional republic from the perceived threat of unbridled democratic principles. Rather than run for reelection in 1800, 17 of 60 House Federalists retired, and two others (Georgia's James Jones and Benjamin Taliaferro) were reelected as Republicans. Senate Federalists Goodhue, Lloyd, Schuerman, and Watson joined Laurance in resigning their seats, while Dexter traded his for a brief stint in Adams's lame-duck cabinet. Senator Read resigned for a last-minute federal judgeship, but Senate moderates James Gunn and Humphrey Marshall (Kentucky) were shown the door by their respective state legislatures. Arch-Federalist Theodore Sedgwick, whose quest for strong federal government stretched all the way back to 1780 as delegate to the Continental Congress, retired after learning that Jefferson had won. William Bingham sailed to Bermuda with his dying wife when his term expired in March 1801, and Samuel Livermore resigned due to ill health that June. By mid-1801, the pronounced Federalist senate majority that helped steer the Washington and Adams administrations had melted away into a two-vote minority.

As to party rank and file, Troup sighed that, "Public spirit seems to have spent its force among the Federalists. They are wearied out with the warfare in which we have been engaged ever since our general constitution has been framed. And they seem to pant so much for repose that they are ready to submit to any state of things short of Parisian massacres."[75] Rudderless after Adams's defeat, and unable to recruit leaders outside of established and aristocratic families, Federalists would never again seriously contend for the presidency. And Alexander Hamilton, his judgment now suspect, was in Troup's own words "considered an unfit head of the party."[76] If Hamilton's failed campaign to undermine President Adams didn't amount to political suicide, his adulterous affair with Maria Reynolds and subsequent hush-money payments certainly did. Although Hamilton publicly recanted over the Reynolds transgression, Republicans held an electoral trump card that precluded future public office. Aged 46, the Federalist fountainhead had, in the words of biographer Ron Chernow, "acquired the uncomfortable status of a glorified has-been."[77]

And John Laurance? Out of office, reputation tarnished for abandoning his party in its hour of need, law practice neglected, and mourning his deceased wife, it would be easy to surmise that our protagonist had reached wits' end. But Washington's former judge advocate general—incredible as it may seem—stepped from the personal and electoral wreckage a new man! Unburdened by public service obligations or party pressures, he emerged remarkably intact from under the twin clouds of Elizabeth's death and his own sporadic ill health. No longer compromised by playing good Federalist soldier, John was free at last to focus entirely on self and children. "Laurance is again with us," observed an amazed Troup as the new year of 1801 approached, "and in perfect health and is getting more money from his lands than all his friends put together. He appears firmly resolved against every species of public life but a permanent office."[78]

EIGHTEEN

The Consolation of Wealth

THE DISTRICT OF COLUMBIA, MARCH 4, 1801. Shortly before noon, 57-year-old President-elect Thomas Jefferson exited Conrad and McMunn's New Jersey Avenue boarding house and walked some 200 muddy paces to the crowded Senate wing of the still-unfinished United States Capitol. Wearing the clothes "of a plain citizen, without any distinctive badge of office," he was sworn in by freshly appointed Supreme Court Chief Justice John Marshall, President Adams's parting last-minute Federalist "gift" to the nation.[1] Hardly had Jefferson delivered his softly spoken inaugural address with its politically healing sentiment, "We are all Republicans, we are all Federalists," than the inevitable distribution of party patronage began. No family shared more in the spoils than the Livingstons of New York. Brockholst was appointed associate justice of the U.S. Supreme Court, Edward was made New York district attorney, and Chancellor Robert Livingston—on Jefferson's second day in office—was named minister plenipotentiary to France. With Schuyler and Hamilton negated, the very family that dominated pre-Revolutionary New York politics was a quarter-century later back in the driver's seat.

Despite the Livingston ascendancy, despite Elizabeth's passing, despite his election vanishing act, despite everything, ex-Senator Laurance had one last political card yet to play. Five years earlier, it may be remembered, he resigned his federal judgeship to keep Rufus King's vacated Senate seat safely in Federalist hands. To square the deal, New York Governor Jay, now in the waning months of his second and final term of office, maneuvered delicately with an overwhelmingly Republican legislature to secure Laurance a state judgeship. "Governor Jay," wrote Robert Troup in late March to Ambassador King, "has resolved if possible to make a compromise about the office of Chancellor in order to get Lawrance on the [New York] Supreme Court bench."[2] The chancellorship, New York's highest judicial office, was of course synonymous with influential Robert Livingston who wore the position like a custom-tailored waistcoat after helping bring it into being as coframer of the 1777 state constitution. No sooner had Livingston set sail for Paris than his vacated chancellorship became the Empire State's juiciest political plum. Governor Jay's strategy, if Troup's insider account is to be believed, was to nominate sitting state Supreme Court Chief Justice John Lansing Jr. (a Clintonian Republican) as Livingston's successor *if* the Republican-dominated legislative Council of Appointment in turn approved Laurance for the state court.[3] And a seat, as circumstances would have it, indeed was empty due to Egbert Benson's recent appointment to the newly created federal tri-state circuit court.

Laurance, it seems, had laid some preliminary groundwork in Albany with Republican lawmakers to grease the appointment skids. "He thinks himself so popular with the opposite party," wrote Troup, "that if Mr. Jay were now to nominate him for the office of judge, the council would unanimously approve him."[4] Republicans, however, were in no mood for a deal. Determined to rein in gubernatorial appointive powers and dramatically increase headcount in both houses, New York legislators on April 6 called for a statewide constitutional convention. When these changes were made into law that October, Lansing was indeed confirmed chancellor, but Laurance's quid pro quo fell through. Benson's vacated seat went instead to Republican assemblyman and Livingston protégé Smith Thompson.*

In truth, Laurance—despite Jay's obligatory overture—no longer enjoyed full support of the state legislature's remaining Federalist delegates. His abrupt and premature senate resignation had opened way for Republicans to fill the seat with yet another Livingston disciple: the Chancellor's brother-in-law John Armstrong. Furthermore, Laurance's utter inactivity during the brutally contested national election left former allies filled with indifference, if not disdain. "His withdrawal at this time," observed Troup, "has proven great umbrage and sunk him much in the estimation of his friends."[5]

Laurance burned political bridges altogether when he declined to ante up $25 as one of 25 designated contributors to settle post-election "party funeral expenses."[6] He was far from alone; fellow Federalists Nicholas Fish, Comfort Sands, Nicholas Low, Samuel Bayard, and Matthew Clarkson also neglected to contribute, forcing Troup and Hamilton each to fork over $70 toward the $570 tab.[7] (They only raised $370.) Laurance's reputation sank still lower when rumors swirled in from New Jersey intimating he was "said to be engaged to be married" to Philadelphia widow Sarah (nee Shippen) Lea, sister-in-law to the traitor Benedict Arnold.[8] Six years Laurance's junior, Sarah was a vivacious woman whose 1798 Gilbert Stuart portrait bears an uncanny resemblance to Elizabeth Allen's oldest daughter Nancy.[9] No such engagement ever materialized, but mere whisper of marital connection with the despised Arnold was sufficient to stain the name of George Washington's former judge advocate general.

---

*Smith Thompson (Princeton '88) married Susanna Livingston and practiced law until swept into the General Assembly by the Republican landslide of 1800. Later made secretary of the navy by President James Monroe, Thompson campaigned for the Democratic-Republican Party presidential nomination in 1824, losing to Andrew Jackson. Appointed by lame-duck President Monroe to the U.S. Supreme Court, he then served from 1823 to 1843 as a staunch opponent of Chief Justice John Marshall.

After a quarter century of public service, John Laurance, rightly or wrongly, had become a political pariah.

No judgeship sinecure in the offing, he retired unobtrusively to private life. What with pressing estate matters, now five unmarried daughters, and 25-year-old son John McDougall's freshly opened law practice to encourage, John's lower Broadway townhouse buzzed with activity. And New York Society of Cincinnati gatherings could only have been enlivened by son John McDougall's 1798 admission as its first hereditary member.[10] Not about to give up his Bank of the United States New York branch directorship, Laurance also continued as trustee of Columbia University and stepped into a director's shoes at newly founded Marine Life Insurance Company.[11] "He busily engages with his insurance company at £500 or 600 a year," observed old friend Troup. "They have lately been incorporated and put on a footing with the other insurance companies in the city. Laurance is also dealing a little in the law and wishes to go into pretty extensive practice."[12]

But John did not materially resurrect his dormant legal business. For the practice of law in New York had changed significantly since his post-Revolutionary property restitution salad days. No longer were proceedings based on "English books of practice as well as English decisions" geared by a century of legislation toward status quo interests of large landowners like the Livingstons, Schuylers, Beekmans, and Van Zandts.[13] Static, precedent-based interpretation of contract, property, and marine law—at which Laurance had excelled—was giving way to more dynamic forces. Traditional contract law, for example, no longer established damages and worth based on historically "just" value, but rather on current market price. Court judgments were increasingly based on the creativity of a lawyer's argument rather than recitation of precedent. And civil cases once handled *in rem* by individual judges versed in the law were increasing settled by unpredictable juries. Laurance and his Blackstone-based mastery of English legal precedents had become "old school."

The practice of law may have changed, but threat of yellow fever over humid New York City summers had not. For best part of a century, "yellow jack" stalked lower Manhattan's greasy wharves and filthy warehouse back alleys. Only three years earlier, the epidemic of 1798 had claimed 2,000 victims, more than 4 percent of the city's population.[14] Escape to Trout Hall was no longer a summer option, for, as directed by Elizabeth's first husband's 1778 will, the property descended to her two surviving Allen daughters. John therefore pounced immediately when the New Jersey residence of Herr Pieter Johan Van Berckel, first Dutch ambassador to the United States, unexpectedly came available in early 1801. Situated in Newark, two blocks from the (then) scenic Passaic River, the place was really no "summer cottage" at all, but a rather grand six-bedroom estate.

Laurance first came to know Van Berckel in the heady days of 1787–1788 when the polished mahogany table of Confederation foreign affairs secretary Jay hosted the cream of diplomatic society[15] and the Dutch minister kept a lively open house in the old Marston mansion at the northwest corner of Wall and William Streets. Learning of Van Berckel's December 1800 passing, John quickly snapped up the Newark residence from the estate executor, Surrogate Judge Alexander McWhorter. Already one of eastern New Jersey's most promising lawyers, the 29-year-old McWhorter (Princeton '84) endeared himself with the Laurance family. McWhorter's six children not only played hide and seek with John's youngest daughters among the crumbling walls of the ruined stone Academy in Newark's Washington Park, but sons George and Alexander Jr. went on to marry two of the girls.

Turn-of-the-century Newark was a lucrative market for producers of butter, poultry, and grain from miles around to do business with New York dealers. Within a decade, the 1,200-inhabitant village would erupt into a bustling, smelly tanning and shoemaking hub, but in Laurance's day only eccentric temperance advocate Moses N. Combs turned out high-end footwear from his busy Market Street tannery.[16] A few blocks west of Laurance's door was the cabinet-making shop of Newark brothers Caleb and Mathias Bruen. From Caleb, wartime spy for General Washington, John acquired one of his most prized possessions: a fine mahogany lap desk to accompany his many upstate rent-collecting expeditions.[17] Easy access from Newark to lower New York was assured via Archer Giffords's nearby Hunters and the Hounds tavern, terminal for the two-horse, five-passenger coach to Paulus Hook and regular barge service to the city. Center of town life, the Giffords tavern was a popular loitering venue for news of the day or chatting up passengers from Philadelphia between stagecoach comings and goings announced with a grand flourish of fox-hunting horns. Once across the water to Manhattan, Laurance might board a Hudson River schooner or catch the Post Road stagecoach to Albany and his upstate real estate holdings.

Judge Laurance's post-political years were neither lonely nor unpleasant. Family, church, St. John's Lodge where he donned the regalia of "Past Master," and a web of old New York friends guaranteed an active social life despite the frequent political cold shoulder.[18] But dabbling in "the drudgery of the law" (as Troup called it), peddling marine insurance, or fussing over his several residences was not how he passed the days.[19] Rather, it was buying, subdividing, and selling real estate parcels. One of the young Republic's most successful New York land speculators, John on his own and in partnership with Troup, Hamilton, and others would amass as much as a quarter million acres. In 1799 alone he boasted of "an income in excess of $14,000 ($392,840 today) derived solely from his landed investments."[20] Two years later, as Laurance began a comfortable retirement, Troup admiringly allowed, "He is doing better than any among us with his lands; and his estate is very large."[21]

Fortuitously enhanced by the McDougall inheritances, Judge Laurance's respectable estate was the product of nearly three decades of savvy land investments. The first purchase, 1,000 upstate New York acres subsequently incorporated into Vermont, was made shortly after opening his law practice in 1772.[22] Indeed, land was virtually the only investment option after Parliament's Restraining Act of 1764 put an end in King George's colonies to domestic financial institutions and Provincial paper currency instruments. Although hard money remained scarce following independence, speculative opportunity abounded in the form of depreciated government debt certificates and military land bounty warrants. Commercial paper and import/export arbitrage instruments multiplied as the thriving port of New York surpassed Philadelphia to become the young nation's leading exporter. And a raft of private and government securities became tradable when New York's first stock exchange burst to life in 1792 at the Tontine Coffee House. Spawned by the spread of Bank of the United States branches to Boston, Baltimore, Charleston, and Norfolk, a "bancomania" wave by 1801 produced some 32 state banks, each with its varied note instruments. Newly created insurance companies even offered annuities.

Tempting as this investment plethora may have been, Laurance—with an immigrant's tight-fisted fiscal conservatism—plunged virtually all his principal into real estate. "My capital, you know," he confided to Rufus King in 1799, "has gone into land and as far as I get cash I apply it to lessen my debts."[23] Truth be told, few men of means could resist the allure of young America's beckoning speculative real estate money machine. Get-rich fever was rampant. "Were I to characterize the United States," effused one foreign investor in 1796, "it would be by the appellation of the land of speculations."[24] Indeed, was not the entire American experiment itself a gigantic speculative venture? From Maine to Virginia, hundreds of investors formed partnerships and joint stock companies to buy and sell real estate parcels created by Indian treaties and state cessations to the "Western Reserve." Pockets bulging from wartime profiteering, merchant princes Robert Morris, William Bingham, George Clymer, Andrew Craigie, and George Cabot were joined in the speculative rush by prominent public figures ranging from Massachusetts governor John Hancock to Secretary of War Henry Knox and Supreme Court Justice James Wilson. Even President Washington and Congressman Madison indulged in the speculative land mania surrounding America's new capital on the banks of the Potomac.

Pools of European capital fueled the frenzy. "In general there are few rich people in America," observed one Dutch financier, "& Opportunities for investing money [are] very numerous."[25] Drawn by rising land prices and skyrocketing Bank of United States (BUS) stock, foreign bankers eschewed low European interest rates as itinerant capital fled Napoleon's advancing armies in search of opportunity. Opportunistic William Duer as early as 1787 convinced Amsterdam's Nicholas and Thomas van Staphorst and Company, along with the French firm of Delasserts, to capitalize his Scioto Company's preemptive option on some four million Ohio Valley acres.[26] Backed by European sources, private developers such as Duer and Morris really *could* develop million-acre chunks of land more quickly than the nascent federal government. And deep European pockets might also build the backcountry transportation infrastructure neither state nor federal legislatures could afford. "The importance of roads," one agent urged his London backer, "is immense and cannot be too much attended to."[27]

Few of these grand ventures made money. Duer's Scioto Company, for example, went belly-up in 1790, defrauding hundreds of French purchasers who, upon arriving at their Ohio property, discovered the land had to be repurchased from another concern. Like the English South Seas Company stock bubble before it, American backcountry land mania bankrupted overextended speculators by the hundreds. Except during the three-year Bankruptcy Act interregnum, the consequence of bankruptcy until 1833 was debtors' prison. The infamous William Duer was hauled off to jail in 1792, to be followed six years later by bankrupted former Congressional Supervisor of Finance Robert Morris. The latter's partner, Pennsylvania Republican John Nicholson, died in debtors' prison at the age of 43, leaving behind a wife and eight children with debts exceeding $12 million. Massachusetts' speculator Andrew Craigie may have avoided prison by confining himself to his Brattle Street estate, but financially broken New Yorker Alexander Macomb was not so fortunate. Towed from his lavish Broadway mansion in 1792, Macomb spent two years behind bars, never to recover his fortune.

John Laurance did not operate on the grand scale of Morris or Macomb; but neither did he grace a debtors' prison. Borrowing discreetly and buying at advantage, he built his substantial fortune in four portfolios: military bounty lots, confiscated loyalist estates, vacated Native American tracts, and select Manhattan rental properties. To fully appreciate the depth of his financial relationship with Hamilton and Troup—and because he was far from alone in such speculative ventures—a closer look at Laurance's portfolio provides a fascinating lens on how fortunes were made (and unmade) in the frothy decades following independence.

Military Bounty Lands

With a Continental Army officer's depreciating monthly income, Laurance was in no position to expand his initial Vermont property holdings until leaving the service in June 1782. Cashing out with some 582 pounds and 51 pence New York currency plus an indeterminate sum from Continental paymaster general John Pierce, he immediately looked for investment prospects. Father-in-law Alexander McDougall, then New York delegate to the Continental Congress, sniffed profit in snatching up land bounty certificates at bargain prices from discharged soldiers desperate for hard specie. McDougall's military adjutant (Major Richard Platt) monitored Albany street prices of depreciating state notes and certificates, so the canny Scot knew just when to buy. And Laurance joined him.

Land bounties had been offered by the New York legislature as recruiting incentive to men who would serve three years in the Continental Army. After war's end, honorably discharged veterans were awarded 600-acre parcels in the "Old Military Tract" established north of Albany. Because the properties were remotely located and some acreage was substandard, many soldiers happily disposed of their land rights sight-unseen for a pittance in hard specie. In 1788, a second wave of land bounty certificates materialized when the state, responding to congressional directive, established an additional 1,750,000-acre central New York reserve dubbed the "New Military Tract." Rather than wait up to two years for surveyors to subdivide the new tract and organize disbursement procedures, recipients often turned to speculators for cash.

General McDougall and Colonel Laurance opened their purses to financially hard-pressed soldiers as early as November 1783, purchasing 600-acre land warrants from veterans for as little as six pounds New York money.[28] Duly licensed before the New York bar, it was John who prepared the deed transfers, secured witness signatures, and filed the required paperwork with the state clerk's office in Albany. At least 59 such deeds were filed after 1783 under Laurance and McDougall's names.[29] John added to these holdings after the general's death, ultimately amassing some 41,000 acres in 25 of 28 New Military Tract townships.[30] Nor did Colonel Laurance's own wartime sacrifice go unrewarded. A grateful New York General Assembly—as mandated by Congress for qualified Continental officers—in 1792 awarded him 2,000 New Military Tract acres. Sole inheritor to the McDougall estate after wife Betsey's passing, John later received 5,500 acres granted to the deceased general, plus 2,000 acres posthumously awarded to son Ranald Stephen.

What set Colonel Laurance apart from less diligent land speculators was that he held on to bounty warrants until plots were surveyed, and then went the extra mile to visit properties and collaborate with the state clerk to stake out advantageously located acreage. To be sure, purchasing bounty lands was one thing and selling at a profit was another. But with adroit timing, huge gains were to be had. In 1793, for example, John pocketed £200 for 500 acres of a 600-acre lot he purchased a few years earlier for under £8—a profit exceeding 2,500 percent.[31]

Confiscated Loyalist Estates

Its wartime coffers bare and its richest counties in British hands, New York's Provincial Congress in 1777 had little choice but to sequester loyalist property to defray expenses. As the war dragged on, strong measures were adopted for the six southern New York counties still under British control. Within months of British evacuation, New York blatantly ignored Treaty of Paris provisions protecting loyalist lands and proceeded in 1784 to liquidate the 59 estates seized under the Confiscation Act. Clinton-appointed commissioners Isaac Stoutenburgh and Philip Van Cortlandt then raised $3,1000,000 by disposing (for gold, silver, or congressional bills of credit) of all forfeitures in the Southern District of New York.[32] To the auction block came the 52,000-acre Phillipsburg Manor in Westchester County along with James DeLancey's coveted Manhattan estate. Colonel Laurance acquired prime lots in both.

Laurance, as we discovered in chapters Seven and Eight, was extraordinarily well placed when the war concluded. Not only did he sit in the state legislature when several retaliatory property-right measures were crafted, but through his father-in-law's membership on the Council for Temporary Government of the Southern District he was also privy to all administrative measures following the British evacuation. Nor was Forfeitures Commissioner Van Cortlandt a stranger. Briefly John's commanding officer in 1775, the patroon colonel was also a frequent courts-martial board participant during his stint as judge advocate. Clearly Laurance possessed the inside knowledge and personal connections to take full advantage of confiscated property offerings. But from where, in addition to his Continental Army lump sum pension, did the money come to scoop up dozens of lots?

The answer lies in an October 4, 1780, act of New York's state legislature. Having issued state certificates in lieu of Continental currency to pay New York troops, the legislators then resolved that the paper be accepted at full face value as specie toward the purchase of confiscated loyalist estates. Because hundreds of soldiers were either desperate for hard money or doubted the state would ever redeem their pay certificates, they disposed of their certificates to speculators for as little as 10 cents on the dollar. Over the course of some three years, Laurance, General McDougall, and many others accumulated depreciating New York military pay certificates at bargain rates. On a single day (May 13, 1784), Laurance handed over 2,082 pounds, 13 shillings, and 8 pence worth of these state military certificates at full face value to Commissioner Stoutenburgh in return for eight separate forfeited properties.[33] Among his purchases were Westchester County farms in New Rochelle, Rye, and White Plains; a portion of Pelham Manor; and the fine New York City house of John H. Crueger at No. 18 Little Queen Street. Later in the year, Laurance bought loyalist Volker Sprung's 300-acre Long Island farm as well as 731 upstate acres confiscated from notorious Tory John Butler.

No estate liquidation salivated investors more than the 336-acre plot known as DeLancey's Bowery Farm. Heart of present-day Manhattan's Lower East Side, this choice property as early as 1766 was laid out in an intricate street grid by James DeLancey Jr., who hoped to replicate a tony Georgian London residential enclave complete with an elegant central square named after himself. Commissioners Stoutenburgh and Van Cortlandt broke the DeLancey parcel into two pieces, East Farm and West Farm, disposing of each in full city blocks to some 175 investors. Laurance purchased two blocks in West Farm and partnered with Isaac Roosevelt and Henry Kip to acquire a large East Farm lot with coveted waterfront exposure along the East River.[34] At least 16 more nearby Bowery lots were later acquired in partnership with Robert Troup.[35] John next teamed with fellow member of the New York bar John D. Crimshire to purchase George Folliot's confiscated Westchester County lands for £500.[36] When the juiciest plum of all—three-thousand-acre Phillipsburg Manor—went on the auction block in October 1785, John purchased 3 of the 61 lots.[37] Altogether, Colonel Laurance between May 1784 and August 1787 poured more than £13,000 into confiscated New York City and Westchester County properties.[38]

Shortsighted speculators quickly flipped confiscated lots for hard specie (thereby recouping full face value from depreciated certificates), but Laurance chose to create a steady income stream by renting or leasing most of his properties. Typical of John's leases was one structured for a plot acquired from the confiscated estate of James DeLancey:

> 7 Jan. 1786: John Laurance of the city of New York to John O'Connor Esq. lease and let that property late of the estate of James DeLancey with all buildings for seven years for 10 pounds New York money per annum and that O'Connor shall build one small tenement 26 feet × 14 feet and 12 feet high with one door and three windows and leave it as property of Laurance when said lease expires.[39]

In addition to private purchases, Laurance partnered with Robert Troup as early as June 1784 to acquire other confiscated estates in southern New York.[40] "Received of Col. Laurance," wrote Troup, "145 pounds five shillings two pence on account of locations made and places sold—in company."[41] When the commissioners of forfeitures ceased operations in September 1788, Laurance and Troup, together with Alexander Hamilton, brother-in-law John B. Church, and many others, turned their collective financial eyes northward. Upstate New York land ventures promised even more lucrative reward.

Vacated Native American Lands

The ancestral homelands of New York's six-nation Iroquois League—some 20 million acres—went up for grabs in the wake of American independence. Speculators, farmers, and immigrant homesteaders had long lusted after this prime real estate. Standing in their way, however, was

King George III's royal proclamation of 1763 that reserved to his Native American allies all land west of the Alleghenies to the Mississippi River. Twenty years later the Treaty of Paris may have safeguarded loyalist property rights, but Iroquois lands were left to the mercy of the Continental Congress. Because New England's increasing population made unowned property scarce, the younger Yankee generation poised itself to fill any vacuum created by the Treaty of Paris.

British negotiators betrayed their Native American allies completely in the Paris treaty. Without any voice in the matter, all Iroquois homelands were ceded to the United States of America. The Oneida and Tuscarora nations, having sided with the patriots, remained to negotiate treaties retaining at least some of their land, but Seneca and Mohawk warriors under Joseph Brandt had fiercely engaged as British allies. When hostilities ceased, the proud Mohawks fled to Canada, mostly abandoning ancestral homelands north of Albany to the St. Lawrence River and in the fertile Mohawk Valley. It was from these northern lands in 1784 that New York legislators had carved the so-called Old Military Tract. Congressional and New York State negotiators then bargained, buffaloed, and defrauded most remaining Iroquois homelands from the Oneida, Tuscarora, Onondaga, Cayuga, and Seneca nations. Perhaps the most infamous treaty of all was "Clinton's Purchase," a 1788 deal in which the governor persuaded Oneida sachems (his allies during the war) to cede the 1.8 million-acre heart of their central New York homeland for virtually nothing.

Massachusetts in 1786 demanded a piece of Clinton's juicy Native American pie. Waving its original royal charter in New York faces, the Bay State claimed the preemptive right to some six million acres of the western New York Iroquois homelands. Immediately after gaining the property rights (New York retained political sovereignty), Massachusetts in 1788 sold the entire tract for $1,000,000 ($.1667/acre) to an investment consortium headed by two of its citizens, Oliver Phelps and Nathaniel Gorham. Financial troubles forced the pair to default on installment payments to the state of Massachusetts in early 1791, whereupon Philadelphia financier Robert Morris scooped up 3.75 million acres for a little less than 12 cents an acre.[42]

More than doubling his money, Morris two years later conveyed a million-acre piece to a consortium led by British baronet Sir William Pulteney (reputedly the richest man in the world) for roughly 27 and a half cents per acre.[43] And whom should the baronet ultimately name managing agent of his newly acquired empire but Laurance's trusted investment partner, Robert Troup!

Despite conceding six million acres to neighboring Massachusetts, New York still had more land than it knew what to do with. Accordingly, the state legislature in July 1786 appointed Governor Clinton and seven other Albany politicos as commissioners with full power to execute "speedy sale of the unappropriated lands within this state." First on the block were ten 64,000-acre townships laid out in the St. Lawrence River region. Most of this offering was snatched up for a shilling per acre by agents of former war-profiteer Alexander Macomb in a July 1787 deal at Merchants' Coffee House.[44] (Macomb syndicate partners included Henry Knox, Philip Schuyler, Gouveneur Morris, and a dozen others, as well as a small share for Alexander Hamilton.) Eager to open more frontier to settlement, the revenue-hungry legislature in 1791 authorized Governor Clinton and his commissioners to dispose of "such parcels on such terms and in such manner as they shall judge conducive to the interests of the state."[45] Clinton's crony commissioners then went on a selling binge transferring 5,542,170 vacated Iroquois acres between May and September to only 35 grantees. Macomb and two junior partners gobbled up two-thirds of the prize (3,635,200 acres) in one fell swoop for only eight cents per acre and no money down. As speculative interest heightened, Robert Morris closed yet another spectacular deal. Between February 1792 and July 1793, he sold 3,250,000 acres to 13 unincorporated Amsterdam investors known as the Holland Land Company. Title, however, only passed in 1797 when Iroquois leaders at the Treaty of Big Tree blessed the deal in return for 200,000 acres plus $100,000 in BUS stock.[46]

Not all purchasers of vacated Native American lands were absentee speculators like Morris, Duer, and Macomb, out for the short-term windfall. William Cooper, father of novelist James Fenimore Cooper, for example, acquired tens of thousands of acres in Otsego County surrounding present-day Cooperstown. After keeping the choicest land for himself, Cooper made the best remaining property available upfront, sold it as freehold instead of tenancies, and offered long-term financing. Cooper also knew that if he lived among the new settlers and fostered local economic prosperity, his own property values could only rise.[47] As landlord, presiding judge, and local U.S. congressman, William Cooper made himself rich and powerful by turning primitive forest into a thriving community orbiting the town he named for himself.

John Laurance owned land in the proximity, but he was not about to relocate to the wilds of upstate New York—nor was he a mere short-term speculator. Rather, Laurance plowed a middle ground, offering tenancies while improving his holdings with roads and mills until rising property values furnished the opportunity for a handsome sales price. His first significant speculative bet on former Native American land was placed in 1793 by purchasing from Vice President Adams's son-in-law, William S. Smith, the entire 25,780-acre Smyrna Township in central New York's Chenango County.[48] Smith, one step away from debtors' prison, unloaded the parcel to raise desperately needed cash. Within months, Laurance supplemented the Smith purchase with acquired lots in two other Chenango townships, Plymouth and Norwich-New Britain. Together with Robert Troup in 1794, he purchased four full upstate townships totaling 84,804 acres for the sum of £1,765 and 15 shillings New York money.[49] In early 1795,

FIGURE 14 Robert Troup (1857- 1832).
Oil on canvas, attributed to Ralph Earl (1786). University Archives, Rare Book & Manuscript Library. (Courtesy of Columbia University Archives. Reproduced with permission.)

Judge Laurance partnered with Hamilton, Troup, and fellow New York Federalist Nicholas Fish to snap up 21,800 acres of Nobleborough Township.[50] Farther to the west, Laurance could boast of shared ownership of a 39,886-acre parcel[51] with Troup and Federal Marshall Aquila Giles (former Revolutionary War aide-de-camp to Horatio Gates) in Steuben County along the Pennsylvania border.

Judge Laurance could not have chosen a better real estate investment partner than his old friend Troup. Land agent for the massive 12-million-acre Pulteney estate (partly purchased in distressed sale from the aforementioned Phelps and Gorham), the plump and affable Troup was a lobbyist of exceptional skill who befriended virtually any person of importance to peddle their parcels. The fact was that a preponderance of their joint holdings lay in a wilderness of primeval western New York forest whose key to future profitability lay with construction of trunk roads to access the vast Pulteney holdings. Lobbying lawmakers and potential investors alike, Troup not only facilitated the private subscription turnpike from Catskill and Kingston to Jericho Bridge, but he also steered through the state legislature a bill chartering its extension from Bath to Lake Erie.[52]

No deal better demonstrates the high-stakes gamble of often-convoluted land transactions than Laurance's tricky 1796 partnership with Alexander Hamilton and John B. Church to acquire two complete townships in the so-called Scriba Patent. New York merchant George Scriba in late 1793 had purchased 490,136 acres in Oneida and Oswego Counties from John and Nicholas J. Roosevelt. Scriba two years later sold part of the tract to fellow New York merchant Jacob Mark.[53] In January 1796, Laurance, as front man for undisclosed partners Church and Hamilton, contracted with Jacob Mark and Company for the conveyance of townships 15 and 21.[54] When Mark insisted on retaining one-quarter interest in the two townships, Laurance secured the deed on another two-and-a-half Scriba townships (9, 10, and part of 17) as security on the transaction. Unbeknownst to Laurance, however, townships 15 and 21 were under prior mortgage as collateral on a $70,000 debt to Westchester County investor Robert Gilchrist and his New York City partner Theodosius Fowler. Learning of the undisclosed Gilchrist mortgage, Laurance then obtained assurance from Mark that the Gilchrist obligation would be met at maturity.

Expecting to hear that Mark had retired the Gilchrist mortgage, Laurance and his partners in May 1797 instead received a curious missive. "We are sorry to find," Mark explained, "that owing to the embarrassed situation of the Land you purchased from us last year ... we are particularly anxious to remove the most distant hard thought from you towards us."[55] Mark then offered to *sell* his one-fourth ownership of the 42,314 and a quarter-acre Scriba parcel for $2.25 an acre, or $23,801.62. "Should you not think it proper to come into the measures proposed," he concluded, "then be kind enough to set a price on Your Part of the Land at which You will sell."[56]

Taking up Mark's unexpected buy-back offer would net Laurance, Church, and Hamilton 25 cents an acre (almost 13 percent paper profit) because they had shelled out $1.78 an acre plus some 20 cents carrying interest and 2 cents surveying expense. "But," Laurance shrewdly warned Hamilton, "I should be on my guard respecting them—Jacob Mark at least."[57] Suspecting that Mark was far too overextended to offer anything but worthless paper for their shares, John counseled Hamilton and Church to sit tight. "I cannot buy at present," Laurance confided, "and I am not willing to sell, but should I be induced to sell, the money must be paid immediately and the price greater than they mention."[58] Before any such price could be determined, Jacob Mark and Company declared bankruptcy, leaving Gilchrist no choice but in May 1801 to foreclose on the properties. Chancery Court in turn ordered public sale of the Scriba holdings within three months unless Laurance, Church, and Hamilton immediately paid Gilchrist all sums due—a whopping $43,530.33 (more than $1.3 million today) plus accrued interest.[59]

At this point, less patient speculators might have cut and run, hoping to recover some portion of their principal at the court-ordered public sale.

But Laurance, having personally walked the properties, knew real profits were just a matter of time. "Township No. 21," he advised Hamilton, was a "very valuable tract of land, with regard to its soil and timbers, and must command a very good price."[60] The other parcel, John confided, was "well situated, for Settlement" because "the great road to Oswego, will pass through it, in the course of this summer."[61] Therefore he thought it advisable to hold on to the two townships in hope of subdividing them at financial advantage. "I am sorry," he commiserated to Hamilton, "the purchase has been an unprofitable one to you. It has been more so to myself; but I hope the result will be otherwise, when these times, which neither you nor myself could divine . . . have passed away."[62]

Laurance then spared the two Scriba townships from court-ordered public auction by persuading Gilchrist to grant a nine-month mortgage for half the $43,510 judgment, to be repaid in five equal installments with interest by 18 May 1802.[63] The remaining half came straight out of Laurance, Hamilton, and Church's collective pockets. To raise necessary cash, John called in rents, mortgaged two properties, and took out at least two debtor bonds. One was together with Church and Hamilton from Theodosius Fowler,* and the other jointly with Hamilton from James Lenox.[64] When Lenox, in early 1798, unexpectedly called the $6,000 joint bond, Hamilton—who was reluctant to speculate in the first place—asked Laurance to cover it:

> The operation is one very unpromising, and as it turns out, very inconvenient to me. I have never made other speculations to compensate me for the badness of this one . . . I regret any embarrassment which may attend you, but your resources are far greater than mine and you can more safely than me meet the demands. I must entreat you my good friend to lose no time in taking up the bond. I shall be extremely pained if my credit suffers in a case in which I am only nominal.[65]

Laurance indeed took up the bond, preserving both Hamilton's credit and their mutual stakes in the Scriba parcels. Mere weeks before staring down a pistol barrel at Aaron Burr on Weehawken Plain, Hamilton jotted in his 1804 account book that his share of the accumulated Scriba purchases "now stand me in about 33,000 [dollars]."[66] The nagging venture,

---

*Merchant/speculator Theodosius Fowler (1752–1841) was Robert Gilchrist's investment partner. A captain in Henry Livingston's Fourth New York Regiment during the Revolution, Fowler likely became acquainted with Laurance at Valley Forge if not during the Canadian campaign of 1775. After serving (with distinction) for the duration of the war, Fowler inherited his father's huge Eastchester estate and set up shop at 27 Water Street as one of lower New York's wealthier residents. Contracted by Treasury Secretary Hamilton to supply all necessary rations to army posts in the west, Fowler in 1793 was chosen treasurer for the New York chapter of the Cincinnati.

as fate would have it, would not be unwound until three years after Alexander's untimely death.[67] Still, from this episode, it is clear Laurance knew what he was about in sorting out risk and reward in backcountry New York land deals. Profitability for those with deep pockets in capitalist America was only a matter of time.

Laurance, always on the hunt for opportunistic acquisitions at the right price, also turned his eyes to lower Manhattan. Testimony to John's discerning taste in property, both Secretary of State Timothy Pickering and former Secretary of War Henry Knox rented temporary Manhattan addresses from Laurance in 1796.[68] Another five city lots "together with edifices, houses, and buildings" at Broadway and Leonard Street were acquired in late 1804 jointly with Rufus King for a hefty $30,000.[69] Nor was John shy about snapping up distress sale bargains at various U.S. marshal or ordinary sheriff auctions. For but "one cent, lawful money of the United States" a court-ordered bankruptcy sale in 1804 added 1,589 debt-encumbered acres to John's holdings.[70]

By the time Thomas Jefferson's presidential popularity soared with America's largest speculative land acquisition of all time (the Louisiana Purchase in 1803), Laurance and Hamilton had both faded from public view. The mantle of Federalist leadership passed to mutual friend Rufus King, who returned to New York the spring of 1803 after staying on more than two years as Jefferson's minister to the Court of St. James. Rebuffing Hamilton's entreaty to run for governor of New York, King campaigned instead as vice president on the doomed national Federalist ticket of 1804. Neither Hamilton nor Laurance emerged from political retirement to lend a serious hand. Not that Hamilton could ever completely retire. His much sought-after law practice raked in a handsome income while he toyed with politics in his newly founded *New York Post* newspaper venture and leveled scorching, unsigned political broadsides against the detested Aaron Burr. Mostly, however, he reveled in the pleasures of family life with Eliza at their newly completed two-story Federal country house, "The Grange," nine miles north of lower Manhattan.

From time to time Laurance lunched with old friends, but the winter of his years was spent carving township-sized holdings such as the Chenango, Smryna, and Steuben tracts into smaller, more saleable pieces. Turning a profit on rural New York property required more than just a low acquisition price. Unlike "quick-flip" speculators, Troup and Laurance dug into their own pockets to survey and divide township-sized parcels. Sawmills and gristmills were built and paid for; roads were cut, schools erected, and marketing costs incurred to draw prospective buyers. The partners reached out to the general public through offerings in newspapers such as the *Federal Gazette & Baltimore Daily Advertiser:*

> **TO BE SOLD**, Township No. 1, in the 5th range of townships in the county of Steuben, in the state of New-York, containing by actual survey, thirty-nine thousand, eight hundred and eighty-six acres . . . being surveyed and divided into lots generally about three hundred and twenty acres each, having a saw and grist mill built on one of the lots, with plenty of white pine timber adjacent to the mill . . . a pleasant and healthy climate, the land ascending and descending gradually, an excellent soil . . . the timber beach, maple, white pine, white ash, bass wood, hickory, black oak, white oak, some chestnut and wild cherry. . . . the price is not more than two dollars per acre, part cash, and a liberal credit for the remainder.—Enquire of AQUILA GILES, ROBERT TROUP, or JOHN LAWRENCE, in New-York.[71]

Hamilton and Laurance, despite John's tragic opting out of the desperate local political campaign of 1800, had remained on cordial terms. How else to explain Alexander's appointing him, on eve of the fateful Burr duel, one of three trustees to dispose of his 35-acre country estate, The Grange.[72] Trusteeship papers had barely been filed when Laurance learned to his horror that Alexander lay dying in an upstairs bedroom of Bank of New York director William Bayard's North River mansion. Two days later, on July 14, 1804, John and seven fellow pallbearers bore their longtime friend's casket in grand funeral procession to the burial ground of Trinity Church.

To everyone's consternation, Hamilton—despite Jefferson's near-paranoia that he had manipulated public office to fatten his private purse—left Eliza and seven children mired in debt. Gouverneur Morris, perhaps Alexander's closest friend, was appalled to discover Hamilton had "a debt of between fifty thousand and sixty thousand dollars hanging over him, a property which in time may sell for seventy or eighty thousand, but which, if brought to the hammer, would not, in all probability, fetch forty."[73] Appealing to Hamilton's true friends, Morris and Oliver Wolcott Jr. (head of the Merchants Bank of New York) organized more than a hundred subscribers (including Judge Laurance) to establish an $80,000 support fund so confidential that it remained a Bank of New York secret until 1937.[74] Subscriptions would have been larger had it not been for the perceived wealth of Hamilton's father-in-law Philip Schuyler. Sad truth, Wolcott discovered, was that General Schuyler "owes money & has no funds to command."[75]

"Certain gentlemen," revealed Alexander's son James in 1824, went on to buy out Hamilton's share of the "Scriba Patent" partnership for "more than it was worth," then used the proceeds to purchase The Grange from

Eliza for $30,000 and sell it back to her for $15,000.[76] It is inconceivable that pallbearer Laurance, as co-trustee of The Grange and Scriba Patent investment partner, was not one of these clandestine Grange "angels." As to the former treasury secretary's other joint holdings, the association was liquidated and properties partitioned among surviving partners. John's share amounted to 16 separate lots plus interest in another.[77]

With Hamilton's passing, John Laurance's slide into obscurity continued unabated. Only briefly did he make the news in 1807. Not as a political figure but as father of the bride at daughter Ann's wedding. No sooner had Ann (his third child with Betsey McDougall) married New York merchant George Wright Hawkes than the newlyweds removed to Hawkes's native Liverpool, England. Suspecting his daughter might never re-cross the Atlantic, Laurance formalized Ann's dowry with a £3,000 indenture payable in three installments over the following 19 months. Ever the diligent lawyer, he insisted on a provision that should Hawkes predecease Ann, "his estate shall pay to her a life annuity of 500 pounds in quarterly installments."[78] As a special wedding gift, John commissioned one of the day's leading portraitists, Thomas Sully, to render Ann's likeness.[79] Paint barely dry on the 26-inch by 22.5-inch head-to-waist work, Laurance then paid Sully another $50 to render an exact copy for himself. It was a touching, eerily omniscient gesture, for John never again saw Ann or laid eyes upon his namesake grandson Lawrance Hawkes, born February 8, 1808, in Liverpool.[80] Nor is there evidence that he ever met granddaughter Adelaide, who was delivered 11 months later.

Following a brief bout of his old nemesis inflammatory rheumatism, John in mid-1808 could no longer travel by coach. Always one for more land, that summer he disposed of his fine carriage, pair of horses, and harness to John S. Livingston in return for "100 acres to be selected out of my share or part of the seventh township in the county of Chenango."[81] John then gave youngest daughter Margaret his beloved portable mahogany writing desk. Upstate property management expeditions were over for good.

The final vignette we have of Judge Laurance dates from the fall of 1808. Accompanied by devoted friend Troup, John was off to inspect several jointly owned waterfront city lots adjacent to those of sitting New York mayor Marinus Willet. General McDougall's old Liberty Boy co-conspirator received the pair with great cheer. "We drank a glass or two of good wine with him," remembered Troup, "& when the wine had settled we all went with glee to look at our lots."[82] Willet, it seems, had convinced the City Corporation to improve Troup and Laurance's collective waterfront lots with landfill. Arriving on the ground, however, it became all too clear the mayor's own lots were nicely filled while the others remained unimproved. In the ensuing conversation, Willet allowed that being mayor indeed had its privileges, including upward of $13,000 annual emoluments. "The moment he mentioned the sum," Troup chuckled to Rufus

King, "I cast my eyes upon Lawrance's phiz [face], and I need not tell you who know him so well, what an effect the sum had upon it."[83]

In late 1809, Judge Laurance was again struck down with paralysis, from which this time he recovered only partly. Returning to his Broadway home in September 1810 from a restorative visit to the warm mineral springs at Ballston, he felt sprightly enough to write stepson-in-law James Greenleaf that: "my health much improved tho not quite well."[84] Two months later Laurance was dead. Exposed to an inclement November night, he "was seized with a violent chill and died after a short severe illness."[85] Left behind were daughter Elizabeth from his first marriage, three unmarried teenage daughters from second wife Elizabeth Allen,* and son John McDougall who expired 23 years later, unmarried and alone.

Laurance's last will and testament named as executors his son John, son-in-law William Tilghman, Robert Troup, Matthew Clarkson, and Egbert Benson.[86] To each of his four children with Betsey McDougall, he bequeathed $15,000 ($450,100 today). His three daughters with Elizabeth Allen received $6,000, presumably because they had been well provided for by Elizabeth's estate. The remaining estate was bequeathed one-seventh to each child. Invested in real estate, the bulk of Laurance's wealth took years to completely unwind. It was not until 1825 that 79-year-old executor Benson completed affairs by presenting the New York Land Office with 140 ledger-sized pages of individual farms conveyed by the Laurance estate.[87] Totaling several millions of present-day dollars, it was a revealing compendium of the vast property holdings that Judge Laurance legated upon departing this earth 15 years before.

Politically, Laurance had already been dead for a decade, the discarded relic of a spent Federalist party. Shown the door in 1800 by Jefferson and Burr's Republican sweep, America's first political party never recovered. Presidential candidate Charles C. Pinckney was blown away in 1804 by incumbent Thomas Jefferson's 72.8 percent Electoral College margin, followed four years later by James Madison's lopsided 64.7 percent victory. When midterm election ballots of 1810 were counted, only 36 of 140 House seats (25 percent) and 6 of 36 Senate seats (17 percent) remained in Federalist hands. Alexander Hamilton's New York had become a Republican stronghold with the governor, lieutenant governor, chancellor, both legislative houses, and 13 of 17 congressmen in the hands of Jeffersonian successors.

New York was no longer the city that once elected Laurance to Congress. Of its 96,373 inhabitants, more than a third had arrived since he resigned the Senate 10 years before. The 7 polling wards of 1800 had mushroomed to 10. To the city's exploding Irish, German, Italian, and

---

*Eighteen-year-old Emily (1792–1855), 15-year-old Frances (1795–1843), and 13-year-old Margaret (1797–1878), all married, apparently happily, within a decade of John's passing. His third daughter with Betsey McDougall, Elizabeth, apparently died unmarried.

French immigrant population, the War for Independence belonged to a past generation. George Washington's judge advocate general was product of a city whose limits ended where Broadway and Bowery Road came together at present-day 14th Street; by 1810, city planners were mapping out daring blueprints to extend the grid we know today all the way north to 155th Street. Robert Fulton's Hudson River steamship line to Albany was thriving, and the world's first oceangoing steamboat, inventor John Stevens's *Phoenix*, had just steamed out of New York Harbor bound for Philadelphia. Although little more than six years had passed since the grand, city-funded public procession for Hamilton, New York City's first United States congressman was laid to rest in subdued, private fashion. No newspaper reprised his distinguished life and no mention was made in Common Council minutes for the one-time East Ward alderman. A simple obituary in the November 12, 1810, *New York Evening Post* matter-of-factly observed: "Died: yesterday afternoon, John Laurance, esq. His friends are requested to attend his funeral tomorrow afternoon at 4 o'clock."

The New York State Society of Cincinnati, however, was not about to let one of its own depart this earth without proper send-off. President-General Matthew Clarkson directed members "to attend the funeral of the late Col. Laurance from his late residence at 356 Broadway" and "to wear the usual mourning for thirty days."[88] Had Laurance's last testament so instructed, he would have been laid to rest in the yard of his beloved Trinity Church, no doubt in the inescapable lee of Alexander Hamilton's pyramidal white marble monument. But the document directed no such thing. After a lifetime in his fellow immigrant's shadow, John was not about to linger there for perpetuity. Instead, his earthly remains were interred in Alexander McDougall's family vault at First Presbyterian Church's 10 Wall Street burying yard.[89] Alongside first wife Betsey he would repose for eternity.

EPILOGUE

Why John Laurance Matters

HOUSTON, TEXAS, SEPTEMBER 18, 1942. World War II Liberty ship No. 0108 slid unceremoniously down the runway of George and Herman Brown's Green's Bayou Fabrication Yard and splashed into the Houston Ship Channel. One of more than 2,700 armed cargo vessels built from a single wartime template, she was christened the SS *John Laurance* and dispatched to New York Harbor for the treacherous North Atlantic convoy run to Liverpool.[1] The 441-foot transport faithfully served for the duration of its war, sailing in 33 separate convoys before retiring into private service as an oceangoing commercial freighter. Journey's end was Panama City, Florida, where in 1963 SS *Laurance* was broken up for scrap.

John Laurance has vanished as ignominiously as his melted-down namesake Liberty ship. No headstone survives to mark where he went to ground; indeed, a towering Wall Street edifice now occupies First Presbyterian Church burying yard where he was initially interred. Between 1844 and 1846, his remains were displaced along with the McDougall vault when church elders disposed of their century-and-a-quarter Wall Street address in favor of a fine new Gothic Revival structure on Fifth Avenue between 11th and 12th Streets.[2] Although some burying yard relics were anonymously relocated to Brooklyn's Greenwood cemetery, most, including the McDougall vault, were consolidated in a mass unmarked excavation near the new Fifth Avenue entrance and covered with landfill. Today, only a small, inconspicuous, brass plaque hints namelessly at what resides beneath the quiet, shady lawn.

Half a mile to the south, three-block-long King Street memorializes Rufus King, two-time Federalist candidate for vice president. To the north 140 blocks are Hamilton Heights, Hamilton Place, the Alexander Hamilton Playground, and Hamilton Grange National Monument. Other Manhattan streets venerate Jay, Clinton, Duane, McDougall, Morris, van Cortlandt, and Varick. Repentant loyalist John Watts enjoys a commemorative thoroughfare, as does John Broome, defeated by Laurance in the inaugural congressional election of 1789. Even Westchester lawyer Phillip Pell (who ran a distant third behind Broome) is remembered with a two-block Chinatown stretch between the Bowery and Mott Street. But no Laurance Street, Place, Boulevard, Road, or Lane is to be found on New York City maps.

Epilogue

Staring at the tranquil lawn of Presbyterian Church's grassy Fifth Avenue pocket park, one wonders. Why, some two and a quarter centuries later, is the Cornishman's altogether forgotten contribution to our rule of law still relevant? John Laurance matters not just because he is the only non-native-born citizen ever to stand within two heartbeats of the presidency, but also because he personifies an inescapable truth: America's political pie was from the onset baked full of immigrants. Almost one in five of General Washington's Continental Army rank and file were foreign born, along with 22 of his 86 generals and scores of volunteer officers from Canada, France, Poland, and Prussia.[3] Seven of the 40 signers of the Declaration of Independence were immigrants, as were eight delegates to the Constitutional Convention, 23 attendees to the Continental Congress, three of the first eight justices to the Supreme Court, and almost 10 percent of the first United States Congress.

Seven foreign-born citizens* played significant roles in the new federal government, but only Laurance rose primarily through elective office. Yet, he would never would have set foot in the first Congress if Massachusetts delegate Elbridge Gerry had prevailed during the Constitutional Convention; for the prissy Yankee argued that the House of Representatives be restricted to American-born citizens.[4] Pressure to impose second-class citizenship for foreigners did not end with ratification. In 1798, the Massachusetts General Court went so far as to propose amending the founding document to disqualify all naturalized citizens from holding *any* public office lest they "contaminate the purity and simplicity of American character."[5] Five other states were of the same mind. A copy of the Alien Enemies Act of 1798 in hand, federal District Judge Richard Peters confided that: "There are some 'Alien Scoundrels'" that "I want to handle if I can do it legally. One of them is an English Democrat, the worst, if possible, of all."[6] By 1802, even Hamilton harbored reservations about immigrants. "The United States," he warned under the pen name *Lucius Crassus*, "have already felt the evils of incorporating a large number of foreigners into their national mass."[7] Not only did the West-Indian-born Hamilton believe the influx "served very much to divide the community," but he also feared it "likely to compromise the interests of our own country in favor of another."[8] If nothing else, Laurance's long public service career disproves his old friend's xenophobic words.

Colonel Laurance has never received full due for institutionalizing General Washington's judge advocate department and embedding the 1776 Articles of War into America's first professional army. In so doing, he necessarily promulgated a *lex non scripta* (unwritten common law) of "usages or customs of the service" that continues to influence application

---

*Hamilton, Laurance, Secretary of War McHenry, Senator Robert Morris, and Supreme Court justices James Iredell, William Paterson, and James Wilson.

of military law. Determining, for example, whether acts constitute "conduct unbecoming an officer or a gentleman" employs usages of the service dating back to Continental Army experience.[9] In 1786, Laurance left a final mark on the Articles of War by reporting out of the Confederation Congress necessary post-war refinements that kept the Articles essentially in place until 1874.[10] He also established precedent for prosecuting personally at the highest-profile trials, an example followed by Major General Joseph Holt at the 1865 Lincoln assassination trial and Major General Myron Cramer at the 1942 trial of eight German saboteurs.[11] And lest we forget, it was Judge Laurance who put Virginia infantry lieutenant John Marshall on a path that forever altered the United States Supreme Court.

Laurance's vigorous contribution to the important First Federal Congress also merits serious reappraisal. Voice of post-war New York City, he was among the half-dozen key members who—without Washington, Jefferson, Adams, Franklin, or Hamilton in the room—rendered the ratified Constitution into a remarkably resilient federal government. No one played a larger role than Rep. Laurance in chaperoning Treasury Secretary Hamilton's capitalistic financial agenda through the House into law. Indeed, the New Yorker's four-year contest with James Madison over how loosely to interpret the Constitution is a central storyline of the first two federal Congresses. And well after Hamilton departed the government, New York Senator Laurance spearheaded legislation behind America's first real navy in the looming conflict with France. Had he instead of Hamilton crumpled to the ground on Weehawken Plain, immortality would have been ensured. But the Cornish émigré left behind no such signature moment.

A year after Thomas Jefferson assumed the presidency, Robert Troup would ruefully admit: "Laurance has a solid opinion of the Republican system."[12] Had John actually migrated to Republican Party ranks, he may well have capstoned his public career (à la Robert Livingston's ministry to France) with a plum appointment and cracked the first rank of public figures of his day. Instead, disillusioned and distraught after wife Elizabeth's death, he withdrew from politics altogether. It was a regrettably self-interested decision by a man for whom the price of public service had become too steep.

Yet, Laurance's very withdrawal reminds us that America was founded on the fly by a generation of imperfect revolutionaries who juggled family, health, and economic imperatives with public office. Not everyone kept all balls in the air. Battlefield hero "Light Horse Harry' Lee of Virginia went bankrupt and was jailed for it. John Hancock resigned office twice because of his painful gout. Both Hamilton and Henry Knox quit the Washington cabinet to address hemorrhaging personal finances, never again to hold public office. Devoid of post-war employment, naval hero John Paul Jones vanished into the service of Russian Empress Catherine II only to die poverty-stricken in Paris of kidney failure. English-born pamphleteer

Thomas Paine ("Common Sense") struggled with the consequences of his impolitic pen for decades before dying alone in New York City, an impoverished rabble-rousing has-been. And John Laurance conceded to the demands of five motherless unmarried daughters, a neglected law practice, pressing real estate investments, and his own erratic health.

Students of Americana could do worse than to turn their eyes from the dozen or so Capital "F" founding fathers that dominate bookstore windows and look for a moment to the legion of towns, villages, and crossroad communities comprising the 13 original United States. For *there* is where the legacy of a founding generation still endures in rule of law, civic institutions, traditions of community service, and hundreds of landmark buildings that speak across the centuries. And should one's glance find its way to New York City, it's worth a minute to search out John Laurance. From Federal Hall to Fraunces Tavern to Trinity Church to Columbia University to Wall Street itself, his immigrant spirit still roams. Not to mention a small unmarked patch of grass in the lee of Fifth Avenue Presbyterian Church.

APPENDIX A

General Courts-Martial in George Washington's Main Army 1775–1778

The United States Army judge advocate general, or his deputy, was mandated by Section XIV, Article 3 of the September 26, 1776 Articles of War to prosecute all general courts-martial in the name of the United States of America. William Tudor was appointed in July 1775 as the Army's first judge advocate. Upon Tudor's resignation, John Laurance served as judge advocate general from April 10, 1777 until June 6, 1782. From July 4, 1775 until war's end, the commander-in-chief's daily general orders communicated general courts-martial dates, presiding officers, outcomes, and sentences to his Main Army.

Over the first three months of the six-month Valley Forge winter of 1777/1778, courts-martial incidence increased dramatically as General Washington employed military justice to sustain Main Army discipline until Prussian drillmaster Baron von Steuben's parade-ground protocols took hold. To quantify this phenomenon, the author has aggregated general courts-martial incidence in General Washington's Main Army on a quarterly basis from second quarter 1775 through the fourth quarter of 1778, as communicated in Washington's daily general orders. Because Main Army troop count varied widely, quarterly trial aggregates were then indexed to quarterly average fit-for-duty (excluding the sick or otherwise not present) troops to produce a comparable yardstick: quarterly trials per thousand fit-for-duty troops. This metric more clearly depicts the exceptional trial surge that accompanied Judge Laurance's first two quarters in office and during the first quarter of 1778 at Valley Forge. There were 14.9 trials per thousand troops during the first quarter of 1778 (figure 14), almost a five-fold increase versus the prior quarter. When von Steuben's drills began the following quarter, trials per thousand declined to 4.3 and then to 2.8 the subsequent quarter. The author's scholarly article in *Pennsylvania Magazine of History and Biography* (vol. CXLI, no. 1, January 2017) analyzes this symbiotic relationship between courtroom and parade ground discipline.

APPENDIX A

General Courts-Martial in George Washington's Main Army 1775-1778

Period	Present & Fit for Duty	Trials	Convictions	Trials per (000)	Per Cent Convicted
1775					
3rd Qtr.	17,984	117	95	6.5	81.1%
4th Qtr.	15,900	41	31	2.6	75.6
1776					
1st Qtr.	14,644	11	9	.8	81.8
2nd Qtr.	9,608	85	75	8.5	88.2
3rd Qtr.	16,334	82	70	5.0	85.4
4th Qtr.	13,846	20	16	1.4	80.0
1777					
1st Qtr.	1,981*	17	9	8.6	52.9
2nd Qtr.	**7,363**	**122**	**104**	**16.6**	**85.2**
3rd Qtr.	**8,000****	**160**	**118**	**20.0**	**73.8**
4th Qtr.	14,623	42	26	3.1	57.8
1778					
1st Qtr.	**7,656**	**114**	**86**	**14.9**	**75.4**
2nd Qtr.	15,237	65	53	4.3	81.5
3rd Qtr.	20,895	59	42	2.8	71.1
4th Qtr.	22,278	43	31	1.9	72.1

Sources: Officers and soldiers fit for duty are quarterly averages calculated from monthly strength reports of troops under Washington's direct command. *The Sinews of Independence*, ed. Charles Lesser (Chicago: University of Chicago Press, 1976). Trials and convictions are from Washington's daily General Orders (1775-1778). *The Writings of George Washington from the Original Manuscript Sources*, 1745-1799, ed. John C. Fitzpatrick, Varick Transcripts: Continental Army Papers, 1775-1783, General Orders, Letter books 1, 2 & 3.

*Lesser's *The Sinews of Independence* did not contain monthly Main Army strength reports for first quarter 1777. The only hard number is Washington's 4 March 1777 missive to Continental Congress, the postscript of which states the best estimate he could form of fit-for-duty troops was 3000, "all of whom, except nine hundred and eighty-one, were militia."
**In the absence of 3rd quarter 1777 Main Army musters from Lesser, this figure was obtained from Washington's personal correspondence.

FIGURE 15 Chart, "General Courts-Martial in George Washington's Main Army 1776–1778."

(As originally published in *Pennsylvania Magazine of History and Biology* CXLI, no. 1 [January 2017]: 7–29. Reproduced with permission.)

Notes

Introduction

1. "Founding Fathers" is a twentieth-century term. Manufactured by Warren G. Harding's speechwriter for a 1918 Washington's Birthday celebration, the term was little more than a heroic abstraction until historian Kenneth B. Umbreit used it in a 1941 book title describing the lives of John Adams, Samuel Adams, John Hancock, Patrick Henry, Thomas Jefferson, and George Washington. In 1954, Nathan Schachner called his history of the new republic *The Founding Fathers*, but it was Columbia University History professor Richard B. Morris in 1973 who defined the term in *Seven Who Shaped Our Destiny: The Founding Fathers as Revolutionaries* to encompass seven specific men: John Adams, Benjamin Franklin, Alexander Hamilton, John Jay, Thomas Jefferson, James Madison, and George Washington. This "Magnificent Seven" has been loosely expanded to include all who signed the Declaration of Independence, the Continental Association, and Articles of Confederation; attended the Constitutional Convention or the First Federal Congress; or served as senior military officers during the War for Independence. For a succinct discussion of traditional "Founding Father" paternity credentials see John R. Vile's "James Madison and Constitutional Paternity" in *James Madison, Philosopher, Founder, and Statesman*, 35-62.

2. Thomas Jefferson to John Adams, 28 Oct. 1813, in Lester J. Cappon, ed., *The Adams-Jefferson Letters: The Complete Correspondence Between Thomas Jefferson and Abigail and John Adams* (Chapel Hill: University of North Carolina Press, 1959), vol. 2, 388. "I agree with you," wrote Jefferson to Adams, "that there is a natural aristocracy among men . . . the natural aristocracy I consider as the most precious gift of nature, for the instruction, the trusts, and government of society."

3. Lawyers accounted for 28 of 56 signers of the Declaration of Independence, 22 of 48 signers of the Articles of Confederation, 21 of 39 signatories at the Constitutional Convention, 60 percent of the first United States Senate, and 49 percent of the first House of Representatives.

4. Beginning with J. Allen Smith's *Spirit of American Government, a Study of the Constitution: Its Origin, Influence, and Relation to Democracy* (1907), and Charles Beard's landmark *An Economic Interpretation of the Constitution* (1913), through Merrill Jensen and the Wisconsin "School," Progressive historians have questioned the Constitution as an undemocratic document created by and for the aristocratic "better sort." Contemporary proponents of this interpretation include Terry Bouton, *Taming Democracy: "The People," the Founders, and the Troubled Ending of the American Revolution* (2007); and Woody Holton, *Unruly Americans and the Origins of the Constitution* (2007).

5. Charles T. McClenahan, *History of the Most Ancient and Honorable Fraternity of Free and Accepted Masons in New York* (New York: Published by the Grand Lodge, 1888), vol. 1, 201. There is no record of Laurance's specific initiation date, but 1772 lodge by-laws list John Lawrance as Junior Warden, behind Senior Warden William Malcolm and Master Isaac Heron. We can be certain that this "Lawrance" was indeed future Judge Advocate General, United States Congressman and Senator John Laurance because he is identified as such by Masonic historian Peter Ross, *A Standard History of Freemasonry in the State of New York* (New York and Chicago: The Lewis Co., 1899), 143.

6. George C. McWhorter, "Biographical Sketches of the Life of John Laurance," an unpublished presentation to the New York Historical Society: 1869, 8, John Laurance Papers in the New York Historical Society Manuscript Collection. "Family tradition says that General McDougall would have preferred a wealthy connection for his daughter, but she preferred the gallant young officer who was ready to give up his profession for his country." McWhorter was Laurance's grandson.

7. The Presidential Succession Acts of 1792, 1886, and 1947 have designated 91 men and one woman (House Speaker Nancy Pelosi) behind the vice president in line of presidential succession. The first 54 were senate presidents *pro-tempore* (1792–1886), followed by 26 secretaries of state (1886–1947), and 12 speakers of the House (1947–present). Only John Laurance was foreign born. *PRO TEM, Presidents Pro Tempore of the*

United States Senate since 1789 (Washington, DC: U.S. Govt. Printing Office, 2008), 11–20; "Biographies of the Secretaries," Office of the Historian, United States of America Department of State, https://history.state.gov/departmenthistory/people/secretaries; "Speakers of the House (1789 to present)," History, Art & Archives, United States House of Representatives, https://history.house.gov/People/Office/Speakers.

8   General Orders, 20 November 1777, *The Papers of George Washington*, Revolutionary War Series, 12:16, *October 1777–25 December 1777*, ed. Frank E. Grizzard Jr. and David R. Hoth (Charlottesville: University of Virginia Press, 2002), 327–28.

9   John C. Ford, *Calendar of the Correspondence of George Washington, Commander in Chief of the Continental Army, with the Continental Congress* (Washington, DC: U.S. Government Printing Office, 1906), 9. For 62 months (April 1777 to June 1782), Laurance was member of Washington's military family as Army Judge Advocate General. Of Washington's 32 staffers over the eight-year conflict, only Marylanders Tench Tilghman (82 months) and Robert Harrison (65 months) served longer. Alexander Hamilton served from January 1777 through March 1781, some 50 months.

10 Keith Marshall Jones III, "John Laurance and the Role of Military Justice at Valley Forge," *Pennsylvania Magazine of History and Biography* CXLI, no. 1 (January 2017), 7–29. Using a fresh metric—courts-martial per thousand fit-for-duty troops—the author examined Valley Forge's extraordinary trial incidence in context of a 42-month, 586-trial survey.

11 The phrase was first used by William Henry Trescot in 1857 (*The Diplomatic History of the Administrations of Washington and Adams*; Boston: Little, Brown), and later popularized by John Fiske's, *The Critical Period of American History, 1783–1789* (Boston: Houghton Mifflin, 1888) to define these vulnerable postwar years; also E. Wilder Spaulding, *New York in the Critical Period, 1783–1789* (New York: Columbia University Press, 1932).

12 "John Laurance, Representative from New York," *Debates in the House of Representatives: Third Session, December 1790–March 1791, Documentary History of the First Federal Congress*, vol. 14, edited by Charlene Bangs Bickford, Kenneth R. Bowling, William C. di Giacomantonio, and Helen E. Veit (Baltimore: Johns Hopkins University Press, 1996), 718–22.

13 *United States Statutes at Large*, Vol. 1: *Public Acts of the Fifth Congress, 1st Session* (Boston: Little, Brown and Company, 1845), 523–25. The Federalist-controlled Senate took the lead in responding to President Adams's 1797 defense requests largely because a Republican pro-French minority in the House was able to water down or delay any legislation requiring new taxes to support the military build-up. See Roy Swanstrom, *The United States Senate, 1787–1801: A Dissertation on the First Fourteen Years of the Upper Legislative Body* (Washington DC: U.S. Govt. Printing Office, 1962), passim.

14 Stanley Elkins and Eric McKitrick, *The Age of Federalism: The Early American Republic, 1788–1800* (New York: Oxford University Press, 1993), 73. "Madison," wrote Professors Elkins and McKitrick, "was challenged by Representative John Laurance, a merchant of New York City, who insisted that such a policy could only lead to ruinous commercial warfare."

15 For a discussion of common law and early legislation regarding English nationality in terms of *jus soli* (place of birth) and *jus sanguinis* (descent), see Sir Francis Piggott, *Nationality, Including Naturalization and English Law on the High Seas and beyond the Realm*, I (London: William Clowes and Sons, 1907), 41. Also, Sir Alexander Cockburn, *Nationality: Or the Laws Relating to Subjects and Aliens Considered with a View to Future Legislation* (London: Ridgway, 1869), 7, 12.

16 William Blackstone, "Of People, whether Aliens, Denizens or Natives," *Commentaries on the Laws of England*, vol. 1, chap. 10 (Oxford: The Clarendon Press, 1765), 354. Blackstone later reversed himself when it came to "children born out of the King's ligeance, whose fathers were natural born subjects." English naturalization was the only path to secure property rights after death. Applicants were required to take communion in the Protestant tradition and swear allegiance to the Crown, which effectively excluded Catholics, Jews, and other non-Christians. For an examination of British naturalization policies, colonial extensions, and American naturalization policy under the Articles of Confederation and Congressional policies under the Constitution, see Carla L. Reyes, "Naturalization Law, Immigration Flow, and Policy," chap. 7 of *Transforming America*, and also *Perspectives on U. S. Immigration*, vol. 1, edited by Michael C. Le May (Santa Barbara, CA: Praeger, an imprint of ABC-CLIO LLC, 2013), 145–64.

17 David Ramsay, *A Dissertation on the Manner of Acquiring the Character and Privileges of a Citizen of the United States* (Charleston, SC: 1789), 3. Americans, wrote South Carolina physician and historian Ramsay, had "changed from subjects to citizens," and "the difference is immense." On the nature of citizenship created by the Revolution, see James H. Kettner, *The Development of American Citizenship, 1608–1870* (Chapel Hill: University of North Carolina Press, 1978), 173–209.

18   www.census.gov/population/www/documentation/twps0029.html. Also, Aaron Fogleman, "Migrations to the Thirteen British North American Colonies, 1700-1775 and New Estimates," *Journal of Interdisciplinary History* XXII, no. 4 (Spring 1992), 691-709. The first census of the United States was conducted in 1790. It enumerated total population to be 3,929,214, of which 3,140,207 were white. The Naturalization Act of 1790 limited naturalization to immigrants who were "free white persons of good character." Citizenship was therefore excluded for American Indians, indentured servants, slaves, and even free blacks, though the later were allowed to vote in certain states.

Fogleman reviews multiple studies that estimate total white immigration between 1700 and 1790 to have ranged from 435,694 (Galenson) to 485,300 (Gemery) to 663,000 (Fogel et al.). Therefore, if all white immigrants were still alive in 1790 — an impossible case — they would then have represented between 13.9 and 21.1 percent of the total white population. More likely, surviving white immigrants in 1790 represented no more than half the upper number. It was not until 1850 that foreign-born status was measured, at 9.7 percent of total population. It was not until 1870 that foreign-born whites were measured, at 16.4 percent of the white population.

19   John Adams to Treasury Secretary Oliver Wolcott, Jr., quoted in Elkins and McKitrick, *Age of Federalism*, 605. Born in Geneva, Switzerland, Jeffersonian Republican politician, diplomat, secretary of the treasury, and linguist, Albert Gallatin (1761-1849), arrived in America almost a decade after Alexander Hamilton. Adam's comment about Hamilton being foreign born was made in context of the latter's 1798 appointment as major general and second-in-command after Washington in the newly approved "Provisional Army."

20   Thank you, Ron Chernow, *Alexander Hamilton* (New York: Random House, 2004), 250, for this exquisite turn of phrase. "His papers," wrote Chernow, "show that, Mozart-like, he could transpose complex thoughts onto paper with few revisions."

21   Among many others, see Irving Brant, *James Madison*, 6 vols. (Indianapolis and New York, 1941-1961); Ralph Ketcham, *James Madison: A Biography* (New York: Macmillan, 1971); Jack Rakove, *James Madison and the Creation of the American Republic* (New York: Longman, 2002); Garry Wills, *James Madison* (New York: New York Times Books, 2002); Richard LaBunski, *James Madison and the Struggle for the Bill of Rights* (New York: Oxford University Press, 2006); and Robert A. Rutland, *James Madison: The Founding Father* (New York: Macmillan, 1987). Political commentator George F. Will wrote that "if we truly believed that the pen is mightier than the sword, our nation's capital would have been called Madison, D.C. instead of Washington D.C."

22   "An Act to regulate the Collection of the Duties imposed by law on the tonnage of ships or vessels, and on goods, wares, and merchandise imported into the United States," *The Public Statues at Large of the United States of America*, ed. Richard Peters (Boston: Charles C. Little and James Brown, 1845), 29-49.

23   Alexander Hamilton to Alexander McDougall, New York, [1774-1776], *The Papers of Alexander Hamilton*, vol. 26, 1 May 1802-23 October 1804, Additional Documents 1774-1779, edited by George C. Syrett (New York: Columbia University Press, 1979), 353-54. A chagrined Hamilton wrote to McDougall to apologize for losing "Bankrofts treatise, Two volumes of natural philosophy, and a latin author."

24   *Historic U.S. Court Cases: An Encyclopedia*, edited by John W. Johnson (New York: Routledge, 2001). *Rutgers v. Waddington* is listed as one of the six most significant court cases regarding government separation of power.

25   Alexander Hamilton to John Laurance, New York, Monday morning, 178?. John Laurance Papers at New York Historical Society. Laurance had a knack for turning speculative real estate into profit, but Hamilton pedaled hard to stay solvent. When debts significantly exceeded assets as Hamilton's estate was settled in 1804, Laurance was one of perhaps a hundred friends who subscribed to the fund providing for wife Eliza and the family.

26   Laurance and Hamilton were both in lower Manhattan from early 1774 until August 1775 when John marched off to Canada as a New York infantry lieutenant. Returning the following January, Laurance remained in the city together with Hamilton until Washington's evacuation of August 1776. General Alexander McDougall secured Continental Army positions for both men in mid-1776, and they accompanied New York troops in the field until January 1777 when Hamilton joined Washington's personal staff as aide-de-camp. Two months later Laurance was added to His Excellency's staff as judge advocate. It was not until Hamilton's February 1782 resignation that the pair was separated for any significant period of time. In November 1783 they were both back in New York as rising lawyers, dwelling within blocks of one another until the federal government removed in mid-1790 to Philadelphia.

There Laurance's Chestnut Street address was but three blocks from Hamilton's rented Walnut Street quarters. Laurance departed Philadelphia for New York in March 1793 at the expiration of his second congressional term. Hamilton resigned 27 months later and returned to lower New York some six blocks from Laurance's 37 Broad Way address. Except for Laurance's four-year (1796–1800) senatorial stint requiring Philadelphia attendance two-thirds of the time, the pair remained in close New York proximity until Hamilton's tragic July 12, 1804, death.

27 John Laurance to Rufus King, New York, April 16, 1794, Charles King, *Life and Correspondence of Rufus King*, 6 vols. (New York: G. B. Putnam's Sons, 1894), vol. 1, 561-62.

28 Robert Troup to Rufus King, 29 April 1794, Rufus King papers at New York Historical Society.

29 Russell Shorto's *The Island at the Center of the World: The Epic Story of Dutch Manhattan and the Forgotten Colony that Shaped America* (New York: Random House, 2004) was a *New York Times* 2004 book of the year and winner of the New York City Book Award.

30 Benjamin Franklin to Peter Collinson, 9 May 1753, *The Papers of Benjamin Franklin*, ed. Leonard W. Laboree, 40 vols. (New Haven: Yale University Press, 1961), vol. 4, 477-86.

31 Laboree, *Papers of Benjamin Franklin*, 483.

32 John Jay to George Washington, Philadelphia, July 25, 1787, *The Papers of George Washington*, Confederation Series, Vol. 5, *1 February 1787-31 December 1787*, edited by W. W. Abbott (Charlottesville: University of Virginia Press, 1997), 271-72.

33 English-born William Duer (1743-1799) was Hamilton's assistant treasury secretary from 1789 to 1790; Welshman John Nicholson (1757-1800) used his office as Pennsylvania comptroller-general for massive personal speculation; Liverpool native Robert Morris (1734-1806) was Confederated Congress superintendent of finance and U.S. Senator from Pennsylvania; Scottish-born Supreme Court justice James Wilson (1742-1798) was a signer of the Declaration of Independence, two-time member of the Continental Congress, key force in drafting the Constitution, and one of six original Supreme Court justices. All four men became financially overextended casualties of the "Panic of 1792" and its speculative aftermath.

34 The current infatuation with all things Hamilton traces back to Ron Chernow's meticulously researched, masterfully written 2004 biography *Alexander Hamilton*. Inspired by Chernow's telling, playwright/composer/actor Lin-Manuel Miranda's 2015 Broadway production *Hamilton: An American Musical* became an instant pop culture phenomenon, tapping into the present-day societal conversation over immigration, capitalism, and the role of central government.

35 John C. Miller, *Alexander Hamilton: Portrait in Paradox* (New York: Harper & Row, 1959), xi. Miller paraphrased Ralph Waldo Emerson's well-traveled quote from his *Essay on Self-Reliance* (1841) that "An institution is the lengthened shadow of one man."

Chapter One

1 "Benjamin Moore to William Coleman, 12 July 1804," *Founders Online*, National Archives, last modified April 12, 2018, http://founders.archives.gov/documents/Hamilton/01-26-02-0001-0268.

2 Richard Rush to John McDougall Laurence, 19 July 1804, New York Historical Society, Transcript 76531. Twenty-four year-old Richard Rush (1780-1859), third child of noted Philadelphia physician and signer of the Declaration of Independence Benjamin Rush, was a friend of John McDougall Laurance, Judge Laurance's 29-year-old first-born and only son. Richard Rush, no Hamiltonian Federalist, became one of James Madison's most trusted friends, serving under his administration as comptroller of the currency and acting secretary of state before becoming minister to Great Britain and U.S. attorney general (1814-1817). Richard went on to become secretary of the treasury (1825) and minister to France (1847).

3 "General Hamilton's Funeral," *Farmers Museum, or Literary Gazette*, Saturday, July 28, 1804.

4 "Particular and highly interesting account of the Death and Funeral of General Hamilton," *Boston Gazette*, 19 July 1804, 2. Hamilton's eight pallbearers were Gen. Mathew Clarkson, Oliver Wolcott, Esq., Richard Harrison, Esq., Abijay Hammond, Esq., Josiah O. Hoffman, Esq., Richard Varick, Esq., William Bayard, Esq., and Judge Lawrance. Also see W. P. Van Ness, "The Funeral," *The Papers of Alexander Hamilton*, vol. 26, *May 1802-October 1804*, ed. Harold C. Syrett (New York: Columbia University Press, 1979), 322-30.

5   *Boston Gazette*, 19 July 1804, 2. "A more imposing scene," wrote historian Samuel Smucker in 1858 (*The Life and Times of Alexander Hamilton*, Philadelphia: G. G. Evans, p. 135), "had never been witnessed on this continent, than what was then presented."

6   Lieutenant Colonel Hamilton was deposed by Judge Laurance for eyewitness testimony in the courts-martial of Major General Charles Lee, Major General Benedict Arnold, and British Major John André, among others.

7   David B. Ogden, *Four Letters on the Death of Alexander Hamilton, 1804: Found in the Papers of William Meredith of Philadelphia* (Portland, ME: Anthoensen Press, 1980).

8   *New York Evening Post*, 17 July 1804.

9   Receipt, John Laurance Papers at New York Historical Society, folder 1790–1800. Dated June 14, 1790, the receipt is in the amount of £20 from John Lawrence for purchase of pew no. 64 in Trinity Church, John Lewis, collector. Hamilton's name appears in Trinity's 1790 Pew Book registry that July as follows: "Rec. from Alexander Hamilton fourteen pounds, 10 *S* with 90 *S* discount to £30/year subscription paid for rebuilt Trinity Church."

10 *1801 Communicants List*, Trinity Episcopal Church Archives, https://www.trinitywallstreet.org/about/alexander-hamilton-churchman. Elizabeth Schuyler Hamilton was from birth raised as a member of the Dutch Reformed Church. After her marriage to Alexander, she honored her husband's loose Anglican religious orientation and attended Trinity Episcopal Church along with President Washington and much of his administration. Five of Elizabeth and Alexander Hamilton's children were baptized at Trinity between 1788 and 1800. She is buried at Trinity near her husband.

Chapter Two

1   Hugh P. Olivey, *Notes on the Parish of Mylor Cornwall* (Taunton, England: Barnicott & Pearce, Athenaem Press, 1907), 58–59. George Turner, M.A., was Vicar of St. Mylor and Mabe from 1740 until buried at St. Mylor on November 3, 1761.

2   *St Mylor Parish Register and Bishops' Transcripts*, Cornwall Records Office, Old Country Hall Truro, England, TR1 3AY (as researched by parish on-line clerk, Phillip Rodda). Eighteenth-century Anglican bishopric registries recorded only dates of baptism, marriage, and burial. Although family tradition dates our John Lawrence/Laurance's birth to "1750," no specific day is to be found. We can only be certain that he was baptized on February 1, 1751, at St. Mylor under Anglican Vicar George Turner.

3   *St Mylor Parish Register and Bishops' Transcripts*. "John LAWRENCE of Milor" and "Mary Knuckey of Falmouth" were married June 9, 1750, in Redruth parish between Falmouth and Stithians some five miles distant. Mary Knuckey was baptized in Stithians in July 1724 and John Lawrence was baptized in Mylor on 30 July 1722.

4   George Edward Cokayne, *Complete Baronetage, vol. II, 1625–1649* (Exeter, England: William Pollard & Co., 1900), 60. Baptized on 1 December 1588, John Lawrence entered Oxford (St. John's College) on 27 May 1603, received a B.A. from Oriel College in October 1604 and an M.A. from St. Edmunds Hall in 1615. He was knighted on 26 January 1609/10 and made a baronet on 9 October 1628. Sir John purchased a share of stock in the Virginia Company on 23 June 1620, a fact that may entitle his descendants to membership in the Order of First Families of Virginia. He was interred 14 November 1639 at Chelsea Church in Middlesex, England.

5   *Index to Administration in The Prerogative Court of the Archbishop of Canterbury*, vol. III, 1581–1595, ed. Harold C. Ridge (London: British Record Society Ltd., 1954). Ridge compiled 6,645 given names distributed in 345 different forms from wills and last testaments. Also see Douglas A. Galbi, "Long-Term Trends in Personal Given Name Frequencies in the UK" (London: Federal Communications Commission, July 20, 2002), Table 1: Popularity of UK Personal Given Names: 1800–1994. Most genealogies trace to "Lawrence the Monk" who arrived in Britain about A.D. 916 to convert the locals to Christianity, or to Lawrence de Lancaster (1250–1317), whose son John was first to use the Lawrence surname. Others trace to Magister Laurentis (1150), John Lorence of Suffolk (1268), Benedict Laurenz of Huntingdonshire (1292), and Lawrence of Iver (1628). For history of the Lawrence/Lawrance/Laurence name, see John Burke and John Bernard Burke, *The Royal Families of England, Scotland, and Wales with their Descendants, Sovereigns and Subjects*, vol. II (London: E. Churton, 1851); *The Victorian History of the County of Lancaster*, 8 vols., ed. William Farrer and J. Brownbill (London: A. Constable and

Company, 1906–1914); *The Herald and Genealogist* (London: J. G. Nichols and R. C. Nichols, Printers to the Society of Antiquaries, 1863–1874); *Complete Baronetage*, vol. II, 1625–1649 (London: William Pollard & Co, 1902); and Charles A. H. Franklin, *A Genealogical History of the Families of Paulet, Lawrence, and Parker* (Bedford, England: The Foundry Press Ltd., 1963).

6 Charles Sandoe Gilbert, *Historical Survey of the County of Cornwall* (London: J. Congdon, 1820), 187. There were in 1750 only two John Lawrences of sufficient note for mention. One was a lawyer in the village of Launceston; the other was proprietor of Trellissick House (a present-day British National Heritage property) outside Falmouth. Neither was husband of Mary Knuckey or father of a son named John. Our John Lawrence was the namesake great grandson of John Lawrence Sr., who appears in the Mylor Parish Protestation returns of 1641 (Record #22592 in the Cornwall-OPC-Database.org, transcriber Peter Relph). The Protestation was a formal 1641/42 oath of allegiance to King Charles and the Church of England.

7 George C. McWhorter, "Biographical Sketches of the Life of John Laurance," an unpublished 1869 presentation to the New York Historical Society, 3, John Laurance Papers in the New York Historical Society Manuscript Collection. McWhorter was Laurance's grandson. Laurance's father John Lawrence was buried in Falmouth on 26 November 1757 (Cornwall on-line Burials database, record no. 2299939, L. Haywood, transcriber.) when our protagonist was in his seventh year.

8 Nicholas Carlisle, *A Concise Description of the Endowed Grammar Schools in England and Wales* (London, 1818), I:137–51. There were seven public grammar schools in Cornwall County during Laurance's day: Bodmin, St. Ives, Launceston, Liskeard, Penryrn, Saltash, and Truro. Only the latter boasted an endowment or faculty of any significance. Indeed St. Ives, Liskeard, and Saltash may have been shuttered during Laurance's youth. Truro, averaging 50 scholars who entered at age eight or nine and attended for up to seven years at an annual expense of £4–5 exclusive of boarding, employed a system of education based on that of Eton College. Truro Grammar School was reestablished in 1906 as Truro Cathedral School with a focus on teaching choristers for the neo-Gothic Truro Cathedral. It was shut down in 1982 with its 18 remaining choristers assigned to other schools.

9 Walter H. Tregellas, "Truro Grammar School," *Journal of the Royal Institution of Cornwall*, vol. X (Truro, England: Lake and Lake, 1891), 423, 429.

10 Graham Midgely, *University Life in Eighteenth-Century Oxford* (Guildford, England: Biddles Ltd., 1996), 19. From 1334 to 1820, Oxford and Cambridge enjoyed a Crown-enforced duopoly over university education in England. Some £80 per annum was necessary for tuition, tutorial expenses, supplies, room, and board. By contrast, a tradesman needed £40/year to keep a family, while the middling sort could not live comfortably for less than £100.

11 Olivey, *Notes on the Parish of Mylor Cornwall*, 6. "The old semi-feudal system therefore continues," wrote Olivey in 1907, "Every tenement is part and parcel of the lord's demesne or service, either on lease for life or on lease for a term of years."

12 *Bailey's Western and Midland Directory; or Merchants and Tradesman's Useful Companion for the Year 1783* (Birmingham, England: Pearson and Rollason, 1783), 234. Prosperous South Carolina planter and future president of Continental Congress Henry Laurens was a Richard Lawrence trading client.

13 "Uncle R. Lawrance to My Dear Nephew John Laurance, Falmouth, 4 April 1783," John Laurance Papers at New York Historical Society, folder 1784.

14 "July 2, 1802 H.M. packet *Duke of Kent*, William Denner to John Lawrence," John Laurance Papers at New York Historical Society, folder "1800." To Lawrance's inquiry about the family of "the late Mr. Lawrence," Denner replied: "The eldest, Mary Ann is single and keeps a little school for children of the peasantry . . . by which she obtains a very scanty pittance. The second, Alicia, is the widow of Mr. Kempthorne, late a person in the Royal Navy but for many years unemployed who died about a year ago at Plymouth leaving his widow with two children. The third (Jane) is recently married to an attorney named Koppel and lives decent near Portsmouth. The fourth, Elizabeth, is unhappily married to an itinerant dancing master who treats her poorly."

15 John S. Olenkiewicz, "British Packet Sailings–New York–Falmouth: 1755–1790," from data obtained from the newspaper archives of the American Antiquarian Society and Newsbank, 28 December 2011, www.rfrajola.com/resources/falmouthpacket.pdf, 9. By 1767, four sister packets sailed the New York/Falmouth circuit: *Lord Hyde, Harriot, Earl of Halifax*, and *Duke of Cumberland*. Passages to New York in 1767 required between 42 and 77 days at sea, while prevailing west winds shortened the return trip to 24–40 days. Captain of the *Earl of Halifax* from 1759–1770 was John Phillips Boulderson (1717–1797) according to a letter dated 10 Oct 1771 in the Papers of Henry Laurens, fifth president of Continental

Congress. *Papers of Henry Laurens, October 10, 1771 to April 10, 1773* (Charleston: University of South Carolina Press, 1980). In 1771 Boulderson was succeeded by son John Jr.

16 *London Evening Post*, 2 September 1764. Also see Andy Campbell, "Falmouth Packet Archives at the Royal Cornwall Polytechnic Society (est. 1833)," Falmouth, Cornwall, England, falmouth.packet .archives@dial.pipex.com.

17 Benjamin Franklin, *Autobiography* (Dover Publications Inc.: 1996), 62. Reprinted from text edited by John Bigelow (Philadelphia: J.B. Lippincott & Co., 1868). Franklin and fellow packet passenger Kennedy can be placed aboard *Earl of Halifax* according to the *Pennsylvania Gazette* of 32 March 1766: "Yesterday sailed the HALIFAX Packet, Captain Boulderson, for Falmouth. Captain Kennedy, late of the Coventry Man of War, and the Doctor [Franklin], embarked for England."

18 Mary Knuckey, "widow," was buried 26 February 1774 in Stithians parish, where she was also baptized (Cornwall On-Line Burial Database, Record #1967097, M. Bath, transcriber). She would have been 50. No record survives of any correspondence between Laurance and his mother over the seven years between his sailing for New York and her death. Nor according to family tradition and surviving records did Laurance ever return to England.

19 Map of New York prepared in 1767 by Lieutenant Bernd. Ratzen of the 60th Regt. for "His Excellency Sir Henry Moore Bart, Captain General and Gouvenour in Chief in & over the Province of New York," New York Historical Society. Also see the "Metropolitan Transit Authority (MTA) South Ferry Terminal Project Archaeological Report," http://www.mta.info/capconstr/sft/archaeology.htm

20 *New York Journal* (Holt), 26 March 1767. As described in Edward Countryman, *A People in Revolution: The American Revolution and Political Society in New York 1760–1790* (Baltimore: Johns Hopkins University Press, 1981), 41.

21 Edwin G. Burrows and Mike Wallace, *Gotham: A History of New York City until 1898* (New York: Oxford University Press, 1999), 187.

22 Martha J. Lamb, *History of the City of New York: Its Origin, Rise, and Progress*, 2 vols. (New York: A. S. Barnes & Co., 1877), 1:655 56. Archibald Kennedy, Crown-appointed receiver general (customs collector) for New York Province, died in 1763, whereupon the One Broadway property passed to his Royal Navy captain namesake son.

23 I. N. Phelps Stokes, *New York Past and Present: Its History and Landmarks 1524–1939* (New York Historical Society, private printing, 1939), 72; *New York Journal of General Advertisers* (Holt's), May 28, 1767; DeVoe's *Historical Incidents from Newspapers 1696–1800*, vol. I; Countryman, *A People In Revolution*, ix.

24 Burrows and Wallace, *Gotham*, 185.

25 Patrick McRobert, "Patrick McRobert's Tour Through Part of the North Provinces of America," ed. Carl Bridenbaugh, *Pennsylvania Magazine of History and Biography* 59, no. 2, 139.

26 Papers of John Laurance, New York Historical Society, Box I, folder "1771." The two documents linking Laurance to the Queens County Lawrences are A) the *Last Will and Testament of John Lawrence*, dated 11 August 1761 (three years before his demise) appointing four of seven surviving siblings as executors of his estate, and B) a chirograph (meant to be separated at the middle with each party retaining half) *Indenture* made 28 September 1771 in which Ann Lawrence, Thomas Lawrence, Jonathan Lawrence, and Daniel Lawrence, executors of the last will and testament of John Lawrence, deceased, convey for "testament of John Lawrence, deceased for 500 pounds New York money to Abraham Cock and wife Anne, a certain dwelling house and piece of ground lying and being in Montgomery Ward of the City of New York, bounded south by Water Street."

27 There is no reference whatsoever to John Laurance in the most credibly researched genealogy of the Lawrence family in America, Thomas Lawrence's *Historical Genealogy of the Lawrence Family* (New York: Edward O. Jenkins, 1858). Nor is there any reference in John Lawrence, *The Genealogy of the Family of John Lawrence of Wisset in Suffolk, England* (Boston: S.K. Whipple and Co., 1857), or in Mercy Hale, *A Genealogical Memoir of the Families of Lawrences, with a Direct Male Line from Sir Robert Lawrence of Watertown* (Boston: Printed for the Author, 1856).

28 James Riker Jr., *The Annals of Newtown in Queens County New York* (New York: D. Fanshaw, 1852), 282. See also Holgate's *American Genealogy*, 203-204. Two separate John Lawrences immigrated to Massachusetts Colony. The first (born in Suffolk in 1609) arrived in Charlestown on the ship *Arabella* in 1630 and settled in Watertown, his offspring spreading from New Hampshire to Connecticut. See *The Genealogy of the Family of John Lawrence of Wisset in Suffolk, England* (Boston: S.K. Whipple and Co., 1857), 13. The second John Lawrence (1618–1699) hailed from Herefordshire. Aged 17, he arrived in April 1635 on

the ship *Planter* and found his way to New Amsterdam. See Thomas Lawrence, *Historical Genealogy of the Lawrence Family* (New York: Edward O. Jenkins, 1858), 21, 24, 83.

29 Holgate, *American Genealogy*, 204; City of New York Surrogate's Office 1680 Liber No. 22, 24.

30 Riker, *Annals of Newtown*, 284.

31 Edwin Brockholst Livingston, *The Livingstons of Livingston Manor* (New York: The Knickerbocker Press, 1910), 109–111. On 1 October 1715, the great seal of the Province of New York was affixed to the Royal manor grant which was ascertained by a 1714 survey to constitute 160,240 acres.

32 John Laurance Papers, New York Historical Society, Box I, folder "1771." *Indenture* made 28 September, 1771, in which Ann Lawrence, Thomas Lawrence, Jonathan Lawrence, and Daniel Lawrence, executors of the last will and testament of John Lawrence, deceased, convey for "testament of John Lawrence, deceased for 500 pounds New York money to Abraham Cock and wife Anne, a certain dwelling house and piece of ground lying and being in Montgomery Ward of the City of New York, bounded south by Water Street."

33 *Minutes of the Common Council of the City of New York*, 6: 96.

34 McWhorter, p. 4. Grandson McWhorter's assertion that Laurance "read law" under Lt. Governor Cadwallader Colden is bolstered by Laurance's post-Revolutionary War retention as attorney by two separate Colden granddaughters, Jane and Henrietta Maria, in addition to nephew David Colden Willet. See also, Major William F. Fratcher, "Notes on the History of the Judge Advocate General's Department 1775–1941," *The Judge Advocate's Journal*, vol. 1, no. 1, 15 June 1944 (Washington, DC: The Judge Advocates Association), 3.

35 Wayne Bodle, "Review of Books," *William & Mary Quarterly* LX, no. 2, 2003. "He was New York's answer to Benjamin Franklin," wrote Bodle in discussing two primary biographical works on Colden: Alfred R. Hoermann, *Cadwallader Colden: A Figure of the American Enlightenment* (Westport, CT: Greenwood Press, 2002), and Alice Magdalen Keys, dated, amateurish *Cadwallader Colden: A Representative Eighteenth-Century Official* (New York, 1906).

36 Patricia U. Bonomi, *A Factitious People: Politics and Society in Colonial New York* (New York: Columbia University Press, 1971), 237. Bonomi points out that during the decade 1758-1786, when the Livingston's were supposedly in control of the New York General Assembly, the family more often than not was on the losing side of chamber votes. "In all likelihood," she argues, "after the sudden death of James DeLancey the Assembly was temporarily thrown into a state of emergency until new leaders emerged." Also see Leopold S. Launitz-Schürer Jr., *Loyal Whigs and Revolutionaries: The Making of the Revolution in New York* (New York: New York University Press, 1980), 1–96. The author explains differences between Livingston and DeLancey factions as ones of personality and style. With the emergence of the Sons of Liberty in the wake of Parliament's Stamp Act of 1765, leadership became a three-cornered game.

37 Cadwallader Colden to Rt. Honble. Earl of Hillsborough, New York, 7 July 1770. "The Colden Letter Books, Volume 10," *Collections of the New York Historical Society for the Year 1877* (New York: Printed for the Society, 1878), 223–24.

38 Barnet Schecter, *The Battle for New York* (New York: Walker & Company, 2002), 19. For a lively in-depth account of the DeLancey/Livingston rivalry, see pages 15–22. Also L. F. S. Upton, *The Loyal Whig: William Smith of New York and Quebec* (Toronto: University of Toronto Press, 1969), 15–52. A thoroughly researched and highly readable account of the Livingston/DeLancey struggle is to be found in Richard M. Ketchum, *Divided Loyalties: How the American Revolution Came to New York* (New York: Henry Holt and Company, 2003), 187–292.

39 Lt. Gov. Cadwallader Colden to the Earl of Halifax, 22 Feb. 1765, *Documents relative to the Colonial History of the State of New York*, ed. E. B. O'Callaghan (Albany, NY: Weed, Parsons and Company, 1856), VII: 705–06. "Were the people," wrote Colden, "freed from the dread of this Domination of the Lawyers I flatter myself with giving general joy to the people of this Province. I never received the least opposition in my administration except when I opposed the views of this faction."

40 Lt. Gov. Cadwallader Colden to the Lords of Trade, 7 November 1764, *Documents relative to the Colonial History of the State of New York*, ed. E. B. O'Callaghan, VII: 677.

41 Lt. Gov. Cadwallader Colden to the Earl of Halifax, 13 Dec 1764, *Documents relative to the Colonial History of the State of New York*, ed. E. B. O'Callaghan, VII: 698.

42 *Documents relative to the Colonial History of the State of New York*, ed. E. B. O'Callaghan, VII: 682, 685.

43 Hoke P. Kimball and Bruce Henson, *Governor's Houses and State Houses of British Colonial America, 1607–1783* (Jefferson, NV: McFarland & Company, Inc., 2017), 292–93. Built in 1763 near Flushing,

New York, in Queens County, Spring Hill was a boxy two-story, five-bay brick home. Seized as spoils of war by patriots under the Confiscation Act of 1779, Spring Hill ultimately served as office building for Cedar Grove Cemetery in Flushing, Queens County, until demolished in 1930. "A certain ancient burying place" hidden anonymously somewhere nearby contains Colden's mortal remains.

44   Cadwallader Colden to John Colden, 16 July 1749. *Cadwallader Colden Papers, Collections of the New York Historical Society* (New York: Printed for the Historical Society, 1938), vol. LXVIII, 36.

Chapter Three

1. Maturin L. Delafield, "William Smith – The Historian and Chief Justice of New York and of Canada," *The Magazine of American History*, April/June, 1881, 418.

2. William Smith, "Some Directions Relating to the Law," William Smith Papers, New York Public Library, IX, MssCol Ω2796. This essay is attributed to William Smith Jr. in Paul Mahlon Hamlin's "Legal Education in Colonial New York," *New York University Law Quarterly Review* (Washington Square Park: 1939), pp. 61, 62, 82, & 197–200. Hamlin dates the essay to about 1756. However, Milton W. Klein's "Rise of the New York Bar: The Legal Career of William Livingston," 15 *William & Mary Quarterly* 357 (3rd series, 1958) argues that the document was originally prepared much earlier by William Smith Sr. Klein notes that the younger Smith was introduced to the material during his own legal apprenticeship under the elder Smith and in 1747 dispatched a copy to a Connecticut friend.

3. William B. Stoebuck, "Reception of English Common Law in the American Colonies," *William & Mary Law Review* 10, no. 2 (1968/1969): 401. "The assumption that colonial law was essentially the same in all colonies is wholly without foundation," wrote Professor Stoebuck, a point earlier made by George Lee Haskins, *Law and Authority in Early Massachusetts* (New York: Macmillan Inc., 1960), 6–7. Regarding these points, see the classic essay by Julius Goebel Jr., "King's Law and Local Custom in Seventeenth-Century New England," *Columbia Law Review* 31 (1931): 416. Also see Lawrence M. Friedman, *History of American Law* (New York: Simon & Schuster, 2005), 4, 5, 13. For an eyewitness summary of the New York Provincial court system on the eve of Revolution, see "Report of Governor Tryon on the Province of New York to the Earl of Dartmouth London, 11 June 1774," *Colonial History of New York*, vol. XLIV, 444–45.

4. Chester Alden and Edwin M. Williams, *Courts and Lawyers of New York: A History, 1609–1925* (New York: The American Historical Society, Inc., 1925), I: 897–99. Also: James Wilton Brooks, *History of the Court of Common Pleas of the City and County of New York* (New York: Published by subscription, 1896).

5. Anton-Hermann Chroust, "Legal Profession in Colonial America," *Notre Dame Law Review* 33 (1958): 356.

6. *The Charter of the City of New-York*, Printed by Order of the Mayor, Recorder, Aldermen and Commonalty of the City aforesaid (New York: W. Weyman, in Broad Street, 1765). This so-called "Montgomerie Charter" was principally the work of Inner Temple London-trained lawyer James DeLancey Sr. (1703–1760).

7. Chroust, 368. "A distinct bar association, called the New York Bar Association, seems to have been formed in New York as early as 1744 (some authorities claim 1745 or 1747, while one authority suggests the year 1741) and, thus, became the earliest known bar association in colonial America." Also see Albert P. Blaustein, "New York Bar Associations Prior to 1870," *The American Journal of Legal History* 12, no. 1 (January 1968): 50–57.

8. Charles Warren, *A History of the American Bar* (Boston: Little, Brown and Company, 1911), 188. Only five New Yorkers were among the 115 American lawyers that Warren identified as England-educated between 1760 and the Revolution's close. Forty-seven were from South Carolina, 21 from Virginia, 16 from Maryland, and 11 from Pennsylvania.

9. "Agreement of the Bar of New York City, dated Oct. 1756," Hamlin, *Legal Education*, 160–64.

10. Frank Sullivan Smith, "Admission to the Bar in New York," *The Yale Law Journal* 16, no. 7 (May 1907): 514.

11. Hamlin, *Legal Education*, 35–36. See also George William Edwards, *New York as an Eighteenth Century Municipality, 1731–1776* (New York, Longmans, Green and Company, 1917), 32–33.

12. Alden Chester and Edward Melvin Williams, *Courts and Lawyers of New York: A History, 1609–1925*, 3 vols. (New York: The American Historical Society Inc., 1925), 1: 615. In 1769, James Duane was instrumental in convincing Lord Dunmore and four Supreme Court justices (including William Smith Jr.) that some £10,000 in patent fees rightfully belonged to Lt. Governor Colden as acting governor.

13 P. Van Schaack to Henry Van Schaack, Jan. 2, 1769, Henry Van Schaack, *The Life of Peter Van Schaak, LLD* (New York: D. Appleton & Co., 1842), 9.

14 McWhorter, *Biographical Sketches*, 4. Also "John Laurance, Representative from New York," *The Documentary History of the First Federal Congress of the United States 1789-1791* (Model Editions Partnership Digital Age: The Johns Hopkins University Press, 1988–1994).

15 *An Ordinance for Regulating and Establishing the Fees to be hereafter taken by the Officers of the Court of Chancery of the Province of New York*, February 28, 1727/1728 (Bradford printer: Library of the Association of the Bar of the City of New York, 1727).

16 William Smith Jr. Papers, manuscript section 9, New York Public Library, as quoted in *The Law Practice of Alexander Hamilton*, ed. Julius Goebel Jr. (New York: Columbia University Press, 1969), II: 6–7.

17 Walter Stahr, *John Jay, Founding Father* (New York: Hambledon and London, 2005), chap. 2.

18 "Roll of Attorneys of the Supreme Court of the State of New York," McKesson Papers, New York Historical Society; *New York City Directory* (New York: Trow City Directory Co., 1789), 122. Also "John Laurance, Representative from New York," *The Documentary History of the First Federal Congress of the United States* (Model Editions Partnership Digital Age: The Johns Hopkins University Press, 1988–1994).

19 McWhorter, *Biographical Sketches*, 51–52. The exact address of Laurance's first office is not clear. McWhorter names "Broadway & Wall" and an unnamed Broadway boarding house, but either may have been from a later date.

20 Ossian Lang, *History of St. John's Lodge No. 1, 1757–1907* (New York: Published for the Lodge, 1907), 22. Dated December 7, 1757, the St. John's No. 2 Warrant is listed as #272 on the Grand Lodge of England registry.

21 David G. Hackett, *The Religion in Which All Men Agree: Freemasonry in American Culture* (Berkeley: University of California Press, 2014), 21.

22 Ron Chernow, *Washington: A Life* (New York: Penguin Press, 2010), 500. Whatever conspiracy theories," Chernow noted, "later circulated about the group [Freemasonry], the brotherhood provoked no suspicions in eighteenth-century America." For an examination of Freemasonry as a surrogate religion for enlightened men suspicious of Christianity in the formation of early American culture, see: Catherine L. Albanese, *Sons of the Father: The Civil Religion of the American Revolution* (Philadelphia: Temple University Press, 1976), 129–30, and Seven C. Bullock, *Revolutionary Brotherhood: Freemasonry and the Transformation of the American Social Order, 1730–1840* (Chapel Hill: University of North Carolina Press, 1996).

23 *The Universal Masonry Library, a Replication in Thirty Volumes of All the Standard Publications in Masonry*, ed. Robert Macoy (New York: Jno. Leonard & Co., 1855), 6: xii. No record survives of Laurance's exact initiation date into the St. John's No. 2 Masonic Lodge, but pre-Revolutionary lodge records list "John Lawrance" as St. John's No. 2 Secretary on the 1772 subscription list to Wellins Calcott's, "A Candid Disquisition of the Principles and Practices of the most Ancient and Honourable Society of Free and Accepted Masons." 1772 lodge bylaws list "John Lawrance" as Junior Warden, behind Senior Warden William Malcolm and Master Isaac Heron. We can be certain that "Lawrance" is indeed "Laurance" because he is recorded as such in Charles T. McClenahan's *History of the Most Ancient and Honorable Fraternity of Free and Accepted Masons in New York* (New York: Published by the Grand Lodge, 1888), I: 188. Further confirmation that "Lawrance" was "Laurance" is to be found in Masonic historian Peter Ross's *A Standard History of Freemasonry in the State of New York* (New York and Chicago: The Lewis Co., 1899), 186. "Lawrance, who was a Past Master of St. John's Lodge," wrote Ross, "was born in Cornwall, England in 1750 ... presided at the trial of Major André ... served in the state senate and the House of Representatives and crowned a grand career by being elected from New York to the United States Senate."

24 John Adams *Diary*, June 20, 1779, as quoted in *The Founders on the Founders*, ed. John P. Kaminski (Charlottesville: University of Virginia Press, 2008), 268.

25 Stahr, *John Jay, Founding Father*, 62. An experienced lawyer himself, Stahl pored over court and private records to note that Jay over the six-year period beginning in 1770 handled more than 1,300 cases in New York City's Mayor's Court.

26 Robert R. Livingston to John Sargent, May 2, 1766, Livingston Papers, New York Public Library.

27 The Sons of Liberty, according to the papers of John Lamb, were formally organized shortly after Stamp Act passage but did not assume true public character until the fall of 1767. Factions under Joseph Allicocke aligned with the Anglican DeLancey's interests, but others, like oystercatcher's son Isaac Sears and convicted burglar's son John Lamb, broke away from the Delanceys to go their own way, while Alexander McDougall and his followers generally sided with the Livingston camp. See Robert Champagne, "Liberty

Boys and Mechanics of New York City, 1764–1774," *Labor History*, VIII (Spring 1967): 118–21. Also Isaac Q. Leake, *Memoir of the Life and Times of General John Lamb* (Albany, NY: Joel Munsell, 1857), 2–4.

28   Richard M. Ketchum, *Divided Loyalties* (New York: Henry Holt and Company, 2002), 99. Also MacDougall, *American Revolutionary*, 12–15.

29   Pauline Maier, *From Resistance to Revolution: Colonial Radicals and the Development of American Opposition to Britain 1765–76* (New York: Alfred Knopf, 1972), 58.

30   Schecter, *The Battle for New York*, 28; Champagne, *Alexander McDougall and the American Revolution in New York*, 15. On McDougall's attack on the general assembly for approving a supply bill for British troops, see Thomas Jones, *History of New York during the Revolutionary War*, 2 vols. (New York: New York Historical Society, 1879), I: 426–30.

31   Jones, *History of New York During the Revolutionary War*, vol. I: 426. As related in William L. MacDougall's biographical study of Alexander McDougall: *American Revolutionary* (Westport, CT: Greenwood Press, 1977), 25–26.

32   E. B. O'Callaghan, ed., *The Documentary History of the State of New York* (Albany, NY: Weed, Parsons and Company, 1850), vol. III: 317.

33   Sherman Williams, "President's Address," *Proceedings of the New York State Historical Association* (1916), XV: 73. "One citizen was killed, three severely wounded, and a considerable number injured. Many of the soldiers were badly beaten." President of the New York State Historical Association, Williams was also chief school librarian for the University of the State of New York.

34   Lt. Governor Colden to the Earl of Hillsborough, 21 February 1770, *The Papers of Cadwallader Colden*, 13: 208.

35   *Calendar of New York Colonial Manuscript Indorsed Land Papers in the Office of the Secretary of State of New York, 1642–1803* (Albany, NY: Weed, Parsons and Company, 1864), 551–69. For details on Laurance as a land speculator, see Arthur J. Alexander, "Judge John Laurance: Successful Investor in New York State Lands," *New York History*, vol. 25 (1944): 35–44. Laurance likely purchased the 1,000 acres in late 1774–early 1775 when Lt. Governor Colden unilaterally announced that he would freely distribute New York's New Hampshire Grant acres in the Green Mountains area of present-day Vermont. For more on the distribution of New Hampshire Grant land, see William Smith Jr. to Philip Schuyler, 9 July 1774, *William Smith Jr. Historical Memoirs from 16 March 1763 to 25 July 1778*, ed. William H.W. Sabine, 2 vols. (New York Times and Arno Press, 1969), 1: 188–89.

36   McWhorter, *Biographical Sketches*, 8.

37   The Adams Papers, *Diary and Autobiography of John Adams*, vol. 2, *1771–1781*, ed. L. H. Butterfield (Cambridge, MA: Harvard University Press, 1961), 97–118. Hannah Barrett Bostwick (circa 1748–1816) was the 19-year-old daughter of Alexander McDougall's landlady when she became Mrs. McDougall in September of 1767. Only three years older than Betsey, Hannah survived McDougall, going on to marry Presbyterian minister Azel Roe in December of 1796.

38   McWhorter, *Biographical Sketches*, 8.

39   MacDougall, *American Revolutionary*, 20.

40   McWhorter, *Biographical Sketches*, 8

41   Chernow, *Alexander Hamilton*, 48.

42   MacDougall, *American Revolutionary*, 55.

43   Gouverneur Morris to John Penn, 20 May 1774, *American Archives*, 4th series, 6 vols. (Washington, DC: M. St. Clair Clarke and Peter Force, 1837–1846), I: 342–43.

44   Major Isaac Hamilton to Lt. Governor Colden, May 26–June 5, 1775, *Letters and Papers of Cadwallader Colden*, New York Historical Society Collections, LVI (New York: 1922), VII: 299–300. "The loss of our men by Desertion," wrote Hamilton, "is so great and [due to] the Apprehension of losing more, I therefore think it is necessary for the good of the Service to retreat on Board his Majesty's Ship the Asia...." Major Hamilton commanded the British garrison on Manhattan Island.

45   F. B. Heitman, "First New York Regiment, Colonel Alexander McDougall, 30 June 1775–November 1775," *Historical Register of the Officers of the Continental Army During the War of the Revolution, April 1775 to December 1783* (Washington, DC: Rare Book Shop Publishing Company, 1893), 39.

46   Stahr, *John Jay*, 22.

47   McWhorter, *Biographical Sketches*, 48.

Chapter Four

1. "Proceedings of the Second Provincial Congress of New York, Albany, August 11, 1775," *Documents Relating to the Colonial History of the State of New York*, ed. Bernard Fernow (Albany, NY: Weed, Parsons and Company, 1887), vol. XV, 25.

2. "Warrant to John Lawrence 2d Lieutenant issued and dated 3d day of August 1775 instead of Warrant issued to Morris Hazard returned," *Calendar of Historical Manuscripts Relating to the War of the Revolution in the Office of the Secretary of State* (Albany, NY: Weed, Parsons, and Company, 1868), I: 108. Because at least three John Lawrences were of military age in the New York City environs in 1775, it was essential the author had the right man. See Francis Heitman, *Historical Register of Officers of the Continental Army during the War of the Revolution* (Washington, DC: Rare Book Shop Publishing Company, 1914, reissued Genealogical Publishing Co: Baltimore, 1973), 342; William T. Saffell, "Officers Entitled to Half-pay," *Records of the Revolutionary War* (Hot Springs, VA: J.T. McAllister, 1913), 425; Francis J. Sypher Jr., *History of the New York Regiments of the Continental Army* (Fishkill, NY: Society of the Cincinnati, 2008), 11–12; *New York in the Revolution*, ed. Berthold Fernow (Albany, NY: Weed, Parsons and Company, 1887), 529.

3. *The Other New York, The American Revolution beyond New York City, 1763–1787*, ed. Joseph S. Tiedeman and Eugene R. Fingerhut (Albany, NY: State University of New York Press, 2005), 44. The statistics are from Tiedeman's "Response to Revolution: Queens County, New York during the Era of the American Revolution" (Ph.D. diss., The City University of New York, 1977).

4. *HISTORY OF QUEENS COUNTY with illustrations, Portraits & Sketches of Prominent Families and Individuals* (New York: W.W. Munsell & Co., 1882), 329–408.

5. "Journal of the Committee of Safety," August 29, 1775, *Journal of the Provincial Congress of the State of New-York, 1775–1776–1777* (Albany, NY: Thurlow Weed Printer, 1842), I: 137. Lt. Colonel Van Cortlandt on August 28 advised the Committee of Safety that the Fourth Regiment companies of Captains Herrick, Palmer, Horton, and Mills had arrived in Albany to join Captain Livingston's company with "no more than thirty guns with four companies fit for service."

6. *Journal of the Provincial Congress of the State of New-York, 1775–1776–1777*, I: 127: "We earnestly request the favor," wrote Deputy Paymaster Jonathan Trumbull to the Provincial Congress on 29 August 1775, "to advance Col. James Holmes six hundred pounds to enable him to pay his men that they may immediately march." See also I: 138, wherein on 28 August Lt. Colonel Van Cortlandt advised the Committee of Safety that: "The cash I received, I was obliged to pay to the mutinous men in the lower barracks; and I sent by Lieut. Riker to Capt. Woodard, at Newtown, Long-Island some part of it."

7. *Journal of the Provincial Congress of the State of New-York, 1775–1776–1777*, I: 131.

8. Provincial Congress on June 28, 1775, directed Commissary Peter Curtenius to outfit each of New York's four regiments with different-colored (blue, light brown, dark brown, gray) woolen short coats. McDougall's First New York coats were of conventional dark blue, but less-coveted gray coats fell to the least senior regiment, the Fourth New York. In practice, however, the First New York sequestered every available coat, and inventory was in such short supply that the Fourth New York displayed a variety of garb with blue facings.

9. Eric L. Manders, "Those Coats of 1775—A Dissenting View," *Military Collector and Historian Magazine* 33, no. 2 (Summer 1981), 69–71. Manders quotes an unidentified source observing "at Lake George a company Capt Woodward, 25th of grey with blue . . ." Captain Woodward's gray-coated company was likely the final Fourth Regiment company to depart Albany for Ticonderoga and the siege of Fort St. Jean. "The last company proceeded down Lake George the 27th of September," Draught letter of the New York Delegates to Continental Congress, In Provincial Congress at New York, October 4, 1775, Peter Force, *American Archives* (Published by M. St. Clair Clarke and Peter Force under authority of an Act of Congress, 1833), III: 1269.

10. Sypher, *History of the New York Regiments of the Continental Army*, 11–13.

11. Major General Philip Schuyler to George Washington, 6–7 November 1775, *The Papers of George Washington*, Revolutionary War Series, vol. 2, *16 September–31 December 1775*, ed. Philander D. Chase (Charlottesville: University of Virginia Press, 1987), 314–19.

12. Henry Livingston, "Journal of Major Henry Livingston of the Third New York Regiment, 1775," *The Pennsylvania Magazine of History and Biography* 22, no. 1 (1898): 30. Major Livingston described the defenses of Fort St. John: "The forts are abt 100 feet wide each way on the inside; & mounted between them, upwards of 30 Iron Cannon besides Brass fieldpieces (6 pounders) & several mortars . . .

The whole surrounded with a ditch of 7 feet deep & 8 or 9 feet wide—picketed on the Interior side with timbers projecting from the wall & over the Ditch, & a little elevated with their points made very sharp. Between the 2 forts there was a line of pickets placed (or posts) 10 feet high and close together. Its 2-300 yards from the forts to the nearest wood or bushes . . . The wilderness . . . is an impassable Quagmire—low, wet & covered with timber or brush."

13 "Extract of a letter from Montreal, Dated December 17, 1775" (unattributed), *New York Journal* 18 (January 1776) as reproduced in *Americans, 1775–1776*, ed. Mark R. Anderson (New York: State University of New York Press, 2016), 52. "Captain Willet," wrote an unidentified First New York officer, "has the command at St. John's." Willet would remain there until relieved in January 1776 when the enlistments of his men expired. The pension application of private Amon Marshall of Captain Jonathan Platt's Company of Colonel Holmes's regiment "states that he marched to the northward previous to the taking of St. John's, and was then stationed at Ticonderoga." See "Committee on Revolutionary Pensions Reports," *Reports of Committees of the House of Representatives at the First Session of the Twenty-Second Congress, December 7, 1831, in Five Volumes* (Washington: Duff Green, 1831), III: 2.

14 "Lt. Colonel R. Ritzema to Colonel Alexander McDougall, Montreal, November 19, 1775," Alexander McDougall Papers, New York Historical Society, microfilm reel 1.

15 Ibid.

16 Isaac Q. Leake, *Memoir of the Life and Times of General John Lamb* (Albany, NY: Munsell 1857, reprinted by Benchmark Publishing Company, 1970), 124. "From the ice battery, upon which was mounted five guns and a howitzer, Capt. Lamb commenced a well sustained but ineffectual fire upon the walls."

17 www.nycincinnati.org/engagements.htm. The New York State Society of the Cincinnati documents that the "1st, 2nd, 4th, & Lamb's Artillery participated in the invasion of Canada and Battle of Quebec." Montgomery led between 250 and 300 New Yorkers in the Quebec assault according to biographer Michael P. Gabriel, *Major General Richard Montgomery, The Making of an American Hero* (Teaneck, NJ: Fairleigh Dickinson University Press, 2002), 163. Among them were Ulster County private John Van Arsdale and Captain Jacobus Wylnkoop's Eighth Company of the Fourth New York Regiment according to "An Ulster County Boy in the Revolution," *Olde Ulster: An Historical and Genealogical Magazine* 1, no. 9 (September 1905), 271.

18 Riker, *Annals of Newtown*, Riker, 184, 313. "Abraham Riker, of the New York continental line . . . was present at the fall of Montgomery, at Quebec." Although no document places Lt. Laurance on the scene with certainty, the presence of elements of the Fourth New York regiment, and First Lieutenant Abraham Riker, suggests that Laurance was also present.

19 "Major General Philip Schuyler to the New York Provincial Congress, February 27, 1776, and draft letter of the New York Provincial Congress to Continental Congress, February 28, 1776," *New York in the Revolution, Documents Relating to the Colonial History of the State of New York*, ed. Berthold Fernow (Albany, NY: Weed, Parsons & Company, 1887), XV: 76–77. Woodward, Riker, and Lawrence all appear on an undated early 1776 list of officers erased from service due to promotion, death, or resignation on page 43 of vol. II, *Calendar of Historical Manuscripts Relating to the War of the Revolution, in the Office of the Secretary of State* (Albany, NY: Weed, Parsons and Company, 1868).

20 *Journal of the Provincial Congress*, 26 February 1778, I: 326.

21 Ibid.

22 "Vital Records of the First Presbyterian Church, 1776," *New York Genealogical and Biographical Record* (New York: Mott Memorial Hall, 1880), 12: 31.

23 Kenneth Roberts, *March to Quebec* (New York: Doubleday, 1938), 284. See also MacDougall, *American Revolutionary*, 72-73.

24 Henry Phelps Johnston, *The Campaign of 1776 around New York and Brooklyn*, Memoirs of the Long Island Historical Society (New York: S. W. Green, 1878), III: 84–89.

25 Major General Charles Lee to George Washington, February 19, 1776, Johnston, *The Campaign of 1776 around New York and Brooklyn*, III: 54.

26 Matthew I. Davis, *Memoirs of Aaron Burr: With Miscellaneous Selections from His Correspondence*, 2 vols. (Freeport, NY: Books for Libraries Press, 1970) [1836], 1: 307.

27 *Journals of the Provincial Congress of the State of New York*, 23 February 1776.

28 Alexander Hamilton to Colonel Alexander McDougall, New York, 17 March 1776, *The Papers of Alexander Hamilton, 1768–1778*, ed. Harold C. Syrett (New York: Columbia University Press, 1961), I: 181–82.

NOTES

29 "Field Officers and Captains in the First New York Regiment to General George Washington, New York, August 9, 1776," T. W. Eggly, *History of the First New York Regiment* (Hampton, NH: Peter E. Randall, 1981), 31. Also, Francis Heitman, *Historical Register of Officers of the Continental Army during the War of the Revolution* (Washington, DC: Rare Book Shop Publishing Company, 1914), reissued by Genealogical Publishing Company, Baltimore, 1973, 342.

30 "General Orders, 15 August 1776," *The Papers of George Washington*, Revolutionary War Series, vol. 6, ed. Philander D. Chase and Frank E. Grizzard Jr. (Charlottesville: University of Virginia Press, 1994), 27–29.

31 "John Laurance, Representative from New York," *Documentary History of the First Federal Congress of the United States of America*, ed. Charlene Bickford, et al. (Columbia, SC: Model Editions Partnership, 2002). See also Harry M. Ward, "John Laurance," *American National Biography* (Oxford: Oxford University Press, 1999), 1: 256–57.

32 Riker, *History of Queens County*, 193.

33 Chernow, *Alexander Hamilton*, 74.

34 Major Abner Benedict as quoted in Schecter, *Battle for New York*, 125.

35 MacDougall, *American Revolutionary*, 87–88.

36 "General Orders, September 16, 18, 26, 1777," *Papers of George Washington*, VI: 56–57, 71, 120. See also, Eggly, *History of the First New York Regiment 1775–1783*, 32–36.

37 Lt. Governor Colden to the Earl of Hillsborough, New York, 21 February 1770, *Cadwallader Colden Papers*, New York Historical Society, XVI: 208.

38 Henry P. Johnston, *The Battle of Harlem Heights, September 16, 1776, With a View of the Events of the Campaign* (Published for the Columbia University Press by the Macmillan Company, 1887), 94.

39 John C. Hamilton, *Life of Alexander Hamilton*, 1: 128.

40 MacDougall, *American Revolutionary*, 89. Hamilton's first biographer, son John Church Hamilton, places him on a Chatterton Hill ledge spraying the enemy with fire as they crossed the river. See Chernow, *Alexander Hamilton*, 81, and Johnston, *Campaign of 1776 around New York and Brooklyn*, 274. Not all historians, however, agree that John Church's claim is sufficiently documented. Since McDougall's sponsorship led to Hamilton's artillery command and his brigade was accompanied by at least one company of state artillery, the author abides by the assertion of Hamilton's son that he indeed was present.

41 Christopher Ward, *The War of the Revolution*, 2 vols. (New York: The Macmillan Co., 1951), 1: 262. Captain William Hull, as quoted in Maria Campbell, *The Revolutionary Services and Civil Life of General William Hull* (New York: D. Appleton & Co., 1847), 54.

42 Roger Champagne, *Alexander McDougall and the American Revolution* (Schenectady, NY: Union College Press, 1975), 118–19.

43 Alexander McDougall to John Laurance Esq., Haverstraw, New Jersey, 9 December 1776. John Laurance Papers, New York Historical Society, folder "1776."

44 George Washington to McDougall, December 21, 1776, Hawkes Collection at Union College, New York transferred to New York Historical Society. McDougall's letter to General Washington has been lost. However, Washington's reply counseled that this was not the proper time to resign because "Our enemies would probably attribute it to the late unfavorable aspect of our affairs," and he therefore advised "a little rest."

45 John Marshall, *The Life of George Washington*, second edition revised and corrected by the author, 2 volumes (Philadelphia: James Crissy, 1834), 1: 127.

46 George Washington to Alexander McDougall, 28 December, 1776, H. Hawkes Collection at Union College, New York, transferred to New York Historical Society.

47 Eggly, *History of the First New York Regiment 1775–1783*, 47.

48 Col. H.B. Livingston to the New York Committee of Arrangement 26 Nov. 1776, Force, *American Archives*, 5th series, 3: 857–58; Alexander McDougall to John Jay, Peekskill, December 2nd, 1776, *The Correspondence and Public Papers of John Jay*, vol. 1 (1763–1781), ed. Henry P. Johnston (New York: G.P. Putnam's Sons, 1890–1893). "Mr. John Laurance, my son-in-law, is now paymaster to my old regiment, but as it will be soon dissolved, I spoke to Col. Livingston of the 4th to get him appointed for his." The effective date of Laurance's appointment as paymaster to Livingston's Fourth New York Regiment was January 13, 1777. Colonel Livingston refers to Laurance as "Captain Lawrence" in a missive to George Washington, 29 March 1777, *The Papers of George Washington*, Revolutionary War Series, vol. 9, 28 March 1777–10 June 1777, ed. Philander D. Chase (Charlottesville: University of Virginia Press, 1999), 13–14.

49 Alexander Hamilton to John Laurance, Morristown, New Jersey, 1 March–10 April 1777, *The Papers of Alexander Hamilton*, vol. 26, ed. Harold C. Syrett (New York: Columbia University Press, 1979), 355–56.

50 Ibid.

51 Ibid.

Chapter Five

1 Robert K. Wright Jr., *The Continental Army* (Washington, DC: Center of Military History, Unites States Army, U.S. Government Printing Office, 1983), 30–33. Drawing upon the British model, Continental Congress on June 16, 1775 appointed Major General Horatio Gates as adjutant general of the Continental Army. Washington gave the experienced Gates "free hand in establishing administrative procedures," one of which was the creation of staff brigade majors and regimental adjutants for transmission and communication of headquarters orders and unit muster returns. Col. John Womack Wright, *Some Notes on the Continental Army* (Vails Gate, NY: New Windsor Encampment Publication No. 2, 1975), 10, writes: "The daily orders of the Continental Army were given at orderly hour, eleven o'clock in the forenoon, by the Adjutant General." For this purpose, the adjutant general established an orderly office located at the main army headquarters. From mid-January through May of 1777, Washington's headquarters was located at Jacob Arnold's Morristown, New Jersey, tavern. For more on brigade major responsibilities, see Harry M. Ward, *George Washington's Enforcers, Policing the Continental Army* (Carbondale, IL: Southern Illinois University Press, 2006), 52–54.

2 "General Orders, 10 April 1777," *The Papers of George Washington*, Revolutionary War Series, vol. 9, *28 March 1777–10 June 1777*, ed. Philander D. Chase (Charlottesville: University of Virginia Press, 1999), 109–10.

3 George Washington to Colonel Henry Beekman Livingston, 2 April 1777, *The Papers of George Washington*, Revolutionary War Series, *28 March 1777–10 June 1777*, ed. Philander D. Chase, 9: 48–49. "I wish the state of our Treasury," wrote Washington, "admitted of my sending you the Sum of Money you wrote for; But . . . I can only spare you Five thousand Dollars for the present, which I send by Capt. Laurance . . ." Also, Brigadier General Alexander McDougall to George Washington, 29 March 1777, *The Papers of George Washington*, Revolutionary War Series, *28 March 1777–10 June 1777*, 14–19.

4 P. H. Hoffmann, *History of the "Arnold Tavern," Morristown. N.J.: and many incidents connected with General Washington's stay in this place, as his headquarters in winter of 1777: with views of Historic buildings and places of Revolutionary interest* (Morristown, NJ: Chronicle Press, 1903), 1–20. Washington's aides and personal staff were housed together with His Excellency at Arnold Tavern during the spring 1777 Morristown encampment. The practice continued until victory at Yorktown stood down the need for the intimate headquarters staff living arrangement.

5 Wright, *Some Notes on the Continental Army*, 10. The official Valley Forge website (http://www.valley forgemusterroll.org/army.asp) lists 20 staff members, including Judge Advocate Laurance, reporting directly to General Washington.

6 "Instructions to Company Captains [of the Virginia Regiments], 29 July 1759," *The Papers of George Washington*, Colonial Series, vol. 4, *9 November 1756–24 October 1757*, ed. W.W. Abbot (Charlottesville: University of Virginia Press, 1984), 341–46.

7 George Washington to John Hancock, July 21, 1775, *The Papers of George Washington*, Revolutionary War Series, vol. 1, 136–43.

8 William Tudor to John Adams, July 31, 1775, in Taylor et al., *Papers of John Adams*, 3: 107.

9 *Journals of the Continental Congress 1774–1789*, ed. Worthington Chauncey Ford (Washington, DC: Government Printing Office, 1905), vol. V, 1776, June 5–October 8, 8: 442–43, 787–807. On 14 June 1776, the Congressional Committee on Spies was tasked to draft new Articles of War. The Committee consisted of future Presidents John Adams and Thomas Jefferson, future Supreme Court Justice James Wilson (Pennsylvania), future New York Chancellor Robert R. Livingston, and South Carolina lawyer Edward Rutledge. Chiefly the work of Adams and Jefferson, a draft, fiercely championed by Adams, was debated by Continental Congress on August 19 and September 19, then made into law on the 20th.

10 Jesse Lukens to John Shaw Jr., 13 September 1775, *The American Historical Record*, ed. Benson J. Lossing (Philadelphia: John E. Potter and Company, 1873), 1: 547. Tough, self-reliant Jess Lukens was a Virginia frontiersman who rushed to the 1775 siege of Boston with Daniel Morgan's fearsome Rifle Company.

11 Charles Patrick Neimeyer, *America Goes to War: A Social History of the Continental Army* (New York: New York University Press, 1997), 8–26. "What ultimately sustained the Army," wrote Neimeyer after examining state-by-state muster records in detail, "was the sheer volume of Americans who were *temporarily* willing, like Joseph Plumb Martin, to become 'scapegoats' so that others might stay at home."

12 Carolyn Cox, *A Proper Sense of Honor: Service and Sacrifice in George Washington's Army* (Chapel Hill: University of North Carolina Press, 2004), 18. "Given the prevailing racial and social attitudes of the time, it was more likely that the free white men who served were of such low status that they did not see themselves as socially superior to free blacks. In fact, if white soldiers were being drawn from the ranks of local troublemakers, British deserters, vagrants, or convicted criminals, the larger white society probably made little or no distinction either." Cox refers to a 1778 survey by Adjutant General Scammell showing that almost 10 percent of fit-for-duty Continentals were African American, "appearing in regiments from Massachusetts to North Carolina."

13 William F. Fratcher, "The History of the Judge Advocate General's Department, 1775–1941," *The Judge Advocate Journal* 1, no. 1 (15 June 1944): 5. Also see Fratcher's article of the same title in *Military Law Review* IV (1959), 90; and Maurer Maurer, "Military Justice Under General Washington," *Military Affairs* (Spring 1964): 9.

14 Edward F. Sherman, "The Civilianization of Military Justice," *Maine Law Review* 3 (1970): 4. An expert in complex matters of adversarial justice, longtime law professor Sherman was dean of Tulane University School of Law from 1996 to 2005.

15 Maurer, "Military Justice under General Washington," 11.

16 James C. Neagles, *Summer Soldiers: A Survey & Index of Revolutionary War Courts Martial* (Salt Lake City, UT: Ancestry Inc., 1986).

17 William Tudor to John Adams, Morristown, 23 March 1777, *Papers of John Adams*, V: 123–24.

18 United States Articles of War, *Journals of Continental Congress*, 20 September, 1776.

19 *The Army Lawyer: A History of the Judge Advocate General's Corps, 1775–1975* (Washington, DC: U.S. Government Printing Office, 1975), 4, 29.

20 "To John Adams from William Tudor, August 1775," Founders Online, National Archives, last modified April 12, 2018, http://founders.archives.gov/documents/Adams/06-03-02-0072.

21 Keith Marshall Jones III, "John Laurance and the Role of Military Justice at Valley Forge," *The Pennsylvania Magazine of History and Biography* CLXI, no. 1 (January 2017), 17. Of the 918 general courts-martial trials reported in General Washington's daily general orders between July 1775 and December 31, 1778, 78.5 percent of defendants were found guilty.

22 *War Department Collection of Revolutionary War Records*, Record Group 93, National Archives. Whatever transcripts of general courts-martial proceedings that Judge Laurance and his department forwarded to the war office are no longer to be found. Most records from the Revolutionary War in War Department custody were destroyed by fire on November 8, 1800. Much of what remained was lost during the War of 1812.

23 War Office Secy. Richard Peters to Colo. Laurance, 13 May 1777, *The Papers of John Laurance*, New York Historical Society, folder "1777."

24 McWhorter, *Biographical Sketches*, 9.

25 Harry M. Ward, *Major General Adam Stephen and the Cause of American Liberty* (Charlottesville: University of Virginia Press, 1989), 156–72.

26 "General Orders, 26 October 1777," *The Papers of George Washington*, Revolutionary War Series, vol. 12, 26 October 1777–25 December 1777, ed. Frank E. Grizzard Jr. and David R. Hoth (Charlottesville: University of Virginia Press, 2002), 1–2.

27 "General Orders, 20 November 1777," *The Papers of George Washington*, Revolutionary War Series, vol. 12, 26 October 1777–25 December 1777, 327–28.

28 Wayne K. Bodle and Jacqueline Thibaut, *Valley Forge Historical Research Report*, vol. III (Washington, DC: U.S. Department of the Interior, Valley Forge National Historic Park, 1982), 185–90. Bodle and Thibaut's exhaustive study does not place Laurance by name anywhere in the encampment. Since His Excellency's aides-de-camp lodged in upstairs bedrooms of Washington's rented headquarters and Laurance's Valley Forge presence is beyond dispute, one can only conclude that he wintered with the other aides, particularly since the Bake House (venue of military justice) was a short walk away.

29 *Report of the Valley Forge Park Commission* (Philadelphia: James Hogan Company, 1910), 11.

30 Ashbel Green, *The Life of Ashbel Green V.D.M* (New York: Robert Carter and Brothers, 1849), 109. Postwar Divinity graduate of College of New Jersey (later Princeton) and Presbyterian minister, Green was a wartime New Jersey schoolteacher who served sporadically as a militia private. Describing his first impression of Baron von Steuben, Green later wrote: "And never before or since, have I had such an impression of the ancient fabled god of war, as when I then looked on the Baron—he seemed to me to be a perfect personification of Mars."

31 Keith Marshall Jones III, "John Laurance and the Role of Military Justice at Valley Forge." The author introduces a fresh metric (general courts-martial per thousand fit-for-duty troops) to analyze trial incidence between July 1775 and December 1778. Prior to von Steuben's drill regimen commencing, Judge Advocate General Laurance oversaw 114 courts-martial trials in which 75.4 percent of defendants were pronounced "guilty."

32 Charles Patrick Neimeyer, *The Revolutionary War* (Westport, CT: The Greenwood Press, 2007), 9.

33 Charles Royster, *A Revolutionary People at War: The Continental Army and American Character 1775–1786* (Chapel Hill: University of North Carolina Press, 1979), 195. Royster argues that a growing sense of battlefield prowess in the wake of Germantown combined with word of victory at Saratoga to imbue Washington's Valley Forge troops with a sense of competence that with innate character carried them through the winter of privation without the mutinies that emerged in 1780.

34 George Weedon, *Valley Forge Orderly Book of General George Weedon* (Chicago: Arno Press, 1971), 173. Printed from the original manuscript in the library of the American Philosophical Society at Philadelphia.

35 *The Papers of John Marshall*, ed. Herbert A. Johnson (Chapel Hill: University of North Carolina Press, 1974), 1: 15n. Marshall was appointed deputy judge advocate on November 20, 1777 and apparently served as such in some capacity as late as August 1778.

36 John Laurance to George Washington, Camp Great Valley, February 5, 1778, *The Papers of George Washington, Revolutionary War Series*, vol. 13, 26 December 1777–28 February 1778, ed. Edward G. Lengel (Charlottesville: University of Virginia Press, 2003), 458–60.

37 "An account of the number of Persons who have taken the Oath of allegiance from the 30th of September 1777 to the 17th June 1778 . . ." *George Germain Papers*, University of Michigan: William L. Clements Library, vol. 7, item 46. Sir William Howe after entering Philadelphia on September 26, 1777, appointed former Continental Congressman Joseph Galloway as Philadelphia superintendent of police. Galloway, together with fellow Loyalist Enoch Story, prepared this document summarizing monthly influx of Continental Army deserters. Of the 1,134 men who registered with the British, 851 (75 percent) identified themselves as foreign nationals.

38 John Laurance to George Washington, Camp Great Valley, 5 February 1778, *The Papers of George Washington, Revolutionary War Series*, vol. 13, 26 December 1777–28 February 1778, ed. Edward G. Lengel (Charlottesville: University of Virginia Press, 2003), 458 60.

39 Ibid.

40 George Washington to the Committee of Congress with the Army, 29 January 1778, *Writings*, Fitzpatrick, 10, 402. Washington in August 1778 again pressed the case for higher lash limits, but to no avail. George Washington to Henry Laurens, President of Congress, 31 August 1778, *The Papers of George Washington*, Revolutionary War Series, vol. 16, *July 14–September 1778*, ed. David L. Hoth (Charlottesville: University of Virginia Press, 2006), 428 31.

41 Paul H. Smith, et al., ed., *Letters of Delegates to Congress, 1774–1789*, 26 vols. (Washington, DC: Library of Congress, 1976–2000), vol. 9, 105–107.

42 Jos. Reed to Col. Judge Advocate John Lawrance, Camp Valley Forge, February 18, 1778, John Laurance Papers, New York Historical Society, folder "1778."

43 "General Orders, Headquarters Valley Forge, 5 March 1778." *George Washington Papers at the Library of Congress*, Series 3g Varick Transcriptions, letterbook 3, 88 89.

44 George Washington to Colonel Israel Shreve, 6 April 1778, *The Papers of George Washington*, Revolutionary War Series, 14: 413. The commander-in-chief, likely with Laurance's advice, informed New Jersey Colonel Shreve of Congress's new 30-mile resolution and that Billingsport, where two civilian prisoners were captured, lay outside the limit. As late as May 1781, Judge Laurance weighed in to General Washington on court-martial protocol with civilians when the accused resided in Connecticut when apprehended (John Laurance to George Washington, 17 May 1781).

45 Rafael P. Thain, *Legislative History of General Staff of the U.S. Army . . . From 1775 to 1901* (Washington, DC: Government Printing Office, 1901), 124.

46 Timothy Pickering, York Town, 1 April 1778 to John Lawrance Judge Advocate General, Valley Forge. John Laurance Papers, New York Historical Society, folder "1777."

47 Receipt from Hannah McDougall dated Peekskill, 7 April 1777, John Laurance Papers, New York Historical Society, folder "1777."

48 Your affectionate kinsman John McDougall to John Lawrance Esq., 29 1778, John Laurance Papers, New York Historical Society, folder "1777."

49 Ibid.

50 "General Orders, 14 March 1778," *The Papers of George Washington*, Revolutionary War Series, 14: 171–73.

51 John Laurance "Aide-de-Camp" to Captain Nichols, 10 June 1778, John Laurance Papers, New York Historical Society, folder "1778."

52 Broadus Mitchell, *Alexander Hamilton*, 2 vols. (New York, 1957, 1962), 1: 109.

53 James Duane to Alexander Hamilton, 23 September 1779, *Papers of Alexander Hamilton*, ed. Syrett et al., I2: 176–78.

54 James Thomas Flexner, *George Washington in the American Revolution (1775–1783)* (Boston: Little, Brown and Company, 1967), 283–84, quoting John F. Watson, *Annals of Philadelphia*, 3 vols. (Philadelphia, 1907), II: 61.

55 Pierre-Etienne Du Ponceau, "Autobiography," *Pennsylvania Magazine of History and Biography* LXIII (1939): 209, 313.

56 Noel Fairchild Busch, *Winter Quarters, George Washington and the Continental Army at Valley Forge* (New York: Liveright, 1974), 67. Busch writes that "deaths from disease, which during the whole period in winter quarters accounted for some twenty-five hundred men, or twenty-five percent of the force that had arrived in camp at Christmastime." John B. Trussell Jr., *Epic on the Schuylkill: The Valley Forge Encampment* (Harrisburg, PA: Pennsylvania Historical and Museum Commission, 1992),13, estimates that "three thousand soldiers died of disease during the winter of 1777–1778."

57 Captain Abraham Riker ID: NY22242, "The Muster Roll Project," The Friends of Valley Forge Park, *valleyforgemusterroll.org.*

58 T. Pickering to Judge Advocate General John Lawrance, Valley Forge, 3 June 1778, John Laurance Papers, New York Historical Society, folder "1778."

Chapter Six

1 *Papers of Charles Lee*, 4 vols., ed. Sir Henry Bunbury (New York: Printed for the New York Historical Society, 1871), 2, 383. English-born Charles Lee served as Lt. Colonel in the Portuguese army against the Spanish, fought in Poland as aide to King Stanislaus II during the Russo-Turkish war, and in 1773 retired to Virginia. After Lexington and Concord, he offered his services, expecting to be named commander-in-chief. Captured in a New Jersey tavern, Washington's most senior major general spent December 1776–April 1778 in British hands, where he fraternized freely with redcoat officers, going so far as to present Howe a plan for winning the war.

2 *Papers of Charles Lee*, 2, 383–89. "If the Americans," proclaimed Lee to Congress on May 18, 1778, "are servilely kept to the European Plan, they will make an awkward figure, be laughed at as a bad army by their enemy, and defeated in every encounter which depends upon maneuvers."

3 Ibid., 470. See also *Writings of George Washington*, ed. John C. Fitzgerald (Washington, DC: 1931–1944), 12: 143.

4 *Proceedings of a GENERAL COURT MARTIAL held at Brunswick in the State of New-Jersey by order of HIS EXCELLENCY GEN. WASHINGTON for the Trial of Major-General Lee*, July 4th, 1778, Major-General Lord Stirling, President (New York: Privately printed, 1864), 4.

5 Thomas Fleming, "The 'Military Crimes' of Charles Lee," *American Heritage Magazine* 19, no. 3 (April 1968): 4.

6 *Journals of the Continental Congress*, 5 December 1778, 12: 1195. The motion of South Carolina delegate William Drayton to approve the verdict and sentence of General Lee's court-martial was approved and the resolution of Congress ordered to be published. When Lee's 12-month suspension ended, Maryland Congressman James Forbes introduced a resolution that Congress ". . . have no further occasion for his services." The measure was voted down. Nonetheless, Lee dashed off a letter ridiculing Congress for supposing he would ever consider serving. Whereupon, Forbes's reintroduced resolution was carried.

7 Sir Henry Clinton, *Facsimilies of Manuscripts in European Archives relating to America, 1713–1783*, 6 vols. (London: Issued to the subscribers, 1890), 5: 464–564. Clinton's original manuscript now resides in the William L. Clements Collection at the University of Michigan.

8 Major John Clark to Major General Charles Lee, 3 September 1778, Rosenbach Museum and Library, Philadelphia: AMS 785/15. Transcribed by Garry Stone and printed in *Pennsylvania Packet*, 10 December 1778.

9 Ibid.

10 Rule 701 (a) (6) of the *U.S. Government Manual for Courts-Martial* (1998). The Supreme Court in 1963 (*Brady v. Maryland* 373 U.S. 83) ruled that prosecutorial withholding of information that might negate guilt or lessen punishment in civil cases violated the Constitution's due process clause. The requirement was soon extended to discovery protocol in military tribunals as well upon written request by defense counsel.

11 *Journals of the Continental Congress*, 12 June 1778, 11: 603, National Archives. "In Congress, February 5, 1778, Resolved: that the Committee be directed to transmit the evidence by them collected to General Washington, and that he be authorized and directed to appoint a Court Martial for the trial of General Officers who were in the Northern Department when Ticonderoga and Mount Independence were evacuated, agreeable to the Articles of War." The Congressional Committee appointed to draw charges consisted of William Ellery (Rhode Island), James Smith (Pennsylvania), Eliphalet Dyer (Connecticut), and James Lovell (Massachusetts).

12 Extract from the Minutes In Congress, 5 February 1778, *PROCEEDINGS of a GENERAL COURT MARTIAL For the Trial of MAJOR GENERAL St. CLAIR, August 25, 1778, Major General Lincoln, President* (Philadelphia: Hall and Sellers, 1878), 5.

13 "To George Washington from John Laurance 24 August 1778," *Founders Online*, National Archives, last modified April 12, 2018, http://founders.archives.gov/documents/Washington/03-16-02-0400. Laurance asked the commander-in-chief to inform him whether the two "counsellers" named by Congress "have been desired to attend" the court-martial of Major General St. Clair.

14 "From George Washington to John Laurance, 24 August 1778," *Founders Online*, National Archives, last modified April 12, 2018, http://founders.archives.gov/documents/Washington/03-16-02-1401. This reply to Laurance's letter of the same day, in the hand of Washington aide Robert Harrison, advised that Mr. Paterson "declines attending" and "From Mr. Sergeant I have not heard."

15 "From George Washington to John Laurance, 24 August 1778," *Founders Online*, National Archives, last modified April 12, 2018, http://founders.archives.gov/documents/Washington/03-16-02-1401.

16 Warren H. Wilson, "Quaker Hill, A Sociological Study," PhD diss. (New York: Columbia University, 1907), 7.

17 *PROCEEDINGS of a GENERAL COURT MARTIAL Held at Major General Lincoln's Quarters near Quaker Hill in the State of New York By Order of His Excellency General Washington Commander in Chief of the Army of The United States of America For the Trial of MAJOR GENERAL SCHUYLER, October 1, 1778, Major General Lincoln, President* (Philadelphia: Hall and Sellers, 1878), 5–6.

18 Alexander McDougall to George Clinton, 5 November 1779. "Public Papers of George Clinton," State of New York, IV: 248-49.

19 John Laurance to Alexander Hamilton, April 28, 1779, *George Washington Papers* at the Library of Congress, 1741–1799: Series 4, General Correspondence. 1697-1799, 71 of 1125. Washington aide James McHenry wrote to Laurance on 27 April that the general was reluctant to grant Laurance family leave, hinging his "permission on your being perfectly persuaded that the gentleman who you mean to act in your room, is fully competent to the trial of Mr. Hooper, or in cases of the like intricacy which may occur during your absence from the army."

20 Ibid.

NOTES

21 George Washington to John Laurance, HQ. Middlebrook 16 May 1779, *George Washington Papers* at the Library of Congress 1741–1799: Series 4. General Correspondence, 805 of 1125.

22 Silas Deane to Simeon Deane, July 27, 1779, *Silas Deane Papers*, (New York: Published for the New York Historical Society, 1890), 4: 23.

23 Benedict Arnold to the Board of War, Philadelphia, March 19, 1779. *PROCEEDINGS of a GENERAL COURT MARTIAL of the Line... for the Trial of MAJOR GENERAL ARNOLD*, June 1, 1779 (Philadelphia: Francis Baily, 1780), vol. XII.

24 George Washington to John Laurance, Judge Advocate General, 2 December 1779, HQ Morris Town, John Laurance Papers, New York Historical Society, folder "1779."

25 Benedict Arnold to George Washington, 5 May 1779, *The Papers of George Washington*, Revolutionary War Series, vol. 8 April–31 May 1779, ed. Edward G. Lengel (Charlottesville: University of Virginia Press, 2010), 20: 327-29.

26 Willard Sterne Randall, *Benedict Arnold: Patriot and Traitor* (New York: Bodley Head, 1991), chap. 16. Sterne portrays in great detail the economic consequences of a collapsed Continental dollar on Philadelphia food shortages that led political clubs such as Joseph Reed's Constitutional Society to radicalize mobs of street thugs and local militia against wealthy loyalists, conservative merchants, and General Arnold personally. During July of 1779, after he had resigned the Philadelphia command, Arnold and some 30 others retreated inside James Wilson's home outnumbered more than seven to one by a militia-dominated mob. During the subsequent assault, half a dozen were killed and more than a dozen wounded as Arnold blazed away with his pistols from a third-story window.

27 James Flexner, *The Traitor and the Spy: Benedict Arnold and John Andre* (New York: Collier Books, 1962), 279-80.

28 *PROCEEDINGS of a GENERAL COURT MARTIAL OF THE LINE By Order of His Excellency GEORGE WASHINGTON, Esq, for the trial of MAJOR GENERAL ARNOLD, June 1, 1779*. Major General HOWE, President (Philadelphia: Francis Bailey, 1780), 54.

29 Ibid., 145.

30 Jos. Reed to John Laurance, Esq., Feb. 1780, John Laurance Papers, New York Historical Society, folder "1780."

31 Ibid.

32 A. Hamilton to James Duane, Great Egg Harbor Landing, New Jersey, 29 October 1779, Lloyd W. Smith Collection, Morristown Historic Park, Morristown, New Jersey. Laurance followed up his own visit to Continental Congress with a letter to Samuel Huntington, president, asking for an increase in pay dated 18 December 1779. Three days later it was read in Congress, which resolved that his pay be increased to that of full colonel.

33 *Journals of Continental Congress*, XV: 1397. On 21 December 1779, "A letter of 18, from J. Lawrance, judge advocate general was read"; whereupon, "Resolved, that until the further order of Congress, the subsistence of a judge advocate be the same as the present subsistence of a colonel..."

34 E. James Ferguson, *The Power of the Purse* (Chapel Hill: University of North Carolina Press, 1961), 29f. A 1785 statement prepared by Joseph Nourse for the Treasury Board lists $200,000,000 Continental dollars printed, to which he added $16,5000 issued by Congress in 1777 plus another $25,000,000 in 1778. Congress soon exchanged $15,300,000 for other bills, leaving $26,000,000 outstanding.

35 Eric Newman, *The Early Paper Money of America* (Iola, WI: Krause, 1990), 474. In December 1780, a hundred Continental dollars were required to equal one in hard specie. By May 1781 the exchange rate had soared to 280 Continental dollars. At this point, the dollar passed completely out of circulation.

36 Ibid., 50.

37 Ray Raphael, "America's Worst Winter Ever," *American History* 45, no. 1 (April 2010): 52-55. "For the only time in recorded history, all the saltwater inlets, harbors and sounds of the Atlantic coastal plain, from North Carolina northeastward, froze over and remained closed to navigation for a period of a month or more."

38 Joseph Plumb Martin, *Private Yankee Doodle*, ed. George F. Scheer (Boston: Little, Brown and Company, 1962), 171-72.

39 Richard Peters to John Laurance Judge Advocate General, Camp Morristown, 10 January, 1780, John Laurance Papers, New York Historical Society, folder "1780."

40 Benjamin Rush to John Adams, Philadelphia 19 October 1779. *Papers of John Adams*, vol. 8, doc. no. PJA08D158, Massachusetts Historical Society.

41 James Thomas Flexner, *Doctors on Horseback: Pioneers of American Medicine* (New York: Viking Press, 1937), 40–45, 75.

42 George Washington to John Laurance, Judge Advocate General, 2 December 1779, John Laurance Papers, New York Historical Society, folder "1779." Laurance on December 15 (letter not found) replied that the complaints against Dr. Shippen from Congress were not laid with "sufficient certainty and precision." Washington accordingly wrote directly to Dr. Shippen's accuser, Dr. John Morgan, on December 17 requesting more particularly defined charges if the court-martial was to proceed. "From George Washington to John Morgan, 17 December 1779," *Founders Online*, National Archives, last modified April 12, 2018, http://founders.archives.gov/documents/Washington/03-23-02-0487.

43 Whitfield J. Bell Jr., "The Court Martial of Dr. William Shippen Jr., 1780," *Journal of the History of Medicine and Allied Sciences* 19 (1964, July): 218–38.

44 *Journals of Continental Congress*, 18 August 1780, 17: 744–46, National Archives.

45 Wm. Shippen to John Laurance, 27 June 1780, John Laurance Papers, New York Historical Society, folder "1780."

46 James Kirby Martin, *Benedict Arnold, Revolutionary Hero: An American Warrior Reconsidered* (New York: New York University Press, 1997), 525n. As much as £20,000 was discussed with Sir Henry Clinton's go-betweens, but Arnold was paid a lump sum of £6,315 in compensation for lost property. Though a brigadier general in America, he was ranked as a cavalry colonel in the Regular British army with an annual salary of £450. In 1782, Peggy Arnold began receiving an annual pension of £500, with each of her children receiving £100/yr. In 1798 Benedict Arnold also gained title to some 13,400 acres in Canada.

47 George Washington to John Lawrence Esq. Judge Advocate, 26 September 1780, Robinson's House in the Highlands, *Proceedings of the Varick Court of Inquiry to Investigate the Implication of Colonel Varick in the Arnold Treason*, ed. Albert Bushnell Hart (Boston: The Bibliophile Society, 1907), 207–208.

48 *PROCEEDINGS of a BOARD of General Officers, Held by Order of His Excellency Gen. Washington, respecting Major JOHN ANDRE, Adjutant General of the British Army*. September 29, 1780 (Philadelphia: Francis Bailey in Market-Street, 1780), 6. This document was printed by Congress based on Judge Laurance's abstract of the proceedings.

49 Ibid.

50 Ibid., 10.

51 Robert Amory Jr., *John Andre: Case Officer* (Central Intelligence Agency, Center for the Study of Intelligence), Studies Archives Indexes, vol. 5, no. 3, approved for release 22 September 1993. https://www.cia.gov/library/center-for-the-study-of-intelligence.

52 Ibid., 13.

53 James Thatcher, *The American Revolution: From the Commencement to the Disbanding of the American Army Given in the Form of a Daily Journal, with the Exact Dates of all the Important Events* (New York: American Subscription Publishing House, 1860), 227.

54 Richard J. Koke, *Accomplice in Treason: Joshua Hett Smith and the Arnold Conspiracy* (New York: New York Historical Society, 1973), 64: 105–11.

55 Joshua Hett Smith, *Authentic Narrative of the Causes which led to the Death of Major Andre, Adjutant General of His Majesty's Forces in North America* (London: Printed for Matthews and Leigh, 1808), 129.

56 "The Trial of Joshua H. Smith," *American State Trials, A Collection of the Important and Interesting Criminal Trials which have taken place in the United States of America*, ed. John Davison Lawson (St. Louis, MO: F.H. Thomas Law Book Co., 1916) VI: 489.

57 Ibid.

58 Ibid., VI: 512.

59 Charles Worthen Spencer, "John Laurance," *Dictionary of American Biography*, edited by Dumas Malone (New York: Charles Scribner's Sons, 1933), vol. XI, 32. Spencer, Professor of History at Colgate University, neglected to specify source of the quote "humanity and civility" he used to describe Judge Laurance's preparation and performance in the André trial. Spencer most likely based his observation on Winthrop Sargent's *The Life and Career of Major John André* (New York: William Abbat, 1902 reprint of the 1865 original). Of Laurance, Sargent (p. 392) wrote that: "He was a native of Cornwall in England, and by

admission of all a man of humanity and sensibility. His age was about André's own, and his whole conduct evinced his sympathy with the prisoner, whom he warned of the peril in which he stood, and exhorted to preserve his presence of mind; to be cool and deliberate in his answers; and to except freely to any interrogatory that he thought ambiguous." Sargent obtained his information from historian Jared Sparks, who claimed it came directly from Lafayette who sat on the actual trial board of officers.

60 McWhorter, *Biographical Sketches*, 15.
61 Ibid., 16.

Chapter Seven

1 Benedict Arnold, *The Present State of the American Rebel Army, Navy, and Finances. Transmitted to the British Government in October, 1780*, ed. Paul Leicester Ford (Brooklyn, NY: Historical Printing Club, 1891), 9–10. Arnold's comprehensive account of American forces came from a council of general officers held on October 6, 1780, in which Washington stated that his present operating force amounted to 10,400 plus "One Battalion of Continl. Troops at Rhode Island 500" and "Two State Regiments of Continl. Militia at North Castle 500" for a total of 11,400 effectives. "About one half of these Troops are Militia," wrote Arnold to British Lord George Germain, "whose time of service expires on the first day of January next, which will reduce the Army engaged for the war to less than Six Thousand men, exclusive of the Troops in the Southern Department under General Gates."

2 Arnold, *The Present State of the American Rebel Army, Navy, and Finances. Transmitted to the British Government in October, 1780*, 9–11.

3 *The Writings of George Washington from the Original Manuscript Sources 1745–1799*, ed. John C. Fitzpatrick (Washington, DC: U.S. Government Printing Office, 1931–1944), 20: 357, 458, 475.

4 John Laurance to George Washington, 20 February 1781, Peekskill, John Laurance Papers, New York Historical Society, folder "1781."

5 Broadus Mitchell, *Alexander Hamilton, Youth to Maturity 1755–1788* (New York: Macmillan Co., 1957), 199.

6 *Journals of the Continental Congress*, 9 November 1780, National Archives, 18: 1037.

7 Rafael P. Thain, *Legislative History of the General Staff of the Army of the United States from 1775 to 1901* (Washington, DC: Government Printing Office, 1901), 126. Judge Laurance also lobbied Congress on his own financial behalf, "as my future Prosperity depends on their Decision." John Laurance to Samuel Huntington [President of Congress], Philadelphia, 10 November 1780, John Laurance Papers, New York Historical Society, folder "1780."

8 John Laurance to George Washington, 20 February 1781, Peekskill, John Laurance Papers, New York Historical Society, folder "1781."

9 Major General William Heath to George Washington, West Point, 7 April 1781. *The Writings of George Washington from the Original Manuscript*, Fitzpatrick, December 22, 1780–April 26, 1781, 21: 429n.

10 Ibid.

11 "General Orders, 2 October 1781," *George Washington Papers at the Library of Congress*, Varick, letterbook 6, 13.

12 "General Orders, 11 October 1781, *George Washington Papers at the Library of Congress*, Varick, letterbook 6, 22.

13 "General Orders, 3 November 1781," *The Writings of George Washington from the Original Manuscript Sources 1745–1799*, ed. John C. Fitzpatrick (Washington, DC: U.S. Government Printing Office, 1931–1944), August 16, 1781–February 15, 1782, 23: 320–23.

14 "Testimony of John Laurance at the Court Martial of Major General Alexander McDougall," Alexander McDougall Papers, New York Historical Society, microfilm reel #4, 1782.

15 *Memoirs of Major General William Heath By Himself*, ed. Wm. Abbatt (New York: William Abbatt, 1901), 1. Heath described himself as "corpulent and bald-headed" on the first page of his own memoir!

16 "Captain Sumner's deposition, January 22, 1782 at the Court Martial of General Alexander McDougall," Papers of Alexander McDougall, New York Historical Society, microfilm reel #4, 1782.

17 Ibid.

18 Colonel Putnam's narrative, January 16, 1782 at the Court Martial of Major General Alexander McDougall, Papers of Alexander McDougall, New York Historical Society, microfilm reel #4, 1782.

19 Nathan Goodale to Alexander McDougall, January 23, 1782, Papers of Alexander McDougall, New York Historical Society, microfilm reel #4, 1782.

20 General William Heath to Alexander McDougall, January 18, 1782, Papers of Alexander McDougall, New York Historical Society, microfilm reel #4, 1782.

21 Champagne, *Alexander McDougall and the American Revolution in New York*, 178.

22 "General Orders, 28 August 1782," http://rotunda.upress.virginia.edu/founders.defaulst.xgy.

23 John Laurance to George Washington, Newburgh, 16 May 1782, John Laurance Papers, New York Historical Society, folder "1782."

24 George Washington to Benjamin Lincoln, 29 May 1782, George Washington Papers at the Library of Congress, *Writings from Original Manuscript Sources, 1745–1799*, ed. Fitzpatrick, Varick Transcripts Series 3a, letterbook 6, 251.

25 State of New York to John Laurance, Esq., 31 December 1781, Alexander McDougall Papers, New York Historical Society, microfilm reel #3.

26 General Orders 24 January 1782, *The Writings of George Washington*, ed. Fitzpatrick, August 16, 1781–February 15, 1782, 23: 463.

27 Alexander Hamilton to John Laurance, 12 December 1782, *The Papers of Alexander Hamilton*, 1782–1786, ed. Syrett (New York: Columbia University Press, 1962), 3: 211–13.

28 Franklin Benjamin Hough, "Members of the 6th New York State Legislature," *The New York Civil List* (Albany, NY: Weed, Parsons & Company, 1858), 160.

29 Alexander Hamilton to Robert Morris, Albany, 13 August 1782, *The Papers of Alexander Hamilton*, Syrett, 3: 132–43.

30 Robert Morris to Alexander Hamilton, 28 August 1782, *The Papers of Alexander Hamilton*, Syrett, 3: 152–56. Laurance declined Morris's offer as revenue commissioner for either Connecticut or Rhode Island (Hamilton to Morris, 28 September 1782, *The Papers of Alexander Hamilton*, Syrett, 3: 169–71).

31 Alexander Hamilton to Robert Morris, 12 September 1782, *The Papers of Alexander Hamilton*, Syrett, 3: 169–71. "I am flattered," Hamilton wrote, "by the attention you have Obligingly paid to my recommendations of Col. Malcolm and Lawrence. Those Gentlemen are now here: they make you the warmest acknowledgements for your offer, but decline leaving the state; which indeed is not compatible with the present prospects of either of them."

32 Elkins and McKitrick, *Age of Federalism: 1788–1800*, 22–23. Referring to George Washington's army, Elkins and McKitrick wrote: "It was here, and in the experience of those most associated with this side of the endeavor, that a nationalistic vision could exert its greatest attractions."

33 John Marshall to Justice Joseph Story, 30 December 1827, *An Autobiographical Sketch by John Marshall*, ed. John Stokes Adams (Ann Arbor: University of Michigan Press, 1937), 9–10.

34 Merrill Jensen, "The Ideal of National Government during the Revolution," *Political Science Quarterly* 53 (1943): 366–72.

35 James Ferguson, *Power of the Purse* (Chapel Hill: University of North Carolina Press, 1961), 112–115; E. Wayne Carp, *To Starve the Army at Pleasure: Continental Army Administration and American Political Culture 1775–1783* (Chapel Hill: University of North Carolina Press, 1984), 200–202. Longstanding members of Congress with a Continental perspective included John Adams of Massachusetts, New Yorker James Duane, and South Carolinian John Mathews. They were joined in 1780 by James Madison and Joseph Jones of Virginia, Oliver Wolcott of Connecticut, General John Sullivan of New Hampshire, Generals Ezekiel Cornell and James Varnum of Rhode Island, Daniel Carroll and John Hanson of Maryland, and Philip Schuyler and Egbert Benson of New York.

36 Edward Countyman, *A People in Revolution: The American Revolution and Political Society in New York 1760–1790* (Baltimore: Johns Hopkins University, 1981), chap. 9, "The Rise of Conservative Nationalism." Countryman argues persuasively that influential members of the New York manor-ship gentry migrated to Continental roles in 1780–82 in the wake of populist governor George Clinton's middling, yeoman class control of the state political agenda. Benson, Countryman suggests, was intentionally left behind as state attorney general to oversee property-class interests.

37 *Laws of the Legislature of the State of New York in Force Against the Loyalists and Affecting the Trade of Great Britain*, 8 vols. (London: 1786). Between 1778 and 1785 the New York legislature promulgated 24 Tory punishment measures and 8 anti-Tory trade laws aggregating to more than 150 pages of law.

38 "Debt Act of July 12, 1782," 1782 N.Y. Laws, chap. 1, 499.

39 David Colden to H. M. Colden, 15 September 1783, "Letter of David Colden, Loyalist 1783," *JSTOR Early Journal Content*, document #81, http://jstor.org/individuals/early journal-content.

40 Gilbert Colden Willett to John Lawrance, 21 November 1782, John Laurance Papers, New York Historical Society, folder "1782."

41 *New York Laws*, 3, session 1779, 25.

42 *John Murray Land Papers 1734–1828*, New York Historical Society. Among the buyers of Susannah and Gilbert Colden Willett's properties were Connecticut militia major general James Wadsworth and Westchester County landowner William Ogden.

43 Unaddressed letter attributed to John Laurance from Alexander Hamilton (found in the Alexander McDougall Papers), Philadelphia, December 12, 1782, in possession of the New York Historical Society.

44 Headquarters, Newburgh 15th of March 1783, "To the General, field, & other Officers Assembled at the New Building pursuant to the General Order of the 11th Instant March." Washington addressed his assembled officers (who had met to discuss a mutiny petition due to Congress's failure to provide promised pensions) with a nine-page speech that, while sympathetic, denounced their actions.

45 *Journals of the Continental Congress*, 14 April 1783, IV: 178–79.

46 Francis J. Sypher, *New York State Chapter of the Society of the Cincinnati: Biographies of Original Members and other Continental Officers* (Fishkill, NY: New York State Society of the Cincinnati, 2004).

47 Heitman, *Historical Register of the Officers of the Continental Army*, 463–66.

48 Ebenezer Huntington to Andrew Huntington, 7 July 1780, "Letters of Ebenezer Huntington 1774–1781," *American Historical Review* (5 February, 1900), 725–26.

49 John Laurance to James Pierce Paymaster General, December 13, 1783, John Laurance Papers, New York Historical Society, folder "1783."

50 Ibid.

51 "United States in Account with John Laurance, late Judge Advocate General," settled in pursuance of an Act of the First Session of the Second Congress of the United States, 27 March 1792, Joseph Howell, auditor to the Treasury, National Archives and Records Administration, Manuscript File RG93.

52 Joseph Nourse, Registrar to Hon. Richard Rush, Secretary of the Treasury, 16 March 1826. *House Documents, Otherwise Published as Executive Documents, 19th Congress, 1st Session* (Washington: Gales & Seaton, 1826), Document #135, 155–56. See also W. T. R Saffell, *Records of the Revolutionary War, with a list of the officers of the Continental Army who acquired the right to half-pay, commutation and lands* (New York: Pudney & Russell Publishers, 1858). "These certificates, wrote Saffell, "at once reached a depreciation of eight dollars for one in specie; and from the close of the war in 1783 to the organization of the government under the new Constitution in 1787, no man could tell how or when those certificates were to be redeemed." Not until 1790 and 1791 were they funded in a stock bearing 3 percent interest instead of the promised 6 percent.

53 Saffell, *Records of the Revolutionary War, with a list of the officers of the Continental Army who acquired the right to half-pay, commutation and lands*, 425.

54 Harry B. Yoshbe, *The Disposition of Loyalist Estates in the Southern District of the State of New York* (New York: Columbia University Press, 1939), 22. "*An Act of October 4, 1780*," states that certificates issued to pay New York troops defending the United States would in lieu of currency be accepted for the purchase of confiscated estates as the same value as specie.

55 E. Wilder Spaulding, *New York During the Critical Period 1783–1789* (New York: Columbia University Press, 1932), 8. In addition to John Laurance, Wilder's list of 14 prominent New York lawyers at war's end includes Jay, Benson, Duane, Hamilton, Varick, L'Hommedieu, Richard Harrison, John Hobart, Josiah Ogden Hoffman, and Chancellor Livingston. Also see Chancellor James Kent, "Address to the Law Association of the City of New York," quoted in Charles Warren's *A History of the American Bar* (Boston: Little, Brown & Co., 1911), 296. Not mentioned by Kent, but added by Warren were Gouveneur Morris, Edward Livingston, and Abraham Van Vechten.

56 Alexander Hamilton to Major General Nathanael Greene, 10 June 1783, *Papers of Alexander Hamilton*, Syrett, 3: 376.

57 Otto Zeichner, "The Loyalist Problem in New York After the Revolution," *New York History* 21, no. 3 (July, 1940), 286. "In March 1778 they [Tories] were disenfranchised," wrote Zeichner. In October, 1779, Tory lawyers were excluded from the practice of their profession. See also *Laws of the Legislature of New York in Force Against the Loyalists* (London: 1786), 9–30.

Chapter Eight

1 James Riker, *Evacuation Day 1783, It's Many Stirring Events with Recollections of Capt. John Van Arsdale* (New York: Printed for the author, 1883), 3.

2 *Laws of the State of New York Passed at the Sessions of the Legislature in the Years 1777–1801* (Albany, NY: Weed Parsons & Co., 1886), chap. 28, 192–93. On October 23, 1779, the New York Assembly resolved an "Act to Provide for the Temporary Government of the Southern Parts of the State whenever the Enemy shall abandon or be disposed of the same." The Act went on to establish a council composed of the state assemblymen from the five counties in New York's Southern District (New York, Westchester, Queens, Kings, & Suffolk).

3 Colonel Timothy Pickering to John Laurance Esq., Attorney at Law, 21 January, 1783, John Laurance Papers, New York Historical Society, folder "1783." Pickering sent Laurance a power of attorney and requested he prepare a defense against a private suit by securities broker Melancton L. Wolsey against him to obtain payment on Continental certificates signed in his official capacity as quartermaster general. Rather than wait for the Continental Congress to intercede with a resolution insulating Continental officials from private suits, Laurance helped persuade the New York General Assembly to follow the example of Pennsylvania and New Jersey with preemptive legislation. On April 2, the State of New York passed legislation protecting public officers from individual lawsuits regarding public debts. See *The Life of Timothy Pickering* by his son Octavius Pickering (Boston: Little, Brown and Co., 1867), I: 388–89.

4 Leon Bleeker to Colonel John Laurance at Robinson House, January 2, 1783. John Laurance Papers at the New York Historical Society, folder "1783."

5 Along with 54 others, the 600-acre grants of Privates Andrew Rose, Henry Ennis, and Richard Morrison were acquired for £6, 8 shillings apiece between October 11, 1783, and January 6, 1784. List of Deeds deposited in the New York Clerk's Office by "Act of the New York General Assembly, December 28, 1792."

6 Letters to Richard Varick from John Laurance, dated 26 August 1782 and 19 June 1783, in the Richard Varick papers, Series I: Correspondence 1775–1830, at New York Historical Society. As attorney for Daniel Delavan, Laurance represented his client in bail arbitration with Varick as the opposing counsel. Delavan (1757–1835) was a captain of New York light horse during the War for Independence.

7 "Uncle R. Lawrence to my dear nephew John Lawrence," Falmouth 4 April 1783, John Lawrence papers at New York Historical Society. "I recommend my son Richard to your attention," wrote Uncle Richard, adding, "Should any of your acquaintance have any Business to transact here, I shall be happy to do it for them . . ." Young Richard's name appears as witness to the October 11, 1783, sale of war veteran Andrew Rose's 600-acre land grant to Laurance for 6 pounds, 8 shillings on October 11, 1783. He also witnessed Private Henry Ennis's land grant sale to Alexander McDougall on January 6, 1784, Albany County Clerk's Office, Deeds, 1630–present. www.albanycounty.com/Government/CountyClerk/Services/ClerkRecords.aspx.

8 Riker, *Evacuation Day 1783*.

9 Jennifer Steenshorne, "Evacuation Day 1783 and Later," *New York Archives Magazine* 10, no. 2 (Fall 2010), 10–13. See also W. Harrison Bayles, *Old Taverns of New York* (New York: Frank Allaben Genealogical Company, 1915), 307–50.

10 Benjamin Talmadge, *Memoir*, ed. Henry Phelps Johnston (New York: Gilliss Press, 1904), 95.

11 Talmadge, *Memoir*, 95.

12 Colonel Talmadge's personal *Memoirs* only names Knox. Citing von Steuben's letters, Washington biographer Douglas Southall Freeman (*George Washington: A Biography* [New York: Scribner and Sons, 1948], V: 466-68) places the Baron, McDougall, General James Clinton, and Colonel Henry Jackson in the Long Room. Aide Tench Tilghman places himself there in his *Memoirs* (Library of Congress), 42.

Alonzo Chappel's famous 1866 oil painting of the scene (Thomas Phillibrown's engraving of which graces Fraunces Tavern Museum) is pure imagination.

13 Terry Golway, *Washington's General: Nathanael Greene and the Triumph of the American Revolution* (New York: Henry Holt, 2006), 306. Greene bypassed New York and went directly home to Rhode Island when the army was dispersed.

14 Chernow, *Alexander Hamilton*, 185. "There is no proof," wrote Chernow, "that Hamilton attended the historic valedictory, in spite of his being at Washington's side for four years of war."

15 Robert K. Wright Jr., *The Continental Army* (Washington, DC: Center of Military History, United States Army, 1983), 180. Because all enlistments were set to expire in June 1784 and Congress lacked funds to pay them off, General Washington determined not to put the men through another winter. On November 2, 1783, he ordered all but 500 infantry and 100 artillerymen discharged two weeks before Evacuation Day. The 500 infantry regrouped as a single Continental regiment under Colonel Henry Jackson of Massachusetts, and the single artillery company were all New Yorkers under John Doughty.

16 Edwin G. Burrows, *Forgotten Patriots: The Untold Story of American Prisoners During the Revolutionary War*, (New York: Basic Books, 2008); Elizabeth Giddens, "Memorials and the Forgotten," *The New York Times*, September 2, 2011. Also see the dedication plaque at the base of the Prison Ship Martyrs' Monument in Fort Greene Park in the New York City borough of Brooklyn.

17 Henry P. Johnston, "New York After the Revolution, 1783-1789," *Magazine of American History* XXIX, no. 4 (April 1893), 308.

18 Robert Livingston to Alexander Hamilton, 30 August 1783, *Papers of Alexander Hamilton*, Syrett, 3: 434–35.

19 Johnston, "New York After the Revolution, 1783–1789," 320.

20 Anthony Gronowicz, "Political 'Radicalism' in New York City's Revolutionary and Constitutional Eras," *New York in the Age of the Constitution, 1775–1800*, ed. Paul A. Gilje and William Pencak (Plainsboro, NJ: Associated University Presses, 1992), 104.

21 *New York Gazetteer and Country Journal, January 26, 1784*, Collections of the New York Historical Society for the year 1870, Extracts from various Newspapers 1730-1785 (New York: Printed for the Society, 1871), 320–22. Formal minutes of the Temporary Council for the Southern District of New York are no longer to be found; this newspaper advertisement is public record of the Council's seizure of church assets.

22 Morgan Dix, *A History of the Parish of Trinity Church in the City of New York* (New York: G.P. Putnam and Sons, 1901), Part Two, 2–12.

23 Dix, *A History of the Parish of Trinity Church*, 17.

24 "Minutes of the Corporation of Trinity Church," Trinity Wall Street Archives, vol. I, 461–88. Laurance was appointed vestryman on 26 July 1784 and attended vestry meetings as late as 31 October 1786. On 17 November 1784 he was appointed along with fellow vestrymen Stevens and Farquahr to "register files of the Corporation" with city and state authorities.

25 *Journal of the Assembly of the State of New York*, for 1785, 26, 41, 87.

26 Robert A. McCaughey, *Stand, Columbia: A History of Columbia University* (New York: Columbia University Press, 2003), 51–52. For more on the proposed state university system, see Francis P. Hough, *Historical and Statistical Record of the University of the State of New York, 1784–1884* (Albany, NY: Weed, Parsons, and Company 1885).

27 *Laws of the State of New York passed at the Sessions of the Legislature 1785, 1786, 1787, and 1788 Inclusive* (Albany, NY: Weed, Parsons, and Company, 1886), 2: 30–31. Together with friends Hamilton and John Jay, John Laurance was named one of 28 trustees of Columbia College by an Act of the New York Legislature passed November 24, 1784.

28 Scott Reynolds Nelson, *A Nation of Deadbeats: An Uncommon History of America's Financial Disasters* (New York: Random House, 2012), 3.

29 Robert Francis Jones, *The King of the Alley: William Duer—Politician, Entrepreneur, and Speculator 1768–1799* (Philadelphia: American Philosophical Society, 1992), 95.

30 Frederick Trevor Hill, *The Story of a Street: A Narrative History of Wall Street from 1644 to 1908* (New York: Harper & Brothers, 1908), 124. Also I. N. Phelps Stokes, *The Iconography of Manhattan Island 1498–1909* (New York: Robert H. Dodd, 1926), 5: 320–31.

31 John Adams to Abigail Adams, June 10, 1765, *Adams Family Papers*, 3: 20–21.

32 Goebel, *The Law Practice of Alexander Hamilton*, I: 218f. Elizabeth Waldron and her family engaged Laurance to recover damages under the Trespass Act from Michael Chatterton (£180), Joseph Bates (£250), John Dyckman (£1,000), George Mason (£1,000), John DeLancey (£1,000), Jacob Horsa executor for Cornelius Corzine (£1,000), Laurence Kortright (£1,500), Larance Benson (£2,000), Adolph Benson (£2,500), and John Hooper (£6,000), Mayor's Court Box 1784, New York Hall of Records. All dated February 10, 1784, these capiases are on printed forms then obtained from the city recorder.

33 *New York Constitution*, 1777, Article XXXII.

34 Charles Warren, *History of the Harvard Law School and of Early Legal Conditions in America* (New York: Lewis Publishing Co., 1908), I: 96.

35 David Colden to Henrietta Marie Colden, 15 September 1783, "Letter of David Colden, Loyalist, 1783," *The American Historical Review* 25, no. 1 (October 1919), 81. David Colden (Lt. Governor Cadwallader Colden's son) advised his Loyalist niece Mrs. Henrietta Maria Colden, whose maiden name was Bethune, that he had delivered her letter regarding potential property confiscation to John Laurance. "I am informed Mr. Laurance supports a favorable character — is pushing himself forward, and bids fair to rise in his profession. He will probably be a useful man to you."

36 Thomas E. V. Smith, *The City of New York in the Year of Washington's Inauguration 1789* (New York: Anson D. F. Randolph & Co., 1889), 8.

37 John Laurance, 10 January 1785, "New York Mayor's Court: Elizabeth Waldron, Peter Waldron, John Waldron v. Estate of Cornelius Corzine, deceased," OCLC #71015007, The Library of Congress, Washington, DC.

38 Richard B Morris, "The Salzer Collection of Mayor's Court Papers," *Columbia Library Columns*, vol. 7, no. 3 (New York: Friends of the Columbia Libraries, 1958), 17. Morris detailed 2,500 chestnut trees, 3,000 hickories, 2,200 white oaks 2,100 black oaks, 1,500 red cedars, 1,800 maples, 1,900 ash, 2,000 birch, and 5,000 apple trees.

39 John Lawrence, attorney for plaintiff in *Helena Brasher et al v. Daniel Ebbets*, New York Mayors Court, 1784, Trespass Act records, Municipal Archives and Records Center, New York City.

40 Ibid.

41 H. P. Nash, "Origins of the Grand Lodge of New York," *Transactions of the American Lodge of Research* 3, no. 2, 291. For details on Lodge Master William Walter, see *Collections of the New Brunswick Historical Society*, vol. 7 (St. John, N.B: The Telegraph Publishing Company, 1907), 270–93. William W. Walters, former rector of Trinity Church in Boston, fled with the British army to New York in 1776 to become chaplain in the Third Battalion of the Loyalist DeLancey's Brigade. He accompanied fellow Loyalists to Shelburne, British Columbia in September of 1783 to become rector of the local Trinity Church. In late 1790, he returned with his family to Boston to accept charge of Christ Church.

42 Mark A. Tabbert, *American Freemasons: Three Centuries of Building Communities* (New York: New York University Press, 2005), 41. American Union Lodge (known as "Washington's Lodge"), writes Tabbert, was "Organized within a Connecticut Regiment during the siege of Boston and chartered by a Massachusetts provincial grand lodge, the travelling lodge operated throughout the war . . . By war's end, hundreds of officers had become Masons in the ten or more regimental lodges, and at least 33 of the Continental Army's 78 generals were Freemasons."

43 Lang, *History of St. John's Lodge No. 1, 1757–1907* [New York], 39.

44 Ibid., 42. "St. John's No. 2," writes Lang," was reorganized as No. 1 under the Warrant dated June 9th 1789." The Master was Jacob Morton, John Laurance having progressed to "Past Master" status.

45 Peter Ross, *A Standard History of Freemasonry in the State of New York* (New York and Chicago: The Lewis Publishing Co., 1899), V: 143. On March 3, 1784, John Laurance (Lawrence) was identified as Master of St. John's No. 1. On June 25, 1801, Laurance was addressed as Past Master when deputed by outgoing Grand Master Robert R. Livingston to install successor Jacob Morton.

46 Werner Hartmann, "History of St. John's Lodge No. 1," *www.stjohns1.org/portal/lodge_history*. "At that same commission of the Grand Lodge, John Lawrence, Master of St. John's, and James Giles, Senior Warden, were appointed joint Grand Secretaries, thus demonstrating the full acceptance of the Lodge by the Grand Lodge."

47 "Freemasonry in America," *The Illustrated American* III, no. 23 (New York: for the week ending August 2, 1890), 107. The article goes on to describe the anti-Masonic agitation that by 1830 decimated New York membership to "75 lodges and 3000 members," and the subsequent recovery by 1860 to "432 lodges and 30,000 members."

48 Arthur Everett Peterson, *Minutes of the New York City Common Council*, 10 June 1784 (City of New York: 1917), vol. 1 (1784–1831), 10.

49 Alexander Hamilton, John Laurance, Morgan Lewis, and Richard Varick to Thomas Mifflin, President of Congress December 10, 1783, *The Papers of Alexander Hamilton*, Syrett, 3: 478–79. Mifflin replied to their joint letter on December 17th promising, " I will transmit to you an authenticated copy of the Ratification the moment Congress shall put it into my power."

50 "Treaties in Force, A List of Treaties and Other International Agreements of the United States in Force on January 1, 2016" (United States Department of State, United States Government), 463.

51 John W. Johnson, ed., *Historic U.S. Court Cases: An Encyclopedia* (New York: Routledge, 2001). *Rutgers v. Waddington* is listed as one of the six most significant United States court cases regarding separation of power. Most other legal anthologies echo Columbia Law School Professor Julius Goebel's 1964 assertion that the case was a "marker on the long road that led to the ultimate formation of judicial review."

52 Goebel, *The Law Practice of Alexander Hamilton*, I: 301. Also, *Selected Cases of the Mayor's Court of New York City 1674–1784*, ed. Richard B. Morris (Washington, DC: The American Historical Association, 1935), 302.

53 Goebel, *The Law Practice of Alexander Hamilton*, 1: 220–75, "People of the State of New York v. Nicholas Hoffman," NY Supreme Court, 1783–1784 (Confiscation Act); "Lewis DuBoys v. James DesBrosses Acting Exec of Elias DesBrosses," NY Mayors Court, 1784–1786 (Citation Act); "William Elsworth v. Rebecca Aspinwall Executrix of John Aspinwall," NY Mayor's Court, 1784–1785 (Citation Act).

54 Alexander Hamilton to Robert Livingston, 13 August 1783, Goebel, *The Law Practice of Alexander Hamilton*, 2: 216.

55 Sir William Blackstone, *Commentaries on the Laws of England* (London: Routledge-Cavendish, 2001), ed. Wayne Morrison, 4 vols., I: 91.

56 *Rutgers v. Waddington*, Opinion, Mayor's Court Proceedings, 27 August 1784 (New York: Printed by Samuel Loudon, 1784), New York Hall of Records.

57 Ibid.

58 James Kent, *Address to the Law Association of the City of New York* (1836), reprinted in part in Warren, *A History of the American Bar* (1913), 295– 97. Kent, who at the time clerked in Attorney General Benson's office, recalled the speaking manner of all the participating attorneys.

59 James Hughes to James Kent, March 20, 1784, James Kent Papers, Manuscript Section, Library of Congress.

60 Kent, *Address to the Law Association of the City of New York*, footnote #37. Kent's description here of Laurance and Hamilton is from another Trespass Act confrontation between the two. The contrast between a genteel litigator (Laurance) and passionate Constitutional lawyer (Hamilton) was matter of personal character, not a single courtroom appearance.

61 Goebel, *The Law Practice of Alexander Hamilton*, 1: 312.

62 Ibid., I: 415.

63 George Washington to James Duane, April 10, 1785, James Duane Papers, New York Historical Society.

64 *New York Assembly Journal*, 8th Assembly Meeting (Oct 4–Nov 29, 1784), 34.

65 Hough, "Members of the General Assembly, 8th Session," *The New York Civil List*, 100. Together with Aaron Burr, William Denning, Daniel Dunscomb, William Goforth, Peter Livingson, Thomas Randall, Henry Remsen, and Comfort Sands, John Laurance was elected on April 29, 1784, as New York County representatives to the State General Assembly. The body first met at the Old City Hall on October 12, then from January 27–April 27, 1785, at the Royal Exchange, both but a few blocks from Laurance's Wall Street residence.

66 Arthur Everett Peterson, *Minutes of the New York City Common Council,* 6 January 1785 (New York: City of New York, 1917), I: 1784–1831.

67 Alexander Hamilton to John Laurance, undated. John Laurance Papers, New York Historical Society, folder "1785." This incompletely dated note is one of several from Hamilton asking to borrow from Laurance.

68 Alexander Hamilton to John B. Church, March 10, 1784, Henry W. Domett, *A History of the Bank of New York, 1784–1884* (New York: G. P. Putnam's Sons, 1884), 8–9.

69 Domett, *A History of the Bank of New York, 1784–1884*, 9.

70 Robert E Wright, *Origins of Commercial Banking in American 1750–1800* (New York: Rowman & Littlefield Publishers, 2001), 91.

71 Jacob E. Cooke, *Alexander Hamilton* (New York: Charles Scribner's Sons, 1982), 45.

72 Alexander Hamilton to John Church, 10 March 1784, Domet, *A History of the Bank of New York*, 10. "I shall hold it [the bank directorship] til Wadsworth and you come out," wrote Hamilton, "and if you choose to become parties to the bank, I shall make a vacancy for one of you." Wadsworth indeed came aboard to become the bank's second president after Alexander McDougall stepped down.

73 Laurance's investment was richly rewarded. The bank paid a 3 percent cash dividend semi-annually after 1785, which was increased to 3.5 percent in November 1788 (7 percent per annum). By 1791, John's shares were earning 7 percent every *six months,* or $70 per share annually. Domett, *A History of the Bank of New York, 1784–1884* (New York: G. P. Putnam's Sons, 1884), 29: 130.

74 Robert Troup to John Laurance, receipts dated 30 June 1784, and 2 July 1784. Robert Troup received of John Laurance "monies on account of locations made, and places sold—in company." John Laurance Papers, New York Historical Society, folder "1784." Several similar transactions took place with Hamilton.

75 "From Alexander Hamilton to Richard Varick, 23 July 1784," *Founders Online*, National Archives, last modified April 12, 2018, http://founders.archives.gov/documents/Hamilton/01-03-02-0369. "Mr. Laurance and myself who have been retained by Mr. R. Smith," wrote Hamilton to City Recorder Varick, "being about to leave Town, I have recommended Mr. Smith to you in our absence."

76 *Minutes of the Manumission Society of New York*, vol. 1, 2, Papers of John Jay, Item 3630, New York Historical Society. Laurance in 1789 was among six members of the Society's Standing Committee according to *The New York Directory* (New York: Hodge, Allen & Campbell, 1789), 121.

77 Noah Webster, *New York City Directory, 1786* (New York: Trow City Directory Co., 1886), 6: 46–77. Undamaged by the 1776 fire and seven years of British occupation, Wall Street was one of post-Revolutionary New York's most desirable addresses. State Supreme Court Chief Justice Richard Morris resided at 1 Wall Street.

78 Allan McLane Hamilton, *The Intimate Life of Alexander Hamilton* (New York: Scribner's Sons, 1910), 270. It is curious to note that the copy of this book in the Harvard College Library was donated a century after John Laurance's death by one J. L. Lawrance.

Chapter Nine

1 Noah Webster, *New York Directory—1786* (New York: Trow City Directory Co., 1886), 6–12. Webster, in his preface to the first post-war directory of New York City, described the "more strong than elegant" City Hall and the New York streetscape in some detail. Members of the Congress "sat in carved mahogany chairs trimmed with red morocco leather, each with a small 'bureau table' in front," according to James Grant Wilson, ed., *The Memorial History of the City of New York*, 4 vols. (New York, 1892–1893), III: 26–7.

2 *Journals of the Continental Congress 1774–1789*, ed. John Fitzpatrick (Washington DC: Government Printing Office, 1912), 28: 209. John Lawrance (Laurance), John Haring, and Melancton Smith were on March 26 appointed by Governor George Clinton to represent the State of New York until November 1, 1785. Later in the year, anti-federalists Peter Yates and Zephaniah Platt increased the New York delegation to five.

3 Alfred F. Young, *The Democratic Republicans of New York: The Origins, 1763–1797* (Chapel Hill: The University of North Carolina Press, 1967), 27. To finance Patriot New York's war effort, the legislature in late 1777 "levied a tax of three cents a pound on improved land and a half cent a pound on personal property."

4 Hough, *The New York Civil List*, 112, 162. The Eighth New York Senate consisted of 25 seats from 4 districts. Nine came from the Southern District that included New York County and City. Seven of the nine, including Senators Duane and McDougall, were pronounced nationalists. In the Assembly, Walter, James, and Peter Van Brugh Livingston advanced Duane and McDougall's downstate agenda.

5 Charles Rappleye, *Robert Morris, Financier of the American Revolution* (New York: Simon & Schuster, 2010), 380.

6 *Journals of the Continental Congress*, Fitzpatrick, 28 April 1785, 28: 316; 8 August 1785, 28: 619.

NOTES

7 *Journals of the Continental Congress*, 20 May, 1785, 28: 375.

8 *Papers of the Continental Congress*, No. 19, III, folio 623, National Archives.

9 *Papers of the Continental Congress*, No. 41, III, folio 542.

10 *Papers of the Continental Congress*, No. 19, VI, folio 135.

11 *Journals of the Continental Congress*, 30 May 1785, 28: 404. Brockholst Livingston was captured at sea by British cruisers on 25 April 1782 and paroled in early May by newly arrived British commander Edward Carlton. There is no evidence that Livingston was compensated for his time in captivity.

12 *Journals of the Continental Congress*, 2 November 1781, 21: 1090.

13 *Journals of the American Congress from 1774 to 1788* (Washington, DC: Way and Gideon, 1823), 18 July 1785, IV: 547–49.

14 *Journals of the American Congress from 1774 to 1788*, 2 August 1785, V: 60. "A division was called for by Mr. Lawrance; and on the question to agree to the first clause, as far as the public treasury ... So it was Resolved that the board of treasury, on the first Monday in every month lay before Congress an abstract of the receipts and expenditures of the preceding month, with the balance remaining in the public treasury."

15 *Journals of the Continental Congress*, 17 September 1785, 29: 771–74.

16 *Journals of the Continental Congress*, 28 December 1785. 29: 905; *Papers of the Continental Congress*, No. 23, folio 369.

17 Robert Ernst, *Rufus King: American Federalist* (Chapel Hill: University of North Carolina Press, 1968), 69.

18 *Journals of the Continental Congress*, 25 February 1786, 30: 84.

19 *Journals of the Continental Congress*, 3 February 1786, 30: 47.

20 *Journals of the Continental Congress*, 30: 45.

21 *Journals of the Continental Congress*, 30: 48–49.

22 John P. Kaminski, "The Reluctant Pillar," *The Reluctant Pillar*, ed. Stephen L. Schecter (Troy, NY: Russell Sage College, 1985), 52. Between 1783 and 1788, annual New York revenue from impost collections ranged from $125,000 to $225,000 New York dollars.

23 Allan Nevins, *The American States During and After the Revolution, 1775–1789* (New York: Macmillan, 1927), 283. For an unsurpassed account of Governor Clinton's rise to office and his anti-loyalist and tariff schemes, see pages 260–87.

24 Burrows and Wallace, *Gotham*, 279.

25 *Connecticut Courant*, 16 October 1786.

26 *New York and the Union*, Schechter Bernstein, 277.

27 *Journals of the Continental Congress 1774–1779*, 16 August 1786, 30: 439–44, 31: 511–14. Also "James Monroe to George Clinton, New York, Augt. 16, 1786," Smith, *Letters of delegates to Congress*, 1774–1789, 23: 480–81.

28 John H. Hazelton, "Trumbull's 'Declaration of Independence,'" *The Pennsylvania Magazine of History and Biography* 31, no. 121 (1907): 39–40. "Comparing the picture with the Declaration on parchment," wrote Hazelton, "we find that Trumbull has represented Clinton, Willing, R. R. Livingston, and Dickinson, whose names do not appear on the instrument ..." The painting now resides in the United States Capitol Rotunda, while a smaller predecessor is held by the Yale University Art Gallery.

29 Robert Troup to Alexander Hamilton, 15 June 1791, *The Papers of Alexander Hamilton*, Syrett, 8: 478–79. In paying a $200 note for Hamilton, Troup advised Hamilton of no need to repay him. "I shall never be indifferent to ... the wishes of *those in our circle* who have proved themselves worthy of confidence." There is little doubt the circle included Laurance, who also subsidized Hamilton's cash flow exigencies and shared speculative real estate investments with both men.

30 Webster, Noah. *New York City Directory – 1786*, 146.

31 Last Will and Testament of Alexander McDougall. *New York Historical Society Collections 1905*, Abstracts of Wills 1786–1795, 14–15. "To my daughter Elizabeth Laurance, during her natural life, a negro man, called Coleraine, and all the issues and profits of a certain farm I now rent, late the property of Peter Corney. ... All the rest of my real estate shall be sold by my executors, the money arising shall be divided into three equal parts: son Ranald, daughter Elizabeth Laurance, and wife Hannah. John Laurance, Esq. to receive those parts given to his wife and son from the estate of my nephew, Lieutenant John McDougal, lately deceased."

32 Webster, *New York City Directory – 1786*, 152–153.

33 *Journals of Continental Congress 1774–1789*, 27 June 1786, 30: 365.

34 *Journals of Continental Congress 1774–178*, 30: 382.

35 "An Address from the United States Congress assembled, to the Legislatures of the several States," 6 October 1786, *Journals of the Confederated Congress*, 31: 967.

36 Woody Holton, *Unruly Americans and the Origins of the Constitution* (New York: Hill and Wang, 2007). Bancroft Prize winning University of South Carolina history professor Holton makes a persuasive case that agrarian revolt in New England, together with middle state unrest from state tax legislation (to cover their share of Confederation Congress expenditures) played a "critical" role in precipitating the Constitutional Convention of 1787.

37 *Journal of the Senate of the State of New York*, at their Tenth Session, begun and holden in the City of New York, the Twelfth Day of January, 1787 (New York: Samuel and John London, 1787), 15. New York's 1787 delegates to the Confederation Congress were holdovers John Haring, John Lansing, Melancton Smith, and Abraham Yates. John Laurance was replaced by Egbert Benson.

38 *Journals of the Continental Congress 1774–1789*, 17 January 1787, 32: 1.

39 General Accounts of the Treasurers Receipts and Payments from January 1, 1784 to December 31, 1787, *Votes and Proceedings of the New York General Assembly*, 11 Session, 16 January 1788, 23; General Accounts of the Treasurers Receipts and Payments from January 1, 1788 to December 31, 1788, *Votes and Proceedings of the New York General Assembly*, 12 Session, 13 January 1789, 56.

40 Webster, *New York Directory – 1786*, iv.

41 I. N. Phelps Stokes, *The Iconography of Manhattan Island*, 6 vols. (New York: Robert H. Dodd, 1915–1918), 6. The genial John Simmons's 1795 obituary noted: "He was said to be the most corpulent man in the United States." His tavern doorway, according to tradition, had to be enlarged to admit passage of his coffin.

42 Augustus Van Cortlandt to John Laurance, 3 April 1787, John Laurance Papers, New York Historical Society, folder "1787."

43 James Madison to George Washington, New York, 18 March 1787, *The Papers of James Madison*, ed. Robert A. Rutland and William M. E. Rachal (University of Virginia Press: Charlottesville, 1975), 9: 315.

44 "Constitutional Convention, 1787," *Historical Magazine*, 1st series, 5 (January 1987), 18, as quoted in ed. John W. Vile, William D. Pederson, and Frank J. Williams, *James Madison: Philosopher, Founder, and Statesman* (Athens, OH: Ohio University Press, 2008), 60. None of the four most detailed surviving accounts of the Philadelphia Convention (James Madison, Rufus King, William Pierce, and Robert Yates) credit Hamilton with a leading role in the debates. The "gentleman from New York," declared Delegate Samuel Johnson, "has been praised by everybody, he has been supported by none." The most vocal participants were Gouverneur Morris, who is recorded as speaking 173 times, followed by James Wilson (168 times), James Madison (161), Roger Sherman (138), George Mason (136), and Elbridge Gerry (119).

45 George Washington to Benjamin Harrison, 18 January 1784, *George Washington Papers*, Congressional Series, edited by Dorothy Twohig, et al., I: 57. Washington was the first of 39 delegates (from the original 55) to sign the final document. Twenty-two, along with Convention Secretary William Jackson, were members of the Society of the Cincinnati. David O. Stewart, *The Summer of 1787* (New York: Simon & Schuster, 2007), 244.

46 Jackson Turner Main, *The Antifederalists: Critics of the Constitution 1781–1788* (New York: W. W. Norton, 1961), viii–xii. As Main painstakingly explains, the term *antifederalist* in the 1780s implied a hostility toward the Articles of Confederation and the corresponding Congress. Accordingly, the Federalists (or *nationalists* as they were then sometimes called) were actually *antifederalist*; conversely, defenders of the Confederation were called *Federalist*.

47 Main, *The Antifederalists: Critics of the Constitution 1781–1788*. Also see Cecilia M. Kenyon, *The Anti-federalists* (Indianapolis: Bobbs-Merrill, 1966), and Morton Borden, *The Antifederalist Mind* (East Lansing: Michigan State University Press, 1965). Kenyon in an earlier work ("Men of Little Faith: The Anti-Federalists on the Nature of Representative Government," *The William and Mary Quarterly* 12, no. 1, 3rd series [January 1955]: 11), summarizes the fundamental anti-federalist objection to the Constitution was: "because of the small size of the House of Representatives, the middle and lower classes would not be elected to that body, and that consequently this, the only popular organ of the government, would not be democratic at all." Republican government, then, must be limited to the comparatively small geographical and political individual states.

48 Clarence E. Miner, *The Ratification of the Federal Constitution by the State of New York* (New York: Columbia University, 1921), 121–22.

49 At the New York Ratifying Convention, middling opponents to ratification pounded away at Livingston, Schuyler, and Hamilton as aristocratic "high-fliers," as Abraham Yates dubbed them. See Gordon Wood, *Empire of Liberty*, 35–36; "Debate in the New York Ratifying Convention, 17 June–26 July 1788" in Bailyn, ed., *Debate on the Constitution*, 778–79; and Young, *Democratic Republicans of New York*, 45.

50 *The Correspondence and Public Papers of John Jay*, edited by Henry Phelps Johnston, 4 vols. (New York: G.P. Putnams's Sons, 1890-1892), 1: 262–64. Also see E. Wilder Spaulding, *New York During the Critical Period 1782–1789* (New York: Columbia University Press, 1932), 211, stating that "perhaps most successful [pro-ratification] tract was Jay's January 20, 1788 'Address to the People of New York.'" Citing Spaulding and Frank Monaghan, Alfred F. Young, *The Democratic-Republicans of New York* (Chapel Hill: University of North Carolina Press, 1967) asserts on page 111 that Jay's essay "probably made more converts" than Hamilton's *Federalist Papers*.

51 Alexander Hamilton to Robert Morris, Albany 13 August 1782. *Papers of Alexander Hamilton*, Syrett., 3: 140–42. In this long letter to Revolutionary War financier Morris, Hamilton offers character insights of the men running New York State. Identifying Laurance as one of five leading members of the General Assembly, he described his war-time friend: "Laurance is a man of good sense and good intentions—has just views of public affairs—is active and accurate in business. He is from conviction an advocate of strengthening the Federal government and for reforming the vices of our interior administration."

52 Charles A. Beard, *An Economic Interpretation of the Constitution of the United States* (New York: Macmillan Company, 1913), 23. "The chief obstacle in the way of the rapid appreciation of these lands," wrote Beard, "was the weakness of the national government, which prevented the complete subjugation of the Indians . . ." Beard cites a letter from North Carolina member of the Constitutional Convention, land speculator Hugh Williamson, to James Madison to make the persuasive case for the Constitution as a document created by and for the upper economic class.

53 *New York Daily Advertiser*, 8 February 1788.

54 "Proceedings of the New York General Assembly, Thursday, 31 January, 1788," pp. 705–707, *The Documentary History of the Ratification of the Constitution Digital Edition*, edited by John P. Kaminski, Gaspare J. Saladino, Richard Leffler, Charles H. Schoenleber, and Margaret A. Hogan (Charlottesville: University of Virginia Press, 2009). Assembly debates were reported in the *Daily Advertiser*, 12 February 1788; *Country Journal*, 19 February; the *New York Journal*, 21 February; and reprinted in the *Boston American Herald*, 6 March.

55 *Proceedings of the Commissioners of Indian Affairs, appointed by Law for the Extinguishment of Indian Titles in the State of New York* (Albany, NY: Joel Munsell, 1891), 252–60.

56 *New York Journal*, 13,17, 22 March, and 22, 24 April 1788. Laurance/Lawrence was on tickets proposed in letters from the pen names "Freeman," "Marcus," and "Citizens to the Independent Electors of the city and county of New York."

57 *The Debates in the Convention of The State of New York on the Adoption of the Federal Constitution*, Wednesday, June 23rd, http://www.constitution.org/rc/rat_ny.htm.

58 *The Debates in the Convention of The State of New York on the Adoption of the Federal Constitution*, Friday, July 17, 1788.

59 Brooks McNamara, *Day of Jubilee: The Great Age of Public Celebrations in New York, 1788–1909* (New Brunswick, NJ: Rutgers University Press, 1997), 17. George C. McWhorter claims his grandfather Laurance led the parade bearing a copy of the Constitution, but he was not alone. Robert Troup and John Corzine bore similar copies.

60 Virginia Congressman John Randolph, quoted in I. N. Phelps Stokes, *Iconography of Manhattan Island, 1490-1909*, 5: 1230.

61 *Minutes of the Common Council of the City of New York–1784–1831* (New York: City of New York, 1917), 1: 420.

62 Thomas Edward Vermilye Smith, *The City of New York in the Year of Washington's Inauguration* (New York: W.D. F. Randolph & Co., 1889), 41.

63 Smith, *The City of New York in the Year of Washington's Inauguration*, 43.

64 New York *Morning Post and Daily Advertiser*, 14 March 1789.

65 Representative Frederick Muhlenberg of Pennsylvania to Benjamin Rush, 5 March 1789, Frederick Muhlenburg Papers, Historical Society of Pennsylvania.

66 Richard Hofstadter, *The Idea of a Party System: The Rise of Legitimate Opposition in the United States, 1780-1840* (Berkeley: University of California Press, 1969), 2. Chapter 1 summarizes two centuries of Anglo-American thought on political faction leading up to the First Federal Congress.

67 V. W. Franklin Crane, "The Internal State of America," *William and Mary Quarterly* 15 (1958): 226.

68 Jefferson to Francis Hopkinson Paris, 13 March 1789, *The Papers of Thomas Jefferson*, edited by Julian P. Boyd (Princeton, NJ: Princeton University Press, 1958), 14: 650.

69 *The New York Journal*, and *Daily Patriotic Register*, 18 April 1788.

70 Cooke, *Alexander Hamilton*, 68-70. The New York Federalist campaign of 1788, from determining state and federal candidates to developing campaign strategy and publicity, was run by Hamilton. He established correspondence with other state Federalist committees and advised President-elect Washington on matters of appointment and etiquette. See also *The Documentary History of the First Federal Elections, 1788-1790*, edited by Merrill Jensen and Robert Becker, 6 vols. (Madison, WI: University of Wisconsin Press, 1976), 3: 455-60.

71 "John Laurance, Representative from New York," *Documentary History of the First Federal Congress of the United States of America*, edited by Charlene Bickford, et al. (Columbia, SC: Model Editions Partnership, 2002), http://adh.sc.edu. See also *The Documentary History of the First Federal Elections, 1788-1790*, Jensen and Becker, 3: 425.

72 "New York City Federalist Committee of Correspondence to Their Fellow Citizens," 26 February 1789, Alexander Hamilton, Chairman; *Daily Gazette*, and also the *Daily Advertiser*, 27 February 1789; and *The Documentary History of the First Federal Elections: 1788-1790*, Jensen, 3: 206, 454.

73 *The Documentary History of the First Federal Elections: 1788-1790*, ed. Jensen and Becker, 457.

74 Ibid., 476.

75 *New York Packet*, March 3, 1789. The writer signed himself "A Spectator."

76 *The Documentary History of the First Federal Elections: 1788-1790*, ed. Jensen and Becker, 460.

77 John Lamb to John Smith, 11 February 1789. John Smith Papers, New York Historical Society; New York *Daily Advertiser*, February 24, 26, 1789.

78 The claims that Pell was on Washington's staff, or his judge advocate general, are completely without documentation. Neither U.S. Army Judge Advocate Corps (JAG) records nor the Journals of Continental and Confederation Congress document any such service. According to JAG records, Thomas Edwards of Massachusetts was judge advocate general when the department was discharged on November 3, 1783. Pell, according to Bernard Fernow, *New York in the Revolution*, vol. XV, 537, finished the war as a commissary of prisoners. He may, however, briefly have filled in as emergency regimental judge advocate in 1777 (Heitman, *Register of Continental Officers*, 434).

79 Campaign flyer in support of John Laurance for the First United States House of Representatives, reproduced in *The Documentary History of the First Federal Elections, 1788-1790*, Jensen, 3: 462.

80 McWhorter, *Biographical Sketches*, 26. See also *Documentary History of the First Federal Congress of the United States of America*, Bickford, Bowling, et al., XIV: 718-22.

81 *First Census of the United States Taken in the Year 1790, New York* (Washington, DC: Government Printing Office, 1908).

82 Milton Lomask, *Aaron Burr, the Years from Princeton to Vice President 1756-1805* (New York: Farrar, Strauss & Giroux, 1979), 138. Lomask attributes the phrase to Burr's earlier biographer James Parton (1822-1891).

Chapter Ten

1 *The Diary of William Maclay and Other Notes on Senate Debates, March 4, 1789–March 3, 1791*, edited by Kenneth R. Bowling and Helen E. Veit (Baltimore: The Johns Hopkins University Press, 1988), 11.

2 Lang, *History of St. John's Lodge No. 1, 1757-1907*, 68. "No Bible was on the crimson cushion prepared for it to rest upon. General Jacob Morton, Master of St. John's No. 2, who was also Marshall of the Day, suggested the Bible at the lodge might be readily obtained. The Tyler of the Lodge was dispatched to bring it."

3 *Journal of the Senate of the United States of America*, Thursday, 30 April 1789, 1: 18.

4 "Recollections of Captain John Van Dyke," *Official Program of the Centennial Celebration of the Inauguration of George Washington as first President of the United States* (Washington, DC: Celebration Committee, Clarence Winthrop Bowen Secretary, 1889), 7. Captain Van Dyke commanded the artillery battery at President Washington's inauguration.

5 Rufus Griswold, *The Republican Court, or American Society in the Days of Washington* (New York: D. Appleton Co.: 1864), 173.

6 *Documentary History of the First Federal Congress*, ed. Bickford, Bowling et al., 3: 31–32. Laurance and Boudinot, together with New York representatives Egbert Benson, Virginian Richard Bland, Thomas Tudor Tucker of South Carolina together with their Senate counterparts met the president-elect in Elizabeth Town and "then embarked for this city, where they arrived about three o'clock in the afternoon of the same day, and accompanied him to the house appointed for his residence."

7 Elias Boudinot to Hannah Boudinot, 24 April 1789.

8 *The Diary of William Maclay*, Bowling and Veit, 13.

9 McWhorter, *Biographical Sketches*, 47–48.

10 Ibid., 48.

11 "Collection Circulation Records 1789–1792," New York Society Library, p. 361. Laurance (Lawrance) and wife Betsey's readings included *Sully's Memoirs*, *Pindar's Works*, *Macpherson's History*, *Hawksworth's Voyages*, the novels *Emilia*, *Louisa*, and *Fair Syrian*, plus *Swinburne's Travels*, *Chastellux's Travels*, and the curiously titled *Female Stability*.

12 *New York Packet*, 3 March 1789. Hamilton's speech at the political meeting is also reported in *The Papers of Alexander Hamilton*, Syrett, 5: 276–77.

13 *The Memorial History of the City of New York*, edited by James Grant Wilson (New York: New York History Company, 1893), 63. There was no shortage of rooms for transient lawmakers and public officials in the surrounds of Federal Hall. At least four boarding houses graced Wall Street alone, and rooms were to be had in many of New York's 330 taverns paying the 30-shilling city license fee.

14 George Galloway, *History of the House of Representatives* (New York: Thomas Y. Crowell, 1961), 75–78. The Joint Committee on Enrolled Bills was created on July 31, 1789. Congressman Laurance was not a member.

15 Jeffrey A. Jenkins and Charles Stewart III, *Fighting for the Speakership, The House and the Rise of Party Government* (Princeton, NJ: Princeton University Press, 2013), 57. "The first Speaker," observed Jenkins and Stewart, "was a policy moderate who did not aspire to use his position in a distinctly partisan manner. This was in keeping with the fluidity in the House, as partisan sorting was still in its infancy."

16 Ralph Ketcham, *James Madison: A Biography* (Charlottesville: University of Virginia Press, 1971), 112.

17 James Madison to Edmund Randolph, May 31, 1789, Madison, *Writings*, 5: 372–4n; to Edmund Pendleton, June 21, 1789, 405–406n. See also, "Vices of the Political System of the United States," (1787) Madison, *Writings*, 5: 75. "The danger of undue power in the President from such a regulation [power of cabinet member removal] is not to me formidable. I see and *politically feel* that that will be the weak branch of the Government." For an interpretation of Madison's "Nationalist Decade," see Irving Brant, *James Madison the Nationalist 1780–1787*, 2 vols. (New York: Bobbs-Merrill, 1948–1949); Garrett Ward Sheldon, *The Political Philosophy of James Madison* (Baltimore: The Johns Hopkins University Press, 2001); James E. Ferguson, "The Nationalists of 1781–1783; and the Economic Interpretation of the Constitution," *The Journal of American History* 56, no. 2 (September 1969), 241–61.

18 *Annals of Congress*, 1st Congress, 1st session, 6 May 1789, *Gales & Seaton's History of Debates in Congress*, 280. "If the constitution is the supreme law of the land," Laurance argued, "consequently every general declaration it contains is the supreme law. But then these general declarations cannot be carried into effect without particular regulations adapted to the circumstances. These particular regulations are to be made by Congress," he continued, "who, by the constitution have power to make all laws necessary or proper to carry the declarations of the constitution into effect." It would be hard to imagine a more sweeping broad-constructionist interpretation of congressional power under the Constitution.

19 Madison Speech on Import Duties, 8 April 1789, *Papers of James Madison*, Congressional Series, 12 vols. (www.upress.virginia.edu/rotunda#rotcoll), 12: 65.

20 *Documentary History of the First Federal Congress*, ed. Bickford, Bowling et al., 10: 246.

21 Frank W. Taussig, *The Tariff History of the United States* (New York: The Knickerbocker Press, 1910), 9. Between 1787 and 1790, 87 percent of American import trade in manufactures was conducted with

Great Britain. Huge available credit resources, low product costs, and return-cargo shipping options all favored the British trade. As to the prohibited British West Indies trade, American smuggling ingenuity took care of business.

22 Taussig, *The Tariff History of the United States*, 9.
23 *Annals of Congress*, House of Representatives, 1st Congress, 1st session, April 21, 1789, 190.
24 Ibid., 131–32.
25 Fisher Ames to George R. Minot, 3 May 1789, as cited in Nathan Schachner, *The Founding Fathers* (New York: G. P. Putnam's Sons, 1954), 41.
26 *The Diary of William Maclay*, ed. Bowling and Veit, 50. Pennsylvania senator Maclay was deeply suspicious of New York, New Jersey, and New England Federalists, none more so than John Laurance, whom he thought a puppet for Hamiltonian aristocrats, land speculators, and special merchant interests.
27 *Magazine of American History*, April 1893, 324 ff. in Charles Beard, *An Economic Interpretation of the Constitution* (New York: Macmillan Company, 1913), 46ff. Progressive historian Beard points out that the protection of New York manufacturers, merchants, and shippers led to that state's adoption of the Constitution. Indeed, a petition from Rep. Laurance's New York mercantile community asking for tariff protection landed on the House floor in its first month.
28 *Annals of Congress*, House of Representatives, 1st Congress, 1st session, 114–15, 115–19, 153–54 (steel), 174 (paper), 158.
29 Bickford and Bowling, *Birth of the Nation*, 32.
30 George Washington as quoted in David P. Currie, *The Constitution in Congress: The Federalist Period 1789–1801* (Chicago: University of Chicago Press, 1997), 33.
31 *Annals of Congress*, House of Representatives, 1st Congress, 1st session, June 25, 1789, 659.
32 Ibid., June 16, 1789, 475.
33 Ibid., 492.
34 Ibid., 530.
35 *Annals of Congress*, House of Representatives, 1st Congress, 1st session, June 17, 1789, 504. Laurance spoke at length in favor of vesting executive department appointment and removal with the president, 500–505. On this occasion, he and James Madison were in agreement.
36 "Declaration of Rights and Form of Ratification" in Convention, Saturday July 26, 1788, *Poughkeepsie County Journal*, 29 July 1788. As a condition of ratification of the Federal Constitution, delegates to the New York ratifying convention, listed 21 rights reserved to the people, and directed that "until a Convention shall be called and convened for proposing amendments to said Constitution" a number of actions were prohibited by Congress in the state of New York. On February 5–7, 1789, the New York Assembly followed up with a resolution to Congress for a second convention, a copy of which Governor Clinton transmitted on May 5 to his Antifederalist counterpart in Virginia.
37 *Annals of Congress*, House of Representatives, 1st Congress, 1st session, 1789, June 8, 1789, 468.
38 Carol Berkin, *The Bill of Rights, The Fight to Secure America's Liberties* (New York: Simon & Schuster, 2015), 58. Berkin backs up her assertion that Madison's amendments were a vehicle for crushing Antifederalist opposition by referring to his March 1789 letter to Jefferson. "I hope and expect that some conciliatory sacrifices will be made, in order to extinguish opposition to the system, or at least break the force of it, by detaching the deluded opponents from their designing leaders." While North Carolina and Rhode Island indeed quickly joined the union, University of Chicago Professor of Constitutional Law David P. Currie attributes the action to customs taxes both states faced on all goods "brought into the United States" as if they were foreign countries. David P. Currie, *The Constitution in Congress, The Federalist Period 1789–1801* (Chicago: The University of Chicago Press, 1997), 98.
39 *Gazette of the United States*, 15 August 1789; *Documentary History of the First Federal Congress 1789–1791*, vol. XI, *Debates in the House of Representatives*, ed. Bickford, Bowling, and Veit, 1211.
40 *Documentary History of the First Federal Congress 1789–1791*, vol. XI, *Debates in the House of Representatives*, ed. Bickford, Bowling, and Veit, 1214.
41 *Annals of Congress*, House of Representatives, 1st Congress, 1st session, 15 August 1789, 774.
42 Ibid., 25 June 1789, 613.
43 Ibid., 616.

44 Ibid., 621.
45 Ibid., 626.
46 Ibid., 628.
47 John R. Vile, *The Constitutional Convention of 1787: A Comprehensive Encyclopedia of America's Founding*, 2 vols. (Santa Barbara, CA: ABC-CLIO Inc., 2005), 1: 382-93. Also see Max Farrand, ed., *The Records of the Federal Convention*, 4 vols. (New Haven, CT: Yale University Press, 1937), and Robert J. Steamer, "The Legal and Political Genesis of the Supreme Court," *Political Science Quarterly* 77 (December 1962), 546-69.
48 James Madison to Edward Pendleton, 14 September 1789, James Madison Papers at the Library of Congress. "The Judiciary is now under consideration," Madison wrote. "I view it as you do, as defective both in its general structure, and many of its particular regulations . . . . The most I hope is that some offensive violations of Southern jurisprudence may be corrected . . . and that the system may speedily undergo a reconsideration under the auspices of the Judges who alone will be able perhaps to set it to rights."
49 *Annals of Congress*, House of Representatives, 1st Congress, 1st session, 24 August 1789. For a thorough treatment of debate on the Judiciary Act of 1789, see Maeva Marcus and Natalie Weeks, "The Judiciary Act of 1789: Political Compromise or Constitutional Interpretation." In *Origins of the Federal Judiciary: Essays on the Judiciary Act of 1789*, edited by Maeva Marcus (New York: Oxford University Press, 1992), 14-30.
50 Ibid., 31 August 1789, 864.
51 Thornton Anderson, *Creating the Constitution* (University Park, PA: Penn State University Press, 1993), 219. University of Maryland Professor Emeritus Anderson argues that in addition to "nationalist" and "states-rightist" factions in the First Federal Congress, a third group, the "state Federalists" provided the swing vote.
52 Thomas Jefferson to Benjamin Harrison, November 11, 1783, *Letters of Delegates to Congress, 1774-1789*, edited by Paul H. Smith, 26 vols. (Washington, DC: Library of Congress, 1994), 21: 152-53. See also *Journals of Congress*, October 21, 1783.
53 *Papers of Continental Congress*, No. 78, XII: 283-86. See also Carlos E Godfrey, *The Mechanic's Bank* (Trenton, NJ: Privately Printed, 1919), 25-26.
54 *New Jersey Gazette*, 23 December 1783. Dr. David Cowell, "a physician of respect, and extensive practice" died on December 18, 1783, leaving "the first legacy we recollect to have been given to the United States and is respectable for a person of middle fortune."
55 *Journals of Congress*, 20, 23, 24 December 1784, XXVII: 710
56 Ibid.
57 *The Papers of George Washington (Confederation Series)*, ed. W. W. Abbot (Charlottesville: University of Virginia Press, 1992), 2: 332. Washington helped crush the Trenton plan. Writing to Richard Henry Lee on February 8, 1785, the future president observed: "By the time your Federal buildings on the banks of the Delaware . . . are fit for the reception of Congress, it will be found that they are improperly placed for the seat of the empire, and will have to undergo a second erection in a more convenient site."
58 *Journals of Congress*, 23 December 1784, XXVII: 707-708.
59 John Jay, "Notes of Debates New York Rarifying Convention," 11 July 1788, John McKesson Papers, New York Historical Society.
60 *The Daily Advertiser*, 3 September 1789, reporting House debate of September 1st, *Documentary History of the First Federal Congress*, ed. Bickford, Bowling et al, XI: 1397. A full account of Laurance's speech was printed in the *New Jersey Journal*, 16 September 1789.
61 *Annals of Congress*, House of Representatives, 1st Congress, 1st session, September 1, 1789, I: 825.
62 H. W. Crew, *Centennial History of the City of Washington D.C.* (Dayton, OH: W. J. Shuey Publisher, 1892), 82. As late as seven days before Residence Act passage, Laurance moved to derail momentum for a Potomac location by motioning to substitute "Baltimore" as permanent seat of government. When his motion only garnered 26 yeas against 34 nays, he later (unsuccessfully) moved to cap appropriations by adding the words: "<u>Provided</u> the buildings shall not exceed the sum of _____ dollars."
63 *The Daily Advertiser*, 4 September 1789. *Documentary History of the First Federal Congress*, ed. Bickford, Bowling, Veit, XI: 1408.

64 *The New York Daily Gazette*, 11 June 1790, *Documentary History of the First Federal Congress*, ed. Bickford, Bowling, Veit, XI: 1554.

65 Rufus King Papers at New York Historical Society, 26 September 1789; *Documentary History of the First Federal Congress*, ed. Bickford, Bowling, and Veit, XIX: 1619.

66 *Documentary History of the First Federal Congress*, ed. Bickford, Bowling, and Veit, IV: 1858.

67 James Madison to Tench Coxe, 18 September 1789, *The Papers of James Madison*, edited by Charles F. Hobson and Robert A Rutland (Charlottesville: University of Virginia Press, 1979), 12: 409-10.

68 *Annals of Congress*, Senate, 1st Congress, 1st session, September 24, 1789, I: 88. Vice President Adams voted in the affirmative to break a nine-to-nine Senate tie to include land in Bucks' County around Germantown into HR-25. New York Senators King and Schuyler voted with Morris to carry the amended measure.

69 Rufus King Papers at New York Historical Society, 26 September, 1789; *Documentary History of the First Federal Congress*, ed. Bickford, Bowling, and Veit, XIX: 1620.

70 David P Currie, *The Constitution in Congress: The Federalist Period 1789-1801* (Chicago: University of Chicago Press, 1997), 3. Distinguished Professor of Law at the University of Chicago, Currie (1936-2007) was noted for both casebooks on the federal courts and histories on the early Congress and Supreme Court.

71 Abigail Adams to John Adams, 20 October 1789, *Adams Family Correspondence*, 8: 427, The Adams Papers Digital Edition, The University of Virginia Press, 2008.

72 Douglas Southall Freeman, *George Washington, A Biography. Vol. 6: Patriot and President* (London: Eyre and Spottiswood, 1954), VI: 226, 252, 253. President Washington set a lavish table in New York, ordering as many as 26 dozen bottles of claret and champagne at a time.

73 *The Diaries of George Washington*, ed. Donald Jackson and Dorothy Twohig (Charlottesville: University of Virginia Press, 1979), V: 509.

Chapter Eleven

1 Thomas K. McCraw, *The Founders and Finance: How Hamilton, Gallatin, and Other Immigrants Forged a New Economy* (Cambridge, MA: The Belknap Press of Harvard University Press, 2012), 387n.5. Nominal GDP % is a twentieth-century invention that can be re-created for past years in which both the numerator (total public debt) and the denominator (total public income) are available. Harvard Business School professor and Pulitzer Prize winner McCraw calculated the debt as a percentage of gross domestic product as: 1790, 31 percent; 1795, 18 percent; 1800, 15 percent. The strong growth of national income following ratification of the Constitution combined with Hamilton's fiscal policies to result in a spectacular decline of public debt as a percentage of national income.

2 Alexander Hamilton, *Report Relative to a Provision for the Support of Public Credit*, Treasury Department, January 9, 1790, in *The Papers of Alexander Hamilton*, Syrett et al., 6: 51-96. Hamilton overestimated the amount of state debts. The issue authorized to cover them was $21,500,00, and the amount actually dispersed was $18,275,786.47. Also see www.treasurydirect.gov/govt/reports/pd/histdebt/histdebt.htm, 1791-1849. The size of the national public debt was a moving target. As of January 1 of each year it was as follows: 1791, $75.5 million; 1792, $77.2 million; 1793, $80.4 million. The best analyses of Hamilton's plan are those of modern financial historians who understand its technical components better than eighteenth-century contemporaries. Standing out in the literature are the works of James Ferguson, Richard Sylla, Robert F. Wright, Donald E. Swanson, and Andrew P. Trout.

3 Donald F. Swanson and Andrew P. Trout, "Alexander Hamilton's Hidden Sinking Fund," *William and Mary Quarterly* 49 (1992), 108-16. Swanson and Trout argue that, because the debt was so massive, the sinking fund was primarily of symbolic importance at the time but was included for important political reasons. Tying it to Postal Service revenues gave the fund ironclad provenance.

4 Aedanus Burke to Samuel Bryan, 3 March 1790, Record Group 59, National Archives.

5 Forest McDonald, *Alexander Hamilton: A Biography* (New York: W. W. Norton & Company, 1979), 172-75.

6 John F. Hoadley, *Origins of American Political Parties 1789-1803* (Lexington, KY: The University Press of Kentucky, 1986), 51. Hoadley contends that Hamilton relied on Massachusetts reps. Fisher Ames and Theodore Sedgwick along with South Carolinian William Smith as his lead spokesmen in the First Federal Congress. Close reading of *Gales & Seaton's History of Debates in Congress*, however, indicates

NOTES 323

that more often than not, Hamilton's friend John Laurance rose with them to counter James Madison's forceful opposition to Hamilton's financial program.

7   Glyn Davies, *A History of Money, From Ancient Times to the Present* (Cardiff: University of Wales Press, 1994), 238.
8   *Annals of Congress*, House of Representatives, 1st Congress, 2nd session, 9 February 1790, 1192.
9   Ibid., 1193.
10 The gold standard of period financial understanding is James Ferguson, *Power of the Purse*, 297–300. Ferguson attributes Madison's stunning funding reversal to "political expediency rather than concern for the common man." Elkins and McKitrick generally accept Ferguson's rationale in their definitive *Age of Federalism*, 139–40. Ferguson, however, goes a step further (p. 299) when he suspects Madison of arguing to pay 6 percent interest on the entire public debt purely as a strategy to block assumption of state debt due to insufficient funds.
11 James Madison to Edmund Pendleton, March 4, 1790, *The Papers of James Madison*, ed. Charles F. Hobson and Robert Rutland (Charlottesville: University of Virginia Press, 1981), 13: 85–7.
12 *Annals of Congress, House of Representatives*, 1st Congress, 2nd session, 15 February 1790, 1250. Laurance rebutted Madison at length on the issue of discrimination among domestic debt holders for repayment on pages 1250–53.
13 *Annals of Congress, House of Representatives*, 1st Congress, 2nd session, 15 February 1790, 1251.
14 Ibid.
15 Ibid., 1252.
16 Ibid., 1253.
17 New York Loan Office Books in the Treasury Department, and *State Papers: Finance*, I: 165, as quoted in Charles Beard, *Economic Origins of Jeffersonian Democracy* (New York: Macmillan, 1915), 183n. "Of the three [Benson, Laurance, and Sylvester]," wrote Professor Beard, "Lawrence was a security holder, and among the large operators in public stocks in New York."
18 Beard, *Economic Origins of Jeffersonian Democracy*, 193–94. Professor Beard documents that 29 of 64 House members were holders of government securities.
19 *Annals of Congress, House of Representatives*, 1st Congress, 2nd session, 22 February 1790, 344. Nine of the 13 votes in favor of discrimination were from the Virginia delegation.
20 Representative Theodorick Bland of Virginia to [St. George Tucker?], 6 March 1790, *Documentary History of the First Federal Congress*, Bickford, Bowling, et al., 18: 747.
21 Thomas J. DiLorenzo, *Hamilton's Curse: How Jefferson's Arch Enemy Betrayed the American Revolution—and What It Means for Americans Today* (New York: Three Rivers Press, 2008), 48. Antifederalist Virginia agrarian political philosopher (and future secessionist) John Taylor served in the Virginia House of Delegates (1779–1781, 1783–1785, 1796–1800) and the U.S. Senate (1792–1794, 1803, 1822–1824). A close friend of Jefferson, he was a prolific political writer and author of one of America's first books on agriculture.
22 Thomas Jefferson, *The Anas of Thomas Jefferson*, ed. Franklin B. Sawvel (New York: DaCapo Press, 1970), 32.
23 Paul Jennings, *A Colored Man's Reminiscences of James Madison* (Brooklyn: George C. Beadle, 1865); Rachel L. Swarms, "Madison and the White House through the Memoirs of a Slave," *The New York Times*, 15 August 2009; "Chronology and Dolley Madison," *The Dolley Madison Project*, Virginia Center of Digital History. Upon Madison's death in 1836, his will left educated valet Paul Jennings to widow Dolley, who sold him in 1846 for $200.
24 *Annals of Congress*, House of Representatives, 1st Congress, 2nd session, 11 February 1790, 1225.
25 Ibid.
26 Ibid., 1226.
27 Ibid., 1228.
28 David Brion Davis, *The Problem of Slavery in the Age of Revolution, 1770–1823* (New York: Oxford University Press, 1999), 131–32.
29 Ibid., 132.
30 *Annals of Congress*, House of Representatives, 1st Congress, 2nd session, 23 February 1790, 1355–56.
31 Ibid.

32 Ibid., 1356.

33 "William Smith, Representative from South Carolina," *Documentary History of the First Federal Congress of the United States of America*, ed. Bickford, Bowling, and Veit (Columbia, SC: Model Editions Partnership, 2002), http://adh.sc.edu.

34 "An Act making provision for the payment of the Debt of the United States," 1 *United States Statutes at Large*, 1st Congress, 2nd session, chap. 34, 12. Passed on August 4, 1790, this act assumed South Carolina debt in the amount of $4,000,000 out of a total state debt assumption of $21,500,00. As early as January 20, the South Carolina legislature passed legislation in favor of assumption.

35 Joseph Ellis, *Founding Brothers: The Revolutionary Generation* (New York: Vintage Books, 2000), 58; John C. Miller, *The Federalists: 1789–1801* (New York: Harper & Row, 1960), 46–47.

36 *Annals of Congress*, House of Representatives, 1st Congress, 2nd session, 23 February 1790, 1389.

37 Ibid., 1394.

38 "Report of the Commissioners of the Public Debt," June 29, 1795. LXXXIII, Record Group 53, Fiscal Records Sec., National Archives.

39 Mark Grossman, *Political Corruption in America: An Encyclopedia of Scandals, Power, and Greed* (Chicago: ABC-CLIO, 2003), 106.

40 Anthony J. Connors, "Andrew Craigie, Brief life of a patriot and a scoundrel 1754–1819," *Harvard Magazine*, November–December, 2011. Also see Bleecker to Andrew Craigie, December 15, 26, 1789, Craigie Papers at the American Antiquarian Society, Worcester, MA.

41 Jones, *King of the Alley*, 130.

42 Elkins and McKitrick, *Age of Federalism,*" 138.

43 Kaminski, *George Clinton: Yeoman Politician of the New Republic*, 199.

44 *The Diaries of George Washington*, edited by Donald Jackson and Dorothy Twohig (Charlottesville: University of Virginia Press, 1979), 6: 44–45.

45 *The Diary of William Maclay*, Bowling and Veit, 241–42.

46 McDonald, *Alexander Hamilton*, 184.

47 Rufus King, *The Life and Correspondence of Rufus King: Comprising His Letters, Private and Official, His Public Documents and His Speeches*, edited by Charles R. King (New York: G.P. Putnam's Sons, 1894), 384. According to King's diary entry of 30 June 1790, Treasury Secretary Hamilton called on "Col. Lawrance" and informed him that "the funding System, including the assumption is the primary national object; all subordinate points which oppose it must be sacrificed." Laurance, nonetheless, voted against relocating the seat of government out of New York.

48 Receipt dated June 14, 1790, in the amount of £20 from John Lawrence for purchase of pew #64 in Trinity Church from John Lewis, collector. John Laurance Papers, New York Historical Society, folder "1790–1800."

49 "John Laurance esq. Bank Paper Book," June 26, 1790, Bank of New York, 1,296 pounds. John Laurance Papers at New York Historical Society. Other than portions of his wartime account ledger, Laurance left behind no comprehensive personal or professional financial records. His only surviving bank statement for the year 1790 is referenced above, which may or may not represent the average daily balance.

50 William L. Livingston to John Lawrence, 22 November 1790, John Laurance Papers, New York Historical Society, folder "1790–1800."

51 James R. Perry and James M. Buchanan, "Admission to the Supreme Court Bar, 1790–1800: A Case Study of Institutional Change," *Supreme Court Historical Society Yearbook* (1983), 11. Laurance was one of nine congressmen among the 27 lawyers admitted to the Supreme Court bar during the Court's first term in February 1790.

52 John Adams to John Laurance, 19 September 1790, Library of Congress, Adams Personal Manuscripts, Reel 115. "I send my son to you, Sir," wrote Adams, "in order to know upon what conditions You will take him into your Office.... He will board with me and attend your office as he did Col. Hamilton's, from ten in the morning – til – three in the afternoon."

53 *The Adams Papers*, Adams Family Correspondence: January 1790–December 1793, edited by Margaret A. Hogan et al. (Cambridge: Massachusetts Historical Society, 2009), 9: 296–97. Charles Adams died in dire financial straits of alcoholism at the age of 30 on November 30, 1800.

NOTES

54 William Nisbet Chambers, *Political Parties in a New Nation: The American Experience 1776-1809* (New York: Oxford University Press, 1963), 39-40.

55 Roy F. Nichols, *The Invention of the American Political Parties: A Study of Political Improvisation* (New York: Macmillan, 1967), 199-247. There is considerable evidence to suggest the lack of a viable party system in the early republic. See also Ronald P. Formisano, "Deferential Participant Politic: The Early Republic's Political Culture, 1789-1840," *American Political Science Review* 6 (September 1974):473-87.

56 McDonald, *Alexander Hamilton*, 24.

57 William Jay, *The Life of John Jay* (New York: J & J Halper, 1833). Jay's son William wrote that his father had told him: "By this constitution (NY State 1777) the right of suffrage was, in several instances, restricted to freeholders; It being a favorite maxim with Mr. Jay that those who own the country ought to govern it."

58 John J. Beckley to James Madison, 10 September 1792, *The Papers of James Madison*, ed. Robert A. Rutland and Thomas A. Mason (Charlottesville: University of Virginia Press, 1983), 14: 361-63.

59 *Documentary History of the First Federal Congress of the United States of America*, ed. Linda Grant De Pauw, Charlene Bangs Bickford, LaVonne Marlene Siegel (Baltimore: Johns Hopkins University Press, 1977), 3: 619.

60 "The Second Annual Address of the President of the United States, Philadelphia, 8 December 1790," *A Compilation of the Messages and Papers of the Presidents Prepared under the Direction of the Joint Committee on printing, of the House and Senate Pursuant to an Act of the 52nd Congress of the United States* (New York: Bureau of National Literature Inc., 1897).

61 Ibid.

62 Act of Incorporation, February 25, 1791, quoted from John T. Holdsworth and Davis R. Dewey, *The First Bank of the United States (1910)* (Washington, DC: Kessinger Publishing, 2008), 126-32.

63 Congress, despite Hamilton's protests, never appropriated funds to pay off its $2,000,000 debt to the BUS. As a result, the government disposed of over half its borrowed BUS stock, with a steady gravitation of bank shares to European ownership. President Jefferson in 1802 sold the last 2,220 shares to the English banking house of Baring.

64 *Annals of Congress*, House of Representatives, 1st Congress, 3rd session, 1 February 1791, 1891.

65 Ibid., 1892.

66 Ibid., 3 February, 1791, 1945.

67 Ibid., 4 February 1791, 1964.

68 Ibid.

69 *General Advertiser*, 8 February 1791; *Documentary History of the First Federal Congress, 1789-1791, Debates of the House of Representatives Third Session Dec. 1790-Mar. 1791, and Biographies of Members*, ed. Bickford, Bowling, Veit, and Di Giacomantonio, XIV: 382-83.

70 *Documentary History of the First Federal Congress, 1789-1791, Debates of the House of Representatives Third Session Dec. 1790-Mar. 1791, and Biographies of Members*, ed. Bickford, Bowling, Veit, and Di Giacomantonio, XIV: 383.

71 Ibid.

72 George Washington to David Stuart, 20 November 1791, *The Papers of George Washington*, Presidential Series, vol. 9, *23 September 1791-29 February 1792*, ed. Mark A. Mastromarino (Charlottesville: University of Virginia Press, 2000), 209-14.

73 Bickford and Bowling, *Birth of a Nation*, 73-75. The authors suggest President Washington wanted Alexandria included in his pet federal district project so badly that he was willing to risk reopening the divisive capital location issue resolved by the compromise of 1790. The bank bill, which Washington may have been inclined to veto, was the "unexpected price" he paid.

74 *Annals of Congress*, House of Representatives, First Congress, 3rd session, 1891-92.

75 *Annals of Congress*, House of Representatives, First Congress, 3rd session, 25, 27 January 1791, 1931-33.

76 Philip Schuyler to Rufus King, "Profile of Rufus King, Senator from New York," *Documentary History of the First Federal Congress: 1789-1791*, vol. XIV, *Debates of the House of Representatives Third Session Dec. 1790-Mar. 1791, and Biographies of Members*, ed. Bickford, Bowling, Veit, and Di Giacomantonio, 708.

Chapter Twelve

1. "Col. Quarry and others to Governor Nicholson, Philadelphia, 18 January 1698," *Historical Collections Relating to the American Colonial Church: Pennsylvania*, ed. William Stevens Perry (Hartford, CT: The Church Press, 1871), 5–6. The "wicked and damnable principles and doctrines" of William Penn's Philadelphia Society of Friends included the presence of women in church councils, justice and charity toward Native Americans, pacifism, and omission of the sacraments of baptism and the Lord's Supper from a clergy that was neither ordained nor paid. Penn's "holy experiment" also produced the first slavery ban in America.

2. Thomas Edward Vermilye Smith, *The City of New York in the Year of Washington's Inauguration*, 195–96. George Wright of Trinity College, Dublin was in 1784 made "able assistant" in Dr. William Cochran's private school at 23 Maiden Lane. In May of that year, Cochran was elected Professor of Greek and Latin at Columbia College and his school became the "Columbia College Grammar School." Tuition was one guinea for admission, and seven dollars a school quarter.

3. "Marriage Records of Christ Church, Philadelphia, PA," *Record of Pennsylvania Marriages Prior to 1810* (Clarence M. Busch, State Printer of Pennsylvania, 1895) vol. 1, record no. 1709N1806, Pennsylvania Archives Second Series, vol. 8. "John Lawrence and Elizabeth Allen, June 30, 1791." In the words of historian E. F. DeLancey, "The name of Allen, for more than a century" was the "synonym for high ability, political power, great wealth, and the first social position." Charles Rhoads Roberts, *History of Lehigh County, Pennsylvania*, 2 vols. (Allentown, PA: Lehigh Valley Publishing Company, Inc., 1914), 1: 409.

4. Tobias Lear to George Washington, Philadelphia, 27 September 1791, *The Papers of George Washington*, Presidential Series, 23 September 1791–29 February 1792, ed. Mark A. Mastromarino (Charlottesville: University of Virginia Press, 2000), 9: 27–29. "The marriage of Colo. Lawrence & Mrs. Allen is at length avowed by the parties—and this week She received her Company in form."

5. John K. Heyl, "James Allen and Trout Hall," *Lehigh County Historical Society, Volume 24, Proceedings* (Allentown, PA: Lehigh County Historical Society, 1962), 89–91.

6. Currently administered by the Lehigh County Historical Society, Trout Hall was acquired by the town of Allentown in 1908 and listed 70 years later on the National Register of Historic Places. The first home to Muhlenberg College in 1667, the two-and-a-half-story manor house also served as a Lutheran seminary.

7. "Mapping West Philadelphia, landowners in October 1777," www.archives.upenn.edu/WestPhila1777/view-parcel.php. Among the six West Philadelphia properties owned by Elizabeth's father, John Spratt Lawrence, were two parcels on the north side of Chestnut Street between Fourth and Fifth Streets. To the west of the Chestnut Street properties owned by Daniel Williams and Charles Moore were two large parcels owned by Elizabeth's father-in-law William Allen. The Chestnut Street residence of James and Elizabeth Allen, given by her father, no longer survives. It is specifically referred to in the "Diary of James Allen, Esq., of Philadelphia," *The Pennsylvania Magazine of History and Biography* 9, no. 2 (July 1885): 179, and "probably stood on the site of the present [late nineteenth century] Farmers' and Mechanics' Bank."

8. Anne Hollingsworth Wharton, *Social Life in the Early Republic* (Philadelphia: J. B. Lippincott Company, 1903), 30. Elizabeth (Allen) Laurance was so strongly vested in Trout Hall as a family asset that she instigated a movement to designate a new county with Allentown as its seat. "With respect to any expenses which may be incurred in this business," she wrote to Judge Peter Rhoades in November 1792, "my children will very willingly pay a large proportion of them." Charles Rhoades Roberts, *History of Lehigh County, Pennsylvania*, 2 vols. (Allentown, PA: Lehigh Valley Publishing Co., 1914), I: 212.

9. Allen McLane Hamilton, *The Intimate Life of Alexander Hamilton*, 314. Among the ladies of the Washington Federalist "Court," according to Alexander Hamilton's grandson, were the "Misses Allen." See also Rufus Griswold, *The Republican Court*, 270.

10. Wharton, *Social Life in the Early Republic*, 30–31.

11. Francois Furstenberg, *When the United States Spoke French: Five Refugees Who Shaped a Nation* (New York: Penguin Books, 2014), 201.

12. Duke de la Rochefoucauld-Liancourt, *Travels through the United States of North America . . . in the years 1795, 1796, and 1797* (London: B. Phillips, 1799) as quoted in Wharton, *Social Life in the Early Republic*, 35.

13. Frances Seney to Hanna Nicholson, 12 January 1791, Albert Gallatin Papers, New-York Historical Society. Frances Seney was wife of Maryland Representative to Congress Joshua Seney (1756–1798).

14 Abigail Adams to Abigail Adams Smith, 26 December 1790. Charles Francis Adams, *Letters of Mrs. Adams, the Wife of John Adams* (Boston: Charles Little and James Brown, 1840), 408–409.

15 Abigail Adams to Cotton Tufts, Philadelphia, 6 February 1791, Adams Family Papers, Massachusetts Historical Society.

16 Wharton, *Social Life in the Early Republic*, 30–31.

17 Ibid., 31.

18 Griswold, *The Republican Court*, 270.

19 Abigail Adams to Abigail Adams Smith, Philadelphia, 25 January 1791, *Abigail Adams, Letters*, Charles Francis Adams, 353–55.

20 McWhorter, *Biographical Sketches*, 49.

21 Miss Franks to her older sister, Mrs. Andrew Hamilton, Griswold, *The Republican Court*, 23.

22 Abigail Adams, quoted in Griswold, *The Republican Court*, 250.

23 Robert E. Wright, *The First Wall Street: Chestnut Street, Philadelphia, and the Birth of American Finance* (Chicago: The University of Chicago Press, 2005), 2–3.

24 Benjamin Rush to Tench Coxe, 15 August 1790, quoted in Cooke, *Tench Coxe*, 166.

25 John T. Holdsworth and Davis R. Dewey, "The First and Second Banks of the United States," *National Monetary Commission Report to the United States Senate* (Washington, DC: Government Printing Office, 1910), 24. Additional BUS shares made available at the Bank of New York were sold out as well, but 2,400 shares allocated to the Bank of Massachusetts in Boston required four days to sell in the entirety.

26 James O. Wettereau, "New Light on the First Bank of the United States," *Pennsylvania Magazine of History and Biography* 61 (July 1937): 274. This article reproduces the substance of a paper read before the American Historical Association and the Business Historical Society at Providence, RI, December 29, 1936.

27 David J. Cowen, Richard Sylla, and Robert E. Wright, *The U.S. Panic of 1792: Financial Crisis Management and the Lender of Last Resort*, prepared for the NBER DAE Summer Institute, July 2006, and the XIV International Economic History Congress Session 20, "Capital Market Anomalies in Economic History," Helsinki, August 2006, 11.

28 William Seton to Alexander Hamilton, 12 September 1791, *The Papers of Alexander Hamilton*, Syrett, IX: 202–203.

29 To George Washington from Tobias Lear, 27 September 1791, *The Papers of George Washington*, Presidential Series, vol. 9, *23 September 1791–29 February 1792*, edited by Mark A. Mastromarino (Charlottesville: University of Virginia Press, 2000), 27–29.

30 Wharton, *Social Life in the Early Republic*, 31.

31 Holdsworth and Dewey, *National Monetary Report to the United States Senate*, 34. The first 25 elected directors of the Bank of the United States (BUS) were: Thomas Willing, Joseph Ball, James C. Fisher, Archibald McCall, Israel Whelen, Joseph Anthony, William Bingham, Robert Smith, Isaac Wharton, George Cabot, Tristram Dalton, Andrew Cragie, Samuel Breck, James Davenport, John Lawrence, Nicholas Low, James Watson, Rufus King, Herman LeRoy, John Watts, Henry Nichol, James McClurg, Samuel Johnson, and William Smith.

32 *Annals of Congress*, House of Representatives, 2nd Congress, 1st session, 142.

33 Ibid., 24 July 1789, 696.

34 Ibid., 1258.

35 James Madison, "Notes on Remarks on the Bank Bill to the House of Representatives," 2 February 1791, *The Papers of James Madison, 20 January 1790–31 March 1791*, ed. Charles F. Hobson and Robert A. Rutland (Charlottesville: University of Virginia Press, 1981), 13: 372–81. Madison enlarges upon his *Federalist Paper 41* by arguing that expansive interpretation of the Necessary and Proper Clause ran counter to its essential composition of limited and enumerated powers. See also Richard S. Arnold, "How James Madison Interpreted the Constitution, *New York University Law Review* 72, no. 2 (May 1997): 271–76; Peter Zavodnyk, *The Age of Strict Construction: A History of the Growth of Federal Power, 1789–1861* (Washington, DC: The Catholic University Press, 2007), 42–50; and Kevin R. C. Gutzman, *James Madison and the Making of America* (New York: St. Martin's Press, 2012), 256–60.

36 David J. Siemers, *After Ratification: Antifederalists and Federalists in Constitutional Time* (Stanford, CA: Stanford University Press, 2002), 47. Siemers, Chair of the University of Wisconsin–Oshkosh

Department of Political Science, explores the Antifederalist subterfuge of strict-constructionism in some detail in chap. 3, "Refuge of the Resigned."

37 *Annals of Congress*, House of Representatives, 2nd Congress, 1st session, 221, 1258–1259. Representative Parker was exaggerating. Laurance's proposed 1792 budget of $1,059,222 represented less than a 43 percent increase versus 1791. Still, proposed 1792 federal operating expenditures were substantially higher than for 1791 ($740,233). Furthermore, interest on foreign and domestic debt would increase to $2,849,194 versus $2,060,861 in 1791.

38 *Annals of Congress*, House of Representatives, 2nd Congress, 1st session, 221, 1258–59.

39 Ibid.

40 Ibid., 223.

41 Ibid.

42 Ibid.

43 Ibid., 227.

44 Elkins and McKitrick, *The Age of Federalism*, 257. "The twelve-month period from the fall of 1791 to the fall of 1792," wrote Elkins and McKitrick, "was marked by the emergence of what could be for the first time clearly discerned as an opposition ... in reaction to the rising influence of the Treasury over Administration policy, and to the fierce urge of Jefferson and Madison to prevent completion of Hamilton's grand design." Also see Richard Hofstadter, *The Idea of a Party System: The Rise of Legitimate Opposition in the United States, 1780–1840* (Berkeley: University of California Press, 1970), 3.

45 *Annals of Congress*, House of Representatives, 2nd Congress, 1st session, 228.

46 *A Concise History of the House of Representatives Committee on Appropriations* (Washington, DC: Printed for use of the Committee on Appropriations of the House of Representatives by the U.S. Government Printing Office, 2010), 4.

Chapter Thirteen

1 *Annals of Congress*, House of Representatives, 2nd Congress, 1st session, 8 March 1792, 442.

2 Ibid., 9 March 1792, 444.

3 Ibid., 29 March 1792, 496.

4 Ibid.

5 Richard G. Doty and Eric P. Newman, ed. *Studies on Money in Early America* (New York: American Numismatic Society, 1976), 206. Engraver John Gregory Hancock at the Walker mint in Birmingham, England designed the 1791 coppers and may have also designed the 1792 gold eagle presented to Washington as a pattern coin. Between 1783 and 1795, more than a dozen coins were struck by private minters in various denominations bearing Washington's likeness. See R. S. Yeoman, *A Guide Book of United States Coins*, 68th edition (Racine, WI: Western Publishing Company, 2015), 51–56.

6 *Annals of Congress*, House of Representatives, 2nd Congress, 1st session 24 March 1792, 484. "It had been a practice," Page said, "of monarchies to exhibit the figures or heads of their Kings upon their coins ... I am certain it will be more agreeable to citizens of the United States to see the head of Liberty on their coin, than the heads of Presidents."

7 *Annals of Congress*, House of Representatives, 2nd Congress, 1st session, 26 March 1792, 486. Laurance was among the 32–22 majority approving "An Act Establishing a Mint and regulating the coins of the United States."

8 *A Century of Population Growth from the First Census to the Twelfth, 1790–1900*, United States Bureau of the Census (Washington, DC: Government Printing Office, 1909), 42–93. Of a total population of 3,893,635, free persons accounted for 3,268,355 and slaves totaled 694,280. Virginia, with 292,627 slaves, accounted for 42.1 percent of the nation's slave population. Because of its slaves, Virginia's total population (747,610) greatly exceeded Pennsylvania (434,373), the next most populous state. Massachusetts, with zero slaves, ranked third with 378,787 free persons. New York ranked fourth with a total census population of 340,120, of which 21,324 were slaves.

9 *Annals of Congress*, House of Representatives, 2nd Congress, 1st session, 31 October 1791, 148.

10 Ibid., 149.

11   *Annals of Congress*, House of Representatives, 2nd Congress, 1st session, 16 February 1792, 409–11.

12   Wood, *Empire of Liberty*, 105–115. "The Federalists," writes Wood (p. 105), "were good republicans, in that they believed in election as the source of political leadership, but they also believed that election ought to result in government by patrons and by the wise and virtuous, in other words, by men like themselves."

13   Charles M. Biles, *The History of Congressional Apportionment* (Arcata, CA: Humboldt State University Press, 2017), 7–27. Humboldt State University Professor of Mathematics Emeritus Biles provides a definitive exposition of the competing formulas used by the House, Senate, and President Washington's Cabinet in crafting the Apportionment Act of 1792.

14   *Annals of Congress*, House of Representatives, 2nd Congress, 1st session, 15 November 1791, 191.

15   Ibid., 24 November 1791, 210.

16   Ibid., 26 March 1792, 331–36, 403–405, 407–14.

17   David P. Currie, "The Constitution in Congress," *Northwestern University Law Review* 90, no. 2 (1995–1996): 612. Professor Currie analyzes in detail (pp. 607–15) the legislative debates leading to the Apportionment Act of 1792. President Washington asked Cabinet members Hamilton, Jefferson, Knox, and Randolph for written opinions on the constitutionality of the congressional apportionment bill he received in February 1792. The president sided with Jefferson and Randolph to veto the measure based on the argument that the Constitution provided that the number of representatives "shall not exceed one for every thirty thousand," and therefore the fractional measure allotted to eight states unconstitutionally increased their individual representation to more than 1 for every 30,000. Curiously, the bill that Washington finally signed was a more flagrant violation of the ratio than the bill he vetoed, and it denied two extra seats to his home state of Virginia. For a succinct account of Cabinet input to Washington's veto, see Jefferson's "Opinion of Apportionment Bill, 4 April 1792," *Founders Online*, National Archives, last modified April 12, 2018, http://founders.archives.gov/documents/Jefferson/01-23-02-0324.

18   *Annals of Congress*, House of Representatives, 2nd Congress, 1st session 9 April 1792, 541, 542, 543.

19   Ibid., 10 April 1792, 548–49.

20   "An Act for apportioning Representative among the several States, according in the first enumeration," April 14, 1792, 1 Stat. 253.

21   For balanced insight into the convoluted financial schemes of William Duer, see Robert E. Wright and David J. Cohen, *Financial Founding Fathers: The Men Who Made America Rich* (Chicago: University of Chicago Press, 2006), chap. 4, "The Sinner"; Robert Francis Jones, *King of the Alley: William Duer: Politician, Entrepreneur, and Speculator, 1768–1799* (Philadelphia: American Philosophical Society, 1992), chap. VII, "The Speculator Fallen: March 1792–May 1799"; and Scott Reynolds Nelson, *A Nation of Deadbeats: An Uncommon History of America's Financial Disasters* (New York: Random House, 2012), chap. 1 and 2.

22   William Constable to Alexander Macomb, 12 February 1792, William Constable Papers, New York Public Library.

23   Elkins and McKitrick, *The Federalist Age*, 262–63. The SUM scrip prices were sourced from Joseph S. Davis, *Essays in the Early History of American Corporations* (Cambridge, MA: Harvard University Press, 1917), 1: 408.

24   Wright and Cohen, *Financial Founding Fathers*, 79.

25   Jones, *King of the Alley*, 172–78. John Pintard endorsed notes in Duer's venture in the neighborhood of a million dollars according to James Grant Wilson, "John Pintard, Founder of the New York Historical Society: An address Delivered before the New York Historical Society, December 3, 1901" (New York: Printed for the Society, 1902), 21–22.

26   Joseph Standish Davis, "William Duer, Entrepreneur, 1747–99," *Essays in the Earlier History of American Corporations*, 2 vols. (Cambridge, MA: Harvard University Press, 1918), 2: 281–316. Also see Jones. *King of the Alley*, 185–206.

27   *New York Assembly Journal 1792*, 31–32, 46, 49. In an attempt to combine the "Million Dollar Bank," the "State Bank," and the "Merchant's Bank," an "Act to incorporate a State Bank" was introduced in the New York General Assembly on February 4, 1792, by assemblyman Nathaniel Laurance (no apparent relation to John Laurance).

28   Macomb to Duer, January 1, 1792, and Macomb to William Constable, January 11, 1792, William Duer Papers at New York Historical Society.

29 Richard Sylla, Robert E. Wright, and David J. Cohen, "Alexander Hamilton, Central Banker: Crisis Management and the Lender of Last Resort in the U.S. Panic of 1792," *Business History Review* 83 (Spring 2009): 11, 61–86. See also Davis, "William Duer Entrepreneur," 280–82.

30 Alexander Hamilton to William Seton, 10 February 1792, Syrett, *Papers of Alexander Hamilton*, 11: 27–29.

31 Miller, *Alexander Hamilton*, 305. "The Livingstons," Miller wrote, "cornered all the gold and silver in New York, then drawing the specie from the banks they forced down the price of securities, prevented the banks from discounting and obliged them to call in their loans. Duer and his associates having gone heavily in debt to the banks were caught in the middle of a ruinous credit squeeze."

32 *The Daily Advertiser* (New York), 31 January 3 1792.

33 Davis, "William Duer, Entrepreneur, 1747–99," 285. Professor Robert Francis Jones, *King of the Alley*, 188, suggests that estimates of Duer's debts at three million dollars were too high, and that *The Gazette of the United States* was closer to the mark at $1,583,000. Robert Troup, who assembled a group of friends to help ease Duer's predicament, on 19 March 1792 advised Hamilton that Duer's debts were "about half a million dollars." *Papers of Alexander Hamilton*, Syrett, 11: 155–58.

34 Cohen, Sylla, and Wright, 24–27.

35 Ibid., 21–22.

36 Walter Livingston to Philip H. Livingston, April 17, 1792, Robert R. Livingston Papers, series 6, 1761–1885.

37 H.M. Colden to John Lawrence, Esq., 11 April 1792. John Laurance Papers, New York Historical Society, folder "1790–1800."

38 McWhorter, *Biographical Sketches*, 46. We are at the mercy of Laurance grandson George McWhorter's second-hand information regarding both Duer's borrowing request and Laurance's correspondence with John Jay on the matter. Since Duer and Laurance knew one another intimately through shared public service and Trinity Church, the desperate Duer could not have avoided pleading for financial help. And given Laurance's tight financial fists, it's equally probable he refused.

39 *The National Gazette*, Philadelphia, 19 April 1792.

40 Massachusetts clergyman Manasseh Cutler, quoted in Jones, *King of the Alley*, 96. "Lady Kitty," crowed Reverend Cutler, "performed the honors of the table most gracefully, was constantly attended by two servants in livery. I presume he had not less than fifteen sorts of wine at dinner, and after the cloth was removed, besides most excellent bottled cider, porter, and several other kinds of strong beer."

41 Elkins and McKitrick, *The Federalist Era*, 279.

42 Thomas Jefferson to George Washington, 9 September 1792, quoted in George Tucker, *The Life of Thomas Jefferson*, 2 vols. (London: Charles Knight and Co., 1837), 1: 438. "I was duped into it by the Secretary of the Treasury ... and of all the errors of my political life this has occasioned me the deepest regret." For more on Jefferson's antipathy with debt, see Herbert F. Sloan, *Principle and Interest: Thomas Jefferson and the Problem of Debt* (Charlottesville: The University of Virginia Press, 1995).

43 Hamilton to Edward Carrington, 26 May 1792, *Works of Alexander Hamilton*, edited by Henry Cabot Lodge, 12 vols. (New York: G. P. Putnam's Sons, 1904), 8: 264.

44 *Annals of Congress*, House of Representative, 2nd Congress, 3rd session, 5 November 1792, 571.

45 George Washington, "The State of the Union Address," delivered to Congress on Tuesday, November 6, 1792.

46 *Annals of Congress*, House of Representatives 2nd Congress, 2nd Session, February 4, 1793, 1413–14.

47 Burrows and Wallace, *Gotham*, 347.

48 *United States Census of 1790*, 23.

49 Lloyd Stewart, *A Far Cry From Freedom: Gradual Abolition (1799–1827)* (Bloomington, IN: Author House, 2005), 122–23.

50 Erica Armstrong Dunbar, "George Washington, Slave Catcher," *The New York Times*, February 16, 2015. When 22-year-old slave Ona Judge fled the Philadelphia presidential mansion in May 1796 for freedom in New Hampshire, Washington unsuccessfully pursued her until his dying day. Dunbar is an associate professor of black studies and history at the University of Delaware.

51 Ralph E. Weber, *United States Diplomatic Codes and Ciphers 1775–1938* (Chicago: Precedent Publishing, 1979), 121–22. Gouveneur Morris was formally received in Paris as United States minister to France in June 1792. He suggested to Hamilton that they devise a confidential communication system to escape

prying Gallic eyes. Twenty-five code names were developed to cover President Washington (Scavola) and members of the Cabinet, Senate, and the House. Laurance was designated "Solon." The code served as much to protect private communication among Hamilton's Federalist circle from Jeffersonian Republicans.

52 John Adams to John Quincy Adams, 3 January 1793, *The Adams Papers*, Family Correspondence, vol. 10, *January 1793–June 1795*, ed. Margaret A. Hogan, C. James Taylor, Sara Martin, Gregg l. Lint, and Sara Georgini (Cambridge, MA: Harvard University Press, 2011), 3–4. "The Attorney General is not yet nominated," wrote Vice President Adams. "Mr. Lewis, Mr. Lawrence, Mr. Benson, Mr. Gore, Mr. Potts &c have been mentioned in conversation."

53 "An Act making Appropriations for Government for the year one thousand seven hundred and ninety-three," *Annals of Congress*, House of Representatives, 2nd Congress, 2nd session, Appendix, 1437–38.

54 Chernow, *Alexander Hamilton*, 426–27. In the Hamilton biography of our present generation, Ron Chernow refers to a document that surfaced in 1895 in Thomas Jefferson's hand supplying Giles with a list of proposed censures against Treasury Secretary Hamilton. Chernow asserts that they were slipped to Representative Giles for the purpose of discrediting Hamilton in Congress. For a taut synopsis of the Giles and Jefferson Resolutions, see "Editorial Note: Jefferson and the Giles Resolutions," *Founders Online*, National Archives, last modified April 12, 2018, http://founders.archives.gov/documents/Jefferson/01-25-02-0259-0001.

55 "Editorial Note: Jefferson and the Giles Resolutions," *Founders Online*, National Archives, last modified April 12, 2018, http://founders.archives.gov/documents/Jefferson/01-25-02-0259-0001.

56 *Papers of Alexander Hamilton*, Syrett, 8: 451–62.

57 *Annals of Congress*, House of Representative, 2nd Congress, 3rd session, 923.

58 Ibid., 925.

59 Alexander Hamilton to John Steele, 15 October 1792, *The Papers of Alexander Hamilton*, Syrett, 12: 567–69. "My apprehension is excited," wrote Hamilton, "when I see so many valuable members dropping off. Mr. Laurance & Mr. Benson will not serve again. The house will I fear lose more of its talents than it can spare."

60 *Annals of Congress*, House of Representatives, 2nd Congress, 3rd session, Appendix, 1287–88.

61 Fisher Ames to William Tudor, 24 November 1791, Massachusetts Historical Society Collection, 2nd set, 8: 325.

62 James Madison to Edmund Randolph, 1 March 1789, *The James Madison Papers at the Library of Congress*, http://hdl.loc./gov/loc.mss/mjm.03_0942_0944.

63 *Annals of Congress*, House of Representatives, 2nd Congress, 2nd session, 16 February 1792, 408–409. Rep. Laurance's remarks were made as the House debated chamber reapportionment of seats in light of 1790 census results. He believed House members should adopt a national rather than local perspective in revising the population formula underlying representative districts.

64 *Annals of Congress*, House of Representatives, 2nd Congress, 2nd session, 16 February 1792, 408–409.

65 Robert Troup to Alexander Hamilton, 15 June 1791, *The Papers of Alexander Hamilton*, Syrett, 8: 478–79.

66 John Laurance to Rufus King, New York, 16 April 1794, *Life and Correspondence of Rufus King*, ed. Charles R. King, 6 vols. (New York: G. B. Putnam's Sons, 1894), I: 561–62.

67 Richard Hofstadter, *The Idea of a Party System: The Rise of Legitimate Opposition in the United States 1780–1840* (Berkeley: University of California Press, 1969), 9. In 1749, anti-party English political gadfly Henry St. John Bolingbroke wrote: "Faction is to party what the superlative is to the positive: party is a political evil and faction is the worst of all parties." *Letters on the Spirit of Patriotism: on the IDEA of a PATRIOT KING and on the STATE of PARTIES* (London: Printed for T. Davies, 1749), 46.

68 Robert Troup to Rufus King, New York, 1 January 1794, King, *Life and Correspondence*, 540.

69 McDonald, *Alexander Hamilton*, 251. Secretary Jefferson in May, 1792 wrote to President Washington that the "ultimate objective" of his adversary was "to prepare the way for a change from the present republican form of government to that of a monarchy."

70 John Hancock coined the term "junto" in 1778 to label Massachusetts reactionaries in wealthy commercial Essex outside of Boston. President John Adams would later dub these Hamilton devotees "a Junto of incorrigible Aristocrats." Its core included Fisher Ames, George Cabot, Tristram Dalton, Francis Dana, Nathan Dane, Benjamin Goodhue, Stephen Higginson, Jonathan Jackson, John Lowell, Harrison Gray Otis, Robert Treat Paine, Theophilus Parsons, Joshua Quincy, Theodore Sedgwick, and Caleb Strong. As an organized political entity, however, David Hackett Fisher argues, in "The Myth of

71. Hamilton to Edward Carrington, 26 May 1792, *Works of Alexander Hamilton*, Lodge, 8: 264. " I said that I was affectionately attached to the republican theory," wrote Hamilton, adding: "this is the real language of my heart . . . I have strong hopes for the success of that theory; but, in candor, I ought to add that I am far from being without doubts."

72. Gordon S. Wood, *Empire of Liberty: A History of the Early Republic, 1789-1815* (New York: Oxford University Press, 2009), 231.

73. Alyn Brodsky, *Benjamin Rush: Patriot and Physician* (New York: St. Martin's Press, 2004), 337-43. When Dr. Rush in 1800 sued William Cobbett for libel in the amount of $5,000, the latter fled to New York then to Nova Scotia and back to his native England, where in 1810 he was found guilty of treasonous libel (for objecting to public floggings) and thrown in notorious Newgate Prison.

74. Martin S. Pernick, "Politics, Parties, and Pestilence: Yellow Fever in Philadelphia and the Rise of the First Party System," *William & Mary Quarterly* XXIX, 3rd ser. (October 1972): 559-86.

75. Rufus King to John Laurance, 21 December 1793, Philadelphia, John Laurance Papers, New York Historical Society, folder "1790-1800."

76. Robert Troup to Rufus King, New York, 1 January 1794, *Life and Correspondence of Rufus King*, ed. Charles R. King, I: 562.

77. Robert Troup to Rufus King, New York, 13 January 1794, *Life and Correspondence of Rufus King*, ed. Charles R. King, I: 542.

Chapter Fourteen

1. John Laurance to Alexander Hamilton, New York, 25 December 1793, *The Papers of Alexander Hamilton*, Syrett, 15: 586-87. Hamilton had earlier written Laurance asking for his written oath to support his defense in Congress against charges from former treasury employee, Andrew Fraunces. For a detailed description of the Fraunces affair, see *The Papers of Alexander Hamilton*, Syrett, 14: 460-70.

2. "Introductory Note from Andrew G. Fraunces, 16 May 1793," Founders Online, National Archives, http://founders.archives.gov/documents/Hamilton/01-14-02-0307-0001.

3. To George Washington from Andrew G. Fraunces, 30 July 1793, *The Papers of George Washington*, Presidential Series, vol. 13, *1 June-31 August 1793*, ed. Christine Sternberg Patrick (Charlottesville: University of Virginia Press, 2007), 303-308.

4. Andrew Fraunces to George Washington, 19 August 1793, *The Papers of George Washington,* Presidential Series, vol. 13, *1 June-31 August 1793*, ed. Christine Sternberg Patrick (Charlottesville: University of Virginia Press, 2007), 493-96.

5. John Laurance to Alexr Hamilton Esqr, New York, 25 December 1793, *The Papers of Alexander Hamilton*, Syrett, 15: 586-7. Also see John Laurance to Rufus King, 18 December 1793, Rufus King Papers, New York Historical Society. Hamilton had earlier written Laurance asking for his written oath to support his defense in Congress against charges from former treasury employee Andrew Fraunces.

6. Laurance's affidavit, on file in the National Archives, verifies that treasury policy toward Confederation-era warrants had changed prior to Fraunces's submissions (due to Assistant Secretary Duer's neglect in submitting warrant payment accounts prior to entering debtors' prison in March 1792) and that he (Laurance) could therefore not possibly have advanced Fraunces the $2,000 in question.

7. Edmond Randolph to John Laurance, 30 April 1794, W. Wright Hawkes Collection, Union College of Schenectady, NY. Laurance was offered the position as Federal Judge for the District of New York after fellow New York Attorney Richard Harrison earlier refused President Washington's nomination for the position.

8. John Laurance to Edmond Randolph, 2 May 1794, George Washington Papers at the Library of Congress, Digital Edition, ed. Theodore J. Crackel (Charlottesville: University of Virginia Press, 2008).

9. Appointment, "United States Judge of the Federal District of New York," dated May 6, 1794, John Laurance Papers, New York Historical Society, folder "1790-1800."

10. Wharton, *Social Life in the Early Republic*, 31.

11 Justin Kaplan, *When the Astor's Owned New York* (New York: Viking Penguin, 2006), 9.

12 Duc François-Alexandre-Frèdèric La Rochefoucauld-Liancourt, *Travels through the United States of North America, the Country of the Iroquois, and Upper Canada . . . with an Authentic Account of Lower Canada*, 2 vols. (London: Printed for R. Phillips, 1799), 2: 132.

13 Charles Hamilton, *Life of Alexander Hamilton*, 5: 532-33.

14 John Lawrance to Rufus King, 23 March 1794, *Life and Correspondence of Rufus King*, ed. Charles R. King, 1: 556.

15 John Lawrance to Rufus King, New York 24 April 1794, *Life and Correspondence of Rufus King*, ed. Charles R. King,1: 564.

16 Charles Merrill Hough, *The United States District Court for the Southern district of New York, 1789-1919* (Maritime Law Association of The United States, Document No. 194, June, 1934), 7. Hough was federal district judge from 1906 to 1916, and circuit judge from 1916 to 1927.

17 "Profile of John Laurance," *The 154 District Judges: Biographies, Writings and Cases*, United States District Court Southern District of New York, http://history.nysd.uscourts.gov.judges.php.

18 Christopher H. Pyle, *Extradition, Politics, and Human Rights* (Philadelphia: Temple University Press, 2001), 21-22. Professor of Politics at Mount Holyoke College, Pyle has frequently testified before Congress on the subject of extradition and deportation.

19 *United States v. Lawrence* (United States Supreme Court Cases, vol. 3, U.S. 42), argued 18 February 1795, decided 3 March 1795.

20 *United States v. Lawrence*, 43.

21 *United States v. Lawrence*, 45.

22 Edmond Randolph to John Laurance, 12 August 1794, *The Documentary History of the Supreme Court of the United States, 1789-1800*, ed. Maeva Marcus, 8 vols. (New York: Columbia University Press, 1998), 6: 527-28.

23 Edmond Randolph to William Bradford Jr. 7 October 1794, *The Documentary History of the Supreme Court of the United States, 1789-1800*, ed. Maeva Marcus, 528-29.

24 William Bradford Jr. to John Laurance, 31 January 1795, *The Documentary History of the Supreme Court of the United States, 1789-1800*, ed. Maeva Marcus, 529-30.

25 *Writings of George Washington from the Original Manuscript Sources*, 1745-1799, edited by John C. Fitzpatrick, and David Maydole, 39 vols. (Washington, DC: U.S. Government Printing Office, 1931-1944), XXIV: 293-95; Josiah T. Newcomb, "New Light on Jay's Treaty," *American Journal of International Law* XXVIII (1934): 687; "Edmund Randolph on the British Treaty," edited by W. C. Ford, *American Historical Review* XII (1907), 587-99; and John C. Miller, *The Federalist Era*, 169-70. Thomas P. Slaughter, *The Whiskey Rebellion* (New York: Oxford University Press, 1986), however, suggests nothing in the captured Fauchet dispatches supports bribery implications against Randolph, although he clearly had not shared Washington and Hamilton's enthusiasm for military suppression of the so-called Whiskey Rebellion.

26 John Laurance to William Bradford Esq., 3 February 1795, *Writings of George Washington from the Original Manuscript Sources*, ed. Fitzpatrick and Maydole, XXIV: 530-31.

27 Alexander Dallas, "Minutes of the Supreme Court, February 18 and March 3, 1795," *Docket of the Supreme Court*, vol. 3: 53, reproduced in *The Documentary History of the Supreme Court of the United States, 1789-1800*, ed. Maeva Marcus (New York: Columbia University Press, 1998), 6: 526.

28 Pyle, *Extradition, Politics, and Human Rights*, 22.

29 Harry Clinton Green and Mary Wolcott Green, *Wives of the Signers: The Women behind the Declaration of Independence*, excerpted from *The Pioneer Mothers of America* originally published in 1912 (Aledo, TX: Wallbuilder Press, 1997), 206. Wealthy signer of the Declaration of Independence and Supreme Court Justice James Wilson was entranced by 19-year-old Hannah Gray upon meeting her in Boston in June 1793. Two days later he proposed and they were shortly married. It was a rocky marriage punctuated by Wilson's two brief debtors' prison stints in wake of the financial "Panic of 1798."

30 James Iredell to Hannah Iredell, 8 April 1795, *The Documentary History of the Supreme Court*, ed. Marcus, 2: 24.

31 *The Daily Advertiser*, 28 February 1795. In attendance were "the Chancellor of the State, the Judges, the Speaker of the Assembly, the Recorder of the City, and the President of Columbia College," according to Alan McLane Hamilton, *Intimate Life of Alexander Hamilton*, 205.

32 John Laurance to Alexander Hamilton, 13 January 1795, *Papers of Alexander Hamilton*, ed. Syrett, 18: 39-40. "Colonel [Jeremiah] Wadsworth," wrote Laurance, "mentioned to me he had paid you some money on account of Mr. Church, which you might wish in New York." The funds may have been related to an early January transaction in which Hamilton and Laurance, in partnership with Robert Troup and Nicholas Fish, acquired 21,800 acres of Nobleborough Township. That same day of 13 January, Hamilton wrote " a bank check payable to Col. John Laurance & endorsed by him" (sold by C. F. Libbie and Company, May 8, 1894, Item 982).

33 Alexander Hamilton to Angelica Church, 18 December 1794, *Papers of Alexander Hamilton*, ed. Syrett, 17: 428.

34 Alexander Hamilton to John Jay, 24 April 1798, *The Papers of Alexander Hamilton*, ed. Syrett, 21: 447.

35 Paul A. W. Wallace, *The Muhlenburgs of Pennsylvania* (Philadelphia: University of Pennsylvania Press, 2018), 291. Professor Wallace, for 25 years on the faculty of Lebanon Valley College, is consultant to the Pennsylvania Historical and Museum Commission.

36 *The Trade Winds: A Study of British Overseas Trade During the French Wars, 1793-1795*, ed. C. Northcote Parkinson (London: 1948), 204n. A total of 91.3 percent of the U.S. trade was carried in U.S. ships in 1795, versus only 58.6 percent five years earlier.

37 "The United States v. La Vengeance," *Condensed Reports of Cases in the Supreme Court of the United States*, edited by Richard Peters, 6 vols. (Philadelphia: Thomas Cowperthwait & Co., 1844), 2: 132-34.

38 "Minutes and Rolls of the U.S. District Court for the Southern District of New York 1789-1811," National Archives and Records Services, General Services Administration: Records of District Courts of the United States Record Group 21, microfilm roll #1, located at the Alexander Hamilton U.S. Customs House, 1 Bowling Green, New York.

39 "Minutes and Rolls of the U.S. District Court for the Southern District of New York 1789-1811."

40 Alexander Hamilton to Rufus King, January, 1796, *The Life and Correspondence of Rufus King*, ed. Charles R. King, 2: 54.

41 *The Life and Correspondence of Rufus King*, ed. Charles R. King, 2: 54.

Chapter Fifteen

1 A. Hamilton to Rufus. King, 5 May 1796. King, *The Life and Correspondence*, 2: 49. "If such things be," Hamilton wrote, "you cannot leave the senate. Jay is against it, at all events until the European storm is over." Hamilton later reversed himself once ratification of the Jay Treaty was assured.

2 Rufus. King to Alexander Hamilton, 2 May 1796, *The Papers of Alexander Hamilton*, ed. Syrett, 20: 151-52.

3 John Laurance to R. King, London, from New York, 15 October 1796, *The Life and Correspondence of Rufus King*, ed. Charles R. King, 2: 208.

4 John Laurance to George Washington, 30 November 1796, *The Founding Era Collection*, University of Virginia Press. rotunda.upress.virginia.edu. DNA: R6-ML.

5 Robert. Troup to Rufus King, New York, 16 November 1796, *The Life and Correspondence of Rufus King*, ed. Charles R. King, 2: 110.

6 Robert Troup to Rufus King, New York, 23 March 1801, *The Life and Correspondence of Rufus King*, ed. Charles R. King, 3: 410. Troup's letter alludes to an indeterminate previous commitment from Federalist leaders (Jay, Hamilton, Schuyler, King) to find a place for Laurance in the state judiciary at the end of his Senate term.

7 John Y. Kohl and Helen W. Kohl, "Introducing . . . The Livingstons," *Proceedings of the Lehigh County Historical Society*, ed. Mildred Rowe Trexler (Allentown, PA: Lehigh County Historical Society, 1968), 27: 112.

8 Isaac Weld, *Travels Through North America*, 2 vols. (London: Printed for J. Stockdale, 1807), 1: 10.

9 William Plumer on Samuel Livermore, from James McLachlan, *Princetonians: A Biographical Directory, 1748-1768* (Princeton, NJ: Princeton University Press, 1976-1991), I: 52. Livermore, wrote Plumer, was distinguished by the "force of talents, and the reputation for integrity, and not by the mildness of his temper, or the amenity of his manners . . . and had a vein for severe satire."

NOTES

10 *Annals of Congress*, 4th Senate, 2nd session, 1524.

11 John Ferling, *John Adams: A Life* (New York: Henry Holt, 1966), 326.

12 Senator Henry Tazewell to Thomas Jefferson, 1 February 1797, *The Papers of Thomas Jefferson*, vol. 29, *1 March 1796-31 December 1797*, ed. Barbara B. Oberg (Princeton, NJ: Princeton University Press, 2002), 281-83. Tazewell suspected potential Federalist foul play in the selection of Federalists Laurance, Sedgwick, and Read "as a thing of concert" in the Senate committee for developing electoral vote counting procedure.

13 George Washington, "The President of the United States to John Laurance, Senator for the State of New York," March 1, 1797, circular letter sold at auction in Boston on October 30, 2016 by Skinner Inc. for $23,985. www.skinnerinc.com/auctions/2950B/lots/31.

14 Undated text by an unknown hand titled "Extract of a letter from a correspondence," *Thomas Jefferson Papers*, 96: 42162. Massachusetts Senators Goodhue and Sedgwick invited "the federal part of the Senate" to a February 14 meeting at Bingham's nearby mansion "to arrange measures for chusing a president of the Senate pro tempore." Laurance and Sedgwick received some votes, but Bingham tallied the majority.

15 Theodore Sedgwick to Rufus King, London, Stockbridge, 12 March 1797, *The Life and Correspondence of Rufus King*, ed. Charles R. King, 2: 156-59.

16 Jeffrey L. Pasley, *The First Presidential Contest: 1796 and the Founding of American Democracy* (Manhattan, KS: University Press of Kansas, 2016), 254-72. Popular vote by district determined electors in Kentucky, North Carolina, Virginia, and Maryland. All went for Washington in 1792, but only Maryland backed Adams in 1796. New Hampshire, Georgia, and Pennsylvania chose electors by statewide popular vote, the latter two shifting from Washington in 1792 to Jefferson in 1796. The new state of Tennessee (employing a hybrid popular/legislative approach to selecting its first electors), cast all three votes for Jefferson.

17 Manning J. Dauer, *The Adams Federalists* (Baltimore: The Johns Hopkins University Press, 1953). American political scientist Dauer (1909-1987) chaired the University of Florida political science department and was key consultant to the state Constitutional Revision Commission.

18 As Professors Elkins and McKitrick, *The Age of Federalism* (pp. 538-39), explain, French interference with American shipping had sporadically occurred since outbreak of hostilities with Great Britain in 1793. The May 9, 1793 law authorizing French privateers to confiscate neutral ships was rescinded and restored four times, culminating in a modified decree of July 2, 1796 that was put into effect that October. "Throughout this entire time," wrote Elkins and McKitrick, "French actions had been arbitrary, erratic, and unpredictable."

19 Greg H. Williams, *The French Assault on American Shipping 1793-1813* (Jefferson, NC: McFarland & Co., 2009), 22-23.

20 Roy Swanstrom, *The United States Senate, 1787-1801: a dissertation on the first fourteen years of the upper legislative body* (Washington, DC: U.S. Govt. Printing Office, 1962), 293.

21 *Annals of Congress*, 5th Senate, 1st Session, 29 May 1797, 15-16.

22 *Annals of Congress*, 5th Senate, 1st Session, 29 May 1797, 16. Also: Walter Stubbs, *Congressional Committees 1789-1982: A Checklist* (Westport, CT: Greenwood Press, 1985).

23 Jeffrey L. Pasley, *The Tyranny of Printers: Newspaper Politics in the Early American Republic* (Charlottesville: University of Virginia Press, 2001), 3, 48-77. "Newspapers and their editors," wrote Pasley, "were purposeful actors in the political process, linking parties, voters, and the government together, and pursuing specific political goals."

24 Connecticut Representative Chauncey Goodrich to Oliver Wolcott Sr., May 20, 1796, *Memoirs of the Administrations of Washington and John Adams*, edited from the papers of Oliver Wolcott by George Gibbs, 2 vols. (New York: William Van Norden, 1846), I: 341.

25 Swanstrom, 292-95.

26 *Annals of Congress*, 5th Senate, 1st Session, 7 June 1797, 18.

27 Ibid., 9 June 1797, 20.

28 Ibid., 14 June 1797, 22.

29 Ibid., 19 June 1797, 23, "An Act to provide for the further Defense of the ports and harbors of the United States."

30 Ibid., 15 June 1797, 22.

31 "Public Acts of the Fifth Congress, 1st session," *United States Statutes at Large,* edited by Richard Peters (Boston: Little, Brown & Company, 1845), 523–25.

32 John Adams to Samuel Adams, London, 26 January 1786, *Bulletin of the New York Public Library*, January to December, 1906, X: 241.

33 Alexander Hamilton to James McHenry, March 1797, *The Papers of Alexander Hamilton,* ed. Syrett, 20: 574–75. Hamilton's letter detailed a specific eight-point military build-up plan, even suggesting that McHenry recommend Adams's call for a day of national prayer (which he did).

34 *Aurora General Advertiser*, July 14, 1797.

35 Adams, *Works*, IX, pp. 301–302, quoted in Joseph P. Harris, *The Advice and Consent of the Senate: A Study of the Confirmation of Appointments by the United States Senate* (Berkeley: University of California Press, 1953), 45.

36 Alexander Hamilton to James McHenry, March 1797, *The Papers of Alexander Hamilton*, ed. Syrett, 20: 574–75.

37 *The Papers of Alexander Hamilton*, ed. Syrett, 20: 574–75.

38 Ibid.

39 John Adams, *The Boston Patriot*, May 29, 1809. Hamilton's letter was originally sent to Connecticut Federalist senator Uriah Tracy who shared it with Adams. "I despised and detested the letter too much to take a copy of it," wrote Adams in 1809.

40 Dauer, *The Adams Federalists*, 120–28. See also Bernard Christian Steiner, *The Life and Correspondence of James McHenry* (Cleveland, OH: The Burrows Brothers Company, 1907), 212–22; Karen E. Robbins, *James McHenry, Forgotten Federalist* (Athens, GA: University of Georgia Press, 2013), 170–85.

41 John Adams to Harrison Gray Otis, 4 April 1823, Samuel Eliot Morrison, *The Life and Letters of Harrison Gray Otis, Federalist, 1765–1848* (Boston: Houghton Mifflin Company, 1913), I: 158.

42 *Journal of the Executive Proceedings of the Senate of the United States of America 1789–1805*, Monday, 5 June 1797, 241–44.

43 Laurance to Hamilton, 13 January 1796 ($1,500 cash transfer to Bank of New York); Hamilton to Laurance, 1 June 1797 (receipt of a letter no longer found); Laurance to Hamilton, 3 June 1797 (re: property purchase from J. Mark & Co.); Laurance to Hamilton, 10 December 1797 (re: $2,000 payment on joint bond to Robert Lenox); Hamilton to Laurance, 26 December 1798 (re: joint bond for $6,000 to Robert Lenox); Laurance to Hamilton, 28 December 1798 (re: Joint bond payment to Robert Lenox), *Founders Online*, National Archives, http://founders.archives.gov/documents.Hamilton.

44 Alexander Hamilton to William Smith, with enclosure, 10 April 1797, *The Papers of Alexander Hamilton*, ed. Syrett, 5: 29–41.

45 Richard H. Kohn, *Eagle and Sword: The Federalists and the Creation of the Military Establishment in America, 1783–1802* (New York: The Free Press, 1975), chap. X–XVII.

46 Ibid., 157–70. On the Whiskey Rebellion, see Leland D. Baldwin, *Whiskey Rebels: The Story of a Frontier Uprising* (Pittsburgh, PA: University of Pittsburgh Press, 1939), and Thomas P. Slaughter, *The Whiskey Rebellion: Frontier Epilogue to the American Revolution* (New York: Oxford University Press, 1988).

47 "I sincerely hope." Laurance wrote to Senator King on April 3, 1794, "you will not relax from the system which had begun to show itself. I mean fortifying our ports, having a competent select body of Militia ready, supplying the deficiency in the Army & providing for its increase on the contingency of war." *The Life and Correspondence of Rufus King*, ed. Charles R. King, 1: 558–59.

48 Max A. Edling, *A Revolution in Favor of Government: Origins of the U.S. Constitution and the Making of the American State* (New York: Oxford University Press, 2003), Part Two, Military Power, 71–146. "Military strength," writes Edling, "was needed in order to enforce commercial regulations, which would secure treaties. Treaties, in turn, would promote trade, which would be the major object of federal taxation and therefore the national government's main source of income," 76.

49 John G. B. Hutchins, *American Maritime Industries and Public Policy, 1789–1914: An Economic History* (Cambridge, MA: Harvard University Press, 1941), 224–25.

50 Michael A. Palmer, *Stoddert's War: Naval Operations During the Quasi-War with France* (Columbia, SC: University of South Carolina Press, 1987), 6.

51 Charles O. Paullin, *Navy of the American Revolution* (Chicago: University of Chicago Press, 1906), 217. On recommendation of delegate Alexander Hamilton, Confederation Congress elected Major General

McDougall to the new post of secretary of the Marine. He served from February 7 to August 29, 1781, resigning when forced to choose between his army commission and the new secretary position.

52 *Observations on Certain Documents Contained in No. V & VI of "The History of the United States for the Year 1796," in Which the Charge of Speculation Against Alexander Hamilton, Late Secretary of the Treasury, is Fully Refuted. Written by Himself." Papers of Alexander Hamilton*, ed. Syrett, 21: 238, "The Reynolds Pamphlet."

53 Robert Troup to Rufus King, 3 September 1797, Robert Troup Papers at New York Historical Society.

54 Entry in Cash Book of Alexander Hamilton, 1795-1808, for 29 December 1797, "John Laurance Dr to Cash paid R Lenox at his request by way of loan 1500," Alexander Hamilton Papers, Library of Congress. Laurance was the lead partner with Hamilton and John B. Church in the purchase of upstate New York property from J. Mark & Co.

Chapter Sixteen

1 Dumas Malone, *Jefferson and the Ordeal of Liberty* (Boston: Little, Brown & Company, 1962), 360. The vice president, already estranged from the president, was delayed at Monticello until December 12. Not only had newly wedded daughter Maria (Eppes) been injured in a fall, but Jefferson also suffered a "rare cold" during "a period of uncommonly bad weather, which also rendered the rivers unfordable." Between July 6, 1797, and December 12, 1797, Senators William Bradford and Jacob Read presided over the Senate for 45 days in the vice president's absence. Senators Sedgwick and Laurance would do the same for almost six months of 1798.

2 Robert Troup to Rufus King, New York, June 8, 1798, *Life and Correspondence of Rufus King*, ed. Charles R. King, 2: 283.

3 *Annals of Congress*, 5th Senate, 2nd session, 526.

4 John Laurance to Rufus King, Phila., 5 June 1798, *Life and Correspondence of Rufus King*, ed. Charles R. King, 2: 332.

5 "An Act to Provide Additional Armament for Further Protection of the Trade; and for Other Purposes." *United States Statutes at Large*, vol. I: 5th Congress, 2nd session, 27 April 1798, chap. 31, 552

6 "An Act to Authorize the President to cause to be purchased or built, a number of small vessels to be equipped as Galleys, or otherwise," *Annals of Congress*, 5th Senate, 2nd session, 4 May 1798, 556.

7 "An Act supplementary to the Act providing for the further defense of the ports and harbors, of the United States," May 3, 1798, *Annals of Congress*, 5th Senate, 2nd session, 3 May 1798, 544.

8 Alexander Hamilton, *Works of Alexander Hamilton*, ed. Lodge, 8: 63.

9 Oliver Wolcott Jr. to Alexander Hamilton, 18 May 1798, *The Papers of Alexander Hamilton*, ed. Syrett, 21: 456–57.

10 Ian W. Toll, *Six Frigates: The Epic History of the Founding of the U.S. Navy* (New York: W. W. Norton & Company, 2006), 98.

11 *Naval Documents Related to the Quasi-War between the United States and France: Naval Operations from February 1797 to October 1798* (Washington, DC: U.S. Government Printing Office, 1935), 59–60. Also see Charles Paullin, *History of Naval Administration 1775 1911* (Annapolis: Naval Institute Press, 1968), 1796–99.

12 *Annals of Congress*, 5th Senate, 2nd session, June 19, 1798, 583. Only five warships were actually purchased: *Philadelphia* (44 guns), *New York* (40 guns), *Boston* and *Essex* (36 guns each), and *John Adams* (32 guns). After an uneventful career, *New York* was retired from service in 1804 and ultimately burned at the Washington, DC, Navy Yard in 1814 to avoid seizure by the invading British.

13 Timothy Pickering to John Pickering, Philadelphia, 16 June 1798, Gerard H. Clarfield, *Timothy Pickering and the American Republic* (Pittsburgh: University of Pittsburgh Press, 1980), 195.

14 "Draft to British minister to the United States Robert Liston, Downing Street, London, June 8, 1798, no. 12, Mayo, *Instructions to British Ministers*, 155ff," Dauer, *The Adams Federalists*, 182. A similar draft was communicated to Liston on January 27, 1797.

15 Clarfield, *Timothy Pickering*, 200.

16 Allan McLane Hamilton, *Intimate Life of Alexander Hamilton*, 323.

17   Robert C. Alberts, *The Golden Voyage: The Life and Times of William Bingham (1752-1804)* (Boston: Houghton Mifflin Co., 1969), 341. Thomas Jefferson, *Anas of Thomas Jefferson, Works*, IX, 195-96, confirms this meeting by alluding to three different sources, including Federalist congressman Harrison Gray Otis (CT).

18   Theodore Sedgwick to Rufus King, July 1, 1798, *Papers of Rufus King*, II: 352.

19   Dauer, *The Adams Federalists*, 170.

20   John C. Fitzpatrick, *Writings of George Washington*, 7: 336f. "He was," wrote Fitzpatrick of Timothy Pickering, "a captious critic of George Washington and acted a part in the infamous Conway Cabal." See also Edward G. Lengel, *A Companion to George Washington* (New York: John Wiley & Sons), chap. 12. "Timothy Pickering," wrote Lengel, "openly criticized Washington's generalship at Brandywine, especially his indecisiveness."

21   "An Act to declare the treaties heretofore concluded with France, no longer obligatory on the United States," 1 *Stat.* 578, July 7, 1798. The Senate committee (Laurance, Bingham, Goodhue, Gunn, and Tracy) that was appointed on November 29, 1797 to recommend: "measures being adopted for the security and protection of the commerce of the United States," on June 21, 1798 "reported a bill, declaring void the treaties between the United States and the French Republic." It was amended in the House to pass on July 6 by a 47 to 37 margin, *Annals of Congress*, 5th House, 2nd Session, 6 July 1798, 2127-28.

22   *Annals of Congress*, as quoted by the Philadelphia *Aurora* of July 6, 1798; Richard N. Rosenfeld, *American Aurora* (New York: St. Martin's Press, 1997), 182-83.

23   "President John Adams to all commanders of armed vessels belonging to the United States of America, Philadelphia, July 10, 1798," *Naval Investigation: Hearings before the Subcommittee on Naval Affairs United States Senate, Sixty-Sixth Congress Second Session* (Washington, DC: Government Printing Office, 1921), 1: 1273.

24   "An Act to make a further appropriation for the advancement of naval armament," 16 July 1798, *United States Statutes at Large*, Peters, 608.

25   "An Act authorizing the President of the United States to raise a Provisional Army," May 28, 1798, *Statutes II, Fifth Congress, Session II, Chapter XLVII*, 1798, 558-61; "An Act providing Arms for the Militia throughout the United States," July 6, 1798, *Chapter LXV*, 1798, 576-77.

26   George Washington to John Adams, President of the United States, 13 July 1798, *Annals of Congress*, Senate, 5th Congress, 2nd session, 18 July 1798, 621-22.

27   *Documents relating to New England Federalism 1800-1815*, edited by Henry Adams (Boston: Little, Brown & Company, 1905), 335; *Writings of* George *Washington*, ed. Fitzpatrick, XXXVI, July 4, 1798.

28   "Candidates for Army Appointments from New York," *Papers of Alexander Hamilton*, ed. Syrett, 22: 100-101.

29   Alexander Hamilton to James McHenry, 21 August 1798 with enclosures, *Papers of Alexander Hamilton*, ed. Syrett, 22: 89-108.

30   Alexander Hamilton to James McHenry, 20 December 1798, *Papers of Alexander Hamilton*, ed. Syrett, 22: 380.

31   *Certificate of Commission by the State of New York*, John Laurance Papers at Oswego County Historical Society. John McDougall Laurance was not among the federal officer corps in an "Additional Army" that never approached half-strength and a "Provisional Army" that never mobilized. He was, however, commissioned a "Captain in the 3rd Regiment of Militia in the City and County of New York" on 5 July 1804.

32   James Ross to George Washington, 2 February 1798, *Writings of George Washington*, ed. Fitzpatrick, XXXVI: 164.

33   Leonard W. Levy and Merrill D Peterson, *Major Crises in American History* (New York: Harcourt, Brace and World, 1962), I: 200; James Morton Smith, *Freedom's Fetters: The Alien and Sedition Laws and American Civil Liberties* (Ithaca, NY: Cornell University Press, 1956), 103.

34   James Lloyd to George Washington, Philadelphia, 4 July 1798, *The Papers of George Washington*, Retirement series, vol. 2, *2 January 1798-15 September 1798*, ed. W.W. Abbot (Charlottesville: University of Virginia Press, 1998), 375-76.

35   Philadelphia *Aurora* of 12, 15, and 19 February 1800, as communicated to the Senate by New Jersey senator Jonathan Dayton on 14 March 1800, *American State Papers, Documents, Legislative and Executive of the Congress of the United States* (Washington, DC: Gales and Seaton, 1834), vol. I, document 126. *Aurora* editor William Duane stated that the information came from two senators who were present

at the Bingham conclave; and that a dozen senators as well as Speaker Sedgwick would swear to the meeting if put under oath. The veracity of the *Aurora*'s information is reinforced by its use by an outraged Federalist Senator Dayton to later bring charges against the paper for seditious language in the hearings of editor William Duane in March of 1800.

36 John Adams to Harrison Gray Otis, 4 April 1823, Morrison, *The Life and Letters of Harrison Gray Otis*, 1: 97n.

37 Alberts, *The Golden Voyage*, 337; Philadelphia *Aurora*, 19 February 1800.

38 John F. Hoadley, *Origins of American Political Parties, 1789–1803* (Lexington, KY: University Press of Kentucky, 1986), 153. In chap. 7, Duke University assistant professor of political science Hoadley presents an extensive multi-variable statistical analysis of voting patterns in both houses of the Fifth United States Congress. "It would be a mistake," he concludes, " to consider High Federalists a major factor . . . There is no evidence from spatial analysis of any substantial division within the Federalist bloc." Both Bell (1973) and Dauer (1953) disagree. The latter argues that a serious split occurred between so-called High Federalists and the Adams moderates, while the former identified 10 different factions with distinct voting alignments that shifted depending upon the issue.

39 Frank M. Anderson, "The Enforcement of the Alien and Sedition Laws," *Annual Report of the American Historical Association for the Year 1912* (Washington, DC: Smithsonian Institution, 1914), 120. Although instantly considered unconstitutional by public opinion, the four acts never received Supreme Court review. Five leading Republican newspapers were targeted, and all but the Philadelphia *Aurora* were effectively shut down. Altogether some 25 people were arrested under the Alien and Sedition Acts, 15 of whom were indicted. Eleven came to trial and 10 (including Kentucky congressman Matthew Lyon) went to jail.

40 Samuel Eliot Morrison and Henry Steele Commager, *The Growth of the American Republic*, 2 vols. (New York: Oxford University Press, 1962), 1: 359. Secretary of State Pickering would have received both messages via personal meeting with Liston.

41 "From Thomas Jefferson to John Taylor, 4 June 1798," *Founders Online*, National Archives, last modified June 13, 2018, http://founders.archives.gov/documents/Jefferson/01-30-02-0280. "A little patience," Jefferson wrote, "and we shall see the reign of witches pass over, their spells dissolve, and the people recovering their true sight, restore their government to its true principles."

42 *Annals of Congress*. 5th Senate, 2nd session, 575–623.

43 Ibid., 26 April 1798, 523.

44 Theodore Sedgwick to Rufus King, 9 April 1798, *Life and Correspondence of Rufus King*, ed. Charles R. King, 2: 311.

45 Alexander Hamilton to Oliver Wolcott Jr., 29 June 1798, *Papers of Alexander Hamilton*, ed. Syrett, 21: 522.

46 Robert Troup to Rufus King, New York, 2 October 1798, *Life and Correspondence of Rufus King*, ed. Charles R. King, 2: 428–29.

47 *Life and Correspondence of Rufus King*, ed. Charles R. King, 2: 428–29.

48 *Annals of Congress*, 5th Senate, 3rd session, 3 December 1798, 2189.

49 James A. Richardson, *A Compilation of the Messages and Papers of the Presidents*, 11 vols. (Washington, DC: Bureau of National Literature 1897), I: 276.

50 *Extracts from the Journal of the United States Senate in All Cases of Impeachment Presented by the House of Representatives 1797–1904* (Washington, DC: Government Printing Office, 1912), 5.

51 *Annals of Congress*, 5th Senate, 3rd session, 16 February 1799, 2222.

52 McWhorter, *Biographical Sketches*, 50.

53 "An Act for the Augmentation of the Navy," *Annals of Congress*, 5th Senate, 3rd session, 19 February 1799, 2225.

54 Palmer, *Stoddert's War*, 126.

55 Nathan Miller, *The U.S. Navy, A History* (Annapolis: Naval Institute Press, 1997), 40.

56 Charles G. Goldsborough, *United States Naval Chronicle* (Washington, DC: J. Wilson, 1824), 109–11. Goldsborough served as chief navy clerk for more than 40 years.

57 Elkins and McKittrick, *Age of Federalism*, 658.

58 John Adams, *Works*, X: 152. Adams had no doubt in his own mind as to who sired the Navy. In his old age he boasted: "I humbled the French Directory as much as all Europe has humbled Bonaparte . . . I built frigates, manned a navy, and selected officers with great anxiety and care."

59 Robert Troup to Rufus King, New York 6 May 1799, Rufus King Papers, New York Historical Society, vol. 47, Robert Troup letters.

60 Robert Troup to Rufus King, New York, 5 June 1799, Rufus King Papers, New York Historical Society, vol. 47, Robert Troup letters.

61 Robert Troup to Rufus King, New York, 6 November 1799, Rufus King Papers, New York Historical Society, vol. 47, Robert Troup letters.

62 Harrison Gray Otis to Sally Foster Otis, 26 December 1799 from the House of Representatives, Morrison, *The Life and Letters of Harrison Gray Otis*, I: 141.

Chapter Seventeen

1 Robert Troup to Rufus King, New York, 9 March 1800, Rufus King Papers, New York Historical Society, vol. 47, Robert Troup letters. The letter from Laurance to which Troup refers is not to be found.

2 *Annals of Congress*, 6th Senate, 1st session, 12–151. Between January 1 and May 14 when the 1st session of the Sixth United States Senate adjourned, John Laurance was assigned to committees to consider and report on: relief of persons imprisoned for debt; salvage of vessels in cases of recapture; valuation of unseated lands, dwelling house, and the enumeration of slaves; compensation increase for members of Congress; provisions for results of disputed elections; drawing jurors by lot in federal courts; uniform system of bankruptcy in the United States; settling financial balances of the states; laying duties on manufacture of snuff; regulating the medical department; and reforming the Superior Court of the U.S. territory northwest of the Ohio River.

3 James I. Brownson, *The Life and Times of Senator James Ross* (Washington, PA: Printed for the Washington County Historical Society, 1910), 19. "On January 19, 1799," wrote Ross biographer Brownson, "Thomas Jefferson jotted down the fact that W. C. Nicholas had told him that in a conversation with Ross . . . Ross had said 'that he saw no good in any kind of election.'" For a thorough account of the "Ross Bill," see J. Hampden Dougherty, *The Electoral System of the United States* (New York: G. P. Putnam's Sons, 1906), 63–72.

4 Thomas Jefferson to James Madison, 8 March 1800, *The Papers of James Madison*, Rutland, 17: 368.

5 Philadelphia *Aurora*, Feb. 19, 1800.

6 Susan Dunn, *Jefferson's Second Revolution: The Election of 1800 and the Triumph of Republicanism* (New York: Houghton Mifflin Company, 2004), 170–71. The author refers to a newspaper piece in the Frankfort, KY *Palladium* of 10 April 1800 quoting an unidentified senator, most likely outspoken Kentucky Federalist Humphrey Marshall.

7 *Annals of Congress*, Sixth Senate, 1st session, Wednesday, 27 March 1800, 122–23.

8 Ibid., 28 March 1800, 125–26. Passing the House by a single vote margin, "An Act for uniform system of bankruptcy throughout the United States," arrived with Senator Laurance's select committee on February 20, 1800. The proposed bill was read on the Senate floor on March 4, 10, and 17 before passage on March 28 with a 16 to 12 margin.

9 *Journal of the House of Representatives*, 1 June 1789, I: 43; 8 November 1791, I: 451; 21 November 1792, I: 623: and 10 December 1792, I: 636. On 10 December 1792 Rep. Smith from the committee presented a bill to "establish a uniform system of bankruptcies throughout the United States," which was read the first and second time and committed to a committee of the whole House (H.B. 205) on the second Monday of January 1793 but was not acted upon.

10 For an understanding of congressional efforts to create a uniform bankruptcy system from 1789 to 1800, see *Annals of Congress*, 9: 2649–2677; Kathryn Turner, "Federalist Policy and the Judiciary Act of 1801," *William and Mary Quarterly* 22, 3rd series (January, 1965): 3–32; Charles Warren, *Bankruptcy in United States History* (Washington, DC: reprinted by Beard Books by arrangement with Harvard University Press from the 1935 original, 1999), 10–19; and Peter J. Coleman, *Debtors and Creditors in America: Insolvency, Imprisonment for Debt, and Bankruptcy, 1697–1900* (Madison: State Historical Society of Wisconsin, 1974), 7–19, 269–75.

11 *Annals of Congress*, 6th Senate, 1st session, 4 March 1800, 68.

12 Ralph Brubaker, "On the Nature of Federal Bankruptcy Jurisdiction: General Statutory and Constitutional Theory," *William & Mary Law Review* 41 (March 2000): 758-59. See also Charles Jordan Tabb, "The History of Bankruptcy Laws in the United States," *ABI Law Review* 3, no. 5 (1995): 10-15. For insight into state-by-state debtor insolvency practices, see Coleman, *Debtors and Creditors in America*, passim.

13 Bruce H. Mann, *Republic of Debtors: Bankruptcy in the Age of American Independence* (Cambridge, MA: Harvard University Press, 2002), 6-34. Litigation, Mann observes, was the creditor's last resort. Debtors unable to find a bondsman to stand bail then faced imprisonment, not as punishment but to guarantee they would appear in court.

14 *Annals of Congress*, 6th Senate, 1st session, 28 March 1800, 146. No Senate Republican voted in favor of the bill, two moderate Federalists voted against it, and John Laurance abstained.

15 Ibid., 25 February 1799, 2993.

16 Marcus, *The Documentary History of the Supreme Court of the United States*, 4: 246. "By early 1800," writes Marcus, "the Jeffersonian opposition was actively engaged in seeking a solution to extrajudicial office holding." Accordingly, Senator Pinckney on February 3 introduced a constitutional amendment to preclude such activity on pain of removal from the bench. Pinckney had also unsuccessfully proposed a similar measure during the Constitutional Convention of 1787. See also *Senate Legislative Journal* 3: 10, 43, 63.

17 Marcus, *The Documentary History of the Supreme Court of the United States*, vol. 4, 246, n16. The absent John Laurance was the only member of the committee that did not vote against the proposed Pinckney amendment. See *Senate Legislative Journal* 3: 66.

18 J. Hampton Dougherty, *The Electoral System of the United States* (New York: G. P. Putnam's Sons, 1906), 70. Without attributing the source, Dougherty quoted Jefferson as writing that the Ross Bill "underwent a revolution in the House of Representatives."

19 "Record of Pennsylvania Marriages Prior to 1810," *Pennsylvania Archives*, 2nd series, vol. 8 (Clarence M. Busch, State Printer of Pennsylvania, 1895), 11.

20 Bob Amebeck, "Tracking the Speculators: Greenleaf and Nicholson in the Federal City," *Washington History* 3, no. 1 (Spring/Summer 1991): 112-25. See also, Allen C. Clark, *Greenleaf and Law in the Federal City* (Washington, DC: Press of W. F. Roberts, 1901); and Daniel M. Friedenburg, *Life, Liberty, and the Pursuit of Land: The Plunder of Early America* (Buffalo, NY: Prometheus Books, 1992), 344.

21 Mann, *Republic of Debtors*, 201. Together with Robert Morris and John Nicholson, Greenleaf formed the North American Land Company on February 20, 1795, acquiring some six million acres. Interpersonal difficulties led to Greenleaf selling out his share to the other partners on December 24, 1795; but the entire $10 million enterprise went under when much of the land turned out to be barren and worthless and the federal city materialized more slowly than anticipated. All three men ended up in debtors' prison.

22 Carol B. Wickkiser, "The Allen Family and Trout Hall," *Chapters from the History of the Lehigh County Historical Society* (Allentown, PA: November 1976), 9.

23 Brian Phillips Murphy, "'A very convenient instrument': The Manhattan Company, Aaron Burr, and the Election of 1800," *William and Mary Quarterly* LXV, no. 2, 3rd series (April 2008): 233-34. Incorporated by the state as a water company in April 1799, the Manhattan Company was infiltrated by Burr, who quietly amended the charter, took over the board of directors, enlarged its capitalization, and turned the company into a lending bank. "To Federalists and Republicans alike, Jefferson's election—the revolution of 1800—had been financed by a reservoir of Manhattan Company cash."

24 Alfred F. Young, *The Democratic Republicans of New York: Origins, 1763-1797* (Chapel Hill: University of North Carolina Press, 1967), 394-96.

25 Jason K. Duncan, *Citizens or Papists? The Politics of Anti-Catholicism in New York 1685-1821* (New York: Fordham University Press, 2005), 100.

26 Duncan, *Citizens or Papists*, 97.

27 Burrows and Wallace, *Gotham: A History of New York City to 1898*, 328. "Burr," wrote Burrows and Wallace, "also introduced 'fagot' or 'bundle' voting into the party's political repertoire . . . enfranchising scores of working people who failed to meet the property requirement for voters by making them joint owners of a single piece of property."

28 Robert Troup to Rufus King, 30 April, 1800, as cited in Susan Dunn's *Jefferson's Second Revolution: Election Crisis of 1800 and the Triumph of Republicanism* (New York: Houghton Mifflin Company, 2004), 180.

29 Robert Troup to Rufus King, New York, 1 March 1800, Rufus King Papers, New York Historical Society, vol. 47, Robert Troup letters.

30 Larson, *A Magnificent Catastrophe*, 95.

31 Elkins and McKittrick, *Age of Federalism*, 733. The quote is from an unnamed Republican stalwart upon first reading the list of Federalist candidates for New York City's 13 General Assembly seats.

32 The documented facts surrounding Senator and Mrs. Laurance's hurried last week of April trip to New York are these: 1) Elizabeth Laurance was in her Philadelphia home as of 9 March 1800 per letter that date from Robert Troup to Rufus King; 2) Senator Laurance, after attending the session of 24 April 1800 was absent from Senate business until May 5, 1800, a period of 11 days, per *Annals of Congress*, 6th Senate, 1st session, April 24, 1800–May 6, 1800, 165–84; 3) The May 3, 1800 *Daily Advertiser* (New York, NY), reported: "Died in this city, on Tuesday morning the 29th Inst., Mrs. Elizabeth Lawrence, wife of the hon. John Lawrence, a Senator of the United States"; 4) Twenty-two days after her New York death, Elizabeth's body was interred at Philadelphia's Christ Church burying yard on 20 May 1800, per *Christ Church Historical Collections Online*, Book 1795–1800, p. 3581; 5) Laurance after an absence of 11 days was present in the Senate on May 5, 1800 per *Journals of the U.S. Senate*, 6th Congress, 1st session, 86.

33 J. Hardie, *The Philadelphia Directory & Register* (1793), 214.

34 *Daily Advertiser* (New York, NY), Saturday, 3 May 1800. "Died in this city, on Tuesday morning the 29th Inst., Mrs. Elizabeth Lawrence, wife of the hon. John Lawrence, a Senator of the United States."

35 Benjamin Rush, *Travels Through Life or Sundry Incidents in the Life of Dr. Benjamin Rush*, ed. Louis Alexander Biddle (Philadelphia: Published privately, 1905), 162. Under the date of April 29, 1800, Dr. Benjamin Rush wrote of Mrs. Allen that "She made one of her physicians declare a few days before she died upon his honor she was not dying."

36 Rush, *Travels Through Life*, 162.

37 Dunn, *Jefferson's Second Revolution*, 180.

38 Edward Channing, *A History of the United States, Federalists and Republicans 1789–1815* (New York: The Macmillan Company, 1917), vol. 4, 237.

39 McCullough, *John Adams*, 550.

40 Larsen, *A Magnificent Catastrophe*, 104; Duncan, *Citizens or Papists?*, 100. John Laurance acquired a dozen Seventh Ward properties in partnership with Robert Troup some time before July 1790 (John Laurance to Robert Troup, 26 July 1790, Robert Troup Papers at New York Public Library, box I, folder 7). After selling his share in eight of the lots over to Troup for "7500 dollars lawful money of the United States of America" on 13 September 1798, Laurance and wife Elizabeth retained half share of the remaining four lots situated "between Grand and Bullock Street in the Bowery" (John Laurance to Robert Troup, 26 July 1790, Deed of Indenture dated 13 September 1798, Robert Troup Papers at New York Public Library, box I, folder 7).

41 John Ferling, *Adams vs. Jefferson: The Tumultuous Election of 1800* (New York: Oxford University Press, 2004), 131. "Republicans," wrote Ferling, "took over 65% of the votes in the Sixth and Seventh Wards combined, and that was sufficient to sweep them to victory."

42 John C. Miller, *Alexander Hamilton: Portrait in Paradox* (New York: Harper & Row, 1959), 531.

43 *Christ Church Historical Collections Online* (www//christchurchphila.pastperfectonline.com) Book 1795–1800, 3581. Charles Peirce, *Meteorological Account of the Weather in Philadelphia from January 1, 1790 to January 1, 1847* (Philadelphia: Lindsay & Blakiston, 1847), 89. According to Peirce, May of 1800 was "the warmest May we have yet on record."

44 John Hill Martin, *Bench and Bar of Philadelphia* (Philadelphia: R. Welsh & Co., 1883), 288. John Laurance was inducted to the Philadelphia bar on June 7, 1780. Most likely Dr. William Shippen or Executive Council President Joseph Reed had something to do with it, since both expressed their gratitude to Judge Advocate Laurance for his even-handed 1780 prosecution in the respective trials of Shippen and former Philadelphia Military District commander Benedict Arnold.

45 Fisher Ames to Timothy Pickering, Dedham, 19 October 1799, *Works of Fisher Ames*, edited by Seth Ames and John Thornton Kirkland (Boston: Little, Brown and Co., 1854), 257.

46 Gouverneur Morris to George Washington, 9 December 1799, Alexander Johnson, *American Political History 1763–1876*, 2 vols. (New York: G. P. Putnam's Sons, 1913), 1: 230.

47 James McHenry to George Washington, undated, Steiner, *James McHenry*, 420.

48 William Garrott Brown, *The Life of Oliver Ellsworth* (New York: Macmillan Company, 1905), 311. An anonymous letter of March 11, 1800, to President Adams claimed that Hamilton, Pickering, Wolcott, McHenry, et al. were collaborating behind his back to elect Ellsworth. See also *1896 Report of the American Historical Association*, 1: 824–35.

49 Philadelphia *Aurora*, May 16 and May 20, 1800. Most sources suggest this inaugural caucus took place in the Senate chamber rather than Read's home. See John J. Patrick, Richard M. Pious, and Donald Ritchie, *Oxford Guide to the United States Government* (New York: Oxford University Press, 1993, 1994, 1998, 2001), 93.

50 Francis B. Heitman, *Historical Register and Dictionary of the United States Army, From Its Organization, September 29, 1789, to March 2, 1903* (Washington, DC: U.S. Government Printing Office, 1903), vol. II, 568. By the time that Adams left office the following February, the United States Army consisted only of the general staff, four regiments of infantry, two of artillery, and two troops of light dragoons, a total of 4,436 men.

51 Chernow, *Alexander Hamilton*, 620. Two years after Hamilton's passing, Adams described him in an 1806 letter to Benjamin Rush as "a bastard brat of a Scotch peddler."

52 John Laurance to John Jones, 12 March 1800, Thomas Addis Emmet Collection, New York Public Library. Laurance confided to Jones that he had asked Adams the personal favor of considering mutual friend W. W. Morris for a government post.

53 McDougall, *American Revolutionary*, 51–53.

54 Alberts, *The Golden Voyage*, 342–43. See also Robert Troup to Rufus King, 2 October 1798, ed. Charles R. King. *Life and Correspondence of Rufus King*, III: 430.

55 *Journal of the Executive Proceedings of the 5th United States Senate*, 2nd session, 303. President Adams in July 1798 submitted son-in-law Smith's name as candidate for brigadier general alongside major general's commissions for Henry Knox, C.C. Pinckney, and Alexander Hamilton. The Senate rejected Smith for brigadier, but later approved him as lieutenant colonel of the Twelfth Regiment of Infantry on 8 January 1799.

56 Robert Troup to Rufus King, New York, 24 June 1800, Rufus King Papers at New York Historical Society, box 47, Robert Troup letters.

57 Jerry W. Knudson, *Jefferson and the Press: Crucible of Liberty* (Columbia: University of South Carolina Press, 2006), 52.

58 *Gazette of the United States*, September 9, 1799; Phillip I. Blumberg, *Repressive Jurisprudence in the Early American Republic* (New York: Cambridge University Press, 2010), 37.

59 Robert Troup to Rufus King, New York, 9 August 1800, Rufus King Papers at New York Historical Society, box 47, Robert Troup letters.

60 *Annals of Congress*, 6th Senate, 1st session, 14 May 1800, 183–84.

61 Dauer, *The Adams Federalists*, 200.

62 Ferling, *Adams Versus Jefferson*, 140.

63 James Madison to Thomas Jefferson, 1–3 November 1800, Thomas Jefferson Papers, Library of Congress.

64 Jedediah Morse to Oliver Wolcott Jr., 27 October 1800, Oliver Wolcott Papers, Connecticut Historical Society.

65 John Lawrance to Rufus King, New York, 12 January 1801, Rufus King Papers at New York Historical Society, vol. 47, Robert Troup letters.

66 Alexander Hamilton to James Bayard, 16 January 1801, *The Papers of Alexander Hamilton*, Syrett, 25: 319–24. See also Hamilton to Gouverneur Morris, 9 and 13 January 1801, Harrison Gray Otis, 23 December 1800, John Rutledge, 4 January 1801, Theodore Sedgwick, 21 January 1801, and Oliver Wolcott Jr., 16 December 1800.

67 Chilton Williamson, *American Suffrage from Property to Democracy, 1760–1860* (Princeton, NJ: Princeton University Press, 1960), 174.

68 http://www/archives.gov/exhibits/charters/charters_of_freedom_13.htm. "Expansion of Rights and Liberties—The Right of Suffrage," *On-line Exhibit: The Charters of Freedom*, National Archives. "At the time of the first Presidential election in 1789, only 6 percent of the population—white male property owners—was eligible to vote."

69 *Historical Statistics of the U.S., Colonial Times to 1970* (U.S. Department of Commerce, Bureau of the Census, 1975), 8. The United States population of adult white males increased from 3,929,214 in 1790 to 5,308,483 in 1800, a gain of 35.1 percent. See also Donald Ratcliffe, "The Right to Vote and the Rise of Democracy, 1787-1828," *Journal of the Early Republic* 33 (Summer 2013): 221, 230, 232.

70 Wood, *Empire of Liberty*, 74–83. "England, for example," writes Professor Wood, "had become for Adams as much of a republic as America was, a 'monarchical republic it is true, but still a republic'... so too, he said was the new national government a 'limited monarchy' or 'a monarchical republic' like England," 82. Wood goes on to detail how comfortable voters and legislators alike were with the expectation that President Washington, with his "republican court," would become an elected version of King George.

71 Seth Cotlar, *Tom Paine's America: The Rise and Fall of Transatlantic Radicalism in the Early Republic* (Charlottesville: University of Virginia Press, 2011), 120. Willamette University Professor Cotlar uses the writings of Delaware librarian/schoolteacher/pamphleteer Robert Coram (1761-1796) to illustrate how democratic visions of economic justice refuted the concept of exclusive property rights promulgated by Sir William Blackstone's *Commentaries on the Laws of England*. Coram spoke for many when he advocated a public-funded system of universal education and questioned the economic stranglehold of the propertied elite on the common man. For a broader account of the vast divide between the Federalist elite and the everyday citizen that fueled the Jeffersonian triumph of 1800, see David Waldstreicher, Jeffrey L. Pasley, and Andrew W. Robertson, *Beyond the Founders: New Approaches to the Political History of the Early American Republic* (Chapel Hill: The University of North Carolina Press, 2004), particularly "Part One: Democracy and Other Practices," 31–106, and Seth Cotlar's "The Federalists' Transatlantic Cultural Offensive of 1798 and the Moderation of American Democratic Discourse," 272–302.

72 Elkins and McKitrick, *The Age of Federalism*, 754.

73 Thomas J. Scharf, *The Chronicles of Baltimore* (Baltimore: Trumbull Brothers, 1874), 281ff. See also, *Original Election Returns*, Maryland State Archives, Annapolis, and *The Federalist Gazette and Baltimore Daily Advertiser*, November 18, 1796, and *The Federalist Gazette*, November 11, 1800.

74 *1986 Fact Book of United States Agriculture, Compiled from Departmental Sources by the Office of Information* (Washington, DC: U.S. Government Printing Office, 1985), 114–15. The census of 1790 showed 90 percent of U.S. residents were farmers. Urban population of 202,000 in towns of 2,500 or more was only 5 percent of the total 3.9 million population. Income from agriculture in 1800 was $266 million, or 39.3 percent of national income.

75 Robert Troup to Rufus King, New York, 1 Oct. 1800, Rufus King Papers at New York Historical Society, vol. 47, Robert Troup letters.

76 Robert Troup to Rufus King, 31 December 1800, *The Life and Correspondence of Rufus King*, ed. Charles R. King, III: 359.

77 Chernow, *Alexander Hamilton*, 665.

78 Robert Troup to Rufus King, New York, 15 December 1800, Rufus King Papers at New York Historical Society, vol. 47, Robert Troup letters.

Chapter Eighteen

1 *The National Intelligencer*, 5 March 1801. President Jefferson was described in similar language that appeared in that day's *Alexandria Times*. Virginia Representative Marshall took office as secretary of state in June 1800 and officially took office as chief justice on March 4, 1801. "My gift of John Marshall to the people of the United States was the proudest act of my life," John Adams reputedly said 25 years later to Marshall's son.

2 Robert Troup to Rufus King, New York, 23 March 1801, *Life and Correspondence of Rufus King*, ed. Charles R. King, 3: 410.

3 Robert Troup to King, New York, 23 March 1801, *Life and Correspondence of Rufus King*, King, 3: 410.

4 Robert Troup to Rufus King, 5 April 1801, Rufus King Papers at New York Historical Society, box 47, Robert Troup letters.

5 Robert Troup to King, 23 March 1801, *Life and Correspondence of Rufus King*, King, 3: 410.

6 Robert Troup to Rufus King, New York, 5 December 1801, Rufus King Papers at New York Historical Society, vol. 47, Robert Troup letters.

NOTES

7   Wendell Edward Tripp Jr., *Robert Troup: A Quest for Security in a Turbulent New Nation (1775–1832)* (New York: Arno Press, 1982), 249–50.

8   Robert Troup to Rufus King, New York, 27 May 1801, Rufus King Papers, New York Historical Society, vol. 47, Robert Troup letters.

9   Gilbert Stuart's 1798 29 1/8 inch by 23 15/16 inch oil on canvas of Sarah Shippen Lea was acquired in 2014 by the National Gallery of Art in Washington, DC. The portrait is strikingly, even eerily, similar to Stuart's circa 1795 portrait of Elizabeth Allen Laurance's daughter Ann Penn Allen in hair color and style, facial features, and pose.

10   John Schuyler, *Institution of the Society of the Cincinnati* (New York: Douglas Taylor, 1896), 260. John McDougall Laurance "was the first hereditary member admitted by the New York State Society in 1798."

11   *Officers & Graduates of Columbia College, General Catalogue 1754–1900* (New York: For the University, 1900), 17. Laurance served as Columbia trustee from 1784 until his death in 1810, a period of 26 years.

12   Robert Troup to Rufus King, New York, 9 April 1802, Rufus King Papers, New York Historical Society, vol. 47, Robert Troup letters.

13   James Kent, "Address to the Law Association of New York City" (1836), quoted in Charles Warren, *A History of the American Bar* (Boston: Little, Brown & Co., 1911), 295.

14   Ira Rosenwaike, *Population History of New York City* (Syracuse, NY: Syracuse University Press, 1972), 17.

15   Griswold, *The Republican Court*, 99. The Broadway home of John and Mrs. Jay was the undisputed center of New York high society during Jay's 1787–1788 term as the Confederated States' minister of foreign affairs. Reproduced on pages 98–99, Mrs. Jay's social invitation list of some hundred names included John Lawrence as well as Mr. van Berckel and his unmarried daughter.

16   Frank John Urquhart, *A Short History of Newark* (Newark, NJ: Baker Printing Company, 1910), 64.

17   Presently in the New York Historical Society artifact collection, Laurance's 4 5/8 inch by 15 5/8 inch by 9 3/8 inch wooden lap desk features a flat hinged lid, green textile writing surface, and compartments for ink bottle, sand shaker, wax seals, and writing paper.

18   Peter Ross, *A Standard History of Freemasonry in the State of New York* (New York and Chicago: The Lewis Co., 1899), 143. On June 25, 1801, Laurance donned his Masonic regalia as "Past Master" and acted in the stead of out-going Grandmaster Robert R. Livingston to install General Jacob Morton as successor in an elaborate ceremony at the Assembly Room of the Tontine Hotel.

19   Robert Troup to Alexander Hamilton, 15 June 1791, *Papers of Alexander Hamilton*, ed. Syrett, 8: 223. As early as June 1791, Laurance's friend Robert Troup had quit the practice of law in favor of land investment management, advising Hamilton by letter of "Collecting a little modicum to enable me to quit the drudgery of the law." There is little doubt that Laurance harbored similar thoughts, despite a profusion of unmarried daughters.

20   Robert Troup to Rufus King, 9 August 1800, Arthur J. Alexander, "Judge John Laurance: Successful Investor in New York State Lands," *New York History* 25 (1944): 35.

21   Robert Troup to Rufus King, May 21, 1801, Rufus King Papers, New York Historical Society, vol. 47, Robert Troup letters.

22   *Calendar of New York Colonial Manuscripts, Indorsed Land Papers in the Office of the Secretary of State of New York, 1642–1803* (Albany, NY: Weed, Parsons & Co., 1864), 551–69.

23   John Laurance to Rufus King, Philadelphia, 4 June 1799, Rufus King Papers, New York Historical Society, 3: 28.

24   A. M. Sakolski, *The Great American Land Bubble* (New York: Harper & Brothers, 1932), 30.

25   Peter Stadnitski, "Preliminary Information respecting a Negotiation on Lands in America" (1792), a typescript in the archives of ING Bank in London, quoted in Francois Furstenberg, "An Economic Interpretation: Reflections on European Investment in the Post-Revolutionary American Backcountry," 12. The paper was prepared for "Foreign Confidence: International Investment in North America, 1700–1860," a conference sponsored by the Rothschild Archive in Philadelphia, October 11–12, 2012.

26   Archer Butler Hulbert, "The Methods and Operations of the Scioto Group of Speculators," *The Mississippi Valley Historical Review* 1.4 (1915), 507–10. For background on Staphorst and the first Dutch loan, see Paul Demund Evans, *The Holland Land Company* (Buffalo, NY: Buffalo Historical Society, 1924), 3. Also Pieter Jan van Winter, *American Finance and Dutch Investment, 1780–1805: With an Epilogue to 1840*, edited by James C. Riley, 2 vols. (New York: Arno Press, 1977), 1: 247–56.

27 Alexander Baring to Hope & Co., 3 December 1796, in Frederick Scouller Allis, *William Bingham's Maine Lands 1790–1820* (Boston: Colonial Society of Massachusetts, 1954), 792.

28 Bounty right of Jacob Albright assigned to John Laurance, 8 November 1783 (Dept. of State, Division of the Land Office, Albany, NY, Book of Deeds, XXIV: 285). See also William Burnham to John Laurance, 10 November 1783, Book of Deeds, XXIV: 286.

29 New York State Archives, series AO447 Military Patents, 1764–1797, vols. 4–8. The numbered lots assigned to each veteran are listed in *The Balloting Book* (Albany: The State of New York, 1825). For example: "Richard Morrison, private soldier in the late 1st NY Regt for the sum of 6 pounds, 8 shillings of John Laurance all lands due Jan. 1, 1784," witnessed by Alexander McDougall and Ranald McDougall.

30 Arthur J. Alexander, "Judge John Laurance: Successful Investor in New York State Lands," *New York History* 25 (1944): 38.

31 Deed, June 26, 1793, John Laurance to James Geddis and William Sawyer, Dept. of State, Division of the Land Office, Albany, NY, Book of Deeds XXV: 123.

32 Harry B. Yoshpe, *The Disposition of Loyalist Estates in the Southern District of the State of New York* (New York: Columbia University Press, 1939), passim. The State of New York raised $3,100,000 from selling 2.5 million acres confiscated from 941 loyalist estates.

33 *Sales Records of the New York State Commissioners of Forfeitures for the Southern District, 1784–1787*, 2 vols, 1: 43 49, New York Historical Society Collection.

34 Eric Homberger, *The Historical Atlas of New York City* (New York: Henry Holt & Company, 1994), 60–61. John Laurance bought two West Farm lots, one at Broome and Coliver Streets, the other at Houston and Ridge Streets. Together with Isaac Roosevelt and Henry Kip, he also acquired a large parcel just west of Corlear's Hook bordered by Columbia Street and the East River. Taken from the Certificate of Commissioners of Forfeiture for the Southern District of the State of New York.

35 John Laurance to Robert Troup, 26 July 1790, Robert Troup papers at the New York Public Library, box 1, folder 7. "I do hereby declare," wrote Laurance, "that Robert Troup Esquire is equally indentured with me in four lots of Ground Situated in the City of New York between Grand and Bullock Street in the Bowery, purchased by me from Benjamin Sexias . . . also Eight lots of ground purchased by me from Money situated on Bullock Street, and in four lots of Ground adjacent to these purchased from Mr. Dohrman, which were purchased from Melancton Smith."

36 Alexander, "Judge John Laurance," 37.

37 "Abstracts of Sales by the Commissioners of Forfeitures in the Southern District of New York State," copied and contributed by Theresa H. Bristol, *New York Genealogical and Biographical Record* 59, no. 3 (October 1928), 251.

38 Alexander, "Judge John Laurance," 37.

39 Property Lease dated 8 Jan. 1786 of John Laurance to John O'Connor, John Laurance Papers, New York Historical Society, folder "1786."

40 Robert Troup, fellow officer of the Revolution, Federalist lawyer, and long-time personal friend, was Laurance's primary real estate investment partner. Among the Troup Papers at New York Public Library is an 1806 ledger sheet summarizing 15 separate properties then held in partnership.

41 Receipt from Robt. Troup, 30 June 1784, John Laurance Papers, New York Historical Society, folder "1784." A second receipt dated 2 July 1784 for 18 pounds four shillings is in the same folder.

42 Blake McKelvey, "Historical Aspects of the Phelps & Gorham Treaty of July 4–8, 1788," *Rochester History Magazine* 1, no. 1 (January 1939).

43 George S. Conover, *The Genesee Tract: Cessions between New York and Massachusetts; The Phelps and Gorham Purchase; Robert Morris; Captain Charles Williamson and the Pulteney Estate* (Geneva, NY: George S. Conover, 1889), 2–3.

44 Franklin B. Hough, *A History of St. Lawrence and Franklin Counties, New York, from the Earliest Period to the Present Time* (Albany, NY: Weed, Parsons & Co., 1853), reprinted by Regional Publishing Company, Baltimore, 1970, 237–41.

45 Proceedings of the New York State Legislature, Albany, March 1791, quoted in John P. Kaminski, *George Clinton: Yeoman Politician of the New Republic* (Madison, WI: Madison House Publishers, Inc., 1993), 196.

46 Charles E. Brooks, *Frontier Settlement and the Market Revolution: The Holland Land Purchase* (Ithaca, NY: Cornell University Press, 1996), 13–14. For more about Robert Morris's New York real estate

ventures see: Barbara A. Chernow, "Robert Morris: Genesee Land Speculator," *New York History* 58 (1977): 195–220; Paul Evans, "The Pulteney Purchase," *Proceedings of the New York State Historical Society* 20 (1922): 83–103; and Manfred Jonas and Robert V. Wells, eds., *New Opportunities in a New Nation: The Development of New York after the Revolution* (Schenectady, NY: Charles W. Jones, 1982), 35–68.

47 Alan Taylor, *William Cooper's Town: Power and Persuasion on the Frontier of the Early American Republic* (New York: Vintage Books, 1995), 101.

48 Alexander, "Judge John Laurance," 42–43.

49 Indenture, 17 October 1794 between Thomas A. and Catherine Cooper of the City of New York and Hon. John Laurance, Papers of Robert Troup, New York Public Library, box 1, folder 7. "I hereby certify that Robert Troup is jointly and equally interested with me in the land and letters mentioned, the said Robert Troup having paid half of the consideration money."

50 Alexander, "Judge John Laurance," 43; Deed, A. Noble to John Laurance and Nicholas Fish, June 30, 1795 (Land Office Records, XXVIII: 191); Alexander Hamilton, "Statement of my property and Debts" of July 1, 1804, Alexander Hamilton Papers, New York Historical Society. "My ¼ purchase in Nobleborough together with JLaurance Robert Troupe & N. Fish being 5450 acres computed now to stand me in abt. 9000 [dollars]."

51 Partition Deed, John Laurance, Robert Troup, and Aquila Giles, 27 June 1798, Land Office Records, XXX: 367.

52 Tripp, *Robert Troup*, 260.

53 George Scriba paid the Roosevelts £77, 917, 6s (N.Y. Colonial Manuscripts, 980). For the Scriba to Mark transaction see Oneida County Clerk's Office, Deeds, X: 499–502, Utica, New York.

54 Alexander, "Judge John Laurance," 40; Mortgage, Jacob Mark to John Laurance, Jan. 15, 1796 (Oneida County Clerk's Office, Libers of Mortgages, II: 72, 101). Mr. Mark retained an undivided one-fourth interest in Scriba townships 15 and 21 that was held in trust (Chancery Papers, Copied Libers, 1: 507–10, Hall of Records, New York City). For a detailed original source accounting of this mortgage and its financial and legal aftermath, see *The Papers of Alexander Hamilton*, Syrett, 26: 38–39.

55 Jacob Mark and Company to John B. Church, Alexander Hamilton, and John Laurance, New York, 30 May 1797, *Papers of Alexander Hamilton*, Syrett, XX: 93-95.

56 Ibid.

57 John Laurance to Alexander Hamilton, 3 June 1797, *Papers of Alexander Hamilton*, Syrett, XX: 97.

58 Ibid.

59 Alexander, "Judge John Laurance," 41. Deed, Gilchrist to John Laurance, Aug. 20, 1802 (Oneida County Clerk's Office, Conveyances X, p. 314). To protect the investment already made in Townships 15 and 21, Laurance and Church purchased the residue of Mark's holdings still subject to mortgage (Townships 9, 10, and a portion of 17) for the total of $43,530.33 according to decree, 30 May 1802 (Chancery Papers, Copied Libers, 420: 401–403, 404–406, Hall of Records, New York City). Also see Final Chancery Decrees March 7, 1803 (Chancery papers, Copied Libers, 128: 522-33, Hall of Records, New York City).

60 John Laurance to Alexander Hamilton, 3 June 1797, Papers of Nathanael Pendleton, Yale University Library Manuscript and Archives Collection. Also see *Papers of Alexander Hamilton*, Syrett, XXI: 97.

61 Laurance to Hamilton, 3 June 1797, Papers of Nathanael Pendleton, Yale University Library Manuscript and Archives Collection. Also see *Papers of Alexander Hamilton*, Syrett, XXI: 97.

62 John Laurance to Alexander Hamilton, 28 December 1798, *The Papers of Alexander Hamilton*, Syrett, XXII: 395–97.

63 Mortgage from John Laurance, John Barker Church, and Alexander Hamilton to Robert Gilchrist, New York, 21 August 1802, Oneida County Clerk's office, *Mortgages*, III: 500–501, Utica, New York.

64 Mortgage note, Laurance, Church and Hamilton to Theodosius Fowler, August 21, 1802, Oneida County Clerk's Office, *Mortgages*, III: 501.

65 Alexander Hamilton to John Laurance, Esq., Senate of the U.S., New York, 26 December 1798, John Laurance Papers, New York Historical Society, folder "1798."

66 "Statement of my Property and debts, July 1, 1804", *The Papers of Alexander Hamilton*, Syrett, XXI: 95.

67 John Laurance to Nathaniel Pendleton, esq., New York, 29 August 1807, Papers of Nathaniel Pendleton, Yale University Library Manuscript and Archives Collection. Former Federal district judge Pendleton was a Duchess County lawyer who was "second" to Hamilton in the duel with Aaron Burr.

68 John Laurance to Henry Knox, New York, 26 Sept. 1796, Gilder Lehman collection at New York Historical Society, item #02437.06826. Laurance was forced to pursue Knox for delinquent rent to the tune of £33, 6 shillings/ month plus minor property damage.

69 Deed, David Clarkson to Rufus King and John Laurance, 14 December 1804, New York County Register's Office (NYC), Libers of Conveyances LXX: 293.

70 Deed, John Jones to John Laurance, 28 January1804, Oneida County Clerk's Office, Conveyances, XIII: 6.

71 *Federal Gazette & Baltimore Daily Advertiser*, 13 June 1801.

72 Deed of Trust, *Papers of Alexander Hamilton*, Syrett, XXV: 38. The conveyance to trustees, John Laurance, B. Church, and Mathew Clarkson is dated July 6, 1804. Certified copy recorded Jan. 7, 1805, Conveyances in the Offices of the Register, City of New York, Libers 71: 347–49, Hall of Records, New York City. Hamilton's "The Grange" consisted of 35 acres, a farmhouse, a barn, and several outbuildings.

73 Gouverneur Morris to Rufus King, *Life and Correspondence of Rufus King*, ed. Charles R. King, 4: 403–404.

74 Chernow, *Alexander Hamilton*, 725.

75 Broadus Mitchell, *Alexander Hamilton, The National Adventure 1788-1804* (New York: The Macmillan Company, 1962), 72.

76 James A. Hamilton to Major William Popham, Oct. 14, 1824, *Reminiscences of James A. Hamilton: Or Men and Events at Home and Abroad . . .* (New York: Charles Scribner & Co., 1868), 9. "Mr. Pendleton . . . informed me with reluctance that my father's lands in Scriba's Patent had been taken by certain gentlemen in this city, whose names he would not mention, at prices which, he said, were perhaps a little more than they were worth at the time. These gentlemen hoped with the amount thus raised, and the sums due my father, to pay his debts and leave the Grange clear to my mother." Although James Hamilton does not specifically name Laurance as one of the benefactors, it is inconceivable that, as co-trustee of the Grange and Alexander's Scriba deal partner, he was not involved.

77 Partition Deed, John Laurance, Robert Troup, John Church, and others, July 6, 1805, New York Land Office, Libers XXVIII: 191.

78 Letter of Indenture between John Laurance and George W. Hawkes of Liverpool, Great Britain, 15 May 1807, John Laurance Papers, New York Historical Society, folder "1800–1810."

79 Edward Biddle and Mantle Fielding, *The Life and Works of Thomas Sully (1783–1972)* (Philadelphia: Wickersham Press, 1921), 205. Six years into a long and prolific career as society portraitist, Sully (1783–1872) completed "Miss Ann Lawrance" on March 27, 1807, just before her April marriage to Hawkes. A 1921 publication of Sully's lifeworks listed the original painting in the New York hands of the Hon. McDougall Hawkes with a valuation of $30,000. Still under private ownership, the painting may be found in the Smithsonian's National Portrait Gallery cataloged under reference number PC991540.

80 St. George Parish Records, Liverpool, Lancashire, England. Baptisms 1797–1813, 13, Entry 8, LDS Film 1656155. Born on Feb. 8, 1808, Lawrance Hawkes was baptized on Feb. 25.

81 John S. Livingston to John Laurance, 23 August 1808, John Laurance Papers, New York Historical Society, folder "1800–1810."

82 *Life and Correspondence of Rufus King*, ed. Charles R. King, 5: 184.

83 Ibid.

84 John Laurance to James Greenleaf esq., Allentown, Pa., 11 September 1810, John Laurance Papers, New York Historical Society, folder "1800–1810."

85 McWhorter, *Biographical Sketches*, 52.

86 Will and Testament of John Laurance, 28 February 1808, John Laurance Papers, New York Historical Society.

87 Alexander. "Judge John Laurance," 45; Deed, Egbert Benson, Executor of John Laurance's Last Will and Testament to Gabriel A. Ludlow, 5 January 1825, New York Land Office, XLI: 372–512.

88 *New York Daily Advertiser*, November 12, 1810.

89 McWhorter, *Biographical Sketches*, 53. See also, *Genealogical Record, Saint Nicholas Society of the City of New York* (New York: Saint Nicholas Society, 1905), 136.; Charles Edwards, *Reports of Chancery Cases Decided in the First Circuit of the State of New-York by The Hon. William T. McCoun* (New York: Gould, Banks & Co., 1843), 160. Alexander McDougall took advantage of the 5 June 1769 resolution of First Presbyterian Church trustees to "grant vaults in their churchyard . . . for vaults thirteen and a half feet by ten and a half in the clear with room for the steps in fee forever of £15, subject to all the usual charges for burial."

Epilogue

1. John G. Bunker, *Liberty Ships: The Ugly Ducklings of World War II* (Annapolis, MD: Naval Institute Press, 1973), 208. The SS *John Laurance* completed four New York-to-Liverpool convoy round-trips between January 1943 and February 1944, suffering weather damage in two. Complete wartime convoy records may be found at: http://www.convoyweb.org.uk/hague/index.html.

2. McWhorter, *American Revolutionary*, 53. Specifics of the multi-parcel sale of First Presbyterian Church of the City of New York's Wall Street property may be found in Liber 450 of the *Deeds of New York City*, 428, 430, and 453–56; Liber 451: 499–502; Liber 452: 411–14; and Liber 462: 147–50.

3. Washington's foreign-born generals were: Major Generals Horatio Gates, Marquis de Lafayette, Charles Lee, Baron de Kalb, and Baron von Steuben; Brigadier Generals Armstrong, de Borre, Conway, Coudray, Duportail, de Fermoy, Hand, Hazen, Irvine, Kosciuszko, Maxwell, McIntosh, Montgomery, Pulaski, Sullivan, Thompson, and von Woedke. Lt. Colonel François Fleury, battlefield hero at Brandywine, Newport, Stony Point, and Yorktown, was one of only 11 men to earn congressional medals during the War for Independence.

4. James Madison, *Notes of Debates in the Federal Convention of 1787 Reported by James Madison* (Athens, Ohio: Ohio University Press, 1966), 438.

5. Miller, *The Federalist Era*, 230.

6. Richard Peters to Timothy Pickering, 24 August 1798, Pickering Papers at Massachusetts Historical Society, as quoted in James Morton Smith, *Freedom's Fetters: The Alien and Sedition Laws and American Civil Liberties* (Ithaca, NY: Cornell University Press, 1956), 163–64. Although Peters had clashed with Judge Laurance over the Barrè extradition matter, the latter was definitely *not* the Englishman in Peter's sights.

7. Alexander Hamilton under the nom de plume *Lucius Crassus*, "The Examination, Number VIII," *New York Evening Post*, January 12, 1802.

8. Hamilton as *Lucius Crassus*, "The Examination, Number VIII," *New York Evening Post*, January 12, 1802.

9. William Winthrop, *Military Law and Precedents*, 2 vols. (Boston: Little, Brown & Co., 1896), I: 40–43. In a work that was adopted by the War Department in 1920, Colonel Winthrop wrote: "The regulations, for example, on such subjects as discipline, precedence, command, arrests, and the procedure of courts-martial, are in great part but the specific expressions of usages of more or less early date; whether certain acts amount to 'conduct unbecoming an officer or a gentleman,' or 'conduct to the prejudice of good order or discipline' . . . *will constantly recur* to the general usage of the service as understood and acted upon by military men."

10. Francis H. Heller, "Military Law in the Continental Army," 25 *University of Kansas Law Review* (1976–1977): 360. "No major revision was then necessary until the Civil War produced new experience that led to the first major revision in 1874."

11. Major William F. Fratcher, "Notes on the History of the Judge Advocate General's Department, 1775–1941," *The Judge Advocate Journal* I, no. 1 (15 June 1944): 6.

12. Robert Troup to Rufus King, 9 April 1802, Rufus King Papers, New York Historical Society, volume 47, Robert Troup's letters, 1796–1802.

Bibliography

Manuscript Collections

John Adams Papers, Massachusetts Historical Society.

John Adams Personal Manuscripts, Library of Congress.

Thomas Addis Emmet Collection, New York Public Library.

Cadwallader Colden Papers, New York Historical Society.

Chancery papers, Copied Libers, vol. 128, Hall of Records, New York City.

George Clinton Public Papers, State of New York Archives.

Sir Henry Clinton Public Papers, William L. Clements Collection at the University of Michigan.

William Constable Papers, New York Public Library.

Daniël Crommelin and Sons Company archives (since 1859), Amsterdam City Archives.

Benjamin Franklin Letters, Library of Congress.

Alexander Hamilton Papers, New York Historical Society.

John Jay Papers, New York Historical Society.

James Kent Papers, Library of Congress.

Rufus King Papers, New York Historical Society.

John Laurance Papers, New York Historical Society.

Charles Lee Papers, New York Historical Society.

Robert R. Livingston Papers, New York Public Library.

Alexander McDougall Papers, New York Historical Society.

John McKessson Papers, New York Historical Society.

Robert Murray Land Record Papers, New York Historical Society.

Benjamin Rush Papers, Historical Society of Pennsylvania.

William Smith Jr. Papers, New York Public Library.

Robert Troup Papers, New York Public Library.

Tudor Family Papers, Massachusetts Historical Society.

Richard Varick Papers, New York Historical Society.

Oliver Wolcott Papers, Connecticut Historical Society.

Selected Books, Pamphlets, and Dissertations

A Compilation of the Messages and Papers of the Presidents Prepared under the Direction of the Joint Committee on Printing, of the House and Senate Pursuant to an Act of the 52nd Congress of the United States (New York: Bureau of National Literature Inc., 1897).

A Concise History of the House of Representatives Committee on Appropriations (Washington, DC: Printed for use of the Committee on Appropriations of the House of Representatives by the U.S. Government Printing Office, 2010).

Adams Family Correspondence: January 1790–December 1793, Margaret A. Hogan, et al. editors (Cambridge: Massachusetts Historical Society, 2009).

Alberts, Robert C. *The Golden Voyage: The Life and Times of William Bingham (1752–1804)* (Boston, MA: Houghton Mifflin Co., 1969).

Alexander, DeAlva Stanwood. *A Political History of the State of New York*, three vols. (New York: Henry Holt and Company, 1906), vol. I.

Allen, Frederick James. *The Law as a Vocation* (Cambridge, MA: Harvard University, 1919).

The Army Lawyer: A History of the Judge Advocate General's Corps, 1775–1975 (Washington, DC: U.S. Government Printing Office, 1975).

Bayles, Harrison. *Old Taverns of New York* (New York: Frank Allaben Genealogical Company, 1915).

Beard, Charles A. *An Economic Interpretation of the Constitution of the United States* (New York: Macmillan Company, 1913).

Beard, Charles A. *Economic Origins of Jeffersonian Democracy* (New York: Macmillan Company, 1915).

Berkin, Carol. *The Bill of Rights, The Fight to Secure America's Liberties* (New York: Simon & Schuster, 2015).

Berkin, Carol. *A Sovereign People, The Crises of the 1790's and the Birth of American Nationalism* (New York: Basic Books, an imprint of Perseus Books, LLC, 2017).

Bickford, Charlene Bangs, and Kenneth R. Bowling. *Birth of the Nation: The First Federal Congress 1789–1791* (Lanham, MD: Madison House Publishers, Inc., 1989).

Biles, Charles M. *The History of Congressional Apportionment* (Arcata, CA: Humboldt State University Press, 2017).

Blackstone, Sir William. *Commentaries on the Laws of England*, 4 vols. edited by Wayne Morrison (London: Routledge-Cavendish, 2001).

Bloomfield, Joseph. *Citizen Soldier: The Revolutionary War Journal of Joseph Bloomfield*, edited by Mark E. Lender and James Kirby Martin (Newark: New Jersey Historical Society, 1982).

Blumberg, Philip I. *Repressive Jurisprudence in the Early American Republic* (New York: Cambridge University Press, 2010).

Bodle, Wayne K., and Jacqueline Thibaut. *Valley Forge Historical Research Report*, 3 vols. (U.S. Department of the Interior: Valley Forge National Historic Park, 1982).

Bond, Beverley W., Jr. *The Quit-Rent System in the American Colonies* (New Haven, CT: Yale University Press, 1919).

Bonomi, Patricia U. *A Factitious People: Politics and Society in Colonial New York* (New York: Columbia University Press, 1971).

Bowen, Clarence Winthrop, ed. *Official Program of the Centennial Celebration of the Inauguration of George Washington as first President of the United States* (New York: D. Appleton and Company, 1892).

Bowling, Kenneth R. *The Creation of Washington, D.C.: The Idea and Location of the American Capital* (Fairfax, VA: George Mason University Press, 1991).

Bowling, Kenneth R., and Donald R. Kennon, ed. *Neither Separate nor Equal: Congress in the 1790's* (Athens, OH: Ohio University Press, 2000).

Boyd, Julian, ed. *The Papers of Thomas Jefferson* (Princeton, NJ: Princeton University Press, 1958).

Brands, H. W. *The First American: The Life and Times of Benjamin Franklin* (New York: Doubleday, 2000).Brookhiser, Richard. *Gentleman Revolutionary: Gouverneur Morris, The Rake Who Wrote the Constitution* (New York: Free Press, 2003).

Brooks, Charles E. *Frontier Settlement and the Market Revolution: The Holland Land Purchase* (Ithaca, NY: Cornell University Press, 1996).

Brownson, James I. *The Life and Times of Senator James Ross* (Washington, PA: Printed for the Washington County Historical Society, 1910).

Bunker, John G. *Liberty Ships: The Ugly Ducklings of World War II* (Annapolis, MD: Naval Institute Press, 1973).

Burrows, Edwin G. *Forgotten Patriots: The Untold Story of American Prisoners During the Revolutionary War* (New York: Basic Books, 2008).

Burrows, Edwin G., and Mike Wallace. *Gotham: A History of New York City until 1898* (New York: Oxford University Press, 1999).

Cadwallader Colden Papers, Collections of the New York Historical Society (New York; Printed for the Historical Society, 1938), vol. LXVIII.

Calcott, Wellins. "A Candid Disquisition of the Principles and Practices of the most Antient and Honourable Society of Free and Accepted Masons," *The Universal Masonry Library, a Replication in Thirty Volumes of All the Standard Publications in Masonry*, edited by Robert Macoy, vol. 6 (New York: Jno. Leonard & Co., 1855).

Calendar of New York Colonial Manuscript Indorsed Land Papers in the Office of the Secretary of State of New York, 1642–1803 (Albany, NY: Weed, Parsons and Company, 1864).

Chambers, William Nisbet. *Political Parties in a New Nation: The American Experience 1776–1809* (New York: Oxford University Press, 1963).

Champagne, Roger J. *Alexander McDougall and the American Revolution in New York* (Schenectady: New York State American Revolution Bicentennial Commission, in conjunction with Union College Press, 1975).

Channing, Edward. *A History of the United States, Vol. IV, Federalists and Republicans 1789–1815* (New York: Macmillan Company, 1917).

Chernow, Ron. *Alexander Hamilton* (New York: Penguin Group, 2004).

Chernow, Ron. *Washington: A Life* (New York: Penguin Press, 2010).

Chester, Alden, and Edwin M. Williams. *Courts and Lawyers of New York: A History, 1609–1925*, 6 vols. (New York: The American Historical Society Inc., 1925).

Clarfield, Gerard H. *Timothy Pickering and the American Republic* (Pittsburgh, PA: University of Pittsburgh Press, 1980).

Clark, Allen C. *William Greenleaf and Law in the Federal City* (Washington, DC: Press of W. F. Roberts, 1901).

Cohen, David J., Richard Sylla, and Robert E. Wright. *The U.S. Panic of 1792: Financial Crisis Management and the Lender of Last Resort*, prepared for the NBER DAE Summer Institute, July 2006, and XIV International Economic History Congress Session 20, "Capital Market Anomalies in Economic History," Helsinki, August 2006.

Coleman, Peter J. *Debtors and Creditors in America: Insolvency, Imprisonment for Debt, and Bankruptcy, 1697–1900* (Madison, WI: State Historical Society of Wisconsin, 1974).

Conover, George S. *The Genesee Tract: Cessions between New York and Massachusetts; The Phelps and Gorham Purchase; Robert Morris; Captain Charles Williamson and the Pulteney Estate* (Geneva, NY: George S. Conover, 1889).

Cooke, Jacob E. *Tench Coxe and the Early Republic* (Chapel Hill: University of North Carolina Press, 1978).

Cooke, Jacob E. *Alexander Hamilton* (New York: Charles Scribner's Sons, 1982).

Cotlar, Seth. *Tom Paine's America: The Rise and Fall of Transatlantic Radicalism in the Early Republic* (Charlottesville: University of Virginia Press, 2011).

Countryman, Edward. *A People in Revolution, The American Revolution and Political Society in New York 1760–1790* (Baltimore, MD: Johns Hopkins University Press, 1981).

Cox, Carolyn. *A Proper Sense of Honor: Service and Sacrifice in George Washington's Army* (Chapel Hill: University of North Carolina Press, 2004).

Crew, H. W. *Centennial History of the City of Washington D.C.* (Dayton, OH: W. J. Shuey Publisher, 1892).

Currie, David P. *The Constitution in Congress: The Federalist Period 1789–1801* (Chicago: University of Chicago Press, 1997).

Custis, George Washington Parke. *Recollections and Memoirs of Washington* (Philadelphia: J. W. Bradley, 1861).

Dangerfield, George. *Chancellor Robert Livingston of New York: 1746–1813* (New York: Harcourt, Brace & Company, 1960).

Dauer, Manning. *The Adams Federalists* (Baltimore, MD: Johns Hopkins University Press, 1953).

Davies, Glyn. *A History of Money, From Ancient Times to the Present* (Cardiff: University of Wales Press, 1994).

Davis, David Brion. *The Problem of Slavery in the Age of Revolution, 1770–1823* (New York: Oxford University Press, 1999).

Davis, Joseph. "William Duer, Entrepreneur, 1747–99," *Essays in the Earlier History of American Corporations*, 2 vols. (Cambridge, MA: Harvard University Press, 1918).

Davis, Matthew I. *Memoirs of Aaron Burr: With Miscellaneous Selections from his Correspondence* (Freeport, NY: Books for Libraries Press, 1970) [New York: 1836].

Debates and Proceedings in the Congress of the United States, First, Second, and Third Sessions of the First United States Congress, The Library of Congress (Washington, DC: Gales and Seaton, 1837).

Department of the State of New York, Division of the Land Office, Albany, NY, *Book of Deeds* XXIV.

DePauw, Linda G. *The Eleventh Pillar: New York State and the Federal Constitution* (Ithaca, NY: Cornell University Press, 1966).

DiLorenzo, Thomas J. *Hamilton's Curse, How Jefferson's Arch Enemy Betrayed the American Revolution — and What it Means for Americans Today* (New York: Three Rivers Press, 2008).

Dix, Morgan. *A History of the Parish of Trinity Church in the City of New York* (New York: G. P. Putnam's Sons, 1901).

Documentary History of the First Federal Congress of the United States of America March 4, 1789–March 3, 1791, edited by Charlene Bangs Bickford, Kenneth R. Bowling, Linda G. DePauw, Helen E. Veit, and William C. di Giacomantonio, 22 vols. (Baltimore, MD: Johns Hopkins University Press, 1972–2014).

The Documentary History of the First Federal Elections: 1788–1790, edited by Gordon Den Boer, Merrill Jensen, et al. (Madison: University of Wisconsin Press, 1986).

Documents Relative to the Colonial History of the State of New York, edited by E. B. O'Callaghan (Albany, NY: Weed, Parsons and Company, 1856), vol. VII.

Domett, Henry W. *A History of the Bank of New York, 1784–1884* (New York: G. P. Putnam's Sons, 1884).

Dougherty, J. Hampton. *The Electoral System of the United States* (New York: G. P. Putnam's Sons, 1906).

Duncan, Jason K. *Citizens or Papists? The Politics of Anti-Catholicism in New York 1685–1821* (New York: Fordham University Press, 2005).

Dunn, Susan. *Jefferson's Second Revolution: Election Crisis of 1800 and the Triumph of Republicanism* (New York: Houghton Mifflin Company, 2004).

Edling, Max A. *A Revolution in Favor of Government: Origins of the U.S. Constitution and the Making of the American State* (New York: Oxford University Press, 2003).

Edwards, George William. *New York as an Eighteenth-Century Municipality, 1731–1776* (New York: Longmans, Green and Company, 1917).

Eggly, T. W. *History of the First New York Regiment* (Hampton, NH: Peter E. Randall, 1981).

Egnal, Marc. *A Mighty Empire: The Origins of the American Revolution* (Ithaca, NY: Cornell University Press, 1988).

Elkins, Stanley, and Eric McKitrick. *The Age of Federalism: The Early American Republic 1788–1800* (New York: Oxford University Press, 1993).

Ellis, Joseph. *Passionate Sage, The Character and Legacy of John Adams* (New York: W.W. Norton & Company, 1993).

Ferguson, E. James. *The Power of the Purse* (Chapel Hill: University of North Carolina Press, 1961).

Ferling, John. *Adams vs. Jefferson: The Tumultuous Election of 1800* (New York: Oxford University Press, 2004).

Fernow, Berthold. *New York in the Revolution* (Albany, NY: Clearfield Company, 1887).

First Census of the United States Taken in the Year 1790, New York (Washington, DC: U.S. Government Printing Office, 1908).

Fitzpatrick, John C. *Calendar of the Correspondence of George Washington, Commander in Chief of the Continental Army, with the Continental Congress* (Washington, DC: U.S. Government Printing Office, 1906).

Flexner, James Thomas. *The Traitor and the Spy: Benedict Arnold and John André* (New York: Collier Books, 1962).

Flexner, James Thomas. *George Washington, Anguish and Farewell (1793–1799)* (Boston: Little, Brown & Co., 1969).

Fowler, William F. *American Crisis: George Washington and the Dangerous Two Years After Yorktown, 1781–1783* (New York: Walker & Company, 2011).

Franklin, Benjamin. *Autobiography* (Dover Publications Inc.: 1996), section 62, reprinted from text edited by John Bigelow (Philadelphia: J.P. Lippincott & Co., 1868).

Freeman, Douglas Southall. *George Washington, A Biography, Vol. 6: Patriot and President* (London: Eyre and Spottiswood, 1954).

Frehen, Ric (Tilburg University), William N. Goetzmann (Yale School of Management), and K. Geert Rouwenhorst (Yale School of Management). "Dutch Securities for American Land Speculation in the Late-Eighteenth Century." Draft paper dated July 3, 2013.

Friedenburg, Daniel M. *Life, Liberty, and the Pursuit of Land: The Plunder of Early America* (Buffalo: Prometheus Books, 1992).

Friedman, Lawrence M. *History of American Law* (New York: Simon & Schuster, 2005).

Furstenberg, Francois. *When the United States Spoke French: Five Refugees Who Shaped a Nation* (New York: Penguin Books, 2014).

Gabriel, Michael P. *Major General Richard Montgomery* (Teaneck, NJ: Fairleigh Dickinson University Press, 2002).

Galloway, George. *History of the House of Representatives* (New York: Thomas Y. Crowell, 1961).

Gilbert, Charles Sandoe. *Historical Survey of the County of Cornwall* (London: J. Congdon, 1820).

Goebel, Julius Jr. *The Law Practice of Alexander Hamilton*, 6 vols. (New York: Columbia University Press, 1964–1968).

Griswold, Rufus. *The Republican Court; or American Society in the Days of Washington* (New York: D. Appleton & Company, 1864).

Grossman, Mark. *Political Corruption in America: An Encyclopedia of Scandals, Power, and Greed* (Chicago: ABC-CLIO, 2003).

Grubb, Farley. *State Redemption of the Continental Dollar, 1779–1790*, Working Paper No. 2011-08, University of Delaware Alfred Lerner College of Business & Economics.

Hackett, David G. *The Religion in Which All Men Agree: Freemasonry in American Culture* (Berkeley: University of California Press, 2014).

Hamilton, Alexander. *The Papers of Alexander Hamilton*, 27 vols, edited by Harold Syrett et al. (New York: Columbia University Press, 1979).

Hamilton, Allan McLane. *The Intimate Life of Alexander Hamilton* (New York: Scribner's Sons, 1910).

Hamilton, James. *Reminiscences of James A. Hamilton: Or Men and Events at Home and Abroad . . . .* (New York: Charles Scribner & Co., 1868).

Harlow, Ralph Volney. *The History of Legislative Methods Before 1825* (New Haven, CT: Yale University Press, 1917).

Harris, Joseph P. *The Advice and Consent of the Senate: A Study of the Confirmation of Appointments by the United States Senate* (Berkeley: University of California Press, 1953).

Hart, Albert Bushnell, ed. *Proceedings of the Varick Court of Inquiry to Investigate the Implication of Colonel Varick in the Arnold Treason* (Boston: The Bibliophile Society, 1907).

Heitman, Francis. *Historical Register of Officers of the Continental Army during the War of the Revolution* (Washington, DC: Rare Book Shop Publishing Company, 1914), reissued by Genealogical Publishing Co.: Baltimore, 1973.

Hill, Frederick Trevor. *The Story of a Street: A Narrative History of Wall Street from 1644 to 1908* (New York: Harper & Brothers, 1908).

History of the "Arnold Tavern," Morristown. N.J.: and many incidents connected with General Washington's stay in this place, as his headquarters in winter of 1777: with views of Historic buildings and places of Revolutionary interest (Morristown, NJ: Chronicle Press, 1903).

HISTORY OF QUEENS COUNTY with illustrations, Portraits & Sketches of Prominent Families and Individuals (New York: W.W. Munsell & Co., 1882).

Hoadley, John F. *Origins of American Political Parties 1789–1803* (Lexington, KY: The University Press of Kentucky, 1986).

Hofstadter, Richard. *The Idea of a Party System: The Rise of Legitimate Opposition in the United States, 1780–1840* (Berkeley: University of California Press, 1969).

Holdsworth, John T., and Davis R. Dewey. "The First and Second Banks of the United States," *National Monetary Commission Report to the United States Senate* (Washington, DC: U.S. Government Printing Office, 1910).

Holgate, Jerome B. *American Genealogy, being a History of some of the Early Settlers of North American and their Descendants* (Albany, NY: Joel Munsell, 1848).

Holton, Woody. *Unruly Americans and the Origins of the Constitution* (New York: Hill and Wang, 2007).

Homberger, Eric. *The Historical Atlas of New York City* (New York: Henry Holt & Company, 1994).

Hough, Charles Merrill. *The United States District Court for the Southern District of New York, 1789–1919* (Maritime Law Association of The United States, Document No. 194, June 1934).

Hough, Franklin B. *A History of St. Lawrence and Franklin Counties, New York, from the Earliest Period to the Present Time* (Albany, NY: 1853) reprinted by Regional Publishing Company, Baltimore, 1970.

Hünemörder, Markus. *The Society of the Cincinnati: Conspiracy and Distrust in Early America* (London: Berghahn Books, 2006).

Hutchins, John G. B. *American Maritime Industries and Public Policy, 1789–1914, An Economic History* (Cambridge, MA: Harvard University Press, 1941).

Jackson, Donald, and Dorothy Twohig, ed. *The Diaries of George Washington* (Charlottesville: University of Virginia Press, 1979).

Jay, William. *The Life of John Jay* (New York: J & J Halper, 1833).

Jefferson, Thomas. *The Anas of Thomas Jefferson*, edited by Franklin B. Sawvel (New York: Da Capo Press, 1970).

Jenkins, Jeffrey A., and Charles Stewart III. *Fighting for the Speakership, the House and the Rise of Party Government* (Princeton, NJ: Princeton University Press, 2013).

Johnson, Alexander. *American Political History 1763–1876*, 2 vols. (New York: G. P. Putnam's Sons, 1913).

Johnson, Herbert A., et al., ed. *Papers of John Marshall*, vol. 1 (Chapel Hill: University of North Carolina Press, 1974).

Johnston, Henry Phelps. *The Battle of Harlem Heights, September 16, 1776, With a View of the Events of the Campaign* (Published for the Columbia University Press by the Macmillan Company, 1887).

Johnston, Henry Phelps. *The Campaign of 1776 around New York and Brooklyn: Memoirs of the Long Island Historical Society* (New York: S. W. Green, 1878), vol. III.

Jonas, Manfred, and Robert V. Wells, ed. *New Opportunities in a New Nation: The Development of New York after the Revolution* (Schenectady, NY: Union College Press, 1982).

Jones, Keith Marshall III. *Congress As My Government: Chief Justice John Marshall in the American Revolution (1775–1781)* (Baltimore, MD: Gateway Press for Connecticut Colonel Publishing Co., 2008).

Jones, Robert Francis. *King of the Alley: William Duer: Politician, Entrepreneur, and Speculator, 1768–1799* (Philadelphia: American Philosophical Society, 1992).

Jones, Thomas. *History of New York During the Revolutionary War*, edited by Edward S. DeLancey, 2 vols. (New York: New York Historical Society, 1879).

Kaminski, John P. "The Reluctant Pillar." In *The Reluctant Pillar*, edited by Stephen L. Schecter (Troy, NY: Russell Sage College, 1985).

Kaminski, John P. *George Clinton: Yeoman Politician of the New Republic* (Madison, WI; Madison House Publishers, Inc., 1993).

Kaminski, John P., ed. *The Founders on the Founders* (Charlottesville: University of Virginia Press, 2008).

Kaplan, Justin. *When the Astors Owned New York* (New York: Viking Division of Penguin Press, 2006).

Keith, Charles P. *The Provincial Counselors of Pennsylvania* (Philadelphia: W. S. Sharp Printing Co., 1883).

Kent, James. *Address to the Law Association of the City of New York* (1836), reprinted in part in Warren, *A History of the American Bar* (1913).

Kenyon, Cecilia M. *The Anti-federalists* (Indianapolis, IN: Bobbs-Merrill, 1966).

Ketcham, Ralph. *James Madison: A Biography* (Charlottesville: University of Virginia Press, 1971).

Ketchum, Richard M. *The Winter Soldiers: The Battles for Trenton and Princeton* (New York: Holt Paperbacks, Owl Books First edition, 1999).

Ketchum, Richard M. *Divided Loyalties: How the American Revolution Came to New York* (New York: Henry Holt and Company, 2003).

Kimball, Hoke, and Bruce Henson. *Governor's Houses and State Houses of British Colonial America, 1607–1783* (Jefferson, NV: McFarland & Company, Inc., 2017).

King, Charles R., ed. *Life and Correspondence of Rufus King*, 6 vols. (New York: G. B. Putnam's Sons, 1894).

Knudson, Jerry W. *Jefferson and the Press: Crucible of Liberty* (Columbia: University of South Carolina Press, 2006).

Kohl, John Y., and Helen W. Kohl. "Introducing... The Livingstons," *Proceedings of the Lehigh County Historical Society*, vol. 27, edited by Mildred Rowe Trexler (Allentown, PA: Lehigh County Historical Society, 1968).

Kohn, Richard H. *Eagle and Sword: The Federalists and the Creation of the Military Establishment in America, 1783–1802* (New York: The Free Press, 1975).

Labunski, Richard. *James Madison and the Struggle for the Bill of Rights* (New York: Oxford University Press, 2006).

Lamb, Martha J. *History of the City of New York: Its Origin, Rise, and Progress*, 2 vols. (New York: A. S. Barnes & Co., 1877).

Lang, Ossian. *History of St. John's Lodge No. 1, 1757–1907* (New York: Published for the New York Grand Lodge, 1907).

Larson, Edward J. *A Magnificent Catastrophe: The Election of 1800* (New York: Free Press Division of Simon and Schuster, 2007).

Laurens, Henry. *Papers of Henry Laurens* (Charleston: University of South Carolina Press, 1980).

Laurens, John. *Army Correspondence of Colonel John Laurens in the Years 1777–8* (New York: Bradford Club, 1867)

Lawrence, Thomas. *Historical Genealogy of the Lawrence Family: from their First Landing in this Country, 1635 to the Present Date* (New York: Edward O. Jenkins, 1858).

Laws of the State of New York Passed at the Sessions of the Legislature in the Years 1777–1801 (Albany, NY: Weed, Parsons & Company, 1886).

Leake, Isaac. *Life and Times of General Lamb* (Albany, NY: Joel Munsell's Sons, 1857), reprinted in 1970 by Benchmark Publishing Company.

Leibiger, Stuart. *Founding Friendship: George Washington, James Madison and the Creation of the American Republic* (Charlottesville: University of Virginia Press, 1999).

Levy, Leonard W., and Merrill D. Peterson. *Major Crises in American History* (New York: Harcourt, Brace and World, 1962).

Livingston, Edwin Brockholst. *The Livingstons of Livingston Manor* (New York: The Knickerbocker Press, 1910).

Lomask, Milton. *Aaron Burr: The Years from Princeton to Vice President 1756–1805* (New York: Farrar, Strauss & Giroux, 1979).

Lossing, Benson J., ed. *The American Historical Record*, vol. 1 (Philadelphia: John E. Potter and Company, 1873).

MacDougall, William L. *American Revolutionary: A Biography of General Alexander McDougall* (Westport, CT: Greenwood Press, 1977).

Maclay, Edgar S. *The Diary of William Maclay and Other Notes on Senate Debates*, edited by Kenneth R. Bowling and Helen E. Veit (Baltimore, MD: The Johns Hopkins University Press, 1988).

Madison, James. *Notes of Debates in the Federal Convention of 1787 Reported by James Madison* (Athens, OH: Ohio University Press, 1966).

Madison, James. *The Papers of James Madison*, vol. 10, edited by Robert A. Rutland, et al. (Chicago: University of Chicago Press, 1977).

Madison, James. *The Papers of James Madison*, vol. 11, edited by Charles F. Hobson, et al. (Charlottesville: University of Virginia Press, 1977).

Madison, James. *The Papers of James Madison*, Vols. 12, 13, edited by Charles F. Hobson, et al. (Charlottesville: University of Virginia Press, 1979, 1981).

Maier, Pauline. *From Resistance to Revolution: Colonial Radicals and the Development of American Opposition to Britain 1765–76* (New York: Alfred A. Knopf, 1972).

Main, Jackson Turner. *The Antifederalists: Critics of the Constitution 1781–1788* (New York: W. W. Norton, 1961).

Majerus, Gloria, and Laurie Postoris. *Memoir of Lieut. Col. Tench Tilghman, Secretary and Aid to Washington* (Albany, NY: Munsell & Co., 1876).

Malone, Dumas. *Jefferson and the Rights of Man* (Boston: Little, Brown & Co., 1951).

Malone, Dumas. *Jefferson and the Ordeal of Liberty* (Boston: Little, Brown & Co., 1962).

Mann, Bruce H. *Republic of Debtors: Bankruptcy in the Age of American Independence* (Cambridge, MA: Harvard University Press, 2002).

Manual for Courts-Martial, United States Government (Washington, DC: U.S. Government Printing Office, 1998).

Marcus, Maeva, ed. *The Documentary History of the Supreme Court of the United States, 1789–1800* (New York: Columbia University Press, 1998).

Marshall, John. *The Life of George Washington*, Second edition revised and corrected by the author, 2 vols. (Philadelphia: James Crissy, 1834).

Martin, James Kirby. *Benedict Arnold, Revolutionary Hero: An American Warrior Reconsidered* (New York: New York University Press, 1997).

Martin, Joseph Plumb. *Private Yankee Doodle, Being a Narrative of some of the Adventures, Dangers and Sufferings of a Revolutionary Soldier*, edited by George E. Scheer (Boston: Little Brown & Co., 1962).

McCaughey, Robert A. *Stand Columbia: A History of Columbia University* (New York: Columbia University Press, 2003).

McCraw, Thomas K. *The Founders and Finance, How Hamilton, Gallatin, and other Immigrants forged a New Economy* (Cambridge, MA: The Belknap Press of Harvard University Press, 2012.

McCullough, David. *John Adams* (New York: Simon & Schuster, 2001).

McCullough, David. *1776* (New York: Simon & Schuster, 2005).

McDonald, Forest. *Alexander Hamilton: A Biography* (New York: W. W. Norton & Company, 1979).

McLachlan, James. *Princetonians: A Biographical Directory, 1748–1768* (Princeton, NJ: Princeton University Press, 1976–1991).

McNamara, Brooks. *Day of Jubilee: The Great Age of Public Celebrations in New York, 1788–1909* (New Brunswick, NJ: Rutgers University Press, 1997).

McWhorter, George C. "Biographical Sketches of the Life of John Laurance," Unpublished presentation to the New York Historical Society, New York, 1869.

Meredith, William. *Papers of William Meredith* (Portland, ME: Anthoensen Press, 1980).

Midgely, Graham. *University Life in Eighteenth-Century Oxford* (Guildford, England: Biddles Ltd., 1996).

Miller, John C. *Alexander Hamilton: Portrait in Paradox* (New York: Harper & Row, 1959).

Miller, John C. *The Federalist Era 1789–1801* (New York: Harper & Brothers, 1960).

Miller, Nathan. *The U.S. Navy, A History* (Annapolis, MD: Naval Institute Press, 1997).

Miner, Clarence E. *The Ratification of the Federal Constitution by the State of New York* (New York: Columbia University, 1921).

Mintz, Max M. *Gouverneur Morris and the American Revolution* (Norman, OK: University of Oklahoma Press, 1970).

"Minutes and Rolls of the U.S. District Court for the Southern District of New York 1789–1811," National Archives and Records Services, General Services Administration: Records of District Courts of the United States Record Group 21.

Mitchell, Broadus. *Alexander Hamilton: Youth to Maturity, 1755–1788* (New York: Macmillan & Co., 1957).

Mohl, Richard. *Poverty in New York, 1783–1825* (New York: Oxford University Press, 1971).

Morrison, Samuel Eliot. *The Life and Letters of Harrison Gray Otis, Federalist, 1765–1848*, vol. I (Boston: Houghton Mifflin Company, 1913).

Morrison, Samuel Eliot, and Henry Steele Commager. *The Growth of the American Republic*, vol. 1 (New York: Oxford University Press, 1962).

Morrissey, Brendan. *Quebec 1775: The American Invasion of Canada* (Oxford, England: Osprey Publishing, 2003).

Neagles, James C. *Summer Soldiers: A Survey & Index of Revolutionary War Courts Martial* (Salt Lake City, UT: Ancestry Inc., 1986).

Nevins, Allan. *The American States During and After the Revolution, 1775–1789* (Reprint of the 1924 original, New York: Augustus M. Kelley, 1969).

New York and the Union, edited by Schechter, Stephen L., and Richard B. Bernstein (New York: New York State Commission on the Bicentennial of the United States Constitution, 1990).

New York City Directory (New York: Trow City Directory Co., 1789).

The New York Civil List (Albany, NY: Weed, Parsons and Company, 1858).

New York State Archives, series AO447 Military Patents, 1764–1797, vols. 4–8.

Newman, Eric. *The Early Paper Money of America* (Iola, WI: Krause, 1990).

Nichols, Roy F. *The Invention of the American Political Parties: A Study of Political Improvisation* (New York: Macmillan & Co., 1967).

Norway, Arthur H. *History of the Post-Office Packet Service Between the Years 1793–1815* (London: Macmillan & Co., 1895).

O'Callaghan, E. B., ed., *The Documentary History of the State of New York*, vol. III (Albany, NY: Weed, Parsons and Company, 1850).

Officers & Graduates of Columbia College, General Catalogue 1754–1900 (New York: Printed for the University, 1900).

Olivey, Hugh P. *Notes on the Parish of Mylor, Cornwall* (Taunton, England: Barnicott & Pearce, Athenaem Press, 1907).

The Other New York: The American Revolution Beyond New York City, 1763–1787, edited by Joseph S. Tiedeman and Eugene R. Fingerhut (Albany, NY: State University of New York Press, 2005).

The Papers of Thomas Jefferson, vol. 29, *1 March 1796–31 December 1797*, edited by Barbara B. Oberg (Princeton, NJ: Princeton University Press, 2002).

Pasley, Jeffrey L. *The Tyranny of Printers: Newspaper Politics in the Early American Republic* (Charlottesville, VA: The University of Virginia Press, 2001).

Pasley, Jeffrey L. "1800 as a Revolution in Political Culture," *The Revolution of 1800: Democracy, Race, and the Republic*, edited by James P. P. Horn, Jan Ellen Lewis, and Perter S. Onuf (Charlottesville: University of Virginia Press, 2002).

Paullin, Charles Oscar. *Navy of the American Revolution* (Chicago: University of Chicago Press, 1906).

Paullin, Charles Oscar. *Paullin's History of Naval Administration 1775–1911* (Annapolis, MD: Naval Institute Press, 1968), a reprint of essays written between 1905 and 1944.

Peirce, Charles. *Meteorological Account of the Weather in Philadelphia from January 1, 1790 to January 1, 1847* (Philadelphia: Lindsay & Blakiston, 1847).

Peters, Richard, ed. *Condensed Reports of Cases in the Supreme Court of the United States*, 6 vols. (Philadelphia: Thomas Cowperthwait & Co., 1844).

Peterson, Arthur Everett. *Minutes of the New York City Common Council* (City of New York: 1917), vol. 1, 1784–1831.

PROCEEDINGS of a BOARD of General Officers, Held by Order of His Excellency Gen. Washington, respecting Major JOHN ANDRE, Adjutant General of the British Army, September 29, 1780 (Philadelphia: Francis Bailey in Market-Street, 1780).

PROCEEDINGS of a GENERAL COURT MARTIAL for the Trial of MAJOR GENERAL ARNOLD (New York: Munsell & Company, 1865).

PROCEEDINGS of a GENERAL COURT MARTIAL held at Brunswick in the State of New-Jersey by order of HIS EXCELLENCY GEN. WASHINGTON for the Trial of Major-General Lee, July 4th, 1778, Major-General Lord Stirling President (New York: Privately printed, 1864).

PROCEEDINGS of a GENERAL COURT MARTIAL For the Trial of MAJOR GENERAL St. CLAIR, August 25, 1778, Major General Lincoln, President (Philadelphia: Hall and Sellers, 1878).

PROCEEDINGS of a GENERAL COURT MARTIAL Held at Major General Lincoln's Quarters near Quaker Hill in the State of New York By Order of His Excellency General Washington Commander in Chief of the Army of The United States of America For the Trial of MAJOR GENERAL SCHUYLER, October 1, 1778, Major General Lincoln, President (Philadelphia: Hall and Sellers, 1878).

Pyle, Christopher H. *Extradition, Politics, and Human Rights* (Philadelphia: Temple University Press, 2001).

Rappleye, Charles. *Robert Morris, Financier of the American Revolution* (New York: Simon & Schuster, 2010).

Record of Pennsylvania Marriages Prior to 1810, vol. 1 (Clarence M. Busch, State Printer of PA, 1895).

"Report of Governor Tryon on the Province of New York to the Earl of Dartmouth London, 11 June 1774," *Documents Relevant to the Colonial History of New York*, vol. XLIV, edited by E. B. O'Callaghan (Albany, NY: Weed, Parsons and Company, 1853–1887).

Richardson, James A. *A Compilation of the Messages and Papers of the Presidents*, vol. I (Washington DC: Bureau of National Literature, 1897).

Riker, James Jr. *The Annals of Newtown in Queens County New York* (New York: D. Fanshaw, 1852).

Riker, James Jr. *Evacuation Day 1783, Its Many Stirring Events with Recollections of Capt. John Van Arsdale* (New York: Printed for the author, 1883).

Robbin, Karen E. *James McHenry, Forgotten Federalist* (Athens: University of Georgia Press, 2013).

Roberts, Charles Rhoads. *History of Lehigh County, Pennsylvania*, 2 vols. (Allentown, PA: Lehigh Valley Publishing Company, Inc., 1914).

Roberts, Kenneth. *March to Quebec* (New York: Doubleday, 1938).

Rolls and Documents Relating to Soldiers in the Revolutionary War, vol. XVII, edited by Isaac W. Hammond (Manchester, NH: John B. Clarke, Public Printer, 1889).

Rosenfeld, Richard N. *American Aurora* (New York: St. Martin's Press, 1997).

Rosenwaike, Ira. *Population History of New York City* (Syracuse, NY: Syracuse University Press, 1972).

Ross, Peter. *A Standard History of Freemasonry in the State of New York* (New York: The Lewis Publishing Co., 1899).

Royster, Charles. *A Revolutionary People at War: The Continental Army and American Character 1775–1786* (Chapel Hill: University of North Carolina Press, 1979).

Rush, Benjamin. *Travels Through Life or Sundry Incidents in the Life of Dr. Benjamin Rush*, edited by Louis Alexander Biddle (Philadelphia: Published privately, 1905).

Rutland, Robert A., and William M. E. Rachel, ed. *The Papers of James Madison* (Charlottesville: University of Virginia Press, 1975).

Rutland, Robert A. *James Madison: The Founding Father* (New York: Macmillan, 1987).

Saffell, William T. *Records of the Revolutionary War, with a list of the officers of the Continental Army who acquired the right to half-pay, commutation and lands* (New York: Pudney & Russell Publishers, 1858).

Sakolski, A. M. *The Great American Land Bubble* (New York: Harper & Brothers, 1932).

Sales Records of the New York State Commissioners of Forfeitures for the Southern District, 1784–1787, 2 vols., New York Historical Society Collection.

Schachner, Nathan. *The Founding Fathers* (New York: G. P. Putnam's Sons, 1954).

Scharf, J. Thomas. *The Chronicles of Baltimore* (Baltimore, MD: Trumbull Brothers, 1874).

Scharf, J. Thomas. *History of Westchester County, New York*, 2 vols. (Philadelphia: L. E. Preston & Co., 1886).

Schecter, Barnet. *The Battle for New York* (New York: Walker & Company, 2002).

Schuyler, John. *Institution of the Society of the Cincinnati* (New York: Douglas Taylor, 1896).

Scott, Henry Wilson. *The Courts of the State of New York: Their History, Development and Jurisdiction* (New York: Wilson Publishing Company, 1909).

Siemers, David J. *After Ratification: Antifederalists and Federalists in Constitutional Time* (Stanford, CA: Stanford University Press, 2002).

Simms, William. *Life of John Taylor* (Richmond, VA: The William Byrd Press Inc., 1932).

Slaughter, Thomas P. *The Whiskey Rebellion: Epilogue to the American Revolution* (New York: Oxford University Press, 1986).

Smith, James Morton. *Freedom's Fetters: The Alien and Sedition Laws and American Civil Liberties* (Ithaca, NY: Cornell University Press, 1956).

Smith, Joshua Hett. *Authentic Narrative of the Causes which led to the Death of Major Andre, Adjutant General of His Majesty's Forces in North America* (London: Printed for Matthews and Leigh, 1808).

Smith, Paul H., ed. *Letters of Delegates to Congress, 1774–1789*, vol. 21 (Washington, DC: Library of Congress, 1994).

Smith, Thomas Edward Vermilye. *The City of New York in the Year of Washington's Inauguration* (New York: W. D. F. Randolph & Co., 1889).

Spaulding, Ernest W. *New York During the Critical Period, 1783–1789* (New York: Columbia University Press, 1932).

Spencer, Charles Worthen. "John Laurance," *Dictionary of American Biography*, edited by Dumas Malone, vol. XI (New York: Charles Scribner's Sons, 1933).

Stadnitski. Peter. "Preliminary Information respecting a Negotiation on Lands in America" (1792)," a typescript in the archives of ING Bank in London.

Stahr, Walter. *John Jay, Founding Father* (New York: Hambledon and London, 2005).

Stanley, George. *Canada Invaded 1775–1776* (Toronto: Hakkert Press, 1973).

Steiner, Bernard Christian. *The Life and Correspondence* of *James McHenry* (Cleveland: The Burrows Brother's Company, 1907).

Stewart, David O. *The Summer of 1787* (New York: Simon & Schuster, 2007).

Stewart, L. Lloyd. *A Far Cry From Freedom: Gradual Abolition (1799–1827)* (Bloomington, IN: Author House, 2005).

Stille, Charles J. *Major-General Anthony Wayne and the Pennsylvania Line in the Continental Army* (Philadelphia: J.B. Lippincott Company, 1893).

Stokes, I. N. Phelps. *Iconography of Manhattan Island, 1490–1909* (New York: Robert H. Dodd, 1915–1928).

Stokes, I. N. Phelps. *New York Past and Present: Its History and Landmarks 1524–1939* (New York Historical Society, private printing, 1939).

Stubbs, Walter. *Congressional Committees 1789–1982: A Checklist* (Westport, CT: Greenwood Press, 1985).

Swanstrom, Roy. *The United States Senate, 1787–1801: A Dissertation on the First Fourteen Years of the Upper Legislative Body* (Washington, DC: U.S. Govt. Printing Office, 1962).

Sypher, Francis J. *History of the New York Regiments of the Continental Army* (Fishkill, NY: Society of the Cincinnati, 2008).

Tabbert, Mark A. *American Freemasons: Three Centuries of Building Communities* (New York: New York University Press, 2005).

Talmadge, Benjamin. *Memoir*, edited by Henry Phelps Johnston (New York: Gilliss Press, 1904).

Taylor, Alan. *William Cooper's Town: Power and Persuasion on the Frontier of the Early American Republic* (New York: Vintage Books, 1995).

"Testimony of Professor John Yinger," *United States Senate Committee on the Judiciary*, October 5, 2004.

Thain, Rafael P. *Legislative History of the General Staff of the Army of the United States from 1775 to 1901* (Washington, DC: U.S. Government Printing Office, 1901).

Thatcher, James, M.D. *The American Revolution: From the Commencement to the Disbanding of the American Army Given in the Form of a Daily Journal, with the Exact Dates of all the Important Events* (New York: American Subscription Publishing House, 1860).

Toll, Ian W. *Six Frigates: The Epic History of the Founding of the U.S. Navy* (New York: W. W. Norton & Company, 2006).

Tripp, Wendell Edward Jr. *Robert Troup: A Quest for Security in a Turbulent New Nation (1775–1832)* (New York: Arno Press, 1982).

Tucker, George. *The Life of Thomas Jefferson*, 2 vols. (London: Charles Knight and Co., 1837).

Upton, L. F. S. *The Loyal Whig: William Smith of New York and Quebec* (Toronto: University of Toronto Press, 1969).

Van Winter, Pieter Jan. *American Finance and Dutch Investment, 1780–1805: With an Epilogue to 1840*, edited by James C. Riley, 2 vols. (New York: Arno Press, 1977).

Vile, John R. *The Constitutional Convention of 1787: A Comprehensive Encyclopedia of America's Founding*, 2 vols. (Santa Barbara, CA: ABC-CLIO Inc., 2005).

Vile, John R., William D. Pederson, and Frank J. Williams, ed. *James Madison: Philosopher, Founder, and Statesman* (Athens, OH: Ohio University Press, 2008).

Wallace, Paul A. W. *The Muhlenburgs of Pennsylvania* (Philadelphia: University of Pennsylvania Press, 2018).

Ward, Christopher. *The War of the Revolution*, 2 vols. (New York: John R. Alden, 1952).

Ward, Harry M. *Major General Adam Stephen and the Cause of American Liberty* (Charlottesville: University of Virginia Press, 1989).

Ward, Harry M. *George Washington's Enforcers: Policing the Continental Army* (Carbondale: Southern Illinois University Press, 2006).

Warren, Charles. *History of the Harvard Law School and of Early Legal Conditions in America* (New York: Lewis Publishing Co., 1908).

Warren, Charles. *A History of the American Bar* (Boston: Little, Brown & Co., 1911).

Washington, George. *The Writings of George Washington*, 39 vols., edited by John C. Fitzpatrick (Washington, DC: U.S. Government Printing Office, 1931–1944).

Washington, George. *The Diaries of George Washington*, edited by Donald Jackson and Dorothy Twohig, 6 vols (Charlottesville: University of Virginia Press, 1975–1979).

Washington, George. *The Papers of George Washington*, Colonial Series, vol. 4, 9 November 1756–24 October 1757, edited by W. W. Abbot (Charlottesville: University of Virginia Press, 1984).

Washington, George. *The Papers of George Washington*, Revolutionary War Series, vol. 6, edited by Philander D. Chase and Frank E. Grizzard Jr. (Charlottesville: University of Virginia Press, 1994).

Washington, George. *The Papers of George Washington*, Revolutionary War Series, vol. 9, 28 March 1777–10 June 1777, edited by Philander D. Chase (Charlottesville: University of Virginia Press, 1999).

Washington, George. *The Papers of George Washington*, Presidential Series, vol. 9, *23 September 1791–29 February 1792*, edited by Mark A. Mastromarino (Charlottesville: University of Virginia Press, 2000)

Washington, George. *The Papers of George Washington*, Revolutionary War Series, vol. 12, 26 October 1777–25 December 1777, edited by Frank E. Grizzard Jr., and David R. Hoth (Charlottesville: University of Virginia Press, 2002).

Washington, George. *The Papers of George Washington, Revolutionary War Series*, vol. 13, 14, 20, 26 December 1777–28 February 1778, edited by Edward G. Lengel (Charlottesville: University of Virginia Press, 2003–2010).

Washington, George. *The Papers of George Washington*, Revolutionary War Series, vol. 16, *July 14–September 1778*, edited by David L. Hoth (Charlottesville: University of Virginia Press, 2006).

Washington, George. *The Papers of George Washington*, Presidential Series, vol. 13, edited by Christine Sternberg Patrick (Charlottesville: University of Virginia Press, 2007).

Webster, Noah. *1786 New York City Directory* (New York: Trow City Directory Co., 1886).

Weedon, George. *Valley Forge Orderly Book of General George Weedon* (Chicago: Arno Press, 1971). Printed from the original manuscript in the library of the American Philosophical Society at Philadelphia.

Westcott, Thompson. *The Historic Mansions and Buildings of Philadelphia* (Philadelphia: Porter & Coates, 1877).

Wharton, Anne Hollingsworth. *Social Life in the Early Republic* (Philadelphia: J. B. Lippincott Company, 1903).

Williams, Greg H. *The French Assault on American Shipping, 1793–1813* (North Carolina: McFarland Co., 2009).

Williams, Nathan B. *The American Post Office* (61st Congress, 2nd Session, Senate Document No. 542).

Wilson, James Grant. "John Pintard, Founder of the New York Historical Society: An Address Delivered before the New York Historical Society, December 3, 1901" (New York: Printed for the Society, 1902).

Wilson, Warren H. "Quaker Hill, A Sociological Study." PhD diss., Columbia University, 1907.

Winthrop, William. *Military Law and Precedents*, 2 vols. (Boston: Little, Brown & Co., 1896).

Wolfe, Gerard R. *New York: A Guide to the Metropolis: Walking Tours of Architecture and History*, revised edition (New York: McGraw-Hill Book Company, 1983.)

Wood, Gordon S. *Empire of Liberty* (New York: Oxford University Press, 2009).

Wright, John Womack. *Some Notes on the Continental Army* (Vails Gate, NY: National Temple Hill Association, 1975).

Wright, Robert E. *Origins of Commercial Banking in America 1750–1800* (New York: Rowman & Littlefield Publishers, 2001).

Wright, Robert E. *Hamilton Unbound: Finance and the Creation of the American Republic* (Westport, CT: Greenwood Press, 2002).

Wright, Robert E. *The First Wall Street: Chestnut Street, Philadelphia, and the Birth of American Finance* (Chicago: The University of Chicago Press, 2005).

Wright, Robert E., and David J. Cohen. *Financial Founding Fathers: The Men Who Made America Rich* (Chicago: University of Chicago Press, 2006)

Wright, Robert K. Jr. *The Continental Army* (Washington, DC: Center of Military History, United States Army, 1983).

Yoshpe, Harry B. *The Disposition of Loyalist Estates in the Southern District of the State of New York* (New York: Columbia University Press, 1939).

Young, Alfred F. *The Democratic Republicans of New York: Origins, 1763–1797* (Chapel Hill: University of North Carolina Press, 1967).

Ziegler, Phillip. *The Sixth Great Power: A History of One of the Greatest of All Banking Families, the House of Barings, 1762–1929* (New York: Alfred A. Knopf, 1988).

Selected Print Articles

"Abstracts of Sales by the Commissioners of Forfeitures in the Southern District of New York State," copied and contributed by Theresa H. Bristol, *New York Genealogical and Biographical Record* 59, no. 3 (October 1928).

Alexander, Arthur J. "Judge John Laurance: Successful Investor in New York State Lands," *New York History* 25 (1944).

Allen, James. "Diary of James Allen, Esq., of Philadelphia," *The Pennsylvania Magazine of History and Biography* 9, no. 2 (July 1885).

Amebeck, Bob. "Tracking the Speculators: Greenleaf and Nicholson in the Federal City," *Washington History* 3 (Spring/Summer 1991): 1.

Anderson, Frank M. "The Enforcement of the Alien and Sedition Laws," *Annual Report of the American Historical Association for the Year 1912* (Washington, DC: Smithsonian Institution, 1914).

"An Ulster County Boy in the Revolution," *Olde Ulster: An Historical and Genealogical Magazine* 1, no. 9 (September 1905).

Atkinson, Paul Jr. "The System of Military Discipline and Justice in the Continental Army: August 1777–June 1778," *The Picket Post* (Valley Forge Historical Society, Winter 1972–1973).

Bell, Whitfield J., Jr. "The Court Martial of Dr. William Shippen Jr., 1780," *Journal of the History of Medicine and Allied Sciences* 19 (July 1964): 218–238.

Brandt, Claire. "Robert R. Livingston, Jr.: The Reluctant Revolutionary," *The Hudson Valley Regional Review* 4, no. 1 (March 1987).

Brooks, Lynn Matluck. "The Philadelphia Dancing Assembly in the Eighteenth Century," *Dance Research Journal* 12, no. 1 (Spring 1989).

Brubaker, Ralph. "On the Nature of Federal Bankruptcy Jurisdiction: General Statutory and Constitutional Theory," *William & Mary Law Review* 41 (March 2000).

Champagne, Roger. "Liberty Boys and Mechanics of New York City, 1764–1774," *Labor History* VIII (Spring 1967).

Chernow, Barbara. "Robert Morris: Genesee Land Speculator," *New York History* 58 (1977).

Chroust, Anton-Hermann. "Legal Profession in Colonial America," *Notre Dame Law Review* 33 (1958).

Connors, Anthony J. "Andrew Craigie, Brief Life of a Patriot and a Scoundrel 1754–1819," *Harvard Magazine* (November–December 2011).

Crane, V. W. "Franklin's 'The Internal State of America,'" *William and Mary Quarterly* 15 (1958).

Currie, David P. "The Constitution in Congress," *Northwestern University Law Review* 90, no. 2 (1995–1996).

Davis, Wallace Evans. "The Society of the Cincinnati in New England 1783–1800," *William & Mary Quarterly*, 3rd Series, 5 (1948).

Delafield, Maturin L. "William Smith—The Historian and Chief Justice of New York and of Canada," *The Magazine of American History* (April and June 1881).

Dunbar, Erica Armstrong. "George Washington, Slave Catcher," *The New York Times*, February 16, 2015.

Du Ponceau, Pierre Etienne. "Autobiography," *Pennsylvania Magazine of History and Biography* LXIII (1939).

Evans, Paul. "The Pulteney Purchase," *Proceedings of the New York State Historical Society* 20 (1922).

Fleming, Thomas. "The 'Military Crimes' of Charles Lee," *American Heritage Magazine* 19, no. 3 (April 1968).

Fogleman, Aaron. "Migrations to the Thirteen British North American Colonies, 1700–1775 and New Estimates," *Journal of Interdisciplinary History* XXII, no. 4 (Spring 1992).

Fratcher, Colonel William F. "Notes on the History of the Judge Advocate General's Department, 1776–1941," *Judge Advocate Journal* 1, no. 1 (June 15, 1944).

Fratcher, Colonel William F. "History of the Judge Advocate General's Corps, United States Army," *Military Law Review* IV (1959).

Giddens, Elizabeth. "Memorials and the Forgotten," *The New York Times*, September 2, 2011.

Goebel, Julius Jr. "King's Law and Local Custom in Seventeenth-Century New England," *Columbia Law Review* 31, no. 3 (1931): 416.

Hamlin, Paul Mahlon. "Legal Education in Colonial New York," *New York University Law Quarterly Review* (Washington Square Park: 1939).

Hazelton, John H. "Trumbull's 'Declaration of Independence,'" *The Pennsylvania Magazine of History and Biography* 31, no. 121 (1907).

Heller, Francis H. "Military Law in the Continental Army," *University of Kansas Law Review* 25 (1976–1977).

Heyl, John K. "James Allen and Trout Hall," *Lehigh County Historical Society Proceedings* 24 (Allentown, PA: Lehigh County Historical Society, 1962).

Holton, Woody. "Far From Lexington and Concord," *The New York Times Book Review*, July 5, 2015.

Johnston, Henry P. "New York After the Revolution, 1783–1789," *Magazine of American History* XXIX, no. 4 (April 1893).

Jones, E. Alfred. "Letter of David Colden, Loyalist, 1783," *The American Historical Review* 25, no. 1 (October 1919).

Jones, Keith Marshall III. "John Laurance and the Role of Military Justice at Valley Forge," *Pennsylvania Magazine of History and Biography* CXLI, no. 1 (January 2017).

"Journal of Major Henry Livingston of the Third New York Regiment, 1775," *The Pennsylvania Magazine of History and Biography* 22, no. I (1898).

Manders, Eric I. "Those Coats of 1775 – A Dissenting View," *Military Collector and Historian Magazine* 33, no. 2 (Summer 1981).

Maurer, Maurer. "Military Justice Under General Washington," *Military Affairs*, 28, no. 1 (Spring 1964).

McKelvey, Blake. "Historical Aspects of the Phelps & Gorham Treaty of July 4–8, 1788," *Rochester History Magazine*, 1, no. 1 (January 1939).

McRobert, Patrick. "Patrick McRobert's Tour Through Part of the North Provinces of America," edited by Carl Bridenbaugh, *Pennsylvania Magazine of History and Biography* 59, no. 2 (April 1935).

Minutes of the Common Council of the City of New York — 1784–1831 (New York: City of New York, 1917).

Morris, Richard B. "The Salzer Collection of Mayor's Court Papers," *Columbia Library Columns* 7, no. 3 (New York: Friends of the Columbia Libraries, 1958).

Murphy, Brian Phillips. "'A very convenient instrument': The Manhattan Company, Aaron Burr, and the Election of 1800," *William & Mary Quarterly*, 3rd series, LXV, no. 2 (April 2008).

Naval Investigation: Hearings before the Subcommittee on Naval Affairs United States Senate, Sixty-sixth Congress Second Session (Washington, DC: U.S. Government Printing Office, 1921), vol. 1.

Olenkiewicz, John S. "British Packet Sailings–New York–Falmouth: 1755–1790," from data obtained from the newspaper archives of the American Antiquarian Society and Newsbank, December 28, 2011.

Pernick, Martin S. "Politics, Parties, and Pestilence: Yellow Fever in Philadelphia and the Rise of the First Party System," *William & Mary Quarterly* XXIX (3rd Ser., October 1972): 559–86.

Perry, James R., and James M. Buchanan. "Admission to the Supreme Court Bar, 1790–1800: A Case Study of Institutional Change," *Supreme Court Historical Society Yearbook* (1983).

Risch, Erna. "Supplying Washington's Army," Center of Military History, United States Army, Washington, DC, 1981.

Smith, Frank Sullivan. "Admission to the Bar in New York," *The Yale Law Journal* 16, no. 7 (May 1907).

Steenshorne, Jennifer. "Evacuation Day 1783 and Later," *New York Archives Magazine* 10, no. 2 (Fall 2010).

Sylla, Richard, Robert E. Wright, and David J. Cohen. "Alexander Hamilton, Central Banker: Crisis Management and the Lender of Last Resort in the U.S. Panic of 1792," *Business History Review* 83 (Spring 2009).

Tabb, Charles Jordan. "The History of Bankruptcy Laws in the United States," *ABI Law Review* 3, no. 5 (1995).

"Vital Records of the First Presbyterian Church, 1776," *New York Genealogical and Biographical Record*, vol. 12 (New York: Mott Memorial Hall, 1880).

Ward, Harry M. "John Laurance," *American National Biography*, vol. 13 (Oxford: Oxford University Press, 1999).

Wettereau, James O. "New Light on the First Bank of the United States," *Pennsylvania Magazine of History and Biography* 61 (July 1937).

Winthrop, Clarence Bowden. "The Inauguration of Washington," *Century Magazine* (April 1889).

Zeichner, Otto. "The Loyalist Problem in New York After the Revolution," *New York History* 21, no. 3 (July 1940).

Newspapers

Baltimore Gazette

Boston Gazetteer

Connecticut Courant

Farmers Museum or Literary Gazette

Federal Gazette & Baltimore Daily Advertiser

Gazette of the United States

National Intelligencer

New Jersey Gazette

New York Commercial Advertiser

New York Daily Advertiser

New York Daily Gazette

New York Daily Patriotic Register

New York Evening Post

New York Journal

New York Packet

New York Post Boy

Philadelphia Aurora

Philadelphia General Advertiser

Poughkeepsie Country Journal

Selected Online Materials

Annals of Congress. https://memory.loc.gov/ammem/amlaw.lwac.html.

On-line Exhibit: The Charters of Freedom, National Archives. https://www.archives.gov/exhibits/charters/charters_of_freedom_13.htm, "Expansion of Rights and Liberties – The Right of Suffrage," www.archives.upenn.edu/WestPhila1777/view-parcel.php.

"Biographies of the Secretaries," Office of the Historian, United States of America Department of State, https://history.state.gov/departmenthistory/people/secretaries.

Campbell, Andy. "Falmouth Packet Archives at the Royal Cornwall Polytechnic Society" (est. 1833), Falmouth, Cornwall, England (falmouth.packet.archives@dial.pipex.com).

www.census.gov/population/www/documentation/twps0029.html.

Journals of the Continental Congress 1774–1789. https://memory.loc.gov/ammem/amlaw/lwjclink.html.

Convoy Web. Arnold Hague Convoy Database: www.convoyweb.org.uk/hague/index.html.

Cornwall Parish Records. http://www.cornwall-opc-database.org/.

Founders Online – National Archives, https://founders.archives.gov

"John Laurance, Representative from New York." In *The Documentary History of the First Federal Congress of the United States 1789–1791* (Model Editions Partnership Digital Age: The Johns Hopkins University Press, 1988–1994.). http://adh.sc.edu.

Metropolitan Transit Authority (MTA) South Ferry Terminal Project Archaeological Report: http://www.mta.info/capconstr/sft/archaeology.html.

Notes of the Founding Fathers, "Letters of the Delegates to Congress 1774–1789. https://www.loc.gov/lclb/0010/delegates.html.

"Record of Engagements," New York Society of the Cincinnati. www.nycincinnati.org/engagements.htm.

Olenkiewicz, John S. "British Packet Sailings–New York–Falmouth: 1755–1790," from data obtained from the newspaper archives of the American Antiquarian Society and Newsbank, December 28, 2011, www.rfrajola.com/resources/falmouthpacket.pdf.

The Debates in the Convention of The State of New York on the Adoption of the Federal Constitution, Wednesday, June 23rd, www.constitution.org/rc/rat_ny.htm.

Papers of Alexander Hamilton. https://founders.archives.gov/documents/Washington/Hamilton.

"The Muster Roll Project," The Friends of Valley Forge Park. http://valleyforgemusterroll.org.

United States District Court Southern District of New York, *The 154 District Judges: Biographies, Writings and Cases*, "Profile of John Laurance," https://history.nysd.uscourts.gov.judges.php.

The Papers of George Washington Digital Edition, edited by Theodore J. Crackel (Charlottesville: University of Virginia Press, Rotunda, 2008). www.senate.gov/artandhistory/history/common/briefing/Commitees.htm.

"William Smith, Representative from South Carolina." In *Documentary History of the First Federal Congress of the United States of America*, edited by Charlotte Bickford, et al. (Columbia, SC: Model Editions Partnership, 2002), http://adh.sc.edu.

"Speakers of the House (1789 to present)," History, Art & Archives, United States House of Representatives, https://history.house.gov/People/Office/Speakers.

www.stjohns1.org/portal/lodgehistory.

www.treasurydirect.gov/govt/reports/pd/histdebt/histdebt.htm.

Index

fn denotes footnotes; n, notes.
Subentries are listed in chronological order and are not alphabetical.

Act for establishing a Marine Corps (1798), 234, 241
Act for providing a Naval Armament (1797), 4, 224
Act to provide for the further Defense of the ports and harbors of the United States (1797), 224, 234, 231
Adams, Abigail, 152, 176, 179, 251
Adams, Abigail, "Nabby" (Mrs. William S. Smith), 255
Adams, Charles, 166, 255
Adams, John, 1, 53, 91fn, 95fn, 102, 258
   Continental Congress, in, 38; and JL, 166, 239, 255
   Vice President, as, 136, 146, 152, 179, 180, 188, 195, 199, 204, 219, 221, 243
   President, as, 4, 5, 7, 221, 222, 223, 225, 226, 230, 231, 233, 234, 235, 237, 241, 242, 254, 257
Adet, Pierre, 8, 220, 237
agrarian political interests, 148–151, 169, 193, 246, 316 n.36
Albany, NY, 28, 267
   War for Independence, in, 41, 42, 83
   JL land business, in, 239, 241, 256, 264
Alexander, James, 27, 30, 31
Alexander, William (Lord Stirling), 65, 77, 102, 107
Alien and Sedition Acts (1798), 8, 237–238, 281
   Alien Act, 237
   Alien Enemies Act, 237, 281
   Naturalization Act, 237
   Sedition Act, 238, 246, 259
Allen, Anne Penn (Mrs. William Greenleaf), 176, 177, 247, 248, 249, 251, 262
   portrait of, 248
Allen, Elizabeth Lawrence (Mrs. John Laurance)
   portrait of, 175
   James Allen marriage and children, 174, 175, 238
   failing health, death and funeral, of, 7, 239, 241, 243, 252, 253, 254
   JL marriage and children, of, 174, 192, 197, 203, 206, 218, 228, 233, 239, 247
   New York City, in, 7, 203, 204, 209, 251, 252
   Philadelphia, in, 174–197, 206, 218, 239, 241
Allen, James, 174, 253, 263
Allen, James, Jr., 253
Allen, Margaret (Mrs. William Tilghman), 206, 238
Allen, Mary Masters (Mrs. H. Walter Livingston), 176, 180, 203, 218
Allentown, PA, 174, 238, 239
American Revolution. *See* individual events
Ames, Fisher, 4, 6, 254, 257, 259
   congressman, as, 142, 150, 157, 159, 164, 167, 169, 184, 187, 188, 196, 197
   political observer, as, 204, 205, 259
Anglophile-Francophile political animosity, 198, 211, 223, 235, 236, 237, 238, 240
Annapolis Conference, 123, 134
Andrè, John (British major), 72, 83, 85
anti-administration faction, 167, 182, 185, 195, 196. *See also* Maclay, William
antifederalism
   description of, 126
   pre-*Federalist Papers*, 114, 120, 126, 128, 316 n.47
   post-*Federalist Papers*, 131, 132, 140, 143, 145, 146, 156, 182, 186, 197
   New York proponents of
      Haring, Thomas, 114, 120
      Hathorn, John, 97
      Lansing, John, 120, 125, 261, 261
      Smith, Melancton, 114, 119, 120, 126, 132, 166
      Yates, Robert, 125, 126, 131

antifederalism *(Continued)*
  other leading proponents of
    Adams, Sam, 69, 126, 225
    Burke, Aedenus, 143, 144, 156
    Henry, Patrick, 126, 160
    Jones, Willie, 126
    Lee, Richard Bland, 143, 160, 170
    Lee, Richard Henry, 33, 114, 126
    Mason, George, 126.
    See also Clinton, George, and Lamb, John
Apportionment Act of 1792, 186–188
Arnold, Benedict, Continental Army, in, 41, 43–5, 62
  courts-martial of, 3, 70, 71–3
  treason of, 76, 77–80, 262
  British service, in, 83
Arnold, Jacob, tavern of, 52, 53, 56
Articles of Confederation, 92, 109, 116, 118, 119, 126
Articles of War (1776), 53, 55, 57, 59, 67, 68, 300 n.9
  JL interpretation of, 60, 67, 68, 281, 282
Asia, HMS, 39, 45
assumption of state wartime debts, 148, 155–164, 165
Astor, John Jacob, 203
Attorney General (United States), 170, 203, 212
Aurora, Philadelphia, 210, 223, 225, 228, 233, 236, 237, 244, 245, 247, 254
  Bache, Benjamin, editor of, 225, 244
  Duane, William, editor of, 8, 244, 245

bancomania, 265
banks, land vs. money banks, 112; fear of, 181
Bank of England, 157, 168
Banks, state
  Maryland, Bank of, 189, 191
  Massachusetts, Bank of, 189
  New York, Bank of, 111, 112, 129, 148, 152, 180, 276
  Panic of 1792, in, 189, 190, 191, 250
Bank of North America, 92, 112, 152, 169, 181, 189, 191
Bank of the United States (BUS), 168–171, 190, 196, 238, 265
  scrip and stock prices, 180, 265
  shareholders and directors, 181, 200, 212, 229, 327 n.31
  branches, 188, 201, 213, 250, 265
Banque de France, 157

bankruptcy, and the Bankruptcy Act of 1800 (An Act to establish a uniform system of bankruptcy throughout the United States), 245, 246, 246fn, 249
  JL role in, 245
Barré, Jean-Baptiste-Henri, 4, 206–209
Beekman, Gerard, 85, 86
Benson, Egbert
  postwar New York, in 91fn, 92, 103, 107, 108, 114, 124, 128
  Federalist congressman, as, 134, 145, 152, 164, 171, 192, 195
  state/federal judge, as, 217
  co-executor of JL estate, as, 134, 278
Beverly (Robinson House), 77, 85
Bill of Rights, 144, 145
  JL role in, 144
  James Madison role in, 5, 144
Bingham, William, 163, 176, 177, 181, 327 n.31
  senator, as, 221, 223, 224, 232, 233, 236, 241, 255, 259, 265
Blackstone, Sir William, 5, 107, 109, 263
Bleeker, Leonard (major), 97
Board of War, Congressional 59, 61, 64, 74, 255
Bolingbroke, Henry St. John, 1st viscount, 95fn, 131, 331 n.67
Bonaparte, Napoleon, 157, 236, 265
Boston, HMS, frigate, 205
Boston Tea Party, 37, 38
Boudinot, Elias (congressman), 6, 137, 144, 145, 157, 170, 183, 195, 196
Brandywine Creek, battle of, 3, 56, 69
Brooklyn, battle of, 47
Broome, John, 132, 133, 250, 280
Burr, Aaron, American Revolution, in, 90
  New York lawyer, as, 96, 103
  Federalist, as, 131
  Hamilton, rivalry with, 13, 274, 275
  U.S. senator, as, 171, 219, 247
  election of 1800, in, 7, 249–254, 257, 258

Canada, American invasion of, 41–5, Lord Dorchester as governor, 204
Capital, U.S. *See* seat of government
Carleton, Sir Guy, 43, 44, 47, 96
census of 1790, House of Representatives reapportionment, from, 187, 188, 194
Chatterton's Hill, battle of, 49
Church, John Barker, 13, 111, 112, 269, 273, 274

INDEX

Cincinnati, Society of, 13fn, 15, 44, 94, 96, 105, 123, 129, 279; JL member, of, 13, 94, 105, 263, 279
Clark, John Jr. (major), 67
Clarkson, Matthew (Society of Cincinnati), 262, 278, 279
Clinton, George, portrait of, 115
    Continental Army general, as, 97, 120
    New York governor, as, 70, 92, 97, 113, 114, 120, 121, 125, 137, 210, 252, 270, 271
        deterrent to national unity, 114, 119, 120, 125, 126
        Schuyler, Philip, feud with, 126, 134
        New York ratifying convention, at, 128
        election of 1789, in, 133, 134
Clinton, James (colonel), 99, 311 n.12
Clinton, Sir Henry, 47, 48, 65, 72, 78, 83, 86
Coinage Act of 1792, 186
Coke, Sir Edward, 28, 29
Colden, Cadwallader, portrait of, 25
    early life of, 24–6, 93
    lt. governor, as, 5, 25–8, 32, 36, 37, 39, 48
    Provincial Crown prerogative defender v. lawyers, 1, 27, 286 n.3, 293 n.39
    JL mentor, as, 1, 24, 26. 28, 31, 32
    Spring Hill, at, 27, 28, 39, 48, 294 n.43
Colden, Henrietta M., 92 n.39, 191
Columbia College/University, JL as trustee, 101, 283.
See also King's College
common law, English, in New York, 27, 30, 103, 108, 294 n.3
"commutation" certificates (1783), 95, 309 n.52
Consumption (pulmonary tuberculosis), 243, 254fn
Congress, Chesapeake, and *President,* frigates, 234
Confederation Congress, 114–124, 169, 228, 282
    insolvency of, 117, 118, 123, 142
    JL delegate to, 114–124
Connecticut trade war with New York, 119, 120
Constellation, U.S.S., frigate, 4, 225, 228, 231
Constitution, U.S.S., frigate, 4, 225, 228, 231
Constitution, U.S. (1789), 125. 126, 157, 161, 186, 244, 245
    ratification of, 128, 129

Constitutional Construction, Madison v. Laurance
    executive powers, 140
    imposts, duties, and tariffs, 141, 142
    British import discrimination, 141, 142
    revenue collection, 142, 143, 144
    President's salary, 143
    appointment and removal powers, 143, 144
    Bill of Rights vs. amendments to, 144, 145
    treasury department powers, 145, 146
    Federal judiciary, 146, 147
    seat of federal government, 147, 148, 149, 150, 151
    retiring domestic debt at par, 4, 156, 157
    sinking fund, 158
    assumption of state debts, 4, 158, 160–164
    discrimination between original and subsequent debt holders, 158, 159
    slave trade, 160–162
    Bank of the United States (BUS), 4, 168–170
    power to borrow money, 169
    "General Welfare" clause, 182
    re-apportionment of House seats, 186–188
Constitutional Convention, 8, 123, 125, 126, 146, 316 n.44
    proposed second convention, 144
Continental Army: organization of, 51, 53, 54, 58, 85
    New York regiments, in, 40–53
    Philadelphia campaign, of, 56, 57
    Valley Forge, at, 58–64
    battle of Monmouth, in, 65
    Yorktown, at, 86–88
    Hudson Highlands, at, 83–6, 89–94
    officer pensions, in, 92, 94, 95
    Evacuation Day, on, 97, 98, 99
Continental Army Judge Advocate General Department, 53–55, 281–282
    Tudor, William, judge advocate general, 52, 53, 54, 55
    Laurance, John, judge advocate general, 52–64, 65–80, 83
    JL staff, 1777–1782:
        Edwards, Thomas, 85, 89, 90
        Marshall, John, 59
        Purcell Henry, 69
        Purcell, Henry D., 69
        Strong, Caleb, 85, 89, 147, 223
        Taylor, John, 59, 69, 160

Continental Congress
  First (1774), 39
  Second (1775–1781), 40, 41, 53, 59, 68, 69, 71, 74, 85
  Congress of the Confederation (1781–1788), 91, 94
Conway Cabal, 67, 76, 234
Cooper, William (father of Cooperstown, NY), 271
Cornwall, England, 16, 17–19, 135
Cornwallis, Charles, 1st marquess Cornwallis (lord), 51, 86, 87
Council of the Southern District of New York, 97, 98, 99, 100, 268
  JL member of, 97, 268
courts-martial in General Washington's Main Army 1775–1778, 60, 285, 286. 301 n.22
courts-martial, JL as prosecutor
  John Andrè (British major) of, 77–80, 306 n.59
  Benedict Arnold (major general), 3, 70–73
  Friedrich Enslin (ensign), 61
  Charles Lee (major general), 65–7, 304 n.6
  William Maxwell (brigadier general), 56, 57
  Alexander McDougall (major general), 89
  Phillip Schuyler (major general), 69
  William Shippen (medical director), 75, 76, 306 n.42
  Arthur St. Clair (major general), 67, 68
  Adam Stephen (major general), 3, 56, 57
  John Sullivan (major general), 56
  Anthony Wayne (brigadier general), 56
courts-martial, protocols, 55, 56, 59–61, 284, 302 n.44
courts-martial, venues
  Boston, 53
  Morristown, 56
  Philadelphia campaign, 55–7, 75
  Middlebrook, 70–73
  New Brunswick, 65
  North Castle, NY, 65
  Peekskill, 65
  Quaker Hill, 69
  Valley Forge, 58–63
  White Plains, 67–9
  Hudson Highlands, 77–80
  Yorktown, 86, 87
Cramer, Myron (judge advocate general), 282

Currency
  Continental Dollar, 61, 74, 90
  JL wartime compensation, in, 61, 74, 85, 90, 95, 266–269
  coins, minting of, 117
  New York money, 74. 90, 98, 119, 120, 268
  British Restraining Act (1764) impact on, 265

Dana, Francis, 60, 226
debt, public
  Continental notes and obligations, 74, 155, 158
  Federal debt, 156, 157, 158, 171, 182, 185, 240, 322 n.1
  foreign loans, 155, 168, 171, 191, 195, 196
  discrimination among holders of, 158, 159
  state debt component of, 155–165, 324 n.34
  See also assumption of state debt
  JL views on, 157, 158, 159, 161, 162, 165, 169, 170, 171, 182
  debtor's prison, 8, 191, 192, 199
  See also immigrant speculators incarcerated in: Duer, William, Macomb, Alexander, Morris, Robert, Wilson, James
Decatur, Stephen, 231
Declaration of Independence, 5, 23, 36, 53
  New York celebration of, 122, 123
De Grasse, Francois, Joseph Paul, 86, 88
DeLancey, James, 25, 30, 35
DeLancey, James Jr., 26, 35, 36, 39
  estate of, 268, 269
Delancey/Livingston rivalry, 26, 27, 34
Delavan, Daniel (captain), 98
democracy, 258
  Federalist fears about, 142, 187, 199, 258, 269
Democratic-Republican Party. *See Republicans, Republican Party*
Democratic ("Republican") Societies, 204, 237
d'Estaing, Jean-Baptiste-Charles-Henri-Hector, comte, 206
Duane, James, 26, 32, 74, 102, 217, 280
  portrait of, 110
  congressional delegate, as, 62, 90, 91fn, 92
  Federal district judge, as, 134, 203
  New York City mayor, as, 100, 101, 102, 104, 114, 123, 124, 129, 137, 159

Rutgers v. Waddington, in, 107–110
   state legislator, as, 111, 125, 127
Duer, William, 101
   Trinity Church, and, 100, 101
   JL, and, 101, 120, 123, 191, 202
   federalist, as, 127, 131
   treasury dept., at, 124, 163
   speculative ventures, of, 8, 159, 163, 189–192, 248, 265, 266, 271, 330 n.33
   debtor's prison, 192
"Duke's Laws," 29, 30
Du Ponceau, Pierre–Etienne, 63
Du Portail, Louis Lebecque, 206
Dwight, Timothy, 237

Earl of Halifax, packet (Boulderson, John Phillips, captain), 19
Electoral College, 199, 221, 243.
   See also Ross bill
Elections, national
   1789, of, 132, 133
   1792, of, 222
   1796, 220, 221, 222
   1800, of 7, 243, 244, 249–254, 257–259
   1804, of 278
Embuscade, French frigate, 205
Episcopal Church of America, 173, 174, *See also* Philadelphia, Christ Church, and Trinity Church NYC
Essex Junto, 199, 254, 331 n.70
Evacuation Day (New York City), 97, 98
executive branch powers. *See* Constitutional construction
extradition, U.S., JL policy role, in, 206–209

Falmouth, England, 17–19, 203
farmers, 54, 269
   banks feared by, 169, 259
   political beliefs, 114, 121, 258, 259
   uprisings of, 123, 227
Fauchet, Jean Antoine, 4, 206–209
Federal Government power vs. states, 146, 147, 161, 185–187, 198, 199
Federal Hall (New York City), 15
   First Federal Congress venue of, 129, 130, 136, 165, 178, 283
   Federal District Court of New York venue of, 206
   JL at, as congressman, 136–147, as district judge, 203, 210
Federal Judiciary, establishment of (Judiciary Act of 1789), 147, 148, 205

Federalist Papers, 106, 127, 131, 146, 169
Federalism, 1, 95, 111, 126, 168, 193, 197, 199, 205, 207, 222, 227, 231, 233, 240, 251
   Adams Federalists, 222, 233, 234, 254
   High Federalists, 198, 199, 222, 225, 232, 233, 236, 254
   New York as stronghold of, 131–134, 217, 218, 244, 249–254, 260
Federalist capitalism and the English model, 155–157, 198, 199
Federalist financial revolution of 1790–1792, 155–161, 163–165, 168–171
   treasury initiatives:
      Report Relative to a Provision for the Support of Public Credit (1790), 155
      Second Report on the Public Credit (1790 Report on a National Bank), 168
      Report on the Establishment of a Mint (1791), 171
   legislative acts: Funding Act of 1790, 165, National Bank Act (1791), 70, 171, Whiskey Excise Act (1791), 171, and the Coinage Act (1792), 186. (*see also* John Laurance; Hamilton's legislative champion)
Federalist moneymen
   Bayard, Samuel, 262
   Bayard, William, 159, 276
   Cabot, George, 223, 257, 258, 265, 327 n.31
   Clymer, George, 142, 150, 164, 265
   Constable, William, 131, 159, 163, 189
   Craigie, Andrew, 163, 189, 190, 265, 266, 327 n.31
   Fish, Nicholas, 96, 262, 272
   Higginson, Stephen, 331 n.70
   LeRoy, Herman 159, 327 n.31
   Low, Nicholas, 189, 327 n.31
   Sands, Comfort, 262
   Wharton, Thomas, 179, 213
   Willing, Thomas, 177, 179, 181, 189. *See also* Duer, William
Federalist Party, 131, 167, 198, 210, 223, 233, 234, 235, 236, 244, 259, 278
   Adams/Hamilton schism, 254, 257, 258
   decline and fall, 199, 246, 252, 253, 258–260, 278
   New York ratifying convention, and, 126, 127, 128

Federalist public figures
  Allen, John (congressman), 234
  Baldwin, Alexander (congressman), 156
  Bayard, James, 193, 199
  Carrington, Edward, 193, 199
  Carroll, Daniel, 142
  Chase, Samuel (judge), 212
  Coit, Joshua (congressman), 233
  Corzine, John (lawyer), 129
  Dayton, Jonathan (congressman), 236, 245, 254
  Dexter, Samuel (senator), 244, 259
  Ellsworth, Oliver (senator and judge), 146, 147, 209, 212, 221, 223, 247, 254
  Fenno, John (newspaperman), 19
  Fitzsimmons, Thomas (congressman), 160, 183
  Goodhue, Benjamin, 150, 219, 223, 224, 225, 226, 260
  Griswold, Roger (congressman), 238
  Gunn, James (senator), 223, 259
  Harper, Robert G. (congressman), 198, 254
  Hartley, Thomas (congressman), 161
  Heister, Daniel (congressman), 142
  Hillhouse, James (senator), 219, 224, 238, 254
  Hobart, John Sloss (judge), 217
  Iredell, James (Supreme Court justice), 209
  Johnson, William Samuel, 125
  Livermore, Samuel, 146, 147, 161, 187
    as senator, 219, 223, 224, 238, 244, 259
  Lloyd, James (senator), 236, 259
  Lyman, Samuel, 257
  Marshall, Humphrey (senator), 247, 259
  Moore, Andrew (congressman), 142
  Morse, Jedediah (high federalist pastor), 257
  Otis, Harrison Gray, 236,
  Parker, Josiah, 182, 183, 231
  Peters, Richard (judge), 55, 74, 75, 206, 281
  Read, Jacob (senator), 219, 221, 223, 224, 230, 238, 254, 259
  Ross, James, 224, 235, 243, 244
  Schureman, James (senator), 259
  Seney, Joshua (congressman), 188
  Sherman, Roger (congressman), 145
  Silvester, Peter congressman), 134
  Stockton, Richard (senator), 224
  Tracy, Uriah (senator), 223, 224
  Taliaferro, Benjamin (senator), 259
  Trumbull, Jonathan (congressman), 199
  Varick, Richard (mayor), 33, 96, 106, 109, 129, 217, 250, 280
  Vining, "Jack" (senator), 144, 219
  Wadsworth, Jeremiah (congressman), 111, 112, 163, 167, 199
  White, Alexander (congressman), 161, 181, 187
  Williamson, Hugh, 187. *See also* Ames, Fisher, Benson, Egbert, Bingham, William, Boudinot, Elias, Duane, James, Jay, John, Laurance, John, McDougall, Alexander; McHenry, James, Morris, Gouverneur, Morris, Robert; Muhlenberg, Frederick, Paterson, William; Peters, Pickering, Timothy, Pinckney, Charles Cotesworth, Schuyler, Philip; Sedgwick, Theodore, Smith, William Loughton, Troup, Robert, Wolcott, Oliver Jr
First Federal Congress, the, 15, 138–152, 155–172, 173–197, 245, 283
  legislative acts of:
    Coasting Act (1789), 142
    Collection Act (1789), 142
    Tariff Act (1789), 141, 142
    Tonnage Act (1789), 141, 142
    Judiciary Act (1789), 146, 147, 205, 230, 238
    Funding Act (1790), 165. *See also* Great Compromise of 1790
    Residence Act (1790), 165
    Northwest Territory Ordinance, 117
First Presbyterian Church of New York City, 45, 122, 166, 279, 280, 281, 283
Fish family, 22, 23, 96, 262, 272
Flushing, NY, Lawrence Point, 21, 22
Forsey v. Cunningham, 27
Fort George, 20, 45, 129
Fort Saint-Jean, 42, 43, 297 n.12
Fort Ticonderoga, 41, 43, 51, 67, 68
Founding Fathers, 1, 283, 286 n.1. *See also* Adams, John; Franklin, Benjamin; Hamilton, Alexander; Jay, John; Jefferson, Thomas, Madison, James, Marshall, John, Washington, George

INDEX 381

France, American ally, 86, 87, 88, 94
   Jacobin Directory, under, 206, 222, 230, 234, 237
   enmity with Great Britain, 204, 232
   quasi-war with the U.S., 222–256
   Napoleonic, 255, 256
Franklin, Benjamin, 8, 19, 24, 33, 131, 161, 179
Fraunces, Andrew, 202, 203
Freemasonry, Fraternal Order of, 2, 33, 105
   Continental Army, in, 52fn, 76, 105
   New York, in, 33, 104, 105, 264. See also St. John's Masonic Lodge #2 of New York City
Fugitive Slave Act of 1793. See slavery

Gardiner, Lion, 22
Genêt, Edmund Charles (Citizen Genêt), 8, 204, 207, 237
George II, King of England, 26, 246
George III, King of England, 26, 27, 231, 270
Georgia, in the American Revolution, 58; in Confederation Congress, 118, 119
Germantown, battle of, 3, 56, 57, 69
Gerry, Elbridge, 126, 143, 146, 152, 159, 161, 281; XYZ Affair, in, 226, 230
Giles, Aquila, 211, 272, 276
Giles, W. B. and Jefferson resolutions against Hamilton's Treasury Dept., 196, 331 n.54
Golden Hill, "battle" of, 36
Grange, The (Hamilton residence), 275, 277
   JL as executor of, 6, 277
Grasse, Francois Joseph Paul, comte de, 86, 88
Gray, Hannah, 209, 209fn
Great Compromise of 1790, 164, 165, 165fn, 193
"Great Man" theory, 5, 9, 283
Greene, Nathanael, 65, 77, 78, 83, 88, 96
Greenleaf, James, 247, 248, 278

Hamilton (miniature frigate), 129
Hamilton, Alan McLane, 113
Hamilton, Alexander, collegian, as, 38, 39
   Alexander McDougall, and, 38, 39, 46, 94, 112, 123
   artillery captain, as, 46, 47, 48, 49, 51
   Washington's aide-de-camp, as, 51, 53, 62, 63, 66, 77, 78, 84
   Yorktown, at, 87, 90
   JL friend, as, 8, 39, 48, 51, 53, 70, 74, 91, 94, 106, 111, 112, 113, 138, 152, 195, 196, 209, 213, 227, 235, 276, 288/289 n.26
   Bank of New York, and, 111, 112, 180
   post-war lawyer, as, 90, 91, 94, 96, 101, 102, 103, 106–111, 125, 136
   Federalist Papers, and, 106, 127, 131
   fight for the Constitution, and, 125, 126, 128
   treasury secretary, as, 4, 134, 145, 152, 155–172, 180, 181, 183, 190, 192–197, 200, 202, 210
   post-treasury dept. legal practice, of, 210, 211, 275
   JL investment partner, as, 6, 112, 210, 227, 229. 272–275
   Federalist leader, as, 217, 223, 225, 226, 227, 231, 232, 242, 254, 257, 260, 261, 262
   Jefferson, Thomas, political adversary of, 5, 165, 167, 193, 195, 196
   adulterer, as, 228, 229, 229fn, 260
   quasi-war with France, and, 233. 235, 255
   John Adams, feud with, 254, 255, 257
   election of 1800, and, 7, 249–254, 258
   death and funeral, of, 13–16, 276
   legacy of, 9, 280, 281, 282
Hamilton, John Church, 38, 48
Hancock, John, 33, 118, 265, 282
Hand, Edward, 76
Harlem Heights, battle of, 48
Harrison, Richard (lawyer), 103, 134, 332 n.7
Heath, William, 85, 88, 89
Helena Brasher et al v. Daniel Ebbets, 104
Henderson, Thomas (doctor), 217
Hoffman, Josiah (district attorney), 211, 212
Holmes, James (colonel), 41–3
Holt, Joseph (judge advocate general), 282
Howe, Robert (general), 72, 77
Howe, Sir William, 24, 45, 47, 48, 49, 51, 56, 57, 65, 77, 107, 175
Hudson Highlands, 84, 88–96
Hunters and Hounds Tavern, Archer Giffords, of, 264

immigration and immigrants, 4, 212, 241, 250, 251, 253, 258, 269, 279
   bias against, 8, 200, 237–239, 281
   Continental Army, in, 54, 59, 281
   immigrant newspapermen: Burk, John D., 8, Cobbett, William, 200, Cooper, Thomas, 8, Callender, James, 8, 228; Continental Army, in, 54, 59, 281

immigration and immigrants *(Continued)*
  founding fathers, as, 281, 349 n.3. *(see also* Hamilton, Alexander, Iredell, James, Laurance, John, McHenry, James, Morris, Robert, Patterson, William, Wilson, James)
  land speculators, as, 289 n.33. *(see also* Duer, William, Laurance, John, Macomb, Alexander, Morris, Robert, Wilson, James)
implied powers, doctrine of, 169
  JL views of, 140, 169, 196, 319 n.18
impost duties and tariffs:
  Confederation Congress, in, 118, 119, 120
  Federal Congress, in 141, 142
  New York State, in 119, 120, 124, 142
  JL and Madison conflicted, over, 140, 141, 142
interest rates, 156, 190; Federal notes, on, 156, 168, 185, 186, 190, 323 n.10

Jackson, Henry (colonel), 79, 99, 310 n.12
Jackson, James (congressman), 143, 144, 156, 161, 169
Jay, John, 280
  Provincial lawyer, as, 32, 34, 40, 107
  American Revolution, in, 46, 71
  Confederation Congress, in 91, 92, 114
  secretary of foreign affairs, as, 103, 116, 124, 264
  Trinity Church, and, 100, 152
  JL, and, 34, 37, 191, 261
  Federalist leader, as, 8, 106, 127, 128, 167, 198
  Supreme Court chief justice, as, 134, 152, 180, 203, 207
  envoy to England, as, 205, 217
  governor of New York, as, 210, 250, 261
Jay Treaty (1795). *See* treaties
Jefferson, Thomas, 1, 95fn, 131
  American Revolution, in, 53
  "Compromise of 1790" and, 160, 164, 165
  Secretary of State, as, 164, 167, 170, 171, 180, 188, 19i
  Democratic-Republican Party, and, 192, 193, 221, 228
  Vice President, as, 221, 222, 230, 237, 239, 240, 245
  election of 1800, and, 243, 244, 257, 258, 259
  President, as, 198, 261, 275

John Laurance, S.S., Liberty Ship No. 0108, 280
Jones, John Paul, 282
Judge advocate general. *See* Continental Army Judge Advocate General Department
judicial review, concept of, 6, 106, 109
  Marbury v. Madison, in reference to, 6, 109
Judiciary Act (1789), 146, 147, 205, 230, 238

Kean, John, 181
Kempe, John (Provincial attorney general), 27
Kennedy, Archibald (Eleventh Earl of Cassilis), 19, 21
Kent, James (New York lawyer), 103, 109
Kentucky, 187, 258, 259
King, Rufus, 6, 280
  portrait of, 122
  JL, and, 7, 120, 121, 150, 152, 202, 203, 204, 205, 213, 230, 265, 275
  Confederation Congress, in, 116, 118, 121, 125
  Federalist leader, as, 171, 198, 201, 223, 238, 275
  BUS Director, as, 201, 213, 327 n.31
  New York senator, as, 4, 134, 150, 151, 159, 161, 179, 181, 200, 232
  minister to England, as, 217, 223, 231, 261, 275
  Robert Troup, correspondence with (*see* Robert Troup)
King's College (later Columbia College), 21, 24, 34, 101, 107, 134
Knox, Henry
  War for Independence, in, 51, 79, 94, 98, 99, 124, 213
  secretary of war, as, 170, 195
  quasi-war with France, during, 235
  financial affairs of, 192, 199, 265, 271, 275, 282
Knuckey, Mary (JL's mother), 17, 292 n.18
Kuhn, Adam (Philadelphia physician), 200

La Concorder, French frigate, 206–209
Lafayette, Marie-Joseph Paul Yves Roch Gilbert du Motier, marquis de, 63, 65, 76, 77, 79, 206
Lamb, John, 35, 36, 37, 44; as antifederalist, 126, 132

land grants
   Federalist era, in 265, 266, 268, 270, 271
   New York speculators, and,
      Fowler, Theodosius, 190, 273, 274, 274fn
      Gilchrist, Robert, 273, 274
      Kip, Henry, 269
      Lenox, James, 229, 274
      LeRoy, Herman, 159, 327 n.31
      Mark, Jacob, 273–275
      Platt, Jonathan, 43
      Roosevelt, Isaac, 269. *See also* Craigie, Andrew, Duer, William, Greenleaf, John Laurance, 266–276, James, Macomb, Alexander, McDougall, Alexander, Morris, Robert, Scriba patent, Smith, William S

Landesdowne (mansion), 249
Laurance, Ann (Mrs. George Wright Hawkes), 277
Laurance, Elizabeth Allen. *See* Allen, Elizabeth (Mrs. John Laurance)
Laurance, Elizabeth "Betsey." *See* McDougall, Elizabeth (Mrs. John Laurance)
Laurance, John
   physical description of, 40, 138, 177, 260
   portraits of, 116, 164, 219
   birth and youth of, 17–19, 23, 27, 290 n.2
   passage to America, 1, 18–19, 291 n.15:
   law education of 24, 27, 28, 29–32, 293 n.34
   Trinity Church, and, 3, 32, 33, 101, 105, 125, 137, 152, 203, 264, 279, 311 n.24
   New York Bar, and, 3, 32, 166, 264
   freemason, as, 2, 3, 33, 52, 105, 264, 286 n.5
   McDougall, Alexander, and, 2, 6, 35, 38, 46, 47, 49, 51, 70, 84, 98, 166, 219, 228, 255, 266, 267
   McDougall, Alexander, court-martial of, 88, 89
   McDougall, Betsey, and, 2, 6, 7, 37, 38, 46, 70, 85, 122, 138, 166, 255, 279:
      children of, and, 44, 56, 70, 85, 166, 174, 277, 278
   Hamilton, Alexander's friend, as, 6, 8, 13–16, 51, 53, 70, 74, 91, 102, 106, 111, 113, 167, 196, 209, 218, 235
   Continental Army infantry officer, as, 21, 40, 42–51, 52, 297 n.2, 299 n.48
   state legislator, as, 3, 91, 92, 93, 94, 100, 111, 125, 127, 128, 313 n.65, 317 n.51
   judge advocate general, as, 2, 3, 52–64, 65–80, 83–87, 89, 90, 281, 284, 285
      Valley Forge, at, 301 n.28, 301 n.31
   George Washington, and, 40, 52, 53, 59, 60, 62, 71, 77, 78, 84, 89, 152, 203, 205, 219, 221, 242
      assassination plot on, 85, 86
      resignation to, 89
   post-war lawyer, as, 6, 92, 93, 96, 97, 98, 99, 102, 103, 104, 106, 125, 166, 263
      Rutgers v. Waddington, and, 6, 106–111
   Duer, William, and, 100, 101, 102, 202, 203
   Columbia College trustee/State University regent, as, 3, 101, 105, 263
   Confederation Congress delegate, as, 3, 114–123
   City Alderman, as, 3, 15, 129, 130
   abolitionist, as, 3, 112, 150, 160, 161, 172, 195
   Rufus King, and, 7, 120, 121, 150, 152, 202, 203, 204, 205, 213, 230, 234, 261, 265, 275
   Federalist, as, 119, 120, 127, 129, 171, 172, 198, 218, 236, 237, 261, 262
   "Complete" Federalist, as, 134, 135, 167
   U.S. congressman, as, 3, 132, 133, 134, 138–152, 156–199
      House Appropriations Committee, on 3, 181–184, 195
      Hamilton's legislative champion, as, 4, 6, 156–172, 180–197, 219, 227
      James Madison, and, 4, 15, 150, 163, 170, 182, 184, 188, 193, 194, 219 (*see also* Constitutional Construction, *Laurance v. Madison*)
   Allen, Elizabeth, marriage to, children with, Philadelphia Society, and, 174–180, 192, 197, 218, 228, 239, 247, 251, 252, 264, 278
   Bank of the United States, director of, 181, 201, 212, 213, 263
   state legislator, as, 3, 91, 92, 93, 94, 100, 111, 125, 127, 128, 313 n.65, 317 n.51
   Federal judge, district of New York, as, 4, 203–214, 218
      United States v. Lawrence, defendant in, 4, 206–209

Laurance, John *(Continued)*
  U.S. senator, as, 7, 132, 217–257
    senate midwife to U.S. Navy, as, 4, 224, 231–236, 241
    Alien & Sedition Acts, and, 8, 237, 238
    senate president, *pro-tempore*, as, 2, 239–240
    bankruptcy legislation, and, 245, 246
  "High" Federalism, disaffection with, 7, 198, 200, 238, 246, 247, 255–257
  John Adams, and, 166, 195, 239, 255
  election of 1800, and, 244, 249–254, 257
  real estate speculator, as, 2, 37, 210, 212, 228, 260, 264–280
  Hamilton, Alexander's investment partner, as, 112, 210, 212, 227, 229, 272–275, 277
  Robert Troup, friend/co-investor of, 7, 48, 113, 121, 198, 201, 217, 239, 269, 271, 272, 275
  inflammatory rheumatism, struggle with, 230, 239, 240, 241, 256, 277, 278
  final years, 260, 263–278
  last will and testament of, 278, 348
  relevance today of, 9, 280–283
Laurance, John McDougall, 7, 13, 44, 45, 174, 235, 278
Laurens, Henry, 63
La Princessa de Asturias, vessel, 211–212
La Vengeance, privateer, 211–212
Lawrence/Lawrance family genealogy, 17
Lawrences of Long Island
  Ann (Sackett), 23
  Daniel, 24, 47, 70
  Jonathan, 23, 37, 41, 47, 70
  John (of New York City), 22
  John Jr. (grandson of Thomas), 23
  John (of Queens County, NY), 23
  Richard, 24, 47
  Samuel (captain), 24
  Thomas (major), 22, 23
  William, 22, 24, 47
Lawrence, John (of Philadelphia), 32
Lawrence, "John of Milor" (JL's father), 17
Lawrence, John (of Westchester, NY), 32
Lawrence, Sir John, 17
Lawrence, John Spratt (Elizabeth Allen's father), 174, 174fn
Lawrence Point/Neck, NY, 21, 27
Lawrence, Richard (Cornwall, England), 18, 98
Lear, Tobias, 174, 180
Leavenworth, Jesse, 68

Lee, Charles (major general), 3, 14, 45, 49, 65–7, 303 n.1
Lee, Henry (Light Horse Harry), 160, 227, 282
L'Enfant, Pierre Charles (Peter), 129, 165, 238
LePerdrix, frigate, 207–209
Lewis, Morgan, 96, 103, 107, 108
Lincoln, Benjamin, 68, 90
Liston, Sir Robert, 232, 233
Livingston family, 23, 26, 134, 217, 218, 247, 250, 261
Livingston, Brockholst, 45, 96, 103, 107, 108, 117, 189, 190, 191, 210, 250, 261
Livingston, Catherine (daughter of Philip), 23
Livingston, Edward, 190, 210, 250, 261
Livingston, Henry B., 51, 189
Livingston, Henry Walter, 218
Livingston, John R., 190
Livingston, John S., 277
Livingston, Peter R., 26, 206
Livingston, Peter van Brugh, 39
Livingston, Philip, 23, 26, 46, 47, 189, 192, 210
Livingston, Robert R., 26, 34
Livingston, Robert R. Jr., 1
  Provincial lawyer, as, 26, 33, 34, 37, 46
  Chancellor, as, 92, 100, 102, 103, 111, 126, 134, 136, 203
  freemason, as, 105
  New York ratification convention, at 128
  Clinton Republican, as, 134, 198, 250, 261
Livingston, Sarah (Mrs. John Jay), 34, 176
Livingston, Walter C., 114, 191
Livingston, William, 26, 29, 34, 103, 138fn, 149
Lynn, William (reverend), 152

Maclay, William, 137, 142, 163, 164
Macomb, Alexander
  land speculator, as, 152, 189, 189fn, 190, 191, 192, 203, 235, 271
  debtor's prison, in, 266
Madison, James, 5, 91fn, 95fn, 278
  Constitutional Convention, in, 125, 140
  federalist, as, 106, 127, 131, 140, 172, 193;
  slavery, and, 160, 182
  Virginia politics, and, 156, 162
  House of Representatives, in, 140–152, 155–172, 181, 182, 183, 204, 224, 265

INDEX

Laurance, John, and, 15, 150, 159, 163, 170, 182, 188, 193, 194. *See also* Constitutional construction, Madison v. Laurance
Democratic-Republican Party, and, 183, 192, 193, 228
Manhattan Company, Republican bank masquerading as water utility, 250
Manufacturing. *See* Society for Establishing Useful Manufacturing (SEUM)
Marshall, John, 3
   American Revolution, in, 50, 59, 91, 109
   XYZ Affair, in, 226, 230
   Congressman, as, 247
   Supreme Court chief justice, as, 261, 282
Maryland
   War for Independence, in, 92
   Confederation Congress, in, 118
   election of 1800, in, 258, 259, 260
Massachusetts
   land grants to, 259, 270
   battle of Lexington and Concord, in, 39
   Constitution, ratification by, 144
Masters' Mansion (president's house), 175, 179
Maxwell, William (general), 56, 57
McDougall, Alexander, 35, 280
   portrait of, 50
   New York Sons of Liberty, and, 2, 35, 36, 37, 38
   Hamilton, Alexander, and, 38, 46, 112
   Continental Army, in. 2, 40, 42, 47, 49, 50, 52, 70, 88, 89, 91
   Confederation Congress, in, 85, 92
   New York legislature, in, 43, 114, 120, 228
   Council for Temporary Government of the Southern District of New York, in, 97, 99, 102
   speculative investor, as, 266, 267
   physical demise of, 120, 120fn, 121, 122, 279
McDougall, Elizabeth "Betsey" (Mrs. John Laurance), 2, 6, 7, 37, 38, 46, 70, 85, 122, 138, 166, 255, 279
   children with JL, and, 44, 56, 70, 85, 166, 174, 277
McDougall, Hannah, 38, 61
McDougall, Jack, 33, 34, 37, 40, 43
McDougall, John, 61, 122
McDougall, Stephen ("Stevey"), 40, 45, 56, 122

McHenry, James (secretary of war), 84, 225, 226, 231, 232, 233, 235, 254
McWhorter, Alexander, 264
McWhorter, George C., 80, 138, 177, 264
military bounty lands
   Old Military Tract, 266, 267, 270
   New Military Tract, 267
   JL holdings, in, 98, 266, 267
Mifflin, Thomas, 67, 69
Million Dollar Bank, the, 189, 190
Mint, U.S., 170, 171, 186, 196
Monmouth, battle of, 3, 65–67, 69
Montgomery, Richard General), 42, 43, 44
Monroe, James, 116, 118, 120, 228
Moore, Benjamin, 13–15, 24, 100, 101
Morgan, Daniel (general), 66
Morgan, John (physician), 75
Morris, Gouverneur, 28
   Hamilton, Alexander's friend, as, 13, 14, 33, 254, 276
   Provincial lawyer, as, 39
   American Revolution, in, 46, 60, 92, 102
   Confederation Congress, in, 103, 125
   foreign minister, as, 195, 217, 218
   land speculator, as, 159, 271
Morris, Lewis, 46, 103
Morris, Richard, 100, 124
Morris Robert
   congressional superintendent of finance, as, 91, 115, 155
   Bank of North America, and, 92
   U.S. senator, as, 150, 151, 165, 174, 177
   real estate speculator, as, 8, 223, 247, 265, 271
   debtor's prison, in, 266
Morristown, NJ, 49, 52, 55, 56, 75, 83, 84
Morton, Jacob, 14
Muhlenberg, Frederick, 130
   House Speaker, as, 136, 139, 151, 156, 163, 169, 183, 188, 202, 210

National Bank. *See* Bank of the United States
Nationalists, 1, 91, 91fn, 92, 94, 115, 308 n.35, 308 n.36
Nations, Law of, 107–111
natural-born v, naturalized American citizen, 5, 287 n.16, 287 n.17, 287 n.18; *See also* Naturalization Act (1790), 5, 212, and Alien and Sedition Acts (1798)

Navy, U.S., 182, 224–229, 231, 232, 241
   Adams, John's views on, 225
   JL's role, in establishing, 224, 227,
      231–236, 241
   Cabinet department, of, 232, 241, 243
Neutrality policy, U.S., 205, 227, 234
Newburgh, NY, Continental officer mutiny
   of, 94
Newtown, NY, American Revolution, in, 41
New England
   political interests of, 67, 69
   seat of government negotiations, in, 148,
      150
New Hampshire, 35, 39, 43, 128, 258
New Jersey, 22, 149, 258, 259
   American Revolution, in, 50, 51, 56, 65,
      66, 83
   New York trade war, with, 120
   JL, Newark residence of, 263, 264
New Netherlands, British conquest of by
      James Stuart, Duke of York, 22, 30
Newton, Sir Isaac, 25
New York, U.S.S., frigate, 232
New York Bar Association and practice of
   Crown colony in, 2, 26, 30, 31, 33, 70, 90,
      263, 294 n.7
   State constitution of 1777, under, 309 n.55
   Confederation Congress, during, 118,
      119–121
New York City Chamber of Commerce,
   132, 210
New York City coffeehouses, 21, 265
   Merchants' coffee house, 21, 37, 111,
      112, 271
   Tontine coffee house, 210
New York City Common Council, 129, 130
New York City elections:
   1784, 111
   1787, 125
   1789, 129, 131–134
   1800, 249–253
New York City newspapers: *New York Daily
      Advertiser*, 126, 165; *New York
      Evening Post*, 5, 165, 275, 279;
      New York Gazette, 252; *New York
      Packet*, 112
New York City, population of, 20, 124, 149,
   264, 278
New York City, streets and structures of:
   Battery, 19, 20, 21
   Bowling Green, 20, 21, 100, 203
   Broad Way/Broadway, 7, 13, 21, 123, 124,
      129, 137, 203, 204, 266, 275, 278, 279

   City Hall, 20, 32, 114, 124, 314 n.1
   common (the fields), 36, 38, 98
   Hanover Square, 129
   John Street Theater, 21, 123, 150
   JL residences:
      Broadway, 203, 204, 279
      McDougall Nassau Street home, 102
      Wall Street, 15, 32, 102, 113, 121, 124
   lower Manhattan, map of (1789), 139
   Wall Street, 15, 21, 32, 48, 98, 102, 113,
      122, 124, 136; 139, 283
   Whitehall Slip, 20. 48, 99
New York City, taverns of
   Bardin, Edward, 8, 131, 132
   Bull's Head, 97
   Cape, John, 98, 99, 123
   City Tavern, 21, 98, 99
   Corre's, 123
   Fraunces, Samuel, 21, 34, 98, 99, 202, 283
   Hull's, 40
   Montayne's, 34
   Simmons, John's, 100, 109, 124
New York City in the War for Independence:
   Committee of One Hundred, 39
   Provincial Congress, 39, 41
   battle for Long Island and Manhattan,
      45–48
   British occupation of, 48, 99, 100, 102
   Evacuation Day, 97, 98; rising from the
      ashes, 97–113 passim
New York City, yellow fever, in, 200, 239,
   263
New York Constitution of 1777, 70, 100,
   102, 103
   rule of law, under:
      General Assembly, 70, 92, 100, 127,
         249, 267, 268
      Mayor's Court, 30, 102, 103, 107–110
      post-war judiciary structure, 102, 103
      State Supreme Court, 90, 103, 104
New York Continental Army regiments, 40
   1st NY, 46, 51, 97
   2nd NY, 63
   3rd NY, 42
   4th NY, 41–8, 51, 52, 63, 297 n.6, 297 n.8
New York, Crown colony, rule of law in,
   19–22, 26–32, 34, 35, 103
   Provincial General Assembly, 20, 26, 30,
      35, 37, 39, 45
   Provincial Judiciary/King's Courts, 26,
      27, 29–31,103
   Whig parliamentarianism v. the Crown,
      in, 26, 32, 39

INDEX

New York elections
  1789, 133
  1800, 249–254
New York state finances
  debt of, 92, 124
  imposts and tariffs, 119, 120, 124
  land grant sales, 98, 266–269, 270
New York Historical Society, 7, 21, 23
New York Manumission Society, 3, 112, 160, 195
New York merchants, 119, 131, 141, 227, 228, 241, 320 n.27
  JL as voice of, 119, 120, 132, 141, 166, 227
New York Sons of Liberty, 34–40
New York tories (loyalists), 92, 96, 133
  confiscated estates of, 267–269
  legislation against, 92, 93, 96, 111, 121
    Citation Act (New York's Debt Act of 1782), 92, 111
    Confiscation Act (1779), 93, 106, 268
    Trespass Act (1783), 93, 98, 100, 104, 106, 107, 108
New York ratification of U.S. Constitution, 127, 128, 144
New York Society Library, 121, 138, 138fn
New York Stock Exchange, 148, 265
North v. South, political schism between, 160, 161, 163, 167, 169, 181, 186, 187, 194
Nicholson, John, 8, 249, 266
North Carolina, 230, 258, 259
Northwest Territory Ordinances, 117

Osgood, Samuel (postmaster general), 250
Otis, Samuel Allyn, 218

Packet routes of England, 18, 19
Palfrey, William, 52, 55
Panic of 1792, 189–192, 245
Palmer, David, 44
Paoli, Pennsylvania, battle of, 56
Parker, James, 36, 37
Parliament, British, 20, 26, 34, 37, 141
  laws of
    British Restraining Act (1764), 265
    Stamp Act (1765), 20, 27, 36
    Quartering Act (1765), 20, 35
    Tea Act (1773), 27, 37
    Coercive "Intolerable Acts" (1774), 37
    Townshend Act (1774), 34
    Navigation Act (1783), 141
Paterson, William, 68, 91, 147

Pell, Philip, 33, 103, 132, 133, 280
Pendleton, Edmund, 158
Penn, William, family of, 173, 174, 218, 249
Pennsylvania, American Revolution, in, 56–64, 71, 83
  Supreme Executive Council of, 60, 70, 71, 73
  Confederation Congress, in, 120
  election of 1800, in, 243, 244, 246, 258, 259
Philadelphia, PA, 149, 149fn, 179
  map (1790) of, 178
  American Revolution, in, 56, 59, 69, 70, 71, 73, 88, 90, 94
  belles of, 175–176:
    Allen, Elizabeth, Ann, and Margaret, 175
    Bingham, Anne Willing, 176, 186, 233, 254
    Powel, Eliza, 176
  Carpenter's Hall, in, 178, 180
  Chestnut Street, in, 168, 174, 178, 179, 218, 249
  Christ Church, in, 173, 174, 206, 218, 247; Congress Hall, 168, 177, 181, 218, 219, 230, 239, 242
  Independence Hall, in, 177
  temporary U.S. capital, as, 130, 149, 150, 151, 168, 170, 176–190
  U.S. Mint, as home of, 170, 171, 186
  yellow-fever epidemics in, 199–201, 228, 239
Pickering, Timothy, 275
  in American Revolution, 61, 64, 97
  as secretary of state, 225, 226, 232, 233, 234, 236, 254, 255
Pierce, John, 74, 90, 266
Pinckney, Charles, 1, 116, 244, 244fn, 246, 247
Pinckney, Charles Cotesworth, 198, 221, 226, 230, 235, 254, 278
Pinckney, Thomas, 222
Pintard, John, 189, 191, 191fn, 329 n.25
Pintardo, Don Diego, 210
political parties. *See also* Federalist Party, and Republican Party
  emergence of, 130, 167, 198
  negative view of, 131, 198, 331 n.67
Polk, James, E. (President), 233
Postal Service Act (1792), 19
Presidential Succession Act (1792), 2, 286 n.7

press, of the period, 127, 132, 192, 221, 223, 236, 256
  Sedition Act persecution of, 246, 339 n.39
  pro-Federalist newspapers
  Federal Gazette, 236, 276
  Gazette of the United States, 193, 223, 236
  pro-Republican newspapers
  American Citizen, 251
  National Gazette, 167, 192, 193, 223. See also *Aurora*, Philadelphia
Price, William, 99
Privy Council, His Royal British Majesty's, 27, 103
pro administration/pro government political view, 1, 131, 167, 183
Progressive/Neo-Progressive historiography, 1, 126, 286 n.4
"Provisional" Army (1797–1800), 225, 226, 232, 234, 235, 246, 255
Provoost, Samuel (reverend), 15, 32, 101, 137, 152
Publius (Alexander Hamilton pen-name), 127
Pulteney, Sir William (British baronet), 270, 272
Putnam, Rufus (colonel), 89

Quaker Society of Friends, 15, 69, 173 326 n.1; the slave trade, and, 160, 161
Quaker Hill, NY, 69
Quasi-War. See France, quasi-war with
Quebec, battle of, 43, 44
Queens County, NY, 21, 22, 40; War for Independence, and, 41, 42

Randolph, frigate, 61
Randolph, Edmund, 170, 180, 188, 195, 203, 207, 208, 232
Real estate speculation. See land speculation in the Federalist era
Reed, Joseph, 60, 67, 69, 71, 73
"Reign of Witches," 8, 230–242
"Republican Court" of President Washington, 233–254, passim
Republican Party, 1, 5, 192, 194, 235, 240, 261
  Jefferson/Hamilton feud, and, 193, 195, 196
  pamphlet wars, and, 193, 235
  public debt, and, 193, 195, 196
  election of 1796, and, 220, 221
  election of 1800, and, 244, 249–254, 256, 257, 258, 260
  election of 1804, and, 278
  Revolutionary France, and, 207, 223, 226, 235, 236, 237

Republican Party public figures:
  Beckley, John, House Clerk, as, 167, 183, 199, 221
  Bloodsworth, Timothy (congressman), 126, 219
  Blount, William (senator), 240, 240fn
  Butler, Pierce (congressman), 247
  Findley, William (congressman), 187, 227
  Freneau, Philip (newspaperman), 193
  Gallatin, Albert, 5,
  Gates, Horatio (general), 62, 63, 67, 250
  Giles, William Branch, 185, 186, 187
  Jackson, Andrew, 230
  Jones, James (senator), 259
  Lee, Richard Henry, 33, 114, 126
  Lyon, Matthew (congressman), 236
  McKean, Thomas (governor), 243, 244, 247
  Page, John (congressman), 145, 186
  Pinckney, Charles (senator), 1, 116, 244, 244fn, 246, 247
  Scott, Thomas (congressman), 157
  Thompson, Smith, 261, 261fn
  Tucker, Thomas Tudor (congressman), 143, 145, 161. *See also* Burr, Aaron, Clinton, George, Jefferson, Thomas, Livingston, Brockholst, Livingston, Edward, Livingston, Robert R., Madison, James, Monroe, Rush, Benjamin Reynolds, Maria affair, 228, 260
Rhode Island
  American Revolution, in, 50, 88
  Confederation Congress, in, 118
  Constitution, ratification by, 145
Riker, Abraham, 41, 44, 63, 64
Riker, family, 23, 44
Ritzema, Rudulphus (colonel), 43, 43fn
Rochambeau, comte de, 86, 206
Rochefoucald-Liancourt, duc la, 176, 203
rôle d'équipage, 207–209, 222
Rouge, Jacques, 211, 212
Royal Governors of New York Province
  Burnett, William, 25
  Colden, Cadwallader (acting), 30
  Cosby, William, 30
  Leisler, Jacob, self-appointed governor, 22
  Montgomerie, John, 30
  Monckton, Robert, 26
  Moore, Sir Henry, 29, 32
  Tryon, William, 39, 45

Royal Navy, British, and American
  protectionism, 157, 227, 228, 231,
  232, 233
rule of law, early Republic, in, 3, 9, 283,
  chapters, 11–17
  JL, interpretation of contracts under,
    159. *See also* New York rule of
    law under the Constitution of
    1777, and New York rule of law
    as Crown colony
Rush, Benjamin, 13, 75, 179, 199, 200,
  200fn, 252, 289 n.2
Rush, Richard (son of Benjamin), 13, 289
  n.2
Rutgers, Elizabeth, 106, 107, 109
Rutgers v. Waddington, 6, 106–111, 119, 134,
  313 n.51

Saratoga, battle of, 62, 63
Schuyler, Elizabeth "Eliza" (Mrs. Alexander
  Hamilton), 15, 84, 276, 290 n.10
Schuyler, Philip
  in War for Independence, 42, 44, 67, 69,
    84, 91, 126
  Confederation Congress, in, 91fn, 101
  state legislator, as, 126, 217
  Federalist leader, as, 127, 134, 261, 276
  US senator, as, 134, 151, 159, 172
Scott, Charles (general), 49, 66, 67
Scott, John Morin, 26, 27, 33, 37, 45, 103
Scriba Patent (JL and Hamilton, and
  Church land purchase from
  Jacob Mark), 273–275, 277, 336
  n.43, 337 n.54, 348 n.76
scrip bubble of 1791, 180
Seabury, Samuel (reverend), 32, 38, 38fn
Sears, Isaac, 37, 39
seat of U.S. government
  debates in Congress, 147–152
  Annapolis as seat; Trenton as seat, 148,
    150
  New York as seat; 129, 147, 148, 149, 150,
    151, 165, 238
  Philadelphia as seat, 130, 149, 150, 151,
    170, 176–190, 255
  Potomac banks as seat, 148, 149, 150,
    151, 170, 265
  Washington, D.C. as seat, 170, 171,
    171fn, 255, 256
Secretary of State
  Thomas Jefferson, as, 168–172,
    173–201
  Edmund Randolph, as, 211, 212
  Timothy Pickering, as, 225–232

Sedgwick, Theodore, 4, 6
  congressman, as, 147, 157, 159, 164, 169,
    184, 185, 187, 188,195, 196, 245,
    254, 259
  senator, as, 219, 223, 224, 238
Senate president, *pro-tempore,* 221, 230; JL,
  as, 2, 239–240
Senate Ross bill and the Electoral College,
  7, 243, 244, 246, 247
  JL role, in, 244, 246
  Philadephia *Aurora,* and, 245
Seney, Frances, 176
Serjeant, Jonathan, 68
Seton, William, 180, 191
Sewall, Samuel, 233
Shippen, Margaret, "Peggy" (Mrs. Benedict
  Arnold), 71, 77, 84
Shippen, Edward, IV, 71
Shippen, Sarah (rumored Laurance
  fiancé), 262
Shippen, William, 75, 75fn, 76, 79
sinking fund, Federal, 156, 156fn, 157, 158,
  180, 191, 240
Six Nations (Iroquois league), 117
  New York land grab from, 269–274
slavery, 160, 161, 231, 328 n.8
  in New York, 195, 258
  JL views on, 160, 161, 162, 195, 247,
    257
  Fugitive Slave Act (1793), 194, 195
  Judge, Ona (Washington's slave), 195
  free blacks, 258
smallpox, 28, 55, 63, 85
Smith, Adam (Wealth of Nations), 157
Smith, George, 69
Smith, Jeremiah, 188
Smith, Joshua Hett, 79, 80
Smith, William, 30
Smith, William Jr., 26, 27, 29, 31, 32, 33, 45,
  79, 103, 203
Smith, William Loughton, 6, 162, 327
  n.31
  congressman, as, 147, 157, 161, 181, 183,
    196, 199, 222, 225, 227, 245
Smith, William S., 134, 152, 255, 271
Society for Establishing Useful
  Manufacturing (SEUM), 189,
  192
Sons of Liberty (New York), 2, 6, 20, 34, 35,
  36, 37, 38, 39, 295 n.27
South Carolina
  American Revolution, in, 35, 58
  election of 1796, in, 222
  election of 1800, in, 257, 258

St. Aubyn, Sir John (5th baronet of Clowance), 135
St. Clair, Arthur, 67, 68, 87, 184, 195
St. Clair, Sir John (colonel), 20
St. John's Masonic Lodge #2 of New York City, 2, 33, 105, 136
   JL as member of, 2, 105, 264, 295 n.23
St. Mylor parish, England, 17–19
   Turner, George, Ninth vicar of, 17, 18
St. Simon, marquis de, 86
Stamp Act (1765), 20, 27, 36
Stephen, Adam, 3, 56, 57
Stoutenburg, Isaac (confiscation commissioner), 268, 269
Steuben, Frederick William August von, 3, 58, 59, 63, 77, 94, 99, 118, 123, 166, 192
Stirling, Lord. *See* William Alexander
Stoddert, Benjamin, 232
Stuart, Gilbert, 176, 249, 262
Sullivan, John (general), 56, 91fn
Sully, Thomas, 277
Sumner, Ebenezer (captain), 89

Talleyrand, Périgord, Charles-Maurice de, 230, 231, 231fn
Talmadge, Benjamin, 99
tariffs. *See* import duties and tariffs
Tennessee, 187, 230, 232, 240
Tilghman, William, 206, 207, 249
Treasury Department
   powers, of, 145, 152
   Hamilton, Alexander, secretary of, 145, 152, 155–172, 173–201
   House investigation of, 195, 196
   Fraunces, Andrew's affair, with, 202, 203
   Wolcott, Oliver, Jr., secretary, of, 226, 231, 232, 233, 240, 254
treaties
   Amity and Commerce with France (1778), 207, 222, 234, 237, 338 n.21
   Native American, 117, 195, 270, 271
   Treaty of Paris (1783), 106, 107, 109, 268, 270
   Jay Treaty with Great Britain (1795), 210, 211, 217, 223, 227, 237, 259
   Convention of Môrtefontaine (1800), 256
Trellissick House, Cornwall, 17
Trenton, NJ
   War for Independence, in, 50, 63
   seat of government, as, 148, 150
Trinity Church of NYC, 13–16, 21, 48, 100, 101, 152, 279
   JL and, 2, 32, 101, 152, 173, 264, 283, 311 n.24
   St. Paul's Chapel of, 137, 152, 203

Troup, Robert
   portrait of, 272
   King's College, at, 46
   JL friend, as, 7, 48, 113, 121, 198, 201, 217, 239, 282
   American Revolution, in, 40, 46, 48, 62, 62, 94
   post-war New York, in, 101, 120, 124, 192
   legal practice, of, 90, 96, 107, 108, 192
   Federalist, as, 129, 131, 134, 198
   Federal judge, as, 218
   real estate co-investor of JL, as, 112, 269–277
   Rufus King correspondence, with, 200, 201, 218, 229, 230, 239, 241, 242, 243, 256, 260, 261, 262, 263, 264, 277, 278, 282
Trout Hall (Allen residence), 174, 180, 192, 228, 238, 263
Trumbull, John, 121, 16
Truro Grammar School (Cornwall), 18
Tuthill, Barnabas (major), 42, 43, 44

United States, U.S.S., frigate, 4, 225, 228, 231
United States District Court of New York, 205, 206
United States House of Representatives
   1st U.S. Congress, 138–152, 155–172, 245. (*See Also* First Federal Congress)
   committees and protocols, of, 138, 181
   JL and Appropriations committee, of 181–184, 195
   2nd U.S. Congress, 181–197, 245
   JL, census of 1790 re-apportionment, of, 186–188
   3rd U.S. Congress, 194
   5th U.S. Congress, 234
United States v. La Vengeance (1796), 211–212
United States v. Lawrence (1795), 4, 206–209
United States mint, 117
   Philadelphia, in, 170, 171, 186
   Report on the Establishment of a Mint (Hamilton), 171
   Coinage Act of 1792, and, 186
United States Senate, 142, 219
   First U.S. Senate, 138–172
   Second U.S. Senate, 173–197
   Fourth U.S. Senate, 219–223
   Fifth U.S. Senate, 223–242
      Federalist policy nursery, as, 223, 224, 226, 230–241, 287 n.13
   Sixth U.S. Senate, 242–257
United States Supreme Court, 178, 206–212, 230
   establishment of, 146–148

Valley Forge, PA, 57–64, 67, 69; JL as JAG, at, 3, 57–64
Van Arsdale, John, 98
Van Berckel, Pieter Johan (Dutch minister to U.S.), 263
Van Cortlandt, Augustus, 125
Van Cortlandt, Philip, 42, 63, 268, 269
Van Cortlandt, Pierre Jr. (lt. governor), 97, 131, 280
Van Dyke, John (militia captain), 136
Van Schaik, Gozen "Goose" (colonel), 51
Van Staphorst and Company (Amsterdam bank), 266
Van Zandt, Peter, 125
Vermont, 194, 258, 265
Virginia, 128
   American Revolution, in, 86
   assumption-related debt of, 162
   ratification of the Constitution by, 128, 144
   census of 1790 voting power, in, 186–188, 194
   campaign to rein in Hamilton, Alexander's treasury initiative, 185, 195–197
   election of 1800, in, 259

Waddington, Benjamin, and Evelyn Pierrepont, 107
Walcut, Thomas, 117
Waldron family (JL clients), 102, 104
Wall Street. *See under* New York City, streets and structures, Wall Street
Warner, Seth, 43
Washington, D.C. *See* seat of Government; Washington, D.C.
Washington, George
   Addresses by, 94, 168, 199
   American Revolution, in, 33, 40, 46, 47, 48, 49, 50, 51, 52, 54, 55, 56, 57, 59, 62, 63, 67, 77, 78, 86, 89, 94, 234
   general orders of, 3, 55, 57, 300 n.1
   Newburgh mutiny, confronts, 94
   British evacuation of New York City, in, 97–100
   Fraunces Tavern, farewell to officers, 99
   Constitutional Convention, at, 125
   District of Columbia as seat of government, and, 148, 150, 170, 171, 265
   President, first term, as, 136, 138, 143, 163, 174, 179, 188, 195, 196
   President, second term, as, 2, 196, 204, 205, 207, 221, 222, 231
   Jefferson/Madison-Hamilton feud, and, 194, 196, 198, 202
   quasi-war with France, and, 233, 234, 236
   JL, correspondence with, 7, 59, 71, 77, 84, 85, 89, 221
   JL, relationship with, 46, 57, 59, 62, 84–86, 152, 163., 203, 205, 242
   death and funeral, of, 14, 242, 254
Washington, George's wartime headquarters aides, 287 n.9
   Harrison, Robert, 62, 67, 84
   Laurens, John, 62, 63, 66, 84, 87
   Meade, Richard Kidder, 62, 63, 66, 84
   Scammell, Alexander, 63, 78, 84
   Tilghman, Tench, 62, 88, 310 n.12. *See also* Hamilton, Alexander, and Laurance, John Washington,
   Martha Dandridge Custis, 63, 83, 176, 242
Watts, John (lawyer), 103, 280, 327 n.31
Wayne, Antho (general), 56, 66, 87, 227
Weedon, George (general), 52, 86
Webster, Noah Jr., 122, 124, 249
West Point, 77, 78, 79, 83
   Congressional Act of July 1790, 172, 172fn
West Indies trade, 88, 141, 204, 231, 241
Whigs. *See* New York City, Whigs
whiskey excise tax, 155, 171
   JL role in, 171
   Whiskey Rebellion against, 207, 227
White, William (reverend), 173, 174, 218. 242
White Hart Tavern, of Minnie Vorhees, 65
Wilcox, William, 107
Willet, Gilbert Colden, 92, 93
Willet, Marinus, 39, 43, 100, 104, 132, 277, 278
Wilson, James
   Constitutional Convention, at, 125
   Supreme Court Justice, as, 199, 209, 209fn
   speculative excess, of, 8, 199
   debtor's prison, in, 265
Wolcott, Oliver, Jr., 91fn 198, 226, 231, 232, 233, 240, 254, 257, 276. *See also* Treasury Department; Wolcott as Secretary
Woodward, Nathaniel (captain), 41, 43
Wooster, David (general), 44
Wright, George (tutor), 174

XYZ Affair, 230, 231, 231fn

Yellow fever. *See* New York, yellow fever, 228, 232, 263
   Philadelphia, yellow fever, 199–201, 228, 239
Yorktown campaign, 86, 87, 95

Zedtwitz, Herman (colonel), 46, 46fn

www.ingramcontent.com/pod-product-compliance
Lightning Source LLC
Chambersburg PA
CBHW050738110426
42814CB00006B/300